Anonymous Security Systems and Applications:

Requirements and Solutions

Shinsuke Tamura
University of Fukui, Japan

Information Science
REFERENCE

Managing Director:	Lindsay Johnston
Senior Editorial Director:	Heather A. Probst
Book Production Manager:	Sean Woznicki
Development Manager:	Joel Gamon
Acquisitions Editor:	Erika Gallagher
Typesetter:	Nicole Sparano
Cover Design:	Nick Newcomer, Lisandro Gonzalez

Published in the United States of America by
Information Science Reference (an imprint of IGI Global)
701 E. Chocolate Avenue
Hershey PA 17033
Tel: 717-533-8845
Fax: 717-533-8661
E-mail: cust@igi-global.com
Web site: http://www.igi-global.com

Library of Congress Cataloging-in-Publication Data

Tamura, Shinsuke.
Anonymous security systems and applications: requirements and solutions / by Shinsuke Tamura.
p. cm.
Includes bibliographical references and index.
Summary: "This book outlines the benefits and drawbacks of anonymous security technologies designed to obscure the identities of users, solve various privacy issues and encourage more people to make full use of information and communication technologies"-- Provided by publisher.
ISBN 978-1-4666-1649-3 (hardcover) -- ISBN 978-1-4666-1650-9 (ebook) -- ISBN 978-1-4666-1651-6 (print & perpetual access) 1. Computer security. 2. Data encryption (Computer science) I. Title.
QA76.9.A25T345 2012
005.8--dc23
2012002869

British Cataloguing in Publication Data
A Cataloguing in Publication record for this book is available from the British Library.

All work contributed to this book is new, previously-unpublished material. The views expressed in this book are those of the authors, but not necessarily of the publisher.

Table of Contents

Section 3
Developing Secure Anonymous Systems

Preface

Recent advances of information and communication technologies are making societies highly efficient and convenient. When the Internet and credit card systems are combined, people can buy various things without going out from their homes or offices, and if their buying articles are home appliances or manufacturing machines for example, monitoring systems can remotely trace these appliances or machines and monitor their operational states to provide their users with suggestions so that they can be operated in more efficient, safe, and environmentally friendly ways. However, currently these systems are available only on an exchange with privacy disclosure risks of individuals. For example, because all kinds of purchase records of individuals are stored in databases of credit card companies, all privacies of individuals will be revealed if the card companies are not operated adequately. These risks exist also in organizations, e.g. companies must disclose sensitive information including their top secrets to fully utilize latest e-business systems. Threats of these privacy or secret disclosures are becoming more and more serious as people are extending their activities while being supported by the advancing information and communication technologies.

Here, among information about individuals and organizations, identities of entities are one of the most sensitive data on the one hand, i.e. as many books about security refer the phrase "spy agencies acquire more information from the traffic of messages than the messages themselves (Wright, 1987)," sometimes identities of owners and/or users of the information are more sensitive than the information itself. On the other hand, things people can conceal are only their identities in many applications. For example, people cannot conceal messages themselves when they want to inform others of them, also when people buy articles, they cannot conceal articles or their prices from stores. Therefore, establishments of technologies that enable secure handlings of identities of individuals and organizations are one of the keys to make our societies further convenient, efficient, safe, and environmentally friendly. Namely, technologies to conceal owners or users of data and objects reduce risks of privacy and secret disclosures, and as a consequence, encourage many people to reap benefits from advancing information and communication technologies.

Anonymous systems and anonymous security technologies are concerned with information systems and mechanisms that conceal identities of entities at the minimum cost. Here, it is not so difficult to develop anonymous systems when absolutely trustworthy entities can be assumed. For example, if a credit card company is ensured absolutely not to disclose purchase records of its customers to others, cardholders can easily conceal their individual purchases from others. However the costs for maintaining these trustworthy entities become extremely high, because no entity is absolutely trustworthy in the real world, credit card companies must maintain highly educated staffs, and they must protect their maintaining information from every kind of threats regardless they are intentional or accidental. By making use of anonymous security technologies, it becomes possible to exclude these absolutely trustworthy entities from information systems as much as possible so that people can receive services from them securely at less cost.

Since the pioneering works of Chaum (1985), many researchers and practitioners had been continually making progresses in developing anonymous security technologies, and currently, at least theoretically, it is possible to develop communication systems, in which people can securely exchange information without disclosing their identities to others including senders or receivers of their messages and managers of communication systems. Also cardholders of credit card systems can make purchases without disclosing their identities to any other entities while enabling credit card companies to correctly calculate total expenditures of individual cardholders, and maintenance companies can monitor running states of home appliances while preserving privacies of the users.

This book discusses requirements for anonymous systems in various application fields, and based on currently available technologies, develops anonymous systems so that anonymous security technologies are applied more extensively and people are encouraged to develop more efficient and effective anonymous security technologies that exclude trustworthy entities as much as possible. The book consists of 3 sections: "Introduction," "Data and Communication Security in Anonymous Systems," and "Developing Secure Anonymous Systems." All sectionss are for every kind of readers who have interests in anonymous systems from non-experts to experts. Only fundamental mathematical knowledge is assumed.

The 1st section introduces requirements for anonymous security technologies in various applications together with fundamental security components such as encryption functions and digital signatures, and the 2nd section discusses schemes for protecting data owned by anonymous entities from their illegitimate modifications, deletions, additions, etc. Schemes for exchanging messages without disclosing identities of senders and/or receivers to others, and calculating aggregate values of data without knowing their individual values are also discussed. Then finally in the 3rd section, anonymous authentication systems, and as applications of anonymous security technologies, electronic payment (e-payment), electronic procurement (e-procurement) and electronic governance (e-governance) systems are developed. In detail, e-payment systems include credit card and electronic cash (e-cash) systems, and e-procurement systems include auction, object delivery and object monitoring systems. Regarding e-governance systems, an electronic voting (e-voting) system is developed as a typical example.

However, it must be noted that although several application systems can be developed without assuming any trustworthy entity (i.e. for an entity in them entities that it can trust is only itself), as far as for currently available technologies, there are still many important applications in which trustworthy entities cannot be excluded completely. Therefore, in these cases, trusts are distributed into multiple independent authorities, and entities can believe that their identities are concealed from others unless all authorities conspire, in other words, when at least one of authorities is honest.

Topics of individual chapters are shown below.

SECTION 1

This section consists of 4 chapters. The first chapter discusses requirements for anonymous security technologies while introducing typical applications. Namely, to preserve privacies of individuals and to protect secrets of organizations, communication systems must enable entities to send or receive messages without disclosing their identities even to managers of communication systems and receivers or senders of messages, and credit card systems must enable cardholders to make their purchases without disclosing their identities to others while ensuring that card companies can collect exact expenditure amounts from cardholders. Also, service providers in cloud computing must be able to calculate various functions of data owned by clients without knowing values of individual data. Moreover, to protect voters from coercers who are forcing the voters to choose their supporting candidates, e-voting systems must conceal correspondences between voters and their votes even from voters themselves. Secure anonymous system technologies must cope with these requirements.

The 2nd chapter defines encryptions and decryptions as the most fundamental security components for developing security enhanced systems. Also, homomorphic (additive or multiplicative), probabilistic, commutative and verifiable features are highlighted as the desirable ones of encryption algorithms for developing secure anonymous systems, and typical encryption algorithms are evaluated in terms of these features. Then, the 3rd chapter, about schemes for protecting data from their illegitimate modifications and forgeries, follows, i.e. hash functions, MACs (Message Authentication Codes) and digital signatures are introduced. Hash functions, MACs, and digital signatures protect data by detecting illegitimate modifications while attaching redundant values to the data, namely, when an entity illegitimately modifies the data, the modified results become inconsistent with the attached values, and among them, digital signatures enable anyone including third parties to convince others that its owning data with signatures are legitimate ones.

In the last chapter of the section, linear equation based encryption functions and re-encryption and threshold encryption schemes are discussed as ones that play important roles in anonymous systems. Linear equation based encryption functions enable entities to calculate sums of data owned by others without knowing individual values, and by using probabilistic, commutative and verifiable re-encryption schemes, entities can encrypt data while concealing the correspondences between encrypted data and their decrypted forms from anyone including the owners of the data. Threshold ElGamal encryption functions disable entities to decrypt encrypted data without the cooperation among t out of n authorities ($t \leq n$), while ensuring correct decryptions when at least t-authorities are honest. All encryption schemes will be extensively used in the following sections of this book, e.g. for developing anonymous communication systems, anonymous authentication systems, anonymous payment systems, and e-voting systems.

SECTION 2

This section also consists of 4 chapters. After discussing approaches to implementing secure anonymous systems, discussions about schemes for maintaining integrities of data in anonymous environments and exchanging messages with anonymous entities follow. Schemes for anonymous statistics calculation that enable entities to calculate aggregate values of data without knowing their individual values are also discussed.

The 1st chapter summarizes how homomorphic and commutative features of encryption functions solve various problems appear in satisfying requirements of anonymous systems. Commutative encryption functions can be used to detect illegitimate modifications and forgeries of data without knowing data themselves, and homomorphic encryption functions can be used to calculate functions of data without knowing their individual values, to detect dishonest deletions of data maintained by other entities and to identify dishonest entities without knowing any secret of honest entities. Here, frequently entities can maintain their encryption keys as their secrets in anonymous systems, therefore there are opportunities not only for modern public key based encryption schemes but also for secret key based ones, and legacy encryption algorithms such as linear equation based ones play important roles.

The 2nd chapter relates to schemes for detecting illegitimate modifications and forgeries of data without knowing data themselves. Blind signature schemes enable entity P to obtain the signature of other entity on its data *M* without disclosing *M*, therefore later on P can prove the authenticity of *M* without disclosing its identity. Unlinkable signatures on data ensure that signers had honestly signed on only and all eligible data while disabling anyone including data owners and signers to know correspondences between the data and their signed forms, and implicit transaction links (ITLs) can be used to detect deletions of data maintained by other entities without knowing the data themselves. They also enable the developments of anonymous tokens and homomorphic anonymous tokens by which entities can prove their eligibilities while maintaining their anonymities. As another approach to enabling anonymous entities to prove their eligibilities, anonymous tag-based credentials are also discussed, where anonymous tags are attached to physical or logical objects so that entities can identify their objects while disabling others to identify them. Anonymous tokens, homomorphic anonymous tokens, and anonymous credentials can be used also to identify dishonest entities while preserving privacies of honest entities. In addition to tokens and credentials, as schemes to convince others that an entity is honest (knows secrets) without disclosing its secrets, well known cut and choose protocols and zero knowledge proofs (ZKPs) are also discussed.

Schemes of anonymous communication that enable entities to send and/or receive messages without disclosing their identities to others are discussed in the 3rd chapter. Here, anonymous communications are bases for almost all kinds of anonymous application systems because current computer supported services are implemented as networks of service providing servers and clients, and without anonymous communications identities of entities are easily revealed from their network addresses. Among various existing schemes this chapter introduces Crowds, DC net, Mix-net, ESEBM (Enhanced Symmetric key Encryption Based Mix-Net), and Onion Routing. Mechanisms to protect anonymous communication systems from malicious entities are also discussed. However, different from many other schemes in this section that completely exclude trusted entities, current technologies cannot exclude trusted entities completely from anonymous communications, i.e. all of the above mechanisms consist of multiple independent message transferring servers, and senders and/or receivers are ensured to be anonymous only when at least one of multiple servers is honest.

Finally, the last chapter of this section discusses schemes for anonymous statistics calculations, in which entities calculate various functions of data owned by anonymous or non-anonymous entities without knowing their individual values. Employees of a company do not mind even if their average salary is disclosed, but they do not want to disclose their individual salaries for example, and mechanisms in this chapter cope with these requirements. Currently, companies are shifting to achieve their tasks while using resources owned and operated by others, but still they must use their own computing resources to process their secret data. Schemes discussed in this chapter play important roles in accelerating these shifts and consequently to reduce total energy and resource consumptions. However, although theoretically there are schemes to calculate any function of data without knowing their individual values, their implementations are not practical, i.e. too complicated and time consuming. Therefore, this chapter discusses methods based on encryption functions with homomorphic features, they are blind sum/product calculation schemes, partial computation based multi party computation schemes, and re-encryption based multi party computation schemes. Although they are not for general purposes, they enable efficient calculations of averages, variances, auto and mutual correlations, etc. of given data.

SECTION 3

This section analyses requirements of various applications of anonymous system technologies and develops systems that satisfy the requirements while using security components discussed in Section 1 and 2. In the 1st chapter, anonymous authentication systems are developed based on various different approaches, then as anonymous payment systems, an anonymous credit card system and an e-cash system are developed in the 2nd chapter based on ITLs and anonymous tags, respectively. Here, both anonymous authentication and payment systems offer the most fundamental services for almost all kinds of anonymous systems as same as anonymous communication schemes do. The 3rd chapter develops anonymous auction, object delivery, and monitoring systems as components of e-procurement systems, and the last chapter concerns e-governance systems, and an e-voting system is developed. The important thing that must be reminded is every system cannot assume absolutely trustworthy neutral entities faithful to all participants. An entity that each participant in many of the above systems can trust is only the participant itself. Unfortunately it is not possible to develop object delivery or e-voting systems while completely excluding neutral and trustworthy entities at least for technologies developed until now. Therefore, the object delivery and voting systems in this section are constructed while assuming multiple mutually independent authorities. Namely, participants can convince themselves that they are anonymous when at least one of the authorities is honest.

Anonymous authentication schemes enable managers of systems to determine whether entities accessing them are authorized ones or not without knowing identities of the entities. An important thing is that schemes must be able to handle entities that lose their eligibilities or forget their secrets (e.g. passwords) without invading privacies of honest entities in addition to simple authenticating functions, e.g. passwords of expelled entities must be invalidated. Also although entities to be authenticated are anonymous, they must identify dishonest entities when dishonest events happen. As schemes that satisfy these requirements, anonymous tokens, ITLs, ID-lists, and anonymous credential based ones are developed in the 1st chapter while completely excluding trusted entities. Anonymous token, ITL, and anonymous credential based systems have advantages in protecting systems from ineligible entities, i.e. different from password based systems in which eligible entities can tell their passwords to others, entities in these systems cannot give their secrets to others without losing their eligibilities (in ITL based systems, an entity cannot use secrets of others even if it steals them). On the other hand, ID list based systems have advantages in handling entities those forget their secrets or those are expelled from systems.

In the 2nd chapter, an anonymous credit card system in which cardholders can make purchases while concealing their identities is developed without assuming any absolutely trustworthy entity. A difficult thing is that the system must enable the card company to correctly calculate total expenditures of individual cardholders at the same time. Therefore, in the developed system, cardholders maintain their purchase records by themselves, and report only their total expenditure amounts to the card company.

Then mechanisms to force cardholders to honestly report their total expenditures are necessary. ITLs successfully implement these mechanisms. As an e-payment system, an e-cash system is also developed based on anonymous tag based credentials, and entities in the developed e-cash system can use also e-cash that had been paid to them by others, and they can receive changes from others in e-cash, under both online and offline environments.

An e-procurement system is one in which people can choose their favorite articles, obtain them, and receive maintenance services through networks without going out from their homes or offices, and preserving privacies of individuals is the one of the most urgent issues to be addressed for making people accept this kind of systems. In the 3rd chapter, anonymous English auction system and an anonymous Vickrey auction system are developed based on ITLs and homomorphic re-encryption schemes respectively, so that people can sell or buy articles without disclosing their identities. In both systems, although sellers and buyers are anonymous, sellers are forced to sell their articles to the auction winners at the prices determined by the auctions, on the other hand, buyers are forced to buy their winning articles. Here, the English auction system assumes no absolutely trustworthy entity, but the Vickrey auction system ensures the anonymity of entities when at least one of multiple authorities is honest.

Participants of the above auctions can receive their winning articles also without disclosing their identities through anonymous object delivery systems, i.e. as same as anonymous communication systems, anonymous object delivery systems enable people to send or receive physical objects without disclosing their identities. But different from electric signals conveyed in anonymous communication systems, long durations are necessary to transport physical objects and it is difficult to re-send them when they disappear in the delivery channel. Therefore, object delivery systems must enable senders or receivers to identify their objects in the delivery channel and liable entities when accidents happen on them of course while concealing correspondences between the objects and their senders or receivers. Anonymous tags successfully satisfy these requirements.

Anonymous object monitoring systems are ones that monitor states of objects owned by anonymous entities so that they can use them efficiently, safely and environmentally friendlily, and in this chapter, they are developed based on anonymous memories, anonymous statistics calculation schemes, and ITLs. Here, an anonymous memory is a set of memory sections that are assigned to entities, and owners of the sections can maintain their data securely and efficiently without disclosing their identities. Also anonymous statistics calculation schemes and ITLs enable monitoring stations to calculate statistics of operational states of the objects without knowing their individual values and to identify dishonest users without invading privacies of honest users when dishonest events happen on the objects. By these mechanisms, it is expected that more people will accept various kinds of remote software services, e.g. companies will ask service providers to execute even tasks that require their top secrets.

E-voting system is a typical example of e-governance systems, and e-voting is one of the most promising applications of anonymous security technologies. While being supported by computers and networks e-voting systems make elections more convenient, efficient, and accurate. Actually, e-voting systems are widely used already in the real world. However, current e-voting systems cannot preserve privacies of voters successfully enough. For example, it is not trivial to convince voters that election authorities never know votes of individual voters because all information is computerized and the way computer programs are processing votes cannot be seen from the outside. To make e-voting systems be accepted more widely, in the last chapter, an e-voting system is developed so that the following requirements are satisfied: no one except voters can know votes of voters, anyone can verify that all and only eligible votes are counted, no one can know partial tally before ends of elections, no one coerce voters, and no one can disrupt elections. Then together with a fact that the system does not require much computations all major requirements of e-voting systems can be successfully satisfied in a practical way. However, it must be noted that these requirement are satisfied under the assumption that at least one of multiple authorities is honest.

As mentioned already, although advances in information and communication technologies had been making human activities efficient and convenient, privacy issues still make many people reluctant to reap benefits from them. Anonymous security technologies solve various problems about privacies, and it is expected that application systems enhanced by these technologies encourage more people to make full use of information and communication technologies aiming at the establishments of more secure, convenient, efficient, and environmentally friendly societies. However, although theoretically it is possible to make anonymous security technologies satisfy various kind of requirements, there are big arguments about the practicality of anonymous systems. For example, it is difficult to convince people that these anonymous systems are reliable enough. Anonymities may easily make people behave dishonestly, also various unforeseen events may happen in the real world, but in anonymous systems it is difficult to limit damages of individuals and authorities even if liable entities can be identified. Effective and unavoidable things to make anonymous systems practical are gathering and systematization of knowledge that is proven through various experiences in real applications. Only these experiences, beginning from ones in simple and small systems used by closed communities, enable enhancements of anonymous security technologies so that anonymous systems for larger and more complicated and important applications can be accepted.

Shinsuke Tamura
University of Fukui, Japan

REFERENCES

Chaum, D. (1985). Security without identification: Transaction systems to make big brother obsolete. *Communications of the ACM, 28*(10), 1030–1044. doi:10.1145/4372.4373

Wright, P. (1987). *Spycatcher: The candid autobiography of a senior intelligence officer*. Viking Penguin.

Acknowledgment

This book is based on many efforts from students and colleagues in department of information science at university of Fukui, and I think this book could not be completed without their efforts.

First of all I express my gratitude to associate Professor Dr. Shuji Taniguchi and former Associate Professor Dr. Tatsuro Yanase for their supports in conducting research on anonymous systems. Regarding individual topics, materials about anonymous communication systems were enhanced through discussions with Mr. Kazuya Kouro, Dr. Hazim Anas Haddad, Mr. Hiroya Tsurugi, and Ms. Hazuki Okuno. Their developments of various prototype systems had enlarged the initial ideas about ESEBM, and also ideas about anonymous tags had emerged thorough discussions with them. Performance of ID list based anonymous authentication schemes had been improved by Mr. Keisuke Ikuta and Mr. Masatoshi Sasatani. Many defects and weaknesses of anonymous credit card systems (including anonymous record agreement protocol) and anonymous auction systems had been removed through discussions and prototype system developments with Mr. Yusuke Ohashi and Ms. Hazuki Okuno, and Mr. Kazem Hasan and Mr. Masatoshi Sasatani, respectively. Discussions with Mr. Kazuya Kouro, Mr. Masaki Yamaguchi, and Mr. Ryou Akioka had given me various ideas about anonymous object delivery and monitoring systems. About e-voting systems, discussions with Mr. Arturo Valencia Milian had inspired me to start the development, initial ideas had emerged from these discussions, and they had been realized through discussions and prototype system developments with Dr. Kazi Md. Rokibul Alam.

I express my gratitude also to IGI Global and anonymous reviewers of this book. IGI Global gave me an exciting opportunity, and suggestions of the reviewers substantially improved the book. Lastly, I'm grateful to my wife Yuri, and daughters Youko and Tomoko for their supports and encouragements.

Shinsuke Tamura
University of Fukui, Japan

Section 1
Introduction

Chapter 1
Secure Anonymous Systems and Requirements

ABSTRACT

To understand the importance of secure anonymous system technologies, this chapter introduces communication, electronic payment, cloud computing, and electronic governance systems as their applications, and discusses roles of secure anonymous system technologies in these systems. To preserve privacies of individuals and to protect secrets of organizations, communication systems must enable users to send or receive messages without disclosing their identities even to managers of communication networks and receivers or senders of their messages, and credit card systems must enable cardholders to make their purchases without disclosing their identities while ensuring card companies to collect their exact expenditure amounts. Also, service providers in cloud computing must be able to calculate various functions of data owned by their clients without knowing values of individual data. Moreover, to protect voters from coercers who are forcing the voters to choose their supporting candidates, computerized voting systems must conceal correspondences between voters and their votes even from voters themselves. Secure anonymous system technologies enable developments of systems that satisfy these requirements.

INTRODUCTION

Anonymity is becoming one of the most important issues in developing and using information and communication systems.

Advancement of information and communication technologies is continually making our societies convenient and efficient. The Internet enables people to communicate with others and to know every event in the world at anytime while staying in their homes or offices, and people can make their purchases or accomplish their business tasks without visiting shops or their business partners. Also, a company can accomplish its every task without maintaining expensive resources when technologies such as cloud computing are exploited. However, currently people and companies cannot reap these benefits without risks about disclosures of their secrets. For example,

DOI: 10.4018/978-1-4666-1649-3.ch001

network managers or internet providers can know friends and acquaintances or hobbies and life styles of people when they know senders or receivers of e-mails flowing in networks or identities of entities that access web pages. If communication partners are a company and its customer or a part supplier, business strategies of the company may leak out to its rival companies. Even top secrets of a company may be leaked to its rivals when the company commissions other organizations that are not trustworthy enough to accomplish its tasks while exploiting cloud computing technologies.

Therefore, information and communication systems must be endowed with anonymous features so that they can be used more widely and effectively, i.e. people and companies must be able to use them without disclosing their identities. Here, a difficult thing is that anonymous systems must be secure enough as usual systems are despite that their users are anonymous, e.g. they must be able to detect dishonest events and to identify entities liable for those events. If they are less secure, compensations for damages caused by dishonest events become extremely difficult because liable entities are anonymous.

This chapter discusses desirable anonymous features of systems in various applications as the background of secure anonymous systems. One more thing that must be stated here is that establishments of secure anonymous technologies that provide these features lead us to the sustainable society while encouraging more people to use information and communication systems in their daily activities. For example, when cloud computing is widely used, enormous materials and energies necessary for maintaining information systems in individual companies can be reduced.

COMMUNICATION SYSTEMS

Mechanisms for communication among entities are the most important components of every information system, e.g. all of electronic mailing, web browsing and electronic banking systems are based on communication mechanisms. To enable users to securely exchange their messages, recent communication systems extensively adopt advanced encryption technologies, i.e. even when an entity eavesdrops on messages it cannot use them illegitimately because the entity that does not know the encryption scheme cannot understand the messages. However encryptions of messages are not enough. If the above entity can know identities of persons who are frequently communicating with each other, it can easily estimate that those persons like or hate each other and know their privacies. When these persons are replaced by companies, risks involved become more understandable. In this case, communication partners are manufactures and their customers, manufactures and their part suppliers, or manufactures and banks for example, and identities of these communication partners can be used to know business strategies of the manufactures. Here, it must be noted that theoretically at least communication system managers can know identities of these communicating partners in the most of current communication systems.

There are also cases where identities of message senders or receivers must be concealed not only from the 3rd parties including system managers but also even from the receivers or senders of messages. For example in an electronic voting system, an election authority can easily know candidates that individual voters had chosen if identities of entities that had cast their votes through the communication system are not concealed, and if an internet provider can know identities of users that are accessing it, it can know hobbies and life styles of the users by analysing information that the users had fetched. On the other hand, the internet provider must send reply information back to users without knowing their identities when their users are anonymous.

Then, anonymous communication systems must be able to conceal identities of message senders and/or receivers from anyone except the senders or the receivers (Chaum, 1981). At the same time they must be able to protect themselves from various threats such as DOS (denial of service) attacks, message forgeries and deletions without disclosing identities of honest message senders and/or receivers. Here, anonymity of senders and/or receivers make communication systems more vulnerable to various threats, e.g. people can send fake messages to deceive their receivers or send dummy messages as attempts of DOS attacks more easily because their identities are not known. In the same way, system managers can modify or delete messages without being noticed because in many cases receivers of anonymous messages do not expect their arrivals. Although it is not so difficult to develop almost complete (but incomplete) anonymous communication systems, in which many efforts are required to identify senders or receivers of messages (Reiter, 1998), they cannot be used in important applications in the real world. When voters in an electronic voting system or users of an internet provider maliciously claim their votes or hobbies were revealed to others while intentionally disclosing them, the election authority or the internet provider must compensate the voters or the users for their fake damages.

ELECTRONIC PAYMENT

Almost all activities of our society include payments; therefore when all payment systems are computerized and connected all privacies of individuals will be revealed if they are not anonymous. For example, when databases of multiple credit card companies and banks are connected, it is not difficult to know details about every purchase of a person and this knowledge will reveal occupations, friends, hobbies, life styles, economical conditions, etc. of the person. When a person in the above is replaced by a company, business strategies of the company leak out to its rival companies, in the same way as in the previous section.

This situation does not change even electronic cash (e-cash, digital cash) is used. E-cash is actually data in portable memories, and forging e-cash or making its copies is not so difficult especially for insiders. Therefore, a bank may issue individual e-cash while embedding information about its owners in it so that it can detect forged ones or can identify persons who had used same e-cash repeatedly (currently available e-cash is not so cautious about these risks because it is used only for small purchases). As a consequence the bank can know details of purchases also made by e-cash by examining the information embedded in it.

A simple way to make individual purchases anonymous is to assume banks or credit card companies as absolutely trusted entities that do not disclose any privacy of their customers. However, tremendous efforts are necessary to maintain these entities, e.g. many kinds of regulations, checking systems, education systems for employees, etc. are necessary for maintaining absolutely trustworthy entities. They must protect themselves also from various kinds of attacks made by outsiders. Actually, it is not rare that privacies of customers are leaked from banks or credit card companies despite their efforts to protect them. To make anonymous payment systems practical enough these absolutely trustworthy entities must be removed.

As same as in communication systems, difficulties for developing anonymous payment systems are they must be able to detect malicious events and identify their liable entities despite they are anonymous. In e-cash systems, individual e-cash cannot include any information about its owner; nevertheless owners of e-cash must be identified when they use same e-cash repeatedly (Eslami, 2011). In cases of anonymous credit card systems, to conceal individual purchases of cardholders, individual purchase records are necessarily maintained by cardholders themselves and they do not disclose their records, but card companies must calculate the total expenditure of each cardholder correctly.

CLOUD COMPUTING

Cloud computing makes various business activities agile, efficient and economical, it also reduces resource and energy consumptions. Namely in cloud computing, companies accomplish their business tasks by outsourcing them to different organizations equipped with information systems established already; therefore the companies do not need to develop their own information systems dedicated to their new businesses, they do not need personnel for maintaining the systems, and common computing resources (hardware software and energies) can be shared among different companies.

However, companies must take serious risks to use cloud computing, i.e. they must disclose even their top secrets to the outside to accomplish their important tasks. Therefore, to use cloud computing in more effective ways, at least identities of its users must be concealed from anyone except the users themselves. Here, even when users are anonymous, in many cases they can be identified by the data that they disclose for accomplishing the tasks. For example, identities of companies can be estimated by their sales amounts, customers, part suppliers, etc. Then, ideal cloud computing must enable companies to outsource their tasks even without disclosing their data.

Although the above situation is almost same as in anonymous credit card systems where card companies must calculate total expenditures of individual cardholders without knowing their individual purchases, in this case, individual tasks cannot be accomplished by simple additions of data; they require much more complicated calculations. Therefore compared with in electronic payment systems, more sophisticated schemes for various calculations based on secret data become necessary in cloud computing (Naor, 1999).

ELECTRONIC GOVERNANCE

Although many data maintained by government offices such as family records are intrinsically non-anonymous, technologies about secure anonymous systems play important roles also in activities around governments. Typical examples are opinion poll and voting. Different from usual opinion polls, people who put individual opinions are identified easily and accurately when poll systems are computerized, therefore electronic polling systems must be strictly anonymous (Bruschi, 2005). Although it is easy to make people anonymous when anonymous communication systems are available, at least 2 problems arise. The one is to inhibit ineligible people to put opinions or inhibit people to put their opinions repeatedly, and the other is to ensure that opinions are correctly counted. In the same way, electronic voting systems (computerized voting systems) must ensure that eligible voters put their votes only once and voting authorities honestly counted votes from only and all eligible voters despite voters are anonymous (Sampigethaya, 2006).

In addition to these features, electronic voting systems must be incoercible. Namely, although voters must be able to know that their votes are certainly included in a set of votes finally disclosed by a voting authority, at the same time, voters must be disabled to identify their votes in the disclosed set. If a voter can identify its vote, a coercer who is forcing the voter to choose a candidate that it is supporting can easily confirm whether the voter had chosen the candidate or not, and as a consequence the coercer can achieve its aim in more successful ways. The further difficult thing is that the coercer may ask the voter to put an invalid candidate name unique to it, and in this case the coercer can confirm the performance of the voter by simply examining whether the finally disclosed votes include the invalid name or not.

Before ending this subsection, it must be noted that although many individual governmental tasks cannot be accomplished without knowing identities of individuals, yet there are many opportunities for anonymous security technologies also in these systems, e.g. although it is desirable that every kind of data about people are combined to provide them with better services, links among these data must be concealed from government offices to preserve privacies of people.

CONCLUSION

As discussed in this chapter, privacy is one of the most important issues to effectively and safely computerize our activities and to make our society more convenient, efficient and environmentally friendly, and anonymous systems are solutions to protect relevant entities from their privacy leaks. But anonymity of entities bring various threats to information and communication systems, and without mechanisms for protecting systems from these threats anonymous systems cannot be used in the real world applications.

There are 3 kinds of approaches to implementing these mechanisms. The easiest one is to assume absolutely trustworthy entities that are responsible for preserving privacies of all relevant entities. However, it is impossible to establish absolutely trustworthy entities in the real world, e.g. it is not rare that organizations assumed to be trustworthy such as credit card companies accidentally or intentionally disclose privacies of cardholders. Even if it is possible, tremendous efforts are necessary to maintain these entities. Therefore, many anonymous security technologies are trying to remove these absolutely trustworthy entities as much as possible, and this book also discusses mechanisms that try to exclude these entities.

In anonymous systems based on the 2nd approach, absolutely trustworthy entities are excluded completely. Namely in these systems, for an arbitrary entity, the entity that it can trust is only itself, and the costs for maintaining trusted entities can be reduced at the minimum. However, as far as for the state of the art technologies, there are many important applications in which trustworthy entities cannot be excluded completely. For these applications the 3rd approach is adopted, in which trusts are distributed to multiple independent entities. Namely, in systems based on the 3rd approach, entities involved in systems can believe that their anonymities are maintained as long as at least one of the multiple trusted entities is honest.

In later chapters in this book, mechanisms about electronic payments will be developed while completely excluding absolutely trustworthy entities, however, systems about communication and electronic voting will be developed through the 3rd approach.

REFERENCES

Bruschi, D., Fovino, I., & Lanzi, A. (2005). A protocol for anonymous and accurate e-polling. *Proceedings of the International Conference on E-Government: Towards Electronic Democracy,* (pp. 112-121).

Chaum, D. (1981). Untraceable electronic mail, return address and digital pseudonyms. *Communications of the ACM, 24*(2), 84–90. doi:10.1145/358549.358563

Eslami, Z., & Talebi, M. (2011). A new untraceable off-line electronic cash system. *Electronic Commerce Research and Applications, 10*(1), 59–66. doi:10.1016/j.elerap.2010.08.002

Naor, M., Pinkas, B., & Sumner, R. (1999). Privacy preserving auctions and mechanism design. *Proceedings of the 1st ACM Conference on Electronic Commerce*, (pp. 129-139).

Reiter, K., & Rubin, A. D. (1998). Crowds: Anonymity for Web transactions. *ACM Transactions on Information and System Security*, *1*(1), 66–92. doi:10.1145/290163.290168

Sampigethaya, K., & Poovendran, R. (2006). A framework and taxonomy for comparison of electronic voting schemes. *Elsevier Computers and Security*, *25*, 137–153.

Chapter 2
Encryption and Decryption

ABSTRACT

As the foundation of all security enhanced systems, encryptions and decryptions are defined, and homomorphic (additive or multiplicative), probabilistic, commutative, and verifiable features are extracted as the desirable ones of encryption and decryption algorithms for developing secure anonymous systems. Also encryption and decryption algorithms are classified and onetime pad, permutation and substitution, RSA, and ElGamal are introduced as typical algorithms. Among them, onetime pad, RSA, and ElGamal are extensively used to develop secure anonymous systems in the remainder of this book.

INTRODUCTION

As the bases of the following chapters, this chapter discusses various kinds of encryption and decryption algorithms. A typical example, in which encryption and decryption algorithms are required, is communication between two entities. When entity Q wants to receive messages from entity P, while protecting them from wiretappings, Q informs P of the algorithm to encrypt messages through usually an expensive and inefficient communication channel that is protected from wiretappings (e.g. an isolated private channel) in advance. After that, P encrypts its message M by the encryption algorithm received from Q so that no one except Q that knows the decryption algorithm can understand the meaning of M even someone eavesdrops on it, and sends M in its encrypted form through a usual inexpensive and efficient communication channel, e.g. through the Internet. Then, only Q can decrypt the message sent from P, and consequently can understand the meaning of M. The important thing here is that the encryption algorithm must be transferred more easily than M itself. If the encryption algorithm and the message are equally difficult to transfer, P may send M directly to Q through the expensive and inefficient communication channel in the same way as Q sends the encryption algorithm. Namely, P does not need to encrypt M.

DOI: 10.4018/978-1-4666-1649-3.ch002

Figure 1. Encryption and decryption

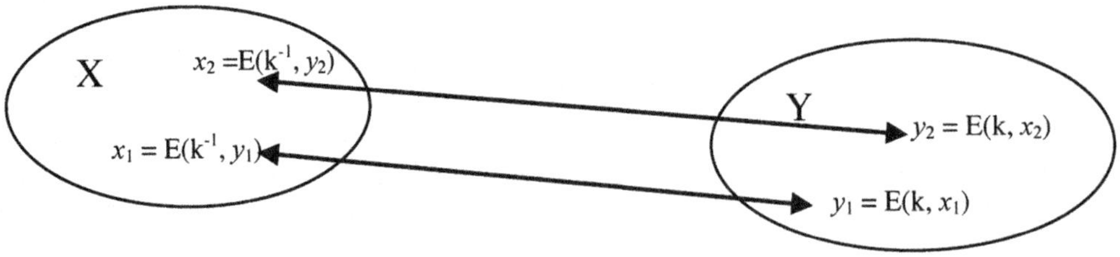

Encryption and decryption algorithms used in the above communication are the most fundamental component of information security, i.e. they are used not only in protecting messages from wiretappings but also in protecting information from unauthorized modifications, in confirming honest behaviours of entities and almost in every security enhanced activity in both non-anonymous and anonymous information systems as shown in later chapters. However in anonymous systems, encryptions and decryptions are carried out under environments different from in usual non-anonymous systems, e.g. frequently information is both encrypted and decrypted by same entities, also, it is not rare that entities must ask not completely trusted other entities to encrypt their information, or all entities are required not to know correspondences between information and their encrypted forms. Therefore encryption and decryption algorithms for anonymous systems are required to have different features from the ones required in usual non-anonymous systems. There are cases where important constraints of encryption and decryption algorithms (e.g. algorithms must be transferred easily as just mentioned above) can be relaxed, and contrarily, some other requirements that are not important in usual systems become important. Consequently, not only the modern encryption and decryption algorithms but also various legacy ones can be or must be exploited to develop practical anonymous application systems. To confirm these circumstances, this chapter firstly summarizes desirable features of encryption and decryption algorithms; then in later sections, various kinds of algorithms are discussed especially in terms of these features.

DEFINITION AND DESIRABLE FEATURES

Encryption and Decryption Functions

A one to one function pair E(k, x) from set X to set Y, and E(k^{-1}, y) from Y to X is called an encryption and decryption function pair, when there exists element k^{-1} of set K^{-1} for every k in set K, and E(k^{-1}, y) is an inverse function of E(k, x). Here, X is a set of plain data x to be encrypted, Y is a set of encrypted data y = E(k, x), and k and k^{-1} are encryption and decryption keys, respectively. Namely function E(k, x) transforms (encrypts) plain data x in set X into encrypted data y = E(k, x) in set Y, and function E(k^{-1}, y) transforms (decrypts) encrypted data y = E(k, x) in Y to plain data x in X, as shown in Figure 1 (Amoroso, 1994; Katz, 2007; Koblitz, 1994: Pieprzyk, 2003; Trappe, 2005; Vaudenay, 2006).

To disable unauthorized entities to know x from its encrypted form E(k, x), and to enable authorized entities to easily calculate E(k, x) and

x from x and E(k, x), respectively, E(k, x) and E(k^{-1}, y) are defined so that entities that do not know k or k^{-1} cannot easily calculate E(k, x) from x or calculate x from E(k, x) even they know the encryption or the decryption function, and at the same time, entities that know k or k^{-1} can easily calculate E(k, x) or x from x or E(k, x), respectively. Therefore, it is not necessary to conceal the form of the encryption function even from unauthorized entities if encryption key k and decryption key k^{-1} are not known to them, and usually encryption and decryption functions are publicly disclosed. In the communication example in the introduction, when P calculates E(k, M) from M and sends E(k, M) instead of M while being informed of k by Q in advance, only Q that knows k^{-1} can reconstruct M from E(k, M). Therefore, P can send M to Q, while disabling other entity R to understand the meaning of M even if R eavesdrops on it. Here, usually the size of key k is much smaller than message M; therefore Q can securely inform P of k efficiently and economically even through a highly guarded secure communication channel, which may be expensive and inefficient, and after receiving k from Q, P can also securely send message M to Q efficiently and economically even if its volume is large without using the highly guarded communication channel while encrypting M by using k. In the remainder of this book, the word encryption algorithm is used also to represent an encryption and decryption algorithm pair, when there is no confusion.

When encryption algorithms are implemented in computer systems, both sets X and Y consist of all possible bit strings of length less than or equal to L (L is the finite number). Theoretically, it is not necessary to limit length of bit strings to be encrypted; however in physical computer systems, their length is limited at the value determined by their underlying system designs.

Homomorphic, Probabilistic, Commutative, and Verifiable Encryption Functions

Because bit strings are considered as integers, addition, multiplication and other operations can be defined on sets X and Y in Figure 1, i.e. a set of plain data to be encrypted and a set of encrypted data. Provided that operation ^ (^ is addition or multiplication for example) is defined in sets X and Y, encryption function E(k, x) is called homomorphic under the operation ^, when the relation E(k, x_1^x_2) = E(k, x_1)^E(k, x_2) is satisfied for arbitrary x_1 and x_2 in X. Apparently decryption function E(k^{-1}, y) corresponding to homomorphic encryption function E(k, x) also satisfies the relation E(k^{-1}, y_1^y_2) = E(k^{-1}, y_1)^E(k^{-1}, y_2) for arbitrary y_1 and y_2 in Y; namely, when it is assumed that E(k, x_1) = y_1 and E(k, x_2) = y_2, because y_1^y_2 = E(k, x_1)^E(k, x_2) = E(k, x_1^x_2) is decrypted into x_1^x_2, relation E(k^{-1}, y_1^y_2) = E(k^{-1}, y_1) ^ E(k^{-1}, y_2) is also satisfied. In the following, encryption algorithms that are homomrphic under addition or multiplication are called additive or multiplicative, respectively.

The additive and multiplicative properties play important roles in developing anonymous systems. One of the important operations in anonymous systems is to calculate the sum of the data that are given in their encrypted forms. When encryption algorithms are additive, the sum of the decrypted data can be calculated by decrypting the sum of encrypted data without decrypting individual data, i.e. many cumbersome decryption operations can be removed. More importantly, entities can calculate sums of the data without knowing individual data that may include privacies of the data owners.

Other features of encryption algorithms that are important in developing anonymous applications are probabilistic, commutative, and verifiable properties. An encryption algorithm is called probabilistic when bit string M is transformed into different bit strings in different encryptions even if the same encryption key is used. For example, let entity V be a voter in an electronic voting system, where V encrypts its vote by using an encryption key of the voting authority to conceal its decision. However, if the encryption function is not probabilistic other voters can identify V's decision easily provided that candidates are publicly announced in advance. Because candidate C selected by voter V is encrypted into the same form in every encryption, from the encrypted vote of V, other voters who had selected C can easily know that V also had selected C. Probabilistic encryption algorithms can solve this kind of problems.

Here, any encryption algorithm can have the probabilistic feature by mixing information to be encrypted with random factors. If bit string M is encrypted while being accompanied by secret random bit string r, e.g. $M\|r$ is encrypted instead of M ($M\|r$ is the concatenation of bit strings M and r, i.e. when M= 01001100 and r = 1011, $M\|r$ is bit string 010011001011), individual encrypted forms of M differ each other, provided that r is changed in every encryption. Nevertheless, each encrypted form of M can be decrypted successfully, by decrypting the encrypted form into $M\|r$, and by removing r from it. Although probabilistic encryption functions seem not one to one mappings, when the random factors are taken into account (in the above example random bit string r), they are still one to one.

A probabilistic encryption function E(k, x) may not satisfy the exact relation E(k, x_1^x_2) = E(k, x_1)^E(k, x_2) even if E(k, x_1)^E(k, x_2) is decrypted into x_1^x_2 for arbitrary x_1 and x_2 in set X, because it encrypts a same bit string into different forms. However, the important thing of homomorphic encryption function E(k, x) is not that any encrypted form of x_1^x_2 exactly coincides with a given instance of E(k, x_1)^E(k, x_2), it is that all instances of encrypted form E(k, x_1)^E(k, x_2) are decrypted into x_1^x_2 for any x_1 and x_2 in X. Therefore, to treat probabilistic encryption functions, the definition of homomorphic encryption functions must be relaxed. In the relaxed definition, an encryption function E(k, x) is homomorphic under operation ^ when E(k, x_1)^E(k, x_2) is decrypted into x_1^x_2 for any x_1 and x_2 in X. It must be noted that although E(k, $x_1\|r_1$)^E(k, $x_2\|r_2$) = E(k, ($x_1\|r_1$)^($x_2\|r_2$)) is satisfied when encryption function E(k, x) is homomorhic, there are cases where additional operations are required to decrypt E(k, $x_1\|r_1$)^E(k, $x_2\|r_2$) to x_1^x_2. For example, when ^ is the multiplication E(k, $x_1\|r_1$)^E(k, $x_2\|r_2$) is decrypted to ($x_1\|r_1$)^($x_2\|r_2$), but lengths of bit strings x_1 and x_2 must be taken into account to extract x_1^x_2 from ($x_1\|r_1$)^($x_2\|r_2$).

Regarding the commutative property, when bit string M is encrypted repeatedly by multiple entities S_1, S_2, ---, S_Q while applying their encryption keys k_1, k_2, ---, k_Q in this order, M is encrypted into E(k_Q, E(k_{Q-1}, --- E(k_2, E(k_1, M)) ---)) = E(k_*, M) as shown in Figure 2, and usually M is reconstructed from E(k_*, M) only when E(k_*, M) is repeatedly decrypted by applying decryption keys in the order k_Q^{-1}, k_{Q-1}^{-1}, ---, k_1^{-1}. Here, {k_q, k_q^{-1}} is a pair of encryption and decryption keys of entity S_q. Namely, E(k_*, M) can be decrypted as E(k_1^{-1}, E(k_2^{-1}, --- E(k_{Q-1}^{-1}, E(k_Q^{-1}, E(k_*, M))) ---)) = M. However, when the encryption functions are commutative, E(k_*, M) can be decrypted into M regardless of the order of encryption and decryption key applications. In the followings, encryption and decryption processes shown in Figure 2 are called re-encryption and re-decryption, or repeated encryption and repeated-decryption, respectively.

One of important objectives of the re-encryption scheme is to disable entities other than P that owns bit string M to know M that they are going to encrypt. To achieve this, a sequence of entities S_1, S_2, ---, S_Q (they are different from P) repeatedly encrypt M to E(k_*, M) = E(k_Q, E(k_{Q-1}, ---, E(k_1, M) ---)), so that no one can calculate M from E(k_*, M) unless all the entities conspire. Namely, there is no entity that knows all decryptions keys k_1^{-1}, k_2^{-1}, ---, k_Q^{-1}. However, S_1 that receives M directly from P easily can know P's secret M, therefore P asks the entities to encrypt M while

Figure 2. Re-encryption process

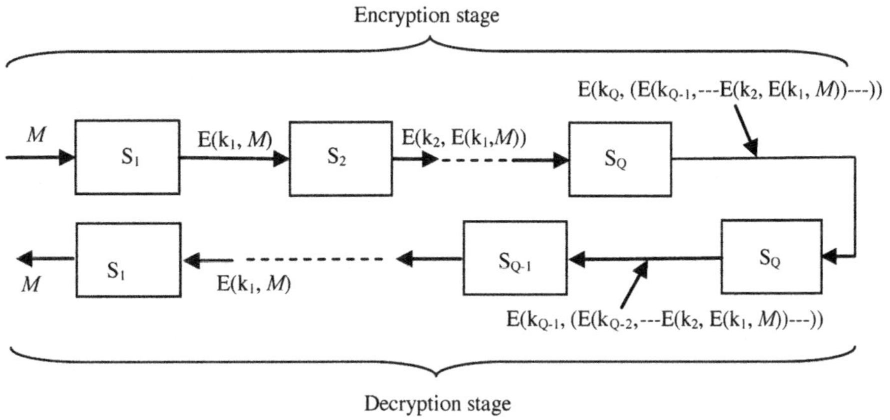

encrypting M to E(p, M) by its encryption key p. Then, S_1, S_2, ---, S_Q repeatedly encrypt E(p, M) to E(k_Q, E(k_{Q-1}, ---, E(k_1, E(p, M)) ---)) to be decrypted to E(k_Q, ---, E(k_1, M) ---)) by P itself, and consequently no one except P can know P's secret M unless all S_1, S_2, ---, S_Q conspire. Here, it must be noted that P cannot decrypt E(k_Q, ---, E(k_1, E(p, M)) ---)) to E(k_*, M) if the encryption functions are not commutative.

Verifiability is also important in anonymous systems. It is the property of encryption algorithms that enables owners of bit strings (or their representatives) to convince themselves the correctness of encrypted forms of their bit strings that are calculated by others while using encryption keys unknown to the owners. For example in an electronic voting system, to preserve its privacy each voter may ask an election authority to encrypt its vote without knowing the encryption key of the authority. Therefore, voters must verify the correctness of the authority's encryptions without knowing either the encryption or the decryption key of the authority. Provided that the encryption algorithm is not probabilistic, when the disclosure of the encryption key is possible (it is possible when an asymmetric key encryption algorithm is used as discussed in the next subsection), it is trivial i.e. voters can verify the correctness of the encryptions by simply encrypting their votes again by themselves to compare the results with the ones encrypted by the authority. But, in cases where encryption keys cannot be disclosed, verifying the correctness of encryptions is not trivial.

Homomorphic encryption functions solve this problem as follow. Let P be an entity that asks Q to encrypt its bit string M to E(q, M) by using encryption key q owned by Q and unknown to P. To convince P the honest encryption of Q, firstly, Q registers a set of test bit strings $\{T_1, T_2, ---, T_m\}$ and their encrypted forms {E(q, T_1), E(q, T_2), ---, E(q, T_m)} in advance, and when P receives $\underline{M}$ as the value of E(q, M), the encrypted form of M, P calculates $test$ = E(q, T_1)^{r1}E(q, T_2)^{r2}---E(q, T_m)$^{rm}\underline{M}^{r}$, where r_1, r_2,---, r_m, r are bit strings (integers) secret of P, and it is assumed that E(q, x) is homomorphic under multiplication. Then, P asks Q to decrypt $\underline{test}$ by Q's decryption key q^{-1}, and determines that $\underline{M}$ is the correct encrypted form, i.e. $\underline{M}$ = E(q, M), when the decryption result coincides with $test$ = $T_1^{r1}T_2^{r2}$---$T_m^{rm}M^{r}$. Because Q does not know r_1, r_2,---, r_m, r, it cannot calculate $test$ from $\underline{test}$, when it encrypt M to $\underline{M}$ dishonestly. On the other hand, when $\underline{M}$ = E(q, M), Q can calculate $test$ easily by simply decrypting $\underline{test}$ without knowing r_1, r_2,---, r_m, r, i.e. E(q^{-1}, $\underline{test}$) = E(q^{-1}, E(q, T_1^{r1}))---E(q^{-1}, E(q, T_m^{rm}))E(q^{-1}, E(q, M^{r})) = T_1^{r1}---$T_m^{rm}M^{r}$. Verification of bit strings encrypted by additive encryption functions also can be carried out in the same way.

Classification of Encryption Algorithms

There are 2 kinds of encryption algorithms; they are symmetric key and asymmetric key encryption algorithms. When symmetric key encryption algorithms are used, anyone can easily calculate decryption key k^{-1} from encryption key k and vice versa; i.e. an entity that knows encryption key k can decrypt the bit string encrypted by k, therefore k and k^{-1} can be considered as the same. On the other hand when asymmetric key encryption algorithms are used, it is practically impossible to calculate k^{-1} from k (and to calculate k from k^{-1}), and consequently, k and k^{-1} are considered different.

Asymmetric key encryption algorithms have advantages over symmetric ones at least in terms of the following 3 aspects. Firstly, asymmetric key encryption algorithms can reduce cumbersome key exchanging processes between entities that share secrets. When entity P wants to send message *M* to entity Q while encrypting *M* to protect it from wiretappings, P must know encryption key k that corresponds to decryption key k^{-1} of Q. Therefore, Q informs P of k in advance through a secure communication channel, e.g. through an isolated private channel; and usually these secure channels are slow to exchange information and also expensive to develop and maintain them, and as a consequence key exchanging processes become complicated, slow and expensive. However, when an asymmetric key encryption algorithm is used, because it is practically impossible to calculate k^{-1} from k, Q can send k to P through a usual fast and inexpensive channel without being afraid that someone eavesdrops on it. Even if k is known by other entities, they cannot calculate k^{-1} from k in practical time. While exploiting this property, in communication systems based on asymmetric key encryptions, usually encryption keys of entities are not protected, i.e. they are publicly disclosed; therefore asymmetric key encryption algorithms are frequently called public key encryption algorithms. On the other hand symmetric key algorithms are called secret key encryption algorithms. Then, when asymmetric key encryption algorithms are used, expensive and complicated key exchanging processes can be simplified. This is a significant advantage of asymmetric key encryption algorithms. Nevertheless symmetric key encryption functions play important roles in anonymous systems, i.e. in anonymous systems, frequently same entities carry out encryptions and decryptions, and key exchanging processes are not necessary from the beginning.

The other advantage of asymmetric key encryption algorithms is that many existing asymmetric key encryption algorithms are much more secure than symmetric ones, more intuitively, calculating *M* from E(k, *M*) without knowing decryption key k^{-1} is much more difficult for asymmetric key encryption algorithms than for symmetric ones. Also, obviously asymmetric key encryption algorithms have an advantage regarding the verifiability. Because encryption keys are publicly disclosed, anyone can confirm the correctness of encryptions, provided that the algorithm is not probabilistic (when the algorithm is probabilistic, only entities that know the random factors used in the encryptions can confirm the correctness except cases where the decryption key is known). On the other hand, an advantage of symmetric key encryption algorithms is they require much less computations. Generally, asymmetric key encryption algorithms require more computations for both encryptions and decryptions than symmetric ones do.

In developing computer and information systems, encryption algorithms must be chosen while considering advantages and disadvantages of them for satisfying various requirements of the systems. Among them, security strength, operability, and efficiency are important. Firstly as the most fundamental requirement, encryption and decryption algorithms must be secure enough, in other words, it must be difficult enough to decrypt data that are encrypted by the algorithms without knowing the decryption keys. However, to apply algorithms to real systems, they must be not only secure but also practical, i.e. they should be operable and efficient. Regarding the operability and efficiency, encryption key exchanging processes must be simple enough, and computation volumes required for data encryptions and decryptions must be small enough, respectively. Encryption algorithms that require a lot of efforts for exchanging keys are not practical even they are secure enough, also algorithms that require a lot of time for encryptions and decryptions cannot be used in the real world applications. However, it must be noted that especially in anonymous systems there are cases where key exchanging is not necessary from the beginning, e.g. as discussed already, there are applications in which data are both encrypted and decrypted by same entities, and also there are cases where time consuming encryption and decryption processes are allowed. For example, even complicated algorithms can work efficiently for small volume of information, and in several cases, encryptions and decryptions of small portion of information satisfy given security requirements even the volume of the whole information is extremely large.

According to the above discussions, generally, symmetric key encryption algorithms are efficient but not so secure or operable; on the other hand, asymmetric key encryption algorithms are secure and operable, but not so efficient. A hybrid approach mixes the advantages of symmetric and asymmetric key encryption algorithms to establish secure, operable and efficient encryptions. In a communication system based on the mixed approach, keys of symmetric key encryption algorithms are exchanged by using asymmetric key encryption algorithms, and messages themselves are exchanged by using symmetric key encryption algorithms, both through usual inexpensive and efficient communication channels. Namely, entities can exchange encryption keys securely while simplifying cumbersome key exchanging processes by exploiting asymmetric key encryption algorithms; although asymmetric key encryption algorithms are used, the entities can maintain the efficiency because volumes of encryption keys are not so large. Also they can exchange large volume of messages efficiently while exploiting symmetric key encryption algorithms. Although symmetric key encryption algorithms are not secure enough as asymmetric ones, they can satisfy the security requirements of the message themselves by frequently changing encryption keys.

SYMMETRIC KEY ENCRYPTION ALGORITHMS

Onetime Pad

One of the most simple symmetric key encryption algorithms is onetime pad (Kahn, 1996). Encryption keys of onetime pad are random secret bit strings that have the same lengths as bit strings to be encrypted, i.e. onetime pad encrypts bit string M by calculating bitwise XOR of M and key P, a random secret bit string of the same length as M, and decrypts the encrypted bit string by calculating bitwise XOR of the encrypted bit string and same key P as shown in Equation (1). Therefore, encryption and decryption keys are exactly the same. For example, when $M = \{0, 0, 1, 1, 0, 1, 0, 1\}$ and $P = \{1, 0, 0, 1, 1, 0, 1, 1\}$, the encrypted form of M is $M \oplus P = \{0, 0, 1, 1, 0, 1, 0, 1\} \oplus \{1, 0, 0, 1, 1, 0, 1, 1\} = \{1, 0, 1, 0, 1, 1, 1, 0\}$, and the decrypted form of $M \oplus P$ is $(M \oplus P) \oplus P = \{1, 0, 1, 0, 1, 1, 1, 0\} \oplus \{1, 0, 0, 1, 1, 0, 1, 1\} = \{0, 0, 1, 1, 0, 1, 0, 1\}$.

$$E(P, M) = P \oplus M,$$

$$E(P^{-1}, E(P, M)) = E(P, E(P, M)) = P \oplus (P \oplus M) = M \quad (1)$$

Provided that the length of bit strings M and P is n, all possible n-bits bit strings can be generated from equation $M \oplus P$ by changing values of

P, therefore for an entity, which does not know P, all meaningful bit strings of length n have the equal possibility to be a decrypted form of E(P, M). In other words, E(P, M) does not provide entities that do not know P with any information about M. An apparent advantage of onetime pad is its efficiency, i.e. computations required for encryptions and decryptions are only simple bit-wise XOR calculations. Its commutative feature is the other advantage. When M is encrypted repeatedly to $\underline{M}$ = E(P_N, E(P_{N-1}, ---, E(P_1, M) ---)) = (--- (($M \oplus P_1$)$\oplus P_2$)$\oplus$ ---)$\oplus P_N$ by using multiple keys P_1, P_2, ---, P_N, M can be decrypted into M regardless of the order in which the decryption keys are applied, e.g. $\underline{M}$ can be decrypted by either way ((--- (($M \oplus P_1$)$\oplus$---)$\oplus P_8$)$\oplus P_5$ or ((--- (($M \oplus P_8$)$\oplus$ ---)$\oplus P_5$)$\oplus P_1$.

A serious drawback of onetime pad is that it is weak against plain text attacks. When a bit string and its encrypted form pair {M, E(P, M)} is known, anyone can calculate key P easily by the simple calculation, i.e. $M \oplus$E(P, M) reveals P. In the above example, bitwise XOR of the original bit string {0, 0, 1, 1, 0, 1, 0, 1} and the encrypted bit string {1, 0, 1, 0, 1, 1, 1, 0} coincides with key {1, 0, 0, 1, 1, 0, 1, 1}, i.e. {0, 0, 1, 1, 0, 1, 0, 1} $\oplus$ {1, 0, 1, 0, 1, 1, 1, 0} = {1, 0, 0, 1, 1, 0, 1, 1}. Therefore, key P cannot be used repeatedly. When an entity knows pair {M, E(P, M)} by chance, it can decrypt all encrypted forms if same P is used repeatedly. The same key cannot be used for encrypting long bit strings either, i.e. when a bit string of length s is divided into a sequence of substrings of length q (here, q is the length of keys, and q < s), different keys must be applied to different substrings; if the same key is applied to these substrings, encryption results of individual substrings become good suggestions to calculate the key. Another drawback of onetime pad is that key lengths are prone to being long. They must be strictly equal to that of the bit strings to be encrypted. Therefore, onetime pad is not appropriate for exchanging confidential messages. To use onetime pad for exchanging messages, senders and receivers of messages must exchange keys before every message transfer. This means that the receiver must send secret bit strings (keys) to the sender through secure channels for every message, moreover the length of these secret bit strings are equal to that of the messages the sender wants to send. Obviously it is more efficient to send the original messages directly through secure channels, instead of sending encryption keys. Efforts required to securely sending keys and messages are totally the same.

In conclusion, onetime pad is not secure or operable for sharing secrets among multiple entities, because it is weak against plain text attacks and entities must exchange long encryption keys while frequently changing them. However, in applications where same entities encrypt and decrypt bit strings, it is secure, efficient, operable and also commutative. Therefore, despite of the above serious drawbacks about security strength and operability, onetime pad plays important roles in anonymous systems.

Permutation and Substitution

Typical symmetric key encryption algorithms are constructed as the combinations of permutation and substitution operations. A permutation operation on a given bit string M changes positions of individual bits in bit string M. For example, permutation operation P, which exchanges the 1st and the 6th bit positions with the 3rd and the 7th positions of given bit strings of length 8, transforms 8 bits bit string M = {0, 0, 1, 1, 0, 1, 0, 1} into 8 bits bit string M^* = {1, 0, 0, 1, 0, 0, 1, 1}. A substitution operation maps a bit string of length n_1 to that of length n_2, according to the rule defined in advance. When substitution operation

Q that transforms 2-bits bit strings {0, 0}, {0, 1}, {1, 0} and {1, 1} into 3-bits bit strings {1, 0, 1}, {0, 1, 0}, {1, 0, 0} and {0, 0, 1}, respectively, is applied to 8-bits bit string M^*, firstly M^* is divided into four 2-bits substrings, i.e. {1, 0}, {0,1}, {0, 0}, {1, 1}, then individual substrings are transformed into 3-bits bit strings according to the above substitution rules, and finally the transformed substrings {1, 0, 0}, {0, 1, 0}, {1, 0, 1}, {0, 0, 1} are combined into a 12-bits bit string M^{**} = {1, 0, 0, 0, 1, 0, 1, 0, 1, 0, 0, 1}. Therefore, when permutation operation P and substitution operation Q are combined, 8-bits bit string M = {0, 0, 1, 1, 0, 1, 0, 1} is encrypted into 12-bits bit string M^{**} = {1, 0, 0, 0, 1, 0, 1, 0, 1, 0, 0, 1}.

For an entity that knows permutation and substitution rules, it is easy to reconstruct original bit strings from given permuted and substituted bit strings. However, it is difficult for entities that do not know the permutation or substitution rules. Permutation and substitution based encryption algorithms, encrypt bit strings by applying these 2 operations iteratively. Therefore, the encryption and decryption keys of this type of algorithms are the permutation and substitution rules, and the encryption and the decryption keys can be considered same. The well known encryption algorithm DES (Data Encryption Standard) (FIPS, 1977) is constructed based on permutation and substitution operations.

About the performance of this type of algorithms, an advantage is they do not require much computation. However, they are not secure as modern asymmetric key encryption algorithms discussed in the next section are, and because encryption keys must be kept confidential among secret sharing entities they are not so operable. They are not verifiable either, and do not have any distinctive feature as commutative property of onetime pad. Therefore, there is not a positive reason to use permutation and substitution based algorithms in anonymous systems, except the cases where specific constraints exist.

ASYMMETRIC KEY ENCRYPTION ALGORITHMS

Asymmetric key encryption and decryption algorithms use pairs of different keys, the ones for encryptions and the others for decryptions. Usually, decryption keys are secrets of key owners, but encryption keys are publicly disclosed. Therefore encryption and decryption keys are also called public and private or secret keys, respectively. As the word "public" implies, anyone can generate encrypted forms of given bit strings, however, as the word "private/secret" implies, only entities that know the decryption keys can decrypt them. Then, cumbersome and expensive key exchanging processes between entities that are sharing information can be removed.

Two typical asymmetric encryption key algorithms are RSA and ElGamal encryptions. Primitive operations included in these algorithms, are multiplications and divisions of integers (bit strings). However, different from usual arithmetic calculations, all operations are carried out based on modulo arithmetic. Here, $x_{\mathrm{mod\,p}} = m$, when integer x satisfies relation $x = n\mathrm{p} + m$ for some non-negative integers n and m (< p), and $(x+y)_{\mathrm{mod\,p}}$, $(xy)_{\mathrm{mod\,p}}$ and $(x/y)_{\mathrm{mod\,p}}$ can be calculated as $x_{\mathrm{mod\,p}}+y_{\mathrm{mod\,p}}$, $x_{\mathrm{mod\,p}}y_{\mathrm{mod\,p}}$ and $x_{\mathrm{mod\,p}}/y_{\mathrm{mod\,p}}$, respectively. It must be noted that results of divisions under modulo arithmetic are always integers, namely, $(x/y)_{\mathrm{mod\,p}}$ is integer c (< p) that satisfies relation $cy = n\mathrm{p} + x$. Therefore, to divide x by y, integer c and n that satisfy relation $cy = n\mathrm{p} + x$ must be found. This calculation can be carried out efficiently by exploiting well known Euclidean algorithm (Menezes, 1996). In the remainder of this book, modulo notations are omitted when confusions can be avoided.

RSA

RSA is the combination of initials of Rivest, Shamir and Adelman the inventors of the algorithm (Rivest, 1978). For appropriately selected integer p, there are pairs of integers {e, d} that satisfy relation $(M^e)^d{}_{\text{mod p}} = M^{ed}{}_{\text{mod p}} = M$ for any integer $M (0 \leq M < p)$. Also, when p is large enough (e.g. when p is about 2^{1000}), it is practically impossible to calculate M from M^e for entities that do not know d. Therefore, when M is an original bit string, M^e can be considered as its encrypted form, and e and d correspond to encryption and decryption keys, respectively. For prime number p, integer pair {e, d} satisfies the above relation when ed $_{\text{mod(p-1)}}$ = 1. For example when p is 17, relation $(x^3)^{11} = x$ is satisfied for any integer x $(1 \leq x < 17)$; therefore, {3, 11} can be used as an encryption and a decryption key pair. Fortunately, when p is a product of 2 different sufficiently large prime numbers v and w (i.e. when p = vw), an integer pair {e, d} also has the above property provided that the pair satisfies relation $ed_{\text{mod (v-1)(w-1)}} = 1$. The important thing is that although calculating d from e (and p) is not so difficult when v and w are given, it is practically impossible unless both v and w are known, in other words, it is practically impossible to decompose the given large integer p into a product of 2 prime numbers v and w. Therefore, provided that person Q keeps 2 prime numbers v and w as its secrets, Q can disclose encryption key e while maintaining decryption key d as its secret. Then, Q who wants to receive messages from another person P can inform P of key e by simply disclosing it to the public without any protection.

Based on the above settings, RSA encrypts bit string M by public encryption key e into E(e, M) = $M^e{}_{\text{mod p}}$, and decrypts E(e, M) by secret decryption key d as E(d, E(e, M)) = $(E(e, M))^d = M^{ed}{}_{\text{mod p}}$ = $M_{\text{mod p}}$, namely $E(e^{-1}, y) = E(d, y)$. To calculate M from E(e, M) is practically impossible when d is not known. To decrypt E(e, M), an entity that does not know d must multiply m^e by m^e itself d times while examining the results whether they are meaningful or not. For example, if d is set to about 2^{1000}, 2^{1000} times of multiplications must be carried out in the worst case. However, when keys are known, encryption and decryption processes are rather easy. When e or d is known, times of multiplication can be reduced to the order of $(\log_2 e)^2$ or $(\log_2 d)^2$, e.g. 1000^2 when e or d $\approx 2^{1000}$. For example, when it is known that the key is 2^{1000}, $x^{2\exp(1000)}$ can be obtained by calculating x^2, $(x^2)^2 = x^4$, $(x^4)^2 = x^8$, ---.

It must be noted that in order to maintain RSA secure enough, only a single encryption and decryption key pair can be used for single prime number pair {v, w} that is given for constructing the base of modulo arithmetic. When 2 public and secret key pairs $\{e_1, d_1\}$ and $\{e_2, d_2\}$ are used for a single prime number pair {v, w}, for an entity that knows $\{e_1, d_1\}$, it is straightforward to calculate d_2 from publicly known e_2 because relations $(e_1d_1)_{\text{mod x}} = 1$ and $(e_2d_2)_{\text{mod x}} = 1$ are satisfied for integer x = (u-1)(w-1), i.e. it is easy to estimate x = (u-1)(w-1) from $(e_1d_1)_{\text{mod x}} = 1$, and d_2 can be calculated as $d_2 = (1/e_2)_{\text{mod(u-1)(w-1)}}$. However, when encryption keys (public keys) are not disclosed to others, multiple key pairs can be used even for single prime number pair {v, w}. Entities that do not know e_2, cannot calculate d_2 from $\{e_1, d_1\}$ even they know relation $(e_1d_1)_{\text{mod (u-1)(w-1)}} = (e_2d_2)_{\text{mod (u-1)(w-1)}}$.

Advantages of RSA are that not only it excludes cumbersome encryption key exchanging processes between entities that share information, but also it is much more secure than symmetric key encryption algorithms; according to the above discussion, when key is set to about 2^{1000}, in the worst case about 2^{1000} times of multiplications are necessary to break the encryption algorithm. Therefore, RSA is secure and operable. RSA is also verifiable; because encryption keys can be disclosed to the public, any entity can confirm the correctness of encryptions. A disadvantage of RSA is the large computation volume. Even for entities that know keys, encryption and decryption processes require many times of multiplications of long bit strings. Therefore, RSA is practical when the volume of information to be encrypted is small; however times required for encryptions and decryptions are not negligible when the volume of the information is large.

As a component of anonymous security, RSA has another advantageous feature; that is RSA is homomorphic (multiplicative), i.e. it preserves multiplications. Encrypted forms of M_1, M_2 and M_1M_2 are E(e, M_1) = M_1^e, E(e, M_2) = M_2^e and E(e, M_1M_2) = $(M_1M_2)^e$, respectively, and relation E(e, M_1)E(e, M_2) = $M_1^eM_2^e$ = $(M_1M_2)^e$ = E(e, M_1M_2) holds. Therefore, RSA encryption functions can be made verifiable even when encryption keys are not publicly disclosed. It must be noted that there exists function $f(x)$ that satisfies relation $f(M_1)f(M_2)$ = $f(M_1+M_2)$. For example, when function $f(M)$ is defined as $f(M) = B^M{}_{\mathrm{mod}\ p}$, $f(M_1+M_2)$ is represented as the product of 2 numbers $f(M_1) = (B^{M1})_{\mathrm{mod}\ p}$ and $f(M_2) = B^{M2}{}_{\mathrm{mod}\ p}$ (i.e. $B^{M1+M2}{}_{\mathrm{mod}\ p} = B^{M1}B^{M2}{}_{\mathrm{mod}\ p}$). In the above, B is a constant integer that satisfies relation $B^y{}_{\mathrm{mod}\ p} = 1$ only for $y > X$, where, X is the maximum integer to be encrypted. Therefore the product of encrypted forms of B^{M1} and B^{M2} is decrypted to B^{M1+M2}, in other words, E(e, $f(M_1)$) E(e, $f(M_2)$) = E(e, B^{M1})E(e, B^{M2}) = E(e, $B^{M1}B^{M2}$) = E(e, B^{M1+M2}) = E(e, $f(M_1+M_2)$). Then, when E(e, $f(x)$) is considered as encryption function E'(e, x), the product of encrypted forms E'(e, x) and E'(e, y) is decrypted to $x+y$, and sometimes this property is also called additive.

Here, it is easy for entities that know decryption key d to decrypt E'(e, x) = E(e, B^x) to x, i.e. firstly E'(e, x) is decrypted to y, and x that satisfies $B^x{}_{\mathrm{mod}\ p} = y$ is found from a look up table, where if the maximum integer X to be encrypted is known in advance, the size of the look up table also can be suppressed. Namely, it is enough for the look up table to maintain values {B^1, B^2, ---, B^X}. Also, for a given integer $y \in$ {B^1, B^2, ---, B^X}, integer x that satisfies $B^x = y$ can be found quickly by binary search when {B^1, B^2, ---, B^X} are arranged in the descending or the ascending order in the table. But it must be noted that encryption function E(e, x) must have probabilistic feature when a finite set of bit strings to be encrypted is known in advance. For example, when it is known that encrypted forms are decrypted to integer x ($0 \leq x \leq X$), any entity can know the decrypted value of E'(e, x) by encrypting all non-negative integers that do not exceed X by the publicly known encryption key.

About the commutative property, RSA is not commutative, when individual encryptions are carried out based on different modulo arithmetic. Namely, if p_1 and p_2 are different, $(x^{e1}{}_{\mathrm{mod}\ p1})^{e2}{}_{\mathrm{mod}\ p2}$ can be decrypted to x only when keys d_2 and d_1 are applied in this order, i.e. $(x^{e1}{}_{\mathrm{mod}\ p1})^{e2d2}{}_{\mathrm{mod}\ p2} = x^{e1}{}_{\mathrm{mod}\ p1}$, and $(x^{e1})^{d1}{}_{\mathrm{mod}\ p1} = x_{\mathrm{mod}\ p1}$. Here, {$e_j$, d_j} is an encryption and decryption key pair for j = 1 and 2, and it is assumed that p_2 is larger than p_1 of course. However, when individual encryptions are carried out based on the same modulo arithmetic, RSA becomes commutative. Namely, E(e_2, E(e_1, x)) = $(x^{e1}{}_{\mathrm{mod}\ p})^{e2}{}_{\mathrm{mod}\ p} = x^{e1e2}{}_{\mathrm{mod}\ p}$ can be decrypted into x regardless of the decryption key application orders; x can be calculated from E(e_2, E(e_1, x)) by either way, i.e. $((x^{e1e2})^{d1})^{d2} = x$, or $((x^{e1e2})^{d2})^{d1} = x$. Because multiple public keys enable calculation of secret keys as discussed before, commutative property can be exploited only when data are encrypted by multiple public keys of a single entity, or when all encryption keys are kept as secrets of individual key owners.

Commutative and homomorphic properties of the above RSA encryption function enable entities to generate numbers that are secret from all entities as follows. In the following, it is assumed that multiple entities P_1, P_2, ---, P_N have their encryption and decryption key pairs {e_1, d_1}, {e_2, d_2}, --- {e_N, d_N}, and they share the same modulo arithmetic p to make encryption algorithms commutative and homomorphic. Also each encryption key e_j is kept as P_j's secret to protect its decryption key d_j from other entities. Under these assumptions firstly, individual independent entities P_1, P_2, ---, P_N generate their secret numbers r_1, r_2, ---, r_N and each entity P_j encrypts r_j by its encryption key e_j to r_j^{ej}, after that P_j asks other entities to repeatedly encrypt r_j^{ej} to E(e_*, r_j) = E(e_N, E(e_{N-1}, --- E(e_1, r_j))) = $r_j^{e1e2\text{---}eN}$ by their encryption keys e_1, e_2, ---, e_{j-1}, e_{j+1}, ---, e_N. Then, because of homomorphic property, the product of $E(e_*, r_1)$, $E(e_*, r_2)$, ---, $E(e_*, r_N)$ coincides with $E(e_*, r_1r_2\text{---}r_N)$, the repeatedly encrypted form of $r_1r_2\text{---}r_N$. Here, each P_j knows only its secret bit string r_j, therefore, no one can know the value of $R = r_1r_2\text{---}r_N$ until all P_1, P_2, ---, P_N agree to decrypt $E(e_*, r_1r_2\text{---}r_N)$ or to disclose their secret numbers r_1, r_2, ---, r_N. This mechanism plays important roles in later chapters.

ElGamal

In an ElGamal encryption algorithm, a public encryption key is pair $\{Y, g\}$ and a secret decryption key is integer X that satisfy Equation (2), and bit string M is encrypted and decrypted as shown in Equation (3) and (4), respectively (Elgamal, 1985).

$$Y = g^X{}_{\text{mod p}} \quad (2)$$

$$E(\{Y, g\}, M) = \{g^k{}_{\text{mod p}}, MY^k{}_{\text{mod p}}\} = \{g_*, M_*\} \quad (3)$$

$$E(X, \{g_*, M_*\}) = M_*/g_*{}^X{}_{\text{mod p}} \quad (4)$$

Here, p is a sufficiently large prime number (bit string), and g is a number that satisfies relation $g^z{}_{\text{mod p}} = 1$ only for $z = (p - 1)$ (any number b satisfies $b^{(p-1)} = 1$). k is a secret random number selected by an entity that encrypts the bit string. From Equation (2) and (3), $M_* = MY^k = Mg^{kX}$, therefore, an entity that knows secret key X can decrypt $E(\{Y, g\}, M)$ into M successfully by calculating $Mg^{kX}/g_*{}^X = Mg^{kX}/g^{kX} = M$. ElGamal encryption algorithms are constructed based on the fact that it is difficult to calculate logarithms of given integers (this fact is referred as the difficulty of discrete logarithm problems). In this case it is practically impossible to know X even when $Y = g^X{}_{\text{mod p}}$, g and p are disclosed if p is sufficiently large.

ElGamal encryption algorithms are homomorphic under multiplication as same as RSA. Because $E(\{Y, g\}, M_1) = \{g^k, M_1Y^k\}$ and $E(\{Y, g\}, M_2) = \{g^h, M_2Y^h\}$, relation $E(\{Y, g\}, M_1)E(\{Y, g\}, M_2) = \{g^{k+h}, (M_1M_2)Y^{k+h}\}$ holds; and $\{g^{k+h}, (M_1M_2)Y^{k+h}\}$ is just $E(\{Y, g\}, M_1M_2)$. As same as RSA, ElGamal can be made satisfy also relation $E(\{Y, g\}, M_1)E(\{Y, g\}, M_2) = E(\{Y, g\}, M_1+M_2)$ by defining the encrypted and decrypted forms of M as in equations (5 - 7) while choosing appropriate constant integer B (provided that X is the maximum integer to be encrypted, integer B must be defined so that $B^y = 1$ is satisfied only when $y >$ X), i.e. the encrypted form of the addition of M_1 and M_2 coincides with the product of 2 encrypted forms $E(\{Y, g\}, M_1)$ and $E(\{Y, g\}, M_2)$. Because $E(\{Y, g\}, M_1) = \{g^k, B^{M1}Y^k\}$ and $E(\{Y, g\}, M_2) = \{g^h, B^{M2}Y^h\}$, when they are multiplied, the result is equal to $\{g^{k+h}, B^{M1+M2}Y^{k+h}\}$, and this is decrypted to $B^{M1+M2}g^{X(k+h)}/g^{(k+h)X} = B^{M1+M2}$.

$$Y = g^X{}_{\text{mod p}} \quad (5)$$

$$E(\{Y, g\}, M) = \{g^k{}_{\text{mod p}}, B^MY^k{}_{\text{mod p}}\} = \{g_*, M_*\} \quad (6)$$

$$E(X, \{g_*, M_*\}) = M_*/g_*{}^X{}_{\text{mod p}} = B^M \quad (7)$$

As the conclusion, ElGamal has good performance about security strength, operability and verifiability, and it is homomorphic as same as RSA. When compared with RSA, it has an additional distinctive feature, i.e. it provides public key re-encryption schemes with commutative feature as discussed in subsection "ElGamal based Commutative Re-encryption Scheme" in this section. Different from ElGamal, RSA can provide re-encryption schemes with the commutative feature only when encryption keys are kept as secrets of individual key owners. Also ElGamal is probabilistic. Because random secret number k is used in the encryption process, encryption results change every time even if same data are encrypted by a same key. Although any encryption algorithm can have the probabilistic feature by adding random factors to bit strings to be encrypted, ElGamal provides probabilistic features in much more comprehensive and systematic ways.

CONCLUSION

After the definitions of encryptions and decryptions, this chapter introduced homomorphic, probabilistic, commutative and verifiable features of encryption and decryption algorithms as the desirable ones especially for developing anonymous application systems. Also various encryption and decryption algorithms were evaluated mainly according to these features.

In anonymous systems, frequently there are cases where usual important constraints of encryption and decryption algorithms can be relaxed, and contrarily, some additional requirements that are not important in usual systems become important. As a consequence, there are opportunities for not only the modern encryption and decryption algorithms but also various legacy ones to be incorporated. Onetime pad and linear equation based encryption functions discussed in this chapter and in the last chapter of this part respectively are examples of legacy ones that play important roles in developing anonymous applications.

REFERENCES

Amoroso, E. (1994). *Fundamentals of computer security technology*. Prentice Hall.

Elgamal, T. (1985). A public-key cryptosystem and a signature scheme based on discrete logarithms. *IEEE Transactions on Information Theory*, *31*(4), 469–472. doi:10.1109/TIT.1985.1057074

FIPS. (1977). *Data encryption standard. FIPS pub 46*. FIPS.

Kahn, D. (1996). *The codebreakers – The comprehensive history of secret communication from ancient times to the Internet – Revised and updated*. New York, NY: Scribner.

Katz, J., & Lindell, Y. (2007). *Introduction to modern cryptography*. Boca Raton, FL: CRC Press.

Koblitz, N. (1994). *A course in number theory and cryptography* (2nd ed., p. 114). New York, NY: Springer-Verlag Graduate Texts in Mathematics.

Menezes, A. J., van Oorschot, P. C., & Vanstone, S. A. (1996). *Handbook of applied cryptography*. CRC Press.

Pieprzyk, J., Hardjono, T., & Seberry, J. (2003). *Fundamentals of computer security*. Springer-Verlag.

Rivest, R., Shamir, A., & Adleman, L. (1978). A method for obtaining digital signatures and public-key cryptosystems. *Communications of the ACM*, *21*(2), 294–299. doi:10.1145/359340.359342

Trappe, W., & Washington, L. C. (2005). *Introduction to cryptography with coding theory*. Englewood Cliffs, NJ: Prentice-Hall.

Vaudenay, S. (2006). *A classical introduction to cryptography, applications for communication security*. New York, NY: Springer-Verlag.

Chapter 3
Schemes for Digital Signatures

ABSTRACT

Integrity is the property of information concerning protection against its unauthorized modifications and forgeries. This chapter discusses bulletin board (BB), hash functions, MACs (Message Authentication Codes) and digital signatures, as schemes for maintaining integrity of data. BBs protect data by simply disclosing them to the public, i.e. an entity cannot modify them without being watched by others. Hash functions, Macs, and digital signatures protect data by detecting illegitimate modifications while attaching values to the data. Namely, when an entity illegitimately modifies the data, the modified results become inconsistent with the attached values. When hash functions, MACs and digital signatures are compared regarding the ability to convince entities that the data are authorized ones, hash functions cannot enable entities to convince others, and by MACs, entities can convince others only when relevant secrets are properly protected. On the other hand, digital signatures enable anyone to convince others without constraints.

INTRODUCTION

This chapter discusses mechanisms for maintaining integrity of data, where, integrity is the property of information about protection of itself against its unauthorized modifications and forgeries. However, protecting data from unauthorized modifications or forgeries is difficult without dedicated hardware that physically disables modifications of data (read only memories completely protect data from unauthorized modifications for example, but even it cannot protect the data from disruptions), therefore usually, integrity of information is defined as the capability of detecting unauthorized modifications and forgeries of the information. Bulletin boards (BBs), hash functions, MACs (Message Authentication Codes) and digital signatures are the typical mechanisms for detecting unauthorized modifications and forgeries of data.

Bulletin boards firstly discussed in this chapter disable entities to modify or delete data in unauthorized ways by simply publicly disclosing the data, i.e. an entity that tries to modify or delete data in the BB in unauthorized ways must take risks that it is being watched by someone else. Then, Hash functions, MACs and digital signatures that are discussed next to BBs, enable entities to

DOI: 10.4018/978-1-4666-1649-3.ch003

detect unauthorized modifications and forgeries of data by calculating values that are functions of the data themselves. Namely, the modifications and forgeries are detected by checking the consistency between the data and the calculated values.

BULLETIN BOARD (BB)

A bulletin board (BB) is a set of memory sections that are disclosed to relevant entities (Cramer, 1997). Where, only authorized entities can write data in particular sections of the BB, but any relevant entity can read the data at arbitrary positions in the BB at any time. Therefore all relevant entities can share the same states of the data in the BB, and consequently the data are protected from unauthorized modifications, deletions and additions. Entities cannot modify, delete or add the data in the BB in unauthorized ways without taking risks of being watched by someone else. A disadvantage that secrets of entities are revealed through the disclosed data in the BB can be mitigated when entities disclose their data in the BB while encrypting them by appropriate encryption schemes. When re-encryption schemes are adopted, no one can understand the meanings of data in the BB unless all relevant entities conspire with each other.

The integrity of data in the BB can be enhanced more when digital signatures of appropriate entities discussed in the next section are combined. Anyone can convince itself that validity of data in the BB had been certainly verified by authorized entities when the data are accompanied by signatures of authorities, because no one except the entities that had generated the signatures can consistently forge or modify the signatures.

HASHES, MACS AND DIGITAL SIGNATURES

Although various mechanisms exist for maintaining integrity of bit strings, many of them share the common idea. That is to add redundant information to the bit strings to be protected so that their modifications can be detected by examining the relations between the bit strings and the added redundant information. A Hamming code for error detection shown in Figure1 is an example (Hamming, 1980). In the figure, a redundant bit P is added to bit string M so that the total number of 1s in bit string M and P becomes even. Therefore, when erroneous behaviours of hardware or software disrupt M, changes in M can be detected by counting the number of 1s in M and P, provided that the errors change values only in a single bit position of the given bit string, i.e. when erroneous behaviours of hardware or software change M, the number of 1s in M and P becomes odd. Many exiting mechanisms that maintain data integrity behave in the same way. However, the redundant information must be constructed in more sophisticated ways, because different from Hamming codes that detect modifications made by hardware or software failures, mechanisms for maintaining data integrity must detect data modifications and disruptions also made intentionally by malicious entities.

There are 3 kinds of schemes, i.e. hash functions (NIST, 1993), MACs (Message Authentication Codes) (Krawczyk, 1997) and digital signatures (Rivest, 1978). A hash function $h(x)$ is a function that maps element x in X, a set of all bit strings of arbitrary length, to element y in Y, a set of bit strings of length N. It is similar to an encryption function in the aspect that although it is easy to calculate $y = h(x)$ from x, it is difficult to

Figure 1. Hamming code

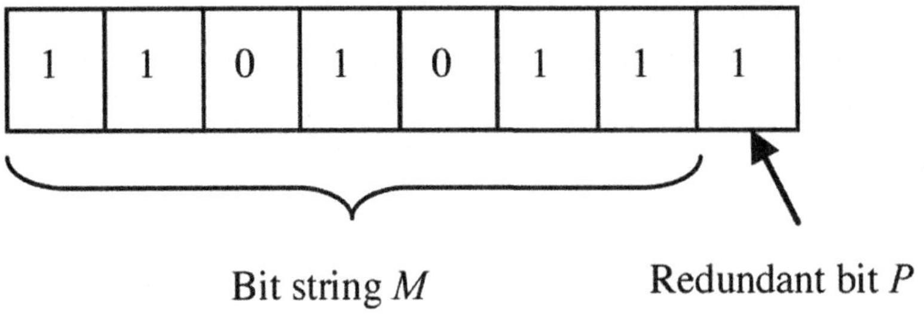

find x that satisfies relation $y = h(x)$ for given y. Because of this property, a hash function is called a one way function. But different from encryption functions, it is not necessarily a one to one mapping, i.e. different bit strings x_1 and x_2 in X may have the same value (this is called a collision). As same as in encryption functions, it is not necessary to limit the length of bit strings in X, but when a hash function is implemented in computer systems, X is a set of bit strings of which length is less than or equal to some finite value L. Anyway because of the property of the one way function, protection of bit string M can be achieved by the protection of $h(M)$. When M is accompanied by $h(M)$ and $h(M)$ is protected from modifications, entity P, which tries to modify M to M^* without being detected, must generate M^* so that $h(M^*)$ has the same value as h(M), however to generate M^* so that $h(M^*)$ coincides with $h(M)$ is practically impossible. The important thing is that the length of $h(M)$ is much shorter than that of M, therefore efforts for protecting long bit string M can be reduced to that for protecting the shorter bit string $h(M)$. However, because anyone who knows function $h(x)$ can calculate $h(M^*)$ from M^*, malicious entities can modify M to M^* without being detected while attaching $h(M^*)$ to it when $h(M)$ in not protected properly. Therefore, mechanisms to disable malicious entities to modify or forge $h(M)$ are necessary. MAC is a solution.

A MAC is a hash function with secret keys, i.e. it is a function $h(\mathrm{k}, x)$, where $h(\mathrm{k}, x)$ is a hash function for each k, and $h(\mathrm{k}_1, x)$ and $h(\mathrm{k}_2, x)$ are not necessarily the same when $\mathrm{k}_1 \neq \mathrm{k}_2$. Namely, k is a key, and when key k is shared only among entities that generate and use bit string M, they can protect M by only attaching $h(\mathrm{k}, M)$ to it, without an additional mechanism to protect $h(\mathrm{k}, M)$. No one except entities that share M can modify M to M^* while attaching consistent $h(\mathrm{k}, M^*)$, because only entities that know k can calculate $h(\mathrm{k}, M^*)$ consistently. However, MAC does not work effectively when 2 entities P and Q that generates bit string M and that uses M cannot trust each other. Namely, P or Q that knows k can change M to M^* while attaching consistent $h(\mathrm{k}, M^*)$ after they agreed about M. Also because modifications can be detected only by entities that know the key (in the above case only P and Q can detect modifications), it is difficult for third parties to mediate disputes between the entities about liability for the modifications.

The digital signature is a solution to cope with the above difficulties, namely as same as the written signature, it satisfies the following requirements. In the remainder, the word "signature" is used to represent "digital signature," when confusions can be avoided. Requirements for digital signatures are,

1. Only signer S can generate its valid signature on bit string *M*, and
2. Anyone can verify the validity of the signature of S on *M*.

It is apparent that when the 1st and the 2nd requirements are satisfied, anyone including third parties can convince itself that bit string *M* with the consistent signature was certainly generated by the signer and it was not modified by others. However, to protect signatures from cut and paste attacks, in which an attacker uses a signature on one bit string as a signature on another bit string, the signature of S on bit string *M* must differ from that on other bit string M^* even if values of *M* and M^* are actually the same. This can be achieved by attaching additional information to bit strings to be signed. When *M* is concatenated with bit string *R* that is unique to *M* (e.g. *R* is the date when *M* was created), the result $M \| R$ becomes unique, therefore S(d, $M \| R$), the signature on $M \| R$, disables entities to use it as the signature on other bit string M^* even *M* and M^* have the same value.

The digital signature can be implemented by exploiting asymmetric key encryption algorithms, namely, when signer S encrypts bit string *M* by its secret key d, the result E(d, *M*) is the digital signature of S on *M*, where signature E(d, *M*) is valid when it is successfully decrypted into *M* by public key $e = d^{-1}$. Because key d is known to only S, only signer S can generate consistent signature E(d, *M*). On the other hand, because key e is publicly disclosed, anyone can calculate *M* from E(d, *M*) as E(e, E(d, *M*)) = *M* and convince itself that E(d, *M*) was generated by S, i.e. anyone can verify the validity of E(d, *M*). In the remainder of this book, to explicitly represent signatures, notations S(d, *M*) and S(e, S(d, *M*)) are also used instead of E(d, *M*) and E(e, E(d, *M*)), respectively. Also, the words "verification key" and "signing key" are used to represent "public encryption key" and "secret decryption key."

Because asymmetric key encryption algorithms require much computation volumes to encrypt and decrypt long bit strings, usually a signer signs on *h*(*M*) instead of *M* itself. Here, *h*(*M*) is the hash value of *M* and its length is much shorter than that of *M*. By combining the facts that calculating M^* that satisfy $h(M) = h(M^*)$ is difficult, and that the digital signature on *h*(*M*) ensures *h*(*M*) was generated by the signer, entities can believe that *M* was generated by the signer when *h*(*M*) is consistent with *M* and the signature on *h*(*M*) is valid.

When RSA is adopted as the base encryption algorithm, implementation of digital signature schemes is straightforward. Let e and d be public encryption and secret decryption keys, respectively, then signature on bit string *M* can be constructed as M^d. Only the signer that knows d can generate M^d, on the other hand, because encryption key e is publicly known, anyone can verify the validity of the signature by calculating $(M^d)^e = M^{de} = M$, i.e. e and d are the verification and the signing keys, respectively.

Combined with publicly disclosed hash function *h*(*M*), digital signature schemes can be implemented also by ElGamal encryption functions (Elgamal, 1985). Let *x* and $y = g^x$ be secret decryption and public encryption keys of an ElGamal encryption function, and *h*(*z*) be a hash function, then pair $\{r = g^k, s = (h(M)\text{-}xr)k^{-1}\}$ is the signature on bit string *M*, where k is a secret integer of the signer. Namely, only the signer that knows *x* can generate $s = (h(M)\text{-}xr)k^{-1}$, on the other hand, anyone can verify that (r, s) is the signature on *M* based on relation $y^r r^s = g^{h(M)}$, i.e. from $s = (h(M)\text{-}xr)k^{-1}$, $ks + xr = h(M)$ and $y^r r^s = g^{xr}g^{ks} = g^{h(M)}$ are concluded.

An advantage of the digital signature is that anyone can verify the validity of it. In other words, entity Q that has the signature of signer S on *M* can convince any entity X that *M* was generated by S. On the other hand, when a MAC is used, Q cannot convince X that *M* was generated by S even the associated MAC is valid. The reasons are that Q can inform X of key k dishonestly, and even when Q honestly informs X of k, Q that knows key k can easily calculate valid MAC *h*(k, *M*) while generating *M* by itself. Then, MAC enables Q to convince X that *M* was generated by S, only when S does not disclose key k to others except X. Hash functions cannot enable Q to convince X in any condition because anyone can calculate *h*(*M*) while generating *M* by itself. In conclusion when a hash function, a MAC and a digital signature are compared regarding the ability to convince entities that S had generated bit string *M*, a hash function cannot enable entity Q to convince others, and by a MAC, Q can convince others only when the key is properly protected. On the other hand, a digital signature enables anyone to convince others without constraints.

Digital Signatures of Multiple Signers

As discussed above, digital signature schemes have substantial advantages compared with other schemes. However, digital signatures ensure validity of bit strings only when signers themselves are honest, i.e. dishonest signers who know their signing keys can forge or modify bit strings with their consistent signatures by themselves. A set of signatures of multiple independent signers on bit string *M* protects *M* also from dishonesties of signers. When entity S_1 and S_2 sign on *M* to generate $S(d_1, M)$ and $S(d_2, M)$ by their signing keys d_1 and d_2, respectively, it is practically impossible to modify $S(d_1, M)$ and $S(d_2, M)$ to $S(d_1, M^*)$ and $S(d_2, M^*)$, or forge $S(d_1, M^*)$ and $S(d_2, M^*)$ so that both $S(d_1^{-1}, S(d_1, M^*))$ and $S(d_2^{-1}, S(d_2, M^*))$ become M*, unless S_1 and S_2 conspire with each other. Re-signing mechanisms also protect signatures from dishonesties of signers. When S_1 and S_2 sign on *M* repeatedly as $S(d_2, S(d_1, M))$ by their signing keys d_1 and d_2, either S_1 or S_2 cannot modify *M* to *M** while calculating $S(d_2, S(d_1, M^*))$ so that it is decrypted to *M** without the help of S_2 or S_1. On the other hand, anyone can verify the validity of $S(d_2, S(d_1, M))$ while decrypting it to *M* by using 2 public verification keys d_2^{-1} and d_1^{-1} of S_2 and S_1. Re-signing schemes become essential for developing unlinkable signature schemes in Section 2.

CONCLUSION

This chapter introduced schemes to protect information from illegitimate modifications and forgeries. Namely, hash functions, MACs and digital signatures that are widely used in various applications were discussed. Although these schemes cannot be directly applied to anonymous systems, and they cannot protect information from their deletions, they will be extended in Section 2 to enable entities to protect data even without knowing their values, or to detect deletions of data and to identify their liable entities without knowing identities of honest entities.

REFERENCES

Cramer, R., Gennaro, R., & Schoenmakers, B. (1997). A secure and optimally efficient multi-authority election scheme. *Advances in Cryptology '97 –EUROCRYPT'97 . LNCS, 1233*, 103–118.

Elgamal, T. (1985). A public-key cryptosystem and a signature scheme based on discrete logarithms. *IEEE Transactions on Information Theory, 31*(4), 469–472. doi:10.1109/TIT.1985.1057074

Hamming, R. W. (1980). *Coding and information theory*. Prentice-Hall.

Krawczyk, H., Bellare, B., & Canetti, R. (1997). *HMAC: Keyed-hashing for message authentication. RFC 2104*. IETF.

National Institute of Standards and Technology. (1993). *Secure hash algorithm*. FIPS180-1.

Rivest, R., Shamir, A., & Adleman, L. (1978). A method for obtaining digital signatures and public-key cryptosystems. *Communications of the ACM*, *21*(2), 294–299. doi:10.1145/359340.359342

Chapter 4
Encryption Schemes for Anonymous Systems

ABSTRACT

As encryption schemes useful in developing secure anonymous systems, linear equation based encryption, probabilistic, commutative and verifiable re-encryption, and threshold ElGamal encryption schemes are introduced. Linear equation based encryption functions are additive, and they enable entities to calculate sums of data owned by others without knowing individual values, and probabilistic, commutative and verifiable re-encryption functions enable entities to encrypt data while concealing the correspondences between encrypted data and their decrypted forms from anyone including the owners of the data. Finally, threshold ElGamal encryption functions disable entities to decrypt encrypted data without the cooperation among t out of n authorities ($t \leq n$), while ensuring correct decryptions when at least t authorities are honest. All encryption schemes are extensively used in the following parts of this book, e.g. for developing anonymous communication systems, anonymous authentication systems, electronic payment, procurement, and voting systems.

INTRODUCTION

This chapter discusses various encryption algorithms important especially in developing anonymous systems, i.e. algorithms with additive, multiplicative, probabilistic, commutative, or verifiable feature are introduced. In anonymous systems, to maintain privacies of data owners for example, entities are frequently required to calculate averages, variances, etc. of data without knowing the individual data, or to encrypt data in the ways where no one including the data owners and entities that encrypt the data can know the correspondences between the encrypted data and their decrypted forms. These requirements are satisfied by encryption algorithms with the above features. Firstly additive encryption functions that enable entities to calculate sums of data without knowing individual values are discussed. Then discussions about probabilistic, commutative and verifiable re-encryption schemes, which enable entities to encrypt data while concealing the correspondences between encrypted data and their decrypted forms from anyone including the

DOI: 10.4018/978-1-4666-1649-3.ch004

owners of the data, follow. The threshold ElGamal encryption schemes discussed in the last section disable entities to decrypt encrypted data without the cooperation among t out of n authorities ($t \leq n$), while ensuring correct decryptions when at least t authorities are honest.

LINEAR EQUATION BASED ENCRYPTION SCHEME

Basic Mechanism

An encryption algorithm based on linear equations consider bit strings as numbers (not limited to integers), and encrypts a vector of bit strings $M = \{m_1, m_2, ---, m_H\}$ to vector $M_* = \{m_{*1}, m_{*2}, ---, m_{*H}\}$ by calculating weighted sums of individual elements in vector M while using secret coefficient (H x H)-matrix $Q = \{q_{ij}\}$ as shown in Equation (1). When, the data to be encrypted consist of a single bit string, vector M can be constructed by dividing it into H substrings $\{m_1, m_2, ---, m_H\}$ as shown in Figure 1. H-dimensional vector M can be generated also by adding (H-1)-dummy bit strings instead of dividing M, i.e. M can be constructed as $M = \{m, d_1, ---, d_{H-1}\}$, where, $d_1, d_2, ---, d_{H-1}$ are dummy bit strings.

$$m_{*1} = q_{11}m_1 + q_{12}m_2 + ---- + q_{1H}m_H$$

$$m_{*2} = q_{21}m_1 + q_{22}m_2 + ---- + q_{2H}m_H \qquad (1)$$

$$m_{*H} = q_{H1}m_1 + q_{H2}m_2 + ---- + q_{HH}m_H$$

Then, an entity that does not know coefficient matrix Q cannot calculate M from M_*; however when Q is disclosed, anyone can calculate M from M_* by solving linear Equation (1), provided that Q has its inverse. Therefore in linear equation based encryption, vector M_* is the encrypted form of vector M, and coefficient matrix Q and Q^{-1} are an encryption key and a decryption key, respectively. Here, elements of matrix Q are not necessarily limited to integers.

The distinctive feature of the linear equation based encryption algorithm is the additive property (the algorithm is homomorphic under addition), i.e. when M_1 and M_2 are encrypted into, $E(Q, M_1)$ and $E(Q, M_2)$, $sE(Q, M_1)+tE(Q, M_2)$ is decrypted into sM_1+tM_2, where operator + represents addition of vectors, s and t are arbitrary numbers, and sM_1 represents the product of number s and vector M_1. However this advantage introduces a serious drawback, i.e. a linear equation based encryption algorithm is weak against plain text attacks (Anderson 2001). When H-mutually independent H-dimensional vectors $A_{1*}, A_{2*}, ---, A_{H*}$ are known as encryption results of known vectors $A_1, A_2, ---, A_H$, because arbitrarily given H-dimensional vector x_* is represented as $x_* = g_1A_{1*} + g_2A_{2*} + ---- + g_HA_{H*}$, x_* can be easily decrypted into $x = g_1A_1 + g_2A_2 + ---- + g_HA_H$ even when coefficient matrix Q is not known. Nevertheless, linear equation based encryption algorithms play important roles in anonymous systems, because in various anonymous applications entities that encrypt data do not need to disclose their decrypted forms to others, i.e. entities that try to breach encryptions cannot

Figure 1. Decomposition of bit string M

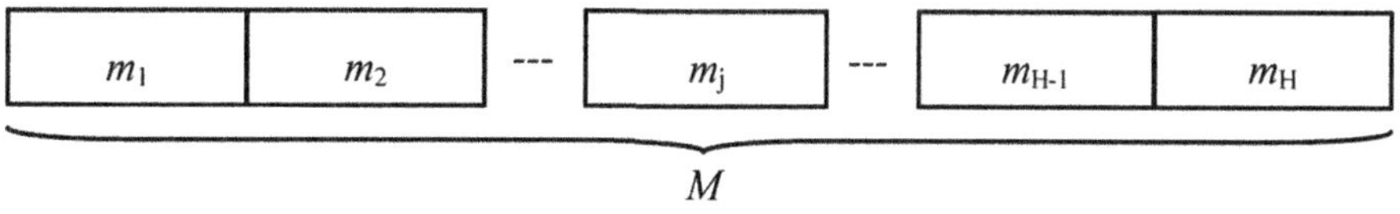

know plain texts, therefore plain text attacks are impossible from the beginning.

An anonymous credit card system is an example, where card company S gives each transaction record *T* to cardholder C while encrypting it to E(k, *T*) and calculates C's total expenditure without knowing each record by decrypting the sum of encrypted records provided by C. Here, the objective of the encryption is not to conceal *T* from C, i.e. even if S conceal it C knows its transaction details e.g. the date, the place and the transaction amount, from the beginning of course. The objective is to disable C to modify *T* illegitimately, and to achieve this objective, S constitutes the transaction data as pair {*T*, *F*} to encrypt it to E(k, {*T*, *F*}) while adding secret element *F* to *T*. Then, to deceive S by illegitimately modifying E(k, {*T*, *F*}) to X, C must generate X so that its decrypted form E(k^{-1}, X) includes *F*. Namely, if E(k^{-1}, X) does not include *F* consistently, S can determine that X was illegitimately generated as discussed later in this section, but it is practically impossible for C that does not know encryption key k to consistently include *F* in X. The important thing in this example is that same entity S both encrypts {*T*, *F*} and decrypts E(k, {*T*, *F*}) (an anonymous credit card system is a typical example of anonymous systems, in which information is encrypted and decrypted by same entities); therefore S does not need to disclose *F* to other entities. Then, plain text attacks to modify E(k, {*T*, *F*}) becomes impossible for C.

In the remainder of this book, M_1, a part of information *M* that should be kept secret from entities other than the ones that encrypt *M*, is called the confidential part of *M*. On the other hand, M_2, a part of information *M* that can be disclosed to others, is called the visible part of *M*. In the above example, *T* is the visible part of {*T*, *F*} and *F* is its confidential part.

Enhancement of the Algorithm

Although entities that use linear equation based encryption algorithms do not disclose complete plain forms of their bit strings to others in many cases, there are cases where they must disclose them, e.g. as explained in the later chapter in conjunction with homomorphic anonymous tokens, therefore coefficient matrices must be defined so that they cannot be calculated even when several plain texts are disclosed in their complete forms. Coefficient matrix calculations can be made difficult by combining the following 3 methods (Tamura, 2007), i.e.

1. By adding secret random elements to a vector to be encrypted, i.e. by adding secret random terms to Equation (1),
2. By inserting secret random dummy elements at random positions in an encrypted vector, and
3. By representing the value of each element in an encrypted vector as the sum of values randomly split into multiple elements.

In the 1st method, G-secret random bit strings r_1, ---, r_G are added to vector of bit strings $M = \{m_1, m_2, ---, m_H\}$ to be encrypted as shown in Figure 2. Therefore, bit strings to be encrypted constitute (H+G)-dimensional vector $\underline{M} = \{m_1, m_2, ---, m_H, r_1, r_2, ---, r_G\}$, and also the secret coefficient matrix Q is extended to {(H+G) x (H+G)}-matrix Q. Then $\underline{M}$ is encrypted to $\underline{M}_* = \{m_{*1}, m_{*2}, ---, m_{*H+G}\}$ according to Equation (2) by using secret coefficient matrix Q, and $\underline{M}_*$ is decrypted into *M* by solving Equation (2) and deleting random bit strings $r_1, r_2, ---, r_G$. Therefore the encryption algorithm becomes probabilistic.

The important thing is that the values of bit strings $r_1, r_2, ---, r_G$ are known only to the entity

Figure 2. Enhanced linear equation based encryption

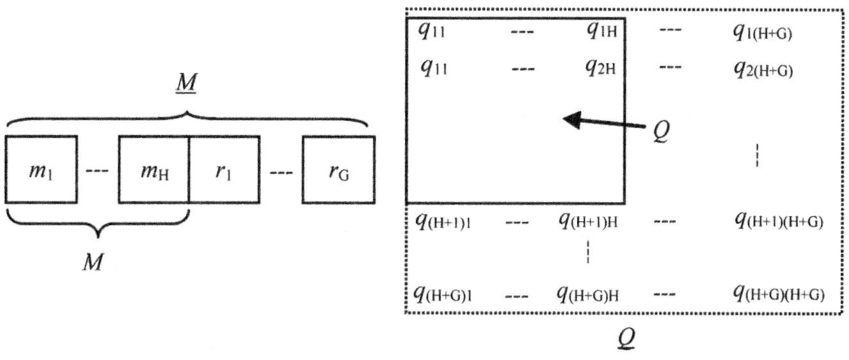

that encrypts bit string M and they are changed at every encryption. Therefore, it is extremely difficult to estimate the encryption key. For example, let $v_{*k}(M_1)$, $v_{*k}(M_2)$ and $v_{*k}(sM_1+tM_2)$ be the k-th elements of (H+G)-dimensional vectors $E(Q, M_1)$, $E(Q, M_2)$ and $E(Q, sM_1+tM_2)$, encrypted forms of bit strings M_1, M_2 and sM_1+tM_2, then relation $sv_{*k}(M_1)+tv_{*k}(M_2) = v_{*k}(sM_1+tM_2)$ exists among $v_{*k}(M_1)$, $v_{*k}(M_2)$ and $v_{*k}(sM_1+tM_2)$ if same secret random bit strings r_1, r_2, ---, r_G are used for calculating $E(Q, M_1)$, $E(Q, M_2)$ and $E(Q, sM_1+tM_2)$. However, values of secret random bit strings r_1, r_2, ---, r_G are changed for every encryption, therefore relation $sv_{*k}(M_1)+tv_{*k}(M_2) = v_{*k}(sM_1+tM_2)$ does not hold, and cannot be used for estimating coefficient matrix Q.

$$m_{*1} = q_{11}m_1 + ---- + q_{1H}m_H + q_{1(H+1)}r_1 + --- + q_{1(H+G)}r_G$$

$$m_{*2} = q_{21}m_1 + ---- + q_{2H}m_H + q_{2(H+1)}r_1 + --- + q_{2(H+G)}r_G \quad (2)$$

$$m_{*H} = q_{H1}m_1 + ---- + q_{HH}m_H + q_{H(H+1)}r_1 + --- + q_{H(H+G)}r_G$$

$$m_{*(H+1)} = q_{(H+1)1}m_1 + ---- + q_{(H+1)H}m_H + q_{(H+1)(H+1)}r_1 + --- + q_{(H+1)(H+G)}r_G$$

$$m_{*(H+G)} = q_{(H+G)1}m_1 + ---- + q_{(H+G)H}m_H + q_{(H+G)(H+1)}r_1 + --- + q_{(H+G)(H+G)}r_G$$

when an entity P that encrypts its data M constructs the data as a combination of its visible part M^V and confidential part M^C, M^C plays the same roles as secret random bit strings r_1, r_2, ---, r_G do, i.e. vector M is a pair of sub-vectors M^V and M^C, and although P discloses elements of M^V to others it maintains elements of M^C as its secrets (in the previous credit card system example M^V and M^C correspond to T and F, respectively). However to make the encryption function secure enough, random secret bit strings r_1, ---, r_G must be used in addition to confidential part M^C when the number of elements in M^C is not large enough. For example, when M^C consists of a single unknown bit string in H-dimensional vector M (therefore, $M^V = \{m_1, m_2, ---, m_{(H-1)}\}$ and $M^C = \{m_H\}$), $E(Q, M)$ provides entities with good suggestions to estimate coefficients $\{q_{1H}, q_{2H}, ---, q_{HH}\}$ that relates to confidential part M^C. Namely, let $M_1 = \{M_1^V, M_1^C\}$, $M_2 = \{M_2^V, M_2^C\}$ be bit strings to be encrypted to $E(Q, M_1) = E(Q, \{M_1^V, M_1^C\})$ and $E(Q, M_2) = E(Q, \{M_2^V, M_2^C\})$, where although M_1^C and M_2^C are secrets of entity P, M_1^V and M_2^V are known to entities other than P; then, if M_1 and M_2 fortunately satisfy relation $M_1^V = aM_2^V$, it is possible to obtain one of encrypted forms of null bit string E(Q, {0, M_1^C-aM_2^C}) as E(Q, {M_1^V, M_1^C}) - aE(Q, {M_2^V, M_2^C}). Therefore, according to Equation (1), E(Q, {0, M_1^C-aM_2^C}) becomes vector (M_1^C-aM_2^C){q_{1H}, q_{2H}, ---, q_{HH}}, which includes many clues for estimating coefficients {q_{1H}, ---, q_{HH}}, although it is not straightforward to calculate them because M_1^C and M_2^C are not known. Multiple secret random bit strings make the coefficient matrix calculations further difficult.

The 2nd method mixes vector {m_{*1}, m_{*2}---, m_{*H}}, which is calculated according to Equation (1) as the encrypted form of M = {m_1, m_2---, m_H}, with secret random dummy vector {w_{*1}, w_{*2}, ---, w_{*T}} while shuffling the elements in M to generate a single (H+T)-dimensional vector; therefore the encryption result becomes to {M_*'} = {w_{*1}, w_{*2}, m_{*3} w_{*3}, m_{*1}---, w_{*4}} for example. As a consequence, positions where m_{*1}, m_{*2}---, m_{*H} are located in {M_*'} must be determined in order to decrypt {M_*'} into M. However, it must be noted that to identify the positions where dummy elements {w_{*1}, w_{*2}---, w_{*T}} are allocated is not so difficult when this method is used without combining with other methods because there are still linear relationships among real elements (non-dummy elements) of encrypted forms of known bit strings. For example, when encrypted forms of known vectors of bit strings M_1, M_2 and sM_1+tM_2 i.e. E(Q, M_1), E(Q, M_2) and E(Q, sM_1+tM_2) are given, the k-th element of the (H+T)-dimensional vector is for a dummy element, if relation sv_{*k}(M_1)+tv_{*k}(M_2) = v_{*k}(sM_1+tM_2) does not hold. Where, v_{*k}(M_1), v_{*k}(M_2) and v_{*k}(sM_1+tM_2) are the k-th elements of (H+T)-dimensional vectors E(Q, M_1), E(Q, M_2) and E(Q, sM_1+tM_2). Then, the number of possibilities that must be examined to remove dummy elements from the (H+T)-dimensional vector can be decreased.

The 3rd method makes coefficient matrix estimations further difficult; it randomly sprits the value of each element m_{*j} in the encrypted vector {m_{*1}, m_{*2}, ---, m_{*H}} into a set of multiple elements {m_{*j1}, m_{*j2}---, m_{*jp}}, i.e. single element m_{*j} is represented as a set of elements {m_{*j1}, m_{*j2}---, m_{*jp}} that satisfy relation m_{*j} = m_{*j1} + m_{*j2} + --- + m_{*jp}, where, each m_{*jh} can take both negative and positive values of course. Then for arbitrary j, j-th elements v_{*j}(M_1), v_{*j}(M_2) and v_{*j}(sM_1+tM_2) of E(Q, M_1), E(Q, M_2) and E(Q, sM_1+tM_2), encrypted forms of known vectors M_1, M_2 and sM_1+tM_2, do not necessarily satisfy relation sv_{*j}(M_1) +tv_{*j}(M_2) = v_{*j}(sM_1+tM_2) and coefficient matrix estimation becomes extremely difficult.

As above, 3 methods in this subsection enable exploitation of the additive property, a distinctive advantage of linear equation based encryption algorithms, while offering enough security strength as modern asymmetric encryption key algorithms do. Because linear relationships among encrypted forms are hidden, values of H^2 = W elements in (H x H)-dimensional coefficient matrix Q must be determined to breach encryptions, even if there is no dummy element. Therefore, Z^W number of possibilities must be examined provided that individual elements in Q can have Z different values, and this number becomes Z^{900} when H = 30 (actually elements in Q are real numbers and the number of their possible values cannot be counted). Also when T-dummy elements {w_{*1}, w_{*2}---, w_{*T}} are added at random positions of H-dimensional vector {m_{*1}, m_{*2}---, m_{*H}} as the encrypted form of {m_1, m_2---, m_H}, ${}_{(H+T)}P_H$ number of possibilities must be examined to remove the dummy elements, and when H and T are set to 50, ${}_{(H+T)}P_H$ becomes ${}_{100}P_{50} > 2^{500}$.

On the other hand, solving Equation (1) or (2) is not difficult when the coefficient matrix is given. For example, LU-decomposition method (Cormen, 2001) solves linear equations with sufficient performance in terms of both computation speed and accuracy. Computation speed is fast enough compared with modern asymmetric encryption key algorithms even the dimensions of coefficient matrices are about 100, and also calculation errors are small enough. Especially in cases where decrypted bit strings are corresponded to finite discrete values (e.g. integers or characters) computation errors can be completely absorbed in truncating processes of fractions.

Protecting the Algorithm from Encrypted Form Forgeries

It must be noted that although the methods discussed in the previous subsection had enhanced linear equation based encryption schemes so that entities that do not know coefficient matrices (encryption/decryption keys) cannot calculate the confidential part values from encrypted forms of bit strings, it is still easy to generate consistent encrypted forms even without knowing encryption keys. By linearly combining known encrypted forms, anyone can generate encrypted forms of variety of bit strings without knowing the key as same as man in the middle attacks (Anderson 2001) in environments where public key encryption algorithms are used. Therefore, entities can behave dishonestly while modifying or forging encrypted forms in unauthorized ways. The following mechanisms disable entities to modify or forge encrypted forms of bit strings in unauthorized ways.

The basic idea is to attach a pair of a check code (CC) and a check value (CV) that is a kind of Hamming code (Hamming, 1980) to vector M to construct vector $\underline{M}$ as shown in Figure 3. Here, M is a bit string to be encrypted, and values of CC and CV are determined as the secret of entity P that encrypts M, and P changes their values randomly in every encryption so that they satisfy the predefined relation. Namely c and v, values of CC and CV, must satisfy $v = f(c)$, therefore when E(Q, $\underline{M}$), the encrypted form of $\underline{M}$, is generated in unauthorized ways, e.g. by lineally combining already known encrypted forms, P can detect that by checking whether $v = f(c)$ is satisfied or not. For entities that do not know CC and CV values of given encrypted forms, it is difficult to generate new encrypted forms by combining these given encrypted forms while maintaining consistent relations between their CC and CV values even if they know function $f(x)$.

Here, it is desireble that function $f(c)$ is non-linear to protect encrypted forms. If $f(c)$ is a linear function, e.g. $v = ac+b$ (a and b are constant values), it is still easy to generate consistent encrypted forms by linealy combining already known encryptrd forms even without knowing the encryption key. For example, let (c_1, ac_1+b), (c_2, ac_2+b) and (c_3, ac_3+b) be CC and CV value pairs of $\underline{M}_1$, $\underline{M}_2$ and $\underline{M}_3$ and E(Q, $\underline{M}_1$), E(Q, $\underline{M}_2$) and E(Q, $\underline{M}_3$) be encrypted forms of $\underline{M}_1$, $\underline{M}_2$ and $\underline{M}_3$, then, any entity can construct a consistent encrypted form of p($\underline{M}_1$-$\underline{M}_2$)+$\underline{M}_3$ as p{E(Q, $\underline{M}_1$)-E(Q, $\underline{M}_2$)}+E(Q, $\underline{M}_3$). Namely, p{E(Q, $\underline{M}_1$)-E(Q, $\underline{M}_2$)}+E(Q, $\underline{M}_3$) is decrypted to p($\underline{M}_1$-$\underline{M}_2$)+M_3 because of the additive property, therefore its CC and the CV value pair becomes {p(c_1-c_2)+c_3, ap(c_1-c_2)+ac_3+b} and satisfies relation ap(c_1-c_2)+ac_3+b = f(p(c_1-c_2)+c_3).

On the other hand, linearity of $f(c)$ is desireble to exploit the advantage of linear equation based encryption functions that they are additive. When $f(c)$ is linear, the consistency of a set of n-encrypted forms can be verified without decrypting individual encrypted forms and consequently without

Figure 3. Check code and check value

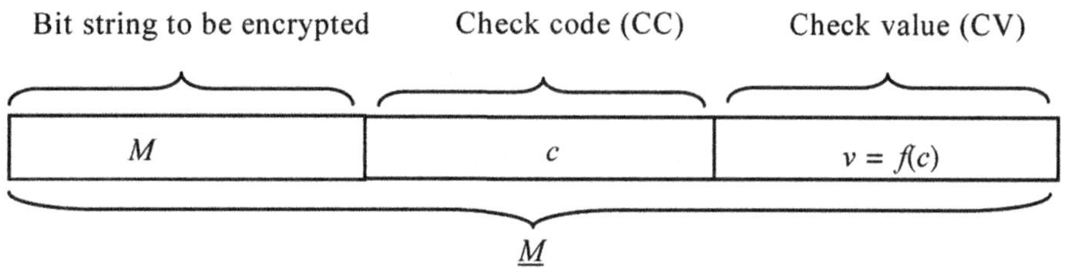

Figure 4 Configuration of CC and CV

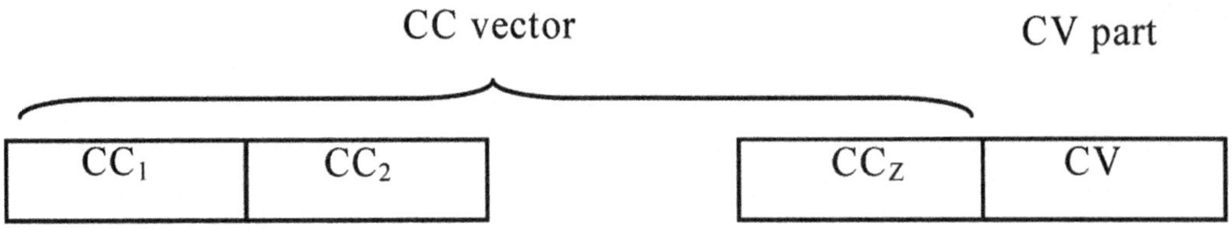

knowing privacies of the owner of the encrypted forms. If $v = f(c) = ac + b$ for example, CC and CV values of the decryption result of each consistent encrypted form E(Q, $\underline{M}_j$) satisfies relation $v_j = ac_j + b$, therefore $\underline{c} = c_1+c_2+ \cdots +c_n$ and $\underline{v} = v_1+v_2+ \cdots +v_n$, the CC and the CV values of the dycrypted form of {E(Q, $\underline{M}_1$)+E(Q, $\underline{M}_2$)+ --- +E(Q, $\underline{M}_n$)} must satisfy relation $\underline{v} = av + nb$. Then, the consistency of individual encrypted forms can be verified by decrypting the sum of the n-encrypted forms without decrypting individual encrypted forms, i.e. when relation $v_j = ac_j + b$ is not satisfied for some j, relation $\underline{v} = a\underline{c} + nb$ does not hold.

CC vectors can satisfy the above requirements. A CC vector is a set of CCs as shown in Figure 4. In the figure, CC vactor is configured as set {CC_1, CC_2, ---, CC_Z}, where each CC_j is a CC that can have 0 or 1 as its value, and P defines their values randomly so that only one of CC_j has 1 as its value. The value of CV is defined accroding to CC_j to which value 1 is assigned. Namely, a set of values v_1, v_2, ---, v_Z are corresponded to CC_1, CC_2, ---, CC_Z in advance, and the CV value is defined as v_j when value 1 is assigned to CC_j. Then, entities cannot generate consistent encrypted forms by combining already known encrypted forms, e.g. when an entity genarates p(E(Q, $\underline{M}_1$)-E(Q, $\underline{M}_2$))+ E(Q, $\underline{M}_3$) as in the above, its CC = {CC_1, CC_2, ---, CC_Z} may have multiple nonzero elements. On the other hand, P can convince itself that a set of n-encrypted forms are consistent ones without checking values of CCs and CVs of decryption results individually. When the sum of the encrypted forms is decrypted, P can extract T_j, the sum of CC_j values for each j, and W, the sum of CV values, and all encrypted forms in the set are consistent when relations $T_1+T_2 + \cdots +T_Z = n$ and $W = T_1v_1+T_2v_2+ \cdots +T_Zv_Z$ hold.

In the same way, entity P can protect encrypted form {m_{*1}, m_{*2}, ---, m_{*H}} from forgeries by defining values of selected elemens {m_{*h1}, m_{*h2}, ---, m_{*hZ}} in the encrypted form so that relation $a_{h1}m_{*h1}+a_{h2}m_{*h2}+ \cdots +a_{hZ}m_{*hZ} = a_0$ is satisfied, where a_{h1}, a_{h2}, ---, a_{hZ}, a_0 are constnt secret numbers of P and m_{*hj} may be a dummy element. Namely, entity Q that does not know h_1, h_2, ---, h_Z or a_{h1}, a_{h2}, ---, a_{hZ}, a_0 cannot modify or forge {m_{*1}, m_{*2}, ---, m_{*H}} consistently. An important thing is as same as in the above P can verify the consistency of a set of encrypted forms without examining individual encrypted forms. Provided that the set includes n-encrypted forms, if each {$m(j)_{*h1}$, $m(j)_{*h2}$, ---, $m(j)_{*hZ}$} satisfies $a_{h1}m(j)_{*h1}+a_{h2}m(j)_{*h2}+ \cdots +a_{hZ}m(j)_{*hZ} = a_0$, the sum of encrypted forms must satisfy $a_{h1}m(j)_{*h1}+a_{h2}m(j)_{*h2}+ \cdots +a_{hZ}m(j)_{*hZ}\} = na_0$.

ITLs (Implicit Transaction Links) discussed in Section 2 are another kind of error detection codes and also enable entities to detect illegitimate modifications or forrgeries of encrypted forms in a given set without examining forms in the set individually. However, different from the above schemes that check consistencies of values embedded in same encrypted forms, the ITL based scheme checks consistencies of ITL values embedded in different encrypted forms in the set.

Verification of Linear Equation Based Encryptions

By using the additive property, linear equation based encryption algorithms can be made also verifiable as discussed in the 2nd chapter of this part. Let P be an entity that verifies the correctness of E(k, M), an encrypted form of bit string vector M calculated by entity Q, without knowing key k. Here, although P knows only M^V, the visible part of M, and generally the dimension of M^V is less than that of E(k, M), to simplify the explanations, M and test bit string vectors $\{T_1, T_2, ---, T_m\}$ appear in the below are assumed to be equal to M^V and $\{T_1^V, T_2^V, ---, T_m^V\}$, respectively, i.e. whole M and $\{T_1, T_2, ---, T_m\}$ are visible to P. However, the verification process below is also applicable to cases where dimensions of M and M^V are different, i.e. M and $\{T_1, T_2, ---, T_m\}$ can be replaced by M^V and $\{T_1^V, T_2^V, ---, T_m^V\}$.

Conceptually the verification of E(k, M) proceeds as follow. Firstly, P generates arbitrary bit string vectors {E(k, T_1), E(k, T_2), ---, E(k, T_m)} as a set of encrypted forms of test bit strings, and asks Q to decrypt them to $\{T_1, T_2, ---, T_m\}$ in advance. Then at a time when P obtains E(k, M^*) as the encrypted form of M, it calculates T_{test} according to Equation (3) while generating random numbers w_0, w_1, ----, w_m secret from Q, and asks Q to decrypt T_{test}. Here, because E(k, x) is additive T_{test} must be decrypted to $T_{test} = w_0M + w_1T_1 + w_2T_2 +$ ---- $+ w_mT_m$ if E(k, M^*) is the correct encryption form of M, on the other hand, if Q had encrypted M to E(k, M^*) dishonestly, Q cannot calculate T_{test} from T_{test} unless it knows the value of w_0.

$$T_{test} = w_0E(k, M^*) + w_1E(k, T_1) + w_2E(k, T_2) + ---- + w_mE(k, T_m) \quad (3)$$

However, when H-dimensional vector E(k, M^*) = {E(k, M^*)$_1$, E(k, M^*)$_2$, ---, E(k, M^*)$_H$} include non-zero element E(k, M^*)$_p$ and the p-th element E(k, T_q)$_p$ of E(k, T_q) = {E(k, T_q)$_1$, E(k, T_q)$_2$, ---, E(k, T_q)$_H$} is 0 for all q = 1, 2, ---, m, Q can estimate w_0 easily and can calculate T_{test} that satisfies $T_{test} = w_0M + w_1T_1 + w_2T_2 +$ ---- $+ w_mT_m$, i.e. Q can know w_0 because the p-th element of T_{test} coincides with w_0E(k, M^*)$_p$, and when the value w_0 is known, T_{test} can be easily calculated as $w_0M^* + w_1T_1 + w_2T_2 +$ ---- $+ w_mT_m + w_0(M - M^*)$. In more generally, M, M^*, T_1, T_2, ---- T_m are H-dimensional vectors, and Q obtains H-equations about (m+1)-variables w_0, w_1, w_2, ---- w_m from Equation (3), therefore it may be possible for Q to calculate w_0, w_1, w_2, ---- w_m when m, the number of test bit string vectors, is small i.e. when $(m+1) \leq H$. On the other hand, it is desirable that m is suppressed as small as possible to make plain text attacks difficult.

To maintain the confidentiality of w_0, w_1, w_2, ---- w_m without increasing the number of test bit strings, for each q = 1, 2, ---, m, P decomposes E(k, M) into {E^q(k, M), E^{qc}(k, M)} so that relation E(k, M) = E^q(k, M) + E^{qc}(k, M) holds, and asks Q to decrypt E^{qc}(k, M) to M_{qc}. Where, E^q(k, M) is the projection of E(k, M) on E(k, T_q), i.e. it is E(k, T_q)-direction component of vector E(k, M), and E^{qc}(k, M) is the component of E(k, M) that is orthogonal to E(k, T_q). Now, P calculates $E_M(T_q) = x_q$E(k, T_q)$+ y_qE^{qc}$(k, M) while maintaining x_q and y_q as its secrets and constructs $T_{test} = w_0$E(k, M)$+ w_1E_M(T_1) + w_2E_M(T_2) +$ ---- $+ w_mE_M(T_m)$, and asks Q to decrypt it. Then, T_{test} must be decrypted to $T_{test} = w_0M + w_1(x_1T_1 + y_1M_{1c}) + w_2(x_2T_2 + y_2M_{2c}) +$ ---- $+ w_m(x_mT_m + y_mM_{mc})$, if Q had calculated E(k, M) honestly. However, when Q had encrypted M to E(k, M^*) dishonestly, it cannot calculate T_{test} from T_{test}, because w_0, w_1, w_2, ---- w_m are not known. Here in a case where $M \neq M^V$, Q discloses only its visible part values as a decryption result of E^{qc}(k, M) of course, therefore Q can maintain the confidential part values as its secret.

Then, P can verify correct encryptions of Q by preparing at least 1 test bit string vector. When it is assumed that $\underline{T}_{test} = w_0$E(k, M^*)$+ w_1E_M(T_1)$ for example, Q can obtain only 2 relations $\underline{T}_{test}^{1} = w_0E^1(k, M^*)+ w_1x_1$E(k, T_1) and $\underline{T}_{test}^{1C} = w_0E^{1C}(k, M^*)+ w_1y_1E^{1C}$(k, M^*), despite that there are 3 unknown values w_0, w_1x_1 and w_1y_1. Where, $\underline{T}_{test}^{1}$ is E(k, T_1)-direction component of $\underline{T}_{test}$ and $\underline{T}_{test}^{1C}$ is the component of $\underline{T}_{test}$ orthogonal to E(k, T_1). Also, the j-th element of the projection of E(k, M) on E(k, T_q) can be calculated as $E(k, T_q)_j\{E(k, T_q)_1E(k, M)_1 + E(k, T_q)_2E(k, M)_2 + \text{---} + E(k, T_q)_HE(k, M)_H\}/\{E(k, T_q)_1^2 + E(k, T_q)_2^2 + \text{---} + E(k, T_q)_H^2\}$. In the remainder of this book, although the correctness of encryptions and decryptions of linear equation based encryption functions is verified as above, only the conceptual procedure based on Equation (3) is described in several places to simplify discussions.

Usually entity P that verifies the encryption checks whether given bit string M is correctly included in the encrypted form to be verified or not, therefore, verifications of only visible part values are enough. Namely, because P does not know the confidential part values, it has no meaning to verify correct encryptions of confidential part values in many cases. Nevertheless, there are cases where encryptions or decryptions of not only the visible part values but also confidential part values must be verified. However in these cases, P is not required to confirm that given bit strings are correctly included in encrypted forms, instead P is required to confirm that encrypted forms do not include given bit strings. Therefore, although more complicated mechanisms become necessary as discussed in subsection "Homomorphic Anonymous Tokens" of Section 2, even in these cases values of the confidential parts can be kept as secrets of Q (in that subsection, P must verify that an encrypted form does not include given bit string M even in forms encrypted by Q).

About verifications of visible part values, in several environments, they can be carried out in more trivial ways. For example, because Q does not need to conceal M^V (visible part values of M are already known to P), Q can give receipt that includes M^V with its signature, and by this receipt P can protect itself even if Q behaves dishonestly while having encrypted M^V incorrectly.

Features of Linear Equation Based Encryption Algorithms

In conclusion, in environments where entities that try plain text attacks cannot obtain complete plain texts, an only remaining drawback of the linear equation based encryption algorithms compared with modern asymmetric encryption key ones is that lengths of encryption keys and encrypted forms become long; their lengths grow longer as security of the algorithms is strengthened, e.g. as more random secret terms are added. Here, the length of an encryption key is a quadratic function of the number of elements in vectors to be encrypted, e.g. when the dimension of a vector is 100, the number of elements in a matrix corresponding to the encryption key is 10,000.

Therefore, linear equation based encryption and decryption algorithms perform well in applications where bit strings are encrypted and decrypted by same entities, i.e. in environments where the operability is not a serious issue, and their additive property plays one of the most important roles in anonymous systems. One of the important operations in anonymous systems is to calculate the sum of the data that are given in their encrypted forms. If encryption algorithms with additive property are not available, every data must be decrypted before calculating the sum of them. When the linear equation based algorithm is used, only a single decryption operation is enough, i.e. decryption of the sum of encrypted data reveals the sum of the decrypted data. More importantly, entities can calculate sums of data without knowing individual data, i.e. without invading privacies of data owners. An anonymous credit card system is an example. In that system, cardholder C makes its purchases without disclosing its identity, therefore individual transaction records of C must be maintained by C itself. Then, card company S gives C its individual transaction records while encrypting them by an encryption key secret from C to disable C to modify its records (encrypted data can be protected from unauthorized modifications, because it is difficult for entities to generate encrypted data consistently without knowing encryption keys). In this setting, S can know the total expenditures of C without knowing individual purchases of C by asking C to calculate the sum of encrypted transaction records and by decrypting the encrypted sum by itself.

Here, it must be noted that an entity may embed information in the data to be encrypted so that it can know privacies of the data holder, therefore additional mechanisms are necessary to preserve privacies of owners of data that are encrypted. In the above anonymous credit card system example, when card company S includes elements, each of which corresponds to a particular store, as the confidential part value of transaction records to be encrypted, as shown in Figure 5, S can know stores that cardholder C had visited even from the sum of C's transaction records. In the figure each element P_j corresponds to the j-th store, and when transaction T_h is carried out at the j-th store, S assigns value 1 to P_j and assigns value 0 to other element P_s, then from the sum of values assigned to P_j that is obtained by decrypting the sum of encrypted transaction records, S can know how many times C had visited the j-th store.

There is another way for S to know stores that C had visited. When the q-th elements of encrypted forms are dummy ones, and S assigns value 1 or 0 to the q-th elements of encrypted forms depending on stores that C visits are the j-th one or not, S can know the number that C had visited the j-th store from the sum of C's encrypted transaction records. For example, if the 3rd element in encrypted form $\{e_1, e_2, ---, e_H\}$ is a dummy element and it is corresponded to the specific store Z, when S obtains $\{a_1+a_2+a_3, b_1+b_2+b_3, 2, ---, h_1+h_2+h_3\}$ as the sum of 3 encrypted transaction records $\{a_1, b_1, 1, ---, h_1\}$,$\{a_2, b_2, 0, ---, h_2\}$ and $\{a_3, b_3, 1, ---, h_3\}$, S can easily know that C had visited store Z twice.

At least for credit card system applications, these problems can be solved easily. Because transaction records themselves are not secrets of S (each cardholder knows its individual transactions from the beginning), provided that S uses different encryption keys for different service periods, C can ask S to disclose its encryption key after all cardholders had paid for their purchases in the past service periods and can confirm that the encrypted forms do not include any information that may disclose its privacy. Another solution will be discussed in Section 2 in conjunction with homomorphic anonymous tokens.

PROBABILISTIC, COMMUTATIVE, AND VERIFIABLE RE-ENCRYPTION

Let Figure 6 be a lottery system that consists of dealer S, players P_1, P_2, ---, P_N and the bulletin boards (BBs), where a BB is a set of memory sections that can be read by anyone at any time as discussed in the previous chapter. In the figure there are 2 BBs, i.e. the applicant and the prize panels, and players choose their favourite letters to put them at positions assigned to the individual players in the applicant panel. However, players put their choosing letters in the applicant panel while writing them on the backsides of cards so that dealer S cannot identify the letters that individual players had chosen. Then, S shuffles these cards, moves each of them to its randomly selecting position in the prize panel, and finally

Figure 5. Transaction record T with elements corresponding to stores

T	P_1	P_2	---	P_N

Figure 6. Simple lottery system

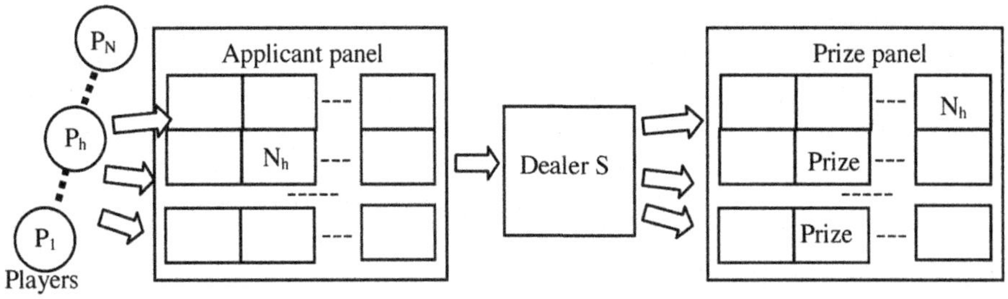

prizes are shared among players of which choosing letters coincide with the ones that are placed at the winners' positions in the prize panel where prizes are allocated by S in advance.

However when the lottery is computerized, players may doubt that S does not fairly shuffle the cards. When S is conspiring with player P_j, it is possible for S to put the card, on which letter N_j that had been chosen by P_j is written, at the winner's position in the prize panel. Also, when some players want to conceal the fact that they are the winners, choices of individual players must be concealed from others (it is assumed that an appropriate mechanism that enables the winners to receive prizes without disclosing their identities is available as discussed in the chapter about object deliveries to anonymous entities in Section 3). Therefore in this case, letters in the applicant panel are not publicly disclosed, and S can pick an arbitrary card, replace letter N_j on it written by player P_j with N_* that was not chosen by any player, and place it at the winner's position in the prize panel. Namely, provided that at least one player other than P_j had chosen N_j, any player including P_j cannot notice the replacement, because N_j still remains in the prize panel and no player knows the number of players who had chosen N_j. As a consequence, any player who had chosen N_* does not appear, and S itself can obtain the prize.

To convince players in the above lottery system that dealer S had fairly selected winners and to preserve privacies of players, the 3 requirements, i.e.

A. No one except a player itself can know the letter chosen by the player,
B. No one can know letters written on backsides of individual cards until they are disclosed in the prize panel, and
C. Anyone can convince itself that only and all letters in the applicant panel are disclosed in the prize panel,

must be satisfied. Re-encryption schemes with probabilistic, commutative and verifiable features in this subsection satisfy requirements (A) and (B), and unlinkable signature schemes discussed in Section 2 satisfy also requirement (C) in addition to (A) and (B).

Figure 7 shows the computerized lottery system that satisfies the 1st and the 2nd requirements. In the figure, the whole system is divided into 2 stages, the encryption and the decryption stages. Also, dealer S is divided into Q mutually independent authorities S_1, S_2, ---, S_Q and they are arranged in the order S_1, S_2, ---, S_Q in the encryption stage and in the order S_Q, S_{Q-1}, ---, S_{z+1} in the decryption stage. Here, each S_q and player P_j have their secret encryption and decryption key pairs $\{k_q, k_q^{-1}\}$ and $\{a_j, a_j^{-1}\}$, respectively, and the

Figure 7 Computerized lottery based on re-encryption scheme

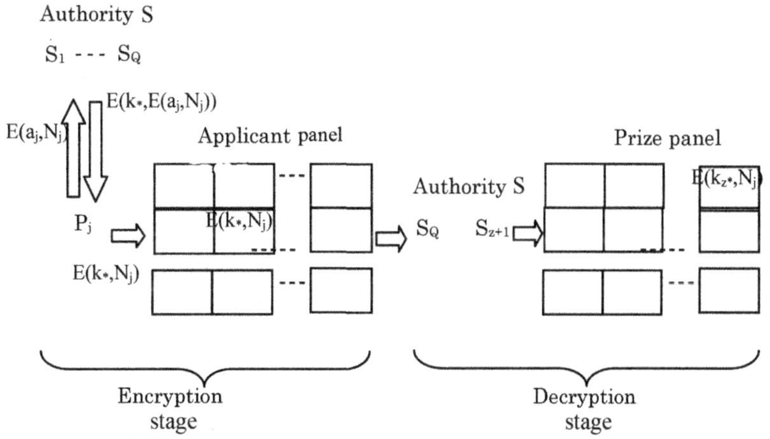

number of authorities in the decryption stage is less than that in the encryption stage (i.e. $z > 1$). Also in some cases, the order of authorities in the decryption stage must be different from S_Q, S_{Q-1}, ---, S_{z+1} in order to satisfy the 2nd requirement, and it is possible because encryption functions $E(k_q, x)$ ($q = 1$, ---, Q) and $E(a_j, x)$ are assumed to be commutative, probabilistic and verifiable.

Now, in the encryption stage, player P_j encrypts its choosing letter N_j to $E(a_j, N_j)$, and asks authorities S_1, S_2, ---, S_Q to repeatedly encrypt $E(a_j, N_j)$ to $E(k_Q$, (---$E(k_2, E(k_1, E(a_j, N_j)))$---)) $= E(k_*, E(a_j, N_j))$. After that, P_j verifies the correctness of $E(k_*, E(a_j, N_j))$, i.e. correct encryptions of the authorities, by using the verifiable feature, and decrypts $E(k_*, E(a_j, N_j))$ to $E(k_*, N_j)$ by its decryption key a_j^{-1} while exploiting commutative features of the encryption functions to put the re-encrypted form $E(k_*, N_j)$ at the position in the applicant panel assigned to it.

The decryption stage begins when all players had put re-encrypted forms of their choosing letters in the applicant panel, and individual authorities decrypt each encrypted letter in the applicant panel while shuffling it with other decryption results. Namely, each S_q ($q > z > 0$) decrypts encrypted letters received from S_{q+1} by its decryption key k_q^{-1}, shuffles the results and forwards them to S_{q-1}, and the last authority S_{z+1} puts each decryption result $E(k_z$, (---$E(k_2, E(k_1, N_j))$---)) $= E(k_{z*}, N_j)$ at its randomly selecting position in the prize panel. Then, remaining authorities S_z, S_{z-1}, ---, S_1 disclose their decryption keys k_z^{-1}, k_{z-1}^{-1}, ---, k_1^{-1} so that anyone can know the letters corresponding to the prize winners by decrypting the letters in the prize panel.

In the above, N_j chosen by P_j is shown to S_1 while being encrypted by P_j itself, and it is disclosed in the applicant panel in the form that are repeatedly encrypted by multiple authorities. Also, each authority S_n knows only its own encryption and decryption key pair $\{k_n, k_n^{-1}\}$, therefore anyone except S_q itself cannot identify the correspondence between $E(k_{q*}, N_j)$ and $E(k_{(q-1)*}, N_j)$, an input and output pair of S_q in the decryption stage, where $E(k_{q*}, N_j) = E(k_q, E(k_{q-1}$, --- $E(k_1, N_j)$ ---)). As a consequence, no one except P_j itself can know that P_j had chosen N_j; no one including P_j and the authorities can know the correspondence between $E(k_*, N_j)$ in the applicant panel and $E(k_{z*}, N_j)$ in the prize panel either. Together with the fact that S_{z+1} cannot decrypt $E(k_{z*}, N_j)$ to N_j until S_z, S_{z-1}, ---, S_1 disclose their decryption keys, this means that S_{z+1} cannot put N_j at the winners' positions in the prize panel even if it is conspiring with P_j, i.e. the requirement (A) and (B) are satisfied.

It must be noted that probabilistic, commutative and verifiable features of the re-encryption scheme are essential to satisfy requirements (A) and (B) in the above. Firstly if the scheme is not probabilistic, when 2 players P_j and P_h had chosen same letter N_j, N_j chosen by the 2 players are encrypted to the same form, therefore P_j can know $c(N_j)$, the number of positions that are filled by the encrypted form of N_j in the applicant panel, and when S_{z+1} is conspiring with P_j, S_{z+1} can put X, the encrypted form of N_j it receives from S_{z+2}, at the winners' positions without knowing decryption keys of other authorities, i.e. S_{z+1} can estimate that X is the encrypted form of N_j when there are exactly $c(N_j)$-encrypted forms that have X as their values. In addition, P_j can know all players who had chosen N_j because N_j chosen by P_j and other players have the same encrypted form, and then privacies of players cannot be preserved.

Secondly, if the scheme is not commutative, P_j cannot decrypt $E(k_*, E(a_j, N_j))$ to $E(k_*, N_j)$ by using decryption key a_j^{-1}, therefore P_j must ask S_1, S_2, ---, S_Q to encrypt N_j to $E(k_*, N_j)$ while disclosing N_j to S_1, and S_1 that receives N_j directly from P_j can know that P_j had chosen N_j. Also, authorities in the decryption stage must be arranged exactly in the order S_Q, S_{Q-1}, ---, S_{z+1}, S_{z+1}, therefore S_{z+1} that had calculated $E(k_{(z+1)*}, N_j)$ from $E(k_{z*}, N_j)$ at the request of P_j in the encryption stage can memorize that $E(k_{z*}, N_j)$ is the encrypted form of the letter chosen by P_j. Then, S_{z+1} can use this memory at the decryption stage to put $E(k_{z*}, N_j)$ in the winners' positions in the prize panel if it is conspiring with P_j. In the same way P_j can inform S_{z+1} of $E(k_{(z+1)*}, N_j)$, encrypted form of its choosing letter, in a case where P_j calculates $E(k_{(z+1)*}, N_j)$ by itself while using public keys of S_1, S_2, ---, S_{z+1} to conceal N_j from others. Although ElGamal re-encryption schemes can remove this difficulty without exploiting the commutative feature of encryption functions (but ElGamal based re-encryption schemes can be made commutative), they have limitations about the performance as will be discussed later in subsection "ElGamal based Commutative Re-encryption Scheme" of this part and in subsection "ElGamal based Verifiable Re-encryption Scheme" of Section 2.

Lastly when the scheme is not verifiable, authorities can easily change N_j chosen by P_j in unauthorized ways while encrypting N_j dishonestly without being detected by others, i.e. even P_j does not notice the replacement when there is at least one player other than P_j who had put N_j in the applicant panel. As a consequence, more importantly, authorities cannot protect themselves even if they are honest when players claim that the authorities had changed their letters.

As discussed in the 2nd chapter, any encryption function can be made probabilistic by mixing a bit string to be encrypted with a secret random bit string. Also when an encryption function is homomorphic, it is possible to make it verifiable. However, additional devices are necessary to make encryption functions commutative. The following subsections construct schemes with not only probabilistic and verifiable but also commutative features to satisfy requirements(A) and (B) based on 2 different ways, i.e. based on RSA and ElGamal encryption functions. About requirement (C), other additional mechanisms are necessary, and will be discussed in subsection "Unlinkable Signatures" and subsection "Verifiable ElGamal based Re-encryption Scheme" in Part II.

Here, the above 3 requirements (A), (B) and(C) can be restated in a more general way (i.e. without being limited to the lottery system) as follows, i.e.

1. No one except an entity that owns a bit string can know the value of the bit string that the entity owns,
2. No one including owners of bit strings and entities that encrypt and decrypt bit strings can identify correspondences between decrypted results of re-encrypted bit strings and their owners at least until decrypted forms of bit strings are completely revealed, and
3. Anyone can confirm that bit strings owned by only and all authorized entities are finally disclosed.

Secret Key Based Commutative Re-encryption Scheme

RSA becomes commutative when multiple entities use the same modulo arithmetic in their encryptions. In this subsection, a re-encryption scheme with probabilistic, commutative and verifiable features is constructed based on this RSA based encryption mechanism while combining bit strings to be encrypted with secret random bit strings. It must be noted that both encryption and decryption keys of individual entities must be kept as their secrets. When multiple entities use the same modulo arithmetic, public keys of the entities reveal their secret keys as discussed in subsection "RSA."

The probabilistic, commutative and verifiable re-encryption scheme discussed here is based on the encryption mechanism that exploits 2 encryption and decryption key pairs, {k, h} for encryptions under modulo p_1 arithmetic and {g, f} for encryptions under modulo p_2 arithmetic (Tamura, 2009). Therefore, {k, h} and {g, f} satisfy relations $x^{kh}{}_{\text{mod p1}} = x_{\text{mod p1}}$ and $y^{gf}{}_{\text{mod p2}} = y_{\text{mod p2}}$ for any integer x $(0 \le x < p_1)$ and y $(0 \le y < p_2)$, respectively, where, p_1 and p_2 are appropriate big integers. Then $E_{k,g}(M)$, the encrypted form of bit string M, is constituted by the data part E(k, *Mr*) $= (Mr)^k{}_{\text{mod p1}}$ and the randomization part E(g, *r*) $= r^g{}_{\text{mod p2}}$ while using random bit string r $(r < p_1, p_2)$ that is a secret of the entity that encrypts M, i.e. $E_{k,g}(M)$ is pair {E(k, *Mr*), E(g, *r*)} as shown in Figure 8. Encrypted form $E_{k,g}(M)$ can be decrypted by decrypting E(k, *Mr*) and E(g, *r*) into *Mr* and *r* by using decryption keys h and f, and by dividing *Mr* by *r*. Here, E(k, *x*) and E(g, *y*) are multiplicative, i.e. $(ab)^k{}_{\text{mod p1}} = a^k{}_{\text{mod p1}} b^k{}_{\text{mod p1}}$ and $(cd)^g{}_{\text{mod p2}} = c^g{}_{\text{mod p2}} d^g{}_{\text{mod p2}}$.

By using the above encryption function $E_{k,g}(x)$, multiple authorities $S_1, S_2, ---, S_Q$ can construct a probabilistic, commutative and verifiable re-encryption scheme to encrypt letter N_j chosen by player P_j as follows. Firstly, each S_q defines 2 encryption and decryption key pairs $\{k_q, h_q\}$ and $\{g_q, f_q\}$, so that both $x^{(kq)(hq)}{}_{\text{mod p1}} = x_{\text{mod p1}}$ and $y^{(gq)(fq)}{}_{\text{mod p2}} = y_{\text{mod p2}}$ are satisfied for every q $(0 < q \le Q)$, x $(0 \le x < p_1)$ and y $(0 \le y < p_2)$. Here, in order to make the re-encryption scheme commutative, each S_q encrypts and decrypts bit strings based on the same modulo arithmetic (i.e. p_1 and p_2), and all k_q, g_q, h_q and f_q are kept as secrets of S_q. Now, P_j generates secret bit strings R_j $(R_j < p_1, p_2)$, Y and Y, where pair {Y, Y} satisfies relation $y = y^{YY}{}_{\text{mod p2}}$ for an arbitrary integer y $(0 \le y < p_2)$, i.e. {Y, Y} is a secret encryption and decryption key pair. Now, P_j asks S_1, ---, S_Q to repeatedly encrypt $(N_jR_j)_{\text{modp1}}$ and $R_j{}^Y{}_{\text{modp2}}$ by their encryption keys, i.e. to calculate $E(k_*, N_jR_j) = E(k_Q, E(k_{Q-1}, --- E(k_1, N_jR_j) ---)) = (N_jR_j)^{(k1)---(kQ)}{}_{\text{mod p1}}$ and $E(g_*, R_j{}^Y) = E(g_Q, E(g_{Q-1}, --- E(g_1, R_j{}^Y) ---)) = (R_j{}^Y)^{(g1)---(gQ)} = R_j{}^{Y(g1)---(gQ)}{}_{\text{mod p2}}$, and based on $E(g_*, R_j{}^Y)$, P_j calculates $E(g_*, R_j{}^Y)^Y = R_j{}^{YY(g1)---(gQ)} = R_j{}^{(g1)---(gQ)} = E(g_*, R_j)$. In this process, although P_j discloses N_jR_j and $R_j{}^Y$, it can maintain N_j as its secret. To estimate N_j from pair N_jR_j and $R_j{}^Y$ is practically impossible because it is difficult to calculate R_j from $R_j{}^Y$ when p_2 is large enough. Namely, requirement (1) is satisfied.

Then, P_j constructs the re-encrypted form of N_j as pair $\{E(k_*, N_jR_j), E(g_*, R_j)\}$, where {E(k*,

Figure 8. Encrypted form of M

Data part	Randomization part
E(k, *Mr*) $= (Mr)^k{}_{\text{mod p1}}$	E(g, *r*) $= r^g{}_{\text{mod p2}}$

N_jR_j), E(g_*, R_j)} is decrypted into N_j, firstly by decrypting E(k_*, N_jR_j) and E(g_*, R_j) to N_jR_j and R_j, i.e. by calculating $(N_jR_j)^{(k1)---(kQ)(h1)---(hQ)} = N_jR_j$ and $R_j^{(g1)---(gQ)(f1)---(fQ)} = R_j$, and by dividing N_jR_j by R_j. Here, each authority does not know decryption keys of other authorities and {E(k_*, N_jR_j), E(g_*, R_j)} is decrypted to {E(k_{z*}, N_jR_j), E(g_{z*}, R_j)} by S_Q, S_{Q-1}, ---, S_{z+1} in the decryption stage while being shuffled with other decryption results, therefore no one can know the correspondence between {E(k_*, N_jR_j), E(g_*, R_j)} and {E(k_{z*}, N_jR_j), E(g_{z*}, R_j)} unless all authorities conspire, i.e. no one can identify that {E(k_{z*}, N_jR_j), E(g_{z*}, R_j)} corresponds to P_j, and requirement (2) is satisfied. This means that, S_{z+1} cannot put {E(k_{z*}, N_jR_j), E(g_{z*}, R_j)} at the position in the prize panel where the prize is allocated even if it is conspiring with P_j.

The above re-encryption scheme is probabilistic, because secret random number R_j that is changed in every encryption is mixed with bit string N_j. Also the scheme is commutative. For example, $E_{(k2)(g2)}(E_{(k1)(g1)}(N_j))$ = {E(k_2, (E(k_1, N_jR_j)), E(g_2, E(g_1, R_j))} = $\{(N_jR_j)^{(k1)(k2)}, R_j^{(g1)(g2)}\}$ can be decrypted to {N_jR_j, R_j} in either the following order, i.e. in order $\{(N_jR_j)^{(k1)(k2)(h2)}, R_j^{(g1)(g2)(f2)}\} = \{(N_jR_j)^{k1}, R_j^{g1}\}$, $\{(N_jR_j)^{(k1)(h1)}, R_j^{(g1)(f1)}\} = \{N_jR_j, R_j\}$ or in order $\{(N_jR_j)^{(k1)(k2)(h1)}, R_j^{(g1)(g2)(f1)}\} = \{(N_jR_j)^{k2}, R_j^{g2}\}$, $\{(N_jR_j)^{(k2)(h2)}, R_j^{(g2)(f2)}\} = \{N_jR_j, R_j\}$. About the verifiability, P_j can verify the correctness of {E(k_*, N_jR_j), E(g_*, R_j)} as follows. Namely, P_j calculates <u>*test*</u>1 = E(k_*, T_1)^{W1}E(k_*, T_2)^{W2}---E(k_*, T_m)^{Wm}E(k_*, N_jR_j)^{W} and <u>*test*</u>2 = E(g_*, T_1)^{W1}E(g_*, T_2)^{W2}---E(g_*, T_m)^{Wm}E(g_*, R_j)^{W}, and asks {S_1, ---, S_Q} to decrypt <u>*test*</u>1 and <u>*test*</u>2 repeatedly, and when the decryption results of <u>*test*</u>1 and <u>*test*</u>2 coincide with $test_1 = T_1^{W1}T_2^{W2}---T_m^{Wm}(N_jR_j)^{W}$ and $test_2 = T_1^{W1}T_2^{W2}---T_m^{Wm}R_j^{W}$, it can believe that the encryption is correct. Here, T_1, T_2, ---, T_m are test bit strings and W_1, W_2, ---, W_m, W are bit strings secret of P_j, and the authorities discloses T_1, T_2, ---, T_m and their re-encrypted forms E(k_*, T_1), E(k_*, T_2), ---, E(k_*, T_m) and E(g_*, T_1), E(g_*, T_2), ---, E(g_*, T_m) in advance. When authorities S_1, ---, S_Q encrypt N_j dishonestly they can calculate neither $test_1$ nor $test_2$ from <u>*test*</u>1 or <u>*test*</u>2 because S_1, ---, S_Q do not know either W_1, W_2, ---, W_m, W. On the other hand when S_1, ---, S_Q honestly calculate E(k_*, N_jR_j) and E(g_*, R_j), they can calculate $test_1$ and $test_2$ by simply decrypting <u>*test*</u>1 and <u>*test*</u>2 without knowing W_1, W_2, ---, W_m, W. Also, to know N_jR_j or R_j from $test_1$ and $test_2$ is practically impossible for the authorities, because they do not know W_1, W_2, ---, W_m, W. Then, P_j can convince itself the validity of encrypted forms as it is using public keys without knowing the encryption or the decryption keys while maintaining N_j and R_j as its secrets.

In the above P_j knows random bit string R_j, but when P_j is a voter in an electronic voting system and if someone Ce is coercing P_j to choose candidate Z that Ce is supporting, Ce can know whether P_j had actually chosen Z or not by asking the value of R_j to P_j, i.e. Ce can know the choice of P_j by identifying R_j attached to the decrypted vote. Therefore, R_j should be concealed from anyone including P_j itself. This can be achieved as already discussed in subsection "RSA." Namely, each S_q encrypts its secret random bit string r_q into E(k_q, r_q) and E(g_q, r_q), and asks other authorities to re-encrypt them into E(k_*, r_q) = E(k_Q, E(k_{Q-1}, ---, E(k_1 r_q)---)) and E(g_*, r_q) = E(g_Q, E(g_{Q-1}, ---, E(g_1 r_q)---)). After that P_j calculates E(k_*, r_1)E(k_*, r_2) ---E(k_*, r_Q) = E(k_*, r_1r_2---r_Q) and E(g_*, r_1)E(g_*, r_2) ---E(g_*, r_Q) = E(g_*, r_1r_2---r_Q) while using the homomorphic property of functions E(k_*, *x*) and E(g_*, *y*), and P_j generates {E(k_*, $N_jR_jr_1r_2$---r_Q), E(g_*, $R_jr_1r_2$---r_Q)}, the encrypted forms of N_j, by calculating E(k_*, N_jR_j) E(k_*, r_1r_2---r_Q) = E(k_*, $N_jR_jr_1r_2$---r_Q) and E(g_*, R_j) E(g_*, r_1r_2---r_Q) = E(g_*, $R_jr_1r_2$---r_Q). Then, because R_j and each r_q are known only to P_j and each S_q, respectively, no one can know the product $R_jr_1r_2$---r_Q, unless P_j and all S_q conspire with each other. Here, values of R_j, r_1, r_2,---, r_Q must be selected so that $R_jr_1r_2$---r_Q < p_1, p_2, i.e. R_j and each r_j must be smaller than some number r_{max}.

About the correct encryption of r_1r_2---r_Q, P_j can verify that E(k_*, r_1r_2---r_Q) and E(g_*, r_1r_2---r_Q) are the encrypted forms of same number r_1r_2---r_Q

that satisfy $R_j r_1 r_2 \text{---} r_Q < p_1, p_2$, by asking authorities S_1, ---, S_Q to decrypt $E(k_*, r_q)$ and $E(g_*, r_q)^X$ for randomly selecting r_q, where X is an integer secret of P_j. Namely, if authorities had honestly calculated $E(k_*, r_q) = u$ and $E(g_*, r_q) = v$, u and v^X are decrypted into s and t that satisfy relations $s < r_{max}$ and $s^X{}_{mod\ p2} = t$. However, if authorities had calculated them dishonestly, they cannot decrypt u and v^X into s and t, or forge s and t so that the relations hold, because the authorities do not know X. Also, although only correct encryptions of r_q are verified, P_j can expect the correct encryptions of other r_m ($1 \leq m \leq Q$), because r_q is selected at random by P_j. To encrypt r_m dishonestly, authorities must take a risk that their dishonesties are revealed when P_j picks r_m. On the other hand, still no one can know the value of $r_1 r_2 \text{---} r_Q$, because r_j is not disclosed for $j \neq q$.

Here, although each $E(k_*, r_q)$ is known to all authorities, no one except P_j knows the correct values of $E(g_*, r_q)^X$ because X is the secret of P_j. Therefore, the above coercer Ce can force P_j to ask authorities to decrypt $E(g_*, r_1\text{--}r_Q)^Y$ instead of $E(g_*, r_q)^X$, while defining Y and Y so that they satisfy relation $y^{YY} = y_{mod\ p2}$ for any y. In this case, Ce can calculate $r_1\text{--}r_Q$ from $(r_1\text{--}r_Q)^Y$, i.e. decryption result of $E(g_*, r_1\text{--}r_Q)^Y$, by calculating $(r_1\text{--}r_Q)^{YY} = r_1\text{--}r_Q$. To cope with this threat, after the correct encryptions of r_q are verified by P_j, authorities ask P_j to disclose X, and check that $t = s^X$ is satisfied or not by itself. Namely, when P_j asked the authorities to decrypt $E(g_*, r_1\text{--}r_Q)^Y$ instead of $E(g_*, r_q)^X$, t does not coincide with s^X.

As the conclusion, P_j can generate $\{E(k_*, N_j R_j r_1 r_2\text{---}r_Q), E(g_*, R_j r_1 r_2\text{---}r_Q)\}$ correctly as follow, i.e. firstly P_j asks authorities S_1, S_2, ---, S_Q to calculate pair $\{E(k_*, N_j R_j), E(g_*, R_j)\}$ while verifying its validity, and at the same time each authority S_m calculates $\{E(k_*, r_m), E(g_*, r_m)\}$ to construct $\{E(k_*, r_1 r_2\text{---}r_Q), E(g_*, r_1 r_2\text{---}r_Q)\}$. Then, P_j verifies the validity of $\{E(k_*, r_q), E(g_*, r_q)\}$ for randomly choosing r_q, and finally construct $\{E(k_*, N_j R_j r_1 r_2\text{---}r_Q), E(g_*, R_j r_1 r_2\text{---}r_Q)\}$ by multiplying $E(k_*, N_j R_j)$ and $E(g_*, R_j)$ by $E(k_*, r_1 r_2\text{---}r_Q)$ and $E(g_*, r_1 r_2\text{---}r_Q)$, respectively.

ElGamal Based Commutative Re-Encryption Scheme

Encryption functions based on ElGamal implement the probabilistic, commutative and verifiable re-encryption schemes more efficiently than the secret key based ones discussed in the previous subsection, i.e. without exploiting secret encryption keys of players (in the previous subsection, player P_j encrypted its secret random number R_j by its secret key Y before asking authorities to repeatedly encrypt it to conceal N_j and R_j from the authorities). However as discussed in subsection "Unlinkable Signatures" and subsection "ElGamal based Verifiable Re-encryption Scheme" in Section 2, different from the secret key based scheme, complicated zero knowledge proof processes are necessary as the additional mechanism to satisfy requirement (3) shown at the beginning of this subsection, i.e. to satisfy the requirement that anyone can confirm that bit strings owned by only and all authorized entities are finally disclosed.

In the ElGamal based scheme, each authority S_q has its encryption and decryption key pair $\{y_q = g^{xq}, x_q\}$. Here, each decryption key x_q is the secret of S_q, however different from the previous subsection encryption key y_q is publicly disclosed, and individual entities can calculate $y_1 y_2\text{---}y_Q = g^{x1+x2+\text{---}+xQ} = g^{x*} = y_*$ as their common public encryption key. Then, each player P_j can conceal its choosing letter N_j simply by encrypting it based on this public encryption key y_* while using its secret random number a_j without using its secret encryption key. The other important difference from secret key based schemes is that each authority shuffles letters in the encryption stage, not in the decryption stage.

ElGamal based re-encryption scheme proceeds as shown in Figure 9. In the encryption stage, firstly, P_j encrypts its choosing letter N_j by public encryption key y_* while using its secret number a_j, i.e. N_j is encrypted to $\{g^{aj}, N_j y_*^{aj}\}$. Then, authorities S_1, S_2, ---, S_Q repeatedly encrypt $\{g^{aj}, N_j y_*^{aj}\}$ to $\{g^{aj+k1+k2+\text{---}+kQ}, N_j y_*^{aj+k1+k2+\text{---}+kQ}\} = E(k_*, N_j)$, where each k_q is S_q's secret random integer. Namely, S_1

Figure 9. ElGamal based re-encryption scheme

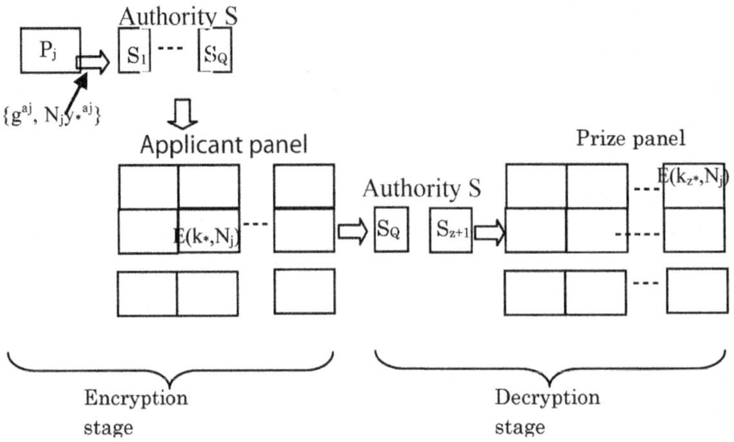

encrypts $\{g^{aj}, N_jy_*^{aj}\}$ received from P_j to $\{g^{aj+k1}, N_jy_*^{aj+k1}\}$ and forwards it to S_2 while shuffling it with other encrypted results, S_2 encrypts $\{g^{aj+k1}, N_jy_*^{aj+k1}\}$ to $\{g^{aj+k1+k2}, N_jy_*^{aj+k1+k2}\}$ and forwards it to S_3 while shuffling it with other encrypted results, and finally S_Q calculates $\{g^{aj+k1+k2+ \cdots +kQ}, N_jy_*^{aj+k1+k2+ \cdots +kQ}\}$.

In the decryption stage, authorities S_Q, S_{Q-1}, ---, S_1 simply decrypts the encrypted letters to N_j by their secret decryption keys, i.e. from $\{g^{aj+k1+k2+ \cdots +kQ}, N_jy_*^{aj+k1+k2+ \cdots +kQ}\}$, S_Q calculates $\{g^{aj+k1+k2+ \cdots +kQ}, N_jy_*^{aj+k1+k2+ \cdots +kQ}/g^{xQ(aj+k1+k2+ \cdots +kQ)}\}$ $= \{g^{aj+k1+k2+ \cdots +kQ}, N_jg^{(x1+x2+ \cdots +xQ)(aj+k1+k2+ \cdots +kQ)}/g^{xQ(aj+k1+k2+ \cdots +kQ)}\} = \{g^{aj+k1+k2+ \cdots +kQ}, N_jg^{(x1+ \cdots +x(Q-1))(aj+k1+k2+ \cdots +kQ)}\}$ by using its secret decryption key x_Q, S_{Q-1} calculates $\{g^{aj+k1+k2+ \cdots +kQ}, N_jg^{(x1+ \cdots +x(Q-1))(aj+k1+k2+ \cdots +kQ)}/g^{x(Q-1)(aj+k1+k2+ \cdots +kQ)}\} = \{g^{aj+k1+k2+ \cdots +kQ}, N_jg^{(x1+ \cdots +x(Q-2))(aj+k1+k2+ \cdots +kQ)}\}$ by using its secret decryption key x_{Q-1}, and S_{Q-2}, ---, S_1 repeat the same operations until S_1 calculates $N_jg^{x1(aj+k1+k2+ \cdots +kQ)}/g^{x1(aj+k1+k2+ \cdots +kQ)} = N_j$ from $\{g^{aj+k1+k2+ \cdots +kQ}, N_jg^{x1(aj+k1+k2+ \cdots +kQ)}\}$ by using its decryption key x_1. However, final decryption results are not directly put in the prize panel to disable the last authority S_1 to put N_j, the letter that had been chosen by P_j with which S_1 is conspiring, in the winner's position in the prize panel. Instead of S_1, S_{z+1} ($z > 1$) puts its calculation result $E(k_{z*}, N_j) = \{g^{aj+k1+k2+ \cdots +kQ}, N_jg^{(x1+x2+ \cdots +xz)(aj+k1+k2+ \cdots +kQ)}\}$ at a random position in the prize panel, and the remaining decryption keys x_1, x_2, ---, x_z are publicly disclosed. Here, as same as in the secret key based scheme the order of authorities in the decryption stage can be changed in arbitrary ways because of the commutative property as discussed later.

In the above, P_j sends N_j to authorities in its encrypted form $\{g^{aj}, N_jy_*^{aj}\}$ so that no single authority can decrypt it, and S_1, S_2, ---, S_Q in the encryption stage repeatedly encrypt $\{g^{aj}, N_jy_*^{aj}\}$ while shuffling it with other encryption results. Therefore, no one except P_j can know N_j, anyone including P_j itself cannot know the correspondence between N_j chosen by P_j and $E(k_*, N_j)$ in the applicant panel either. Namely, requirement (1) and (2) are satisfied. Here, the above scheme is apparently probabilistic and commutative, i.e. encrypted forms of N_j change when the secret random bit strings a_j, k_1, ---, k_Q are changed, also the final decrypted form N_j can be calculated even if keys x_1, ---, x_Q are applied in the order different from x_Q, x_{Q-1}, ---, x_1. About the verifiability, although ElGamal encryption functions can be made verifiable because they are multiplicative, P_j cannot exploit this verifiability as discussed below.

Compared with the secret key based scheme, ElGamal based one is simpler and efficient as long as for satisfying only requirements (1) and (2) in the beginning of this subsection, i.e. when requirement (3) is not considered. To conceal its choosing letter N_j from others, player P_j does not need to prepare its secret encryption and decryption key pair. P_j can conceal N_j by simply encrypting it by the publicly disclosed encryption keys of the authorities. Also each S_q can calculate g^{kq} and y_*^{kq} in advance so that the volume of computations required for encrypting N_j in the encryption stage can be reduced, although the comparable volume of calculations as secret key based schemes are necessary for decrypting re-encrypted forms in the decryption stage.

However the ElGamal based re-encryption scheme has a fatal disadvantage; that is the multiplicative property of ElGamal cannot be exploited for verifying re-encryption results. Because $g^{aj+k1+k2+\cdots+kQ}$ is attached to each decrypted form $\{g^{aj+k1+k2+\cdots+kQ}, N_j g^{(x1+\cdots+xq)(aj+k1+k2+\cdots+kQ)}\}$ in the decryption stage, when they are not shuffled in the encryption stage, letters chosen by individual players are revealed even if each S_q in the decryption stage shuffles its decryption results, e.g. the correspondence between input $\{g^{aj+k1+k2+\cdots+kQ}, N_j g^{(x1+\cdots+xq)(aj+k1+k2+\cdots+kQ)}\}$ and output $\{g^{aj+k1+k2+\cdots+kQ}, N_j g^{(x1+\cdots+x(q-1))(aj+k1+k2+\cdots+kQ)}\}$ of S_q in the decryption stage can be identified by tracing $g^{aj+k1+k2+\cdots+kQ}$. Of course S_q can send its decryption result $\{g^{aj+k1+k2+\cdots+kQ}, N_j g^{(x1+\cdots+x(q-1))(aj+k1+k2+\cdots+kQ)}\}$ to S_{q-1} while encrypting it by the encryption key shared only between S_q and S_{q-1} so that other entities cannot identify $g^{aj+k1+k2+\cdots+kQ}$. However, even in this case any entity can know that $\{g^{aj+k1+k2+\cdots+kQ}, N_j y_*^{aj+k1+k2+\cdots+kQ}\}$ disclosed in the applicant panel belongs to P_j if each S_q in the encryption stage does not shuffle its encryption results. As a consequence, S_{z+1} can know that its decryption result $\{g^{aj+k1+k2+\cdots+kQ}, N_j g^{(x1+x2+\cdots+xz)(aj+k1+k2+\cdots+kQ)}\}$ corresponds to N_j chosen by P_j, and if it is conspiring with P_j it can put $\{g^{aj+k1+k2+\cdots+kQ}, N_j g^{(x1+x2+\cdots+xz)(aj+k1+k2+\cdots+kQ)}\}$ at the prize allocated position in the prize panel. Therefore, to conceal correspondences between players and letters decrypted in the prize panel, each S_q must shuffle its calculation results in the encryption stage, not in the decryption stage. This means that even P_j itself does not know the position in the applicant panel where its choosing letter N_j had been put, and as a result, it cannot verify the correct encryption of N_j in the applicant panel, although ElGamal can be made verifiable by using its homomorphic property. Because of this disadvantage, ElGamal based re-encryption scheme cannot perform efficiently when requirement (3) is considered; time consuming zero knowledge proof procedures must be exploited as discussed in subsection "ElGamal based Verifiable Re-encryption Scheme."

THRESHOLD ELGamal ENCRYPTION SCHEME

The re-encryption scheme discussed in the previous section disables any single entity to decrypt re-encrypted bit strings, i.e. if Q authorities S_1, S_2, ---, S_Q repeatedly encrypt bit string *M* to E(k_*, *M*), E(k_*, *M*) can be decrypted successfully only when all Q authorities S_1, S_2, ---, S_Q agree to decrypt it and behave honestly. This scheme can be generalized as (t, n)-threshold encryption scheme, in which E(k_*, *M*) can be decrypted successfully at least t out of n (in the above case n = Q) authorities agree and behave honestly. The scheme discussed in the previous section is considered as a (Q, Q)-threshold encryption scheme, a special case of (t, n)-threshold ones. (t, n)-threshold encryption schemes are advantageous over (n, n)-threshold ones because they are more reliable; encrypted forms can be decrypted successfully even some of authorities do not work correctly because of malfunctions or they are dishonest. Also because re-encrypted forms can be decrypted by t-authorities ($t < n$), computation volume required for decryptions can be reduced. ElGamal encryption functions efficiently implement (t, n)-threshold encryption schemes as below (Desmedt, 1990).

In a (t, Q)-threshold ElGamal encryption scheme, provided that x_k and $y_k = g^{xk}$ are secret decryption and public encryption keys of authority S_k, and $y_* = y_1 y_2 \text{ --- } y_Q = g^{x1+x2+ \text{ --- } +xQ}$, a single or multiple entities encrypts or repeatedly encrypts bit string N_j to $\{g^k, N_j y_*^k\}$ (here, $k = k_1+k_2 + \text{---} +k_Q$ when N_j is repeatedly encrypted by Q entities), and when t-authorities S_{z1}, S_{z2}, ---, S_{zt} are selected from Q-authorities S_1, S_2, ---, S_Q, they decrypt $\{g^k, N_j y_*^k\}$ in the same way as in the previous subsection, i.e. each S_{zq} calculates $\{g^k, N_j g^{(v(z1)+v(z2)+ \text{ --- } +v(z(q-1)))k}\}$ as $\{g^k, N_j g^{(v(z1)+v(z2)+ \text{---} +v(z(q-1)))k}\} = \{g^k, N_j g^{(v(z1)+v(z2)+ \text{---} +v(zq))k} / (g^k)^{v(zq)}\}$ by using its secret value $v(z_q)$. An important difference from the (Q, Q)-threshold scheme is that although common encryption key y_* is constructed by encryption keys of all Q authorities, the re-encrypted form of N_j can be decrypted by gathering $v(z_1)$, $v(z_2)$, ---, $v(z_t)$, secrets of t-authorities ($t < Q$). To achieve this, authorities S_1, S_2, ---, S_Q defines their encryption keys as follows, i.e.

1. Each S_p randomly generates its secret numbers f_{0p}, f_{1p}, ---, $f_{(t-1)p}$ as coefficients of polynomial $f_p(w) = f_{0p}+f_{1p}w+f_{2p}w^2+ \text{---} +f_{(t-1)p}w^{t-1}$, and calculates $f_p(0), f_p(1)$, ---, $f_p(Q)$,
2. S_p informs each S_h of $f_p(h)$,
3. Each S_p defines its secret key $x_p = f_p(0)$ and discloses $y_p = g^{xp}$ as its public key. Based on $f_h(p)$ given from other S_h, S_p also calculates its secret $v(p) = f(p) = f_1(p)+f_2(p)+ \text{---} +f_Q(p)$.

Then, an entity C that encrypts N_j calculates encryption key $y_* = y_1 y_2 \text{---} y_Q = g^{x1+x2+ \text{ --- } +xQ}$ from publicly disclosed y_1, y_2, ---, y_Q, and N_j is encrypted to $\{g^k, N_j y_*^k\}$, where k is a random integer secret of C. The important thing is that secret decryption key $f(0) = f_1(0)+f_2(0)+ \text{---} +f_Q(0) = x_1+x_2+ \text{--} +x_Q$ can be calculated based on $f(z_1)$, $f(z_2)$, ---, $f(z_t)$, secrets of t-authorities $\{S_{z1}, S_{z2}, \text{---}, S_{zt}\}$ arbitrarily selected from Q-authorities $\{S_1, S_2, \text{---}, S_Q\}$. Namely by Lagrange interpolation formula (Shamir, 1979), when values of polynomial $f(w)$ at any different t-points z_1, z_2, ---, z_t are given, $f(z)$ can be calculated by Equation (4), and as the special case, $f(0)$ is calculated based on (5).

$$f(z) =_j)-z_h)/(z_j-z_h) \tag{4}$$

$$f(0) =z_j)-z_h)/(z_j-z_h) \tag{5}$$

This means that arbitrarily selected t-authorities $\{S_{z1}, S_{z2}, \text{---}, S_{zt}\}$ that know their secrets $\{f(z_1), f(z_2), \text{---}, f(z_t)\}$ can calculate decryption key $f(0)$ as $f(0) = c(z_1)f(z_1) + c(z_2)f(z_2) + \text{---} + c(z_t)f(z_t) = v(z_1) + v(z_2) + \text{---} + v(z_t)$ while maintaining each decryption key x_j as S_j's secret, where $c(z_j) = -z_h)/(z_j-z_h)$. When arbitrary selected t-authorities S_{z1}, S_{z2}, ---, S_{zt} agree to decrypt $\{g^k, N_j y_*^k\}$, firstly, S_{z1} calculates $v(z_1) = c(z_1)f(z_1)$ and decrypts $\{g^k, N_j y_*^k\} = \{g^k, N_j g^{k\{x(1)+x(2)+ \text{ --- } +x(Q)\}}\} = \{g^k, N_j g^{k\{v(z1)+v(z2)+ \text{ --- } +v(zt)\}}\}$ to $\{g^k, N_j g^{k\{v(z1)+v(z2)+ \text{ --- } +v(zt)\}} / g^{kv(z1)}\} = \{g^k, N_j g^{k\{v(z2)+ \text{---} +v(zt)\}}\}$, S_{z2} calculates $v(z_2) = c(z_2)f(z_2)$ and decrypts $\{g^k, N_j g^{k\{v(z2)+ \text{ --- } +v(zt)\}}\}$ to $\{g^k, N_j g^{k\{v(z3)+ \text{ --- } +v(zt)\}}\}$, and finally S_{zt} calculates $v(z_t) = c(z_t)f(z_t)$ and decrypts $\{g^k, N_j g^{kv(zt)}\}$ to $\{g^k, N_j g^{kv(zt)}/g^{kv(zt)}\} = \{g^k, N_j\}$.

CONCLUSION

As encryption and decryption algorithms that play important roles in anonymous application systems, linear equation based encryption algorithms and re-encryption schemes with probabilistic, commutative and verifiable features were discussed. Although linear equation based encryption functions are weak against plain text attacks, and also their encryption keys are prone to being long and consequently key exchanging processes become complicated, they are secure and efficient enough in the environments where data are encrypted and decrypted by the same entity and their confidential part values are never disclosed to others. Then, their additive property enables developments of various kinds of anonymous application systems as discussed in Section 2 and Section 3.

Provided that at least one of multiple authorities is honest, probabilistic, commutative, and verifiable re-encryption schemes ensure correct re-encryptions and decryptions of a set of bit strings while concealing correspondences between bit strings and their owners from any entity including bit string owners and entities that encrypt or decrypt bit strings. This feature will be exploited in developing anonymous communication channels in Section 2 Also, the schemes will be enhanced so that authorities can convince anyone their honest encryptions without knowing the correspondences between encrypted bit strings and their decrypted forms, and will play important roles in developing electronic voting systems in Section 3.

REFERENCES

Anderson, R. (2001). *Security engineering - A guide to building dependable distributed systems*. John Wiley & Sons.

Cormen, T., Leiserson, C., Rivest, R., & Stein, C. (2001). *Introduction to algorithms*. MIT Press and McGraw-Hill.

Desmedt, Y., & Frankel, Y. (1990). *Threshold cryptosystems. Proceedings of Advances in Cryptology - CRYPTO'89, LNCS 435* (pp. 307–315). Springer-Verlag.

Hamming, R. W. (1980). *Coding and information theory*. Prentice-Hall.

Shamir, A. (1979). How to share a secret. *Communications of the ACM, 22*(11), 612–613. doi:10.1145/359168.359176

Tamura, S. Md. Rokibul, A. K., & Haddad, H. A. (2009). A probabilistic and commutative re-encryption scheme. *Proceedings of Asia Simulation Conference 2009.*

Tamura, S., & Yanase, T. (2007). A mechanism for anonymous credit card systems. *IEEJ Transactions in EIS, 127*(1), 81–87. doi:10.1541/ieejeiss.127.81

Section 2
Data and Communication Security in Anonymous Systems

Chapter 5
Approaches to Developing Secure Anonymous Systems

ABSTRACT

This chapter summarizes approaches that are adopted in this book to satisfy various requirements of secure anonymous systems listed in the 1st chapter of Section 1. Homomorphic encryption functions are used to calculate functions of data without knowing their individual values, to detect dishonest deletions of data maintained by other entities, and to identify dishonest entities without knowing any secret of honest entities. Commutative encryption functions are also extensively exploited to maintain integrities of data owned by anonymous entities without knowing the data themselves, e.g. to convince entities that only and all data owned by eligible entities are honestly processed without knowing the values of the data or the identities of their owners.

INTRODUCTION

Anonymous systems must conceal identities of relevant entities while protecting their data and communication from illegitimate modifications, forgeries and deletions. As easily imagined, it is not so difficult to make entities simply anonymous. The difficult thing is to implement mechanisms for protecting information from malicious entities including not only third parties but also ones directly involved in systems while maintaining anonymity of honest entities, and in the course of the implementations, absolutely trustworthy entities that maintain identities of relevant entities confidential must be avoided of course. This chapter summarizes approaches taken in this book to implementing these mechanisms.

As discussed in the previous section, in anonymous systems entities must calculate functions of data without knowing their individual values, they must encrypt bit strings so that no one knows correspondences between the bit strings and their encrypted forms, or they must identify dishonest entities without revealing secrets of honest entities. For example, in electronic cash (e-cash) systems banks must identify entities that had illegitimately made copies of e-cash despite that the entities are anonymous, in anonymous credit card systems card companies must calculate total expenditure of each cardholder without knowing its individual purchases, and election authorities in electronic

DOI: 10.4018/978-1-4666-1649-3.ch005

voting systems must encrypt individual votes so that no one can know correspondences between voters and their votes.

Therefore encryption functions, the most fundamental security components of anonymous systems as same as in usual non-anonymous systems, are required to have additional features. On the other hand, a primary purpose of using encryption functions in anonymous systems is not to conceal data, it is to conceal identities of entities, and one of the most primitive requirements in non-anonymous systems that encryption keys must be transferred securely and efficiently can be removed. For example, in many cases data are encrypted and decrypted by same entities, and consequently, encryption keys can be maintained as secrets of their owners. Then, it becomes possible to use not only modern public key encryption algorithms but also various legacy secret key based ones with desirable features, i.e. with homomorphic, commutative and verifiable properties. This chapter explains how these properties are exploited to implement mechanisms for secure anonymous systems.

HOMOMORPHIC ENCRYPTION FUNCTIONS AND BLIND CALCULATIONS

Blind calculations are processes where an entity or a set of entities calculates functions of data owned by other entity or entities without knowing their individual values, e.g. in an anonymous credit card system, a credit card company calculates the total expenditure of each cardholder without knowing its individual purchases.

When calculations are additions or multiplications of data (only additions of data are considered in this section, but it is possible to blindly carry out other kinds of calculations as discussed later in this section (Goldreich, 1987)), these blind calculation schemes can be easily implemented by exploiting homomorphic property of encryption functions. For example if an additive encryption function is used, although the above card company gives individual purchase records to cardholders while encrypting them by its secret key to disable cardholders to illegitimately modify their records, the card company can know the total expenditure of each cardholder without knowing its individual purchases by decrypting the sum of encrypted records that is calculated by the cardholder itself.

Here, it must be noted that purchase records in the above credit card system are encrypted and decrypted by the same entity, i.e. by the card company. Therefore, secret key encryption functions such as linear equation based schemes with the perfect additive feature become available, without worrying about their cumbersome secret key exchanging procedures. However there are 2 difficulties to use the above scheme. Firstly, although the card company can protect individual purchase records from illegitimate modifications and forgeries by encrypting them while using its secret key, cardholders can easily delete their maintaining records, and secondly, the card company can encrypt purchase records dishonestly because cardholders do not know either the encryption key or the decryption key of the card company.

How to Protect Records from Deletions

Homomophic encryption functions enable implementations of mechanisms for protecting records from their illegitimate deletions. If a check value discussed in section "Linear Equation based Encryption Scheme" of Section 1 is attached to individual records in a given set so that the sum of them satisfies some relation defined in advance, entity P can determine whether other entity Q honestly maintains the set of records that are encrypted by P. Namely, P can convince itself that Q does not delete any record in the set when the decryption result of the sum of encrypted records reveals the consistent check valuc sum.

Figure 1. Detecting record deletions

R(0)	current check value = T(0)	next check value = T(0)+T(1)
R(1)	current check value = T(1)	next check value = T(2)
R(n)	current check value = T(n-1)	next check value = T(n)

Q that does not know the encryption key cannot delete any record while modifying remaining encrypted records so that their check value sum satisfies the relation.

However in subsection "Linear Equation based Encryption Scheme," the number of records in the set was assumed to be known despite that generally entities cannot know it, in addition, records in the set are added or deleted over time, e.g. in an anonymous credit card system, a new purchase record is added every time when a cardholder makes its purchase. Therefore, the above entity Q may dishonestly report the number of records that it maintains. Homomorphic encryption functions can successfully treat also these cases.

Figure 1 is an example, i.e. provided that Q honestly shows its last check values T(n) at its n-th visit to P, if P encrypts Q's j-th record R(j) while attaching pair of check values {current check value = T(j), next check value = T(j+1)} to be given to Q at Q's j-th visit, P can know that Q does not delete any of its records when relation Σ{current check value}+T(n) = Σ{next check value} holds at Q's n-th visit (as an exception the initial next check value is defined as T(0)+T(1)). Here because of the additive property of the encryption function, P can know Σ{current check value} and Σ{next check value} by decrypting the sum of encrypted records reported by Q. Also if check value T(n) is implemented so that Q cannot show same check values repeatedly and Q can have only one check value at a time, P can force Q to honestly show T(n) at its n-th visit. Namely, Q had used T(0), T(1), ---, T(n-1) already and it has only one check value T(n) at its n-th visit. This scheme is applicable also for cases where the number of records decreases over time as will be discussed in Section 3.

Implicit transaction links (ITLs) discussed in this section exploits this mechanism (Tamura, 2007), but in ITLs, entity Q that owns the records also encrypts its next check values by an additive encryption function while using its secret encryption key to disable entity P to know that a same anonymous entity owns records R(j) and R(j+1). Also, entity P multiplies current check value T(j) and next check value T(j+1) in record R(j) by its secret random numbers r_j and r_{j+1} respectively to make current and next check values as its secrets so that Q cannot adjust their values while deleting some of its maintaining records, where secret random values r_j and r_{j+1} are called token concealers.

How to Verify Correct Encryptions

In the above anonymous credit card system, a card company encrypts purchase records of cardholders while using its secret key. Therefore, different from cases where public key encryption functions are used, a cardholder cannot notice even when the card company encrypts its record dishonestly. Homomorphic encryption functions solve also this difficulty, i.e. the encryption function used in the anonymous credit card system is homomorphic (additive) and it can be made verifiable.

As discussed in Section 1, to verify the correct encryption of entity P, P decrypts random bit strings $\underline{\text{Test}_1}$, $\underline{\text{Test}_2}$, ---, $\underline{\text{Test}_Z}$ generated by entity Q as a set of encrypted test bit strings to Test_1, Test_2, ---, Test_Z in advance, and at a time when P encrypts M to E(k, M), Q asks P to decrypt $\underline{\text{Test}} = w_0\text{E}(k, M)+w_1\underline{\text{Test}_1}+w_2\underline{\text{Test}_2}+ \text{---} +w_Z\underline{\text{Test}_Z}$, where w_0, w_1, w_2, ---, w_Z are random numbers secret of Q. Then, Q can determine whether E(k, M) is correct or not, i.e. E(k, M) is correct if P decrypts $\underline{\text{Test}}$ to $w_0M+w_1\text{Test}_1+w_2\text{Test}_2+ \text{---} +w_Z\text{Test}_Z$. Because P does not know w_0, w_1, w_2, ---, w_Z, it cannot calculate $w_0M+w_1\text{Test}_1+w_2\text{Test}_2+ \text{---} +w_Z\text{Test}_Z$ if E(k, M) is not the correct encrypted form of M. On the other hand when E(k, M) is correct, simple decryption of $\underline{\text{Test}}$ reveals $w_0M+w_1\text{Test}_1+w_2\text{Test}_2+ \text{---} +w_Z\text{Test}_Z$. Q can verify the correctness of encryptions in the same way also when encryption functions are multiplicative. Actually, the anonymous credit card system discussed in Section 3 does not require this scheme. Because Q knows details of its purchases in that case, P can give signed purchase records to Q, consequently Q can reveal P's dishonesty even when P encrypts Q's records dishonestly.

How to Identifying Dishonest Entities

Verifiable features also can be used for identifying dishonest entities without revealing secrets of honest entities (Tamura, 2010). Let us assume that entity P detects that bit string M, which was shown by other anonymous entity Q, is incorrect. In this case P must identify Q so that it can correct M, but to preserve privacies of honest entities, P cannot ask relevant entities to disclose their owning bit strings. To identify dishonest entities, as same as in the previous section, P registers Q while generating random bit strings $\underline{\text{Verf}_1}$, $\underline{\text{Verf}_2}$, ---, $\underline{\text{Verf}_Z}$ to be decrypted to test bit strings Verf_1, verf_2, ---, Verf_Z by Q's decryption key k_Q^{-1}, and at a time when Q shows M to P, P asks Q to encrypt M to E(k_Q, M), i.e. P receives pair {M, E(k_Q, M)} from Q. Then, later when P detects M is incorrect, it asks all relevant entities to decrypt E(k_Q, M). Here, entities other than Q cannot decrypt E(k_Q, M) to a consistent value because they do not know decryption key k_Q^{-1}, therefore, P can determine that Q is dishonest when it successfully decrypts E(k_Q, M) to M. On the other hand, although honest entity R decrypts E(k_Q, M) to E(k_R^{-1}, E(k_Q, M)) by its decryption key k_R^{-1} while revealing its identity, R can preserve its privacy because E(k_R^{-1}, E(k_Q, M)) is meaningless and does not include any secret of R.

However, Q may decrypt E(k_Q, M) dishonestly at a time when P detects M is incorrect, or Q may calculate E(k_Q, M) dishonestly from the beginning. Although verifiable feature of E(k_Q, x) easily solves the former problem just as same as in the previous subsection, this verifiability cannot be used for solving the latter problem, i.e. the identity of Q is revealed at a time when Q shows M if it is accompanied by test bit strings Verf_1, Verf_2, ---, Verf_Z. This problem also can be solved successfully when ITLs are combined as discussed in the section about homomorphic anonymous tokens in the next chapter. Namely, when ITLs are combined, Q must honestly decrypt the sum of its encrypted past records at a time when Q shows M to P, therefore P can use the sum of Q's encrypted past records and its decrypted form as test bit strings and their encrypted forms pair {$\underline{\text{Verf}_1}$, ---, $\underline{\text{Verf}_Z}$} and {$\text{Verf}_1$, verf_2, ---, Verf_Z}.

Various zero knowledge proof (ZKP) schemes also enable an entity to prove its honest behaviours to others without disclosing its secrets (in the above case Q can show its honest encryptions to P without disclosing k_Q or M), however they require much more computations as will be discussed in later chapters.

COMMUTATIVE ENCRYPTION FUNCTIONS AND BLIND SIGNATURES

How to Produce Signatures without Knowing Data to be Signed

Blind signature is a scheme, in which signers produce their signatures on given data without knowing the data themselves, and commutative encryption and signing functions successfully implement the scheme (Chaum, 1983). Let encryption function E(a, x) and signing function S(d, y) be commutative, then, entity P that owns bit string M can obtain the signature of signer S on M without disclosing M to S as follow, i.e. firstly P encrypts M to E(a, M) by its encryption key a, then S calculates S(d, E(a, M)) (generates the signature on E(a, M)) by its signing key d, and finally P decrypts S(d, E(a, M)) to S(d, M). Here, S(d, M) is the signature of S on M; only S can generate it because no one except S knows signing key d, and anyone can decrypt it to M if verification key d^{-1} is publicly known, nevertheless S cannot know M, because P shows M to S only in its encrypted form.

Provided that encryption and verification keys of relevant entities can be maintained as their secrets, the above scheme can be extended to unlinkable signature schemes when it is combined with re-encryption and re-signing schemes (Tamura, 2009). Here, an unlinkable signature scheme is a one, in which anyone including signers and bit string owners cannot know correspondences between bit strings and their signed forms. Regarding the verification keys, although they are secrets of signers they are publicly disclosed at a time when the signatures are to be verified of course. The scheme works as described in the chapter "Encryption Schemes for Anonymous Systems" of Section 1 in conjunction with computerized lottery systems, and plays important roles in electronic voting systems as will be discussed in Section 3 for example.

The mechanism consists of 2 stages, i.e. the encryption and the decryption stages, and multiple authorities encrypt and decrypt a set of bit strings on which they are going to sign repeatedly. In the encryption stage, entity P_j firstly encrypts its bit string N_j to E(a_j, N_j) by its secret key a_j and independent multiple authorities S_1, S_2, ---, S_Q repeatedly encrypts E(a_j, M) to E(k_Q, E(k_{Q-1}, ---, E(k_1, E(a_j, M)) ---)) finally to be decrypted to E(k_Q, E(k_{Q-1}, ---, E(k_1, N_j) ---)) by P_j while exploiting commutative features of encryption functions. After that P_j discloses E(k_Q, E(k_{Q-1}, ---, E(k_1, N_j) ---)) in bulletin board BB-1 (applicant panel), and authorities S_Q, S_{Q-1}, ---, Q_{z+1} in the decryption stage repeatedly decrypt it to E(k_z, E(k_{z-1}, ---, E(k_1, N_j) ---)) by using their decryption keys k_Q^{1}, k_{Q-1}^{-1}, ---, k_{z+1}^{-1} to be disclosed in bulletin board BB-2 (prize panel). Here, z and (Q-z) are greater than 1, and each S_q (q > z) in the decryption stage shuffles its decryption results with other decrypted bit strings before transferring them to S_{q-1} so that no one except S_q itself can identify its input and output bit string pairs. Then, at a time when verification keys of S_1, S_2, ---, S_z are publicly disclosed, E(k_z, E(k_{z-1}, ---, E(k_1, N_j) ---)) becomes the signatures of S_z, S_{z-1}, ---, S_1 on N_j. Only S_z, S_{z-1}, ---, S_1 that know k_z, k_{z-1}, ---, k_1 can generate it, and anyone can verify that it is decrypted to N_j by keys k_z^{-1}, k_{z-1}^{-1}, ---, k_1^{-1} when they are disclosed. However, even P_j that owns N_j or authorities S_1, S_2, ---, S_Q cannot know that E(k_Q, E(k_{Q-1}, ---, E(k_1, N_j) ---)) is decrypted to E(k_z, E(k_{z-1}, ---, E(k_1, N_j) ---)) because each S_q (q > z) shuffles its decryption results, and no one knows all encryption or decryption keys k_Q, k_{Q-1}, ---, k_{z+1} or k_Q^{-1}, k_{Q-1}^{-1}, ---, k_{z+1}^{-1}.

In the above, although disclosure of secret verification keys enable entities to calculate also secret signing keys when multiple signing functions share the same modulo arithmetic as discussed in Section 1, disclosures of secret verification keys do not cause any inconvenience if signers do not use their signing keys after the verification keys are disclosed, because no bit string is newly added in BB-2, or no one can change unlinkable signatures disclosed in BB-2. Electronic voting is a typical example that satisfies this assumption; where election authorities do not accept any vote once some of votes are opened so that partial tallying results do not influence decisions of remaining voters. Here, it must be noted that the commutative features of $E(k_1, x)$, $E(k_2, x)$, ---, $E(k_Q, x)$ are essential. If they are not commutative, firstly, P_j cannot decrypt $E(k_Q, E(k_{Q-1}, ---, E(k_1, E(a_j, N_j))---))$ to $E(k_Q, ---, E(k_1, N_j) ---))$ by its decryption key a_j^{-1}. Secondly, in some cases, authorities can know the correspondences between $E(k_Q, E(k_{Q-1}, ---, E(k_1, N_j) ---))$ and $E(k_z, E(k_{z-1}, ---, E(k_1, N_j) ---))$ if authorities in the decryption stage are arranged in the order $S_Q, S_{Q-1}, ---, S_{z+1}$. For example, if authorities $S_Q, S_{Q-1}, ---, S_{z+1}$ are arranged in this order in the decryption stage and S_{z+1} is conspiring with P_j, at a time when S_{z+1} calculates $E(k_z, ---, E(k_1, N_j) ---))$ in the decryption stage, it can easily know that $E(k_z, ---, E(k_1, N_j)) ---))$ corresponds to P_j's encrypted bit string $E(k_z, ---, E(k_1, E(a_j, N_j))---))$ it had received from S_z in the encryption stage, because S_{z+1} can know encryption key a_j by asking P_j. To disable S_{z+1} to know the above correspondence, authorities in the decryption stage must be arranged in orders different from $S_Q, S_{Q-1}, ---, S_{z+1}$.

How to Verify Signatures

To securely use the above unlinkable signature scheme additional mechanisms are necessary, the one is to enable entity P_j to verify the correctness of encrypted signature $E(k_Q, E(k_{Q-1}, ---, E(k_1, N_j) ---))$ in BB-1 that were calculated based on authorities' secrets $k_1, k_2, ---, k_Q$. The other is to ensure the correct behaviours of authorities in the decryption stage, i.e. the scheme must ensure that authorities in the decryption stage correctly decrypt given encrypted signatures and they decrypt only and all encrypted signatures in BB-1 while concealing correspondences between encrypted signatures and their decrypted forms. Provided that the above encryption functions are also homomorphic (multiplicative), to implement the first mechanism is straightforward, i.e. encryption functions can be made verifiable as in the previous section. Also, although to implement the latter mechanism is not trivial, fortunately, an efficient mechanism can be implemented by exploiting confirmation numbers and signature pairs.

A signature pair on bit string N_j is a pair of signatures that are generated while using different signing keys, therefore entities that do not know signing keys cannot forge or modify 2 signed forms consistently. Then, entities can believe that authorities in the decryption stage honestly decrypted encrypted signatures when their 2 decrypted signed forms reveal same bit strings. On the other hand, confirmation numbers are registered bit strings that are unique in the system, and they are repeatedly encrypted so that no one can know correspondences between them and their encrypted forms. Therefore, if authorities in the previous subsection assign different encrypted confirmation numbers to different entities and entities multiply their encrypted signatures by the assigned encrypted confirmation numbers to be repeatedly decrypted, anyone can determine whether there are one to one correspondences between a set of encrypted signatures and their decrypted forms or not. Namely, anyone can believe there are one to one correspondences when each decrypted signature is accompanied (multiplied) by a unique registered confirmation number and all registered confirmation numbers appear as the ones that are attached to signatures.

Verification of Unlinkable Signatures based on Anonymous Tags

If entity P_j in the above can know signed form $E(k_z, E(k_{z-1}, ---, E(k_1, N_j) ---))$ of its bit string N_j, it is easy for P_j to verify whether the authorities had honestly decrypted $E(k_Q, E(k_{Q-1}, ---, E(k_1, N_j) ---))$ to $E(k_z, E(k_{z-1}, ---, E(k_1, N_j) ---))$ or not. Namely, P_j can exploit verifiable features of homomorphic encryption functions. But to preserve its privacy,

P_j must know the correspondence between $E(k_Q, ---, E(k_1, N_j) ---)$ and $E(k_z, ---, E(k_1, N_j) ---)$ while disabling other entities to know that. When the encryption functions are commutative, anonymous tags can achieve this (Tamura, 2008).

An anonymous tag is a pair of bit strings $\{A_{mod\,p}, A^R_{mod\,p}\}$, where A is an arbitrary integer, R is a random integer secret of P_j, and p is a publicly known large prime number. Then, P_j attaches anonymous tag $\{A_{mod\,p}, A^R_{mod\,p}\}$ to its encrypted bit string $E(k_Q, E(k_{Q-1}, ---, E(k_1, N_j) ---))$. Therefore, authority S_Q in the decryption stage receives $\{E(k_Q, E(k_{Q-1}, ---, E(k_1, N_j) ---)), \{A_{mod\,p}, A^R_{mod\,p}\}\}$, and S_Q decrypts it while encrypting the tag part to $\{A^{rQ}_{mod\,p}, A^{R(rQ)}_{mod\,p}\}$, i.e. S_Q calculates $\{E(k_{Q-1}, E(k_{Q-2}, ---, E(k_1, N_j) ---)), \{A^{rQ}, A^{R(rQ)}\}\}$. In the same way S_q $(q > z)$ calculates $\{E(k_{q-1}, E(k_{q-2}, ---, E(k_1, N_j) ---)), \{A^{rQ---rq}, A^{R(rQ---rq)}\}\}$ and S_{z+1} finally calculates $\{E(k_z, E(k_{z-1}, ---, E(k_1, N_j) ---)), \{A^{rQ --- r(z+1)}, A^{R\{rQ --- r(z+1)\}}\}\}$. Here, r_q is a random integer secret of authority S_q, therefore entities other than P_j cannot know that tag $\{A^{rQ --- rq}_{mod\,p}, A^{R(rQ --- rq)}_{mod\,p}\}$ attached to $E(k_{q-1}, E(k_{q-2}, ---, E(k_1, N_j) ---))$ corresponds to tag $\{A, A^R\}$ attached to $E(k_Q, E(k_{Q-1}, ---, E(k_1, N_j) ---))$, provided that p is large enough. But P_j that knows R can know that by calculating R-th power of $A^{rQ --- rq}$, namely, R-th power of $A^{rQ --- rq}$ coincides with $A^{R(rQ --- rq)}$. This means that P_j can trace its bit string in the decryption stage; as a consequence P_j can verify that authorities had honestly decrypted the unlinkable signature on its bit string N_j while concealing the correspondence between N_j and itself. However, it must be noted that P_j cannot verify whether the authorities had honestly decrypted signatures on other bit string N_i $(i \neq j)$ or not.

Anonymous tags can be used also for blind signature schemes, and enable an entity to identify dishonest entities without revealing any privacy of honest entities. If entity P informed signer S of $\{A, A^R\}$ and obtained S's signatures $\{S(d, A), S(d, A^R)\}$ in advance, P can show any entity Q that it was authorized by S while proving that it knows its secret R without disclosing its identity (i.e. without disclosing $\{S(d, A), S(d, A^R)\}$ or R), where, $S(d, x)$ is a multiplicative signing function and d is a signing key of S. Namely, P generates its secret random number W and shows $\{S(d, A)^W, S(d, A^R)^W\}$ to Q. After that, Q verifies that $\{S(d, A)^W, S(d, A^R)^W\}$ is a valid signatures of S on pair $\{A^W, A^{RW}\}$, and informs P of A^{WV} while generating its secret random number V so that P can calculate A^{WVR} from A^{WV}. Then, Q convinces itself that P is eligible, i.e. P knows its secret R, if relation $(A^{WV})^R = (A^{RW})^V$ holds. If P does not know R, it cannot calculate $(A^{RW})^V$ from A^{WV}. On the other hand, other entities including S cannot identify P from either $S(d, A)^W$ or $S(d, A^R)^W$ because W is P's secret. Nevertheless, signer S can identify P when Q finds dishonest events associated with $\{A^W, A^{RW}\}$ without knowing any privacy of honest entities as follows. Namely, at a time when P shows $\{A^W, A^{RW}\}$ to Q, Q asks P to calculate M^R, and when Q finds dishonest events associated with $\{A^W, A^{RW}\}$, S asks all entities to calculate M^R. Then, P is identified as dishonest because only P that knows R can calculate M^R. Mechanisms to force P to honestly calculate M^R and to make R unique to P are discussed in later chapters, and M^R is called a used seal in there.

CONCLUSION

This chapter showed how homomorphic, commutative and verifiable features of encryption functions solve various problems for satisfying requirements in anonymous systems. Verifiability enables entities to verify correctness of encryptions without knowing encryption keys, and as a consequence, it becomes possible to exploit various secret key based encryption functions with desirable features. Then, homomorphic encryption functions enable entities to calculate sums or products of data owned by other entities without knowing their individual values, and commutative encryption functions enable entities to generate signatures on bit strings owned by other entities without knowing their values. It is also possible to generate signatures on bit strings in the way that no one including even the signers and the bit string owners can know the correspondences between the bit strings and their signed forms.

REFERENCES

Chaum, D. (1983). Blind signatures system. *Advances in Cryptology, CRYPTO, 83*, 153–156.

Goldreich, O., Micali, M., & Wigderson, A. (1987). How to play any mental game. *Proceedings of 19th ACM Symposium on Theory of Computing*, (pp. 218-229).

Tamura, S. Md. Rokibul, A. K., & Haddad, H. A. (2009). A probabilistic and commutative re-encryption scheme. *Proceedings of Asia Simulation Conference 2009.*

Tamura, S., Kouro, K., Sasatani, M., Md. Rokibul, K. A., & Haddad, A. S. (2008). An information system platform for anonymous product recycling. *Journal of Software*, *3*(6), 46–56. doi:10.4304/jsw.3.6.46-56

Tamura, S., Ohashi, Y., Taniguchi, S., & Yanase, T. (2010). Detection of dishonest entities. *SMC2010, Proc. of IEEE International Conference on System, Man and Cybernetics*, (pp. 906-911).

Tamura, S., & Yanase, T. (2007). A mechanism for anonymous credit card systems. *IEEJ Transactions on EIS*, *127*(1), 81–87. doi:10.1541/ieejeiss.127.81

Chapter 6
Integrity of Anonymous Data

ABSTRACT

This chapter discusses schemes to confirm that data owned by anonymous entities are legitimate ones, in other words, to protect data owned by anonymous entities from their illegitimate modifications, forgeries, additions, and deletions. Blind Signature schemes enable entity P to obtain the signature of other entity on its data M without disclosing M, therefore later on P can prove the authenticity of M without disclosing its identity. Unlinkable signatures on data ensure that signers had honestly signed on only and all eligible data while disabling anyone including data owners and signers to know correspondences between the data and their signed forms, and implicit transaction links (ITLs) can be used to force entities not to delete their maintaining data without knowing the data themselves. These schemes enable developments of homomorphic anonymous tokens and anonymous credentials, where entities can prove their eligibilities while maintaining their anonymities by showing tokens or credentials. They also enable the identifications of dishonest entities, while preserving privacies of honest entities.

INTRODUCTION

This chapter discusses schemes about blind signatures, unlinkable signatures and implicit transaction links that ensure the integrity of data while preserving privacies of their owners. In conjunction with anonymous credentials, anonymous tags that are attached to physical or logical objects so that owners of the objects can identify the objects while disabling others to identify them are also discussed. Finally, cut and choose protocols and zero knowledge proofs (ZKPs) are discussed. They enable entities to convince others that they know secrets without disclosing them. Although digital signatures enable entities to detect unauthorized modifications and forgeries of data, entities that generate signatures must know the data to be protected, that is sometimes undesirable in anonymous systems. Blind signature and unlinkable signature schemes discussed in this chapter enable entities to generate signatures on data without knowing the data themselves, i.e. entities cannot know the correspondences between the data and their signed forms. In the blind signature scheme, only owners of data can know the correspondences, and in the unlinkable signature scheme, even owners of data cannot know the correspondences. Then, entities

DOI: 10.4018/978-1-4666-1649-3.ch006

become able to convince others that their data are legitimate without disclosing their identities. However, blind signatures and unlinkable signatures are not effective for detecting unauthorized deletions of records in databases; they cannot detect inconsistencies in signatures when records themselves disappear. Implicit transaction links enable entities to detect also unauthorized deletions of data without knowing their individual values.

In addition to detecting dishonest operations on data, entities are frequently required to identify entities liable for these operations or to prove their honesties to others, of course while maintaining confidentiality of the data of honest entities. This chapter also discusses various mechanisms for satisfying these requirements. Homomorphic anonymous tokens, anonymous tag based credentials, cut and choose protocols and zero knowledge proofs satisfy these requirements.

BLIND SIGNATURES

In anonymous systems, frequently signers are required to sign on bit strings without knowing their values. Let us consider tokens that are used to show that their owners are the eligible entities to receive some services. Here, tokens are unique bit strings, on which an authority signs to convince itself that the token owners are the authorized entities, i.e. only authorized entities can have signatures of the authority on their tokens. However, if the authority memorizes tokens and entities to which it had given the tokens, the authority can easily identify entities that show their tokens to receive services. To maintain anonymity of entities, mechanisms that enable the entities to obtain the signatures of the authority on their tokens without disclosing their values are necessary, and schemes of blind signatures enable this.

Blind signature schemes can be developed based on commutative encryption functions, namely, entity P that requires the signature of signer S on its bit string M encrypts M to E(a, M) by its secret encryption key a, and S signs on E(a, M), i.e. S calculates S(d, E(a, M)) by using its signing key d. Then, finally while exploiting the commutative property of the encryption and the signing functions, P decrypts S(d, E(a, M)) to S(d, M) by its decryption key a^{-1}. Here, S(d, M) is the signature of S on M, however, S cannot know the entity that shows S(d, M) because S had signed on E(a, M). There are 2 different ways to implement this scheme, the one is the public key based and the other is the secret key based implementations. In the former implementation, verification keys of signers are disclosed to relevant entities, on the other hand in the latter implementation, verification keys are known only to signers. In anonymous systems there are cases where verification keys are required to be secrets of signers at least during certain periods.

Public Verification Key Based Blind Signature Scheme

A typical blind signature mechanism based on the 1st implementation is the RSA based one shown in Figure 1 (Chaum, 1983). Firstly, entity P that requests the signature of signer S on bit string M generates its secret random bit string R, and multiplies M by R^e, where {e, d} is a verification and signing key pair of S; therefore different from signing key d, P knows publicly disclosed verification key e. After that, P asks S to sign on R^eM, i.e. to calculate $(R^eM)^d$. Then from $(R^eM)^d$, P can calculate M^d by dividing $(R^eM)^d = R^{ed}M^d = RM^d$ by R (P knows its secret bit string R). Here, M^d is the signature of S on M; only S can generate M^d because entities other than S do not know d, and anyone can decrypt M^d to M by using public key e, i.e. $(M^d)^e = M$. On the other hand, P showed S only R^eM at a time when it requested the signature, therefore S cannot know M on which it had signed.

The above scheme enables entity P to make M^d anonymous even S memorizes signature requests from all entities as follows. Let us assume that signer S had calculated $R_1M_1^d$, $R_2M_2^d$, ---,

Figure 1. RSA based blind signature

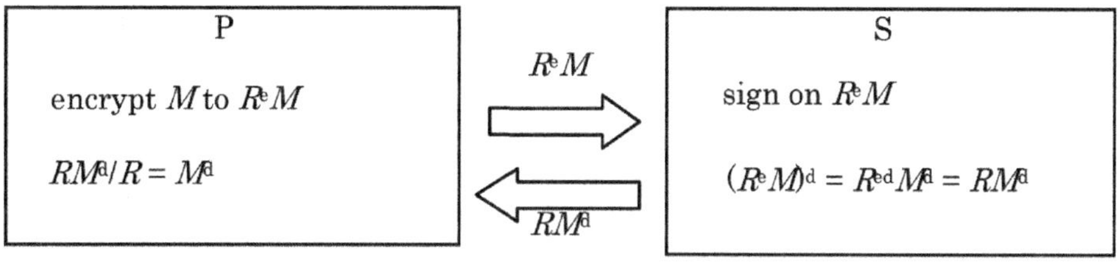

$R_N M_N^d$ at the requests of entities P_1, P_2, ---, P_N to sign on their encrypted bit strings $R_1^e M_1$, $R_2^e M_2$, ---, $R_N^e M_N$, and P_1, P_2, ---, P_N showed S their bit string and signature pairs $\{M_1, M_1^d\}$, ---, $\{M_N, M_N^d\}$ without disclosing their identities (anyone can calculate M_j from M_j^d even P_j showed only M_j^d because verification key e is publicly disclosed). Then, if S memorized triples $\{R_1^e M_1, R_1 M_1^d, P_1\}$, ---, $\{R_N^e M_N, R_N M_N^d, P_N\}$ at times when P_1, P_2, ---, P_N requested the signatures on $R_1^e M_1$, $R_2^e M_2$, ---, $R_N^e M_N$ as shown in Figure 2, S can calculate $R_{jh} = R_j^e M_j / M_h$ and $R_{jh} = R_j M_j^d / M_h^d$ for every triple $\{R_j^e M_j, R_j M_j^d, P_j\}$ in its memory when pair $\{M_h, M_h^d\}$ is shown by P_h. Therefore, it seems that S can know entity P_h by finding pair $\{R_{jh}, R_{jh}\}$ that satisfies relation $R_{jh} = R_{jh}^e$ even if P_h uses $\{M_h, M_h^d\}$ without disclosing its identity. Namely, because $R_{hh} = R_h^e M_h / M_h = R_h^e$ and $R_{hh} = R_h M_h^d / M_h^d = R_h$, pair $\{R_{hh}, R_{hh}\}$ satisfies relation $R_{hh} = R_{hh}^e$. However, because {e, d} is an encryption and decryption key pair, for every pair {j, h}, $R_{jh}^e = (R_j M_j^d / M_h^d)^e = R_j^e (M_j^d / M_h^d)^e = R_j^e M_j / M_h$ coincides with $R_{jh} = R_j^e M_j / M_h$. Therefore, S cannot identify P_h, i.e. the above blind signature scheme conceals identities of bit string owners from the signers. Here, it must be noted that entity P must select different values as its secret random bit string R when it requests signatures on multiple bit strings M_{P1}, ---, M_{Pm}. If P uses same R for these bit strings, S can know P that shows signed bit strings M_{P1}^d, M_{P2}^d, ---, M_{Pm}^d by examining relations between a series of signature requests $\{R^e M_{P1}, RM_{P1}^d, P\}$, $\{R^e M_{P2}, RM_{P2}^d, P\}$, ---, $\{R^e M_{Pm}, RM_{Pm}^d, P\}$ from P and signed bit strings shown by P, i.e. for every signed bit string M_{Pt}^d (t = 1, 2, ---, m) there exists a signature request $\{R^e M_{Pt}, RM_{Pt}^d, P\}$ from P that reveals same R when RM_{Pt}^d is divided by M_{Pt}^d.

In a case where entity P cannot trust signer S, P can obtain blind signatures from multiple signers. Namely a set of blind signatures from multiple signers protect bit string M from also modifications and forgeries made by the signer itself as discussed in Section 1. However, a blind re-signing scheme based on RSA, in which multiple signers S_1, S_2, ---, S_N repeatedly sign on blinded bit string M, does not work efficiently. The scheme works as follow, i.e. firstly, to disable signers to calculate signing keys of other signers, each signer S_j uses modulo p_j unique to it (in the following it is assumed that $p_1 < p_2 <$ --- $< p_N$) and defines its public verification and secret signing key pair $\{e_j, d_j\}$. Then, P encrypts its bit string M to $R_1^{e1} M_{\text{mod } p1}$ to receive signature $(R_1^{e1} M)^{d1}_{\text{mod } p1}$ from S_1 and calculates $M^{d1}_{\text{mod } p1}$ by dividing it by R_1, after that, it encrypts $M^{d1}_{\text{mod } p1}$ again into $R_2^{e2}(M^{d1}_{\text{mod } p1})_{\text{mod } p2}$ to receive $(R_2^{e2}(M^{d1}_{\text{mod } p1}))^{d2}_{\text{mod } p2}$ from S_2 so that it can calculate $(R_2(M^{d1}_{\text{mod } p1}))^{d2}_{\text{mod } p2}/R_{2\,\text{mod } p2} = (M^{d1}_{\text{mod } p1})^{d2}_{\text{mod } p2}$. P repeats the same process until it obtains the signature of S_N, i.e. for each j, P asks S_j to sign on $(R_j^{ej}(---(M^{d1}_{\text{mod } p1})^{d2}_{\text{mod } p2}---)^{d(j-1)}_{\text{mod } (pj-1)})_{\text{mod } pj}$, and obtains $R_j(---(M^{d1}_{\text{mod } p1})^{d2}_{\text{mod } p2}---)^{dj}_{\text{mod } pj}$ from S_j to calculate signature $(---(M^{d1}_{\text{mod } p1})^{d2}_{\text{mod } p2}---)^{dj}_{\text{mod } pj}$. Therefore, P must communicate with all signers sequentially, and this makes the scheme inefficient. The reason why P cannot encrypt its secret random bit string R to $R = (---(R^{e1}_{\text{mod } p1})^{e2}_{\text{mod } p2}{}^{---eN})_{\text{mod } pN}$ in advance by using publicly disclosed verification keys of S_1,

Figure 2. Signature requests from multiple entities

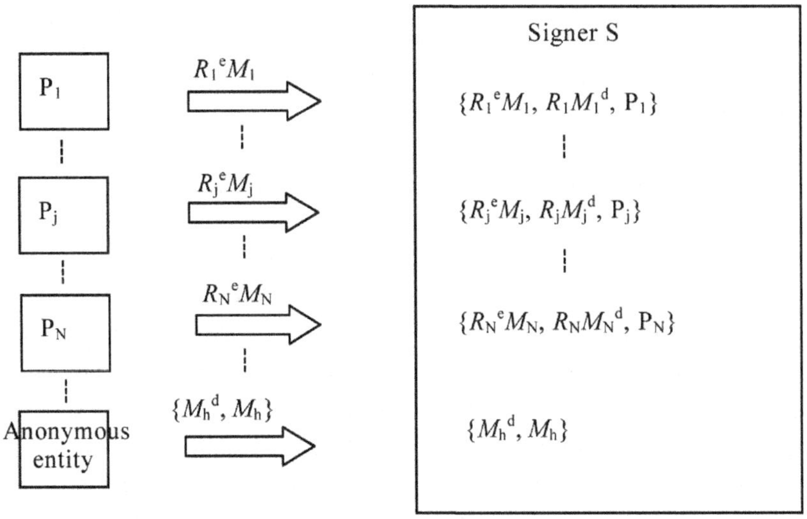

S_2, ---, S_N is that M cannot be multiplied by the repeatedly encrypted result R, because at a time when S_1 signs on M, M is a number of modulo p_1, on the other hand, R is a number of modulo p_N. When this inconvenience is considered, there is no reason to use this re-signing scheme. A simple set of signatures of different signers is more efficient although the length of the set becomes long.

Secret Verification Key Based Blind Signature Scheme

A blind signature mechanism based on the 2nd implementation, in which entities that request signatures do not need to know verification keys of signers, can be constructed by encrypting bit string M and secret bit string R separately. Namely, entity P asks S to sign on pair $\{R^q M_{\mathrm{mod}\ p}, R_{\mathrm{mod}\ p}\}$, and S calculates $\{R^{qd} M^d_{\mathrm{mod}\ p}, R^d_{\mathrm{mod}\ p}\}$. Then, P can generate signature M^d of S by dividing $R^{qd}M^d$ by $(R^d)^q$. Here, q is an arbitrary bit string (integer) secret of P and P may change q for its every signature request, therefore, anyone except P cannot calculate M from $R^q M$ even R is known. In the same way as discussed in the previous subsection, S cannot identify P_h even if it memorizes all signature requests $\{R_1^{(q1)} M_1, R_1, R_1^{(q1)d} M_1^d, R_1^d, P_1\}$, $\{R_2^{(q2)} M_2, R_2, R_2^{(q2)d} M_2^d, R_2^d, P_2\}$, ----, $\{R_N^{(qN)} M_N, R_N, R_N^{(qN)d} M_N^d, R_N^d, P_N\}$ to find request $\{a(h) = R_h^{(qh)} M_h, R_h, b(h) = R_h^{(qh)d} M_h^d, R_h^d, P_h\}$ that satisfies relation $(a(h)/M_h)^d = (R_h^{(qh)} M_h/M_h)^d = R_h^{(qh)d} = b(h)/M_h^d$ at a time when P_h shows signature $\{M_h^d, M_h\}$. Although $\{R_h^{(qh)} M_h, R_h, R_h^{(qh)d} M_h^d, R_h^d, P_h\}$ satisfies the relation, other $\{a(j) = R_j^{(qj)} M_j, R_j, b(j) = R_j^{(qj)d} M_j^d, R_j^d, P_j\}$ also satisfies $(a(j)/M_h)^d = (R_j^{(qj)} M_j/M_h)^d = R_j^{(qj)d} M_j^d/M_h^d = b(j)/M_h^d$.

An advantage of this scheme is that S does not need to disclose its verification key. As discussed in the next subsection, in several anonymous systems entities are required to obtain signatures of authorities without knowing their verification keys. Here, entity P can verify the validity of signature M^d without knowing verification key e, by using T_1^d, T_2^d, ---, T_m^d, signatures on test bit strings T_1, T_2, ---, T_m disclosed in advance. Namely, P asks S to decrypt product $(T_1^d)^{Q1}(T_2^d)^{Q2}$---$(T_m^d)^{Qm}(M^d)^Q$ to $T_1^{Q1} T_2^{Q2}$---$T_m^{Qm} M^Q$, while generating its secret numbers Q_1, Q_2, ---, Q_m, Q in the same way as in subsection "Homomorphic, Probabilistic, Commutative and Verifiable Encryption Functions" of Section 1. Because Q_1, Q_2, ---, Q_m, Q are bit strings secret of P, when S had generated N^d dishonestly as the signature on M instead of M^d, S cannot calculate $T_1^{Q1}T_2^{Q2}$---$T_m^{Qm}M^Q$ from $(T_1^d)^{Q1}(T_2^d)^{Q2}$---$(T_m^d)^{Qm}(N^d)^Q$. On the other hand, S can easily calculate $T_1^{Q1}T_2^{Q2}$---$T_m^{Qm}M^Q$ by decrypting $(T_1^d)^{Q1}(T_2^d)^{Q2}$---$(T_m^d)^{Qm}(M^d)^Q$ when it had honestly generated signature M^d.

UNLINKABLE SIGNATURES

In blind signature schemes, signer S does not know bit string M on which it had signed; therefore S cannot know the correspondence between M and entity P that owns M. But P knows the correspondence and this means that some entity other than P can know the correspondence by coercing P. To preserve privacies of entities, frequently even owners of bit strings are required not to be able to know the correspondences between their owning bit strings and their signed forms. For example, in the lottery system discussed in Section 1, even winners themselves must be disabled to know correspondences between them and their choosing letters in the prize panel to protect the winners from entities that coerce them. The difficult thing is that any entity must be able to verify validities of all signatures even in these situations. Unlinkable signatures satisfy these requirements.

To convince any entity that signatures are authorized ones, namely they are consistent signatures on bit strings owned by authorized entities, under the environment where no one knows the correspondences between bit strings and their signed forms, in unlikable signature schemes, B, a set of bit strings on which signers sign, and G, a set of signatures on bit strings in set B, are publicly disclosed, and also signer S is constituted as a set of mutually independent authorities S_1, S_2, ---, S_Q. But to preserve privacies of individual entities, in many cases, entity P that owns bit string M encrypts it by its encryption key so that no one except P can know M. Then, unlinkable signature schemes must satisfy the following conditions, they are,

A. Only the cooperation of authorities S_1, S_2, ---, S_Q can generate the consistent unlinkable signature on bit string M,
B. Anyone can determine whether B, a set of bit strings to be signed, includes only and all valid bit strings or not, and whether there are one to one correspondences between elements in B and G, a set of unlinkable signatures, or not, and
C. Despite condition (B), anyone except owner P of bit string M in set B cannot know that M is owned by P, and no one including the authorities and owner P of bit string M can know the correspondence between M in set B and its unlinkable signed form in set G.

Condition (A) is same as that of usual digital signatures and in this case ensures that bit strings with consistent signatures in G had been jointly generated by multiple authorities. Condition (C) conceals bit strings that individual entities own on the one hand, and on the other hand, it disables the authorities to handle bit strings dishonestly. In the computerized lottery system example in Section 1, winners can conceal their choosing letters from others, and at the same time, any entity can convince itself that the authorities did not put letters chosen by players they are conspiring with at the winners' positions in the prize panel. There are 2 situations about this condition, in the 1st situation entities are required not to be able to know the owners of bit strings or to prove the correspondences between bit strings and their signed forms until the all signatures are disclosed in set G, and in the 2nd situation entities are required not to be able to know them even after all signatures had been disclosed in G. According to these 2 situations, condition (C) is restated as one of the following 2 conditions, i.e.

a. Until all signatures are disclosed in set G, anyone except owner P of bit string M in set B cannot know that M is owned by P, and no one including the authorities and owner P of bit string M can know the correspondences between M in set B and its unlinkable signed form in set G, or

b. Even after all signatures had been disclosed in set G, anyone except owner P of bit string M in set B cannot know that M is owned by P, and no one including the authorities and owner P of bit string M can know the correspondence between M in set B and its unlinkable signed form in set G.

A distinctive feature of unlinkable signatures is its verifiability. Namely, provided that at least one of authorities is honest, condition (B) ensures the property of digital signatures that "anyone can verify the correctness of signatures" under environments where no one knows correspondences between bit strings to be signed and their signed forms. In detail, by condition (B) validities of individual bit strings in B and the fact that B includes all valid bit strings are ensured, also because signatures in G can be generated only by authorities and there are one to one correspondences between elements in B and G, all bit strings in G are ones that were honestly transformed from bit strings in B. As a consequence, anyone can convince itself that authorities had honestly signed only and all valid bit strings despite that anyone except bit string owners does not know exact bit strings in B or anyone does not know the correspondences between bit strings in B and their signed forms in G

It must be noted that when conditions (A), (B) and (C) in the above are satisfied, all 3 requirements for the probabilistic, commutative and verifiable re-encryption schemes discussed in chapter "Encryption Schemes for Anonymous Systems" of Section 1 in conjunction with the computerized lottery system consists of multiple authorities S_1, S_2, ---, S_Q, players P_1, P_2, ---, P_N, and the applicant and the prize panels are also automatically satisfied, they are,

1. No one except an entity that owns a bit string can know the value of the bit string that the entity owns,
2. No one including owners of bit strings and entities that encrypt and decrypt bit strings can identify correspondences between decrypted results of re-encrypted bit strings and their owners at least until decrypted forms of bit strings are completely revealed, and
3. Anyone can confirm that bit strings owned by only and all authorized owners are finally disclosed.

Namely, when a set of bit strings of individual owners that are disclosed in their encrypted forms and a set of their decrypted forms are corresponded to set B and set G, condition (C) satisfies requirements (1) and (2), and conditions (A) and (B) satisfy requirement (3). As a consequence, by considering owners and their owning bit strings as players of the lottery and their choosing letters, and by considering sets B and G as the applicant and the prize panels, conditions (A),(B) and (C) ensure that authorities of the lottery system in Section 1 not only conceal identities of prize winners but also convince anyone that they had honestly put letters in the prize panel, i.e. they did not give prizes to players they are conspiring with, or they did not modify or forge letters during the decryption stage. Where, although the schemes in Section 1 could satisfy requirements (1) and (2), they could not satisfy requirement (3), i.e. in Section 1, authorities could replace N_j, the letter chosen by player P_j, with other letters without being noticed by others.

Following subsections discuss unlinkable signature schemes that satisfy conditions (A), (B) and (C) while considering the lottery system in Section 1 as an application. Therefore, in the remainder of this subsection, sets B and G appeared in conditions (A), (B) and (C) are corresponded to the applicant and the prize panels in Figure 7 or 9 of chapter "Encryption Schemes for Anonymous Systems" in Section 1.

Temporally Unlinkable Signatures

A temporally unlinkable signature scheme satisfies the conditions (A), (B) and (a) in the previous subsection. When players in the lottery of Section 1 do not mind to disclose their choosing letters to others, they can be publicly disclosed after prize winners had been determined, and re-encryption schemes discussed in subsection "Probabilistic, Commutative and Verifiable Re-encryption" automatically become unlinkable signature schemes. Namely, provided that letters in the applicant panel are finally disclosed publicly in their decrypted forms, repeatedly encrypted form $E(k_{z*}, N_j) = E(k_z, E(k_{z-1}, \text{---} E(k_1, N_j)\text{---}))$ in the prize panel in Figure 7 in chapter "Encryption Schemes for Anonymous Systems" is the unlinkable signature of authorities $S_1, S_2, \text{---}, S_z$ on N_j.

Condition (A) is satisfied because no one knows all signing (encryption) keys $k_1, k_2, \text{---}, k_z$, namely, only the cooperation among authorities $S_1, S_2, \text{---}, S_z$ can generate $E(k_{z*}, N_j)$ so that it is decrypted to N_j. About condition (C) (in this case condition a), no one except P_j can know N_j from encrypted letter $E(k_*, N_j) = E(k_Q, E(k_{Q-1}, \text{---} E(k_1, N_j)\text{---}))$ in the applicant panel until P_j finally discloses it in its decrypted form after prize winners are determined, because P_j asks multiple authorities to repeatedly encrypt N_j while concealing it by its secret random number R_j. Other players that had chosen same N_j cannot estimate the letter chosen by P_j from $E(k_{z*}, N_j)$ either, because $E(k_{z*}, N_j)$ is probabilistic. In addition, because letters in the applicant panel are repeatedly decrypted by mutually independent authorities while being shuffled, anyone including the authorities and P_j itself cannot know the correspondence between $E(k_{z*}, N_j)$ in the prize panel and $E(k_*, N_j)$ in the applicant panel.

Satisfying condition (B) is also trivial. Firstly, each authorized entity verifies its choosing letter and puts it at a position assigned to it in the applicant panel by itself therefore anyone can believe that all encrypted letters in the applicant panel are valid. Also, all encryption and decryption keys of authorities can be disclosed after prize winners had been determined because letters chosen by players are not their secrets. Then, although authorities can disrupt signatures or replace them with the copies of other signatures during the decryption stage, anyone can notice them by decrypting letters in the applicant panel again by itself, while using the disclosed keys. The disclosed decryption keys also enable anyone to identify dishonest entities.

In this way, a temporally unlinkable signature scheme can be easily constructed by using probabilistic and commutative re-encryption schemes. However, the scheme is applicable only to bit strings that are not secrets of their owners. Next subsections discuss schemes that enable owners of bit strings to permanently preserve their privacies. Here, authorities $S_Q, S_{Q-1}, \text{---}, S_1$ in the decryption stage are arranged in this order to simplify notations, but in several cases in this subsection they must be arranged in a different order as discussed in Section 1 or in the previous chapter.

Permanently Unlinkable Signatures

When players in the lottery system do not want to disclose their choosing letters to others, unlinkable signature schemes must satisfy condition (b) instead of (a), i.e. the letters in the applicant panel cannot be disclosed in their decrypted forms even after prize winners had been determined, and consequently decryption keys of authorities cannot be used for verifying signatures in the prize panel. Therefore, the unlinkable signature schemes become more complicated. However, when a set of finite number of letters $\{N_1, N_2, \text{---}, N_T\}$ that players can choose are defined in advance, and disclosures of players that had put disrupted letters in the applicant panel are allowed, a scheme that can satisfy condition (b) can be constructed without major additional mechanisms, provided that the base re-encryption scheme is not only probabilistic and commutative but also verifiable as the secret key based commutative re-encryption scheme in Section 1 was. Therefore a secret key based commutative re-encryption scheme is used in the following.

Here, it must be noted that the secret key based commutative re-encryption scheme is also homomorphic (multiplicative) as discussed in Section 1, therefore it is possible to make the scheme verifiable. On the other hand, although ElGamal (public key) based re-encryption schemes are probabilistic, commutative and homomorphic, it is not possible to exploit their homomorphism to make them verifiable. In ElGamal based schemes, letters are shuffled in the encryption stage, therefore, letter N_j chosen by player P_j is put at a position unknown to P_j in the applicant panel, and consequently, P_j that does not know the encrypted form to be examined cannot verify the encryption even the ElGamal itself can be made verifiable. More complicated mechanisms become necessary as discussed in subsection "ElGamal based Verifiable Re-encryption Scheme" in this chapter.

Let N_j and R_j be a letter chosen by player P_j and a random number secrets of P_j respectively, Y_j and Y_j be secret key pair of P_j that satisfy $x^{YjYj}{}_{\mathrm{mod}\,p2} = x$ for any x ($0 \leq x < p_2$), and $E(k_*, u_j)$ and $E(g_*, u_j)$ be encrypted forms of number u_j unknown to all entities that had been calculated by authorities S_1, S_2, ---, S_Q and verified by P_j as described at the end of subsection "Secret Key based Commutative Re-encryption Scheme." Where, $\{k_q, g_q\}$ is authority S_q's secret encryption key pair of multiplicative encryption functions $E(k_q, x) = x^{kq}{}_{\mathrm{mod}\,p1}$ and $E(g_q, y) = y^{gq}{}_{\mathrm{mod}\,p2}$ (actually $\{k_q, g_q\}$ is S_q's secret signing key pair for $q \leq z$), and $E(k_*, x)$ and $E(g_*, y)$ denote $E(k_Q, E(k_{Q-1}, \text{---} E(k_1, x)\text{---}))$ and $E(g_Q, E(g_{Q-1}, \text{---} E(g_1, y) \text{---}))$, respectively. Also, $E(k_{z*}, x)$ and $E(g_{z*}, y)$ denote $E(k_z, E(k_{z-1}, \text{---} E(k_1, x) \text{---}))$ and $E(g_z, E(g_{z-1}, \text{---} E(g_1, y) \text{---}))$. Then, in the secret key based commutative re-encryption scheme applied to the computerized lottery system, authorities S_1, S_2, ---, S_Q encrypt pair $\{N_jR_{j\,\mathrm{mod}\,p1}, R_j^{Yj}{}_{\mathrm{mod}\,p2}\}$ shown by P_j to $\{E(k_*, N_jR_j), E(g_*, R_j^{Yj})\}$, and P_j verifies the correct encryptions, decrypts $\{E(k_*, N_jR_j), E(g_*, R_j^{Yj})\}$ to $\{E(k_*, N_jR_j), E(g_*, R_j^{Yj})^{Yj}\} = \{E(k_*, N_jR_j), E(g_*, R_j)\}$, and calculates $\{E(k_*, N_jR_ju_j), E(g_*, R_ju_j)\}$ while multiplying $E(k_*, N_jR_j)$ and $E(g_*, R_j)$ by $E(k_*, u_j)$ and $E(g_*, u_j)$, respectively, to put it in the applicant panel. After that, the pair is decrypted by S_Q, S_{Q-1}, ---, S_{z+1} ($z > 1$) to $\{E(k_{z*}, N_jR_ju_j), E(g_{z*}, R_ju_j)\}$ to be put in the prize panel while being shuffled with other decryption results, and finally S_1, S_2, ---, S_z disclose their decryption (verification) keys so that anyone can decrypt $\{E(k_{z*}, N_jR_ju_j), E(g_{z*}, R_ju_j)\}$ to N_j. In the following, R_ju_j is represented as W_j to simplify notations.

Now, $\{E(k_{z*}, N_jW_j), E(g_{z*}, W_j)\}$ in the above becomes the permanently unlinkable signature of authorities S_1, S_2, ---, S_z on N_j, provided that unknown random number W_j for making the re-encryption scheme probabilistic is unique to P_j. Here, authorities can ensure and anyone can confirm the uniqueness of W_j by simply comparing encrypted numbers newly put in the applicant panel with the ones already existed. Namely, at a time when player P_j tries to put $E(g_*, W_j)$, authorities reject it if $E(g_*, W_j)$ was used already by other player and ask P_j to encrypt its choosing letter again by using a secret random number different from W_j. But it must be noted that P_j must show $E(k_*, N_jW_j)$ after all players had shown their encrypted unknown numbers and collisions of the encrypted numbers had been removed, because player P_h that had generated $E(g_*, W_j)$ as its unknown encrypted number can know N_j put by P_j if P_j shows $E(k_*, N_jW_j)$.

It is apparent that conditions (A) and (b) are satisfied, i.e. as same as in the temporally unlinkable signature scheme, $\{E(k_{z*}, N_jW_j), E(g_{z*}, W_j)\}$ can be generated only when S_1, S_2, ---, S_z that know k_1, k_2, ---, k_z agree, also because either encryption or decryption keys of S_{z+1}, S_{z+2}, ---, S_Q or random numbers R_j or u_j is not disclosed, anyone except P_j cannot know N_j from $\{E(k_*, N_jW_j), E(g_*, W_j)\}$. No one including the authorities and P_j can know the correspondence between $\{E(k_*, N_jW_j), E(g_*, W_j)\}$ in the applicant panel and $\{E(k_{z*}, N_jW_j), E(g_{z*}, W_j)\}$ in the prize panel either. About condition (B), because individual players verify correct encryptions of their choosing letters in the applicant panel, the applicant panel includes all letters chosen by authorized players and all letters verified by individual players are valid ones. Therefore, the only ways for authorities to behave dishonestly so that one to one correspondences between letters in the applicant and the prize panels are breached are deletions, additions or modifications of letters during the decryption stage and anyone can detect these dishonesties as follows.

Namely, when authorities delete letters during the decryption stage, anyone can detect the deletions by counting the number of letters put in the applicant and the prize panels. In the same way anyone can detect additions of letters. About forgeries and disruptions of letters, because no entity knows signing keys of all authorities S_1, S_2, ---, S_z, they are detected as meaningless letters (inconsistent signatures). Here, although authority S_q in the decryption stage can consistently forge $\{E(k_{q*}, N_jN_hW_jW_h), E(g_{q*}, W_jW_h)\}$ or $\{E(k_{q*}, (N_j/N_h)(W_j/W_h)), E(g_{q*}, W_j/W_h)\}$ from $\{E(k_{q*}, N_jW_j), E(g_{q*}, W_j)\}$ and $\{E(k_{q*}, N_hW_h), E(g_{q*}, W_h)\}$ while exploiting multiplicative features of the encryption functions, because the decryption result N_jN_h or N_j/N_h is not included in $\{N_1, N_2, ---, N_T\}$, S_q's dishonesty is revealed as a disrupted letter (in the above, $E(k_{q*}, x)$ and $E(g_{q*}, y)$ denote $E(k_q, E(k_{q-1},$ --- $E(k_1, x)$ ---)) and $E(g_q, E(g_{q-1},$ --- $E(g_1, y)$ ---)), respectively). Also, because the number of letters $\{N_1, N_2, ---, N_T\}$ is finite, it is possible to encode letters so that entities cannot find integer v_{j1}, v_{j2}, v_{jm} that satisfy relation $N_{j1}^{v1}N_{j2}^{v2}---N_{jm}^{vm} = N_h$ in a practical time. Simple replacement of $\{E(k_{q*}, N_jW_j), E(g_{q*}, W_j)\}$ by $\{E(k_{q*}, N_hW_h), E(g_{q*}, W_h)\}$ is also detected easily because random number W_h attached to N_h appears multiple times.

However, players may put meaningless letters in the applicant panel from the beginning; therefore a mechanism to determine whether meaningless letters disclosed in the prize panel were meaningless from the beginning or they were the results of illegitimate modifications during the decryption stage is necessary. A procedure shown in Figure 3 satisfies this requirement. The procedure also identifies liable authorities that had illegitimately disrupted, modified or replaced letters during the decryption stage. However, it reveals identities of players that had put meaningless letters.

In Figure 3, $\{E(k_{z*}, N_*W_*), E(g_{z*}, W_*)\}$ disclosed in the prize panel is assumed that it is decrypted to meaningless letter N_*, or W_* attached to N_* appears multiple times. Then, authorities S_{z+1}, S_{z+2}, ---, S_Q detect the liable authorities by repeatedly encrypting $\{E(k_{z*}, N_*W_*), E(g_{z*}, W_*)\}$ again to $\{E(k_{*}, N_*W_*), E(g_{*}, W_*)\}$, namely, each S_q ($z < q \leq Q$) encrypts pair $\{E(k_{(q-1)*}, N_*W_*), E(g_{(q-1)*}, W_*)\}$ that it receives from S_{q-1} to pair $\{E(k_{q*}, N_*W_*), E(g_{q*}, W_*)\}$ by its encryption key k_q and g_q. Then, if S_q had calculated $\{E(k_{(q-1)*}, N_*W_*), E(g_{(q-1)*}, W_*)\}$ dishonestly in the decryption stage, its encrypting results $\{E(k_{q*}, N_*W_*), E(g_{q*}, W_*)\}$ does not coincide with any letter that it had received from S_{q+1} in the decryption stage; therefore S_q is identified as the liable authority that had generated inconsistent $\{E(k_{(q-1)*}, N_*W_*), E(g_{(q-1)*}, W_*)\}$ while having modified letters received from S_{q+1} in the decryption stage. It must be noted that S_q cannot encrypt $\{E(k_{(q-1)*}, N_*W_*), E(g_{(q-1)*}, W_*)\}$ dishonestly in this procedure because encryption functions $E(k_q, x)$ and $E(g_q, y)$ are verifiable. About deletions and additions of letters, their liable authorities can be detected in the decryption stage, i.e. in the decryption stage, each authority S_q can compare the number of letters that it receives from S_{q+1} with that in the applicant panel, and S_{q+1} is dishonest when they differ.

As the conclusion, the above re-encryption scheme satisfies the conditions of the permanently unlinkable signature scheme. However, players cannot choose letters that are not defined in advance. Also, dishonest entity identification procedure shown in Figure 3 reveals identities of players who had put meaningless letters as their choices. Because the procedure in Figure 3 reveals the correspondence between $\{E(k_{(q-1)*}, N_*W_*), E(g_{(q-1)*}, W_*)\}$ and $\{E(k_{q*}, N_*W_*), E(g_{q*},$

Figure 3. Detection of dishonest authorities

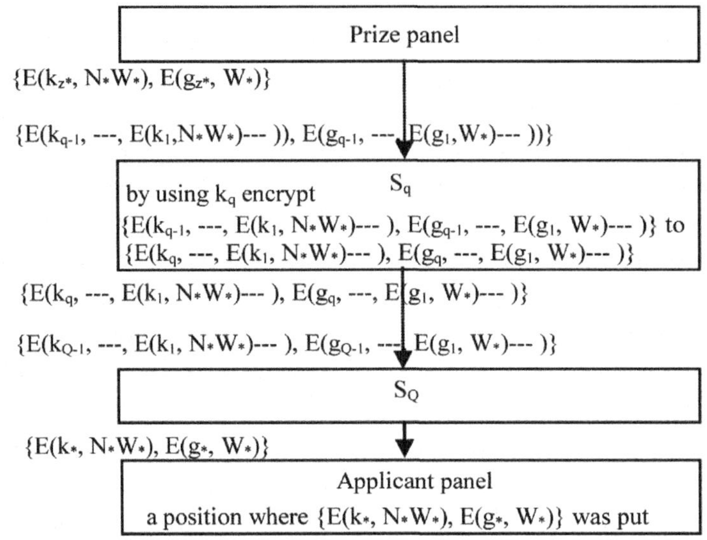

$W_*)\}$ for each q, the correspondence between $\{E(k_{z*}, N_*W_*), E(g_{z*}, W_*)\})$ in the prize panel and $\{E(k_*, N_*W_*), E(g_*, W_*)\}$ in the applicant panel is finally revealed when N_* was meaningless from the beginning (in other words, when all authorities are honest), and anyone can identify the player who had put N_* by the position in the applicant panel where $\{E(k_*, N_*W_*), E(g_*, W_*)\}$ is located. The other undesirable thing is that the procedure shown in Figure 3 must be carried out even if all authorities are honest when there are players who had put meaningless letters as their choices. Confirmation numbers and signature pairs discussed after the next subsection remove all of these inconveniences and constraints.

Dishonest Entity Identification in ElGamal Based Unlikable Signature Schemes

It must be noted that the procedure in Figure 3 cannot be used to identify dishonest authorities when ElGamal based re-encryption schemes are adopted. Let x_q and $y_q = g^{xq}$ be secret decryption and public encryption keys of authority S_q, a_j and k_q be random secret numbers of player P_j and authority S_q, and $x_* = x_1+x_2+ --- +x_Q$ and $y_* = y_1y_2 --- y_Q = g^{x1+x2+---+xQ}$. Then in ElGamal based schemes, letter N_j chosen by player P_j is repeatedly encrypted to $\{g^{aj+k1+---+kQ}, N_jy_*^{aj+k1+---+kQ}\}$ by P_j and authorities $S_1, S_2, ---, S_Q$, but each S_q in the encryption stage shuffles its encryption results. Therefore, P_j does not know the position in the applicant panel where its choosing letter is put, and it cannot verify the correctness of the encrypted form of N_j, although ElGamal encryption functions are homomorphic. Moreover, anyone knows public encryption key y_* and can generate any consistent encrypted form, and as a consequence, any authority S_q can replace $\{g^{aj+k1+---+k(q-1)}, N_jy_*^{aj+k1+---+k(q-1)}\}$ received from its neighbor S_{q-1} (from P_j when q = 1) with other consistent encrypted letter {gkq, N_*y_*kq} at its will to be put in the applicant panel. Also because no one knows all decryption keys, anyone even P_j itself that had chosen N_j cannot detect this dishonesty as long as at least one N_j chosen by other player exists in the prize panel. This means that even a consistent letter in the prize panel is not ensured as the one generated in an authorized way. Therefore, validities of all letters in the prize panel must be verified, and when the procedure in Figure 3 is carried out privacies of all players are revealed. To cope with this difficulty, ElGamal based re-encryption schemes must incorporate a more complicated mechanism as discussed before.

However as temporally unlikable signature schemes, i.e. in cases where players finally can disclose letters they had chosen, ElGamal based schemes work more efficiently than secret key based ones. Namely, while using public keys of authorities players can encrypt their letters with less interaction between the authorities without concealing them by their secret encryption keys. Here, dishonest behaviors during the encryption and decryption stages and authorities liable for them can be easily detected and identified because random numbers used for the encryptions and secret decryption keys of all authorities are finally disclosed.

Unlinkable Signatures with Confirmation Numbers and Signature Pairs

Although the secret key based permanently unlinkable signature scheme discussed before can protect players in the computerized lottery system from various kinds of dishonesties of authorities, disruptions of letters cannot be detected without the risks that identities of players that had put meaningless letters are revealed. Also, dishonest authority identification procedures must be carried out even all authorities were honest when some players had put meaningless letters as their choices. In addition, letters that individual players can choose must be defined in advance. Confirmation numbers and signature pairs remove all of these inconveniences and constraints from the previous scheme, i.e. they prevent dishonest behaviours of authorities without revealing any privacy of players and also exclude cumbersome dishonest authority identification procedures when all authorities are honest (it must be noted that usually authorities are honest because they cannot continue their businesses when their reputations are depraved) while allowing players to choose arbitrary letters that are not defined in advance (Tamura, 2009).

Confirmation numbers (CNs) are registered bit strings that are unique in the system, and they are attached to other bit strings to enable authorities to decide whether the bit strings are the authorized ones or not. For example, when confirmation number C_j is assigned to player P_j in the lottery system and letter N_j chosen by P_j and C_j are combined in the way they cannot be separated or modified, N_j finally disclosed in the prize panel is ensured as the authorized one provided that it is accompanied by unique and consistent C_j. Also, anyone can convince itself that all letters chosen by players are disclosed in the prize panel when all registered confirmation numbers are revealed. Here, to preserve privacies of individual players, CNs assigned to players must be concealed from anyone even from players themselves. As same as unknown random number assigned to P_j in the secret key based commutative re-encryption scheme, when C_j assigned to P_j is known to even P_j itself, entity Ce can ask P_j to tell C_j, and Ce can know N_j chosen by P_j from C_j attached to N_j in the prize panel. Contrarily when P_j does not know C_j, P_j can tell Ce any letter in the prize panel as the one it had chosen. Therefore, CNs are re-encrypted by multiple authorities in advance in the way no one can link individual CNs to their re-encrypted forms based on the mechanism discussed in subsection "Probabilistic, Commutative and Verifiable Re-encryption."

A signature pair on bit string M of authority S is a pair of signatures S(d_1, M) and S(d_2, M) that are generated while using different signing keys {d_1, d_2} of S. Although S(d_1, M) enables entities to confirm that M is the authorized bit string when S(d_1, M) is successfully decrypted into M, if S(d_1, M) is decrypted into a meaningless bit string, no one can prove that S(d_1, M) is the one disrupted by someone or it is the signature on a bit string meaningless from the beginning (here, it is assumed that $S(d_1, M)$ cannot be accompanied by M to maintain the confidentiality of M itself). Signature pairs enable entities to distinguish the above 2 cases. Namely, because entities that do not know 2 signing keys $\{d_1, d_2\}$ cannot forge $S(d_1, M)$ and $S(d_2, M)$ so that their decrypted forms coincide, entities can decide that M is disrupted during the decryption stage when $S(d_1, M)$ and $S(d_2, M)$ are not decrypted into the same bit string. On the other hand, they can convince themselves that the signer signed on a bit string meaningless from the beginning when $S(d_1, M)$ and $S(d_2, M)$ are decrypted into the same bit string. Then, by exploiting the uniqueness of registered CNs and the difficulties of forging consistent signature pairs, it becomes possible to detect all kind of dishonesties in the lottery system while not disclosing any privacy of honest players. Namely, no single entity can consistently generate letters with pairs of signatures accompanied by unique and registered CNs in unauthorized ways.

In the following, authorities $S_1, S_2, ---, S_Q$ are divided into 2 groups, the one is $\{S_1, S_2, ---, S_z\}$ and the other is $\{S_{z+1}, S_{z+2}, ---, S_Q\}$, and for $q > z$, authority S_q has its secret encryption keys k_q and g_q of encryption functions $E(k_q, x)$ and $E(g_q, y)$ for data part and randomization part values respectively. For $q \leq z$, S_q has 2 signing key pairs $\{s_{1q}, t_{1q}\}$ and $\{s_{2q}, t_{2q}\}$ of signing functions $S(s_{1q}, x)$, $S(t_{1q}, y)$ and $S(s_{2q}, x)$, $S(t_{2q}, y)$. Signing keys $\{s_{1q}, s_{2q}\}$ are for data part values and $\{t_{1q}, t_{2q}\}$ are for randomization part values. Here, all encryption and signing functions are multiplicative, commutative, and verifiable because they are RSA based ones that share the same modulo arithmetic. Then, the lottery system based on the permanently unlinkable signature scheme supported by CNs and signature pairs works as below.

Firstly, $C_1, C_2, ---, C_N$ (N is the number of players) are disclosed to all relevant entities as the set of registered CNs, and to disable all entities to know CNs assigned to individual players, each S_q ($q > z$) repeatedly encrypts CNs while shuffling them, i.e. S_{z+1} encrypts each confirmation number C_m to $E(k_{z+1}, C_m)$ and sends it to S_{z+2} while shuffling it with other encryption results, S_{z+2} encrypts $E(k_{z+1}, C_m)$ to $E(k_{z+2}, E(k_{z+1}, C_m))$ to send it to S_{z+3} also while shuffling it with other encryption results, and $S_{z+3}, ---, S_Q$ behave in the same way. As a consequence, S_Q finally generates $E(k_{(z+1)\_Q}, C_m) = E(k_Q, ---, E(k_{z+2}, E(k_{z+1}, C_m))---)$, and S_Q discloses each $E(k_{(z+1)\_Q}, C_m)$ as the encrypted registered C_m. Therefore, although all CNs and their re-encrypted forms are disclosed as shown in Figure 4, anyone cannot calculate C_m from $E(k_{(z+1)\_Q}, C_m)$, i.e. no one knows the correspondences between registered CNs and their re-encrypted forms. Here, $E(k_{(z+1)\_Q}, C_m)$ is not probabilistic; however this does not cause any inconvenience. Because all CNs have different values and each encryption and decryption key pair is secrets of the corresponding authority, no one can know x from $E(k_{(z+1)\_Q}, x)$ by comparing it with other encrypted forms or by encrypting x by itself.

At the same time, each S_q ($q > z$) generates its secret numbers $u_{q1}, u_{q2}, ---, u_{qN}$ and encrypts them to $E(k_q, u_{q1})$, $E(k_q, u_{q2})$, ---, $E(k_q, u_{qN})$ and $E(g_q, u_{q1})$, $E(g_q, u_{q2})$, ---, $E(g_q, u_{qN})$ to ask other authorities $S_{z+1}, ---, S_{q-1}, S_{q+1}, ---, S_Q$ to repeatedly encrypt them to $E(k_{(z+1)\_Q}, u_{q1})$, ---, $E(k_{(z+1)\_Q}, u_{qN})$ and $E(g_{(z+1)\_Q}, u_{q1})$, ---, $E(g_{(z+1)\_Q}, u_{qN})$, where, $E(g_{(z+1)\_Q}, x)$ denotes $E(g_Q, ---, E(g_{z+2}, E(g_{z+1}, x))---)$ as $E(k_{(z+1)\_Q}, x)$ does. Then for each j, S_Q calculates $E(k_{(z+1)\_Q}, u_j) = E(k_{(z+1)\_Q}, u_{1j})E(k_{(z+1)\_Q}, u_{2j})$ --- $E(k_{(z+1)\_Q}, u_{Qj})$ and $E(g_{(z+1)\_Q}, u_j) = E(g_{(z+1)\_Q}, u_{1j})$ $E(g_{(z+1)\_Q}, u_{2j})$--- $E(g_{(z+1)\_Q}, u_{Qj})$ as encrypted forms of $u_j = u_{1j}u_{2j}$ --- u_{Nj}, a number that no one knows.

Then in the encryption stage, encrypted confirmation number $E(k_{(z+1)\_Q}, C_j)$ and encrypted unknown number $\{E(k_{(z+1)\_Q}, u_j), E(kg_{z+1)\_Q}, u_j)\}$ are assigned to player P_j, and P_j generates its secret random number R_j and its secret encryption and decryption key pair Y_j and Y_j to ask authorities $S_{z+1}, S_{z+2}, ---, S_Q$ to encrypt its choosing letter N_j and R_j^{Yj} to $\{E(k_{(z+1)\_Q}, R_jN_j), E(g_{(z+1)\_Q}, R_j^{Yj})\}$ so

Figure 4. Registered CNs and their re-encrypted forms

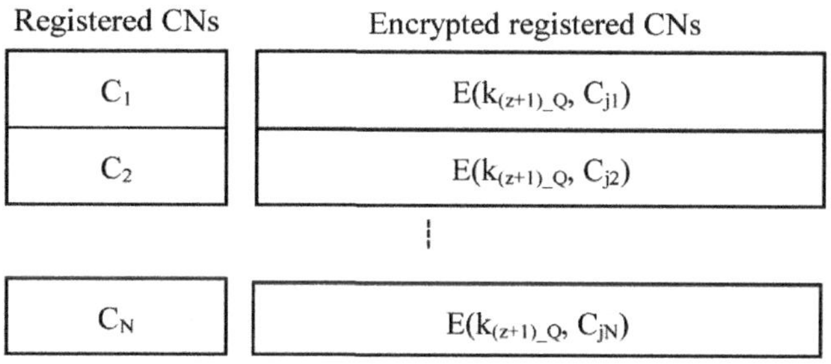
Registered CNs
Encrypted registered CNs
C_1
$E(k_{(z+1)_Q}, C_{j1})$
C_2
$E(k_{(z+1)_Q}, C_{j2})$
C_N
$E(k_{(z+1)_Q}, C_{jN})$

that it can calculate $\{E(k_{(z+1)\_Q}, R_jN_j), E(g_{(z+1)\_Q}, R_j)\}$. Here, P_j can calculate $E(g_{(z+1)\_Q}, R_j)$ from $E(g_{(z+1)\_Q}, R_j^{Yj})$ as $E(g_{(z+1)\_Q}, R_j) = E(g_{(z+1)\_Q}, R_j^{Yj})^{Yj}$. Then, by exploiting the homomorphism of encryption functions $E(k_{(z+1)\_Q}, x)$ and $E(g_{(z+1)\_Q}, x)$, P_j calculates $E(k_{(z+1)\_Q}, R_jN_j)E(k_{(z+1)\_Q}, u_j)E(k_{(z+1)\_Q}, C_j) = E(k_{(z+1)\_Q}, R_ju_jN_jC_j) = E(k_{(z+1)\_Q}, W_jN_jC_j)$ and $E(g_{(z+1)\_Q}, R_j)E(g_{(z+1)\_Q}, u_j) = E(g_{(z+1)\_Q}, R_ju_j) = E(g_{(z+1)\_Q}, W_j)$, and put triple $\{E(k_{(z+1)\_Q}, W_jN_jC_j), E(g_{(z+1)\_Q}, W_j), E(k_{(z+1)\_Q}, C_j)\}$ at the position that is assigned to it in the applicant panel. After that, each S_q $(q \leq z)$ repeatedly signs on individual encrypted letters in the applicant panel by its 2 different signing key pairs $\{s_{1q}, t_{1q}\}$ and $\{s_{2q}, t_{2q}\}$, i.e. provided that $S(s_{h*}, x) = S(s_{hz}, \text{---}\ S(s_{h1}, x)\text{---})$ and $S(t_{h*}, y) = S(t_{hz}, \text{---}\ S(t_{h1}, y)\text{---})$ for h = 1 and 2, each triple $\{E(k_{(z+1)\_Q}, W_jN_jC_j), E(g_{(z+1)\_Q}, W_j), E(k_{(Z+1)\_Q}, C_j)\}$ is transformed into $\{S(s_{1*}, E(k_{(z+1)\_Q}, W_jN_jC_j)), S(t_{1*}, E(g_{(z+1)\_Q}, W_j)), S(s_{1*}, E(k_{(z+1)\_Q}, C_j)), S(s_{2*}, E(k_{(z+1)\_Q}, W_jN_jC_j)), S(t_{2*}, E(g_{(z+1)\_Q}, W_j))\}$. In the above, it must be noted that S_q signs on $W_jN_jC_j$ and W_j by 2 signing key pairs $\{s_{1q}, s_{2q}\}$ and $\{t_{1q}, t_{2q}\}$, but it signs on C_j only by s_{1q}, and although individual encryption and signing keys of the authorities are their secrets, P_j can confirm the correctness of encryption and signing results because the encryption and the signing functions are verifiable. Also, authorities can make each unknown random number W_j unique to P_j as mentioned just before the previous subsection.

In the decryption stage, authorities S_Q, S_{Q-1}, ---, S_{z+1} repeatedly decrypt each $\{S(s_{1*}, E(k_{(z+1)\_Q}, W_jN_jC_j)), S(t_{1*}, E(g_{(z+1)\_Q}, W_j)), S(s_{1*}, E(k_{(z+1)\_Q}, C_j)), S(s_{2*}, E(k_{(z+1)\_Q}, W_jN_jC_j)), S(t_{2*}, E(g_{(z+1)\_Q}, W_j))\}$ to $\{S(s_{1*}, W_jN_jC_j), S(t_{1*}, W_j), S(s_{1*}, C_j), S(s_{2*}, W_jN_jC_j), S(t_{2*}, W_j)\}$ while shuffling their partial decryption results to put the results at the randomly selected position in the prize panel, and final lottery results are opened as the disclosures of all verification keys of S_1, S_2, ---, S_z, i.e. by these keys anyone can decrypt $\{S(s_{1*}, W_jN_jC_j), S(t_{1*}, W_j), S(s_{1*}, C_j), S(s_{2*}, W_jN_jC_j), S(t_{2*}, W_j)\}$ in the prize panel to triple $\{W_jN_jC_j, W_j, C_j\}$ and extract N_j by dividing $W_jN_jC_j$ by W_j and C_j.

Here, $\{S(s_{1*}, W_jN_jC_j)), S(t_{1*}, W_j)), S(s_{1*}, C_j)), S(s_{2*}, W_jN_jC_j)), S(t_{2*}, W_j))\}$ is the permanently unlinkable signature of multiple authorities S_1, S_2, ---, S_z on letter N_j chosen by P_j. As same as the previous permanently unlinkable signature scheme, apparently the above scheme satisfies conditions (A) and (C). The important thing is about condition (B), that is, not only validities of encrypted letters in the applicant panel are ensured because individual players verify them as in the previous scheme, but also supported by CNs and signature pairs, the scheme can perfectly detect deletions, additions, modifications, disruptions and forgeries of letters during the decryption stage without carrying out the dishonest authority identification procedure shown in Figure 3, in other words without revealing any privacy of players. Moreover, players can choose any letter without being restricted to ones that are defined in advance.

Namely, anyone can detect dishonest operations of authorities during the decryption stage as below. In the following, $E(k_{(z+1)\_q}, x) = E(k_q, E(k_{q-1}, \text{---} E(k_{z+1}, x)\text{---}))$ and $E(g_{(z+1)\_q}, y) = E(g_q, E(g_{q-1}, \text{---} E(g_{z+1}, y)\text{---}))$, and to simplify descriptions, input $\{S(s_{1*}, E(k_{(z+1)\_q}, W_hN_hC_h)), S(t_{1*}, E(g_{(z+1)\_q}, W_h)), S(s_{1*}, E(k_{(z+1)\_q}, C_h)), S(s_{2*}, E(k_{(z+1)\_q}, W_hN_hC_h)), S(t_{2*}, E(g_{(z+1)\_q}, W_h))\}$ to S_q in the decryption stage is abbreviated to triple $\{S(s_{1*}, E(k_{(z+1)\_q}, W_hN_hC_h)), S(t_{1*}, E(g_{(z+1)\_q}, W_h)), S(s_{1*}, E(k_{(z+1)\_q}, C_h))\}$ when there is no confusion.

Now, there are 5 ways for authorities to illegitimately generate consistent signatures on letters or to delete or disrupt them without conspiring with all other authorities. The 1st way is to copy authorized signatures from letters put by other players, however, because copies of letters have the same CNs as their original ones do, anyone can detect these dishonesties as multiple appearances of same CNs. As the 2nd way, authorities can multiply an encrypted letter by another one. When authority S_q multiplies encrypted forms of N_h and N_j, i.e. when S_q multiplies $\{S(s_{1*}, E(k_{(z+1)\_q}, W_hN_hC_h)), S(t_{1*}, E(g_{(z+1)\_q}, W_h)), S(s_{1*}, E(k_{(z+1)\_q*}, C_h))\}$ and $\{S(s_{1*}, E(k_{(z+1)\_q}, W_jN_jC_j)), S(t_{1*}, E(g_{(z+1)\_q}, W_j)), S(s_{1*}, E(k_{(z+1)\_q}, C_j))\}$ in the decryption stage, because of the homomorphism of encryption and signing functions, the result becomes $\{S(s_{1*}, E(k_{(z+1)\_q}, W_hW_jN_hN_jC_hC_j)), S(t_{1*}, E(g_{(z+1)\_q}, W_hW_j)), S(s_{1*}, E(k_{(z+1)\_q}, C_hC_j))\}$. Therefore the product constitutes the re-encrypted form of N_hN_j with consistent signatures of authorities. However, anyone can easily notice that C_hC_j, the value of the CN attached to it is invalid, i.e. C_hC_j is not a registered one, it is a repeatedly used one, or it is an unused one. Here, unused CNs are registered ones that had not been assigned to any player, and letters accompanied by unused CNs can be detected easily when the authorities decrypt and disclose also CNs that were not assigned to any player. In the same way, anyone can notice when S_q replaces $\{S(s_{1*}, E(k_{(z+1)\_q}, W_hN_hC_h)), S(t_{1*}, E(k_{(z+1)\_q}, W_h)), S(s_{1*}, E(k_{(z+1)\_q}, C_h))\}$ with $\{S(s_{1*}, E(k_{(z+1)\_q}, W_hN_hC_h))^H = S(s_{1*}, E(k_{(z+1)\_q}, (W_hN_hC_h)^H)), S(t_{1*}, E(k_{(z+1)\_q}, W_h^H)), S(s_{1*}, E(k_{(z+1)\_q}, C_h^H))\}$.

As the 3rd way, authority S_q can replace N_j put by P_j with N_h put by P_h as follows. Namely, when 2 encrypted letters $\{S(s_{1*}, E(k_{(z+1)\_q}, W_jN_jC_j)), S(t_{1*}, E(g_{(z+1)\_q}, W_j)), S(s_{1*}, E(k_{(z+1)\_q}, C_j))\}$ and $\{S(s_{1*}, E(k_{(z+1)\_q}, W_hN_hC_h)), S(t_{1*}, E(g_{(z+1)\_q}, W_h)), S(s_{1*}, E(k_{(z+1)\_q}, C_h))\}$ are given to S_q, because of the homomorphism, $S(s_{1*}, E(k_{(z+1)\_q}, W_hN_h))$ can be obtained as $S(s_{1*}, E(k_{(z+1)\_q}, W_hN_hC_h)/S(s_{1*}, E(k_{(z+1)\_q}, C_h))$, then triple $\{S(s_{1*}, E(k_{(z+1)\_q}, W_jN_jC_j)), S(t_{1*}, E(g_{(z+1)\_q}, W_j)), S(s_{1*}, E(k_{(z+1)\_q}, C_j))\}$ can be modified to the consistent triple $\{S(s_{1*}, E(k_{(z+1)\_q}, W_hN_hC_j)), S(t_{1*}, E(g_{(z+1)\_q}, W_h)), S(s_{1*}, E(k_{(z+1)\_q}, C_j))\}$ by multiplying $S(s_{1*}, E(k_{(z+1)\_q}, W_hN_h))$ and $S(s_{1*}, E(k_{(z+1)\_q}, C_j))$. A signature pair on a letter enables anyone to detect these dishonesties. Because the authorities generates only $S(s_{1*}, E(k_{(z+1)\_Q}, C_j))$, and do not generate $S(s_{2*}, E(k_{(z+1)\_Q}, C_j))$, although S_q can calculate $S(s_{1*}, E(k_{(z+1)\_q}, W_hN_hC_j))$, it cannot calculate $S(s_{2*}, E(k_{(z+1)\_q}, W_hN_hC_j))$, i.e. no one can forge 2 different signatures consistently.

The 4th way is the disruption of letters, i.e. S_q can disrupt N_j during the decryption stage by simply replacing $\{S(s_{1*}, E(k_{(z+1)\_q}, W_jN_jC_j)), S(t_{1*}, E(g_{(z+1)\_q}, W_j)), S(s_{1*}, E(k_{(z+1)\_q}, C_j))\}$ with triple $\{X_1, S(t_{1*}, E(g_{(z+1)\_q}, W_j)), S(s_{1*}, E(k_{(z+1)\_q}, C_j))\}$, where X_1 is an arbitrary bit string. Signature pairs disable also these dishonesties, i.e. no one can generate $\{X_2, S(t_{2*}, E(g_{(z+1)\_q}, W_j))\}$ so that $X_1 = S(s_{1*}, E(k_{(z+1)\_q}, X))$ and $X_2 = S(s_{2*}, E(k_{(z+1)\_q}, X))$ are satisfied for some X, unless all authorities conspire. In the mechanism that does not exploit CNs or signature pairs, dishonesties of this kind are detected as meaningless letters, therefore the procedure in Figure 3 must be carried out to determine whether the meaningless letters are the results of dishonest operations of authorities or not. Finally as the 5th way S_q can simply delete triple $\{S(s_{1*}, E(k_{(z+1)\_q}, W_hN_hC_h)), S(t_{1*}, E(g_{(z+1)\_q}, W_h)), S(s_{1*}, E(k_{(z+1)\_q}, C_h))\}$, however, S_{q-1} that receives decrypted results of S_q in the decryption stage can easily detect the deletions by counting the number of letters in the applicant panel and that it had received from S_q.

As a consequence, all kinds of dishonest decryption results including that were detected as meaningless letters in previous subsections can be detected completely as ones with nonregistered CNs, duplicated CNs or letters with inconsistent signatures, without carrying out the cumbersome dishonest authority identification procedure in Figure 3. Also, when illegitimate letters are detected in the prize panel, the procedure shown in Figure 3 identifies liable entities without revealing any privacy of players. In other words, the procedure identifies dishonest authorities before it reaches players that had chosen letters meaningless from the beginning, i.e. privacies of honest players can be preserved. Moreover as the other important advantage, players can choose arbitrary letters that are not defined in advance.

IMPLICIT TRANSACTION LINKS

Hash functions, MACs and digital signatures discussed in Section 1 were effective for detecting unauthorized modifications, forgeries and disruptions of information. However, when the protection of records in a database system is considered for example, they cannot detect deletions of records or their replacements with other authorized ones. They cannot detect unauthorized additions of records either if they have consistent forms. Actually, hash functions, MACs and digital signatures can protect records in the database system also from these threats, however they need re-calculations of hash functions, MACs or signatures for the whole data in the database every time when individual records are modified, added, or deleted; therefore they are not practical. In the previous subsection, illegal deletions and additions of letters in the applicant panel were detected; however they were not the signatures on letters that detected them. Additions and deletions of letters were detected simply by comparing the numbers of letters disclosed in the applicant and the prize panels, i.e. they were detected by checking the consistency of the whole data in the 2 panels.

Let C_1, C_2, ---, C_N be clients that use some facility managed by server S, where S must calculate total amount of time, during which each client C_h had used the facility, while preserving C_h's privacy. To achieve this objective, S must maintain individual service receiving records of C_h without knowing C_h (here, it is assumed that an appropriate anonymous authentication mechanism is available as discussed in Section 3, and S can check the eligibility of C_h without knowing its identity). Also, individual records of C_h must be constructed so that a sequence of records of C_h cannot be linked each other, because sometimes a sequence of services that C_h had received is the good clue to identify C_h, even if individual records in the sequence do not include any information about C_h. Therefore, S cannot calculate the total service receiving time of C_h even if it maintains C_h's all service receiving records; S must calculate it based on records that C_h itself is maintaining. Then, a problem arises, that is although S can protect unauthorized modifications of individual records maintained by C_h by means of signatures for example, C_h can easily delete its records, and also can replace its records with ones copied from other records to decrease its total service receiving time. Implicit transaction links (ITLs) solve this problem (Tamura, 2007), i.e. ITLs discussed in this subsection enable practical detections of unauthorized deletions, replacements and additions of data included in a set of data without examining the integrity of data in the set individually, and more importantly, without invading privacies of the data owners.

Configuration of an ITL

An ITL is a pair of the current and the encrypted next tokens as shown in Figure 5, and server S generates an ITL at every visit of a client to attach it to a record of the service that it offered to the client,

Figure 5. Configuration of ITL(h, n)

Current token	Next token
v_nT(h, n)	v_{n+1}E(a_h, T(h, n+1))

where as discussed in the next subsection, tokens are bit strings and S signs on them so that clients can prove their eligibilities for receiving services provided by S by showing signatures on them. Also, clients obtain signatures on their tokens without disclosing tokens themselves; therefore they do not need to reveal their identities to receive services. But as an exception, clients make their 1st visit while showing their identities. Therefore S knows the correspondences between clients and their initial tokens, and to preserve their privacies, clients cannot receive any service at their 1st visits, i.e. the 1st service receiving records of individual clients are dummy ones. Here, to prevent tokens from dishonest uses, every token must be unique and clients must be inhibited to use same tokens repeatedly. Mechanisms to inhibit clients to use same tokens repeatedly and to enable server S to issue unique signed tokens to clients without knowing their identities will be discussed in the next subsection.

However, different from tokens discussed in the next chapter that are effective anytime provided that they were not used before, anonymous client C_h in this subsection can use its n-th token T(h, n) only for its n-th visit to server S. Namely at C_h's n-th visit to S, C_h shows its n-th signed token S(g_s, T(h, n)d_n), and S blindly signs on T(h, n+1) shown by C_h in exchange for S(g_s, T(h, n) d_n) while embedding number d_{n+1} in the signature on T(h, n+1) so that C_h can use it only at its (n+1)-th visit. In the above, d_n is a token counter, and S assigns same d_n that is bound to number n as its secret to n-th tokens of all clients to disable clients to use them at their m-th visits (m ≠ n). In more detail, C_h shows signature S(g_s, T(h, n)d_n) at its n-th visit, and S checks whether the signature reveals consistent token T(h, n) when it is divided by d_n, where T(h, n) is consistent when it is accompanied by constant bit string *check* for example. Then if consistent T(h, n) is revealed, S blindly signs on T(h, n+1) while multiplying it by d_{n+1} through the secret verification key based blind signature scheme (this means that S conceals not only signing key g_s of signing function S(g_s, *x*) but also its verification key), therefore C_h obtains S(g_s, T(h, n+1)d_{n+1}) without disclosing T(h, n+1) itself. At the same time, S can conceal d_{n+1} from C_h.

As a consequence, C_h can prove its eligibility without disclosing its identity at its (n+1)-th visit by showing S(g_s, T(h, n)d_{n+1}). Also, C_h can conceal the correspondence between T(h, n) and T(h, n+1) to others. On the other hand, S can disable C_h to use S(g_s, T(h, n)d_n) at its m-th visit (m ≠ n), i.e. C_h cannot forge S(g_s, T(h, n)d_m) from S(g_s, T(h, n)d_n) illegitimately because it does not know either the signing or the verification keys or token counter d_n. In addition, apparently C_h cannot dishonestly declare n, the number of visits that it had made before, at its n-th visit either. Here, although C_h that does not know the verification key or d_n cannot verify that S had signed on T(h, n) correctly or S had used same d_n to all clients at their n-th visits (if S uses different token counters to different clients, it can identify a sequence of tokens shown by a same client by memorizing token counters it had used), S cannot behave dishonestly. Because clients know services that they had received from the beginning their maintaining records are not secrets of S, therefore they can ask S to disclose its verification key and token counters after S had calculated total service receiving times of all clients during its past service periods, and individual clients can easily check whether S is honest or not by decrypting their maintaining records by themselves (it is assumed that S changes signing keys and token counters when its new service periods start).

In the above, a secret verification key based blind signature scheme is essential. If a public verification key based blind signature scheme is used, because client C_j that had used its m-th and n-th tokens $S(g_s, T(j, m)d_m)$ and $S(g_s, T(j, n)d_n)$ can know token counters d_m and d_n by decrypting $S(g_s, T(j, m)d_m)$ and $S(g_s, T(j, n)d_n)$, C_h can generate consistent $S(g_s, T(h, n)d_m)$ at its (n-1)-th visit by asking S to sign on $r^{fs}T(h, n)d_m/d_n$ while obtaining d_m and d_n from C_j, where f_s is the public verification key and r is a random number secret of C_h. Later in this subsection, transaction-wise ITL sum checking mechanism removes the necessity of not only token counters but also the above blind signature process itself.

Now in Figure 5, T(h, n) is the token that C_h showed at its n-th visit to S and T(h, n+1) is the token on which S blindly signed, therefore in ITL(h, n), the ITL of C_h at its n-th visit, T(h, n) and T(h, n+1) constitute the current and the next tokens, respectively. However, C_h encrypts next token T(h, n+1) to $E(a_h, T(h, n+1))$ by its secret key a_h of linear equation based additive encryption function $E(a_h, x)$. Also, S multiplies T(h, n) and $E(a_h, T(h, n+1))$ by token concealers v_n and v_{n+1}, where v_n and v_{n+1} are random numbers common to n-th and (n+1)-th tokens of all clients respectively, and S defines their values as its secrets based on the number of visits C_h had made that is reported by C_h itself (C_h cannot report the number of its visits dishonestly as discussed above).

The important things here are, firstly T(h, n) does not include any information about C_h, and secondly, T(h, n+1) is encrypted to $E(a_h, T(h, n+1))$ by C_h. Therefore no one except C_h can identify C_h from T(h, n), also from pair {T(h, n), $E(a_h, T(h, n+1))$}, no one except C_h can know that the consecutive tokens T(h, n) and T(h, n+1) are owned by a same client. On the other hand as mentioned before, C_h can have only one effective token T(h, n+1) after it had used T(h, n), and it can use T(h, n+1) only for its (n+1)-th visit. Also as discussed later, token concealers disable C_h to illegitimately modify its service receiving records. But although this dishonesty is detected as discussed later, because C_h encrypts T(h, n+1) to obtain blind signature $S(g_s, T(h, n+1)d_{n+1})$ and to generate $E(a_h, T(h, n+1))$ through different mechanisms, C_h can obtain signed (n+1)-th token $S(g_S, T_1(h, n+1)d_{n+1})$ on the one hand and on the other hand encrypt $T_2(h, n+1)$ that is different from $T_1(h, n+1)$ to $E(a_h, T_2(h, n+1))$ to be incorporated as the encrypted next token in its n-th ITL.

Under the above settings, service receiving record L(h, n) of client C_h at its n-th visit to S is configured as triple L(h, n) = {Rec(h, n), v_nT(h, n), $v_{n+1}E(a_h, T(h, n+1))$} as shown in Figure 6. In the figure, Rec(h, n) represents the information about the services that C_h had received at its n-th visit, and pair v_nT(h, n) and $v_{n+1}E(a_h, T(h, n+1))$ is an ITL attached to the record. Here, Rec(h, n) includes at least T(h, n) and $E(a_h, T(h, n+1))$ in addition to service receiving time of C_h. The reason why Rec(h, n) must include T(h, n) and $E(a_h, T(h, n+1))$ is without them C_h cannot confirm that the record is certainly accompanied by ITL(h, n) that includes T(h, n) and $E(a_h, T(h, n+1))$, because S encrypts service receiving records while including ITLs in their confidential parts to maintain them as its secrets as discussed later. But necessity of $E(a_h, T(h, n+1))$ in the service receiving record will be removed later by the transaction-wise ITL sum checking mechanism.

In the above, to preserve privacy of C_h, Rec(h, n) does not include any data those are linked to C_h of course as same as the ITL, therefore, no one except C_h can identify C_h from the record. As discussed before, anyone including S except C_h itself cannot know that the records accompanied by T(h, n) and T(h, n+1) are corresponding to services for a same client either. Then, C_h itself is responsible for maintaining records of services that it had received so that S can calculate the

Figure 6. Structure of service receiving records

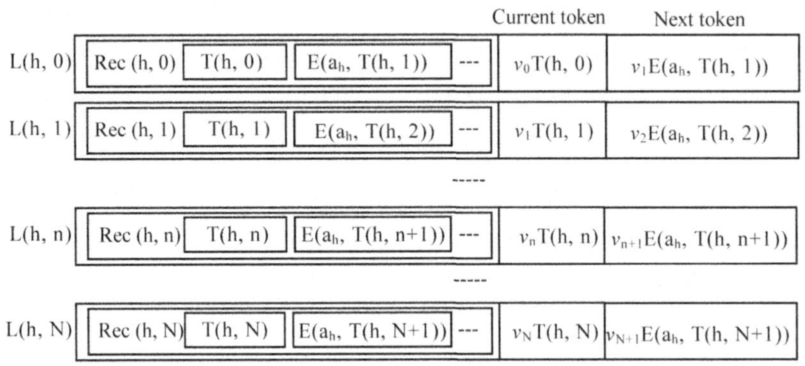

total service receiving time of C_h. Therefore, to disable C_h to modify, delete or replace its maintaining records in unauthorized ways, S gives the records to C_h while encrypting them by its secret encryption key k_S.

Dishonest Record Detection Mechanism

ITLs enable S to detect unauthorized modifications, deletions and replacements of service receiving records maintained by client C_h based on the fact that the sum of current tokens and that of the next tokens included in ITLs of C_h's past service receiving records are the same as shown in Figure 6, provided that the difference between T(h, 0) and T(h, N+1) is compensated, where N is the number of visits that C_h had made before the calculation of its total service receiving time. Here, to enable S to calculate the total service receiving time, and at the same time the sum of current tokens and that of encrypted next tokens without knowing individual service receiving records of C_h, i.e. while preserving privacies of C_h, S uses linear equation based additive encryption function $E(k_S, y)$ for encrypting individual records. Based on relation $E(k_S, y_1) + E(k_S, y_2) = E(k_S, y_1+y_2)$, S can calculate the total service receiving time, the sum of current tokens and that of encrypted next tokens of C_h by decrypting the sum of encrypted service receiving records that is reported by C_h. S can know also the sum of next tokens by asking C_h to decrypt the sum of the encrypted next tokens, provided that C_h encrypts T(h, n+1) to $E(a_h, T(h, n+1))$ also based on additive encryption function $E(a_h, x)$.

In detail, to encrypt next token T(h, n+1) to $E(a_h, T(h, n+1))$, C_h lineally combines T(h, n+1) and its secret random numbers $r_2(h, n+1)$, $r_3(h, n+1)$, ---, $r_g(h, n+1)$ by using C_h's secret (g x g)-coefficient matrix $\{a_{ip}\}$ that corresponds to encryption key a_h. As a consequence, $E(a_h, T(h, n+1))$ becomes g-dimensional vector $\{W_1(h, n), W_2(h, n), ---, W_g(h, n)\}$ calculated by Equation (1). On the other hand, $L(h, n) = \{Rec(h, n), v_n T(h, n), v_{n+1} E(a_h, T(h, n+1))\}$, service receiving record of C_h at its n-th visit, is encrypted into (f+g)-dimensional vector $E(k_S, L(h, n)) = \{L_1(h, n), L_2(h, n), ----, L_{f+g}(h, n)\}$ by linearly combining items in L(h, n) and S's secret random bit strings $R_4(h, n)$, $R_5(h, n)$, ---, $R_f(h, n)$. Namely, the q-th element $L_q(h, n)$ of vector $E(k_S, L(h, n))$ is calculated by Equation (2) while using S's secret {(f+g) x (f+g)}-coefficient matrix $\{k_{qj}\}$ that corresponds to encryption key k_S. Actually, Rec(h, n) consists of multiple items, e.g. service receiving time, T(h, n) and etc. as shown in Figure 6, therefore Rec(h, n) in Equation (2) may be replaced by multiple terms and the dimension of the encrypted forms increases. Also, although they are not shown, random dummy elements may be inserted in vectors $\{W_i(h, n)\}$ and $\{L_q(h, n)\}$ to make encryptions more secure.

As mentioned before, in Equation (2), token concealers v_n and v_{n+1} secret from clients are determined based on the number of visits made by C_h. Also, C_h shows its signed token while declaring the number of visits that it had made before at its every visit to S, therefore S knows n and (n+1) at C_h's n-th and (n+1)-th visits, and it can assign the same value v_{n+1} to token concealers for current token T(h, n+1) in L(h, n+1) and to encrypted next token $W_i(h, n)$ $(1 \leq i \leq g)$ in L(h, n) (S can protect itself from C_h's dishonest report of n as explained already).

$$W_i(h, n) = a_{i1}T(h, n+1) + a_{i2}r_2(h, n+1) + \text{---} + a_{ig}r_g(h, n+1) \ (i=1, \text{---}, g) \quad (1)$$

$$L_q(h, n) = k_{q1}Rec(h, n) + v_n k_{q2}T(h, n) + v_{n+1}\{k_{q3}W_1(h, n) + \text{---} + k_{q(g+2)}W_g(h, n)\} + k_{q(g+3)}R_4(h, n) + \text{---} + k_{q(f+g)}R_f(h, n), \ (q=1, \text{---}, f+g) \quad (2)$$

Here, all information included in Rec(h, n) is known to C_h from the beginning, on the other hand, S never discloses values of $v_nT(h, n)$ or $v_{n+1}E(a_h, T(h, n+1))$. Therefore, Rec(h, n) and pair $\{v_nT(h, n), v_{n+1}E(a_h, T(h, n+1))\}$ constitute the visible and the confidential parts of L(h, n), and pair $\{v_nT(h, n), v_{n+1}E(a_h, T(h, n+1))\}$ can be protected from illegitimate disclosures despite of the fact that linear equation based encryption function $E(k_S, y)$ is weak against plain text attacks. C_h does not disclose the fact that $E(a_h, T(h, n+1))$ is the encrypted form of T(h, n+1) to others either, therefore also C_h can protect $E(a_h, T(h, n+1))$ from plain text attacks. Actually C_h must disclose sums of decrypted next tokens as discussed later, however they are required only at ends of S's individual service periods when S calculates total service receiving times of individual clients, and also C_h changes its encryption key a_h when S's new service periods start, therefore S cannot collect enough number of plain texts to calculate $\{a_{ip}\}$. In addition from the beginning, it is extremely difficult for S to identify service receiving records of C_h among a set of records that were reported from many other clients.

Now, server S can calculate the total service receiving time of client C_h correctly without knowing individual records while protecting service receiving records of C_h from C_h's unauthorized deletions, additions, modifications, replacements and disruptions as follow. Firstly at a time when it calculates total service receiving times of individual clients, S asks C_h (here, C_h is not anonymous at this time of course) to report vector $\underline{L}(h, N) = \{\underline{L}_1(h, N), \underline{L}_2(h, N), \text{---}, \underline{L}_{f+g}(h, N)\}$, the sum of all encrypted service receiving records that C_h maintains, and its initial token and last unused token pair {T(h, 0), T(h, N+1)}, where, $\underline{L}_q(h, N)$, the sum of the q-th elements of C_h's service receiving records encrypted by S's secret coefficient matrix $\{k_{qj}\}$, is calculated as Equation (3). After receiving L(h, N), S calculates the total service receiving time $\sum_{n=0}^{n=N}\{Rec(h, n)\}$ of C_h by solveing the linear Equations (3) about $\sum_{n=0}^{n=N}\{Rec(h, n)\}$ while using coefficient matrix $\{k_{qj}\}$. In the same way, S also calculates $\sum_{n=0}^{n=N}\{v_nT(h, n)\}$ and $\sum_{n=0}^{n=N}\{v_{n+1}W_i(h, n)\}$ $(1 \leq i \leq g)$, and from $\sum_{n=0}^{n=N}\{v_nT(h, n)\}$ and the reported token pair {T(h, 0), T(h, N+1)}, it constructs weighted sum of current tokens $T(h, N+1) = \sum_{n=0}^{n=N}\{v_nT(h, n)\} - v_0T(h, 0) + v_{N+1}T(h, N+1) = \sum_{n=1}^{n=N+1}\{v_nT(h, n)\}$ (S knows its secret token concealers v_0 and v_{N+1}). Then finally, it asks C_h to decrypt vector $\underline{W}(h, N) = [\sum_{n=0}^{n=N}\{v_{n+1}W_1(h, n)\}, \sum_{n=0}^{n=N}\{v_{n+1}W_2(h, n)\}, \text{---}, \sum_{n=0}^{n=N}\{v_{n+1}W_g(h, n)\}]$ to $\underline{T}_*(h, N+1)$ by C_h's secret coefficient matrix $\{a_{ip}\}$. Here, vector $\underline{W}(h, N)$ is the weighted sum of next tokens encrypted by C_h, i.e. $\underline{W}(h, N)$ is the encrypted form of $\underline{T}(h, N+1)$, therefore $\underline{T}_*(h, N+1)$ must coincide with $\underline{T}(h, N+1)$ when C_h maintains its service receiving records honestly. Then, based on this relation S can force C_h to honestly report its total service receiving time $\sum_{n=0}^{n=N}$ {Rec(h, n)}. When C_h attempts to modify, delete or replace its records, it must forget $\underline{T}_*(h, N+1)$ so that relation $\underline{T}_*(h, N+1) = T(h, N+1)$ holds. However, because C_h does not know token concealers v_n (n = 0, ---, N+1) and every record is encrypted by S, C_h cannot know the exact value of any ITL included in its maintaining records, and as a consequence C_h cannot calculate $\underline{T}_*(h, N+1)$ that is consistent with $\underline{T}(h, N+1)$ if it had reported $\underline{L}(h, N)$ dishonestly.

$$L_q(h, N) = \sum_{n=0}^{n=N} \{ {}_q(h, n)] = k_{q1} \sum_{n=0}^{n=N} \{ Rec(h, n)\} + k_{q2} \sum_{n=0}^{n=N} \{ v_n T(h, n)\}$$

$$+ k_{q3} \sum_{n=0}^{n=N} \{ v_{n+1} W_1(h, n)\} + \text{---} + k_{q(g+2)} \sum_{n=0}^{n=N} \{ v_{n+1} W_{m+g}(h, n)\}$$

$$+ kq(g+3) \sum_{n=0}^{n=N} \{ R4(h, n)\} + \text{---} + kq(f+g) \sum_{n=0}^{n=N} \{ Rf(h, n)\} \quad (3)$$

Also C_h must honestly report its initial and last unused token pair {T(h, 0), T(h, n+1)}. When C_h reports T(h, q) (0 < q < N) as its initial token instead of T(h, 0), it can delete {L(h, 0), L(h, 1), ---, L(h, q-1)}, the ealry part of its service receiving records, however C_h can use only T(h, 0) as its initial token because S knows initial tokens of all clients. C_h cannot dishonestly report T(h, m) (m < N+1) as its last unused token instead of T(h, N+1) to reduce its total service receiving time corresponding to records {L(h, m), L(h, m+1), ---, L(h, N)} either. Because C_h can have only one token at a time and it can use $S(g_s, T(h,m)d_m)$ that it obtained at its (m-1)-th visit only for its m-th visit, C_h must show $S(g_s, T(h, N+1)d_{N+1})$ that it had obtained at its N-th visit as its last unused token.

Although C_h can obtain $S(g_s, T(j, m)d_m)$ (m < N+1) from other client C_j while conspiring with it and show $S(g_s, T(j, m)d_m)$ as its consistent last unused token (of course C_h had generated its (m-1)-th ITL while including $E(a_h, T(j, m))$ as its next token value so that T(j, m) becomes consistent with ITL(h, m-1) of C_h), in this case, C_j does not have its last unused token after its (m-1)-th visit because it can have only 1 token T(j, m) that must be reserved for C_h, and C_j is regarded as the client that had received all services correponding to discrepancy between the total service time that S had provided and the sum of total service receiving times that individual clients had reported. Therefore, even if C_h had obtained T(j, m) while conspiring with C_j, C_h and C_j cannot gain anything as the total.

A problem is the case where C_h had stolen T(j, m) from other client C_j. In this case, C_h can continue to receive services from S while obtaining new tokens without payments for example. Namely, either S or C_j cannot trace services that C_h had received after its m-th visit, and as a consequence, C_j is regarded as the client responsible for all damages of S caused by dishonest clients including C_h. Later in this sectin, the dishonest record detection mechanism will be enhanced to transaction-wise ITL sum checking mechanism so that entities cannot use tokens of other entities, and this mechanism will be exploited in Section 3 for authenticating anonymous entities.

In the above dishonest record detection mechanism, the wheigheted sum of current tokens of C_h includes v_0T(h, 0) but does not include v_{N+1}T(h, N+1), on the other hand, C_h's wheigheted sum of next tokens includes v_{N+1}T(h, N+1) but does not include v_0T(h, 0). Therefore, to adjust the difference between the wheigheted sums of current and next tokens in ITLs of client C_h, S must know T(h, 0) and T(h, N+1). Then, C_h is requested to disclose them while showing its identity when S calculates the total service receiving time of C_h, but apparently this information disclosure does not cause any problem. Because C_h does not request any service with T(h, N+1) yet, S cannot link T(h, N+1) to any information about privacy of C_h. C_h

also can disable S to link T(h, 0) to information about its privacy because initial services for individual clients are dummy ones. Here, it is assumed that C_h refreshes its initial token T(h, 0) at its 1st visit in each service period of S.

Preserving Privacies of Frequently Visiting Clients

It must be noted that privacy of C_h may be invaded when it declares n, the number of its past visits, at its n-th visit, despite that n itself does not include any information about C_h. Namely, at a time when S periodically calculates total service receiving times of individual clients, C_h discloses its identity with its last unused token T(h, N+1) and N+1, the number of visits it had made before. Consequently, when N is larger than M, the maximum number of visits that had been made by other clients before the total service reciving time calculation, although service receiving record L(h, n) is anonymous, S can easily know that L(h, n) belongs to C_h if n is greater than M, for example. Therefore, all clients must carry out dummy transactions so that the numbers of their past visits become equal.

Although this inconvenience can be removed if individual clients initialize numbers of their past visits when they reach some relatively small value Z, in this case, S assigns same token concealr v_n to different encrypted next tokens E(a_h, T(h, n)) and E(a_h, T(h, n+Z)) of C_h, as a consequence, C_h can declare that it had visited S only n-times when S calculates C_h's total service receiving time at its (n+Z)-th visit, while having reported E(a_h, T(h, n+Z)) as the encrypted next token value of ITL(h, n-1) at its (n-1)-th visit to delete its service receiving records from L(h, n) to L(h, n+Z-1). Transaction-wise ITL sum checking mechanism discussed later enables server S to initialize the number of visits of each client to remove inconveniences about dummy transactions while protecting S from dishonest clients. Namely, transaction-wise ITL sum checking mechanism forces C_h at its n-th visit to use T(h, n+Z) if it had declared E(a_h, T(h, n+Z)) as its encrypted next token at its (n-1)-th visit.

Integrity of Individual Records

ITLs ensures also the integrity of individual service receiving records of C_h. Namely, C_h cannot modify or forge its encrypted service receiving record E(k_S, L(h, n)) by linearly combining already known encrypted records so that ITL part value ITL(h, n) included in it becomes consistent, because it does not know encryption key k_S or token concealers included in ITL(h, n). Here, the important thing is that S can verify the integrity of individual records by evaluating their encrypted sum, in other words, without decrypting individual records and consequently without invading privacy of C_h, as check codes (CCs) and check values (CVs) discussed in the subsection about linear equation besed encryption scheme in Section 1 did. However, different from the check code and check value based mechanism where S examined relations between CC and CV values included in same records, in the ITL based mechanism, S examines relations between ITLs included in consecutive (i.e. different) records.

Verification of Encryptions

The mechanism in previous subsections includes 2 encryption processes, the one is carried out by client C_h to conceal its next tokens from others and the other is carried out by server S to protect service records from illegitimete modifications and forgeries. About next token T(h, n+1), C_h does not disclose that E(a_h, T(h, n+1)) is decrypted to T(h, n+1), i.e. whole E(a_h, T(h, n+1)) is the confidential part. Therefore, together with the fact that 2 encryption mechanisms, by which C_h obtains the blind signature on T(h, n+1) and by which C_h generates encrypted next token E(a_h, T(h, n+1)), are different, S cannot verify whether T(h, n+1) in E(a_h, T(h, n+1)) is consistent with S(g_s, T(h, n+1)d_{n+1}) that C_h shows at its (n+1)-th visit. However, fortunately verification of $E(a_h, T(h, n+1))$ is not necessary, in other words, C_h cannot use $T(h, n+1)$ at its (n+1)-th visit if it had generated $E(a_h, T(h, n+1))$ dishonestly. If C_h had encrypted $T(h, n+1)$ to $E(a_h, T_1(h, n+1))$ instead of $E(a_h, T(h, n+1))$ and used $T(h, n+1)$ at its (n+1)-th visit, the sum of current tokens and that of next tokens become inconsistent because C_h that does not know token concealers cannot compensate the difference between $T(h, n+1)$ and $T_1(h, n+1)$ (it is assumed that the number of visits that C_h had made before is not initialized until the new service period starts, although this assumption will be removed later by the transaction-wise ITL sum checking mechanism).

About $E(k_S, L(h, n))$, service receiving record $L(h, n)$ encrypted by S, S does not disclose $ITL(h, n) = \{v_n T(h, n), v_{n+1} E(a_h, T(h, n+1))\}$ included in $L(h, n)$, therefore S can insist that sequence $\{E(k_S, L(h, n)), E(k_S, L(h, n+1))\}$ is not consistent while dishonestly calculating $ITL(h, n)$ for example. However, both $T(h, n)$ and $E(a_h, T(h, n+1))$ are included in the visible part of $L(h, n)$ as shown in Figure 6, and based on the additice (verifiable) property of $E(k_S, y)$, C_h can verify that visible parts of $E(k_S, L(h, n))$ and $E(k_S, L(h, n+1))$ include $\{T(h, n), E(a_h, T(h, n+1))\}$ and $T(h, n+1)$, respectivly. Also encryption key a_h proves that $E(a_h, T(h, n+1))$ in $L(h, n)$ and $T(h, n+1)$ in $L(h, n+1)$ are consistent. Then, when the fact that encryption key k_s is known only to S is considered, this means S had authorized that sequence $\{E(k_S, L(h, n)), E(k_S, L(h, n+1))\}$ is consistent, then, C_h can reveal S's dishonesty. Here, C_h must disclose its encryption key a_h and consequently its all privacies may be revealed in this case, however usually S does not behave dishonestly, because S's dishonesty is necessarily revealed and once its reputation is depraved it cannot continue its business.

As discussed in the subsection about the linear equation based encryption scheme, server S can embed data in encrypted forms of client C_h's service receiving records without being noticed by C_h so that it can obtain information about C_h's privacy even from sums of its service receiving records. For example, to know the number of times that C_h had received particular service X, S can define item Z_1 in a confidential part of a record to assign value 1 or 0 to it depending on C_h had received service X or not, also S can add dummy element Z_2 to an encrypted record to assign value 1 or 0 to it in the same way as for Z_1. In the former case, the number of visits in which C_h had received service X coincides with the sum of item Z_1 values in the decrypted records, and in the latter case, it coincides with the sum of element Z_2 values in the encrypted records.

Fortunately, C_h can detect this dishonesty, and more importantly S can easily prove its honesty about this kind of behaviors, by disclosing S's encryption keys after it had calculated total service receiving times of all clients during its last service periods. Namely, every information included in C_h's service receiving records except ITLs is known by C_h from the beginning and also ITLs are not secrets of S after C_h's honesty or dishonesty had been examined, therefore S can disclose the encryption keys used in its past service periods, provided that it uses different encryption keys for different service periods. Then, C_h can convince itself and at the same time S can prove that S did not embed the above kind of information in the service receiving records.

Extended ITLs

Regarding encrypted next tokens in ITLs, C_h can embed information for calculating token concealers $v_0, v_2, ---, v_{N+1}$ so that it can consistently calculate sums of ITLs while using illegitimate tokens. For example, although dummy elements are not explicitly described in this chapter, let $W_z(h, n)$ be a dummy element in C_h's encrypted next token $E(a_h, T(h, n+1)) = \{W_1(h, n), W_2(h, n), ---, W_g(h, n)\}$, then C_h can know token concealer v_{n+1} from the sum of its encrypted next tokens that S calculates from C_h's report about the sum of its encrypted service receiving records. Namely, if C_h generated encrypted next tokens while assigning 1 to z-th element $W_z(h, n)$ in $E(a_h, T(h, n+1))$ and assigning 0 to z-th element $W_z(h, m)$ in other encrypted next token $E(a_h, T(h, m+1))$ ($m \neq n$), the z-th element of encrypted sum of next tokens $\underline{W}(h, N) = v_1E(a_h, T(h, 1)) + v_2E(a_h, T(h, 2)) + \text{---}\ v_{N+1}E(a_h, T(h, N+1))$ coincides with v_{n+1}. Nevertheless, $\underline{W}(h, N)$ is decrypted consistently because the z-th element of each encrypted next token is the dummy one. The following mechanism disables C_h to behave dishonestly in this manner.

That is, S extends ITL(h, n), ITL at C_h's n-th visit to S, from a pair of the current and the encrypted next tokens to a set of current token $v_nT(h, n)$, encrypted next token $v_{n+1}\{E(a_h, T(h, n+1))+p_1(n+1)ext_1+p_2(n+1)ext_2+ \text{---} +p_T(n+1)ext_T\}$, and the 1st, the 2nd, ---, the T-th extended vectors $p_1(n+1)ext_1$, $p_2(n+1)ext_2$, ---, $p_T(n+1)ext_T$ multiplied by token concealer v_{n+1} as shown in Figure 7. Here, $p_1(n+1)$, $p_2(n+1)$, ---, $p_T(n+1)$ are random numbers secrets of S, and ext_1, ---, ext_T are random linearly dependent g-dimensional constant vectors also secrets of S and common to all clients and all records. Then, at a time when S receives $E(a_h, T(h, n+1))$ it does not use $v_{n+1}E(a_h, T(h, n+1))$ directly as the encrypted next token value in ITL(h, n), instead it calculates $v_{n+1}\{E(a_h, T(h, n+1))+p_1(n+1)ext_1+ \text{---} + p_T(n+1)ext_T\}$ as the encrypted next token value, and attaches extended vectors $v_{n+1}p_1(n+1)ext_1$, ---, $v_{n+1}p_T(n+1)ext_T$ as additional elements of ITL(h, n) to encrypt them with other elements in service receiving record L(h, n). Therefore, to calculate the sum of next tokens in C_h's service receiving records, S asks C_h to decrypt $\Sigma[v_{n+1}\{E(a_h, T(h, n+1))+p_1(n+1)ext_1+ \text{---} + p_T(n+1)ext_T\}]$, the sum of the encrypted next token part values, and $r_j(h, n)\Sigma\{v_{n+1}p_j(n+1)ext_j\}$, the sum of the j-th extended vector part values multiplied by S's secret random number $r_j(h, n)$ for each j, to $\Sigma[v_{n+1}\{T(h, n+1)+E(a_h^{-1}, p_1(n+1)ext_1)+ \text{---} +E(a_h^{-1}, p_T(n+1)ext_T)\}]$ and $r_j(h, n)\Sigma\{E(a_h^{-1}, v_{n+1}p_j(n+1)ext_j)\}$, respectively. After that S calculates $\Sigma\{v_{n+1}T(h, n+1)\}$ according to equation (4) while using its secret numbers $r_1(h, n)$, $r_2(h, n)$, ---, $r_T(h, n)$.

$$\Sigma\{v_{n+1}T(h, n+1)\} = \Sigma[v_{n+1}\{T(h, n+1)+E(a_h^{-1}, p_1(n+1)ext_1)+ \text{---} +E(a_h^{-1}, p_T(n+1)ext_T)\}]$$
$$- r_1(h, n)\Sigma\{E(a_h^{-1}, v_{n+1}p_1(n+1)ext_1)\}/r_1(h, n)$$
$$- r_T(h, n)\Sigma\{E(a_h^{-1}, v_{n+1}p_T(n+1)ext_T)\}/r_T(h, n) \quad (4)$$

In the above, C_h cannot estimate values of token concealers even if it had embedded dishonest information in its encrypted next tokens because the embedded information is disrupted by extended vectors that S had added. Here, vectors ext_1, ---, ext_T must take constant values so that S cannot obtain enough number of plain text and encrypted form pairs of encryption function $E(a_h, x)$. Also, it is desirable that constant vectors ext_1, ---, ext_T are linearly dependent so that calculation of $\Sigma\{v_{n+1}E(a_h, T(h, n+1))\}$ becomes difficult for C_h.

Enhancement of the Mechanism for Detecting Dishonest Records

In the previous subsections, when token T(h, n) of client C_h is stolen by other client, C_h was regarded as not only as the client that had received the service corresponding to the stolen token but also as the one that was responsible for all the differences between the total service providing time of S and the sum of total service receiving times that individual clients had reported. This subsection enhances the mechanism for detecting dishonest records so that clients that steal tokens cannot use them to remove damages from honest clients. Different from the mechanism in the previous subsections where client C_h shows sums of its past service receiving records to S only at times when S calculates total service receiving times of individual clients, in this subsection, C_h shows its sum of past records and decrypts the sum of encrypted next tokens at its every visit to S.

Namely, because S examines the consistency between a token shown by C_h and ITLs included in C_h's past service receiving records at its every visit, in more detail, because S compares the sum of current tokens $\underline{T}$(h, n+1) and the sum of decrypted next tokens $\underline{T}_*$(h, n+1) at C_h's (n+1)-th visit, C_h can show T(h, n+1) at its (n+1)-th visit only when it had reported E(a_h, T(h, n+1)) as the encrypted next token at its n-th visit, and consequently, C_h cannot use tokens of other clients. Therefore, clients do not need to worry even their tokens are stolen. At the same time, processes, in which S blindly signs on tokens of clients, also can be removed as discussed just below. However, 2 problems arise if a client shows the sum of its past service receiving records at its every visit. They are firstly, without additional mechanisms, a series of partial sums of tokens not only enable S to identify clients corresponding to individual records but also enable clients to calculate token concealers secrets of S. The 2nd problem is about additive encryption functions of clients that are weak against plain text attacks, i.e. a series of encrypted and decrypted form pairs of next token sums help S decrypt encrypted next tokens without knowing secret keys of clients.

About the 1st problem, when C_h shows the sum of its past records at its every visit, S can memorize $\underline{T}$(h, n) = v_0T(h, 0) + v_1T(h, 1) + --- + v_nT(h, n) for each n =0, 1, 2, ---. Therefore, although C_h shows only T(h, n) and $\underline{T}$(h, n) and does not show T(h, n-1) at its n-th visit, S that knows token concealer v_n can identify $\underline{T}$(h, n-1) that precedes $\underline{T}$(h, n) by finding $\underline{T}$(h, n-1) in its database that satisfies relation {$\underline{T}$(h, n) - $\underline{T}$(h, n-1)} = v_NT(h, n). This means that S can know sequence {$\underline{T}$(h, 0), $\underline{T}$(h, 1), ---, $\underline{T}$(h, n)} and consequently the sequence of tokens {T(h, 0), T(h, 1), ---, T(h, n)} used by C_h. It must be noted that C_h cannot conceal $\underline{T}$(h, n-1) by simply multiplying $\underline{T}$(h, n-1) by its secret number u, because it must inform T(h, n) while multiplying it also by u at its n-th visit so that S can determine whether relation $u\underline{T}_*$(h, n) = $u\underline{T}$(h, n-1)+uv_nT(h, n) holds or not, and consequently S can know the value of u. Also, although it is easy to solve, S can know that {T(h, 0), T(h, 1), ---, T(h, n)} is the token sequence of C_h even without memorizing $\underline{T}$(h, n), because C_h shows its initial token T(h, 0) at its every visit to S. On the other hand, C_h can calculate token concealer v_n, when S asks C_h to decrypt sum of its past encrypted next tokens at its every visit from the same relation {$\underline{T}$(h, n) - $\underline{T}$(h, n-1)} = v_nT(h, n), i.e. v_n= {$\underline{T}$(h, n) - $\underline{T}$(h, n-1)}/T(h, n). The transaction-wise ITL sum checking mechanism (Tamura, 2006) shown below is a solution of this problem.

The distinctive feature of the transaction-wise ITL sum checking mechanism is that validity of token T(h, n) of client C_h is ensured by the consistent relation between T(h, n) and the sum of C_h's past service receiving records, not by S's signature on T(h, n). Therefore, different from the mechanism in previous subsections, in which client C_h acquired signature S(g_S, T(h, n)d_n) from S, the mechanism in this subsection does not require clients to obtain signatures on their tokens. As a consequence, processes for blind signatures and the necessity of token counters can be removed. Also, dummy services that were used to conceal identities of frequently visiting clients become not necessary, i.e. even if S initializes the number of visits that client C_h had made when it reaches the predefined value Z, C_h cannot dishonestly exchange its n-th token T(h, n) and its (n+Z)-th token T(h, n+Z), i.e. it must use T(h, n) and T(h, n+Z) at its n-th and (n+Z)-th visits, respectively. In addition, it is ensured that C_h had encrypted T(h, n+1) honestly to E(a_h, T(n+1)) at its n-th visit when relation T_*(h, n) = T(h, n)+v_{n+1}T(h, n+1) holds, therefore, if C_h verifies that E(k_S, L(h, n)) correctly includes T(h, n) in its visible part, the fact that S had approved the correctness of E(a_h, T(h, n+1)) included in ITL(h, n) is automatically ensured provided that T(h, n+1) is accepted at C_h's (n+1)-th visit. As a consequence, E(a_h, T(n+1)) can be removed from the visible part of L(h, n) shown in Figure 7.

Transaction-wise ITL Sum Checking

Firstly, to enable C_h to visit S without showing T(h, 0) except its initial visit, S constructs the initial ITL of C_h as pair {v_0T(h, 0), v_0E(a_h, T(h, 0))+v_1E(a_h, T(h, 1))} instead of {v_0T(h, 0), v_1E(a_h, T(h, 1))}. Therefore, C_h must inform S of E(a_h, T(h, 0)) in addition to E(a_h, T(h, 1)) at its initial visit. By this modification, the cause of difference between the weighted sums of current and next tokens at C_h's n-th visit becomes T(h, n) only, then, S can compensate the difference without knowing T(h, 0).

Secondly, to disable S to use relation {$\underline{T}$(h, n) - $\underline{T}$(h, n-1)} = v_NT(h, n), client C_h at its n-th visit arbitrarily divides its past service receiving records from the initial to the last ones, i.e. from L(h, 0) to L(h, n-1), into P parts while randomly generating a sequence of secret numbers {$0 = y(0) < y(1) < y(2) <$ ---, $< y(P-1) < y(P) = n$}. Namely, it generates sub-sequences L_*(h, 0) = {L(h, y(0)), L(h, y(0)+1), ---, L(h, y(1)-1)}, L_*(h, 1) = {L(h, y(1)), L(h, y(1)+1), ---, L(h, y(2)-1)}, ---, L_*(h, P-1) = {L(h, y(P-1)), L(h, y(P-1)+1), ---, L(h, y(P)-1) = L(h, n-1)}, and calculates vector $\underline{L}$*(h, n) = {$\sum_{k=0}^{k=p-1}$ {$\underline{L}_1$*(h, k)], $\sum_{k=0}^{k=p-1}$ {$\underline{L}_2$*(h, k)], ---, $\sum_{k=0}^{k=p-1}$ {$\underline{L}_{f+g}$*(h, k)]} as the accumulated encrypted record of C_h at its n-th visit to S instead of $\underline{L}$(h, n) in Equation (3). Here, each $\underline{L}_q$*(h, k) (0≤ k ≤ P-1) is the sum of the q-th elements of C_h's encrypted service receiving records included in subsequence L_*(h, k). However, it must be noted that the sum is multiplied by client token concealer u_k that is a secret of C_h as shown in Equation (5), therefore S cannot know the exact sum of C_h's past records from $\underline{L}$*(h, n). C_h also changes each u_k and the subsequence configuration, i.e. P and sequence {y(0), ---, y(P)}, at its every visit to S.

$$\underline{L}_q\text{*(h, k)} = u_k\{L_q(h, y(k)) + L_q(h, y(k)+1) + \text{---} + L_q(h, y(k+1)-1)\} \quad (5)$$

Then, C_h reports its calculating accumulated encrypted record $\underline{L}$*(h, n), last unused token u_{P-1}T(h, n), sequence {z(1), z(2), ---, z(P-1)} and AD(h, i) = {(u_1 - u_0)W_i(h, y(1)-1), (u_2 - u_1)W_i(h, y(2)-1), ---, (u_{P-1} - u_{P-2})W_i(h, y(P-1)-1)} for each i (1 ≤ i ≤ g) to S. Here, provided that the number of past visits of C_h is initialized when it reaches Z, each z(j) is defined as $z(j) = y(j)_{\text{mod } Z}$, therefore C_h can maintain each y(j) as its secret even z(j) is disclosed. AD(h, i) is token concealer adjusting information, and (u_k - u_{k-1})W_i(h, y(k)-1) enables S to compensate differences between the sum of current tokens and that of next tokens caused by client token concealers u_k and u_{k-1} by which T(h, y(k)) and W_i(h, y(k)-1) are multiplied. Now, S decrypts its receiving accumulated encrypted record $\underline{L}$*(h, n) to calculate Equations (6) and (7) for each i; where W_i(h, -1) in (7) denotes the i-th element of E(a_h, T(h, 0)) included in C_h's initial ITL.

$$\sum_{k=0}^{k=p-1}\{\underline{t}\text{*(h, k)}\} = \sum_{k=0}^{k=p-1}\{u_k\{v_{y(k)}T(h, y(k)) + \text{---} + v_{y(k+1)-1}T(h, y(k+1)-1)\}] \quad (6)$$

$$\sum_{k=0}^{k=p-1}\{\underline{w}_i\text{*(h, k)}\}, \text{ where,}$$

$$\underline{w}_i\text{*(h, 0)} = u_0\{v_0 W_i(h, -1) + v_1 W_i(h, y(0)) + \text{---} + v_{y(1)} W_i(h, y(1)-1)\}, \text{ and for } k > 0,$$

$$\underline{w}_i\text{*(h, k)} = u_k\{v_{y(k)+1} W_i(h, y(k)) + \text{---} + v_{y(k+1)} W_i(h, y(k+1)-1)\} \quad (7)$$

By using (6), (7), {z(1), z(2), ---, z(P-1)}, AD(h, i) and u_{P-1}T(h, n) given from C_h, S also calculates (8) and (9). Here, because S uses same token concealers v_n to C_h's n-th and (n+Z)-th visits, S can know the value of $v_{y(p)}$ for each p (0 ≤ p < P) from z(p) for calculating (9).

$$T^*(h, n) = \sum_{k=0}^{k=p-1} \{t^*(h, k)\} + u_{P-1}v_n T(h, n) = u_0\{v_0 T(h, y(0)) + --- + v_{y(1)-1} T(h, y(1)-1)\}$$

$$+ u_1\{v_{y(1)} T(h, y(1)) + --- + v_{y(2)-1} T(h, y(2)-1)\} + ---$$

$$+ u_{P-1}\{v_{y(P-1)} T(h, y(P-1)) + --- + v_n T(h, n)\} \quad (8)$$

$$\underline{W}^*_i(h, n) = w_i^*(h, y(0)) + \{u_1 v_{y(1)} W_i(h, y(1)-1) - u_0 v_{y(1)} W_i(h, y(1)-1)\}$$

$$+ \underline{w}_i^*(h, y(1)) + \{u_2 v_{y(2)} W_i(h, y(2)-1) - u_1 v_{y(2)} W_i(h, y(2)-1)\} + \underline{w}_i^*(h, y(2)) + ----$$

$$+ \{u_{P-1} v_{y(P-1)} W_i(h, y(P-1)-1) - u_{P-2} v_{y(P-1)} W_i(h, y(P-1)-1)\} + \underline{w}_i^*(h, y(P-1))$$

$$= u_0\{v_0 W_i(h, -1) + v_1 W_i(h, y(0)) + --- + v_{y(1)-1} W_i(h, y(1)-2)\}$$

$$+ --- + u_{P-1}\{v_{y(P-1)} W_i(h, y(P-1)-1) + --- + v_n W_i(h, n-1)\} \quad (9)$$

Therefore, when S asks C_h to decrypt vector $r(h, n)\underline{W}^*(h, n) = r(h, n)\{\underline{W}_1^*(h, n), \underline{W}_2^*(h, n), ---, \underline{W}_g^*(h, n)\}$ while generating its secret random number $r(h, n)$, C_h can decrypt it to $r(h, n)\underline{T}^*(h, n)$ if C_h had reported $\underline{L}^*(h, n)$, $\{z(1), z(2), ---, z(P-1)\}$, AD(h, i) and $u_{P-1}T(h, n)$ honestly. Namely, $\underline{T}^*(h, n)$ and $\underline{W}^*(h, n)$ are the sum of current tokens and the sum of encrypted next tokens weighted by the same token concealers and client token concealers. However, when C_h did not report them honestly, C_h that does not know token concealers cannot calculate $r(h, n)\underline{T}^*(h, n)$ from $r(h, n)\underline{W}^*(h, n)$. Also, random number $r(h, n)$ secret of S disables C_h to calculate token concealer v_{n+1} from the sums of its weighted next tokens at C_h's n-th and (n-1)-th visits, i.e. from r(h, n)$\underline{T}^*(h, n)$ and r(h, n-1)$\underline{T}^*(h, n-1)$ that C_h had obtained from S at its current and previous visit. On the other hand, S cannot know individual tokens of C_h, because individual records are multiplied by client token concealers secret from S. Although $u_{P-1}T(h, n)$ together with T(h, n) reveals u_{P-1}, S cannot calculate any previous token T(h, s) (s < n) from u_{P-1}, T(h, n) and $\underline{T}^*(h, n)$; it does not know $u_0, u_1, ---, u_{P-2}$.

Extended Next Tokens

The second problem also can be solved as follows. Namely, client C_h at its n-th visit to S uses extended next token N(h, n+1) to be incorporated into ITL(h, n) instead of exact next token T(h, n+1). Firstly, C_h constructs the extended next token as Q-dimensional vector N(h, n+1) = $\{N_1(h, n+1), N_2(h, n+1), ---, N_Q(h, n+1)\}$ as shown in Figure 8 while defining intervals {d(q, 1), e(q, 1)}, {d(q, 2), e(q, 2)}, ---, $\{d(q, Z_q), e(q, Z_q)\}$ for each q $(1 \leq q \leq Q)$, where, d(q, j) < e(q, j). Regarding each $N_q(h, n)$, C_h defines its value arbitrarily, but provided that $b_1, b_2, ---, b_Q$ are C_h's secret constant numbers, it assigns value $b_q T(h, n+1)$ to $N_q(h, n+1)$ when n is in interval {d(q, j), e(q, j)} (i. e. when $d(q, j) \leq n \leq e(q, j)$). Also, C_h defines the intervals so that at least one of them includes arbitrarily given integer m ($0 \leq m \leq$ maximum number of visits that individual clients can make). Under these settings, C_h encrypts extended next token N(h, n+1) to a set of g-dimensional vectors $\underline{E}(a_h, N(h, n+1)) = \{E(a_h, N_1(h, n+1)), E(a_h, N_2(h, n+1)), ---, E(a_h, N_Q(h, n+1))\}$, and S incorporates $v_{n+1}\underline{E}(a_h, N(h, n+1))$ into ITL(h, n) as its encrypted next token part value.

While having reported the above encrypted extended next tokens to S at its individual visits, C_h at its n-th visit generates sequence of numbers $\{0 = y(0) < y(1) < y(2) < ---, < y(P-1) < y(P) = n\}$ for dividing the sequence of its past service receiving records as same as in the previous subsection. However, in this case, $y(0), y(1), y(2), --, y(P)$ are defined so that every number from $y(p)$-1 to $y(p+1)$ is included in interval {d(q, j), e(q, j)} at least for one (q, j) pair. Therefore, C_h can calculate partial sum of decrypted original (not extended) next tokens corresponding to every interval $\{y(p), y(p+1)-1\}$ from the sum of $E(a_h, N_q(h, n+1))$

Figure 7. Extended ITL

Current token	Next token	1st extended vector	2nd extended vector	---	T-th extended vector
$v_n T(h, n)$	$v_{n+1}\{E(a_h, T(h, n+1))+ p_1(n+1)ext_1+ --- +p_T(n+1)ext_T\}$	$v_{n+1}p_1(n+1)ext_1$	$v_{n+1}p_2(n+1)ext_2$		$v_{n+1}p_T(n+1)ext_T$

Figure 8. Extended next token N(h, n)

1st next token	2nd next token	------	Q-th next token
$N_1(h, n+1)$	$N_2(h, n+1)$		$N_Q(h, n+1)$

given by S, i.e. $v_{y(p)+1}T(h, y(p)+1)+v_{y(p)+2}T(h, y(p)+2)+ --- +v_{y(p+1)}T(h, y(p+1)) = \{v_{y(p)+1}N_q(h, y(p)+1)+v_{y(p)+2}N_q(h, y(p)+2)+ --- +v_{y(p+1)}N_q(h, y(p+1))\}/b_q$. At the same time, C_h can protect $E(a_h, x)$ from plain text attacks, because linear relationship between encrypted forms of extended next tokens and their decryption results is hidden, e.g. $\{E(a_h, N_1(h, m_1)), E(a_h, N_2(h, m_1)), ---, E(a_h, N_s(h, m_1))\}$ and $\{E(a_h, N_1(h, m_2)), E(a_h, N_2(h, m_2)), ---, E(a_h, N_s(h, m_2))\}$ may have different decrypted values even when $N_q(h, m_1) = N_q(h, m_2)$ for every q. Also, C_h changes its key a_h for every service period of S, and moreover, from the beginning, it is extremely difficult for S to determine whether given 2 encrypted service receiving record sums were reported by a same client or not.

When the above extended next tokens are combined with the extended ITLs shown in Figure 7, Equation (4) must be replaced by Equation (10). In Equation (10), $N_q(h, m)$ is assumed to have value $b_qT(h, m)$ for every m to simplify the representation. Therefore, C_h must report $\Sigma[v_{n+1}\{N_q(h, n+1)+E(a_h^{-1}, p_1(n+1)ext_1)+ --- +E(a_h^{-1}, p_T(n+1)ext_T)\}]/b_q$ and $\Sigma E(a_h^{-1}, v_{n+1}p_j(n+1)ext_j)/b_q$ as decryption result of $\Sigma[v_{n+1}\{E(a_h, N_q(h, n+1)+p_1(n+1)ext_1+ --- + p_T(n+1)ext_T)\}]$ and $\Sigma\{v_{n+1}p_j(n+1)ext_j\}$ instead of $\Sigma[v_{n+1}\{T(h, n+1)+E(a_h^{-1}, p_1(n+1)ext_1)+ --- +E(a_h^{-1}, p_T(n+1)ext_T)\}]$ and $\Sigma\{E(a_h^{-1}, v_{n+1}p_j(n+1)ext_j)\}$.

$$\Sigma v_{n+1}\{T(h, n+1)\} =$$

$$\Sigma[v_{n+1}\{N_q(h, n+1)+E(a_h^{-1}, p_1(n+1)ext_1)+ --- +E(a_h^{-1}, p_T(n+1)ext_T)\}]/b_q$$

$$- [\Sigma\{E(a_h^{-1}, v_{n+1}p_1(n+1)ext_1)\}+ --- +\Sigma\{E(a_h^{-1}, v_{n+1}p_T(n+1)ext_T)\}]/b_q \quad (10)$$

In the remainder of this book, extended next tokens in Figure 8 and extended ITLs in Figure 7 are used as next tokens and ITLs. However to simplify notations, extended next token $N(h, n+1) = \{N_1(h, n+1), N_2(h, n+1), ---, N_s(h, n+1)\}$ is represented as $T(h, n+1)$, also extended vectors in extended ITLs are ommited.

TOKENS

This section describes tokens that enable an authority, which provides other entities with some services, to identify entities that behave or had behaved dishonestly without revealing privacies of honest entities, e.g. their identities and their receiving services. Tokens are bit strings, and when authority S signs on them and gives them only to entities that are eligible to receive its services, entity C that possesses a token with the signature of S can convince S that it is eligible by only showing the token. Usual tokens are not anonymous, i.e. S can identify an entity that shows a token by memorizing the entities to which it had given individual tokens. However, tokens discussed in this section are anonymous, i.e. no one except C can identify C even C uses its tokens. It must be noted that in anonymous systems bit strings assigned to tokens must be unique and they are allowed to be used only once. When same tokens exist or they can be used repeatedly, entity C can easily make copies of its token and give them to ineligible entities without losing its tokens. Because token owners are anonymous, no one can determine whether the tokens shown are copies or not if tokens are not unique or they can be used repeatedly. Provided that tokens are unique and individual tokens can be used only once, S can easily detect copies of tokens as the ones used repeatedly.

Tokens can be made anonymous by 2 schemes, the 1st one is the open token scheme and the 2nd one is the anonymous token scheme. In both schemes any entity except token holder C cannot identify C from its tokens. Therefore, both are anonymous; however because the name "anonymous token" is frequently used for representing the one generated through the 2nd scheme, in this book, the name "open token" is used for representing the one generated in the 1st scheme. In the open token scheme, authority S simply signs on tokens without knowing token holders and possibly without verifying their eligibilities. Therefore, S may know individual tokens that it had given to entities, but does not know the entities to which it had given particular tokens. On the other hand, in the anonymous token scheme, S signs on a token without knowing its value based on blind signature schemes discussed already in this chapter; i.e. S may know the entities to which it had given tokens (depending on situations), but it does not know the tokens that it had given to the entities. In cases where S knows entities, it is possible for S to give tokens to only eligible entities.

Open tokens discussed in the next subsection are simple, and they are used while being combined with other mechanisms e.g. they will be combined with ITLs discussed just before to construct an anonymous authentication scheme in Section 3. In this subsection, open tokens are used to ensure the uniqueness of anonymous tokens and also to implement homomorphic anonymous tokens. Anonymous tokens are usually used for authenticating anonymous entities, although they are not an effective solution as discussed in chapter "Anonymous Authentication" in Section 3. But while assuming that dishonest events occur and can be detected during the entities are receiving services, anonymous tokens enhance authentication mechanisms so that authority S can identify dishonest entities without revealing any privacy of

Figure 9. Token table

token T_A	available
token T_B	used

----

token T_Y	available
token T_Z	used

honest entities. Homomorphic anonymous tokens discussed in the last part of this subsection enable S to identify dishonest entities without revealing any privacy of honest entities even when dishonest events occur or they are detected after the entities had left S. Anonymous tag based tokens discussed in the next subsection also enable S to identify dishonest entities even when dishonest events are detected after the entities had left S.

Open Tokens

An open token scheme is simple, namely authority S only signs on token T that is shown by an anonymous token holder. The scheme does not necessarily require mechanisms for authenticating entities; therefore there are cases where S gives signed tokens even to ineligible entities. For obtaining the signature of S on its token, entity C can hide its identity by accessing S through an anonymous network discussed in the next chapter for example. Uniqueness of open tokens can be achieved by preparing token tables.

A token table shown in Figure 9 maintains available tokens, and authority S publicly discloses this table e.g. through a BB. Then, anonymously accessing entity C picks its tokens from this table, and S signs on the picked tokens. To disable C to choose an already picked token, S attaches a used mark to a token in the table when some entity had picked it, and S checks this mark in the table at every token request from C. Of course, S rejects the request when the token picked by C is accompanied by the used mark. Although it is possible for entity C to pick token T already picked by other entity D, C cannot use it because S did not sign on T shown by C. It must be noted that S must fill the token table with tokens without signatures. When tokens in the token table have signatures from the beginning, entities can obtain already picked tokens by copying the signatures from the table.

Here, because entities are anonymous even ineligible entities can pick tokens from the token table and can obtain signatures on them. Therefore, other mechanisms that protect the token table from unauthorized entities or that invalidate signed tokens given to ineligible entities are necessary. In a mechanism shown in the next subsection, an authority authorizes open tokens as anonymous tokens by signing on open tokens while verifying the eligibilities of entities, for example, where the signing key for anonymous tokens is different from the one for open tokens. Then, open tokens that had been given to ineligible entities become invalid, because they do not have the signatures for anonymous tokens.

Figure 10. Anonymous token

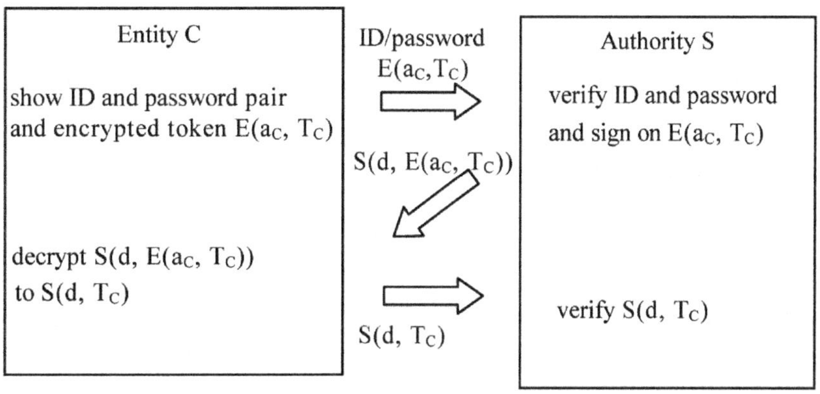

Anonymous Tokens

Entity C can obtain its anonymous token (Chaum, 1983, 1988) from authority S based on a blind signature scheme. As shown in Figure 10, C encrypts its token T_C to $E(a_C, T_C)$ by its secret encryption key a_C and asks authority S to sign on $E(a_C, T_C)$ while convincing S its eligibility by showing its ID and password pair for example. Then after verifying that C is eligible, S signs on $E(a_C, T_C)$ by its signing key d, i.e. calculates $S(d, E(a_C, T_C))$, and finally, C decrypts $S(d, E(a_C, T_C))$ to $S(d, T_C)$, a signed form of T_C, by its secret decryption key a_C^{-1}. As a consequence, entity C can prove its eligibility for receiving some services from authority S by showing anonymous token $S(d, T_C)$ without disclosing its identity i.e. only S that knows signing key d can generate $S(d, T_C)$ so that it is successfully decrypted to T_C, but S cannot identify C from $S(d, T_C)$ because it signed on T_C without knowing T_C itself. In the above, of course it is assumed that the encryption and the signing functions $E(a_C, x)$ and $S(d, x)$ are commutative.

It is also possible for C to receive services repeatedly from S, when it shows its anonymous token in exchange for a new signed token at its every visit to S. Figure 11 shows the token refreshing process (Shigetomi, 2003), i.e. firstly, C obtains the signature of S on its initial encrypted token $E(a_C, T(h, 0))$ while showing its identity as same as in usual blind signature schemes, and afterwards C at its n-th visit to S convinces S that it is an eligible entity by showing its current anonymous token $S(d, T(h, n))$ without disclosing its identity. The important thing is that C shows S not only $S(d, T(h, n))$ but also its encrypted next token $E(a_C, T(h, n+1))$, and S signs on $E(a_C, T(h, n+1))$ to generate $S(d, E(a_C, T(h, n+1)))$ after verifying signature $S(d, T(h, n))$ and confirming that $S(d, T(h, n))$ was not used before so that C_h can calculate $S(d, T(h, n+1))$ from it.

As mentioned before tokens must be unique and their repeated uses must be inhibited, however S may sign on $E(a_C, T)$ and $E(a_D, T)$, i.e. same token T that are encrypted by secret keys a_C and a_D of different entities C and D, because S cannot determine whether $E(a_C, T)$ and $E(a_D, T)$ are encrypted forms of same bit string T or not. As a consequence, when D had used $S(d, T)$ already, C cannot use $S(d, T)$ even if C had obtained $S(d, T)$ legitimately. Open tokens make anonymous tokens unique, and solve this problem. Namely, C anonymously obtains open token $S(\underline{d}, T_C)$ that is prepared by S in advance, and asks S to blindly signs on $S(\underline{d}, T_C)$ to generate $S(d, S(\underline{d}, T_C))$, where, d is the signing key of S for open tokens. Then, uniqueness of anonymous tokens is achieved because open tokens are unique. Of course, S must reject to accept $S(\underline{d}, S(d, T_C))$ when it is repeatedly used or $S(d, S(\underline{d}, T_C))$ cannot be de-

Figure 11. Token refreshing process

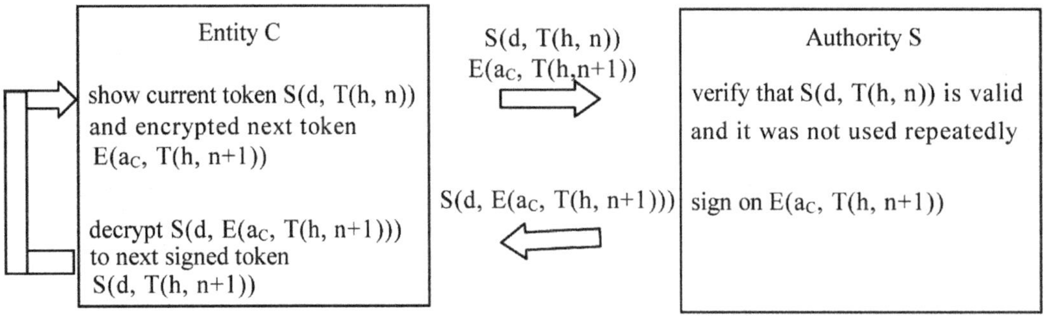

crypted to a consistent value by verification key d^{-1} or $\underline{d}^{-1}$. However, it must be noted that entity C cannot obtain multiple open tokens at a time. If C picks multiple open tokens S($\underline{d}$, T(h, n)) and S($\underline{d}$, T(h, n+1)) at a time, authority S can easily know that anonymous tokens S(d, S($\underline{d}$, T(h, n))) and S(d, S($\underline{d}$, T(h, n+1))) are owned by a same entity, and this fact helps S identify C.

In the remainder of this book notations for representing signatures on open tokens are omitted except in this subsection.

Let C be an entity that rents a machine from authority S while concealing its identity. Here, it is assumed that in addition to an appropriate anonymous authentication mechanism, a mechanism for collecting fees from anonymous entities is available as discussed in Section 3 in conjunction with electronic payment systems. Then, based on these mechanisms, S can collect fees for its providing services from anonymous entity C without knowing any privacy of C. However, S cannot protect itself from dishonest behaviours of C once C is authenticated successfully, e.g. even if C had broken its renting machines C can leave from S without being identified by S, because C is anonymous. If S is allowed to inquire services that it had provided from all entities, dishonest entities can be identified easily; however in this case, privacies of even honest entities are revealed.

Anonymous tokens enable S to identify dishonest entities in the above system without revealing any privacy of honest entities, provided that dishonest events are detected by the time when entities return their renting machines. In the below, it is assumed that S gives only single tokens to individual entities at a time and signs on new tokens encrypted by anonymous entities in exchange for their old ones only when S confirms that not only the old tokens are valid but also the entities had honestly returned their renting machines. Namely, entities cannot obtain new anonymous tokens when they did not return their renting machines honestly. Therefore, although they can leave from the system without any penalty even they had broken machines or did not return them to S, when dishonest events are detected, S can identify the liable entities by asking all entities to show their unused anonymous tokens. Only honest entities can show their unused tokens, on the other hand, S cannot know any privacy of honest entities that showed their unused tokens. Unused tokens do not include any privacy of their owners, because the owners did not receive any service yet by using them.

S can ask entities to show unused tokens without disturbing honest entities by periodically inquiring unused tokens at times when it collects fees for its offering services for example. However, the above mechanism does not work well if S can detect dishonest events only after entities had returned their renting machines. Namely, because S cannot decide whether the entities are honest or not at times when they return the machines to S, S must give new tokens even to dishonest entities.

Homomorphic Anonymous Tokens

A homomorphic anonymous token is a one that is encrypted by a token holder while using a homomorphic (additive) encryption function. Namely, token holder C encrypts its token S($\underline{d}$, T) signed by authority S to E(a_C, S($\underline{d}$, T)) by its encryption key a_C, where, E(a_C, x) is an additive encryption function and $\underline{d}$ is a signing key of S. As same as in previous subsections, S($\underline{d}$, T) must be constructed so that no one except C can identify C from it, however entity C can obtain it with the signature of S not only as a usual anonymous token but also as an open token, i.e. it is not necessary for C to prove its eligibility at times when it obtains signatures on them. In the following, it is assumed that C obtains tokens as open tokens, and the signing key of S is represented as d instead of d to discriminate tokens in this subsection from anonymous tokens.

By using homomorphic anonymous tokens, authority S that offers services to other entities can identify liable entities of dishonest events even if the dishonest events are detected after the completions of the services (Tamura, 2010). S identifies dishonest entity C as follows. Firstly, at anonymous entity C's n-th visit to S, S authenticates C by an appropriate anonymous authentication mechanism, e.g. through one of mechanisms discussed in the chapter "Anonymous Authentication" in Section 3, and before giving services to C, it asks C to show its n-th token S(d, T(C, n)) that is not used before and the encrypted (n+1)-th token, i.e. homomorphic anonymous token $E(a_C$, S(d, T(C, n+1))), where C obtains open tokens S(d, T(C, n)) and S(d, T(C, n+1)) from S separately through the other independent process and encrypts S(d, T(C, n+1)) to $E(a_C$, S(d, T(C, n+1))) by its secret encryption key a_C of additive encryption function $E(a_C, x)$ in advance. Then, C receives services from S, and S memorizes triple {S_{ID}(C, n), S(d, T(C, n)), $E(a_C$, S(d, T(C, n+1)))} as the service record, where S_{ID}(C, n) is the identifier of the service that S had provided.

When dishonest events are detected in the service corresponding to S_{ID}(C, n), S asks all token holders to decrypt $E(a_C$, S(d, T(C, n+1))) that was attached to the service record corresponding to S_{ID}(C, n). Then, C is identified as a dishonest entity when it decrypts it to constant value *check*. Decryption key a_B^{-1} of honest entity B decrypts $E(a_C$, S(d, T(C, n+1))) to an inconsistent value, but C that knows decryption key a_C^{-1} can decrypt it to a consistent value. Here, to enable authority S to determine whether the decryption result is consistent or not, and also to protect $E(a_C, x)$ from plain text attacks, signed token S(d, T(C, n+1))) is constructed as pair {M(C, n+1), *check*} while attaching visible part value *check*, a constant bit string common to all tokens, to confidential part value M(C, n+1). Namely, S(d, T(C, n+1)) is a vector consists of the confidential and the visible parts, and C discloses only visible part value *check* as the decryption result of $E(a_C$, S(d, T(C, n+1))) to prove its honesty.

In the above, S can force C to honestly decrypt $E(a_C$, S(d, T(C, n+1))) to *check* without knowing privacies of honest token holders while exploiting the additive feature of encryption function $E(a_C, x)$. Although additional mechanisms discussed in subsection "Verification of Linear Equation based Encryptions" of Section 1 are required, conceptually, S asks C to decrypt vector Test(C) $= w_0E(a_C$, S(d, T(C, n+1)))$+w_1E(a_C, T_1)+w_2E(a_C, T_2)+ \cdots +w_ZE(a_C, T_Z)$ while generating random numbers $w_0, w_1, \cdots w_Z$ as its secrets. Here, $E(a_C, T_1), E(a_C, T_2), \cdots, E(a_C, T_Z)$ are random bit string vectors of the same dimension as the encrypted forms of tokens, and S generates them at C's 1st visit to S to be decrypted to their visible part values $T_1, T_2, \cdots, T_Z$ by secret decryption key a_C^{-1} of C (i.e. $T_1, T_2, \cdots, T_Z$ are test bit strings), so that S can register pairs $\{T_1, E(a_C, T_1)\}, \{T_2, E(a_C, T_2)\}, \cdots, \{T_Z, E(a_C, T_Z)\}$ as one of information corresponding to C's identity. Then, if C had honestly decrypted $E(a_C$, S(d, T(C, n+1))) to X, it can decrypt Test(C) to $w_0X+w_1T_1+ \cdots +w_ZT_Z$. However, if X is not the correct decryption result, C cannot calculate $w_0X+w_1T_1+ \cdots +w_ZT_Z$ because it does not know $w_0, w_1, \cdots, w_Z$.

To make the above verification scheme effective, S must force C to honestly encrypt S(d, T(C, n+1)) to $E(a_C$, S(d, T(C, n+1))) at its n-th visit. But it must be noted that different from the above case where S verifies the correct decryption of $E(a_C$, S(d, T(C, n+1))) while knowing C's identity, S cannot use encrypted test bit string vectors

Figure 12. Used token record UTR(C, n)

Service identifier	Current token	Encrypted next token
S_{ID}(C, n)	v_nS(d, T(C, n))	$v_{n+1}E(a_C$, S(d, T(C, n+1)))

in this case. When C informs S of its encrypted test bit string vectors, S can easily know that an entity that is requesting its services is C because encrypted test bit string vectors are linked to individual token holders. ITLs force C to encrypt S($\underline{d}$, T(C, n+1)) honestly without using encrypted test bit string vectors. To disable C to dishonestly encrypt S($\underline{d}$, T(C, n+1)) at its n-th visit, instead of triple {S_{ID}(C, n), S($\underline{d}$, T(C, n)), E(a_C, S($\underline{d}$, T(C, n+1)))}, S generates used token record UTR(C, n) consists of the service identifier and the ITL as shown in Figure 12, and encrypts it to E(k_S, UTR(C, n)) by its secret encryption key k_S to be maintained by C. Here, E(k_S, x) is an additive encryption function, and current token S($\underline{d}$, T(C, n)) and encrypted next token E(a_C, S($\underline{d}$, T(C, n+1))) in UTR(C, n) are multiplied by token concealers v_n and v_{n+1} secrets of S so that pair {v_nS($\underline{d}$, {T(C, n)), v_{n+1}E(a_C, S($\underline{d}$, T(C, n+1)))} constitutes an ITL.

Then, provided that the transaction-wise ITL sum checking mechanism in the previous section is adopted, C cannot dishonestly encrypt S($\underline{d}$, T(C, n+1)) to X instead of E(a_C, S($\underline{d}$, T(C, n+1))) in order to decrypt X to inconsistent value X that is different from *check* at a time when dishonest events about S_{ID}(C, n) are detected. Namely to use token S($\underline{d}$, T(C, n)), C must decrypt the sum of ITLs included in its past used token records honestly, then S can use the sum of current tokens and that of encrypted next tokens as a test bit string and its encrypted form pair for verifying C's honest encryption of S($\underline{d}$, T(C, n+1)) without knowing the identity of C. Here, the sum of current tokens and that of next tokens in the above must be calculated as the total of their confidential and visible part values as explained below.

It must be noted that different from in usual verification processes of encryptions where entities verify that encryption results certainly include given bit strings, in the above verification, S must confirm that decryption result of E(a_C, S($\underline{d}$, T(C, n+1))) does not include *check* in its any form. For example, it is possible for C to generate E(a_C, G(n+1)) as the value of E(a_C, S($\underline{d}$, T(C, n+1))) so that its decryption result G(n+1) is configured as real part and presentation part pair {R(h, n+1), P(h, n+1)}, where although real part R(h, n+1) includes enough information for reconstructing S($\underline{d}$, T(C, n+1)), presentation part P(h, n+1) does not include *check* as its visible part value (it must be noted that C can include S($\underline{d}$, T(C, n+1)) in R(n+1) even as the linear combination of multiple confidential part values, so that S cannot identify it even when C discloses all confidential part values). Then, C can calculate the consistent sum of next tokens from the sum of real part values, i.e. R(0)+R(1)+ ---- +R(n+1), and at the same time, it can show P(h, n+1) that does not include *check* as the decrypted from of E(a_C, G(n+1)), so that the above procedure does not identify C as the dishonest entity.

The additive feature of encryption function E(a_C, x) also solves this problem. Namely, when each test bit string vector E(a_C, T_q) is decrypted by decryption key a_C^{-1}, the decryption result reveals T_{qR} and T_{qP} as its real and presentation part values, and C that is deceiving S must prove its correct decryption of E(a_C, S($\underline{d}$, T(C, n+1))) by showing w_0S_P($\underline{d}$, T(C, n+1))+w_1T_{1P}+w_2T_{2P}+ --- +w_ZT_{ZP} as the decryption result of w_0E(a_C, S($\underline{d}$, T(C, n+1)))+w_1E(a_C, T_1)+w_2E(a_C, T_2)+---+w_ZE(a_C, T_Z), where it is assumed that E(a_C, S($\underline{d}$, T(C, n+1))) reveals S_P($\underline{d}$, T(C, n+1)) as its presentation part value when decrypted. However, C must register T_{1R}, T_{2R}, ---, T_{ZR} as its decrypted test bit strings at its initial visit, otherwise C cannot prove correctness of its decryption when S asks C to decrypt the sum of encrypted next tokens included in its past used token records at the end of its previous service period for collecting fees. This means that C must use T_{1R}, T_{2R}, ---, T_{ZR} for proving its correct decryption of E(a_C, S($\underline{d}$, T(C, n+1))), and consequently, it cannot prove that S_P($\underline{d}$, T(C, n+1)) is the correct decrypted form of E(a_C, S(d, T(C, n+1))). Here, it must be noted that C must report the total of confidential and visible part values of encrypted next tokens as the sum of its decrypted next token values.

ANONYMOUS TAGS

Tags are attached to logical objects (e.g. data in computer systems) or physical objects (e.g. parcels in mailing systems) to enable entities to identify and keep track of the objects that are transported to their destinations through communication or physical object transportation channels. Usually, tags include information that suggests the identities of owners of the objects; however, anonymous tags do not include any information that suggests them. Because a sequence of places where a particular object was located may suggest the owner of the object, an anonymous tag attached to the object is required also to disable entities except its owner to identify sequences of locations that the object had visited. Nevertheless, it must enable the owner of the object to keep track of the object that may change its locations.

To conceal identities of owners of objects from any entity other than the owners themselves, owners necessarily encrypt tags by their secret keys. In addition, to disable entities other than the owners to trace objects that are travelling different places, anonymous tags are constructed so that they change their forms at every place where they are located. If a tag has the same form at all places, anyone can easily identify the sequence of places that the object accompanied by the tag was located. Therefore, an anonymous tag attached to an object is necessarily re-encrypted at every place possibly by an entity other than the owner of the object, e.g. by a manager of the place. Then, anonymous tags are characterized by the following features (Tamura, 2008), they are,

1. No one can identify tags owned by other entities,
2. Entities even other than the owner of a tag re-encrypt the tag by their secret keys, and
3. The owner of a tag can identify its tag without knowing any secret (e.g. encryption keys) of entities that had re-encrypted the tag.

RSA Based Anonymous Tags

When a sequence of entities S_Q, S_{Q-1}, ---, S_1 that re-encrypt a tag is fixed, an anonymous tag with the above properties can be successfully implemented by using RSA based re-encryption schemes. Namely, a tag owner C encrypts its tag T that is secret from others repeatedly by using public keys of multiple entities S_1, S_2, ---, S_Q while adding secret random bit string r_j at the j-th encryption, i.e. C calculates $E(k_*, T) = E(k_Q, E(k_{Q-1}, ----, E(k_1, T \| r_1) --- \| r_{Q-1}) \| r_Q)$, and each S_j in the sequence that receives the tag decrypts $E(k_{j*}, T) = E(k_j, E(k_{j-1}, ----, E(k_1, T \| r_1) --- \| r_{j+1}) \| r_j)$ to $E(k_{(j-1)*}, T) = E(k_{j-1}, E(k_{j-2}, ----, E(k_1, T \| r_1) --- \| r_{j-2}) \| r_{j-1})$ by its secret key k_j^{-1} while shuffling the result with other tags. Then, because each S_j knows only its own secret key, no entity except C can trace its tag by linking partially decrypted forms of $E(k_*, T)$ unless all entities conspire with each other. Regarding the identity of the owner of T, no one except C can identify C even after the tag had been decrypted completely, because T is a secret of C.

On the other hand, C can identify its tag even from its partially decrypted forms by memorizing all encrypted forms of T, i.e. T, $E(k_1, T \| r_1)$, $E(k_2, \{E(k_1, T \| r_1) \| r_2\})$, ---, $E(k_*, T)$, at a time when it encrypts T to $E(k_*, T)$. However, the repeatedly encrypted tag must be decrypted by S_Q, S_{Q-1}, ---, S_1 in this order because RSA based re-encryption schemes are not commutative when encryption keys are publicly disclosed, i.e. when different entities use different modulo arithmetic. Therefore the sequence of entities that re-encrypt (in this case, re-decrypt) tags must be fixed in advance. In addition, if $E(k_j, x)$ is defined as $x^{kj}{}_{\mathrm{mod}\, pj}$, p_i must be greater than p_j when $j < i$, and lengths of RSA based anonymous tags prone to being long when many entities are involved in the sequence. Here, secret random bit strings must be added at all stages of re-encryption. When r_j is not added, input $E(k_{j*}, T)$ of S_j can be linked to its output $E(k_{(j-1)*}, T)$ by anyone, i.e. $E(k_{(j-1)*}, T)$ can be encrypted to $E(k_{j*}, T)$ again by using public encryption kcy k_j of S_j.

Although ElGamal based re-encryption scheme can maintain sizes of re-encrypted forms constant even the number of entities becomes large, it cannot be used for implementing anonymous tags. Namely as discussed in subsection "ElGamal based Commutative Re-encryption Scheme" of Section 1, provided that x_j and $y_j = g^{xj}$ are a secret decryption key and a public encryption key of S_j, C re-encrypts tag T to $\{g^{kC}, y_*^{kC}T\}$, where $y_* = y_1 y_2 \cdots y_Q = g^{x1+x2+\cdots+xQ}$ is a common public encryption key, and k_C is a random number secret of tag owner C. Then, the decrypted form of encrypted tag T at entity S_j is calculated as $\{g^{kC}, g^{(x1+x2+\cdots+xj)kC}T/(g^{kC})^{xj}\} = \{g^{kC}, g^{(x1+\cdots+x(j-1))kC}T\}$ that includes g^{kC} common to all encrypted forms of T, therefore anyone can easily trace tag T by identifying g^{kC} included in encrypted T.

Involution Based Anonymous Tags

An anonymous tag shown in Figure 13 is based on commutative encryption functions (Tamura, 2008), and it removes the difficulty of the RSA based anonymous tags discussed just before that the lengths of tags become long as the numbers of entities that re-encrypt the tags increase. Another important thing is that a tag shown in Figure 13 is applicable also in environments where entities that re-encrypt tags cannot be defined in advance. It is configured as a pair of a tag and a associate tag parts, where bit string T is placed in the tag part and T is encrypted to $E(a_C, T) = T^{aC}{}_{\mathrm{mod}\ p}$ by secret key a_C of the tag owner C to be put in the associate tag part, where p is an appropriate integer common to all entities.

Then, every entity S_j separately encrypts the tag and the associate tag parts of individual tags by its secret encryption key k_j when it receives them from other entities. For example, when anonymous tag $t_0 = \{T, E(a_C, T) = T^{aC}{}_{\mathrm{mod}\ p}\}$ is re-encrypted by 3 entities S_1, S_2, and S_3, tag t_0 changes its form to $t_1 = \{E(k_1, T) = T^{k1}, E(k_1, T^{aC}) = T^{(aC)(k1)}\}$, $t_2 = \{E(k_2, T^{k1}) = T^{(k1)(k2)}, E(k_2, T^{(aC)(k1)}) = T^{(aC)(k1)(k2)}\}$ and $t_3 = \{E(k_3, T^{(k1)(k2)}) = T^{(k1)(k2)(k3)}, E(k_3, T^{(aC)(k1)(k2)}) = T^{(aC)(k1)(k2)(k3)}\}$ in this order. Therefore, when each entity shuffles multiple tags, individual entities that know only their own keys cannot identify correspondences between input and output tags of other entities, then no entity other than the tag owner can trace the different forms of T i.e. t_0, t_1, t_2, and t_3 unless all entities conspire with each other.

On the other hand, the owner of the tag can identify it even it is encrypted repeatedly by multiple entities. Namely, when C encrypts the tag part by its encryption key k_C, the encrypted result coincides with the associate tag part even if the tag is encrypted multiple times by other entities, because each $E(k_j, x)$ and $E(a_C, x)$ are commutative. In the above example, C can identify $t_1 = \{T^{k1}, T^{(aC)(k1)}\}$, $t_2 = \{T^{(k1)(k2)}, T^{(aC)(k1)(k2)}\}$ and $t_3 = \{T^{(k1)(k2)(k3)}, T^{(aC)(k1)(k2)(k3)}\}$ as its tag, by relations $(T^{k1})^{aC} = T^{(aC)(k1)}$, $(T^{(k1)(k2)})^{aC} = T^{(aC)(k1)(k2)}$ and $(T^{(k1)(k2)(k3)})^{aC} = T^{(aC)(k1)(k2)(k3)}$, respectively.

Here, it must be noted that each entity can change its key anytime independent of others. But, each S_j must define its key k_j so that $T_x{}^{kj}{}_{\mathrm{mod}\ p}$ or $T_{x*}{}^{kj}{}_{\mathrm{mod} p}$ does not coincides with 1 when it receives tag $\{T_x, T_{x*}\}$. Also, although the onetime pad is commutative, it cannot be used for encrypting anonymous tags. When the onetime pad is adopted,

Figure 13. Structure of anonymous tag

Tag part (T)	Associate tag part ($E(a_C, T)$)

tag $\{T, a_C \oplus T\}$ is encrypted by encryption key k_j of entity S_j to pair $\{k_j \oplus T, k_j \oplus a_C \oplus T\}$. Therefore, XOR of the tag part and the associate tag part coincides with a_C, i.e. $(k_j \oplus T) \oplus (k_j \oplus a_C \oplus T) = a_C$. This relation is satisfied always even when other entities encrypt the tag repeatedly, therefore anyone can easily identify the tag. Namely, when XOR of the tag and the associate tag parts of individual inputs and outputs of entity S_j are calculated, every input and output tag pair $[\{X_{in}, Y_{in}\}, \{X_{out}, Y_{out}\}]$ can be identified as a one that satisfy relation $X_{in} \oplus Y_{in} = X_{out} \oplus Y_{out}$. This is because onetime pad is not safe when it is used repeatedly as discussed in subsection "Onetime Pad" in Section 1.

Anonymous Tokens Based on Anonymous Tags

Involution based anonymous tags can be used also for implementing anonymous tokens. Let S be a server that provides clients with services, and S(d, *x*) and d be an RSA signing function (therefore it is multiplicative) and a secret signing key of server S. Then, signature $S(d, T^{(R+Kg+K+1)W})$ is an anonymous token generated by S and given to client C. Here, T and K are integers defined by S and publicly disclosed, but different from K that is common to all tokens, T is unique to $S(d, T^{(R+Kg+K+1)W})$. R and W are secret random integers defined by C, and g is S's secret integer. In detail, if client C calculates pair $\{T, T^R\}$, and S calculates T^K and T^g and generates signature $S(d, T^{R+Kg+K+1})$ to give it to C together with T^g, provided that C shows triple $\{T^W, T^{gW}, T^{RW}\}$ and $S(d, T^{R+Kg+K+1})^W = S(d, T^{(R+Kg+K+1)W})$ it had calculated while using its secret W, only C can convince others that $S(d, T^{(R+Kg+K+1)W})$ is the signature of S on pair $\{T, T^R\}$. Namely, $S(d, T^{(R+Kg+K+1)W})$ that is decomposed into $\{T^W, T^{KW}, T^{KgW}, T^{RW}\}$ can be generated only by S, and only C that knows R can extract R embedded in pair $\{T^W, T^{RW}\}$, nevertheless, no one except C can identify the correspondence between $S(d, T^{R+Kg+K+1})$ and $S(d, T^{(R+Kg+K+1)W})$ because W is C's secret, i.e. no one can identify C from $S(d, T^{(R+Kg+K+1)W})$.

In other words, $S(d, T^{(R+Kg+K+1)})$ is the blind signature of S on anonymous tag $\{T^W, T^{RW}\}$ consists of tag part value T^W and associate tag part value T^{RW}, and in the above, S informs C of T^g so that anyone can verify the validity of $S(d, T^{(R+Kg+K+1)W})$. Also S generates $\{T^K, T^{gK}\}$ to disable C to extract other tag $\{T^P, T^{QP}\}$ ($Q \neq R$) from $S(d, T^{(R+Kg+K+1)W})$ as discussed later. Here, S cannot know R from T^R, on the other hand, C cannot know g from T^g of course.

Server S verifies the validity of $S(d, T^{(R+Kg+K+1)W})$ as shown in the lower part of Figure 14. In the figure, C calculates $\{T^W, T^{gW}, T^{RW}\}$ to inform S of them together with token $S(d, T^{(R+Kg+K+1)W})$, and to verify its validity, S decrypts $S(d, T^{(R+Kg+K+1)W})$ to $T^{(R+Kg+K+1)W}$ by public verification key d^{-1}, calculates T^{KW} and T^{KgW} based on T^W, T^{gW} and publicly known K, and confirms that $T^{(R+Kg+K+1)W}$ is the product of T^W, T^{KW}, T^{KgW} and T^{RW}. After that, S examines whether C knows R or not. Here, C can convince S that it knows R without disclosing R itself as follow. Namely, S calculates $(T^W)^X$ and $(T^{RW})^X$ while generating its secret random integer X, and C that receives T^{WX} calculates $A = (T^{WX})^R$ by using its secret R, and finally, S determines that C knows R when relation $A = (T^{RW})^X$ holds, because it is practically impossible to calculate T^{RWX} from T^{WX} without knowing R.

In the above, other entities including S cannot extract any tag $\{T^P, T^{QP}\}$ from $S(d, T^{(R+Kg+K+1)W})$. Namely, if $\{T^P, T^{QP}\}$ is consistent with $S(d, T^{(R+Kg+K+1)W})$, relation $T^{(R+Kg+K+1)W} = T^{QP}T^{KgP}T^{KP}T^P$ must hold, and this means $T^{QP} = T^{(R+Kg+K+1)W}/T^{KgP}T^{KP}T^P$. But because R is C's secret, even S that knows both K and g cannot calculate Q from relation $T^{QP} = T^{(R+Kg+K+1)W}/T^{KgP}T^{KP}T^P$. On the other hand, C cannot forge a token by calculating the product of its knowing tokens $S(d, T_1^{(R1+Kg1+K+1)W1})$ and $S(d, T_2^{(R2+Kg2+K+1)W2})$. Because not only T_1 and T_2 but also R_1 and R_2 are defined as unique numbers (uniqueness of R_1 and R_2 will be discussed later), C that does not know g cannot calculate

Figure 14. Generation and verification of anonymous tag based tokens

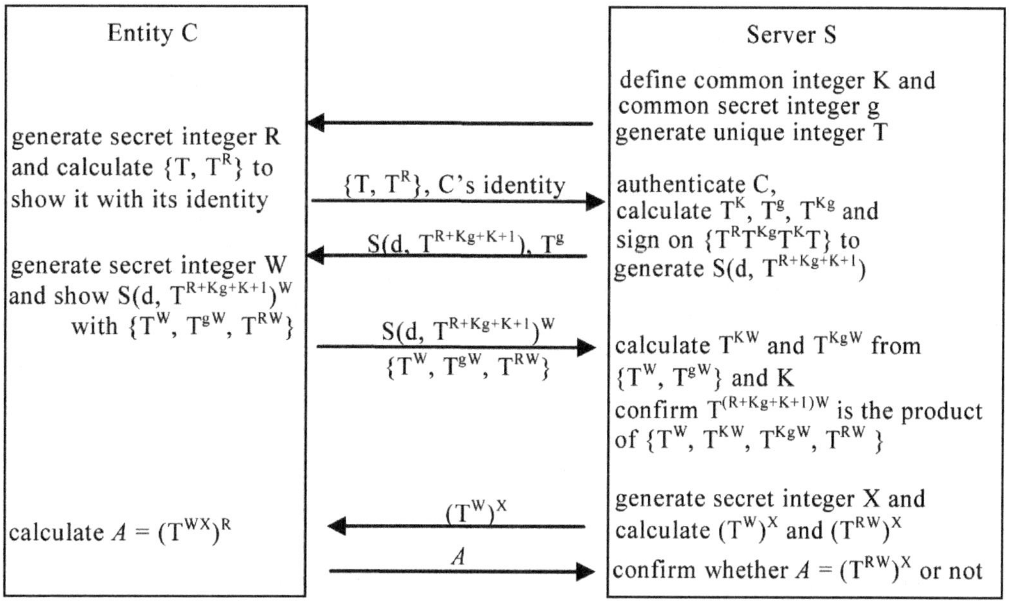

integers T_3 or R_3 from $T_1^{(R1+Kg1+K+1)W1}T_2^{(R2+Kg2+K+1)W2}$ that makes anonymous tag $\{T_3, T_3^{R3}\}$ consistent with $S(d, T_1^{(R1+Kg1+K+1)W1}T_2^{(R2+Kg2+K+1)W2})$.

Advantages of the above scheme is firstly not only S but also anyone can verify the validity of token $S(d, T^{R+Kg+K+1})^W$ because verification key d^{-1} and integer K are publicly known and C discloses T^{gW}, and secondly, C can use $S(d, T^{R+Kg+K+1})^W$ repeatedly while disabling other entities to use it. Namely, entities including the server cannot use $S(d, T^{R+Kg+K+1})^W$ that they obtain by observing tokens exchanged between S and C because C never discloses its secret R. Moreover, no one except C can know that the repeatedly used tokens $S(d, T^{R+Kg+K+1})^{W1}$, $S(d, T^{R+Kg+K+1})^{W2}$, ---, $S(d, T^{R+Kg+K+1})^{WN}$ are owned by a same entity, provided that W_1, W_2, ---, W_N are different. In addition, as shown below, when S detects dishonest events about $S(d, T^{R+Kg+K+1})^W$, it can identify C without knowing any secret of honest entities, and it also can limit numbers of times that C can use $S(d, T^{R+Kg+K+1})^W$.

Dishonest Entity Identification Based on Anonymous Tags

S can identify dishonest entities without knowing any privacy of honest entities as follows. To identify dishonest entities, firstly S memorizes triple $\{T, T^R, C\}$ as a registered token record at a time when it issues token $S(d, T^{R+Kg+K+1})$ to C, and when C requests service *Z* while showing token $S(d, T^{R+Kg+K+1})^W$, it memorizes triple $\{T^W, T^{RW}, Z\}$ as a service record. Under these settings, when S detects dishonest events about service *Z*, it asks all relevant entities to carry out the following procedure. Let $\{T_1, \underline{T}_1\}$ and $\{T_2, \underline{T}_2\}$ be anonymous tags corresponding to registered token record $\{T, T^R, C\}$ and service record $\{T^W, T^{RW}, Z\}$ respectively, i.e. $T_1 = T$, $\underline{T}_1 = T^R$, $T_2 = T^W$ and $\underline{T}_2 = T^{RW}$, then, S firstly prepares a set of tags $\{T_1^{B1}, \underline{T}_1^{B1}\}$, ---, $\{T_1^{BN}, \underline{T}_1^{BN}\}$, $\{T_2^{C1}, \underline{T}_2^{C1}\}$, ---, $\{T_2^{CN}, \underline{T}_2^{CN}\}$ while generating its secret random numbers B_1, ---, B_N and C_1, ---, C_N, and asks C to carry out the procedure shown in Figure 14 for randomly selecting $\{T_1^{Bh}, \underline{T}_1^{Bh}\}$ or $\{T_2^{Cj}, \underline{T}_2^{Cj}\}$. Then, if C is honest it completes the procedure successfully for $\{T_1^{Bh}, \underline{T}_1^{Bh}\}$ but the procedure fails for $\{T_2^{Cj}, \underline{T}_2^{Cj}\}$. On the other hand if C is dishonest, it can complete the procedure successfully for all tags.

Of course if C is dishonest it tries to deceive S while carrying out the procedure incorrectly, but it is impossible for C to know whether $\{T_1^{Bh}, \underline{T}_1^{Bh}\}$ and $\{T_2^{Cj}, \underline{T}_2^{Cj}\}$ were generated based on the registered token record or the service record because B_h and C_j are S's secrets. As a consequence, when S shows $T_1^{(Bh)X}$ while generating its secret integer X, C may calculate $\underline{T}_1^{(Bh)XR^*}$ that is different from $T_1^{B(h)X}$, or it may calculate $T_2^{(Cj)XR}$ that coincides with $\underline{T}_2^{(Cj)X}$ when S shows $T_2^{(Cj)X}$, and S can determine C is dishonest. Also although all entities are required to carry out the procedure, inconveniences caused by S's inquiries are reduced if the procedure is included in payment processes at ends of S's service periods for example.

Limiting Multi-Time Uses of Anonymous Tag Based Tokens

In generating anonymous tag based token S(d, $T^{(R+Kg+K+1)W}$), integers K and g defined by server S (g is a secret of S) are used to force C to calculate $A = (T^{WX})^R$ as T^{WX} to the power of exactly R. For example, if S generates a signature on tag $\{T, T^R\}$ simply as S(d, T^{R+1}), C can know integers P and Q that satisfy relation $T^{(R+1)W} = T^{P+PQ}$ ($Q \neq R$) because it knows both R and W, therefore C can convince others that S(d, $T^{R+1})^W$ is the signature on tag $\{T^P, T^{PQ}\}$ while calculating $A = (T^{PX})^Q$. Token S(d, $T^{R+Kg+K+1}$) disables C to convince others that S(d, $T^{R+Kg+K+1})^W$ is the signature on tag $\{T^P, T^{PQ}\}$ except the case where Q = R, in more precisely, C can show S(d, $T^{R+Kg+K+1})^W$ only with $\{T^W, T^{gW}, T^{RW}\}$, e.g. although $T^{(R+Kg+K+1)W}$ is successfully decomposed into $\{T^{zW}, T^{KzW}, T^{KgzW}, T^{R^*}\}$ even if C defines integer z arbitrarily and calculates $T^{R^*} = T^{(R+Kg+K+1)W}/T^{(K+Kg+1)zW}$, C that does not know g cannot know R* included in tag $\{T^{zW}, T^{R^*}\}$. Generally, it is practically impossible to know both Q and Y that satisfy relations $T^{(R+Kg+K+1)W} = T^{(Q+Y+K+1)P}$ and $T^{YP} = T^{KgP}$ without knowing g.

By exploiting this property, S can limit the number of times that individual entities can use their tokens. To limit the number of effective times of tokens, in Figure 14, C is requested to declare n, the number of visits that it had made before, and S calculates $M(n)(T^{WX})^Y$ in addition to $(T^W)^X$ while generating random secret integer Y and defining integer $M(n)$ unique to n and common to all entities. Then, S asks C to calculate $A = (T^{WX})^R$ and $B = \{M(n)(T^{WX})^Y\}^R$. After that S verifies whether relation $A = (T^{RW})^X$ holds or not, and calculates $B/A^Y = \{M(n)(T^{WX})^Y\}^R/(T^{WX})^{RY} = M(n)^R$. Here, $M(n)^R$ is a number unique to pair {C, n}, therefore if S memorizes pair $\{n, M(n)^R\}$ and rejects request from C when it declares n (> N) as its number of visits or when pair $\{n, M(n)^R\}$ had appeared already, S can disable C to use S(d, $T^{R+Kg+K+1}$) more than N-times. On the other hand, S cannot identify C from $M(n)^R$ or it cannot extract a sequence of tokens used by a same entity, because it is practically impossible to know R from $M(n)^R$. In the remainder of this book, $M(n)^R$ is called a used seal of anonymous tag S(d, $T^{R+Kg+K+1}$).

However there are 2 problems, they are firstly C may calculate $B = \{M(n)(T^{WX})^Y\}^R$ dishonestly, and secondly different entities C and C' may choose same secret random number R. The first problem can be solved if S calculates $T^{WX(1)}, T^{WX(2)}$, ---, $T^{WX(M)}$ while generating its secret integers X(1), X(2), ---, X(M), and asks C to calculate $A_1 = T^{WX(1)R}$, $A_2 = T^{WX(2)R}$, ---, $A_M = T^{WX(M)R}$, and $B = \{M(n)(T^{WX})^Y\}^R$ by showing $\{T^{WX(1)}, T^{WX(2)}$, ---, $T^{WX(M)}, M(n)(T^{WX})^Y\}$ while randomly changing their positions. Namely, if C tries to dishonestly calculates B, it may calculate A_m incorrectly, and A_m does not satisfy relation $A_m = (T^{WX(m)})^R$, as a consequence, C's request is rejected.

The second problem can be solved by a secret number generation process shown below. At a time when C generates its token S(d, $T^{R+Kg+K+1}$), multiple mutually independent authorities S_1, S_2, ---, S_Q generate their secret integers r_1, r_2, ---, r_Q and calculate M^{r1}, M^{r2}, ---, M^{rQ}. Then, S calculates $M^{r1}M^{r2}$---M^{rQ} = $M^{r1+r2+ --- +rQ}$ = M^R, and if M^R did not appear before, S_1, S_2, ---, S_Q inform C of their secret integers r_1, r_2, ---, r_Q so that C can calculate its secret integer R = r_1+r_2+ --- +r_Q, but when M^R appeared already, S_1, S_2, ---, S_Q generates other secret numbers. Here, any entity other than S_h cannot know r_h from M^{rh}, therefore C can make R confidential even when same number R is generated and M^R is disclosed to be unsuccessfully assigned to other entity. Also because *M* is an integer common to all tokens, C can make R unique to it.

In the next section, cut and choose protocols also will be applied to identify anonymous entities that had used same tokens repeatedly, but it will be seen that anonymous tag based mechanisms work more efficiently. Lastly, it must be noted that used seal $M(n)^R$ can be used also as the evidence that C had used its token S(d, $T^{R+Kg+K+1}$) because no one other than C can generate it, then, disputes between S and C about C's visit to S can be resolved by using $M(n)^R$.

CHALLENGE AND RESPONSE PROTOCOLS

Challenge and response protocols are the ones, in which entity V asks entity P questions about information *M* owned by P so that V can convince itself that *M* is correct or P knows *M*. Here, the important thing is that *M* is the secret of P, therefore P must convince V the above fact without disclosing complete information about *M*. The cut and choose protocol in the next subsection enables entity P to convince V the correctness of *M* or P knows *M* by presenting only a part of *M* to V, and Zero Knowledge Proof discussed after the next subsection enables P to convince V that without disclosing any information that suggests *M*, i.e. while disclosing kinds of encrypted forms of *M*.

Cut and Choose Protocol

The cut and choose protocol enables P to convince V that bit string *M* is correct while disclosing only a part of *M* to V (Chaum, 1988). As the word "cut and choose" implies, in the protocol, P divides its secret bit string *M* into 2 parts M_1 and M_2 so that V cannot estimate the value of *M* from either M_1 or M_2 although it can verify the correctness of each part without knowing the other part, and V randomly chooses one of them and verifies the validity of its selecting part M_m (m = 1 or 2). Then, V can believe that both M_1 and M_2 are valid, because P did not know the part that V would select in advance. Namely, P cannot prepare bit strings M_1 and M_2 so that M_1 includes valid information and M_2 does not without the risk that V finds P's dishonesty while selecting M_2. On the other hand, V can know only a part of *M*, therefore P can maintain *M* as its secret.

The probability that V can detect P's dishonesty is 1/2 in the above case; V can increase the probability by dividing *M* into more than 2 parts. When P divides *M* into N parts M_1, M_2, ---,M_N (more generally generates N versions of *M*) so that V can verify the correctness of each version (part) without knowing other versions but it cannot estimate the value of *M* without knowing at least (K+1) versions, V can ask P to show at most K versions while maintaining the confidentiality of *M*. Then the probability that V can detect dishonesties of P becomes greater than K/N. Namely, when P prepares N versions while including at least 1 invalid version, the probability that the invalid version will be selected by V is greater than K/N. Therefore, the probability in which P's dishonesty is detected can be improved by increasing K.

Although mechanisms based on anonymous tags in the previous section are more efficient, a typical situation in which the cut and choose protocol is exploited is the identification of entities that had used their anonymous tokens repeatedly. Namely, the cut and choose protocol enables authority S to identify entities who used same tokens repeatedly while maintaining anonymities of honest entities in environments where online databases about used tokens are not available (Chaum, 1988). In the scheme based on the cut and choose protocol, S identifies entity C by the identifier I(C) of C that is embedded in its token T_C. However, to preserve privacies of honest entities that use their tokens in authorized ways, C encrypts I(C) to form {g(R), g(I(C)R)} by using random number R secret of C, and constructs its token $\underline{T}_C$ as the concatenation of T_C, g(R) and g(I(C)R), i.e. $\underline{T}_C = T_C \| g(R) \| g(I(C)R)$. Where g is a hash function shared between S and C. Then, C encrypts $\underline{T}_C$ to $E(a_C, \underline{T}_C)$ by its encryption key a_C, S blindly signs on it by its signing key d, and finally C decrypts $S(d, E(a_C, \underline{T}_C))$ to $S(d, \underline{T}_C)$ (it is assumed that encryption function $E(a_C, x)$ and signing function $S(d, y)$ are commutative of course). Here, $S(d, \underline{T}_C)$ in the above is anonymous, i.e. hash function $g(x)$ is one way and R is secret of C, therefore anyone except C cannot extract I(C) from {g(R), g(I(C)R)} (it is practically impossible to calculate R from g(R)), also S cannot identify C from $S(d, \underline{T}_C)$ because it had signed on $E(a_C, \underline{T}_C)$ blindly.

Under the above settings, at a time when C requests services by showing $S(d, \underline{T}_C)$ to S, S selects 0 or 1 as the value of *e* at random, and when e = 0, it asks C to show R and accepts the request if g(R) calculated based on the given R coincides with that in {g(R), g(I(C)R)} included in $S(d, \underline{T}_C)$. When e = 1, S asks C to show I(C)R and accepts the request if g(I(C)R) calculated based on the given I(C)R coincides with that in {g(R), g(I(C)R)} included in $S(d, \underline{T}_C)$. Here, in either case S cannot identify C, i.e. C discloses only R or I(C)R. However, when C uses $\underline{T}_C$ 2-times, S can identify C with the probability 1/2. Namely, if C uses T_C 2-times, S can obtain both of R and I(C)R from multiple $S(d, \underline{T}_C)$ in the used token records with probability 1/2, and once both R and I(C)R are obtained, I(C) is extracted by calculating I(C) R/R. Here, C must report R or I(C)R honestly at times when it shows $S(d, T_C)$, i.e. it is practically impossible for C to generate R* or (I(C)R)* so that g(R*) = g(R) or g((I(C)R)*) = g(I(C)R) is satisfied, because $g(x)$ is a one way function.

The probability that S successfully identify dishonest C can be increased by exploiting multiple pairs $\{g(R_j), g(I(C)R_j): j = 1, ---, Z\}$ instead of single pair {g(R), g(I(C)R)}. If $\underline{T}_C$ is constructed as $T_C \| g(R_1) \| g(I(C)R_1) \| g(R_2) \| g(I(C)R_2) \| --- \| g(R_Z) \| g(I(C)R_Z)$ as shown in Figure 15, and S generates a set of random numbers $e_1, e_2, ---, e_Z$, each of which takes 0 or 1 as its value, C must report R_j or $I(C)R_j$ for each j at every use of token $S(d, \underline{T}_C)$. Then, when C uses $S(d, \underline{T}_C)$ 2-times the probability that C reveals both R_j and $I(C)R_j$ at least for one j becomes greater than or equal to $1-(1/2)^Z$, and once S knows both R_j and $I(C)R_j$ at least for one j, it is easy to extract I(C).

However, at the stage where S blindly signs on token T_C in the above procedure, S must convince itself that $\underline{T}_C$ includes {g(R), g(I(C)R)} correctly from its encrypted form $E(a_C, \underline{T}_C)$, i.e. without knowing $\underline{T}_C$, because if C shows T_C to convince S, S can identify C when it uses T_C. The cut and choose protocol solves also this problem. Namely, C generates N versions of $\underline{T}_C$, i.e. it generates $\underline{T}_{C1}, \underline{T}_{C2}, ---, \underline{T}_{CN}$ while constituting each $\underline{T}_{Ck}$ as $T_{Ck} \| g(R_k) \| g(I(C)R_k)$, and encrypts them to $E(a_C, \underline{T}_{C1}), E(a_C, \underline{T}_{C2}), ---, E(a_C, \underline{T}_{CN})$ by its encryption key a_C. Then, S asks C to decrypt its

Figure 15. Structure of token T_C with multiple encrypted identifiers

T_C	$g(R_1)$	$g(I(C)R_1)$	---	$g(R_j)$	$g(I(C)R_j)$	---	$g(R_Z)$	$g(I(C)R_Z)$

Figure 16. Procedure of zero knowledge proof

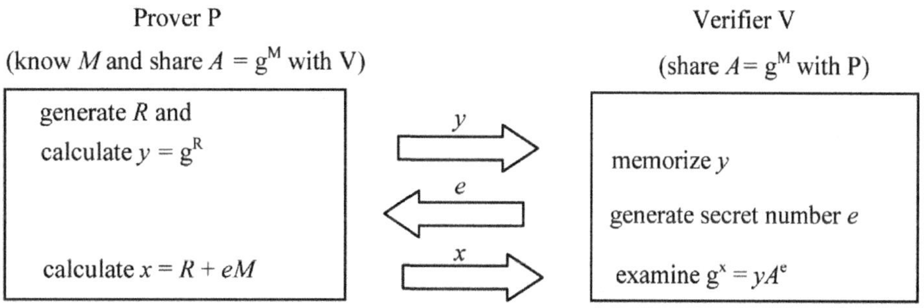

randomly selecting (N-1) versions {$E(a_C, T_{C(p1)})$, $E(a_C, T_{C(p2)})$, ---, $E(a_C, T_{C(p(N-1))})$}, and believes that remaining version $E(a_C, \underline{T}_{Cq})$ is also correct, when every decrypted form $\underline{T}_{C(ps)} = (T_{C(ps)} \| g(R_{Ps}) \| g(I(C) R_{Ps})$ in the selected versions is consistent, i.e. when hash function $g(x)$ generates $g(I(C)R_{Ps})$ and $g(R_{Ps})$ from C's identifier I(C) and its reporting R_{Ps}. After, verifying the correctness of the selected versions of tokens, S signs on the remaining $E(a_C, \underline{T}_{Cq})$ by its signing key d to generate $S(d, E(a_C, \underline{T}_{Cq}))$, and finally C obtains $S(d, \underline{T}_{Cq})$, signed token on the remaining version T_{Cq}. Here, although C can deceive S while not including the information about I(C) in the remaining version $E(a_C, \underline{T}_{Cq})$, it must take risks that S finds its dishonesty with the probability greater than (N-1)/N, and the probability can be improved by increasing N.

As the conclusion, the cut and choose protocol enables S to identify anonymous entities that had used same tokens repeatedly even in environments where online databases about used tokens are not available. However it is not efficient enough because many forms of tokens prepared by C and examined by S are discarded without being used. Although anonymous tag based tokens in the previous section also discards several calculation results, they are for generating used seals at times when C uses tokens. On the other hand, in cut and choose protocols C discards its calculation results both for generating and using tokens.

Also length of tokens becomes long when cut and choose protocols are adopted, because individual tokens must be accompanied by multiple encrypted identity information as shown in Figure 15.

Zero Knowledge Proof (ZKP)

Different from cut and choose protocols, in which P convinces V that it owns or knows bit string M while disclosing the part of M, Zero Knowledge Proof (ZKP) enables entity P to convince V without showing any information that suggests M. Namely in ZKP, although P answers several questions about M made by V, these answers include only encrypted forms of M, and V cannot know M in practical ways. In the following, V and P denote a verifier and a prover, respectively. Then, ZKP satisfies the following 3 properties (Goldwasser, 1989) they are,

1. Completeness: the probability that a verifier accepts the fact that a prover knows M can be made as close as to 1 when the prover actually knows it,
2. Soundness: the probability that a verifier rejects the fact that a prover knows M can be made as close as to 1 when the prover actually does not know it, and
3. Zero knowledge: a verifier cannot know M itself.

Figure 17. Procedure of non interactive zero knowledge proof

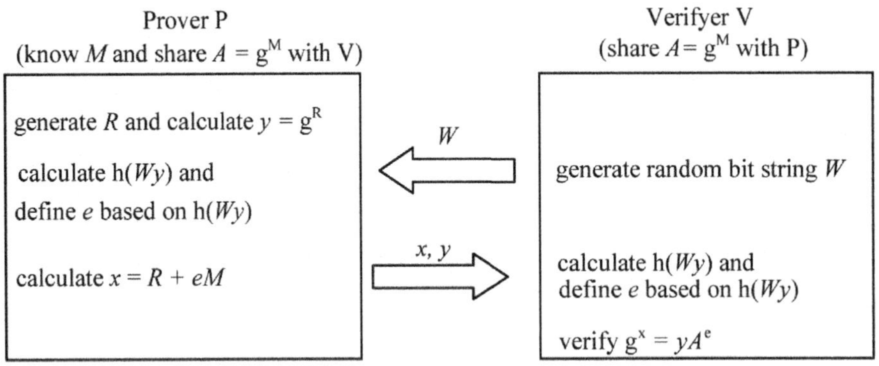

There are many kinds of variations, and this section explains ZKP that exploits the difficulty of calculating discrete logarithms, i.e. when integer p is large enough, to calculate M that satisfies $g^{M}{}_{\mathrm{mod\,p}} = x_{\mathrm{mod\,p}}$ for given x is practically impossible. Figure 16 shows an example of ZKP process, where P and V share $A = g^{M}{}_{\mathrm{mod\,p}}$ so that P can convince V that it knows M. In more detail, P proves that it knows bit string M that satisfies relation $g^M = A$ to V while disclosing $f(M)$; here, it is practically impossible to calculate M from either g^M or $f(M)$.

In the figure, firstly, P generates random secret integer (bit string) R, and calculates $y = g^R$ to send it to V. Then, V that receives y randomly selects integer e from the interval $0 \leq e < p$, asks P to calculate $x = f(M) = (R + eM)$, and finally V decides that P knows M when relation $g^x = yA^e$ is satisfied. On the other hand when the relation is not satisfied V decides that P does not know M. Here, the completeness is satisfied because it is easy for P to calculate x that satisfy $g^x = yA^e$ when it knows M, i.e. $g^x = g^{R+eM} = (g^R)(g^M)^e = yA^e$. About the soundness, when P knows e^*, the value of e, in advance, P can calculate x that satisfies $g^x = yA^e$ without knowing M by selecting an arbitrary value as x and calculating $g^xA^{-e^*}$ as the value of y, i.e. $g^x = (g^xA^{-e^*})A^{e^*} = yA^{e^*}$. However, there are p different values that V can assign to e, therefore, the probability that pair $\{y = g^xA^{-e^*}, x\}$ satisfies $g^x = yA^e$ for given e determined by V is 1/p, i.e. $\{g^xA^{-e^*}, x\}$ satisfies the relation only when V assigns value e^* to variable e out of p different possible values. Then, by iterating the above challenge and response processes, V can make the probability that it determines P does not know M as close as to 1 when P actually does not know it. When N-cycles of challenge and response processes are carried out, the probability of V's correct decision is $(1-1/p^N)$. It is apparent that the above procedure satisfies the zero knowledge property, i.e. V knows only g^M, g^R and $R + eM$, and none of them suggests M.

A drawback of ZKP is that it requires number of interactions between prover P and verifier V to enable V to make correct decisions. The reason why interactions between P and V are necessary is to disable P to calculate y while knowing values of e, if P knows e, it can easily respond so that relation $g^x = yA^e$ holds even if it does not know M as mentioned just above. By exploiting a hash function shared between a prover and a verifier, non-interactive zero knowledge proof (NIZKP) forces P to calculate y while not knowing the value of e without interactions between P and V (Blum, 1988), i.e. it removes the major drawback of ZKP. Figure 17 shows the NIZKP process, where, prover P and verifier V share $A = g^M$ in advance as in usual ZKP, but after generating secret integer R and calculating $y = g^R$, P calculates e by itself instead of obtaining it from verifier V. Namely, by using random integer W given from V and hash function h(z) shared between P and V, P calculates h(Wy), and defines e according to h(Wy) to inform V of y and $x = R + eM$. Then, V calculates h(Wy) and e based on y given from P, and verifies the consistency among A, y, x, and e, i.e. checks whether e is consistent with h(Wy) and relation $g^x = yA^e$ holds or not.

In the above, P must calculate y and e in this order, and cannot change y after e is determined because e is bound to h(Wy), i.e. h(z) is a one way function and it is practically impossible for P to calculate y so that h(Wy) becomes consistent with the given e. But, P can generate x and y in advance so that they satisfy relation $g^x = yA^e$ by examining many possible values. Namely, when P randomly generates a set of triples $\{y_j, x_j, e_j\}$ (j = 1, 2, ---), calculates $y_j = g^{xj}A^{-ej}$ and examines the consistency between e_j and h(Wy_j) to discard inconsistent triples, it can use any pair $\{x_j, y_j\}$ included in the remaining triples as a response because e_j corresponding to y_j is consistent with h(Wy_j). However, the probability that the examined triple $\{y_j, x_j, e_j\}$ is consistent and not discarded is not large, then, Q can convince itself that P knows M, when P replies enough number of consistent pairs. Usually P is required to reply about 80 different pairs (Abe, 2000). Therefore, although NIZKP processes substantially reduce the interactions between provers and verifiers, still they are not efficient enough.

Processes discussed in subsection "Homomorphic, Probabilistic, Commutative and Verifiable Encryption Functions" in Section 1 where an entity proves the correctness of its encryptions by using test bit strings without disclosing its encryption key while exploiting homomorphism of the encryption function can be considered as a kind of ZKP processes, i.e. secret integers r_0, r_1, --- r_m correspond to random integer e in the above. However in processes discussed there, r_0, r_1, --- r_m are maintained as secrets of verifiers different from ZKP and NIZKP processes where verifier V discloses random bit string e; therefore, numbers of verification operations required can be kept much smaller than those required for ZKP or NIZKP processes. Anonymous tag based tokens in the previous section also have the same advantage over ZKP and NIZKP processes.

ElGamal Based Verifiable Re-encryption Scheme

Although the ElGamal based re-encryption scheme discussed in section "Unlinkable Signatures" can satisfy the requirement that no one can know the correspondences between original bit strings and their re-encrypted forms, it cannot satisfy the requirement that anyone can convince itself that re-encrypted forms are correct, i.e. the scheme is not verifiable. ZKP discussed in the previous subsection makes the scheme also verifiable.

The ElGamal based re-encryption scheme consists of multiple authorities S_1, S_2, ---, S_Q, where each authority S_q has its public encryption and secret decryption key pair $\{y_q = g^{xq}, x_q\}$ and secret number k_q, and the re-encryption and decryption processes proceed as follows. In the encryption stage, entity P_j, the owner of bit string N_j, encrypts N_j to $\{g^{aj}, N_j y_*^{aj}\}$ by y_*, the product of encryption keys of the multiple authorities i.e. $y_* = y_1 y_2 \text{---} y_Q = g^{x1+x2+ \text{---} +xQ}$, while using its secret random bit string a_j, and each S_q that receives $\{g^{aj+k1+k2+ \text{---} +k(q-1)}, N_j y_*^{aj+k1+k2+ \text{---} +k(q-1)}\}$ from S_{q-1} (S_1 receives its input from P_j) further encrypts it to $\{g^{aj+k1+k2+ \text{---} +kq}, N_j y_*^{aj+k1+k2+ \text{---} +kq}\}$ by multiplying $g^{aj+k1+k2+ \text{---} +k(q-1)}$ and $N_j y_*^{aj+k1+k2+ \text{---} +k(q-1)}$ by g^{kq} and y_*^{kq}, and shuffles the result with other encrypted bit strings. In the decryption stage, each S_q decrypts encrypted bit strings by its secret key x_q. Namely, each S_q calculates $\{g^{aj+k1+k2+ \text{---} +kQ}, N_j g^{(x1+x2+ \text{----} +xq)(aj+k1+k2+ \text{---} +kQ)}/(g^{aj+k1+k2+ \text{---} +kQ})^{xq}\} = \{g^{aj+k1+k2+ \text{---} +kQ}, N_j g^{\{x1+x2+ \text{----} +x(q-1)\}(aj+k1+k2+ \text{---} +kQ)}\}$ to transfer it to S_{q-1}, and finally S_1 calculates $N_j g^{x1(aj+k1+k2+ \text{---} +kQ)}/g^{x1(aj+k1+k2+ \text{---} +kQ)} = N_j$. Then, because a_j is secret of P_j, each authority S_q shuffles its encryption results and each decryption key x_q is known only to S_q, no one except P_j can know bit string N_j owned by P_j unless all authorities conspire. No one can know the correspondence between original bit string N_j and its re-encrypted form $\{g^{aj+k1+k2+\cdots+kQ}, N_j y_*^{aj+k1+k2+\cdots+kQ}\}$ either. However about the verifiability, although the homomorphism of ElGamal makes the re-encryption scheme verifiable, P_j cannot exploit this property because the scheme shuffles bit strings in the encryption stage and P_j does not know the re-encrypted form to be verified. ZKP or NIZKP makes ElGamal based re-encryption schemes verifiable as below.

Let both $\{g^t, Ny_*^t\}$ and $\{g^s, Ny_*^s\}$ be re-encrypted forms of bit string N. Then, $\{g^t/g^s, Ny_*^t/Ny_*^s\} = \{g^{t-s}, y_*^{t-s}\}$, namely, when 2 parts g^t and Ny_*^t of encrypted form $\{g^t, Ny_*^t\}$ of N is divided by corresponding parts g^s and Ny_*^s of another form $\{g^s, Ny_*^s\}$, the 1st and the 2nd parts of result $\{g^{t-s}, y_*^{t-s}\}$ must be g and y_* to the power of the same number (t-s). Therefore, P_j can convince itself that S_q had honestly re-encrypted $\{g^{aj+k1+k2+\cdots+k(q-1)}, N_j y_*^{aj+k1+k2+\cdots+k(q-1)}\}$ to $\{g^{aj+k1+k2+\cdots+kq}, N_j y_*^{aj+k1+k2+\cdots+kq}\}$ when relation $\{g^{aj+k1+k2+\cdots+kq}/g^{aj+k1+k2+\cdots+k(q-1)}, Ny_*^{aj+k1+k2+\cdots+kq}/y_*^{aj+k1+k2+\cdots+k(q-1)}\} = \{g^r, y_*^r\}$ is satisfied for some r. ZKP enables each S_q to prove this relation without disclosing S_q's secrets k_q or x_q.

Firstly, S_q generates random secret number b_q and calculate $\{g^{bq}, y_*^{bq}\}$, and P_j that receives $\{g^{bq}, y_*^{bq}\}$ generates its random number c_q and calculates $G(c_q) = \{g^{(aj+k1+k2+\cdots+kq)}/g^{(aj+k1+k2+\cdots+k(q-1))}\}^{cq}$ and $Y(c_q) = (Ny_*^{aj+k1+k2+\cdots+kq}/Ny_*^{aj+k1+k2+\cdots+k(q-1)})^{cq}$. After that, S_q that is informed of c_q calculates $d_q = b_q + c_q k_q$, and finally, P_j convinces itself that $\{g^{aj+k1+k2+\cdots+kq}, N_j y_*^{aj+k1+k2+\cdots+kq}\}$ is the encrypted form of $\{g^{aj+k1+k2+\cdots+k(q-1)}, N_j y_*^{aj+k1+k2+\cdots+k(q-1)}\}$ when $g^{dq} = g^{bq}G(c_q) = g^{bq}\{g^{(aj+k1+k2+\cdots+kq)}/g^{(aj+k1+k2+\cdots+k(q-1))}\}^{cq}$ and $y_*^{dq} = y_*^{bq}Y(c_q) = y_*^{bq}(Ny_*^{aj+k1+k2+\cdots+kq}/Ny_*^{aj+k1+k2+\cdots+k(q-1)})^{cq}$ are satisfied for enough number of $\{b_q, c_q\}$ pairs.

In the above, apparently S_q that knows k_q can calculate d_q that satisfies relations $g^{dq} = g^{bq}G(c_q)$ and $y_*^{dq} = y_*^{bq}Y(c_q)$ from b_q and c_q if it is honest, but if S_q is dishonest, i.e. if it had used k_q' instead of k_q to calculate $g^{aj+k1+k2+\cdots+kq}$ or $N_j y_*^{aj+k1+k2+\cdots+kq}$, it is difficult to calculate d_q' so that relations $g^{dq'} = g^{bq}G(c_q)$ and $y_*^{dq'} = y_*^{bq}Y(c_q)$ hold. On the other hand, P_j cannot know k_q from $d_q = b_q + c_q k_q$ because b_q is a secret of S_q.

Although P_j cannot directly use this scheme, because each S_q shuffles its re-encryption results and P_j cannot identify pair of $\{g^{aj+k1+k2+\cdots+k(q-1)}, N_j y_*^{aj+k1+k2+\cdots+k(q-1)}\}$ and $\{g^{aj+k1+k2+\cdots+kq}, N_j y_*^{aj+k1+k2+\cdots+kq}\}$, when shuffling operations are represented by matrices, the above scheme enables P_j to verify the correct re-encryptions even if multiple authorities shuffle their interim re-encryption results (Furukawa, 2001, Nguyen, 2004) (this subsection does not discuss it because the scheme will not be used later). However, although several efforts to reduce computation volumes are being made (Boneh, 2002, Jakobsson, 2002), still the schemes are not so efficient, because ZKP and NIZKP require number of challenge and response processes. It must be noted that ElGamal re-encryption scheme in the above can be replaced with threshold ElGamal without any modification.

CONCLUSION

This chapter introduced schemes to protect information from illegitimate modifications, forgeries, deletions, etc. in environments where relevant entities are anonymous. Mechanisms for identifying dishonest entities or proving honest behaviours of entities while preserving privacies of honest entities were also discussed.

Blind signature schemes enable entities to obtain signatures of authorities on their bit strings without disclosing the bit strings themselves, and many privacy preserving mechanisms can be developed based on them. For example, an unlinkable signature scheme can be implemented based on it. Here, an unlinkable signature scheme is a re-encryption scheme that not only conceals the correspondences between a given set of bit strings and their encrypted forms from any entity, but also ensures that only and all bit strings in the set are honestly encrypted. By exploiting this property, an electronic voting system discussed in Section 3 enables people to verify that only and all votes from eligible voters are counted without disclosing any privacy of voters and as a consequence while completely protecting voters from coercers. ITLs discussed after unlinkable signature schemes enable entity S to convince itself that other entity P honestly maintains a set of data given by S, and can be used for developing anonymous authentication mechanisms and anonymous credit card systems as discussed in Section 3.

As mechanisms for identifying dishonest entities or proving honest behaviours of entities in anonymous environments, firstly tokens were introduced. Anonymous tokens enable identifications of dishonest entities if dishonest events can be detected during anonymous entities are receiving services, and homomorphic anonymous tokens and anonymous tag based tokens enable identifications of dishonest entities even if dishonest events can be detected only after disappearances of the entities. In Section 3, these mechanisms will be incorporated in anonymous authentication schemes and used for developing various application systems. Finally, the cut and choose protocol and the zero knowledge proof (ZKP) enable entities to prove their honest behaviours (e.g. their owning bit strings are legitimate, they had honestly encrypted their bit strings, etc.) without disclosing their secret information.

REFERENCES

Abe, M. (2000). Universally verifiable Mix-net with verification work independent of the number of mix-servers. *IEICE Trans. Fundamentals . E (Norwalk, Conn.)*, *83-A*(7), 1431–1440.

Blum, M., Feldman, P., & Micali, S. (1988). Non-interactive zero-knowledge and its applications. *Proceedings of the 20th Annual ACM Symposium on Theory of Computing* (pp. 103-112).

Boneh, D., & Golle, P. (2002). *Almost entirely correct mixing with applications to voting* (pp. 68–77). ACM Conferences on Computer and Communications Security.

Chaum, D. (1983). Blind signatures system. *Advances in Cryptology, CRYPTO*, *83*, 153–156.

Chaum, D., Fiat, A., & Naor, M. (1988). Untraceable electronic cash. *Advances in Cryptology, - . CRYPTO*, *88*, 319–327.

Furukawa, J., & Sako, K. (2001). An efficient scheme for proving a shuffle. *CRYPTO 2001 . LNCS*, *2139*, 368–387.

Goldwasser, S., Micali, S., & Rackoff, C. (1989). The knowledge complexity of interactive proof system. *SIAM Journal on Computing*, *18*(1), 291–304. doi:10.1137/0218012

Jakobsson, M., Juels, A., & Rivest, R. (2002). Making mix nets robust for electronic voting by randomized partial checking. *USENIX Security*, *02*, 339–353.

Nguyen, L., Sahavi-Naimi, R., & Kurosawa, K. (2004). Verifiable shuffles: S formal model and a Paillier-based efficient construction with provable security. *ACNS 2004 . LNCS*, *3089*, 61–75.

Shigetomi, R., Otsuka, A., & Imai, H. (2003). *Refreshable tokens and its applications to anonymous loans*. SCIS2003.

Tamura, S. Md. Rokibul, A. K., & Haddad, H. A. (2009). A probabilistic and commutative re-encryption scheme. *Proceedings of Asia Simulation Conference 2009*.

Tamura, S., Kouro, K., Sasatani, M., Md. Rokibul, K. A., & Haddad, A. S. (2008). An information system platform for anonymous product recycling. *Journal of Software*, *3*(6), 46–56. doi:10.4304/jsw.3.6.46-56

Tamura, S., Kouro, K., & Yanase, T. (2006). Expenditure limits in anonymous credit card systems. *Proc. of IEEE SMC 2006*, (pp. 1238-1243).

Tamura, S., Ohashi, Y., Tanigichi, S., & Yanase, T. (2010). Detection of dishonest entities. *SMC2010, Proc. of IEEE International Conference on System, Man and Cybernetics*, (pp. 906-911)

Tamura, S., & Yanase, T. (2007). A mechanism for anonymous credit card systems. *IEEJ Transactions in EIS*, *127*(1), 81–87. doi:10.1541/ieejeiss.127.81

Chapter 7
Anonymous Communication

ABSTRACT

Schemes of anonymous communication enable entities to send or receive their messages without disclosing their identities to others including managers of communication systems and receivers or senders of the messages. Among various existing schemes this chapter introduces Crowds, DC net, Mix-net, ESEBM (Enhanced Symmetric key Encryption Based Mix-Net), and Onion Routing. Mechanisms to protect anonymous communication systems from malicious entities are also discussed.

INTRODUCTION

Identities of message senders or receivers are sometimes as sensitive as messages themselves. For example, a company may acquire highly confidential information about its rival companies from identities of their customers and suppliers. Therefore, the importance of anonymous communication is increasing as more people are being involved in network based communication. Anonymous communication mechanisms enable entity S that sends message *M* or entity R that receives *M*, to exchange *M* without disclosing their identities to others. According to subjects to be made anonymous, there are 3 types of anonymous communication schemes, i.e. when S can send *M* without disclosing its identity, the mechanism is called sender anonymous, when R can receive *M* without disclosing its identity, it is called receiver anonymous, and when both S and R can exchange *M* without disclosing their identities it is called mutually anonymous. This chapter mainly discusses sender anonymous communication mechanisms because receiver and mutually anonymous ones can be developed based on them, and except in the last section of this chapter, the word anonymous communication is used for representing the sender anonymous communication.

Now, (sender) anonymous communication mechanisms enable entity S to send message *M* to its receiver R without disclosing the identity of S to any entity except S including R and managers

DOI: 10.4018/978-1-4666-1649-3.ch007

of the communication channel. Here, message M usually reaches R from S while being relayed by multiple entities as shown in Figure 1, because when M reaches R directly from S, R can easily know the source S. In the remainder, entities that send messages and receive messages are called senders and receivers, respectively. Also entities that relay messages are called relay servers or simply servers.

The requirements for sender anonymous communication are summarized as follows, i.e.

1. No one except sender S itself can identify the sender of massage M,
2. No one except sender S itself can know that messages M_1 and M_2 sent from S are the messages sent from the same sender,
3. Sender S can confirm the successful delivery of its message M to receiver R without disclosing its identity to others,
4. Sender S can receive reply messages to its message M from receiver R without disclosing its identity to any other entity, and
5. Communication channels can protect themselves from accesses from unauthorized entities.

Firstly as the most important requirement, sender S must be concealed not only from receiver R but also from any other entities including wiretappers, managers of the communication channels such as relay servers, etc. About the 2nd requirement, although this is satisfied automatically when the 1st one is satisfied in many cases, it is important because a set of messages sent from a same sender usually include a lot of information to identify the sender. The 3rd and the 4th requirements are also important, and especially the 4th one is essential because information exchanges between entities in many kinds of important applications are carried out as conversations between them. Satisfying the 3rd requirement is not so difficult, e.g. senders can confirm the deliveries of their messages when receivers put signals designated by the senders at the specified subs in BBs after the arrivals of their messages so that the senders can notice them. Also, anonymous message reply mechanisms automatically make communication channels satisfy the 3rd requirement, i.e. senders can confirm their message deliveries when they receive replies. However, development of practical mechanisms that satisfy the 4th requirement is not easy as it looks. For example, R, which generates its reply message M_R and knows its contents, can identify sender S by eavesdropping on the communication channel connected to possible senders including S. Namely, R can identify S as the entity to which M_R is delivered, where it must be noted that identifying an entity that receives M_R is not difficult for R when it is conspiring with the server that finally delivers messages. About the 5th requirement, because entities are anonymous,

Figure 1. Configuration of Crowds

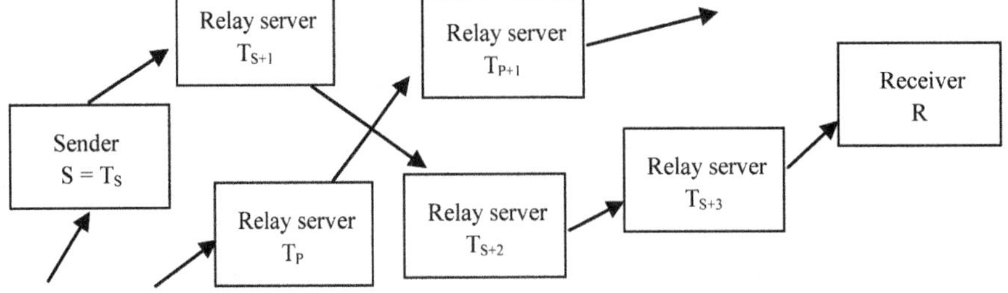

they can behave dishonestly much easier than in usual communication systems, e.g. entities can send spam messages and can illegitimately modify messages in the communication channels more easily. The difficult thing is that even if messages are modified usually their receivers do not notice the modifications because senders are anonymous and consequently receivers do not have enough information to determine whether their receiving messages are correct or not. Therefore anonymous communication mechanisms must be endowed with the ability to protect themselves from various kinds of attacks including DOS (denial of services) attacks, message modifications, etc. The important thing here is that dishonest events must be detected or prevented while maintaining anonymities of honest entities.

Currently 3 approaches are available for developing anonymous communication systems; they are hidden route, hidden message and hybrid approaches. In hidden route based mechanisms, a route through which a message is transferred from its sender to its receiver is constituted as a sequence of mutually independent relay servers so that each server in the route can know only its neighbours, i.e. the ones from which it receives the message and to which it transfers the message. Also, this route is changed for every massage; therefore to trace messages from their senders to their receivers is difficult unless all relay servers conspire. However, theoretically to trace message *M* is possible, i.e. when entity P eavesdrops on incoming and outgoing messages to and from every relay server, it can trace all messages from their sources to their destinations. Also, it is not difficult for receiver R of message *M* to identify the sender if R conspires with the server that receives *M* from the sender. As a consequence, although mechanisms based on the hidden route approach are simple and practical, they cannot conceal message senders completely, and cannot be applied to sensitive applications such as electronic voting systems where elections cannot be conducted without completely preserving privacies of individual voters. When an election system cannot completely protect secrets of voters from some kind of threats, liability for unauthorized leaks of the secrets may be imputed to authorities of the election even when voters themselves intentionally disclose them, and the election itself may be disrupted. Therefore, usually hidden route approaches are combined with other schemes. "Crowds" explained in the next sub is an example of the hidden route approach.

Mechanisms based on the hidden message approach encrypt message *M* by encryption keys of multiple independent servers, and the identities of message senders are concealed completely at least one of the servers is honest. According to the ways in which multiple servers encrypt or decrypt messages, there are 2 different types of methods. The 1st one is the multi path message transfer where multiple servers behave synchronously in parallel to encrypt and forward message *M*, and the other is the single path message transfer where message *M* is repeatedly encrypted by its sender and multiple servers decrypt encrypted message *M* sequentially. Usually mechanisms based on the former method are not flexible, practical or scalable, because they require the multiple servers to behave coherently and synchronously based on mutual agreements among them established in advance (e.g. multiple servers must agree about their encryption keys in advance), and can be applied only to small and closed communications. On the other hand, servers in the mechanisms based on the latter method are not required to agree about their operational parameters in advance; therefore they can be made flexible, scalable and practical. Also it is straightforward to combine them with the hidden route approach. DC-net described after the next sub adopts the multi path message transfer scheme, and Mix-net and ESEBM discussed after that adopt the single path message transfer scheme.

Advantages of both hidden route and hidden message approaches can be exploited by combining them as the hybrid approach, and Onion Routing achieves this. Hidden message and hybrid approaches enable also implementations of receiver anonymous or mutually anonymous communications. Before concluding this chapter, ways to develop receiver anonymous and mutually anonymous communication mechanisms also will be discussed.

CROWDS

Crowds is an anonymous communication network based on the hidden route approach, and consists of mutually independent multiple relay servers T_1, T_2, ----, T_N as shown in Figure 1 (Reiter, 1998). An identity of message sender S is concealed as follows. Firstly, S accesses the network through one of the servers T_S as an anonymous user; and it sends message *M* to T_S while designating message receiver R. However, T_S forwards its receiving message *M* to R only with the probability 1-p(S, *M*), i.e. it transfers *M* to other server T_{S+1} with the probability p(S, *M*), and T_{S+1} behaves in the same way. The important thing is that each server T_j knows only the servers, from which it had received *M* and to which it had forwarded *M*, therefore, no server except T_S can identify S which initially had sent *M* unless all servers conspire with each other.

The advantage of Crowds is it enables the development of highly efficient anonymous networks. Different from many other mechanisms in which messages are encrypted or decrypted repeatedly by encryption or decryption keys of multiple servers, servers in Crowds do not encrypt or decrypt messages, therefore the throughput of the network can be maintained high as same as usual non-anonymous networks. However, when an entity eavesdrops on messages in the network, it can trace a sequence of servers that a particular message had visited, and consequently can identify the sender of the message. Also, it is trivial for T_S that had received *M* from S to identify S as the sender of *M*. Therefore Crowds cannot satisfy the 1st requirement, i.e. the most fundamental requirement for anonymous communication, completely.

DC NET

DC-net is a mechanism based on the multi path message transfer type hidden message approach, and it completely satisfies the first 3 requirements but cannot satisfy other requirements (Chaum, 1988). In DC-net, sender S_q constitutes a group $\{S_1, S_2, ---, S_Q\}$ that includes itself, and entities in the group generate their secret numbers N_1, N_2, ---, N_Q so that the sum of them becomes 0 in advance. While using its generating secret numbers, S_q encrypts its message *M* to $M + N_q$ to send the result to its receiver R. At the same time each S_j in the group also sends its secret number N_j to R. Therefore, R can extract *M* from messages from $\{S_1, S_2, ---, S_Q\}$, i.e. $N_1+N_2+ --- +N_{q-1}+(M+N_q)+N_{q+1}+ --- +N_Q = M + 0 = M$. Namely, receiver R receives *M* through multiple paths, and because the entity that knows the value of N_j is only S_j, entities other than S_q cannot know whether messages in individual paths include *M* or not, i.e. no entity except S_q can identify S_q as the sender of *M* unless all other senders conspire.

Multiple senders $\{S_1, S_2, ---, S_Q\}$ in the above can agree on their random numbers without disclosing their own numbers to others as shown in Figure 2. The procedure in the figure also enables multiple senders to behave coherently at a time when one of the senders sends a message without strict synchronizations. Firstly, coordinator C generates a set of tags $\{t_1, t_2, ---, t_n\}$ and sends the set to S_1. Then S_1 generates a set of secret random numbers $\{\underline{N}_1(t_1), \underline{N}_1(t_2), ---, \underline{N}_1(t_n)\}$ corresponding to individual tags to construct set of tag and random number pairs $\{(t_1, \underline{N}_1(t_1)), (t_2, \underline{N}_1(t_2)), ---, (t_n, \underline{N}_1(t_n))\}$, and encrypts the pairs by the public key of S_2 so that only S_2 can know $\{(t_1, \underline{N}_1(t_1)), (t_2, \underline{N}_1(t_2)), ---, (t_n, \underline{N}_1(t_n))\}$. S_2 that receives the pairs calculates $\{(t_1, \underline{N}_1(t_1)+N_2(t_1)), (t_2, \underline{N}_1(t_2)+N_2(t_2)), ---, (t_n, \underline{N}_1(t_n)+N_2(t_n))\}$ while generating its secret random numbers $\{N_2(t_1), N_2(t_2), ---, N_2(t_n)\}$, encrypts it by the public key of S_3, and sends the result to S_3. S_3, ---, S_Q behave in the same way, and finally S_1 that receives $\{(t_1, \underline{N}_1(t_1)+N_2(t_1)+$

Figure 2. DC-net implementation

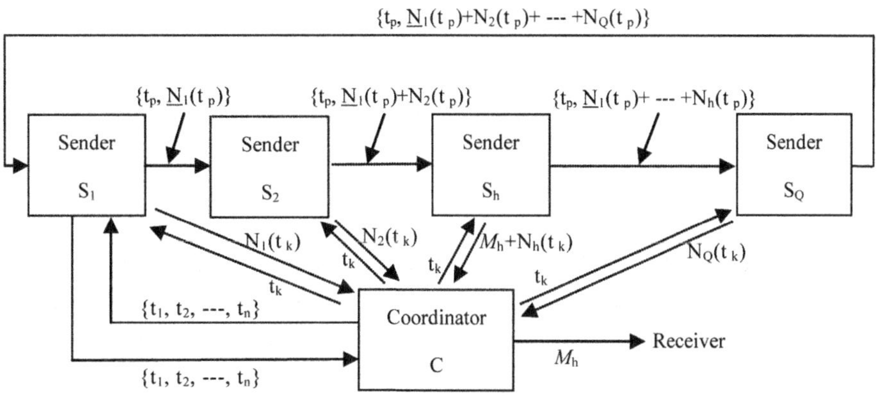

--- $+N_Q(t_1))$, $(t_2, \underline{N}_1(t_2)+N_2(t_2)+ --- +N_Q(t_2))$, ---, $(t_n, \underline{N}_1(t_n)+N_2(t_n)+ --- +N_Q(t_n))\}$ from S_Q replaces it with $\{(t_1, N_1(t_1)), (t_2, N_1(t_2)), ---, (t_n, N_1(t_n))\}$ and sends $\{t_1, t_2, ---, t_n\}$ back to coordinator C, where, $N_1(t_j) = -\{N_2(t_j)+ --- +N_Q(t_j)\}$, therefore the sum of $N_1(t_j), N_2(t_j), ---, N_Q(t_j)$ becomes 0 for each j, also S_1 can calculate $\underline{N}_1(t_j)$ from $N_1(t_j)+N_2(t_j)+ --- +N_Q(t_j)$ because it knows $\underline{N}_1(t_j)$ that it had generated.

After receiving $\{t_1, t_2, ---, t_n\}$ from S_1, C memorizes them and periodically multicasts tags $t_1, t_2, ---, t_n$ in the arbitrary order, and at a time when tag t_k is delivered each S_j sends $\{t_k, N_j(t_k)\}$ to C. As the exception, S_h that wants to send its message M_h sends $\{t_k, M_h+N_h(t_k)\}$ to C. Then, C calculates $N_1(t_k) + N_2(t_k) + M_h+N_h(t_k) + N_{h+1}(t_k) +$ --- $+ N_Q(t_k) = M_h$, and delivers it to its receiver while extracting the destination address from M_h. At the same time C discloses M_h to all $\{S_1, S_2, ---, S_Q\}$ as acknowledgment of the message. Here, each S_j does not know random number $N_h(t_k)$ generated by other S_h, therefore any entity except S_h cannot determine whether $M_h+N_h(t_k)$ is the random number originally generated by S_h or S_h had added M_h to $N_h(t_k)$, i.e. no one except S_h can know the sender of M_h.

In the above, $\{S_1, S_2, ---, S_Q\}$ can behave coherently even if they do not behave synchronously in a strict manner, i.e. tag t_k enables them to choose secret random numbers $\{N_1(t_k), N_2(t_k), ---, N_Q(t_k)\}$ for sending M_h so that $N_1(t_k)+N_2(t_k)+$ --- $+N_Q(t_k)$ becomes 0 even individual senders send their messages in different orders. Also, when different senders S_j and S_h send their massages M_j and M_h while attaching same tag t_k, S_j and S_h can detect this collision by comparing their sending messages with the message that C discloses as the acknowledgement, and when the messages collide S_j and S_h re-sends their messages by using different tags.

Here, it must be noted that each S_j must change random secret number $N_j(t_k)$ at its every message sending. If every S_j uses same random secret number for different messages sent from senders in the group, entity X that eavesdrops on the communications can easily identify senders of the messages. Namely, when S_j sends same number $N_j(t_k)$ as its 1st and 2nd messages, X can know that S_j's random secret number is $N_j(t_k)$. Also, when S_j sends $M_j+N_j(t_k)$ and $N_j(t_k)$ as its 1st and 2nd messages, it is easy for X to extract M_j and to identify the sender.

Fatal drawbacks of DC-net are caused by its synchronous feature. Namely, to enable S_j to send its message, a group of senders $\{S_1, S_2, ---, S_Q\}$

must agree about their secret random numbers in advance and all $\{S_1, S_2, ---, S_Q\}$ must send them even when they do not have messages to send. Also, it is difficult to implement efficient mechanisms for sending reply messages to anonymous senders.

MIX-NET

Configuration of Mix-Net

Mix-net is an anonymous communication channel based on the single path message transfer type hidden message approach, and it is most known among various kinds of anonymous networks (Chaum, 1981, Ingledine, 2001, Golle, 2003). It consists of a sequence of mix-servers T_1, T_2, ---, T_N that encrypt or decrypt their receiving messages and forward the results to mix-servers next to them while shuffling the encryption or decryption results as shown in Figure 3. Mix-net in the figure is a decryption type Mix-net and conceals senders of messages as follow. Firstly, sender S constructs its message as pair $\{M_S, A_R\}$, and it repeatedly encrypts $\{M_S, A_R\}$ to $\{E(k_*, M_S), E(k_*, A_R)\}$ by using public keys $k_N, k_{N-1}, ---, k_1$ of multiple mix-servers $T_N, T_{N-1}, ---, T_1$ to send the result to 1st server T_1. Where, M_S is the content of the message, A_R is the destination address of M_S, i.e. the address of receiver R, and $E(k_*, x) = E(k_1, E(k_2, ---, E(k_N, x) ---))$. Also, it is assumed that each encryption function $E(k_j, x)$ is probabilistic.

After that, T_1 that receives $\{E(k_*, M_S), E(k_*, A_R)\}$ waits for other messages until it receives predefined number of messages, decrypts its receiving messages by using its secret key k_1^{-1} and sends the decrypted results to mix-server T_2 next to it while randomly changing the message sending order from the order that it had received messages from individual senders. Other mix-server T_j behaves in the same way, i.e. it waits for predefined number of messages, decrypts each message $\{E(k_j, E(k_{j+1}, ---, E(k_N, M_S) ---)), E(k_j, E(k_{j+1}, ---, E(k_N, A_R) ---))\}$ received from T_{j-1} to $\{E(k_{j+1}, E(k_{j+2}, ---, E(k_N, M_S) ---)), E(k_{j+1}, E(k_{j+2}, ---, E(k_N, A_R) ---))\}$ shuffles decrypted messages, and sends the results to T_{j+1}. Then, the last mix-server T_N can decrypt message $\{E(k_*, M_S), E(k_*, A_R)\}$ to $\{M_S, A_R\}$, and based on A_R, it can deliver M_S to receiver R. Here, the route through which messages are transferred is fixed and consists of a single path.

Mix-net can completely conceal senders of messages, i.e. satisfy the 1st and the 2nd requirements. Because individual servers know only their own decryption keys and the encryption functions are probabilistic, each mix-server cannot know the correspondences between inputs and outputs of

Figure 3. Configuration of Mix-net

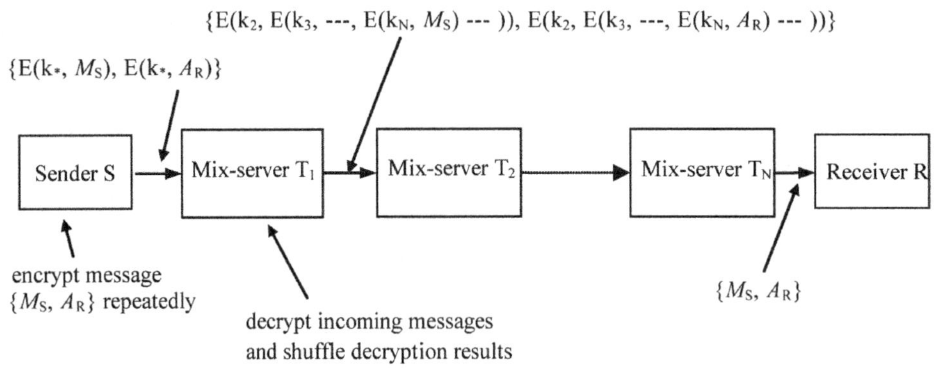

other servers, then, it is not possible for any entity except sender S itself to identify S as the sender of M_S unless all mix-servers conspire. Mix-nets also satisfy the 3rd and the 4th requirements as discussed later; however, because senders must know encryption keys of individual mix-servers, they must adopt asymmetric key encryption algorithms. Therefore although they are appropriate for applications where limited number of rather short messages are exchanged such as in electronic voting systems, it is difficult to use them for general applications with heavy message traffics because of large overheads in encryption and decryption processes of asymmetric key encryption functions.

It must be noted that encryption functions of individual mix-servers must be probabilistic. When they are not probabilistic, receiver R of message $\{M_S, A_R\}$ can easily identify sender S by watching messages in the network sent from possible senders, i.e. because all encryption keys are publicly disclosed, R can encrypt its receiving $\{M_S, A_R\}$ again to $\{E(k_*, M_S), E(k_*, A_R)\}$, the form that S had sent its message to the 1st mix-server T_1, and can identify S as the sender by comparing S's sending message with $\{E(k_*, M_S), E(k_*, A_R)\}$. Also, any entity can know the correspondences between input and output pairs of any mix-server T_j by encrypting its outputs again by the public encryption key k_j to compare the results with the inputs of T_j. Of course, each mix-server T_j or sender S can send its outputs to T_{j+1} while encrypting it by using the key shared only between T_j and T_{j+1} (here S is considered as T_0) to disable other entities to know outputs of T_j, i.e. T_j can encrypt pair $\{E(k_{j+1}, ---, E(k_N, M_S) ---), E(k_{j+1}, ---, E(k_N, A_R) ---)\}$ to pair $\{E(b_{j+1}, E(k_{j+1}, ---, E(k_N, M_S) ---)), E(b_{j+1}, E(k_{j+1}, ---, E(k_N, A_R) ---))\}$ by encryption key b_{j+1} shared only between T_j and T_{j+1}. However even in this case, R can know sender S when it conspires with T_1 that had received $\{E(b_1, E(k_*, M_S)), E(b_1, E(k_*, A_R))\}$ from S and can decrypt it to $\{E(k_*, M_S), E(k_*, A_R)\}$.

Advantages of Mix-net over Crowd or DC-net are firstly different from Crowd it can conceal message senders completely provided that at least one of mix-servers are honest, and secondly, different from DC-net senders can send their messages independently without synchronizing with other senders, i.e. Mix-net is more secure or efficient than them. However, the throughputs of communication channels are limited because asymmetric key encryption functions are used. Also message-traveling times are prone to being long, because individual mix-servers must wait for predefined number of messages before forwarding each message.

Mix-Net Implementation Based on RSA

It is straightforward to implement Mix-net shown in Figure 3 based on RSA encryption functions. Namely, sender S repeatedly encrypts M_S to $E(k_N, M_S \| r_N) = (M_S \| r_N)^{kN}{}_{\mathrm{mod}\ pN}$, $E(k_{N-1}, E(k_N, M_S \| r_N) \| r_{N-1}) = ((M_S \| r_N)^{kN}{}_{\mathrm{mod}\ pN} \| r_{N-1}))^{kN-1}{}_{\mathrm{mod}\ p(N-1)}$, ---, $E(k_1, --- E(k_N, M_S \| r_N) --- \| r_1) = (---(M_S \| r_N)^{kN}{}_{\mathrm{mod}\ pN} --- \| r_1)^{k1}{}_{\mathrm{mod}\ p1}$ by public encryption keys $k_N, k_{N-1}, ---, k_1$ of mix-servers $T_N, T_{N-1}, ---, T_1$ while mixing random numbers $r_N, r_{N-1}, ---, r_1$ secrets of itself. The 1st mix-server T_1 decrypts $(---(M_S \| r_N)^{kN} --- \| r_1)^{k1}$ to $(---(M_S \| r_N)^{kN} --- \| r_1)$ and r_1 is removed to form $(---(M_S \| r_N)^{kN} --- \| r_2)^{k2}$. Then T_1 waits for other messages until it receives predefined number of messages to shuffle the decrypted results. Other mix-servers T_2, ---, T_N behave in the same way until T_N finally calculates $M_S \| r_N$ and removes r_N from it. Here, to simplify descriptions, encryptions and decryptions of receiver address A_R is omitted in this sub and in the next sub.

It must be noted that bases of modulo arithmetic p_j and p_q must be different when $j \neq q$ to maintain confidentiality of secret keys of individual mix-servers as discussed in sub "RSA" in Section 1, and this means that p_j must be larger than p_q when $j < q$. Therefore, the length of messages in RSA based Mix-net is prone to being long. Also, random numbers $r_1, r_2, ---, r_N$ that make the re-encryption scheme probabilistic must be defined corresponding to all mix-servers T_1, T_2, ---, T_N. If r_j is not added to message M_S, anyone can easily know the correspondence between input $E(k_j, E(k_{j+1}, ---, E(k_N, M_S \| r_N) --- \| r_{j+1}))$ and output $E(k_{j+1}, E(k_{j+2}, ---, E(k_N, M_S \| r_N) --- \| r_{j+2}) \| r_{j+1})$ of T_j by encrypting output $E(k_{j+1}, E(k_{j+2}, ---, E(k_N, M_S \| r_N) --- \| r_{j+2}) \| r_{j+1})$ by publicly known key k_j again.

Mix-Net Implementation Based on ElGamal

A straightforward implementation of Mix-net based on ElGamal encryption scheme does not work efficiently. For example when there are 3 mix-servers T_1, T_2, T_3, sender S repeatedly encrypts its message M_S to $\{g^{k3}, M_S y_3^{k3}\}$, $\{g^{k2}, \{g^{k3} y_2^{k2}, M_S y_3^{k3} y_2^{k2}\}\}$, $\{g^{k1}, \{g^{k2} y_1^{k1}, \{g^{k3} y_2^{k2} y_1^{k1}, M_S y_3^{k3} y_2^{k2} y_1^{k1}\}\}\} = E(k_*, M_S)$, and $E(k_*, M_S)$ is decrypted to $\{g^{k2} y_1^{k1}/g^{k1x1}, \{g^{k3} y_2^{k2} y_1^{k1}/g^{k1x1}, M_S y_3^{k3} y_2^{k2} y_1^{k1}/g^{k1x1}\}\} = \{g^{k2}, \{g^{k3} y_2^{k2}, M_S y_3^{k3} y_2^{k2}\}\}$, $\{g^{k3} y_2^{k2}/g^{k2x2}, M_S y_3^{k3} y_2^{k2}/g^{k2x2}\} = \{g^{k3}, M_S y_3^{k3}\}$ and $M_S y_3^{k3}/g^{k3x3} = M_S$. Here, $\{x_3, x_2, x_1\}$ and $\{y_3 = g^{x3}, y_2 = g^{x2}, y_1 = g^{x1}\}$ are secret decryption keys and public encryption keys of mix-servers T_3, T_2, T_1. However, anyone can identify the correspondence between $\{g^{k1}, g^{k2} y_1^{k1}, \{g^{k3} y_2^{k2} y_1^{k1}, M_S y_3^{k3} y_2^{k2} y_1^{k1}\}\}\}$ and $\{g^{k2}, \{g^{k3} y_2^{k2}, M_S y_3^{k3} y_2^{k2}\}\}$, i.e. an input and output pair of T_1, because relation $g^{k3} y_2^{k2} y_1^{k1}/g^{k3} y_2^{k2} = M_S y_3^{k3} y_2^{k2} y_1^{k1}/M_S y_3^{k3} y_2^{k2} = y_1^{k1}$ is satisfied, in the same way, anyone can identify correspondences between inputs and outputs of T_2, and consequently anyone can know the sender of M_S by eavesdropping on the network. Therefore, S must encrypt g^{k3} and $M_S y_3^{k3}$ in $\{g^{k3}, M_S y_3^{k3}\}$ individually to $\{g^{k2}, g^{k3} y_2^{k2}\}$ and $\{gk2, M_S y_3^{k3} y_2 k2\}$ by using 2 different random numbers k_2 and $\underline{k}2$ and 2 different public encryption keys y_2 and $\underline{y}_2$ for example. As a consequence, length of messages becomes further longer, and the scheme becomes complicated and inefficient.

When senders and mix-servers share the same single public encryption key $y_* = y_1 y_2 --- y_N = g^{x1+ --- +xN} = g^{x*}$ as discussed in the sub "ElGamal based Re-encryption Scheme," another type of Mix-net, which is much more efficient than the above, can be implemented, i.e. re-encryption type Mix-net. Here, x_q and $y_q = g^{xq}$ are secret decryption and public encryption keys of mix-server T_q. Figure 4 implements ElGamal based re-encryption type Mix-net. It consists of encryption and decryption stages each of which is configured by mix-servers T_1, T_2, ---, T_N. In the figure, firstly to conceal the correspondence between message M_S and the sender S, S encrypts M_S to $\{g^s, M_S y_*^s\}$ while using its secret random number s before it sends M_S to the 1st mix-server T_1 in the encryption stage. Then, T_1, T_2, ---, T_N in the encryption stage repeatedly encrypt it to $\{g^s g^{k1}, M_S y_*^s y_*^{k1}\} = \{g^{s+k1}, M_S y_*^{s+k1}\}$, $\{g^{s+k1+k2}, M_S y_*^{s+k1+k2}\}$, ---, $\{g^{s+k1+k2+ --- +kN}, M_S y_*^{s+k1+k2+ --- +kN}\} = \{g^{k*}, M_S y_*^{k*}\}$ while shuffling their encryption results with other messages (where, k_1, ---, k_N are random numbers secrets of T_1, T_2, ---, T_N, respectively, and $k_* = s + k_1 + k_2 + --- + k_N$), and mix-servers T_N in the decryption stage decrypts $\{g^{k*}, M_S y_*^{k*}\}$ to $\{g^{k*}, M_S y_*^{k*}/g^{k*xN}\} = \{g^{k*}, M_S g^{k*(x1+x2+ --- +xN)}/g^{k*xN}\} = \{g^{k*}, M_S g^{k*(x1+x2+ --- +x(N-1))}\}$, and T_{N-1} decrypts $\{g^{k*}, M_S g^{k*(x1+x2+ --- +x(N-1))}\}$ to $\{g^{k*}, M_S g^{k*(x1+x2+ --- +x(N-1))}/g^{k*x(N-1)}\} = \{g^{k*}, M_S g^{k*(x1+x2+ --- +x(N-2))}\}$. In the same way, each T_q decrypts its receiving $\{g^{k*}, M_S g^{k*(x1+x2+ --- +xq)}\}$ to $\{g^{k*}, M_S g^{k*(x1+x2+ --- +x(q-1))}\}$, therefore when T_1 decrypts its receiving message the result coincides with the original message M_S. Then, although multiple mix-servers repeatedly encrypt and decrypt message M_S, its length does not change.

It must be noted that each T_q in the decryption stage must know g^{k*} to calculate $\{g^{k*}, M_S g_*^{k*(x1+ --- +x(q-1))}\}$ from $\{g^{k*}, M_S g_*^{k*(x1+ --- +xq)}\}$, therefore g^{k*} is attached to every encrypted form of M_S in the decryption stage. As a consequence, anyone can know the correspondences between inputs and outputs of every T_q in the decryption stage even when T_q shuffles its decryption results. Therefore, re-encryption type Mix-net must shuffle messages in the encryption stage.

Figure 4. Re-encryption type mix-net

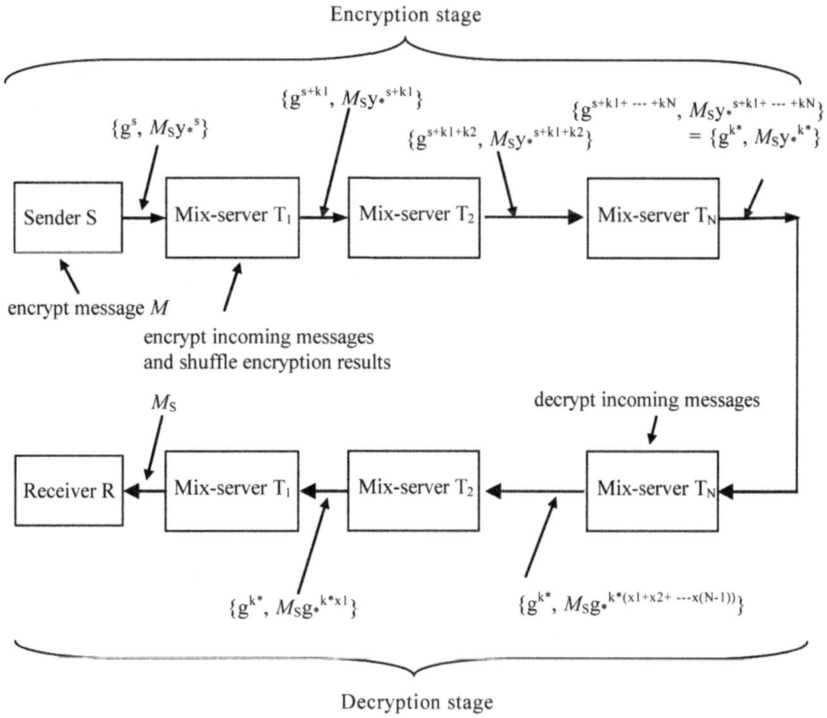

Advantages of re-encryption type Mix-nets over decryption type ones are firstly message lengths can be suppressed short even in Mix-nets consist of many mix-servers. Also the order of mix-servers in both encryption and decryption stages can be determined arbitrarily, because ElGamal encryption functions are commutative. About the computation volume, although it consists of 2 stages, each T_q in the encryption stage can prepare a pair g^{kq} and y_*^{kq} while calculating them in advance, i.e. the pair can be calculated through an off-line process, therefore, computation volume in the encryption stage can be reduced. A disadvantage is, because mix-servers must be arrayed both for the encryption and the decryption stages delays for message arrivals become long.

In the above, Mix-net was constructed by the usual ElGamal based re-encryption scheme, but it is straightforward to construct it also based on the threshold ElGamal re-encryption scheme.

Mechanism for Reply Messages

By using Mix-net, receiver R of message M_S can send reply message M_R to sender S without knowing the identity of S. To enable R to send M_R without knowing S, S in Figure 3 repeatedly encrypts its address A_S to $E(k_1, E(k_2, ---, E(k_N, A_S)---)) = E(k_*, A_S)$ by the public keys k_N, k_{N-1}, ---, k_1 of mix-servers T_N, T_{N-1}, ---, T_1, and constructs triple $\{M_S, A_R, E(k_*, A_S)\}$ as its message instead of $\{M_S, A_R\}$. As a consequence, S sends repeatedly encrypted triple $\{E(k_*, M_S), E(k_*, A_R)), E(k_*, E(k_*, A_S))\}$ to T_1, and T_1, T_2, ---, T_N decrypt it to $\{M_S, A_R, E(k_*, A_S)\}$ to deliver it to R, then R can send its reply M_R to S by sending pair $\{E(k_*, M_R), E(k_*, A_S)\}$ to T_1, i.e. T_1, T_2, ---, T_N repeatedly decrypt $\{E(k_*, M_R), E(k_*, A_S)\}$ to $\{M_R, A_S\}$ and T_N delivers M_R to S according to A_S.

However, receiver R, which had sent $\{E(k_*, M_R), E(k_*, A_S)\}$, knows that its message is finally decrypted to $\{M_R, X\}$ that includes M_R although it does not know the value of X (address of S), therefore, R can know S by observing the network to find the entity that receives M_R. To cope with this type of sender identity leaks, S attaches its secret encryption keys s_1, s_2, ---, s_N to its message while encrypting them by public keys k_N, k_{N-1}, ---, k_1 of mix-servers T_N, T_{N-1}, ---, T_1 (Chaum, 1981, Golle, 2003). Conceptually, provided that $E(k_{q*}, x)$ represents $E(k_1, E(k_2, ---, E(k_q, x) ---))$, S calculates $E(k_*, s_N)$, $E(k_{(N-1)*}, s_{N-1})$, $E(k_{(N-2)*}, s_{N-2})$, ---, $E(k_1, s_1)$, and constructs its message as combination $\{E(k_*, M_S), E(k_*, A_R), E(k_*, E(k_*, A_S)), E(k_*, E(k_*, s_N)), E(k_*, E(k_{(N-1)*}, s_{N-1})), E(k_*, E(k_{(N-2)*}, s_{N-2}))$, ---, $E(k_*, E(k_1, s_1))\}$. As a consequence, the mix-servers decrypt it to $\{M_S, A_R, E(k_*, A_S), E(k_*, s_N), E(k_{(N-1)*}, s_{N-1}), E(k_{(N-2)*}, s_{N-2})$, ---, $E(k_1, s_1)\}$ to deliver it to R.

Then, receiver R constructs its reply message as combination $\{M_R, E(k_*, A_S), E(k_*, s_N), E(k_{(N-1)*}, s_{N-1}), E(k_{(N-2)*}, s_{N-2})$, ---, $E(k_1, s_1)\}$. Therefore, mix-server T_1 can obtain $E(k_{2\_N}, A_S), E(k_{2\_N}, s_N), E(k_{2\_(N-1)}, s_{N-1}), E(k_{2\_(N-2)}, s_{N-2})$, ---, $E(k_2, s_2), s_1\}$ by decrypting $\{E(k_*, A_S), E(k_*, s_N), E(k_{(N-1)*}, s_{N-1}), E(k_{(N-2)*}, s_{N-2})$, ---, $E(k_1, s_1)\}$ while using decryption key k_1^{-1}, and after extracting secret key s_1 from it, it can encrypt M_R to $E(s_1, M_R)$. Namely, T_1 can construct combination $\{E(s_1, M_R), E(k_{2\_N}, A_S)), E(k_{2\_N}, s_N), E(k_{2\_(N-1)}, s_{N-1}), E(k_{2\_(N-2)}, s_{N-2})$, ---, $E(k_2, s_2)\}$ to send it to T_2. Here, $E(k_{q\_j}, x) = E(k_q, E(k_{q+1}, ---, E(k_j, x) ---))$. In the same way, T_2 calculates $\{E(k_{3\_N}, A_S)), E(k_{3\_N}, s_N), E(k_{3\_(N-1)}, s_{N-1}), E(k_{3\_(N-2)}, s_{N-2})$, ---, $E(k_3, s_3), s_2\}$ from its receiving message, and encrypts $E(s_1, M_R)$ to $E(s_2, E(s_1, M_R))$ to construct combination $\{E(s_2, E(s_1, M_R)), E(k_{3\_N}, A_S)), E(k_{3\_N}, s_N), E(k_{3\_(N-1)}, s_{N-1}), E(k_{3\_(N-2)}, s_{N-2})$, ---, $E(k_3, s_3)\}$ so that it can send it to T_3. T_3, T_4, ---, T_{N-1} behave in the same way, and finally T_N receives $\{E(s_{N-1}, E(s_{N-2}, ---, E(s_1, M_R)---)), E(k_N, A_S), E(k_N, s_N)\}$, decrypts $E(k_N, A_S)$ and $E(k_N, s_N)$ to A_S and s_N, and encrypts $E(s_{N-1}, E(s_{N-2}, ---, E(s_1, M_R)---))$ to $E(s_N, E(s_{N-1}, ---, E(s_1, M_R)---))$ to deliver the result to S according to decrypted address A_S. Now, S can decrypt $E(s_N, E(s_{N-1}, ---, E(s_1, M_R)---))$ to M_R by using its secret decryption keys s_N^{-1}, s_{N-1}^{-1}, ---, s_1^{-1}, nevertheless, other entities including receiver R cannot know that S had received M_R. Because mix-servers in the above message transferring process change the form of the reply message from M_R to $E(s_N, E(s_{N-1}, ---, E(s_1, M_R)---))$ by secret encryption keys of sender S, even receiver R cannot identify its message M_R received by S. However, mix-servers can know whether they are transferring reply messages or original ones.

To reduce the number of decryption operations carried out by individual mix-servers in the above, actually, sender S does not encrypt encryption keys s_N, s_{N-1}, ---, s_1 individually to $\{E(k_*, s_N), E(k_{(N-1)*}, s_{N-1}), E(k_{(N-2)*}, s_{N-2})$, ---, $E(k_1, s_1)\}$, instead, S encrypts them as combination $\{s_N, s_{N-1}, ---, s_1\}$. Namely, S firstly encrypts s_N to $E(k_N, s_N)$, and encrypts $\{E(k_N, s_N), s_{N-1}\}$ to $E(k_{N-1}, \{E(k_N, s_N), s_{N-1}\})$. By continuing this process $\{s_N, s_{N-1}, ---, s_1\}$ is finally transformed to $E(k_*, \{s_N, s_{N-1}, ---, s_1\}) = E(k_1, \{E(k_2, \{ --- E(k_{N-1}, \{E(k_N, s_N), s_{N-1}\}) ---, s_2\}), s_1\})$. Here, T_1 can extracts s_1 from $E(k_*, \{s_N, s_{N-1}, ---, s_1\})$ by decrypting it to $\{E(k_2, \{--- E(k_{N-1}, \{E(k_N, s_N), s_{N-1}\}) ---, s_2\}), s_1\}$, and T_2, T_3, ---, T_N also can extracts s_2, s_3, ---, s_N in the same way.

Protecting Mix-Net from Traffic Analysis Attacks

Traffic analysis attacks are general threats for reply message mechanisms, i.e. when receiver R sends many replies to anonymous sender S, it can know S by identifying the entity that receives many messages just after it had sent the replies. Or when R sends reply messages periodically, it can know S as the entity that receives messages periodically. A reply bounding mechanism that limits the number of reply messages that each receiver can send solves this problem (Golle, 2003).

Figure 5 shows the mechanism in which $S(t_1, \{Q, E(k_*, A_S)\})$, signature of mix-server T_1 on

Figure 5. Limiting number of replies

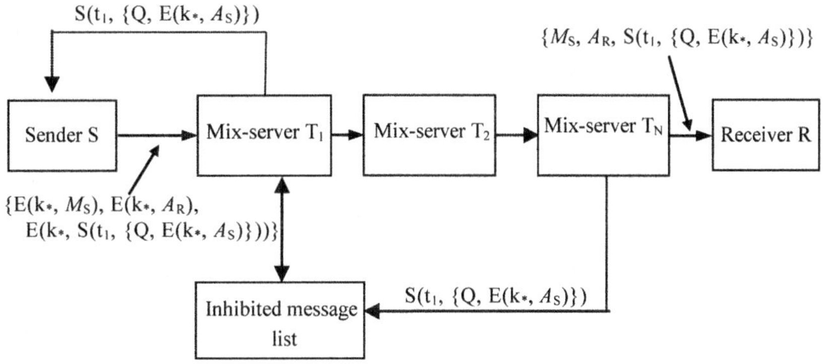

pair {Q, E(k_*, A_S)}, is exploited. Here, A_S is the addresses of sender S, t_1 is the signing key of the 1st server T_1, and Q is the reply bound allowed for receiver R, i.e. by using encrypted address E(k_*, A_S), R can send Q-messages at most as replies to the original message M_S sent from S. Also, sender S of message M_S obtains the signature on {Q, E(k_*, A_S)} in advance without disclosing its value, e.g. through the blind signature scheme. Then, S repeatedly encrypts {M_S, A_R, S(t_1, {Q, E(k_*, A_S)})} to {E(k_*, M_S), E(k_*, A_R), E(k_*, S(t_1, {Q, E(k_*, A_S)}))} to send it to T_1, and mix-servers T_1, T_2, ---, T_N decrypted it to {M_S, A_R, S(t_1, {Q, E(k_*, A_S)})}. But the last mix-server T_N sends it not only to R but also T_1 so that T_1 can register pair {Q, E(k_*, A_S)} in its inhibited message list. Therefore, when R sends more than Q replies to address E(k_*, A_S), T_1 can reject them by comparing the encrypted addresses of the replies with the ones registered in its inhibited message list. It must be noted that nevertheless entities can send replies to other messages of S because encryption functions used are probabilistic and every time address A_S is encrypted into different forms.

Here, although it is possible that T_1 conspiring with receiver R forwards replies more than Q-times, sender S can prove dishonesties of T_1, i.e. S detects T_1's dishonesty when it had received more than Q-replies and it can accuse T_1 by showing the signature on {Q, E(k_*, A_S)}. However, when T_1 and T_N are conspiring, they can identify S without being detected. Namely, T_1 sends reply message M_R multiple times to encrypted address E(k_*, A_S) regardless of Q, and T_N discards messages if their contents coincide with the ones that it had received before. Then, T_1 and T_N can identify S as the destination of the multiple messages with the same contents, but S does not notice that T_1 had sent M_R multiple times because they are discarded. This dishonesty is what is called a replay attack (Anderson, 2001) and can happen for any message (not limited to reply messages). Namely, if an entity X eavesdrops on E(k_*, M_S) sent from S to T_1 and sends it repeatedly to T_1 by itself, X can identify that S is the sender of M_S by observing messages that T_N is repeatedly delivering. Although Mix-nets can protect themselves also from replay attacks, e.g. no one carries out replay attacks successfully unless it conspires with all mix-servers when every mix-server examines its receiving messages to discard repeatedly sent ones, overheads of individual mix-servers for examining messages become large. ESEBM discussed in the next protects communication channels from traffic analysis and replay attacks more effectively and efficiently.

Confirmation of Message Deliveries

When reply message mechanisms are available, sender S easily can confirm the successful delivery of its message. Namely, when it receives a reply to its sending message M_S from receiver R, it can convince itself that M_S had been delivered successfully. Of course it must re-send M_S when it cannot receive any reply, as same as in usual non-anonymous communication channels. However, to hide its identity, S cannot re-send M_S immediately; receiver R can identify S as the sender of M_S if it does not send replies intentionally and S resends M_S many times in a short period as in traffic analysis attacks. Of course, S must resend M_S while encrypting it with different random factors. If S sends the same encrypted messages, R that eavesdrops on the communication channel between senders and the 1st server in Mix-net easily identifies S as the one that is sending same messages repeatedly.

ESEBM (ENHANCED SYMMETRIC KEY ENCRYPTION BASED MIX-NET)

Mix-net discussed in the previous sub has a serious drawback, i.e. it requires tremendous amount of computations to encrypt/decrypt messages that are forwarded from senders to their receivers because asymmetric key encryption/decryption functions are adopted. Enhanced Symmetric key Encryption Based Mix-net (ESEBM) removes this drawback while exploiting symmetric key encryption functions (Haddad, 2011). Symmetric key encryption functions not only make anonymous networks efficient but also enable the development of simple and secure reply message mechanisms.

Configuration of ESEBM

As same as Mix-net, ESEBM is an anonymous network based on the single path message transfer type hidden message approach, and also consists of multiple relay servers. Figure 6 shows the configuration of ESEBM consists of 2 parts; they are the concealing pattern generator (CP generator) and the anonymous channel. In the figure, the CP generator is configured by Z groups $\{G_1, G_2, ---, G_Z\}$ and each group G_g consists of N_g-servers. On the other hand the anonymous channel is a sequence of N-servers. Here, each server in the anonymous channel is corresponded to a single server in the CP generator, and contrarily each server in the CP generator is corresponded to a single server in the anonymous channel; therefore the numbers of servers in the CP generator and the anonymous channel are the same, i.e. $N = N_1 + N_2 + --- + N_Z$. The base algorithm to encrypt and decrypt messages in ESEBM is onetime pad, and it reduces computation volumes required for encrypting and decrypting messages substantially. Also, the complete symmetric feature of onetime pad (not only encryption and decryption keys but also encryption and decryption operations of onetime pad are exactly the same) enables ESEBM to handle original and reply messages in totally the same way, and makes reply mechanisms simple and secure. In the remainder of this sub, notations $T_g(j)$ and T_p are used to represent the j-th server in the g-th group of the CP generator and the p-th server in the anonymous channel, respectively. Notation $T_g(j)$ is also used for representing T_p in the anonymous channel that is corresponded to $T_g(j)$, and vice versa.

In the figure, as an off-line process, sender S of message *M* obtains a concealing pattern (CP) for encrypting *M* from servers in the CP generator in advance. Where at the request of S, the h-th concealing pattern X(h) is generated as the XOR of CP constructors $x_1(h), x_2(h), ---, x_N(h)$ that are secrets of individual servers $T_1, T_2, ----, T_N$ in the CP generator, namely, $X(h) = x_1(h) \oplus x_2(h) \oplus --- \oplus x_N(h)$. Then, S encrypts *M* to $M \oplus X(h)$ and sends it to the first server T_1 in the anonymous channel, and as same as in usual Mix-net, each server in the anonymous channel stores its receiving messages until it receives the predefined

Figure 6. ESEBM configuration

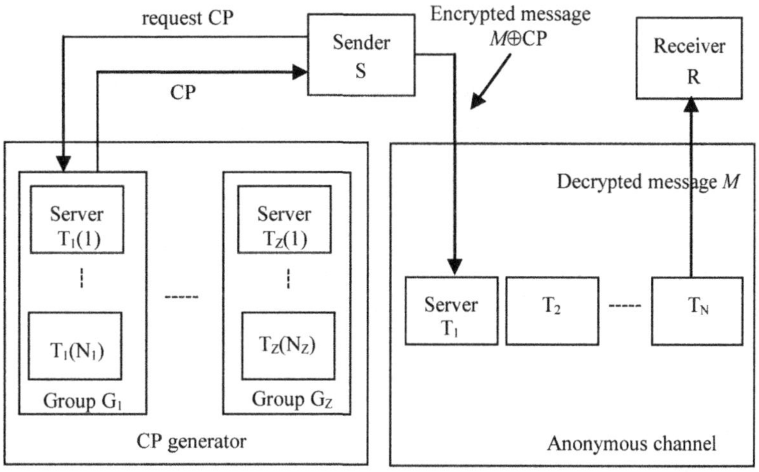

number of messages, and decrypts, shuffles and forwards them to the server next to it finally to be delivered to their receivers. Here, each T_j decrypts its receiving encrypted M by simply XORing it by its secret CP constructor $x_j(h)$ included in X(h) that S had used to encrypt M. Namely, because $X(h) = x_1(h) \oplus x_2(h) \oplus \cdots \oplus x_N(h)$, when each T_j calculates XOR of its receiving message and its CP constructor $x_j(h)$, the final decrypted form of $M \oplus X(h)$ becomes M (i.e. $M \oplus X(h) \oplus x_1(h) \oplus x_2(h) \oplus \cdots \oplus x_N(h) = M$).

Then, as same as in usual Mix-net, anyone except S including the receiver and servers cannot identify the sender of M unless it conspires with all servers. No entity can know all $x_j(h)$ because multiple servers are mutually independent, also, although notations X(h) and $x_j(h)$ are accompanied by h they do not include any information about h. Here, because message M is encrypted to $M \oplus X(h)$, the length of CPs and CP constructors must be same as L_M, the length of messages. When S sends a long message M, it must divide M into multiple frames of length L_M. Also because the one time pad is weak against plain text attacks, S must use different CPs for encrypting different messages. This is also true for a long message, i.e. if a message is divided into multiple frames, these frames must be sent while being XORed by different CPs.

As above, different from Mix-net, in which each server T_j uses a single and fixed secret decryption key for decrypting all messages, each server T_j in ESEBM decrypts different messages by different CP constructors, therefore, a mechanism that enables T_j to identify the CP constructor $x_j(h)$ included in X(h) that S had used for encrypting M is necessary. To implement this mechanism, message M is configured by 2 parts, the message part and the tag part, as shown in Figure 7. The message part maintains encrypted message M, i.e. $M \oplus X(h)$, and the tag part maintains a sequence of tags, i.e. vector $Q(h) = \{Q_1(h), Q_2(h), \cdots, Q_N(h)\}$, where each tag $Q_j(h)$ is the identifier of the CP constructor $x_j(h)$ generated by server T_j in the CP generator to construct X(h). Here, tag $Q_j(h)$ also must be constituted so that no one can trace messages by it or no one except T_j can identify $x_j(h)$ from it.

Behavior of ESEBM

CP Generator

The CP generator generates 2 kinds of secret encryption keys of servers to disable entities to trace messages forwarded through the anonymous channel, i.e. to conceal not only correspondences between the message parts of input and output messages of individual servers but also correspondences between their tag parts. The one is CPs mentioned already and the other is tag concealing vectors (TVs), in more detail, servers in the CP generator generate their secret CP constructors and TV constructors independently of others to constitute CPs and TVs jointly with other servers as shown in Figures 8 and 9. As discussed already, concealing pattern X(h) is calculated as XOR of CP constructors $x_j(h)$ (j = 1, 2, ---, N) generated by each server T_j, and disables anyone except S, which had sent message *M*, to trace the message part of *M* relayed by the servers. On the other hand, TVs disable anyone to trace the tag parts of *M* relayed in the anonymous channel. It must be noted that in Figure 6 senders communicate only with $T_1(1)$, $T_1(2)$, ---, and $T_1(N_1)$ in the 1st group so that servers in the other groups do not know the senders.

Regarding TVs, each element $Q_w(h)$, of N-dimensional tag concealing vector $Q(h) = \{Q_1(h), Q_2(h), ---, Q_N(h)\}$ is constituted as XOR of the w-th element of each N-dimensional TV constructor $q_j(h) = \{0, ---0, q_{j(j+1)}(h), q_{j(j+2)}(h), ---, q_{jN}(h)\}$ generated by T_j (j = 1, ---, N). Therefore, $Q_w(h) = q_{1w}(h) \oplus q_{2w}(h) \oplus --- \oplus q_{Nw}(h) = q_{1w}(h) \oplus q_{2w}(h) \oplus --- \oplus q_{(w-1)w}(h)$. Here for each w, the w-th element $q_{jw}(h)$ of $q_j(h)$, and each tag $Q_w(h)$ are bit strings of length L_T, which is the length of $ID_w(x_w(h), Q_w(h))$, the CP identifier of server T_w discussed later, 0 represents an all zero bit string of the length L_T, and a sequence of j-zero bit strings precede before (N-j)-secret bit strings $\{q_{j(j+1)}(h), q_{j(j+2)}(h), ---, q_{jN}(h)\}$ (the length of CP constructor $x_j(h)$ is equal to the message frame length L_M as mentioned before).

Then, T_1, T_2, ---, T_N calculate XOR of their CP constructors and TV constructors to construct CP and TV as $X(h) = x_1(h) \oplus x_2(h) \oplus --- \oplus x_N(h)$ and $Q(h) = \{0, q_{12}(h), q_{13}(h) \oplus q_{23}(h), ---, q_{1w}(h) \oplus q_{2w}(h) \oplus --- \oplus q_{(w-1)w}(h), ---, q_{1N}(h) \oplus q_{2N}(h) \oplus --- \oplus q_{(N-1)N}(h)\}$. Here, the last server T_N does not generate its TV constructor. In more detail, CPs and TVs above are generated as follows. Provided that $T_1(j)$ in the 1st group of the CP generator corresponds to server T_{j*} in the anonymous channel, firstly, sender S generates a set of private vectors (PVs) $P(h) = \{P_1(h), P_2(h), ---, P_{(N1)}(h)\}$ secrets of itself, and as a request for a CP, sends individual vectors to servers T_{1*}, T_{2*}, ---, T_{N1*}, respectively, as shown in Figure 8. Where, each $P_j(h)$ is vector $\{p_{j0}(h), p_{j1}(h), ---, p_{jN}(h)\}$, and bit string $p_{j0}(h)$ has the same length as CP constructor $x_j(h)$. For w ≠ 0, each $p_{jw}(h)$ is a bit string that has the same length as element $q_{jw}(h)$ in TV constructor $q_j(h)$.

When T_{1*}, the 1st server in the 1st group, receives the request from S with private vector $P_1(h)$, it generates its CP constructor $x_{1*}(h)$ and TV constructor $q_{1*}(h) = \{0, ---, 0, q_{1*(1*+1)}(h), q_{1*(1*+2)}(h), ---, q_{1*N}(h)\}$. It also generates CP

Figure 7. Message structure in ESEBM

Message part	Tag part			
$M \oplus x_1(h) \oplus x_2(h) \oplus --- \oplus x_N(h)$	$Q_1(h)$	$Q_2(h)$	-----	$Q_N(h)$

Figure 8. Servers in the 1st group of CP generator

$p_{10} \oplus x_{1*}(h), Q_1(1, h), ---, Q_N(1, h)$
$Q_w(1, h) =$
for $w < 1*$: $p_{1w}(h)$
for $w = 1*$: $p_{11*}(h) \oplus ID_{1*}(x_{1*}(h), q_{1*}(h))$
for $1* < w$: $p_{1w}(h) \oplus q_{1*w}(h)$

$p_{10} \oplus p_{20} \oplus x_{1*}(h) \oplus x_{2*}(h), Q_1(1, h), ---, Q_N(1, h)$
$Q_w(1, h) =$
for $w < 1*$: $p_{1w}(h) \oplus p_{2w}(h)$
for $w = 1*$: $p_{11*}(h) \oplus p_{21*} \oplus ID_{1*}(x_{1*}(h), q_{1*}(h))$
for $1* < w < 2*$: $p_{1w}(h) \oplus p_{2w} \oplus q_{1*w}(h)$
for $w = 2*$: $p_{12*}(h) \oplus p_{22*}(h) \oplus q_{12*}(h) \oplus ID_{2*}(x_{2*}(h), q_{2*}(h))$
for $2* < w$: $p_{1w}(h) \oplus p_{2w}(h) \oplus q_{1*w}(h) \oplus q_{2*w}(h)$

$T_1(1)$
(T_{1*})

$T_1(2)$
(T_{2*})

$P_1(h)$

$P_2(h)$

S

$P_{N1}(h)$

$P_3(h)$

$T_1(N_1)$
$(T_{(N1)*})$

$T_1(3)$
(T_{3*})

$p_{10} \oplus --- \oplus p_{(N1)0} \oplus x_{1*}(h) \oplus --- \oplus x_{(N1)*}(h), Q_1(1, h), ---, Q_N(1, h)$
for w^* included in the 1st group
$Q_{w*}(1, h) = p_{1w*}(h) \oplus --- \oplus p_{(N1)w*}(h) \oplus q_{1*w*}(h)$
$\oplus --- \oplus q_{(w-1)*w*}(h) \oplus ID_{w*}(x_{w*}(h), q_{w*}(h))$
for i not included in the 1st group
$Q_i(1, h) = p_{1i}(h) \oplus --- \oplus p_{(N1)i}(h)$
$\oplus q_{1*i}(h) \oplus --- \oplus q_{w*i}(h)$, where $w* < i < (w+1)*$.

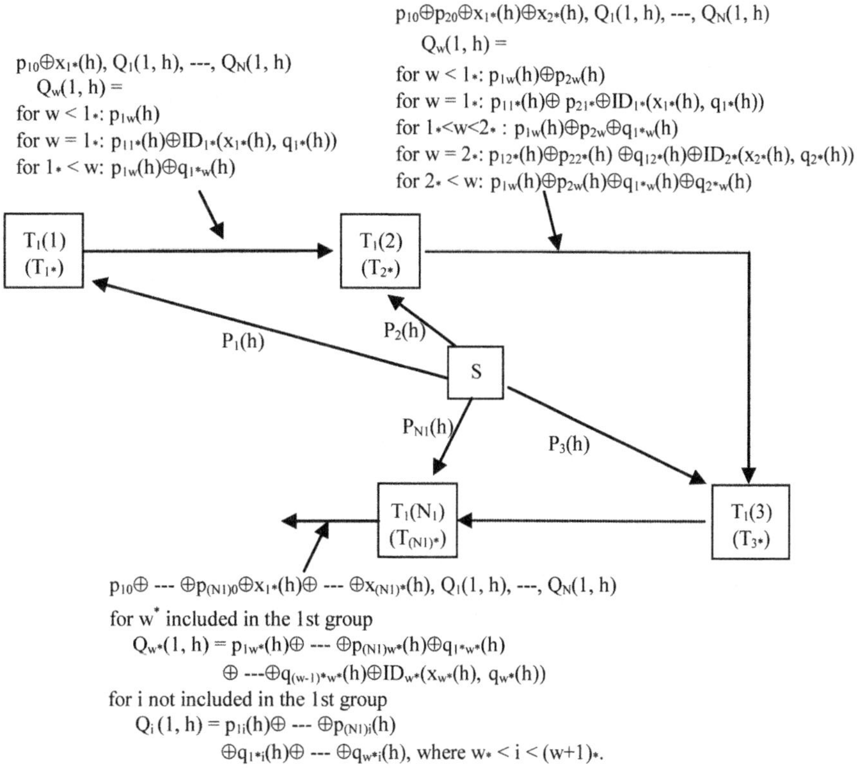

identifier $ID_{1*}(x_{1*}(h), q_{1*}(h))$ to identify $x_{1*}(h)$ and $q_{1*}(h)$ that it generates, and calculates $X(1, h)$ and $Q(1, h)$ as $X(1, h) = p_{10}(h) \oplus x_{1*}(h)$ and $Q(1, h) = \{p_{11}(h), p_{12}(h), ---, p_{11*}(h) \oplus ID_{1*}(x_{1*}(h), q_{1*}(h)), p_{1(1*+1)}(h) \oplus q_{1*(1*+1)}(h), p_{1(1*+2)}(h) \oplus q_{1*(1*+2)}(h), ---, p_{1N}(h) \oplus q_{1*N}(h)\}$, respectively. Here, T_{1*} maintains its CP table, a list of CP and TV constructors that it had generated, and $ID_{1*}(x_{1*}(h), q_{1*}(h))$ is the address of the constructor pair $\{x_{1*}(h), q_{1*}(h)\}$ in this list, and $X(1, h)$ and $Q(1, h)$ are the CP and TV that the 1st group generates. Then finally, T_{1*} encrypts pair $\{X(1, h), Q(1, h)\}$ to $E(k_{1*}, \{X(1, h), Q(1, h)\})$ by secret encryption key k_{1*} shared between T_{1*} and T_{2*} to protect the pair from wiretapping, and forwards the encrypted result to T_{2*}. It is also possible that T_{1*} encrypts $X(1, h)$ and $Q(1, h)$ by using a public key of T_{2*},

but symmetric key encryption function $E(k_{1*}, x)$ reduces the encryption and decryption overheads.

T_{2*} that receives $E(k_{1*}, \{X(1, h), Q(1, h)\})$ modifies its receiving CP and TV as follows, i.e. it decrypts $E(k_{1*}, \{X(1, h), Q(1, h)\})$ to $\{X(1, h), Q(1, h)\}$, generates its CP constructor $x_{2*}(h)$ and TV constructor $q_{2*}(h) = (0, ---0, q_{2*(2*+1)}(h), q_{2*(2*+2)}(h), ---, q_{2*N}(h))$, and by using $x_{2*}(h)$ and $q_{2*}(h)$ together with private vector $P_2(h) = \{p_{20}(h), p_{21}(h), ---p_{2N}(h)\}$ sent from S, calculates the new value of $X(1, h)$ as $X(1, h) = p_{10}(h) \oplus p_{20}(h) \oplus x_{1*}(h) \oplus x_{2*}(h)$. The new value of $Q(1, h)$ is calculated as $Q(1, h) = \{p_{11}(h) \oplus p_{21}(h), p_{12}(h) \oplus p_{22}(h), ---, p_{11*}(h) \oplus p_{21*}(h) \oplus ID_{1*}(x_{1*}(h), q_{1*}(h)), p_{1(1*+1)}(h) \oplus p_{2(1*+1)}(h) \oplus q_{1*(1*+1)}(h), ---, p_{12*}(h) \oplus p_{22*}(h) \oplus q_{1*2*}(h) \oplus ID_{2*}(x_{2*}(h), q_{2*}(h)), p_{1(2*+1)}(h) \oplus p_{2(2*+1)}(h) \oplus q_{1*(2*+1)}(h) \oplus q_{2*(2*+1)}(h), ---, p_{1N}(h) \oplus p_{2N}(h) \oplus q_{1*N}(h) \oplus q_{2*N}(h)\}$. As same

Figure 9. Servers in the r-th group of CP generator

$b_{10}(h) \oplus b_{20}(h) \oplus x_{1'}(h) \oplus x_{2'}(h), Q_1(r, h), ---, Q_N(r, h)$
$Q_w(r, h) =$
for $w < 1'$: $b_{1w}(h) \oplus b_{2w}(h)$
for $w = 1'$: $b_{11'}(h) \oplus b_{21'}(h) \oplus ID_{1'}(x_{1'}(h), q_{1'}(h))$
for $1' < w < 2' =$: $b_{1w}(h) \oplus b_{2w}(h) \oplus q_{1'w}(h)$
for $w = 2'$: $b_{12'}(h) \oplus b_{22'}(h) \oplus q_{1'2'}(h) \oplus ID_{2'}(x_{2'}(h), q_{2'}(h))$
for $2' < w$: $b_{1w}(h) \oplus b_{2w}(h) \oplus q_{1'w}(h) \oplus q_{2'w}(h)$

$b_{10}(h) \oplus x_{1'}(h), Q_1(r, h), ---, Q_N(r, h)$
$Q_w(r, h) =$
for $w < 1'$: $b_{1w}(h)$
for $w = 1'$: $b_{11'}(h) \oplus ID_{1'}(x_{1'}(h), q_{1'}(h))$
for $1' < w$: $b_{1w}(h) \oplus q_{1'w}(h)$

$B_1(h)$ $B_2(h)$ $B_3(h)$

$b_{10} \oplus --- \oplus b_{(Nr)0} \oplus x_{1'}(h) \oplus --- \oplus x_{(Nr)'}(h), Q_1(r, h), ---, Q_N(r, h)$
for w' included in the r-th group
$Q_{w'}(r, h) = b_{1w'}(h) \oplus --- \oplus b_{(Nr)w'}(h) \oplus q_{1'w'}(h) \oplus --- \oplus q_{(w-1)'w'}(h) \oplus ID_{w'}(x_{w'}(h), q_{w*}(h))$
for i not included in the r-th group
$Q_i(r, h) = b_{1i}(h) \oplus --- \oplus b_{(Nr)i}(h) \oplus q_{1'i}(h) \oplus --- \oplus q_{w'i}(h)$, where $w' < i < (w+1)'$

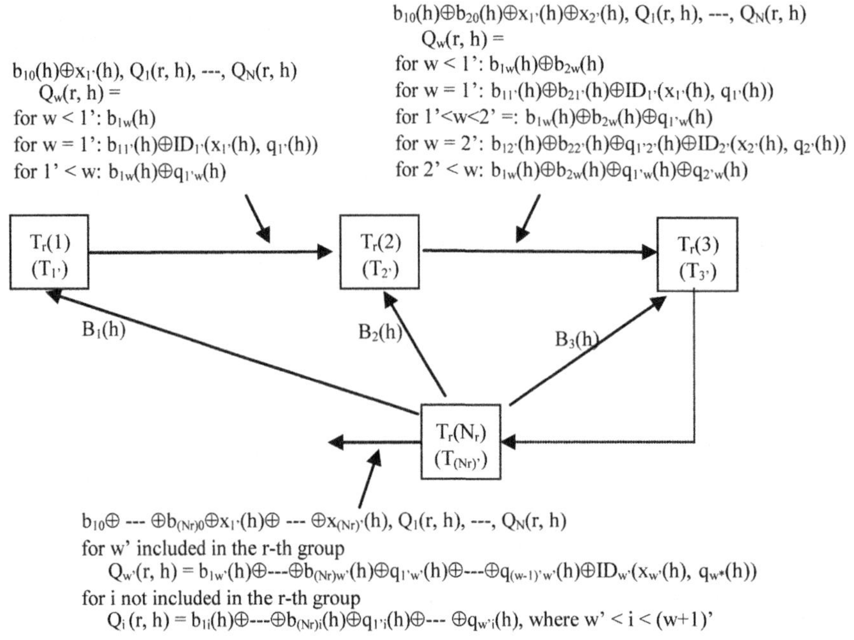

as $ID_{1*}(x_{1*}(h), q_{1*}(h))$, CP identifier $ID_{2*}(x_{2*}(h), q_{2*}(h))$ is the address of $\{x_{2*}(h), q_{2*}(h)\}$ in the CP table that T_{2*} maintains to identify $x_{2*}(h)$ and $q_{2*}(h)$ it generates. Here, it is not necessary but to simplify notations, it is assumed that servers in the anonymous channel are arranged so that $T_g(j)$ comes earlier than $T_g(v)$ when $j < v$, for every g-th group.

Then, calculated $X(1, h)$ and $Q(1, h)$ are sent to T_{3*} while being encrypted by k_{2*}, a shared encryption key between T_{2*} and T_{3*}, and T_{3*}, ---, T_{N1*} continue the same process. Therefore, $X(1, h)$ and $Q(1, h) = \{Q_1(1, h), Q_2(1, h), ---, Q_N(1, h)\}$, the CP and the TV pair generated by the 1st group become as shown in Equations (1), (2) and (3).

$$X(1, h) = p_{10} \oplus p_{20} \oplus --- \oplus p_{(N1)0} \oplus x_{1*}(h) \oplus x_{2*}(h) \oplus --- \oplus x_{(N1)*}(h) \quad (1)$$

for w* included in the 1st group,

$$Q_{w*}(1, h) = p_{1w*}(h) \oplus p_{2w*}(h) \oplus --- \oplus p_{(N1)w*}(h) \oplus q_{1*w*}(h)$$

$$\oplus q_{2*w*}(h) \oplus --- \oplus q_{(w-1)*w*}(h) \oplus ID_{w*}(x_{w*}(h), q_{w*}(h)) \quad (2)$$

for i not included in the 1st group $(w_* < i < (w+1)_*)$

$$Q_i(1, h) = p_{1i}(h) \oplus p_{2i}(h) \oplus --- \oplus p_{(N1)i}(h) \oplus q_{1*i}(h) \oplus q_{2*i}(h) \oplus --- \oplus q_{w*i}(h) \quad (3)$$

Severs in the r-th group (r > 1) behave in the same way as the 1st group as shown in Figure 9. However, different from the 1st group, the r-th group generates CP and TV pairs spontaneously without requests from senders. Therefore, sender S does not inform servers in the r-th group of its private vectors, instead, $T_r(N_j)$, the last server of the r-th group, generates a set of group blinding vectors $B(h) = \{B_1(h), B_2(h), ----, B_{Nr}(h)\}$ and sends individual vectors to $T_r(1), T_r(2), T_r(N_r)$, respectively. Here, as same as private vectors, each $B_j(h)$ is a vector of bit strings $\{b_{j0}(h), b_{j1}(h),$ ---, $b_{jN}(h)\}$ and except $b_{j0}(h)$, $b_{jw}(h)$ has the same length as element $q_{jw}(h)$ in TV constructor $q_j(h)$. Bit string $b_{j0}(h)$ has the same length as CP constructor $x_j(h)$. Then, the r-th group calculates X(r, h) and Q(r, h) as its h-th CP and TV values as shown in equations (4) - (6). Here, it is assumed that server $T_r(j)$ in the r-th group of the CP generator corresponds to server $T_{j'}$ in the anonymous channel.

$$X(r, h) = b_{10} \oplus b_{20} \oplus \text{---} \oplus b_{(Nr)0} \oplus x_{1'}(h) \oplus x_{2'}(h) \oplus \text{---} \oplus x_{(Nr)'}(h) \quad (4)$$

for w' included in the r-th group,

$$Q_{w'}(r, h) = b_{1w'}(h) \oplus b_{2w'}(h) \oplus \text{---} \oplus b_{(Nr)w'}(h) \oplus$$

$$\oplus q_{1'w'}(h) \oplus q_{2'w'}(h) \oplus \text{---} \oplus q_{(w-1)'w'}(h) \oplus ID_{w'}(x_{w'}(h), q_{w'}(h)) \quad (5)$$

for i not included in the r-th group (w' < i < (w+1)')

$$Q_i(r, h) = b_{1i}(h) \oplus b_{2i}(h) \oplus \text{---} \oplus b_{(Nr)i}(h) \oplus q_{1'i}(h) \oplus q_{2'i}(h) \oplus \text{---} \oplus q_{w'i}(h) \quad (6)$$

After X(r, h) and Q(r, h) are calculated as in Equations (4), (5) and (6), the last server $T_r(N_r)$ calculates XOR of {X(r, h), Q(r, h)} and its generating group blind vectors B(h) to remove B(h) from X(r, h) and Q(r, h). As a result, X(r, h) and Q(r, h) are represented as in (7) - (9).

$$X(r, h) = x_{1'}(h) \oplus x_{2'}(h) \oplus \text{---} \oplus x_{(Nr)'}(h) \quad (7)$$

for w' included in the r-th group,

$$Q_{w'}(r, h) = q_{1'w'}(h) \oplus q_{2'w'}(h) \oplus \text{---} \oplus q_{(w-1)'w'}(h) \oplus ID_{w'}(x_{w'}(h), q_{w'}(h)) \quad (8)$$

for i not included in the r-th group (w' < i < (w+1)')

$$Q_i(r, h) = q_{1'i}(h) \oplus q_{2'i}(h) \oplus \text{---} \oplus q_{w'i}(h) \quad (9)$$

$T_r(N_r)$ also receives X(r+1, h) and Q(r+1, h), the CP and TV values generated by the (r+1)-th group, from $T_{r+1}(N_{r+1})$, the last server in the (r+1)-th group, and it calculates X(r, h) = X(r, h)⊕X(r+1, h), and Q(r, h) = Q(r, h)⊕Q(r+1, h) as CP and TV values jointly calculated by servers in the r-th, (r+1)-th, ---, Z-th groups. Then, $T_r(N_r)$ waits for the arrivals of predefined number of CP and TV pairs that servers in the r-th group generate, and shuffles them to sends the results to the last server $T_{r-1}(N_{r-1})$ of the (r-1)-th group. Consequently as the result of the behaviors of all groups, the last server of the 1st group, i.e. $T_1(N_1)$, generates the CP and TV as Equations (10) and (11).

$$X(h) = p_{10}(h) \oplus p_{20}(h) \oplus \text{---} \oplus p_{(N1)0}(h) \oplus x_1(h) \oplus x_2(h) \oplus \text{---} \oplus x_N(h) \quad (10)$$

$$Q_w(h) = p_{1w}(h) \oplus \text{---} \oplus p_{(N1)w}(h) \oplus q_{1w}(h) \oplus \text{---} \oplus q_{(w-1)w}(h) \oplus ID_w(x_w(h), q_w(h)) \quad (11)$$

Then, $T_1(N_1)$ sends X(h) and Q(h) to sender S, and S calculates XOR of {X(h), Q(h)} and its generating private vectors P(h) to remove P(h) from X(h) and Q(h). As the result, finally CP and TV values X(h) and Q(h) become as (12) and (13). Here, it must be noted that because PVs are secrets of sender S and each server T_j does not know CP and TV constructors of other servers, anyone except sender S can know X(h) and Q(h) that S had obtained unless all servers in the 1st group conspire. Also even S cannot know individual CP and TV constructors $x_j(h)$ and $q_j(h)$ included in X(h) and Q(h).

$$X(h) = x_1(h) \oplus x_2(h) \oplus \text{---} \oplus x_{(N-1)}(h) \oplus x_N(h) \quad (12)$$

$$Q_w(h) = q_{1w}(h) \oplus \text{---} \oplus q_{(w-1)w}(h) \oplus ID_w(x_w(h), q_w(h)) \quad (13)$$

Anonymous Channel

The anonymous channel behaves as shown in Figure 10. Provided that $\{X(h), Q(h)\}$ is a concealing pattern and a tag concealing vector pair that sender S had obtained from $T_1(N_1)$, firstly, S calculates $X(h)\oplus M$ as the encrypted form of message M, and attaches $Q(h) = \{Q_1(h), Q_2(h), ---, Q_N(h)\}$ to it. Therefore, S sends its message M in the form $\{\underline{M} = x_1(h)\oplus x_2(h)\oplus --- \oplus x_N(h)\oplus M, Q_1(h), Q_2(h), ---, Q_N(h)\}$ to the 1st server T_1 in the anonymous channel. Here, $Q_w(h) = q_{1w}(h)\oplus --- \oplus q_{(w-1)w}(h)\oplus ID_w(x_w(h), q_w(h))$, and $Q_1(h)$ has value $ID_1(x_1(h), q_1(h))$. Then, T_1 that receives $\{\underline{M}, Q_1(h), Q_2(h), ---, Q_N(h)\}$ retrieves CP constructor $x_1(h)$ and TV constructor $q_1(h)$ from its CP table based on CP identifier $ID_1(x_1(h), q_1(h))$ in $Q_1(h)$, calculates $x_1(h)\oplus\underline{M}$ and $q_{1w}(h)\oplus Q_w(h)$ for each w as new values of $\underline{M}$ and $Q_w(h)$. Therefore, $\underline{M}$ and $Q_w(h)$ become $\underline{M} = x_1(h)\oplus(x_1(h)\oplus x_2(h)\oplus --- \oplus x_N(h)\oplus M) = x_2(h)\oplus x_3(h)\oplus --- \oplus x_N(h)\oplus M$ and $Q_w(h) = q_{1w}(h)\oplus(q_{1w}(h)\oplus q_{2w}(h)\oplus --- \oplus q_{(w-1)w}(h)\oplus ID_w(x_w(h), q_w(h))) = q_{2w}(h)\oplus q_{3w}(h)\oplus --- \oplus q_{(w-1)w}(h)\oplus ID_w(x_w(h), q_w(h))$. After that, T_1 removes $Q_1(h)$ from the tag part, waits for the predefined number of message arrivals, and shuffles them to forward each result $\{\underline{M}, Q_2(h), Q_3(h), ---, Q_N(h)\}$ to server T_2 next to it.

All servers in the anonymous channel carry out the same operations, namely, T_j converts its incoming message $\{x_j(h)\oplus x_{j+1}(h)\oplus --- \oplus x_N(h)\oplus M, Q_j(h), ---, Q_N(h)\}$ to $\{x_{j+1}(h)\oplus x_{j+2}(h)\oplus --- \oplus x_N(h)\oplus M, Q_{j+1}(h), ---, Q_N(h)\}$, where each $Q_w(h)$ is converted from $q_{jw}(h)\oplus --- \oplus q_{(w-1)w}(h)\oplus ID_w(x_w(h), q_w(h))$ to $q_{(j+1)w}(h)\oplus --- \oplus q_{(w-1)w}(h)\oplus ID_w(x_w(h), q_w(h))$. Consequently when T_N, the last server in the anonymous channel, completes its operations on the message, it is converted into M, and T_N can deliver M to its receiver while extracting the address of the receiver from it.

Performance of ESEBM

The above CP generator and the anonymous channel protect identities of message senders from various threats as follows. Firstly, it is impossible for entities including servers except sender S itself to identify the sender of massage $\{\underline{M}, Q_1(h), ---, Q_N(h)\}$ by tracing message parts of individual messages unless all servers conspire. Each server T_j transforms the message part while XORing it by its CP constructor $x_j(h)$, however, anyone except T_j does not know $x_j(h)$ and also T_j assigns different values as CP constructors for transferring different messages. Therefore when T_j shuffles its receiving messages, no one except T_j itself can identify the input and output message pairs of T_j by comparing the message parts of its inputs and outputs.

Figure 10. Behavior of anonymous channel

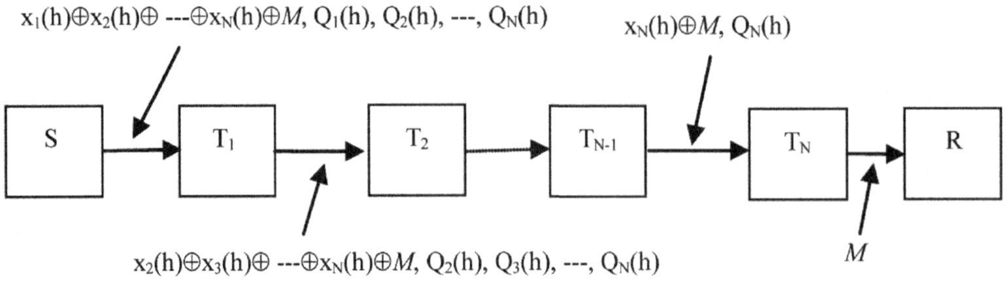

In the same way, any entity other than S cannot trace {M, Q1(h), ---, QN(h)} by examining tag parts of input and output messages of individual servers either. Each Tj assigns different bit strings to individual elements {qj(j+1)(h), ---, qjN(h)} in its TV constructor qj(h), as a consequence, Tj changes individual tags in different ways, and entities other than Tj cannot extract any fixed relation between transitions of different tags in a tag vector to identify correspondences between input and output messages of Tj. For example, there is no fixed relation between transitions from qjv(h)⊕--- ⊕q(v-1)v(h)⊕IDv(xv(h), qv(h)) to q(j+1)v(h)⊕ --- ⊕q(v-1)v(h)⊕IDv(xv(h), qv(h)) and from qjw(h)⊕ --- ⊕q(w-1)w(h)⊕IDw(xw(h), qw(h)) to q(j+1)w(h)⊕ --- ⊕q(w-1)w(h)⊕IDw(xw(h), qw(h)). Although, each server T_j^* in 1st group if the CP generator can know sender S from its CP identifier, because T_j^* is placed at the early position of the anonymous channel, its CP identifiers disappear in the later positions, i.e. the tag parts of {*M*, Q_q(h), ---, Q_N(h)} that is received by server T_q at the later position of the anonymous channel does not include CP identifier of any server in the 1st group, therefore even server T_{j*} conspires with servers at the later positions, it is not possible to identify S. Then, ESEBM successfully conceals identities of message senders as usual Mix-nets do.

As a drawback of ESEBM, a sender must obtain a CP from the CP generator in advance to send its every message. However, by dividing the network into the CP generator and the anonymous channel parts, every time-consuming task can be removed from the anonymous channel part and highly efficient communication becomes possible. Actually it is reported that the throughput of ESEBM can be maintained at more than 25% of usual non-anonymous networks, different from Mix-net, of which throughput is less than 0.7% of non-anonymous networks. This is the substantial advantage of ESEBM over usual Mix-nets, i.e. it can conceal message senders while maintaining the communication efficiency. Also different from Mix-net in which senders must designate their encryption keys to anonymously receive reply messages, in ESEBM, senders can receive reply messages without any additional mechanism as discussed in the next sub. Namely, the complete symmetric feature of onetime pad enables servers to handle original and reply messages in totally the same way. Therefore, servers do not need to carry out additional operations to reply messages on the one hand, and on the other hand, message senders can conceal even the facts that they are receiving reply messages.

Another possible advantage of ESEBM consists of the CP generator and the anonymous channel is the capability of handling forged and/or spam messages. Because message senders are not known, anonymous networks are more vulnerable to forged and spam messages, e.g. in anonymous networks, it is more difficult for receivers to decide whether their receiving messages are the ones sent from their expecting senders or not than in usual networks, also it is easier for anonymous entities to send spam messages. When compared with Mix-net, in which any entity can send meaningful messages while encrypting them by publicly known keys, ESEBM, in which only entities that have consistent CPs can send meaningful messages, is more advantageous. Namely, when an entity X modifies message *M* that is flowing in the network, the modification result is decrypted to a meaningless one because X does not know either *M* or the CP used for encrypting *M*, then, the receiver can know that its receiving message is a fake one even if *M* is from an anonymous sender. Also, when an unauthorized entity that does not have consistent CPs tries to send spam message *M'*, the 1st server in the anonymous channel can discard it because the server cannot find the CP and TV constructors designated by *M'* in its CP table; therefore servers except the 1st one can continue their operations without being disturbed by *M'*. The overheads of the 1st server caused by spam messages also can be reduced when different messages use different servers as 1st servers in anonymous channels, i.e. computa-

Figure 11 Mechanism for reply messages in ESEBM

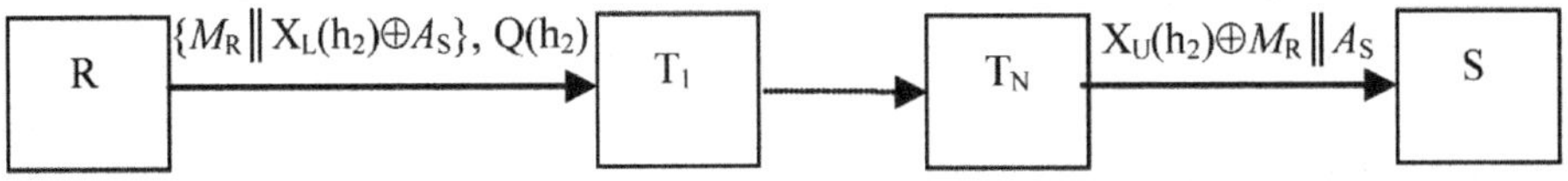

tion load for discarding invalid messages can be distributed over different servers, although tag finding processes of individual servers become complicated.

Reply Messages in ESEBM

In ESEBM senders can efficiently and securely receive reply messages without disclosing their identities as follows. Firstly, sender S obtains 2 CP and TV pairs $\{X(h_1), Q(h_1)\}$, $\{X(h_2), Q(h_2)\}$, and constructs its message while attaching its encrypted address A_S and tag concealing vector $Q(h_2)$ to its sending message *M*. Namely, S calculates $M\|X_L(h_2)\oplus A_S\|Q(h_2)\|A_R$, concatenation of *M*, $X_L(h_2)\oplus A_S$, $Q(h_2)$ and receiver address A_R. Where, bit strings $X_U(h_2)$ and $X_L(h_2)$ are upper and lower bits of bit string $X(h_2)$, in other words $X(h_2) = X_U(h_2)\|X_L(h_2)$. Also, it is assumed that an address of a message receiver is attached at the lowest part of the message as a bit string of the same length as $X_L(h_2)$. Then, S encrypts $M\|X_L(h_2)\oplus A_S\|Q(h_2)\|A_R$ to $\{X(h_1)\oplus(M\|X_L(h_2)\oplus A_S\|Q(h_2)\|A_R), Q(h_1)\}$ and sends it to the 1st server T_1 in the anonymous channel. Therefore, as the decryption result of all servers in the anonymous channel, receiver R receives $M\|X_L(h_2)\oplus A_S\|Q(h_2)\|A_R$, and it can extract message *M*, encrypted address $X_L(h_2)\oplus A_S$ of S and tag concealing vector $Q(h_2)$ to construct its reply message as $\{M_R\|X_L(h_2)\oplus A_S, Q(h_2)\}$. After that, servers in the anonymous channel decrypt (encrypt) $\{M_R\|X_L(h_2)\oplus A_S, Q(h_2)\}$ to $\{X_U(h_2)\oplus M_R\|X_L(h_2)\oplus X_L(h_2)\oplus A_S\} = \{X_U(h_2)\oplus M_R\|A_S\}$, and the last server extracts A_S from it and delivers $X_U(h_2)\oplus M_R$ to S. Therefore, S that knows $X_U(h_2)$ can decrypt $X_U(h_2)\oplus M_R$ to $X_U(h_2)\oplus X_U(h_2)\oplus M_R = M_R$ as shown in Figure 11.

In the above, R receives $M\|X_L(h_2)\oplus A_S\|Q(h_2)\|A_R$ and $X_L(h_2)$ is known only to S, therefore anyone including R cannot know A_S from the original message sent by S. Also, message $\{M_R\|X_L(h_2)\oplus A_S, Q(h_2)\}$ is transformed to $X_U(h_2)\oplus M_R\|A_S$ in the anonymous channel based on CP and TV constructors included in $Q(h_2)$ and each server knows only its CP and TV constructors in $Q(h_2)$, namely, no one except S can know that the message that S had received is reply message $\{M_R\|X_L(h_2)\oplus A_S, Q(h_2)\}$ sent by R. Here it must be noted that servers in ESEBM handle original and reply messages totally in the same way, different from usual Mix-nets where original and reply messages are treated differently. This is a significant advantage of ESEBM, i.e. message reply functions can be implemented without adding any extra mechanism to individual servers, and this means that no one except sender S can know even whether S is receiving messages initiated by others or it is receiving replies to the messages initiated by S itself.

Also it is easy to protect ESEBM from traffic analysis attacks. In ESEBM every message must have different CPs and TVs, and this means that every server deletes CP and TV constructors in its CP table once they are used. Therefore, provided that at least one of the servers is honest, even when R sends multiple replies only one of them is delivered to S, and R cannot identify S. In the same way, ESEBM disables entities to carry out replay attacks. In addition, if each server T_j maintains triple $\{x_j(h), Q_j(h), F(h)\}$ instead of CP and TV constructor pair $\{x_j(h), Q_j(h)\}$ in its CP table, it can deliver (reply) messages accompanied by $\{x_j(h), Q_j(h), F(h)\}$ up to F(h)-times when a mechanism to delete $\{x_j(h), Q_j(h), F(h)\}$ from its CP table after it had received F(h)-messages accompanied by $\{x_j(h), Q_j(h), F(h)\}$ is added. Namely, provided that at least one of the servers is honest, as same as spam messages in the previous sub, (reply) messages accompanied by Q(h) do not reach the destination more than F(h) times.

ONION ROUTING

A drawback of anonymous communication mechanisms based on the sequential encryption type hidden message approach, in which individual servers must wait for arrivals of a number of messages, can be removed by combining them with the hidden route approach. Onion Routing that consists of multiple relay servers called onion routers is an example (Reed, 1998, Dingledine, 2004).

In Onion Routing, to send message M to receiver R, firstly sender S defines a path $\{T_1, T_2, ---, T_N\}$ consists of a sequence of onion routers, and repeatedly encrypts the route with M by $k_1, k_2, ---, k_N$, public encryption keys of $\{T_1, T_2, ---, T_N\}$. As a consequence message M and its destination R are encrypted to $E(k_1, T_2 \| E(k_2, T_3 \| --- E(k_{N-1}, T_N \| E(k_N, M \| R)) ---))$ that is called onion, and S sends the onion to the 1st onion router T_1. Then, T_1 that receives the onion can know that T_2 is the onion router, to which M should be transferred, by decrypting the onion to $T_2 \| E(k_2, T_3 \| --- E(k_{N-1}, T_N \| E(k_N, M \| R)) ---)$ by its secret decryption key k_1^{-1}, and T_1 transfers the decrypted onion $E(k_2, T_3 \| --- E(k_{N-1}, T_N \| E(k_N, M \| R)) ---)$ to T_2. T_2, ---, T_N behave in the same way, i.e. T_j that receives onion $E(k_j, T_{j+1} \| --- E(k_{N-1}, T_N \| E(k_N, M \| R)) ---)$ from T_{j-1} decrypts it to $T_{j+1} \| E(k_{j+1}, T_{j+2} \| --- E(k_{N-1}, T_N \| E(k_N, M \| R))$ by its decryption key k_j^{-1} and sends $E(k_{j+1}, T_{j+2} \| --- E(k_{N-1}, T_N \| E(k_N, M \| R)) ---)$ to T_{j+1}. Therefore, finally T_N can extract message M and its destination R by decrypting $E(k_N, M \| R)$ to $M \| R$ by its decryption key k_N^{-1} to deliver M to R. Here, because each T_j knows only the onion routers next to it, i.e. T_{j-1} and T_{j+1}, and anyone except T_j and sender S cannot know the correspondences between input and output onions of T_j, no one except S can identify S as the sender of message M unless all onion routers conspire.

Then, as an advantage of Onion Routing over Mix-net and ESEBM, each server (onion router) in Onion Routing does not need to wait for arrivals of many messages (onions) before forwarding them to its neighbours. It is also possible to implement reply mechanisms in Onion Routing. However, it must be noted that T_j still must wait for arrivals of several onions although the number of them is small. When T_j forwards onions in the order that it had received them, entities can trace onions from their senders to their receivers by observing inputs and outputs of every onion router. Also, Onion Routing shares the same disadvantage with Mix-net, i.e. because it uses asymmetric key encryption functions it is difficult to maintain throughput of communication channels high.

RECEIVER AND MUTUALLY ANONYMOUS COMMUNICATION

Receiver and mutually anonymous communication channels can be implemented by exploiting the mechanisms for reply messages. Namely, when entity P discloses $E(k_*, A_P)$, its address repeatedly encrypted by a sequence of servers, in the interest list in BBs with other relating information as shown in Figure 12, any entity W that has the same interests as P can send its message to P even if it does not know P. Figure 12 corresponds to a case where ESEBM is used. In the figure, $E(k_*, A_P) = X_L(h) \oplus A_P$, address of P encrypted by bit string $X_L(h)$, in the interest list is accompanied by tag vector Q(h) as the relating information, where, $X(h) = \{X_U(h) \| X_L(h)\}$

Figure 12. Receiver anonymous communication channel

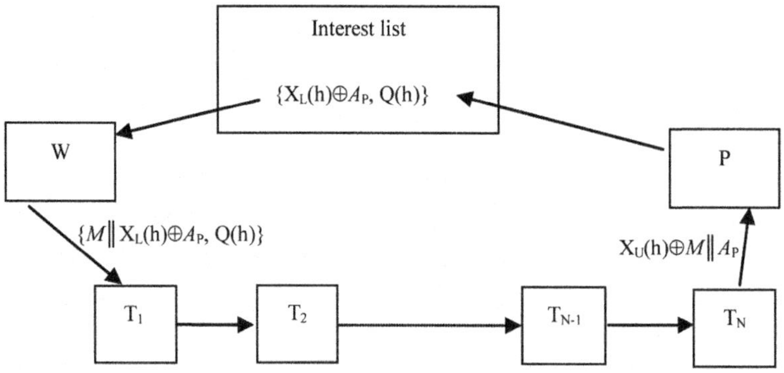

is the concealing pattern corresponding to Q(h) (P must put $\{X_L(h)\oplus A_P, Q(h)\}$ in the interest list thorough an anonymous channel of course). Then, W firstly finds encrypted address $X_L(h)\oplus A_P$ and tag vector Q(h) in the BB, constructs its message as $\{M\|X_L(h)\oplus A_P, Q(h)\}$ and sends it to the 1st server. As a consequence, anonymous network delivers M to P while decrypting (encrypting) $M\|X_L(h)\oplus A_P$ to $\{X_U(h)\oplus M\|X_L(h)\oplus X_L(h)\oplus A_P\}$ $=\{X_U(h)\oplus M\|A_P\}$. Here, W knows only encrypted address $X_L(h)\oplus A_P$ and Q(h), therefore it cannot know receiver P. W cannot identify P by the message that is received by P either, because P receives $X_U(h)\oplus M$, the encrypted form of M.

A mutually anonymous communication channel in which both the sender and the receiver of message M can conceal their identities can be constructed by encrypting message M by 2 concealing pattern and tag vector pairs {X(h), Q(h)} and {X(w), Q(w)}, where {X(h), Q(h)} corresponds to encrypted address and tag vector pair $\{X_L(h)\oplus A_P, Q(h)\}$ disclosed in the BB by anonymous receiver P, and anonymous sender W obtains {X(w), Q(w)} from the CP generator by itself. Namely, W sends its message M in the form $\{X(w)\oplus(M\|Q(h)\|X_L(h)\oplus A_P\|T_1), Q(w)\}$, and the anonymous channel decrypts it to $M\|Q(h)\|X_L(h)\oplus A_P\|T_1$. Therefore the decryption result is transferred to the 1st server T_1 in the anonymous channel, and T_1 constructs message $\{M\|X_L(h)\oplus A_P, Q(h)\}$ to be decrypted (encrypted) to $\{X_U(h)\oplus M\|X_L(h)\oplus X_L(h)\oplus A_P\}$ = $\{X_U(h)\oplus M\|A_P\}$. Then, T_N can deliver it to P and P that knows $X_U(h)$ can decrypt $X_U(h)\oplus M$ to M. In the above, no one except P can know receiver P as just discussed in the receiver anonymous channel. Also because W encrypts M to $X(w)\oplus(M\|Q(h)\|X_L(h)\oplus A_P\|T_1)$ by its secret concealing pattern X(w), even P that knows M cannot identify W from M either.

Receiver anonymous and mutually anonymous communication channels can be constructed in the same way also by Mix-net and Onion Routing.

CONCLUSION

Typical anonymous communication mechanisms had been discussed; they are Crowds, DC-net, Mix-net, ESEBM and Onion Routing. Crowds is practical because it does not include any encryption or decryption process and its throughput is comparable with that of usual non-anonymous communication channels. However, theoretically entities can identify senders of messages by tracing messages flowing in the channels; therefore it cannot be used for sensitive applications such as electronic voting systems. DC-net is a complete solution but it is not practical, it requires large overheads and moreover multiple senders must behave synchronously to send their individual messages. As a consequence, the remaining 3 mechanisms, i.e. Mix-net, ESEBM and Onion Routing are considered as solutions both practical and secure, and among them ESEBM achieves the highest throughput.

Future works include the establishments of more secure and robust anonymous communication mechanisms. About the security, mechanisms that identify dishonest servers or that prove honest behaviors of servers are desirable to make anonymous communications be accepted in more sensitive applications. Zero knowledge proof is a one solution, but this solution is not realistic because of its large overheads. Anonymous tags explained in the previous chapter can achieve this without much overhead, i.e. message senders or receivers can trace their messages by examining anonymous tags attached to them without knowing secret keys of individual servers; however, they cannot be used for mutually anonymous communication. Namely, a sender or a receiver of message *M* that had defined the anonymous tags attached to *M* can trace *M* in the network by examining tags and consequently can identify the receiver or the sender of *M*. This problem will be discussed more as the conclusion of "Object Delivering and Monitoring Systems" in Part-III. Also to make anonymous communications more stable, mechanisms that enable communication systems to continue their operations even when several servers are out of services must be established. One of easy solutions is to duplicate individual servers.

REFERENCES

Anderson, R. (2001). *Security engineering - A guide to building dependable distributed systems*. John Wiley & Sons.

Chaum, D. (1981). Untraceable electronic mail, return address and digital pseudonyms. *Communications of the ACM, 24*(2), 84–90. doi:10.1145/358549.358563

Chaum, D. (1988). The dining cryptographers problem: Unconditional sender and recipient untraceability. *Journal of Cryptology, 1*, 65–75. doi:10.1007/BF00206326

Dingledine, R., & Mathewson, N. (2004). Tor: The second-generation onion router. *Proceedings of the 13th USENIX Security Symposium*, (pp. 303-320).

Golle, P., & Jakobsson, M. (2003). Reusable anonymous return channels. *Proceedings of the 2003 ACM Workshop on Privacy in the Electronic Society, WPES '03*, (pp. 94-100). ACM.

Haddad, H., Tamura, S., Taniguchi, S., & Yanase, T. (2011). Development of anonymous networks based on symmetric key encryptions. *Journal of Networks, 6*(11), 1533–1542. doi:10.4304/jnw.6.11.1533-1542

Ingledine, R., Freedman, M. J., Hopwood, D., & Molnar, D. (2001). A reputation system to increase MIX-net reliability. *Proceedings of the 4th International Workshop on Information Hiding, LNCS 2137*, (pp. 126-141). Springer-Verlag.

Reed, M. G., Syverson, P. F., & Goldschlag, D. M. (1998). Anonymous connections and onion routing. *Selected Areas in Communications, 16*(4), 482–494. doi:10.1109/49.668972

Reiter, K., & Rubin, A. D. (1998). Crowds: Anonymity for web transactions. *ACM Transactions on Information and System Security, 1*(1), 66–92. doi:10.1145/290163.290168

Chapter 8
Anonymous Statistics Calculation

ABSTRACT

This chapter introduces schemes for anonymous statistics calculations, in which an entity or a set of entities calculate functions of data owned by other entities without knowing their values. Although schemes that can be applied to calculate general functions exist, they are not practical enough, therefore schemes applicable only to limited number of functions, e.g. averages, variances, auto-, and cross-correlations are discussed. They are blind sum/product calculation schemes, partial computation based multi party computation schemes, and re-encryption based multi party computation schemes.

INTRODUCTION

Let us consider a case where entity S calculates the average of salaries of persons P_1, P_2, ---, P_N. In this case, usually salaries of persons are their secrets and they do not want to disclose them to others. Therefore mechanisms, which enable S to calculate the average of salaries without knowing those of individual persons, are necessary. Theoretically, there are protocols that enable N entities Q_1, Q_2, ---, Q_N to jointly calculate any function $f(x_1, x_2, ---, x_N)$ while maintaining values of x_1, x_2, ---, x_N as secrets of their owners Q_1, Q_2, ---, Q_N (Goldreich, 1987, Yao, 1986). Then, entity S in the above case, can know the average of salaries while preserving privacies of P_1, P_2, ---, P_N, by asking each P_j to carry out these protocols. However, these protocols are complicated and as a consequence cannot be used in real applications. Although efficient protocols exist, they are applicable only when $f(x_1, x_2, ---, x_N)$ is a Boolean expression (Naor, 1999). As practical schemes, this chapter discusses mechanisms based on encryption functions with the homomorphic property. But it must be noted that they are efficient only for limited kind of anonymous statistics calculations.

In the following, the above requirement is satisfied through 3 ways. The 1st way is the blind sum/product calculation scheme, the simplest one. There are 2 entities P and Q, where P encrypts its data x_1, x_2, ---, x_N to $E(k_P, x_1)$, $E(k_P, x_2)$, ---, $E(k_P, x_N)$ by its encryption key k_P, and Q calculates $f(E(k_P, x_1), E(k_P, x_2), ---, E(k_P, x_N))$ to be decrypted to $f(x_1, x_2, ---, x_N)$ by P that knows decryption key k_P^{-1}. Then, P can calculate $f(x_1, x_2, ---, x_N)$ without

DOI: 10.4018/978-1-4666-1649-3.ch008

disclosing its owning data, and on the other hand, Q can conceal function f. Here, function $f(x_1, x_2, ---, x_N)$ must have the specific forms, e.g. $f(x_1, x_2, ---, x_N) = x_1+x_2+ --- +x_N$, $f(x_1, x_2, ---, x_N) = x_1x_2 --- x_N$, etc. of course.

The 2nd and the 3rd ones are general multi party computation schemes, where multiple entities $P_1, P_2, ---, P_N$ jointly calculate $f(x_1, x_2, ---, x_N)$ while maintaining the secrets of their owning values $x_1, x_2, ---, x_N$. In the 2nd way, each entity P_j that owns x_j (j = 1, 2, ---, N) divides $E(k_C, x_j)$ (here, encrypted form $E(k_C, x_j)$ calculated based on publicly known key k_C is a representation of x_j) into H-parts $E(k_C, x_j)_1$, $E(k_C, x_j)_2$, ---, $E(k_C, x_j)_H$ so that no one can know x_j without knowing all H-parts and anyone that knows k_C can reconstruct x_j when it knows all H-parts, and distributes individual parts $E(k_C, x_j)_1, E(k_C, x_j)_2, ---, E(k_C, x_j)_H$ to H-entities $Q_{w1}, Q_{w2}, ---, Q_{wH}$ selected from $Q_1, Q_2, ---, Q_N$, respectively. Then, each Q_{wh} calculates $f(E(k_C, x_1)_h, E(k_C, x_2)_h, ---, E(k_C, x_N)_h)$, and finally, coordinating entity C gathers calculation results of $Q_{w1}, Q_{w2}, ---, Q_{wH}$ to calculate $f(E(k_C, x_1), E(k_C, x_2), ---, E(k_C, x_N))$, and from that $f(x_1, x_2, ---, x_N)$ is reconstructed, where it is assumed that relation $E(k_C, f(x_1, x_2, ---, x_N)) = f(E(k_C, x_1), E(k_C, x_2), ---, E(k_C, x_N))$ is satisfied.

The 3rd way is based on re-encryption schemes, where coordinator C is constituted by multiple independent authorities $C_1, C_2, ---, C_H$, and each entity P_j in $\{P_1, P_2, ---, P_N\}$ repeatedly encrypts its owning x_j to $E(k_H, E(k_{H-1}, ----, E(k_1, x_j)---)) = E(k_*, x_j)$ by public encryption keys $k_1, k_2, ---, k_H$ of $C_1, C_2, ---, C_H$ so that no entity except P_j can know x_j unless the all authorities conspire. Then, some entity in $C_1, C_2, ---, C_H$ that is defined in advance calculates $f(E(k_*, x_1), E(k_*, x_2), ---, E(k_*, x_N))$ to be decrypted to $f(x_1, x_2, ---, x_N)$ through the collaboration among $C_1, C_2, ---, C_H$. The next section discusses the 1st mechanism, and the 2nd and the 3rd mechanisms are discussed after the next section.

BLIND SUM/PRODUCT CALCULATION SCHEME

Let P and Q be entities that owns data $x_1, x_2, ---, x_N$ and that knows function f, respectively, and P and Q must jointly calculate the value of $f(x_1, x_2, ---, x_N)$. However $x_1, x_2, ---, x_N$ are secrets of P, and f is the secret of Q, therefore P must ask Q to calculate $f(x_1, x_2, ---, x_N)$ without informing Q of exact values of $x_1, x_2, ---, x_N$. When function f has specific forms, homomorphic encryption functions enable P and Q to calculate $f(x_1, x_2, ---, x_N)$ while maintaining the confidentiality of data $x_1, x_2, ---, x_N$ and function f as shown in Figure1.

In the figure, P encrypts its data $x_1, x_2, ---, x_N$ to $E(k_P, x_1), E(k_P, x_2), ---, E(k_P, x_N)$ by its encryption key k_P, asks Q to calculate $f(E(k_P, x_1), E(k_P, x_2), ---, E(k_P, x_N))$, and finally decrypts $f(E(k_P, x_1), E(k_P, x_2), ---, E(k_P, x_N))$ calculated by Q to $f(x_1, x_2, ---, x_N)$ by its decryption key k_P^{-1}. Here, when $f(x_1, x_2, ---, x_N) = x_1x_2 --- x_N$ or $f(x_1, x_2, ---, x_N) = x_1+x_2+ --- +x_N$, $f(E(k_P, x_1), E(k_P, x_2), ---, E(k_P, x_N))$ can be successfully decrypted to $x_1x_2 --- x_N$ or $x_1+x_2+ --- +x_N$, provided that encryption function $E(k_P, x)$ is multiplicative or additive, respectively. Then, P can calculate $f(x_1, x_2, ---, x_N)$ while concealing $x_1, x_2, ---, x_N$ from Q because k_P^{-1} is known only to P, at the same time, Q does not need to disclose f to others because it calculates $f(E(k_P, x_1), E(k_P, x_2), ---, E(k_P, x_N))$ by itself.

Although the situation was somewhat different, the above mechanism had been used already in section "Implicit Transaction Links" to calculate sums of ITLs, i.e. by using an additive encryption function, entity S evaluated the sum of ITLs of other entity C without knowing individual ITLs by decrypting the sum of encrypted ITLs calculated by C itself. However, different from the case where entity S in that section must have used the same encryption key for encrypting ITLs of many entities and also during relatively long

Figure 1. Blind sum/product calculation

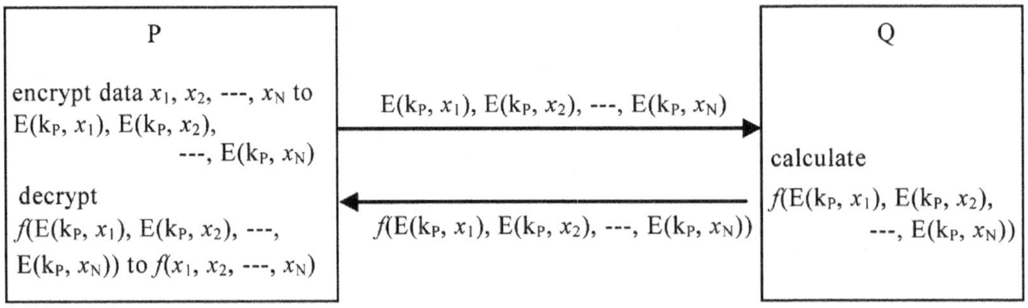

period, entity P in this chapter can change its encryption key at every calculation. Therefore, protecting data x_1, x_2, ---, x_N from their disclosures is not a serious issue, and as a consequence even linear equation based encryption functions that are weak against plain text attacks can be used without deliberated devices discussed in section "Linear Equation based Encryption Functions," such as ones for adding secret random terms, for inserting dummy encrypted items or for splitting encrypted values over multiple terms. Regardless that base encryption functions are multiplicative or additive, the above scheme can be extended to mechanisms to calculate polynomial function $f(x_1, x_2, ---, x_N)$, e.g. $f(x_1, x_2, x_3) = x_1^3 + x_2x_3 + x_1^2x_2x_3^3$ as shown in the following subsections.

Additive Encryption Function

Additive encryption function E(k, x) satisfies relation E(k, x) + E(k, y) = E(k, x+y), therefore it is straightforward for entity P to ask entity Q to calculate function $f(x_1, x_2, ---, x_N) = x_1+x_2+ --- +x_N$, the sum of its owning data x_1, x_2, ---, x_N, without disclosing individual data to Q and also without knowing function f, i.e. P can calculate $f(x_1, x_2, ---, x_N) = x_1+x_2+ --- +x_N$ by decrypting E(k, $x_1+x_2+ --- +x_N$) = E(k, x_1)+E(k, x_2)+ --- +E(k, x_N) which is calculated by Q. Here, even when E(k, x) is implemented as a linear equation based encryption function, P can disclose the calculation results to Q while maintaining the confidentiality of individual x_1, x_2, ---, x_N without complicated mechanisms for protecting bit strings from plain text attacks, provided that P frequently changes its secret encryption key k (Tamura, 2007).

By using linear equation based encryption function E(k, x), P also can ask Q to multiply x_1 by x_2 without disclosing them. Let E($\underline{k}$, x) be another encryption function that transforms x to vector {x(1), x(2), ---, x(z)}, where among z-elements, (z-m)-elements x(h_1), x(h_2), ---, x(h_{z-m}) are dummy ones and their values are defined arbitrarily as secrets of P, on the other hand, the remaining m-elements {x(j_1), x(j_2), ---, x(j_m)} are real ones and their values are defined also as secrets of P in the way that relation x(j_1)+x(j_2)+ --- +x(j_m) = x holds. Under these settings, P informs Q of x_1 and x_2 in their encrypted forms E(k, x_1) and E($\underline{k}$, x_2) = {x_2(1), x_2(2), ---, x_2(z)}, and Q calculates a set of vectors {x_2(1)E(k, x_1), x_2(2)E(k, x_1), ---, x_2(z) E(k, x_1)}, then P can calculate x_1x_2 by decrypting E(k, x_1x_2) that is constructed as E(k, x_1x_2) = x_2(j_1) E(k, x_1) + x_2(j_2)E(k, x_1) + --- + x_2(j_m)E(k, x_1) while selecting m-real elements form {x_2(1)E(k, x_1), x_2(2)E(k, x_1), ---, x_2(z)E(k, x_1)}.

By the mechanism for calculating product x_1x_2, Q can calculate correlation functions of data series {x_1, x_2, ---, x_N} owned by P without knowing their values. For example, auto correlation function of {x_1, x_2, ---, x_N} has the form $x_px_q+x_sx_t+---$, therefore when P shows x_p, x_q, x_s, x_t in their 2-encrypted forms

{E(k, x_p), E($\underline{k}$, x_p)}, {E(k, x_q), E($\underline{k}$, x_q)}, {E(k, x_s), E($\underline{k}$, x_s)}, {E($\underline{k}$, x_t), E($\underline{k}$, x_t)}, Q can calculate vector {$x_q(1)$E(k, x_p) + $x_t(1)$E(k, x_s), $x_q(2)$E(k, x_p) + $x_t(2)$E(k, x_s), ---, $x_q(z)$E(k, x_p) + $x_t(z)$E(k, x_s)}, and from it P can construct E(k, x_px_q+x_sx_t) as $x_q(j_1)$E(k, x_p) + $x_t(j_1)$E(k, x_s) + $x_q(j_2)$E(k, x_p) + $x_t(j_2)$E(k, x_s) + --- + $x_q(j_m)$E(k, x_p) + $x_t(j_m)$E(k, x_s) to decrypt it to $x_px_q + x_sx_t$. In the same way, P can calculate also Fourier transformations of data series; however in this case P cannot disclose the exact results to others because the inverse transformation reveals the original date series.

In the above, encryption function E($\underline{k}$, x) is apparently additive, but when encrypted form of E($\underline{k}$, x) is extended from vector {x(1), x(2), ---, x(z)} to n-dimensional array {x(i_1, i_2, ---, i_n)}, E($\underline{k}$, x) becomes also multiplicative. Therefore, entities P and Q can carry out the above protocol by using only encryption function E($\underline{k}$, x) without using E(k, x). However, E($\underline{k}$, x) includes number of dummy elements and requires additional calculations. On the other hand E(k, x) can be used securely without dummy elements as mentioned just above, and a number of unnecessary operations can be removed when E(k, x) is used.

Here, encrypted form E($\underline{k}$, x) = {x(1), x(2), ---, x(z)} can be extended to 2-dimensional array {x(1, 1), x(1, 2), ---, x(1, z), x(2, 1), x(2, 2), ---, x(2, z), ---, x(z, 1), x(z, 2), ---, x(z, z)}, by distributing the value of each real element x(j_p) to elements {x(j_p, j_1), x(j_p, j_2), ---, x(j_p, j_m)} in the 2-dimensional array. Namely, element x(u, v) of the 2-dimensional array is defined as a real one when u and v coincide with j_p and j_q for some pair (p, q), on the other hand x(u, v) is defined as a dummy element when at least one of u and v coincides with h_p for some p. Of course values of real elements are defined so that relation x = {x(j_1, j_1)+x(j_1, j_2)+ --- +x(j_1, j_m)} + {x(j_2, j_1)+x(j_2, j_2)+ --- +x(j_2, j_m)} + --- + {x(j_m, j_1)+x(j_m, j_2)+ --- +x(j_m, j_m)} holds, therefore, as same as vector {x(1), x(2), ---, x(z)}, 2-dimensional array {x(i_1, i_2)} is successfully decrypted to x. In the same way encrypted form E($\underline{k}$, x) can be extended to an n-dimensional array, and generally, when encrypted form E($\underline{k}$, x) is extended to n-dimensional array {x (i_1, i_2, ---, i_n)}, it is decrypted to x according to Equation (1),.

$$x = \sum_{i1=j1}^{i1=jm} \{\sum_{j1}^{i2=jm} \{--- \sum_{in=j1}^{in=jm} \{ x(i_1, i_2, ---, i_n)\} --- \}\} \quad (1)$$

Now, provided that r < n, let {x_*(i_1, i_2, ---, i_n)} be an n-dimensional array that is constructed by embedding r-dimensional array {x(i_1, i_2, ---, i_r)} in it, namely value of {x_*(i_1, i_2, ---, i_n)} is defined so that element x_*(i_1, i_2, ---, i_r, 1, 1, ---1) has the same value as x(i_1, i_2, ---, i_r) and x_*(i_1, i_2, ---, i_r, i_{r+1}, i_{r+2}, ---, i_n) has value 0 when i_q is greater than 1 for at least one q (r < q ≤ n). Then, apparently {x(i_1, i_2, ---, i_r)} and {x_*(i_1, i_2, ---, i_n)} are decrypted to the same value, therefore, r-dimensional array {x(i_1, i_2, ---, i_r)} and n-dimensional array {x_*(i_1, i_2, ---, i_n)} in which {x(i_1, i_2, ---, i_r)} is embedded are equivalent, and addition and multiplication can be defined in a set of encrypted forms as follows. Namely, addition of r-dimensional array {x(i_1, i_2, ---, i_r)} and n-dimensional array {y(q_1, q_2, ---, q_n)} (r < n) is defined as {x(i_1, i_2, ---, i_r)}+{y(i_1, i_2, ---, i_n)} = {x_*(i_1, i_2, ---, i_n)+y(i_1, i_2, ---, i_n)}. Also, multiplication of {x(i_1, i_2, ---, i_r)} and {y(q_1, q_2, ---, q_n)} is defined as {z(i_1, i_2, ---, i_r, q_1, q_2, ---, q_n)} = {x(i_1, i_2, ---, i_r)y(q_1, q_2, ---, q_n)}. For example, product of {x_1(1), x_1(2), ---, x_1(z)}, encrypted form of x_1, and {x_2(1), x_2(2), ---, x_2(z)}, encrypted form of x_2, is 2-dimensional array {x_1(1)x_2(1), x_1(1)x_2(2), ---, x_1(1)x_2(z), x_1(2)x_2(1), x_1(2)x_2(2), ---, x_1(2)x_2(z), x_1(z)x_2(1), x_1(z)x_2(2), ---, x_1(z)x_2(z)}. Now it is apparent that addition of E($\underline{k}$, x) = {x(i_1, i_2, ---, i_r)} and E($\underline{k}$, y) = {y(i_1, i_2, ---, i_n)} and multiplication of E($\underline{k}$, x) and E($\underline{k}$, y) are decrypted to x+y and xy, respectively, namely, encryption function E($\underline{k}$, x) is both additive and multiplicative.

While exploiting the above additive and multiplicative encryption function E($\underline{k}$, x) and additive encryption function E(k, x), Q can calculate also general polynomials of {x_1, x_2, ---, x_N} owned by

P without knowing them. For example, $f(x_1, x_2, x_3) = x_1^2x_2 + x_2^3x_3$ can be calculated as follows. Firstly, P encrypts x_1, x_2 and x_3 to $\{E(k, x_1), E(\underline{k}, x_1)\}$, $\{E(k, x_2), E(\underline{k}, x_2)\}$ and $E(\underline{k}, x_3)$. Then, provided that linear equation based encryption function $E(k, x)$ encrypts x to vector $\{E(k, x)_1, E(k, x)_2, ---, E(k, x)_H\}$, Q calculates $E(\underline{k}, x_1)E(k, x_2)$ and $E(\underline{k}, x_2)^2E(\underline{k}, x_3)$ to multiply them by scalar values $E(k, x_1)_q$ and $E(k, x_2)_q$ for each q, respectively. As a consequence, Q generates sequences of 2-dimensional and 3-dimensional arrays $\{E(k, x_1)_1E(\underline{k}, x_1)E(\underline{k}, x_2), E(k, x_1)_2E(\underline{k}, x_1)E(\underline{k}, x_2), ---, E(k, x_1)_HE(\underline{k}, x_1)E(\underline{k}, x_2)\}$ and $\{E(k, x_2)_1E(\underline{k}, x_2)^2E(\underline{k}, x_3), E(k, x_2)_2E(\underline{k}, x_2)^2E(\underline{k}, x_3), ---, E(k, x_2)_HE(\underline{k}, x_2)^2E(\underline{k}, x_3)\}$ finally to calculate their sums for each element in the sequences. Therefore, P receives a sequence of 3-dimensional arrays $\{E(k, x_1)_1E(\underline{k}, x_1)E(\underline{k}, x_2)+E(k, x_2)_1E(\underline{k}, x_2)^2E(\underline{k}, x_3), E(k, x_1)_2E(\underline{k}, x_1)E(\underline{k}, x_2)+E(k, x_2)_2E(\underline{k}, x_2)^2E(\underline{k}, x_3), ---, E(k, x_1)_HE(k, x_1)E(k, x_2)+E(k, x_2)_HE(k, x_2)^2E(k, x_3)\}$, and can reconstruct $E(k, x_1^2x_2 + x_2^3x_3)$ from them to decrypt it to $x_1^2x_2 + x_2^3x_3$ by its secret decryption key k^{-1}. Of course it is possible for P to ask Q to calculate polynomials of x_1, x_2, ---, x_N by using only single encryption function $E(k, x)$.

Multiplicative Encryption Function

Both typical asymmetric key encryption algorithms RSA (Rivest, 1978) and ElGamal (Elgamal, 1985) are multiplicative, therefore by using RSA or ElGamal entity P can ask entity Q to calculate the product of its owning data without disclosing them. Namely, when P encrypts its data x_1, x_2, ---, x_N to $E(k, x_1)$, $E(k, x_2)$, ---, $E(k, x_N)$, Q can calculate $E(k, x_1x\ ---\ x_N)$ as $E(k, x_1x\ ---\ x_N) = E(k, x_1)E(k, x_2)\ ---\ E(k, x_N)$, and P can know $x_1x\ ---\ x_N$ by decrypting $E(k, x_1x\ ---\ x_N)$ by its secret decryption key k^{-1}.

RSA and ElGamal can be made also additive as in section "Asymmetric Key Encryption Algorithms" in Section 1. For an appropriate constant integer B, $B^{x+y}{}_{\mathrm{mod\,p}}$ is represented as the multiplication of 2 numbers $B^{x}{}_{\mathrm{mod\,p}}$ and $B^{y}{}_{\mathrm{mod\,p}}$ i.e. $B^{x+y}{}_{\mathrm{mod\,p}} = B^{x}{}_{\mathrm{mod\,p}}B^{y}{}_{\mathrm{mod\,p}}$ (where, p is the base of modulo arithmetic used by encryption function $E(k, x)$), and the product of encrypted forms of B^x and B^y is decrypted to B^{x+y}. In other words, when $E(k, B^x)$ is considered as encryption function $E(k', x)$, product of encrypted forms $E(k', x)$ and $E(k', y)$ is decrypted to $(x+y)$, therefore, P can ask Q also to calculate the sum of x_1, x_2, ---, x_N without disclosing them.

By combining encryption function $E(k', x)$ and additive and multiplicative encryption function $E(k, x)$ defined in the previous subsection, P and Q can calculate general polynomials of $\{x_1, x_2, ---, x_N\}$ in the same way. To jointly calculate polynomial $f(x_1, x_2, x_3) = x_1x_2 + x_2x_3$ firstly, P encrypts x_1, x_2 and x_3 to $E(k, B^{x1}) = B^{k(x1)}$ and $E(k, x_1) = \{x_1(1), x_1(2), ---, x_1(z)\}$, $E(k, B^{x2}) = B^{k(x2)}$ and $E(k, x_2) = \{x_2(1), x_2(2), ---, x_2(z)\}$, and $E(k, B^{x3}) = B^{k(x3)}$ and $E(k, x_3) = \{x_3(1), x_3(2), ---, x_3(z)\}$. Then, Q calculates encrypted forms of x_1x_2 and x_2x_3 as $\{(B^{k(x1)})^{x2(1)}, (B^{k(x1)})^{x2(2)}, ---, (B^{k(x1)})^{x2(z)}\}$ and $\{(B^{k(x2)})^{x3(1)}, (B^{k(x2)})^{x3(2)}, ---, (B^{k(x2)})^{x3(z)}\}$, respectively, and calculates the product $\{B^{k(x1)x2(1)}B^{k(x2)x3(1)}, B^{k(x1)x2(2)}B^{k(x2)x3(2)}, ---, B^{k(x1)x2(z)}B^{k(x2)x3(z)}\} = \{B^{k(x1)x2(1)+k(x2)x3(1)}, B^{k(x1)x2(2)+k(x2)x3(2)}, ---, B^{k(x1)x2(z)+k(x2)x3(z)}\}$ as the encrypted form of $x_1x_2 + x_2x_3$. Then, finally P calculates the product of real elements as $B^{k(x1)\{x2(j1)+x2(j2)+---+x2(jm)\}+k(x2)\{x3(j1)+x3(i2)+---+x3(jm)\}} = B^{k\{(x1)(x2)+(x2)(x3)\}}$, and decrypts it to $B^{\{(x1)(x2)+(x2)(x3)\}}$ by its decryption key k^{-1} to convert it to $x_1x_2 + x_2x_3$. In the above, $x(j_1)$, $x(j_2)$, ---, $x(j_m)$ are real elements of encrypted form $E(\underline{k}, x)$.

The advantage of the mechanism based on multiplicative encryption functions over the ones based on additive encryption functions discussed in the previous subsection is that they are more secure. Because both RSA and ElGamal are not weak against plain text attacks, the above scheme is effective even in cases where P uses a same encryption key for different calculations, however, in cases where P can frequently change its encryption keys, this advantage is not so worthwhile. A disadvantage is mechanisms become complicated when numbers are not limited to integers.

Figure 2. Multi party computation scheme

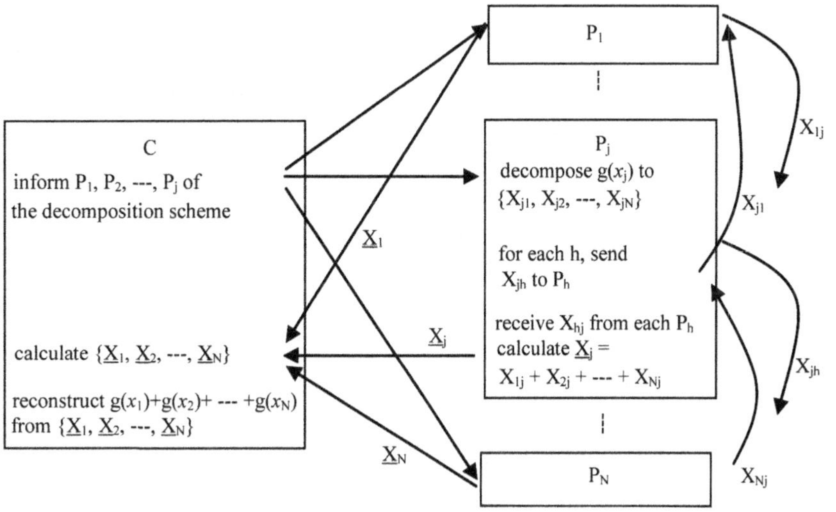

MULTI PARTY COMPUTATIONS

This section discusses mechanisms that enable multiple entities P_1, P_2, ---, P_N to jointly calculate aggregated values of x_1, x_2, ---, x_N, where each x_j is owned by P_j and must be concealed from any entity other than P_j itself. In the previous section, entity P and Q jointly calculate functions of x_1, x_2, ---, x_N owned by single entity P while maintaining them as P's secrets, namely P knows all x_1, x_2, ---, x_N. In this section each entity knows only a part of them.

Partial Computation Based Mechanism

Let us assume that coordinator C calculates $f(x_1, x_2, ---, x_N)$, a function of data x_1, x_2, ---, x_N provided by entities P_1, P_2, ---, P_N, where each x_j is the secret of P_j, therefore C must calculate $x = f(x_1, x_2, ---, x_N)$ while disabling any entity except P_j itself to know x_j. When $f(x_1, x_2, ---, x_N)$ has the form $x = g(x_1)+g(x_2)+ --- +g(x_N)$ or $x = g(x_1)g(x_2) --- g(x_N)$, this requirement can be satisfied as shown in Figure 2 (in the figure $f(x_1, x_2, ---, x_N)$ has the form $g(x_1)+g(x_2)+ --- +g(x_N)$).

Namely, each entity P_j represents $g(x_j)$ as vector $\{X_{j1}, X_{j2}, ---, X_{jN}\}$, and discloses each element X_{jh} to only P_h so that P_h can calculate $\underline{X}_h = (X_{1h}+X_{2h}+ --- +X_{Nh})$ (it is assumed that representation $\{X_{j1}, X_{j2}, ---, X_{jN}\}$ is additive, i.e. $\{X_{j1}+X_{h1}, X_{j2}+X_{h2}, ---, X_{jN}+X_{hN}\}$ represents $g(x_j)+g(x_h)$ when $\{X_{j1}, X_{j2}, ---, X_{jN}\}$ and $\{X_{h1}, X_{h2}, ---, X_{hN}\}$ represent $g(x_j)$ and $g(x_h)$, respectively). Here, $\{Y_1, Y_2, ---, Y_N\}$ is called the minimum representation of y if y can be reconstructed from it but no one can calculate y when any of $\{Y_1, Y_2, ---, Y_N\}$ is missing. Then, if each $\{X_{j1}, X_{j2}, ---, X_{jN}\}$ in the above is the minimum representation of $g(x_j)$, C can know $x = g(x_1)+g(x_2)+ --- +g(x_N)$ from $\{\underline{X}_1, \underline{X}_2, ---, \underline{X}_N\}$ that are calculated by P_1, P_2, ---, P_N. But no one can know $g(x_j)$ without P_j's help, because P_j does not disclose X_{jj} to others.

Representation Based on Linear Equations

Let each x_j be vector $\{x_{j1}, x_{j2}, ---, x_{jH}\}$ owned by entity P_j and $f(x_1, x_2, ---, x_N)$ be also vector $\{g_1(x_{11})+g_1(x_{21})+ --- +g_1(x_{N1}), g_2(x_{12})+g_2(x_{22})+ --- +g_2(x_{N2}), ---, g_H(x_{1H})+g_H(x_{2H})+ --- +g_H(x_{NH})\}$. For example, if x_{j1}, x_{j2} and x_{j3} are the age, the height and the weight of person P_j, then $g_2(x_{12})+g_2(x_{22})+ --- +g_2(x_{N2})$ is the average height of persons when $g_2(x_{j2}) = x_{j2}$, and it is the variance of heights when $g_2(x_{j2}) = x_{j2}^2$. Generally, H is not equal to N but by adding dummy elements $\{x_{j(H+1)}, x_{j(H+2)}, ---, x_{jN}\}$ or assigning multiple numbers j, N+j, 2N+j, --- to P_j if necessary, it is possible to make H and N be equal. Then, additive and minimum representation $\{X_{j1}, X_{j2}, ---, X_{jN}\}$ of $\{g_1(x_{j1}), g_2(x_{j2}), ---, g_N(x_{jN})\}$ can be constituted by N-mutually independent linear combinations of elements of vector $\{g_1(x_{j1}), g_2(x_{j2}) ---, g_N(x_{jN})\}$ shown in Equation (2) (Tamura, 2005).

Namely, firstly it is additive, i.e. provided that $\{g_1(x_{j1}), g_2(x_{j2}), ---, g_N(x_{jN})\}$ and $\{g_1(x_{h1}), g_2(x_{h2}), ---, g_N(x_{hN})\}$ are represented as $\{X_{j1}, X_{j2}, ---, X_{jN}\}$ and $\{X_{h1}, X_{h2}, ---, X_{hN}\}$, $\{X_{j1}+X_{h1}, X_{j2}+X_{h2}, ---, X_{jN}+X_{hN}\}$ is the representation of $\{g_1(x_{j1})+g_1(x_{h1}), g_2(x_{j2})+g_2(x_{h2}), ---, g_N(x_{jN})+g_N(x_{hN})\}$. Also, no one can reconstruct $\{g_1(x_{j1}), g_2(x_{j2}), ---, g_N(x_{jN})\}$ when even one element of $\{X_{j1}, X_{j2}, ---, X_{jN}\}$ is not known, but when all $\{X_{j1}, X_{j2}, ---, X_{jN}\}$ is given any entity that knows coefficient matrix $\{a_{pq}\}$ in Equation (2) can calculate it because $\{a_{pq}\}$ has its inverse. Therefore, coordinator C can calculate $\{g_1(x_{11})+g_1(x_{21})+ --- +g_1(x_{N1}), g_2(x_{12})+g_2(x_{22})+ --- +g_2(x_{N2}), ---, g_H(x_{1H})+g_H(x_{2H})+ --- +g_H(x_{NH})\}$. On the other hand each P_j can conceal $\{g_1(x_{j1}), g_2(x_{j2}), --- g_H(x_{jH})\}$, because it does not disclose X_{jj} to others.

$$X_{j1} = a_{11}g_1(x_{j1}) + a_{12}g_2(x_{j2}) + --- + a_{1N}g_N(x_{jN})$$

$$X_{j2} = a_{21}g_1(x_{j1}) + a_{22}\, g_2(x_{j2}) + --- + a_{2N}\, g_N(x_{jN}) \tag{2}$$

$$X_{jN} = a_{N1}g_1(x_{j1}) + a_{N2}g_2(x_{j2}) + --- + a_{NN}g_N(x_{jN})$$

It must be noted that although entities can protect their data from plain text attacks despite that the above representations are based on linear equations; each entity must add its secret dummy terms to Equation (2). Without the dummy terms, if both entity P_h and P_j have same data $\{g_1(x_{j1}), g_2(x_{j2}), ---, g_N(x_{jN})\}$, P_h can estimate that P_j has $\{g_1(x_{j1}), g_2(x_{j2}), ---, g_N(x_{jN})\}$ when it conspires with several other entities.

By the above scheme, C and $P_1, P_2, ---, P_N$ can calculate not only averages and variances of $x_{j1}, x_{j2}, ---, x_{jN}$ but also their histograms by counting the number of entity P_j that has given v_k as the value of variable x_{jk}, as follows. Namely, each P_j introduces data item Z_{jk} corresponding to data item x_{jk} and assigns value 1 or 0 to it according to the condition that $x_{jk} = v_k$ is satisfied or not, so that the sum of $Z_{1k}, Z_{2k}, ---, Z_{Nk}$ becomes the number of entities that have v_k as values of $x_{1k}, x_{2k}, ---, x_{Nk}$. In this way various kind of functions of $x_{1k}, x_{2k}, ---, x_{Nk}$ can be calculated without invading privacies of the data owners. However, each entity P_j must maintain not only its data x_{jk} itself but also many kinds of functions of x_{jk} to calculate them, e.g. x_{jk}^2 for calculating variances and Z_{jk} for calculating histograms. Also the above scheme is not efficient enough for calculating many kinds of functions, i.e. complicated computations or communications are required. To calculate histograms, C and $P_1, P_2, ---, P_N$ must carry out the above procedure for all possible values of the data for example.

Representation Based on Lagrange Interpolation

Lagrange interpolation formula implements the other type of data representation suitable for partial computation (Shamir, 1979). As discussed in section "Threshold ElGamal Encryption Scheme" of Section 1, when polynomial $f_j(x) = f_{0j} + f_{1j}x + f_{2j}x^2 + --- + f_{(N-1)j}x^{N-1}$ is given, the value of $f_j(x)$ at point q can be calculated from $\{f_j(q_1), f_j(q_2), ---, f_j(q_N)\}$, values of $f_j(x)$ at N different points $\{q_1, q_2, ---, q_N\}$, by Equation (3), and as the special case,

$f_j(0)$ is calculated by Equation (4). On the other hand, it is difficult to know the value of $f_j(q)$ if one of $f_j(q_n)$ is missing. This means that when function $f_j(x)$ is defined so that $f_j(0)$ coincides with $g(x_j)$, a set of values $\{f_j(q_1), f_j(q_2), \text{---}, f_j(q_N)\}$ constitutes the minimum representation of $g(x_j)$, namely, provided that $q_1, q_2, \text{---}, q_N$ are known, any entity can reconstruct $g(x_j)$ from $\{f_j(q_1), f_j(q_2), \text{---}, f_j(q_N)\}$, but cannot know $g(x_j)$ when any $f_j(q_h)$ is missing.

$$f_j(q) = \sum_{h=1}^{N} f_j(q_h) \prod_{p=1(p \neq h)}^{N} (q-q_p)/(q_h-q_p) \quad (3)$$

$$f_j(0) = \sum_{h=1}^{N} f_j(q_h) \prod_{p=1(p \neq h)}^{N} (-q_p)/(q_h-q_p) \quad (4)$$

Then, coordinator C and entities $P_1, P_2, \text{---}, P_N$ can calculate $f(x_1, x_2, \text{---}, x_N) = g(x_1)+g(x_2)+ \text{---} +g(x_N)$ or $f(x_1, x_2, \text{---}, x_N) = g(x_1)g(x_2) \text{---} g(x_N)$, while maintaining each $g(x_j)$ as P_j's secret as follows. Namely, each P_j defines polynomial $f_j(x) = f_{0j} + f_{1j}x + f_{2j}x^2 + \text{---} + f_{(Z-1)j}x^{N-1}$ so that $f_j(0)$ coincides with its secret value $g(x_j)$, and inform each P_h of $f_j(q_h)$. After that, entity P_h that receives $f_1(q_h), f_2(q_h), \text{---}, f_N(q_h)$ from other entities calculates $f(q_h) = f_1(q_h)+f_2(q_h)+ \text{---} +f_N(q_h)$ and $\{\prod_{p=1(p \neq h)}^{N}(-q_p)/(q_h-q_p)\}f(q_h) = F(q_h)$, and informs C of $F(q_h)$. Then, finally C reconstructs $g(x_1)+g(x_2)+ \text{---} +g(x_N)$ as $F(q_1)+F(q_2)+ \text{---} +F(q_N)$. Here, it must be noted that P_j does not disclose $f_j(q_j)$ to others, and C can calculate also $g(x_1)g(x_2) \text{---} g(x_N)$ in the same way.

A disadvantage of this scheme is it cannot be applied to large scale statistics calculations where many entities are involved, because it is difficult for digital computers to calculate numbers $\{x, x^2, \text{---}, x^{N-1}\}$ accurately when N becomes large.

Re-Encryption Based Mechanism

Re-encryption schemes with homomorphic property discussed in Section 1 also enable entities $P_1, P_2, \text{---}, P_N$ and coordinator C to jointly calculate aggregated values of $x_1, x_2, \text{---}, x_N$ while maintaining confidentiality of each x_j owned by P_j. When ElGamal based re-encryption scheme is used, coordinator C is configured as a set of independent authorities $C_1, C_2, \text{---}, C_M$, and each C_j discloses its public encryption key k_j of encryption function $E(k_j, x)$. To calculate the product of $x_1, x_2, \text{---}, x_N$, each P_j repeatedly encrypts x_j to $E(k_*, x_j) = E(k_M, E(k_{M-1}, \text{---} E(k_1, x_j) \text{---}))$, and coordinator C_M gathers $E(k_*, x_1), E(k_*, x_2), \text{---}, E(k_*, x_N)$ to calculate the product $E(k_*, x_1)E(k_*, x_2)\text{--}E(k_*, x_N)$. After that based on the multiplicative property, $C_M, C_{M-1}, \text{---}, C_1$ repeatedly decrypt $E(k_*, x_1)E(k_*, x_2)\text{--}E(k_*, x_N) = E(k_*, x_1x_2\text{--}x_N)$ to $x_1x_2\text{--}x_N$ by their secret keys $k_1^{-1}, k_2^{-1}, \text{---}, k_M^{-1}$. Then, no one except P_j can know x_j unless all $C_1, C_2, \text{---}, C_M$ conspire. Secret key based re-encryption schemes also can be used in the same way, although coordinators $C_1, C_2, \text{---}, C_M$ must maintain their encryption keys as their secrets, and as a consequence each P_j must encrypt x_j by its secret encryption key.

An advantage of re-encryption based mechanisms over partial computation based ones is that they require less communications, i.e. different from in partial computation based mechanisms where entities $P_1, P_2, \text{---}, P_N$ must communicate with each other, in re-encryption based mechanisms $P_1, P_2, \text{---}, P_N$ communicate with only C_M. On the other hand, their disadvantage is that the schemes become complicated when values to be calculated are not limited to integers. Also, they can work based on the stricter assumption about the trustworthiness of entities, i.e. entity P_j can conceal its data when at least one of C_k is honest. In partial computation based mechanisms, P_j can conceal its data even when all other entities are dishonest.

CONCLUSION

Various mechanisms that enable entities to calculate functions of data that are secrets of other entities were discussed. Although several schemes that enable entities to calculate any kind of function without knowing the data owned by others had been proposed already, complicated and large volumes of computations are necessary. Therefore, they cannot be used in real applications, and currently available schemes for practical applications can handle only limited forms of functions, e.g. sums and or products of data, and their auto and cross correlations. To enable calculations of various kinds of functions of data that are required for remotely maintaining home appliances while preserving privacies of their users for example, further investigations to develop more effective and efficient mechanisms are necessary. Also in this chapter, all entities were assumed honest in terms of correctness of their calculations; however, in real applications entities may provide data or may calculate functions dishonestly. Therefore, developments of mechanisms that detect dishonest behaviours and that indentify liable entities are necessary.

REFERENCES

Elgamal, T. (1985). A public-key cryptosystem and a signature scheme based on discrete logarithms. *IEEE Transactions on Information Theory*, *31*(4), 469–472. doi:10.1109/TIT.1985.1057074

Goldreich, O., Micali, M., & Wigderson, A. (1987). How to play any mental game. *Proceedings of 19th ACM Symposium on Theory of Computing*, (pp. 218-229).

Naor, M., Pinkas, B., & Sumner, R. (1999). Privacy preserving auctions and mechanism design. *Proceedings of the 1st ACM Conference on Electronic Commerce,* (pp. 129-139).

Rivest, R., Shamir, A., & Adleman, L. (1978). A method for obtaining digital signatures and public-key cryptosystems. *Communications of the ACM*, *21*(2), 294–299. doi:10.1145/359340.359342

Shamir, A. (1979). How to share a secret. *Communications of the ACM*, *22*(11), 612–613. doi:10.1145/359168.359176

Tamura, S., & Yanase, T. (2005). Information sharing among untrustworthy entities. *IEEJ Transactions in EIS*, *125*(11), 1767–1772. doi:10.1541/ieejeiss.125.1767

Tamura, S., & Yanase, T. (2007). A mechanism for anonymous credit card systems. *IEEJ Trans. EIS*, *127*(1), 81–87. doi:10.1541/ieejeiss.127.81

Yao, A. C. (1986). *How to generate and exchange secrets*. Proc. of the 27th IEEE Symposium on Fo

Section 3
Developing Secure Anonymous Systems

Chapter 9
Anonymous Authentication Systems

ABSTRACT

As the first application of secure anonymous systems, after reviewing conventional schemes, this chapter develops anonymous token, ITL, and ID list based anonymous authentication systems that enable authorities to determine whether entities are eligible or not without knowing their identities. Anonymous token and ITL based systems have advantages in protecting systems from ineligible entities, i.e. different from password based systems in which eligible entities can tell their passwords to others, entities in these systems cannot give their secret to others without losing their eligibilities (in ITL based systems, entity cannot steal secrets of others). On the other hand, ID list based systems have advantages in handling entities those forget their secrets or those are expelled from systems. In the last section of this chapter, an anonymous credential system is also developed based on anonymous tags.

INTRODUCTION

Authentication is a process, in which entity S determines whether entity C_h is an authorized one or not. In this chapter, an entity that authenticates entities is called a server, and entities to be authenticated are called clients. Usually server S authenticates client C_h while identifying it. For example, a computer system authenticates users by asking them to show their identities (IDs) and passwords to protect it from being used by unauthorized persons. Namely, a user can use the computer system when it shows an ID and a password and its showing password coincides with the one that is registered with the ID in advance, therefore the computer system in this example can know the correspondences between the users and the services that the users had received from it. However, there are cases where users want to receive services without disclosing their identities. Although a restroom in an office must be protected from trespassers for safety, employees in the office may not want to show their ID and password pairs for their every use of it, because the number of times they had used the restroom, etc. are privacies of the employees, for example. Anonymous authentication mechanisms enable

DOI: 10.4018/978-1-4666-1649-3.ch009

the development of systems that cope with this kind of requirements, and constitute the foundations of almost all kinds of anonymous systems.

Here, to make authentication mechanisms practical, they must have functions to handle clients that lose their eligibilities and that forget their secrets necessary for the authentications (e.g. passwords), in addition to the basic authentication functions. Also in systems where clients are anonymous they may behave dishonestly after they had authenticated successfully, therefore it is desirable that the mechanisms can identify dishonest clients despite that they are anonymous. Then, requirements for anonymous authentication mechanisms can be summarized as below, they are

1. Only authorized clients are successfully authenticated. This requirement is intensified to untransferability, i.e.
   a. Clients cannot give secrets necessary for authentications to others without losing their eligibilities, or
   b. Anyone cannot impersonate an authorized client by stealing or being informed of secrets necessary for authentications,
2. No one except a client itself can know the identity of the client that is being authenticated,
3. No one except a client itself can link a sequence of its past authentication requests,
4. The server can invalidate eligibilities of clients that secede from the service providing system even without carrying out seceding procedures adequately,
5. The server can handle clients that forget their secrets necessary for their authentications, and
6. Although clients are anonymous, the server can identify clients that behaved dishonestly after they had been authenticated successfully, without revealing any privacy of other honest clients.

Among the above requirements, the 3rd and the 6th requirements are not essential, but strongly desirable. Although S cannot directly identify clients that had requested individual authentications even the 3rd requirement is not satisfied, a set of authentication requests from the same client suggest the identity of the client in many cases. Also, anonymous systems make entities cause various kinds of dishonest events much easier than usual systems do because entities are anonymous; therefore the capabilities of identifying dishonest clients are highly desired. Fortunately, any anonymous authentication mechanism can be made satisfy this requirement by exploiting dishonest entity detection mechanisms discussed in sections "Tokens" and "Anonymous Tags" in Part II. Namely, provided that dishonest events are detectable during clients are receiving services, S can identify dishonest clients by using anonymous tokens, and by using homomorphic anonymous tokens or anonymous tag based tokens S can identify them even if dishonest events are detected after the completions of services.

This chapter discusses mechanisms that satisfy the above requirements without assuming absolutely trustworthy entities. Mechanisms based on anonymous tokens discussed after the next section satisfy the above requirements except the 4th and the 5th ones. The most advantageous feature of them is about the 1st requirement. Different from password based mechanisms, in which a client can tell others its password without any damage to enable them to access the server, in these mechanisms, clients cannot give their tokens to others without losing their eligibilities. Also although any mechanism can be endowed with the capability about the 6th requirement by incorporating dishonest entity detection mechanisms discussed in Part II, anonymous token based mechanisms enable the server to identify clients liable for dishonest events without any additional mechanism provided that dishonest events are detectable during the clients are receiving services. However, the only way to satisfy the 4th and the 5th requirements is to invalidate tokens owned by all clients.

ITL based mechanisms also exploit tokens and enhance capabilities of anonymous token based mechanisms further. Namely, ITL based mechanisms completely exclude possibilities that clients give their tokens or their secrets to others, and this means they disable clients to steal tokens owned by other clients. Also encrypted next tokens in ITL based mechanisms can be considered as homomorphic anonymous tokens discussed in Part II, therefore liable clients for dishonest events can be identified without additional mechanisms even if the dishonest events can be detected only after the services had been completed, i.e. the 6th requirement is satisfied. About the 4th and the 5th requirements, when the server maintains lists of clients that had lost their tokens and that had seceded illegitimately (e.g. without the adequate seceding procedures), ITL based mechanisms can immediately invalidate tokens that are replaced by their spares or that are owned by the seceding clients. However, the 3rd requirement is sacrificed, and also mechanisms to manage the above lists become impractical for systems that include large numbers of potential dishonest clients because examinations of the lists require much computation. When the 3rd requirement is inevitable or the size of the system is large, ITL based mechanisms must invalidate tokens owned by all clients to satisfy the 4th and the 5th requirements, as same as in anonymous token based ones.

ID list based mechanisms following homomorphic anonymous token based ones are based on passwords and satisfy the all requirements of anonymous authentication. The most important feature of them is they can satisfy the 4th and the 5th requirements completely and more easily, i.e. while satisfying the 3rd requirement and without maintaining lists of expelled or secrets forgetting clients. However about the 1st requirement, clients can give passwords to others without any penalty. Therefore ID list based mechanisms are the perfect solutions for applications where authorized clients can receive any number of services at fixed prices during pre-defined periods.

At the end of this chapter, anonymous tag based tokens are applied to implement anonymous credentials. Anonymous credentials are a kind of anonymous tokens, and they enable their owners to efficiently convince not only the server which issued the credentials but also other entities that they are eligible while satisfying the above requirements except the 4th and the 5th ones.

CONVENTIONAL MECHANISMS

The easiest way to authenticate anonymous clients is to use passwords common to all authorized clients. Apparently this approach satisfies the 1st, the 2nd and the 3rd requirements, i.e. server S can reject authentication requests from entities that do not know the common password, and S cannot identify the clients that request authentications because all clients use the same common password. S cannot identify a sequence of authentication requests made by a same client either. However, common passwords have difficulties about the 1st requirement. Namely, eligible client C can give the common password to other unauthorized entities to enable them to receive services from S without any penalty. Although a problem that a client gives the common password to unauthorized entities seems to be same as the one that clients tell their IDs and passwords to unauthorized entities in usual authentication systems, common passwords make the problem much more serious. In the non-anonymous system, S can impute all damages caused by misusing of a password to the password holder, however in anonymous systems, S cannot identify the client to which it imputes the liabilities, and as a consequence, once a password is leaked to an unauthorized entity, it will quickly spread over many unauthorized entities.

The 5th requirement is easy to satisfy, namely, clients that forget the password can know it by simply asking S the common password. Although client C must show its identity when it asks the password to S, there is no inconvenience. S cannot identify C even when C uses the re-issued password because the re-issued password has the same form as the original one that is being used by other clients. However, common passwords have a serious drawback about the 4th requirement. Every time when a client secedes from the system that S is operating, S must change the password to a new one and announce the new password to all other clients immediately; the seceding client can continue to receive services from S if the password is not changed, and when S does not announce the new password, other clients cannot receive services. It must be noted that S must change the common password and announce the new one every time when the password is stolen from a client also; therefore common password based authentication mechanisms are applicable only to small and closed systems.

Group authentication mechanisms mitigate the drawbacks of common password based ones. In the group authentication, a group of clients use the same password with the group ID. Therefore, when client C in group G requests authentication, although server S can identify group G, it cannot identify the exact client in G. The advantage is that different from the common password approach, S can change passwords to new ones by announcing the new passwords only to clients in particular groups. Therefore, new password announcing processes become practical even for large scale systems if sizes of groups are small enough. However, it becomes easier for S to estimate clients that requests authentications when group sizes are too small.

Another easy solution assumes group managers, i.e. group manager M of group G authenticates client C in G on behalf of server S and gives a unique token with its signature to C, and S authenticates C when its showing token was not used before and it has the correct signature of M. Therefore, the anonymity of C is maintained as long as M is honest, and announcement of passwords changes are not necessary even if passwords of clients are stolen, i.e. M can invalidate stolen passwords by simply deleting them from its databases. M also can invalidate stolen tokens by simply informing S of them, and dishonest clients can be identified if M memorizes the correspondences between clients and tokens given to them. Namely it satisfies all requirements of anonymous authentications. However, this solution makes sense only when clients can believe M as an absolutely trustworthy entity, e.g. because C has close relations with M. But in many cases these relations worsen the situation, because usually entities want to hide their identities from entities that have the closer relations with them. Also, it may be easy for S to identify C from M, when C and M are connected by close relations.

ANONYMOUS TOKEN BASED AUTHENTICATION

Basic Mechanism

An anonymous token is given to an eligible client and server S signs on it without knowing its value; therefore S can know that client C_h that owns its anonymous token is an eligible entity by verifying the signature on it; however S cannot identify C_h from its token because S had signed on it without knowing its value. Namely, the 1st, the 2nd and the 3rd requirements of anonymous authentication mechanisms are satisfied. It also satisfies the 6th requirement, although S must detect dishonest events during C_h is receiving services.

$S(k_S, T(h))$, anonymous token $T(h)$ of C_h with the signature of S, can be generated through the blind signature scheme (Chaum, 1983) as described already in subsection "Anonymous Tokens" of Part II, where k_S is the signing key of S. Conditions that ensure anonymous tokens to work well are,

1. Each token is unique, and
2. A client can use each of its token only once.

If clients C_h and C_j can obtain same token $S(k_S, T(h))$ or if C_h can use token $S(k_S, T(h))$ multiple times, server S cannot determine whether $S(k_S, T(h))$ is used in authorized ways by C_h or C_j, or $S(k_S, T(h))$ is a stolen token used by an unauthorized entity. Also, C_h can give its tokens to other entities without any penalty so that other entities can use them. Although anonymous token based mechanisms are not complete solutions for the anonymous authentication because they cannot satisfy the 4th or the 5th requirements as discussed later, under the above 2 conditions they have a substantial advantage over the conventional password based ones in satisfying the 1st requirement, the most important feature of authentication mechanisms. Namely, different from the password based mechanisms, in which eligible entities can tell their passwords to ineligible ones without any penalty so that the ineligible entities can be authenticated successfully, in mechanisms based on anonymous tokens, clients cannot give their tokens to others without losing their eligibilities. When client C_h discloses its token $S(k_S, T(h))$ to other entity C_j, C_j can be authenticated as an authorized one, however, C_h cannot use $S(k_S, T(h))$ anymore, because tokens are unique and they are effective only once. Therefore, C_h's disclosure of $S(k_S, T(h))$ to C_j brings no damage to S. Here, S can easily disable clients to use same tokens repeatedly by memorizing already used tokens; it can reject authentication requests accompanied by repeatedly used tokens by comparing tokens shown by clients with the ones recorded as the used ones, i.e. condition 2 is satisfied.

Token Issuing Mechanism

Token tables discussed in subsection "Open Tokens" of Part II make anonymous tokens satisfy condition (1). A token table is a publicly disclosed table (e.g. through BB discussed in section "Bulletin Board") that maintains available tokens, and any entity can pick tokens from this table while concealing their identities. However, S that manages this table inhibits clients from picking same tokens multiple times so that tokens become unique, namely, tokens in the token table are effective only when they have signatures of S, and S does not sign on tokens that are picked from the token table repeatedly. Here, the signature on token T(h) in the token table is different from the one that S generates through the blind signature scheme, i.e. $S(k_S, T(h))$. It is only for maintaining uniqueness of anonymous tokens, in other words, even unauthorized entities can obtain signed tokens from the token table, but these tokens become effective by the another signatures of S generated through the blind signature scheme, as a consequence, only eligible clients can use them. In the followings, signatures on tokens in the token table are not explicitly shown.

In the above, it must be noted that to satisfy the 3rd requirement, clients cannot pick multiple tokens from the token table at a time. Let T(h, 1), T(h, 2), --- be tokens that had been picked by client C_h from the token table in this order, then, when C_h had picked T(h, n-1) and T(h, n) at a time, S can easily know that authentication requests accompanied by these tokens are from the same client. Therefore, it is desirable for C_h that it can obtain blind signatures of S on tokens without disclosing its identity. If C_h is requested to reveal its identity for every blind signature, it must visit S twice before using its each token $S(k_S, T(h, n))$, i.e. for obtaining open token T(h, n) from the token table and for obtaining the blind signature on it. A token refreshing mechanism (Shigetomi, 2003) shown in Part II, in which C_h shows its token $S(k_S, T(h, n-1))$ in exchange for the signature on new encrypted token $E(a_h, (T(h, n))$, satisfies this requirement (a_h is the secret encryption key of C_h), i.e. C_h can obtain S's signature on T(h, n) at a time when it uses $S(k_S, T(h, n-1))$.

An advantage of the above token issuing mechanism is about the 6th requirement, i.e. as discussed in Part II, anonymous tokens automatically enable S to identify clients liable for dishonest events without knowing privacies of honest clients, provided that dishonest events are detected during clients are receiving services. In detail, if S detects dishonest events during C_h is receiving services S does not give a new token to C_h. Then, although anonymous C_h can leave S without any penalty, it is identified as the dishonest client at a time when S asks all clients to show their unused tokens, because C_h cannot show its unused token. On the other hand, S cannot know services that honest clients had received even they show their unused tokens, because unused tokens are not linked to any service yet. Also not to disturb honest clients, S can ask clients to show their unused tokens at times when it collects fees from individual clients for its services. However, this mechanism is not effective for dishonest events that are detectable only after completions of services. To cope with this kind of dishonesties, anonymous tokens must be made homomorphic.

Limitations of Anonymous Tokens

A serious drawback of anonymous tokens is that server S does not have any information about links between clients and their using tokens or between individual tokens of same clients because S signs on tokens blindly; therefore problems arise when clients lose their eligibilities or lose or pretend to lose their tokens. Namely, firstly client C_h that had lost its eligibility still can use its token, and secondly C_h that obtained its new token as a spare of a token it had lost can use its old token. About the former problem, S can invalidate tokens of clients that secede from the system by carrying out the client deregistration procedures in which clients return their unused tokens, however when clients secede from the system without carrying out the procedures e.g. when they are expelled, they still have effective tokens, and they can obtain new tokens forever by refreshing them. A possible solution for the problem about the 5th requirement is to force C_h to disclose its secret key a_h to invalidate all tokens it had lost, i.e. when a_h is disclosed, server S can know all tokens that it had given to C_h to invalidate them. However this solution is absolutely not desirable because a_h reveals all privacies of C_h. Theoretically the both problems can be solved easily by simply invalidate all tokens on which S had signed before, where, S can find all valid tokens easily by examining the token table. However this solution is impractical as same as common password based authentication mechanisms. All clients are asked to obtain their new tokens while convincing S their eligibilities again e.g. by showing their ID and password pairs. Expiration times attached to tokens may mitigate the problem, but still clients can use invalid tokens until their expiration times. Here, S must assign same values to expiration times of all tokens, because different expiration times may suggest identities of the token holders.

ITL BASED AUTHENTICATION

The advantage of anonymous token based authentication mechanisms that clients cannot give their tokens to other unauthorized entities without penalties can be further enhanced by the ITL based anonymous authentication mechanism (Tamura, 2006, 2007). In addition, they satisfy the 6th requirement more successfully, i.e. based on homomorphic anonymous tokens, they enable server S without additional mechanisms to identify dishonest clients even if dishonest events are detected after the clients had left from S. ITL based mechanisms can satisfy also the 4th and the 5th requirements although in this case the 3rd requirement is sacrificed and computation volumes for authenticating individual clients increase.

Figure 1. ITL based anonymous authentication

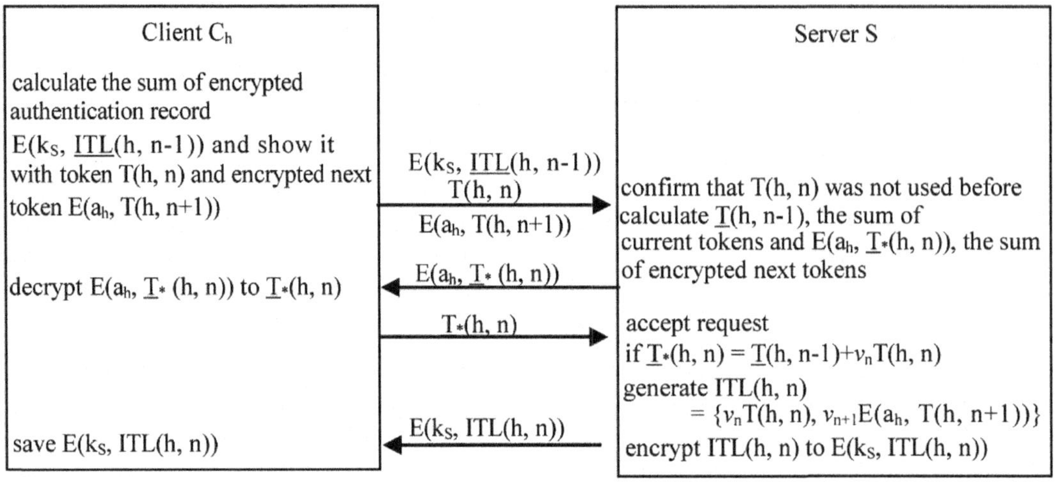

Basic Mechanism

Figure 1 shows the procedure of the ITL based anonymous authentication mechanism. ITL(h, n), the ITL at client C_h's n-th authentication request is pair $\{v_nT(h, n)), v_{n+1}E(a_h, T(h, n+1))\}$, where a_h is the secret encryption key of C_h, T(h, n) and T(h, n+1) are tokens of C_h at its n-th and (n+1)-th authentication requests respectively, and $v_nT(h, n)$ and $v_{n+1}E(a_h, T(h, n+1))$ constitute the current and the encrypted next token parts of ITL(h, n) shown in Figure 5 in chapter "Integrity of Anonymous Data" of Part II. v_n and v_{n+1} are token concealers for the n-th and the (n+1)-th tokens, and S uses same v_n and v_{n+1} for the n-th tokens and the (n+1)-th tokens of all clients as its secrets. Then, S gives ITL(h, n) to C_h at C_h's n-th authentication request, but to disable C_h to modify, add or delete it, ITL(h, n) is encrypted to $E(k_S, ITL(h, n)) = E(k_S, \{v_nT(h, n), v_{n+1}E(a_h, T(h, n+1))\})$ by S. Here, k_S is the secret encryption key of S, and it is assumed that both encryption functions $E(k_S,x)$ and $E(a_h,y)$ are linear equation based ones with the additive feature, i.e. relations $E(k_S, x_1) + E(k_S, x_2) = E(k_S, x_1+x_2)$ and $E(a_h, y_1) + E(a_h, y_2) = E(a_h, y_1+y_2)$ hold. In the above, although they are not explicitly represented to simplify notations, actually ITLs and encrypted next tokens are constituted as extended ITLs and extended encrypted next tokens as discussed in section "Implicit Transaction Links."

Under the above settings, C_h makes its initial visit to S while revealing its identity (i.e. as the exception, C_h is not anonymous at this stage) and shows its initial token T(h, 0) and its encrypted initial and next tokens $E(a_h, T(h, 0))$ and $E(a_h, T(h, 1))$, and if C_h is eligible S gives initial authentication record $E(k_S, ITL(h, 0))$ to C_h, where C_h's initial ITL is defined as $ITL(h, 0) = \{v_0T(h, 0), v_0E(a_h, T(h, 0))+v_1E(a_h, T(h, 1))\}$ as mentioned in Part II. Now after successfully completing its initial visit, C_h requests authentication to S at its n-th visit without disclosing its identity by showing its n-th token T(h, n) and its encrypted (n+1)-th token $E(a_h, T(h, n+1))$ together with $E(k_S, \underline{ITL}(h, n-1))$, the sum of encrypted ITLs from its initial to its (n-1)-th authentication request, and if T(h, n) is valid, S generates $ITL(h, n) = \{v_nT(h, n), v_{n+1}E(a_h, T(h, n+1))\}$ to be saved by C_h in its encrypted form $E(k_s, ITL(h, n))$.

Differences from the anonymous token based scheme in the previous section are firstly, T(h, n) is an open token, i.e. anonymous C_h picks T(h, n) from the token table through the different independent process, and S simply signs on it regardless that C_h is an authorized one or not provided that the picked token is not the one on which it had signed before. More important difference is, together with T(h, n) and E(a_h, T(h, n+1)), C_h shows also E(k_S, $\underline{ITL}$(h, n-1)). Namely, although T(h, n) has the signature of S, this signature is only for ensuring uniqueness of tokens. The validity of T(h, n) is ensured not by the signature of S, instead, the consistent relation between T(h, n) and E(k_S, $\underline{ITL}$(h, n-1)) calculated by C_h ensures the validity. As another difference, encrypted next token E(a_h, T(h, n+1)) constitutes a homomorphic anonymous token because encryption function E(a_h, x) is additive. Here, actually T(h, n) must be represented as S($\underline{d}_S$, T(h, n)) by using S's signing key d_S for open tokens, but this signing key is omitted from notations in this section.

In more detail, S authenticates client C_h at its n-th authentication request as follows. Firstly, C_h calculates the sum of its past encrypted ITLs (authentication records) E(k_S, $\underline{ITL}$(h, n-1)) = E(k_S, ITL(h, 0))+E(k_S, ITL(h, 1))+ --- +E(k_S, ITL(h, n-1)), and shows it to S together with its n-th token T(h, n) and encrypted (n+1)-th token E(a_h, T(h, n+1)) (here actually, C_h calculates E(k_S, $\underline{ITL}$(h, n-1)) according to the transaction-wise ITL sum checking mechanism discussed in Part II). After that, S examines the validity of the signature on open token T(h, n) and whether it was used already before or not, and if it is valid, S decrypts E(k_S, $\underline{ITL}$(h, n-1)) to $\underline{ITL}$(h, n-1) to extract $\underline{T}$(h, n-1) = v_0T(h, 0)+v_1T(h, 1)+ --- +v_{n-1}T(h, n-1), and E(a_h, $\underline{T}_*$(h, n)) = E(a_h, v_0T(h, 0)+v_1T(h, 1)+ --- +v_nT(h, n)), the sum of current tokens and the sum of encrypted next tokens included in C_h's past ITLs, respectively. Then, S asks C_h to decrypt E(a_h, $\underline{T}_*$(h, n)) to $\underline{T}_*$(h, n), and based on C_h's response, S finally accepts C_h's authentication request if $\underline{T}_*$(h, n) coincides with $\underline{T}$(h, n) = $\underline{T}$(h, n-1)+v_nT(h, n). In a case when S accepts the request, S generates ITL(h, n) = {v_nT(h, n), v_{n+1}E(a_h, T(h, n+1))} and encrypts it to E(k_S, {v_nT(h, n), v_{n+1}E(a_h, T(h, n+1))}) as the encrypted n-th authentication record of C_h to be saved by C_h.

In the above, $\underline{T}_*$(h, n), i.e. the decryption result of the sum of encrypted next tokens, coincides with $\underline{T}$(h, n) only when token T(h, n) is consistent with past authentication records that C_h maintains, therefore, other client C_j cannot be successfully authenticated even when C_j stole T(h, n) from C_h. Namely, to successfully decrypt E(a_j, $\underline{T}_*$(j, m)), the sum of past encrypted next tokens of C_j at its m-th request, so that the result $\underline{T}_*$(j, m) coincides with $\underline{T}$(j, m-1)+v_mT(h, n), C_j must compensate the difference between T(h, n) and T(j, m), but it is impossible because C_j does not know S's secret key k_S or token concealer v_n or v_m. On the other hand, S cannot identify C_h from either T(h, n), $\underline{T}_*$(h, n) or $\underline{T}$(h, n-1), because C_h obtains T(h, n) without disclosing its identity and it multiplies its past authentication records by client token concealers that are secret from S and that are changed at every authentication request (client token concealers in the transaction wise ITL sum checking mechanism are not shown explicitly in this section). Also, T(h, n+1) included in ITL(h, n) is encrypted to E(a_h, T(h, n+1)) by C_h, therefore S cannot know that authentication requests accompanied by T(h, n) and T(h, n+1) were made by the same client either. Namely, the scheme in Figure 1 satisfies the 1st, the 2nd and the 3rd requirements of anonymous authentication schemes.

When compared with other mechanisms, ITL based mechanisms have a distinctive advantage in handling stolen tokens or tokens given to unauthorized entities. In anonymous token based mechanisms, when client C_h gives its token T(h, n) to other client C_j, although C_h cannot use T(h, n) anymore because repeated uses of T(h, n) is inhibited, C_j can use T(h, n). On the other hand in ITL based mechanisms, even if C_h gives its token T(h, n) to C_j, C_j cannot use it. Then, C_h does not need to worry even if its token T(h, n) is stolen by other entity C_j. C_j cannot use its stealing T(h, n), and also C_h sill can use T(h, n), because C_j's authentication request accompanied by T(h, n) is rejected and T(h, n) is not registered as an already used token yet. Of course it is possible for S to alert to anonymous client C_h that some client had tried unsuccessfully to use its token T(h, n) at a time when anonymous C_h uses T(h, n) in the authorized way. In this way, different from other mechanisms including anonymous token based ones, ITL based mechanisms successfully protect clients from token thefts without bringing any inconvenience to honest clients.

Satisfying the 4th and the 5th Requirements

ITL based anonymous authentication mechanism can satisfy the 4th and the 5th requirements by 2 ways. The 1st way is token refreshing, in which server S periodically refreshes tokens (for example) at times when it collects fees for its offering services, and the 2nd way is token invalidation, in which S invalidates tokens of clients that had seceded from the system without having carried out the adequate procedures (in other words clients that S had expelled) or that had obtained spares for their lost tokens. The former way does not cause any inconvenience in satisfying other requirements for anonymous authentications, but it cannot disable expelled clients to visit it or clients that had obtained their spare tokens to use their old tokens, until token refreshing times. On the other hand, the latter way can invalidate ineffective tokens immediately, but it sacrifices the 3rd requirement and cannot be applied to large scale systems.

In the token refreshing mechanism, server S periodically invalidates all tokens on which it had signed by assigning expiration times common to all tokens, and clients are asked to obtain their new tokens while showing their identities, as same as in anonymous token based mechanisms. Therefore after the expiration time, expelled clients that do not obtain new tokens cannot be authenticated successfully, and tokens that clients had lost also become ineffective. On the other hand, S cannot obtain any clue about clients by the expiration times attached to tokens; all effective tokens have the same expiration time. However, as a drawback of this token refreshing mechanism, clients can use even invalid tokens until their expiration times.

To immediately invalidate ineffective tokens, in the token invalidation mechanism server S maintains an invalid client list consists of encrypted and decrypted test tokens of clients that had been expelled from the system or that had obtained spare tokens. Namely, at client C_h's each authentication request, in the same way as in the dishonest entity identification process described in subsection "Homomorphic Anonymous Tokens" of Part II, S asks C_h to decrypt each encrypted test token set $\{\underline{check}_1(j), \underline{check}_2(j), ---, \underline{check}_Z(j)\}$ registered in the invalid client list to $\{Y_1(j), Y_2(j), ---, Y_Z(j)\}$ by its decryption key a_h^{-1}, where it is assumed that $\{\underline{check}_1(j), \underline{check}_2(j), ---, \underline{check}Z(j)\}$ is decrypted to a set of visible part values $\{check_1(j), check_2(j), ---, check_Z(j)\}$ by a_j^{-1}, the decryption key of C_j that had been expelled or that had obtained its spare token. Therefore, S can determine the token T(h, n) that C_h is showing is invalid when $\{Y_1(j), Y_2(j), ---, Y_Z(j)\}$ coincides with $\{check_1(j), check_2(j), ---, check_Z(j)\}$ for some j,

In detail at C_h's initial authentication request, S prepares a set of random bit string vectors $\{\underline{check}_1(h), \underline{check}_2(h), ---, \underline{check}Z(h)\}$ that is unique to C_h, and, asks C_h to decrypt them to a set of decrypted test tokens $\{E(a_h^{-1}, \underline{check}_1(h)) = check_1(h), E(a_h^{-1}, \underline{check}_2(h)) = check_2(h), ---, E(a_h^{-1}, \underline{check}Z(h)) = check_Z(h)\}$ by C_h's secret decryption key a_h^{-1}. Then, S registers C_h together with C_h's initial token T(h, 0), initial ITL(h, 0) = $\{v_0 T(h, 0), v_0 E(a_h, T(h, 0)) + v_1 E(a_h, T(h, 1))\}$, encrypted test token set $\{check_1(h), check_2(h), ---, check_Z(h)\}$ and decrypted test token set $\{\underline{check}_1(h), \underline{check}_2(h), ---, \underline{check}_Z(h)\}$. Here, each $\underline{check}_q(h)$ in the encrypted test token set is a bit string vector of the same dimension as encrypted token $E(a_h, T(h, n))$. On the other hand, decrypted test token $check_q(h) = E(a_h^{-1}, \underline{check}_q(h))$ is the visible part value of the token, therefore usually the dimension of $check_q(h)$ is less than that of $\underline{check}_q(h)$. Now, at a time when S expels client C_h or issues a spare token to C_h, it registers $\{\underline{check}_1(h), \underline{check}_2(h), ---, \underline{check}_Z(h)\}$ and $\{check_1(h), check_2(h), ---, check_Z(h)\}$ as a record in the invalid client list. Here, S can identify $\{\underline{check}_1(h), \underline{check}_2(h), ---, \underline{check}_Z(h)\}$ and $\{check_1(h), check_2(h), ---, check_Z(h)\}$ in the registered clients list because it knows C_h when it expels C_h, or C_h discloses its identity when it requests a spare token.

In the above, S can force C_h to use a_h^{-1} for calculating $\{Y_1(j), Y_2(j), ---, Y_Z(j)\}$ without knowing C_h, where, a_h^{-1} is the decryption key that C_h had used to decrypt $\{\underline{check}_1(h), \underline{check}_2(h), ---, \underline{check}_Z(h)\}$ at the time when it was registered as an authorized client. Namely, fortunately S had obtained $\underline{T}_*(h, n)$, the honest decrypted form of $E(a_h, \underline{T}_*(h, n))$, in the authentication process as shown in Figure 1 (if $\underline{T}_*(h, n)$ is not the honest decryption result of $E(a_h, \underline{T}_*(h, n))$, S rejects C_h's authentication request accompanied by $T(h, n)$). Therefore, when C_h decrypts $\{\underline{check}_1(j), \underline{check}_2(j), ---, \underline{check}_Z(j)\}$ by b_h^{-1} other than a_h^{-1}, S can detect this dishonesty by asking C_h to decrypt $\underline{Check} = w_0E(a_h, T_*(h, n)) + w_1\underline{check}_1(j) + --- + w_Z\underline{check}_Z(j)$, while using its secret random numbers $w_0, w_1, ---, w_Z$. If C_h had decrypted $\{\underline{check}_1(j), \underline{check}_2(j), ---, \underline{check}_Z(j)\}$ to $\{Y_1(j), Y_2(j), ---, Y_Z(j)\}$ honestly by using decryption key a_h^{-1}, it can decrypt $\underline{Check}$ to $Check = w_0T(h, n) + w_1Y_1(j) + --- + w_ZY_Z(j)$. On the other hand, if C_h had decrypted $\{\underline{check}_1(j), \underline{check}_2(j), ---, \underline{check}_Z(j)\}$ dishonestly, it cannot calculate *Check* consistently because it does not know any of $w_0, w_1, ---, w_Z$. It must be noted that actually additional operations are required in the process for decrypting $\underline{Check}$ as discussed in subsection "Verification of Linear Equation based Encryptions" of Part I, and S must assign different vectors $\{\underline{check}_1(j), \underline{check}_2(j), ---, \underline{check}_Z(j)\}$ to different clients. If same $\underline{check}_q(j)$ is assigned to C_h and C_j, when C_j behaves dishonestly, at its every authentication request C_h decrypts $\underline{check}_q(j)$ registered in the invalid client list to $check_q(h)$ that it had registered at its initial authentication request, and S can easily identify C_h. Also, to use its spare token, C_h must change its encryption key a_h to a_h that is different from a_h.

However, although the above token invalidation mechanism makes the ITL based anonymous authentication scheme satisfy the 4th and the 5th requirements, it sacrifices the 3rd requirement. Because C_h decrypts same vectors $\{\underline{check}_1(j), \underline{check}_2(j), ---, \underline{check}_Z(j)\}$ in the invalid client list at its every authentication request, S can identify a sequence of authentication requests made by same anonymous client C_h by memorizing decryption result $\{Y_1(j), Y_2(j), ---, Y_Z(j)\}$ at its every visit. Also, the token invalidation mechanism is not practical for large scale systems, where many clients secede from systems without carrying out seceding procedures or lose their tokens. Namely, every time when client C_h requests authentication, C_h must decrypt all encrypted test tokens registered in the invalid client list. Therefore, the token invalidation mechanism can be applied only to small scale systems.

Detection of Dishonest Clients

$E(a_h, T(h, n))$ included in an ITL is a homomorphic anonymous token as mentioned before, therefore the 6th requirement can be satisfied without any additional mechanism, i.e. an ITL based authentication mechanism enables server S to identify dishonest clients without revealing any privacy of honest clients even if dishonest events are detected after the clients had left from S.

ID LIST BASED AUTHENTICATION

An ID list based authentication mechanism removes the drawbacks of anonymous token and ITL based mechanisms and enables the development of anonymous authentication mechanisms that efficiently satisfy all the requirements except the 6th one, in environments where authorized clients can receive services any number of times at a fixed price during each service period of the server. Namely, the ID list based mechanism enables the server not only to successfully authenticate anonymous clients but also securely and timely handle clients that secede from the system in unauthorized ways or forget their passwords, etc. without sacrificing the 3rd requirement and even when the number of clients is large. However, because it is password based, clients can tell their passwords to other entities without losing their eligibilities.

In the mechanism, server S authenticates anonymous client C_h by encrypting a list of passwords of multiple clients including C_h itself while using secret key R of S, and asking C_h to calculate R based on the list of encrypted passwords. Here, when S uses the encryption function that is weak against plain text attacks, authorized C_h that knows its password can calculate R from its own encrypted password included in the list, but an unauthorized client cannot calculate R because it does not know any password in the list. Therefore, S can confirm that C_h is an authorized client when C_h answers the secret key R successfully, however it cannot identify C_h because all clients corresponding to one of the passwords in the list can calculate R. The distinctive feature of this mechanism is that clients are always connected to their ID and password pairs (S authenticates clients based on their IDs and passwords); therefore different from anonymous token or ITL based mechanisms, it can successfully and efficiently handle clients that lose their eligibilities or forget their secrets. It also satisfies the 6th requirement when combined with the dishonest entity detection mechanisms discussed in Part II, and consequently all the requirements of the anonymous authentication mechanisms are satisfied.

Basic Mechanism

Figure 2 shows the procedure of the mechanism in which the server S authenticates client C_h (Tamura, 2005). In the figure, S uses the onetime pad discussed in Part I (Kahn, 1996) as the encryption function that is weak against plain text attacks. The authentication process proceeds as follows. Firstly, C_h that requests authentication generates *D*, a list of IDs of its randomly selecting clients that includes d_h, the ID of C_h itself, and sends *D* to S. After receiving the request with *D*, S generates its random bit strings r and R, and for each d_j in *D*, while finding password p_j that corresponds to d_j from its database, it encrypts p_j to $\underline{p}_j = E(k_S, \{r, p_j\})$ by its public encryption key k_S. Here, $E(k_S, \{r, x\})$ is a probabilistic asymmetric key encryption function and r is a random factor, therefore although C_h can calculate $\underline{p}_h$ from its password p_h and random factor r by publicly known encryption key k_S, it is practically impossible for C_h to calculate p_j, password of other client C_j, from $\underline{p}_j = E(k_S, \{r, p_j\})$. Then, S calculates $q_j = \underline{p}_j \oplus R$ and adds record $\{d_j, q_j\}$ to *P*, a password list consists of ID and encrypted password pair of each client in *D*, to send it to C_h with r and $\underline{R} = E(k_S, R)$. After that, C_h that receives *P*, finds $\{d_h, q_h\}$, an ID and encrypted password pair corresponding to C_h itself, in *P* (individual clients know their own IDs, therefore C_h can find $\{d_h, q_h\}$ in *P*), and calculates $\underline{p}_h' = E(k_S, \{r, p_h\})$ and $R' = q_h \oplus \underline{p}_h'$. Here, if C_h is the authorized client it knows its password p_h, therefore its calculating $\underline{p}_h'$ coincides with $\underline{p}_h$. Then, $R' = q_h \oplus \underline{p}_h' = q_h \oplus \underline{p}_h = \underline{p}_h \oplus R \oplus \underline{p}_h = R$ is satisfied, and S can determine that C_h knows p_h when it receives R as the value of R'. However, an unauthorized entity cannot calculate R because it does not know any password in *P*. On the other hand, S cannot identify C_h provided that S assigns same random bit string R to all clients in *D*, because all clients in *D* know their own passwords and can return R as the value of R'. Here, although C_h can calculate encrypted password $E(k_s, \{r, p_j\}) = \underline{p}_j$ of other client P_j as $q_j \oplus R = \underline{p}_j$, it cannot impersonate

Figure 2. ID list based anonymous authentication

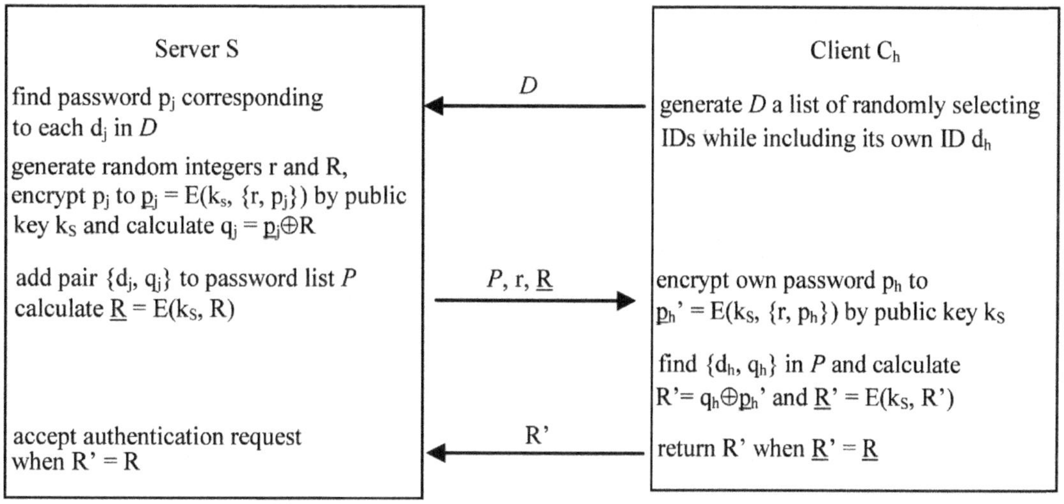

P_j by using $E(k_S, \{r, p_j\})$. Encryption function $E(k_S, \{r, x\})$ is probabilistic, therefore P_j's password p_j will be encrypted to a form different from $E(k_S, \{r, p_j\})$ at its future authentication request.

However, S can identify clients when it encrypts passwords of different clients by different keys. For example, when S assigns R_h to C_h that is unique to C_h, S can easily identify C_h when it receives R_h from C_h as the value of R'. Therefore a mechanism to force S to encrypt passwords of all clients in the ID list by the same key is necessary, and this is implemented by C_h's calculation of $R' = E(k_S, R')$. Namely, when $\underline{R}'$ does not coincide with $\underline{R}$, C_h can determine that S had encrypted passwords of different clients by different keys, but when they coincide, it can believe that S had used the same key R for all clients. Because S does not know the exact client that is requesting the authentication, even when it encrypts p_h, the password of C_h, by encryption key R_h unique to C_h, it cannot send $E(k_S, R_h)$ as the value of R to C_h. It must take risks to send $\underline{R}_j$ that had been assigned to different client C_j to C_h, and in that case $\underline{R}_j$ does not coincide with $E(k_S, R_h)$, then, this dishonesty of S eventually revealed and it cannot continue its business once its reputation is depraved.

Different from anonymous token based mechanisms, ID list based ones can easily handle clients that lose their eligibilities or forget their secrets, because server S checks the eligibilities of clients by their passwords that are linked directly to their identities. When C_h loses its eligibility or forgets its password, the only thing that S must do is to delete d_h, ID of C_h, from the database or replace p_h, password of C_h, in the database with newly declared one. By removing d_h from the database, S can reject C_h's authentication request, because d_h that C_h had included in the ID list cannot be found in its database. In the same way, by replacing p_h in the database with the new password, S can reject C_h's request with its old password p_h. However, ID list based mechanisms can work perfectly only in environment, in which clients can receive services from the server any number of times at a fixed price during its service period; a security gate of a company that permits only its employees to enter is an example. Different from ITL based mechanisms, in which tokens are effective for only once and clients cannot use tokens which they stole from others, in ID list based mechanisms, in which passwords can be used repeatedly, clients can tell their passwords to others without losing their eligibilities and also can use even its stealing passwords.

Possible threats to ID list based anonymous authentication mechanisms that must be considered are (1) password leaks from password lists, and (2) identifications of frequently visiting clients. In terms of password protection, authentication mechanisms based on ID lists are not advantageous, i.e. every time when client C_j requests authentication, a list of passwords of irrelevant clients are disclosed to C_j in the password list. Although server S encrypts each password p_h in the password list into $p_h = E(k_S, \{r, p_h\})$ so that other client C_j cannot calculate p_h from p_h, C_j that knows encryption key k_S and random factor r can try to encrypt possible passwords (e.g. birth date, telephone no.) without any restriction after the authentication communication links between C_j and S are disconnected, i.e. in the ID list based authentication mechanism, C_j can try to encrypt possible passwords of C_h by publicly known key k_S infinite times. Therefore, this threat is more serious than in usual cases, where S can suggest password replacement to C_h when other client C_j fails to access S while using C_h's ID by showing wrong passwords. Regarding the 2nd threat, because IDs of frequently visiting clients appear many times in ID lists, although S cannot identify exact clients that are requesting individual authentications, it can identify clients that visit it frequently. In the following subsections, ID list based anonymous authentication mechanism is enhanced to mitigate the above 2 weaknesses.

Enhancement of ID List Based Anonymous Authentication Mechanism

An apparent way to protect ID list based anonymous authentication mechanisms from the threat that client C_j steals passwords of other clients from password lists is to use longer passwords, not to use passwords that are linked to personal information of clients, such as birth dates or phone numbers, and to change passwords frequently. However, different from usual authentication systems, in this case, C_j can try to estimate passwords of other clients infinite times without being noticed by server S, e.g. C_j includes IDs of its knowing clients in the ID list when it requests authentication, assumes possible passwords of them, and encrypts them by using publicly known key k_S (and random factor r) to compare the results with the values in the password list. To strengthen passwords at least as ones in usual authentication systems, a mechanism to detect events, in which C_j tries to use passwords of other client C_h, is necessary. By this mechanism, S can notify C_h that someone is trying to use its password so that C_h can change its password to protect itself.

Here, it may seem that there is no reason for anonymous C_j that knows its own password to steal passwords of other clients, e.g. instead of stealing a password of other client C_h, C_j can tell its password to others to enable them to visit S without any loss or penalty because C_j is anonymous. However, there are cases where passwords robberies have meanings. For example, if C_j steals a password of other client C_h before it secedes from the system, it can continue to receive services even after its secession. Also when clients use same passwords for other systems, C_j can use its stealing password for visiting them. Therefore, still there exist reasons for C_j to steal passwords of other clients even if it knows its own password.

Aliases are the solution to mitigate the 2nd threat. Namely, by using different alias ID and password pairs at its different visits to S, C_h can decrease the number of appearances of its ID in the ID list even if it requests authentications frequently. Here the difficult thing is, different from non-anonymous systems, in anonymous authentication systems, server S must invalidate all aliases of client C_h without knowing links between C_h and these aliases, at a time when C_h

loses its eligibility, e.g. when C_h secedes from the system. Also, links between aliases of same clients must be hidden from any entity except the clients themselves; when these links are known to S, S can easily know the existences of frequently visiting clients.

Password Protection

This subsection discusses a mechanism that protects clients from unauthorized disclosures of their passwords and detects trials in which anonymous clients steal passwords of other clients. The mechanism exploits function $G(g_h, p_h)$ that transforms passwords so that different passwords may have the same transformed values as shown in Figure 3, where p_h is the password of C_h and g_h is a secret bit string (generally a set of bit strings) shared between S and C_h. Namely, in the anonymous authentication process shown in Figure 2, password p_h is firstly transformed to $G(g_h, p_h)$, after that it is encrypted by the public key of server S to $E(k_S, \{r, G(g_h, p_h)\})$ finally to be XORed by S's secret random bit string R. Therefore, S generates the password list while calculating $q_h = E(k_S, \{r, G(g_h, p_h)\}) \oplus R$. Then, client C_j that knows its own password p_j tries to steal p_h in the following way. Firstly, it calculates $E(k_S, \{r, G(g_j, p_j)\})$ to know $R = E(k_S, \{r, G(g_j, p_j)\}) \oplus q_j$, and extracts $E(k_S, \{r, G(g_h, p_h)\})$ by calculating $E(k_S, \{r, G(g_h, p_h)\}) = q_h \oplus R$, then generates $E(k_S, \{r, G(g_{h1}, p_{h1})\})$ while assuming g_{h1} and p_{h1} as the values of g_h and p_h, to compare the result $E(k_S, \{r, G(g_{h1}, p_{h1})\})$ with $E(k_S, \{r, G(g_h, p_h)\})$. However, because multiple pairs, e.g. $\{g_{h1}, p_{h1}\}$ and $\{g_{h2}, p_{h2}\}$, satisfy relations $E(k_S, \{r, G(g_h, p_h)\}) = E(k_S, \{r, G(g_{h1}, p_{h1})\}) = E(k_S, \{r, G(g_{h2}, p_{h2})\})$, C_j cannot determine whether p_{h1} is the correct password of C_h or not even if $E(k_S, \{r, G(g_h, p_h)\})$ coincides with $E(k_S, \{r, G(g_{h1}, p_{h1})\})$. As a consequence, C_j's authentication request with password p_{h1} may be rejected because S changes g_h at every authentication request from clients. Also C_j's authentication requests with p_{h1} at other server S' are rejected. In addition, at a time when S rejects C_j's request, it can notify C_h that someone is trying to use its ID and password so that C_h can change its password (this will be discussed later). Here, to protect password p_h securely, $N(g_h, p_h)$, the number of passwords that are transformed into the same value $G(g_h, p_h)$, must be large, i.e. the probability that entities successfully use their stealing p_h is less than $1/N(g_h, p_h)$.

An example of functions that satisfies the above property is $G(s, t_h, m_h, p_h) = p_h^{s} \oplus t_h^{mh}$, where p_h is the password of client C_h, t_h and m_h are secret bit strings shared between C_h and S in advance, and s is a bit string that S changes at every authentication request of clients, i.e. g_h is constituted as triple $\{s, t_h, m_h\}$. For a fixed value of s, function $G(s, t_h, m_h, p_h)$ transforms more than 10,000 dif-

Figure 3. Function with collisions

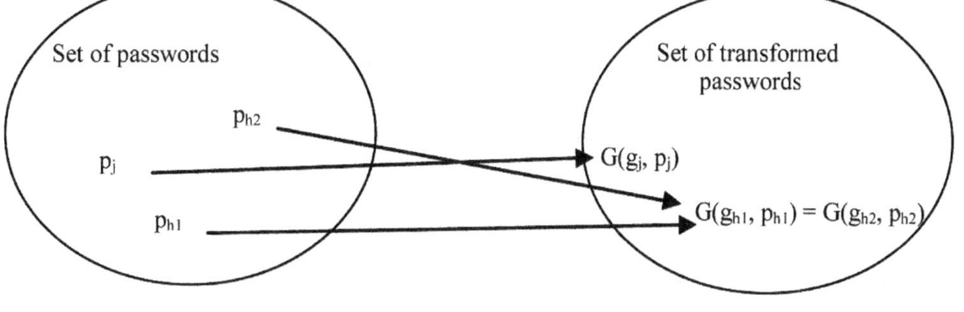

Figure 4. Data structure for registering client C_h

ID part	Password part	1st secret bit string part	2nd secret bit string part
ID_h	p_h	t_h	m_h

ferent triples $\{t_h, m_h, p_h\}$ (h = 1, 2, ---) to same bit string $v = G(s, t_h, m_h, p_h)$, when bit strings s, t_h, m_h, p_h are constituted by 4 digits decimal numbers. Therefore, the probability that C_j can successfully use its estimating password of C_h is less than 1/10,000.

To implement the ID list based authentication mechanism enhanced by $G(s, t_h, m_h, p_h)$, server S must maintain t_h and m_h for each client C_h as shown in Figure 4. Namely, C_h registers itself as an authorized client while showing t_h and m_h in addition to its ID and password pair. At C_h's every authentication request, S generates random bit strings r, R and s, and informs C_h of r and s. Therefore, both S and C_h can calculate $E(k_S, \{r, G(s, t_h, m_h, p_h)\})$. The important thing is that because S changes the value of s at every authentication request from clients, even if C_j finds p_{h1} and bit strings t_{h1} and m_{h1} that satisfy $G(s_1, t_h, m_h, p_h) = G(s_1, t_{h1}, m_{h1}, p_{h1})$ for s_1, C_j cannot use t_{h1}, m_{h1}, p_{h1} at its next visit. Also, S can notify C_h that some client had failed to access S while using C_h's ID by announcing the alert to all clients in the ID list attached to the authentication request of C_j so that C_h can change its password. Although this suggestion mechanism is not practical when the size of ID lists attached to individual authentication requests is large, i.e. S must alert many clients to their password leaks despite that only few of them are relevant. Therefore, although it becomes easier for S to estimate clients that request authentications if sizes of ID lists are small, it is desirable to reduce the size of the ID lists attached to individual authentication requests. Fortunately, aliases discussed below make the sizes of ID lists small while maintaining anonymities of clients.

Alias Management

An alias is a different form of an ID and a password pair of a client; therefore, frequently visiting clients can decrease the appearances of their IDs in the ID lists attached to their authentication requests if they put aliases in their ID lists instead of their original IDs. To make aliases effective and secure, an alias management mechanism must satisfy the following requirements, i.e.

1. Linkages not only between the original ID and its individual aliases but also between the aliases themselves must be concealed from any entity except the owner of the ID, and
2. All aliases that had been generated by an anonymous owner must be invalidated without disclosing the owner of the aliases when the owner secedes from the system.

When linkages between aliases of C_h and $\{d_h, p_h\}$, an original ID and password pair of C_h, are known, S can easily know the number of appearances of d_h in the ID lists even if C_h uses its aliases. Also, when AL(h), a set of aliases of C_h, is identified as a set of aliases owned by a same anonymous client, although S cannot directly know C_h from AL(h), AL(h) reveals the existence of a frequently visiting client, and sometimes this fact helps entities estimate owners of aliases in AL(h). Therefore, links between aliases themselves also must be concealed from others. About the 2nd requirement, to disable already seceding clients to visit the system, at a time when a client secedes from the system, S must invalidate all aliases that the client had generated. However, simple alias invalidation mechanisms reveal owners of aliases, e.g. if C_h had visited S frequently by using its aliases and reveals all of its aliases at a time when it secedes from the system, S can easily know that C_h was a frequently visiting client. ITLs used in the ITL based authentication mechanisms enable the efficient implementation of the alias management mechanism that satisfies the above 2 requirements.

Figure 5 is the procedure, in which C_h generates its r-th alias A(h, r) at its n-th visit to S for registering its aliases. Here, C_h visits S both for generating and deleting its aliases, therefore generally n is larger than r. In the figure, client C_h generates alias A(h, r) while showing its n-th token T(h, n) and encrypted (n+1)-th token $E(a_h, T(h, n+1))$ to constitute ITL(h, n). As same as in the previous section, different from anonymous tokens, properties required for T(h, n) are only its anonymity and uniqueness, therefore T(h, n) is constituted as an open token, i.e. the blind signature scheme is not required.

Firstly, S authenticates anonymous client C_h by an ID list based anonymous authentication mechanism, and when the authentication is completed successfully, C_h asks S to register alias A(h, r) with T(h, n) and $E(a_h, T(h, n+1))$ while encrypting its (n+1)-th token T(h, n+1) by its secret key a_h. Here, T(h, n+1) is a token to be used at C_h's next visit to S for generating or deleting its alias. Then, after confirming that T(h, n) was not used before and it is consistent with C_h's past ITLs, S constructs ITL(h, n) as pair $\{v_nT(h, n), v_{n+1}E(a_h, T(h, n+1))\}$ and generates alias registration record L(h, n) = {A(h, r), ITL(h, n)}, and finally, S registers L(h, n) as an authorized record, and encrypts L(h, n) to $E(k_S, L(h, n))$ by its encryption key k_S to be saved by C_h. Here, v_n and v_{n+1} are token concealers secret from C_h and S assigns values to them according to the number of C_h's visits for alias generations and deletions. Then, because L(h, n) does not include any information about C_h and T(h, n+1)

Figure 5. Alias generation process

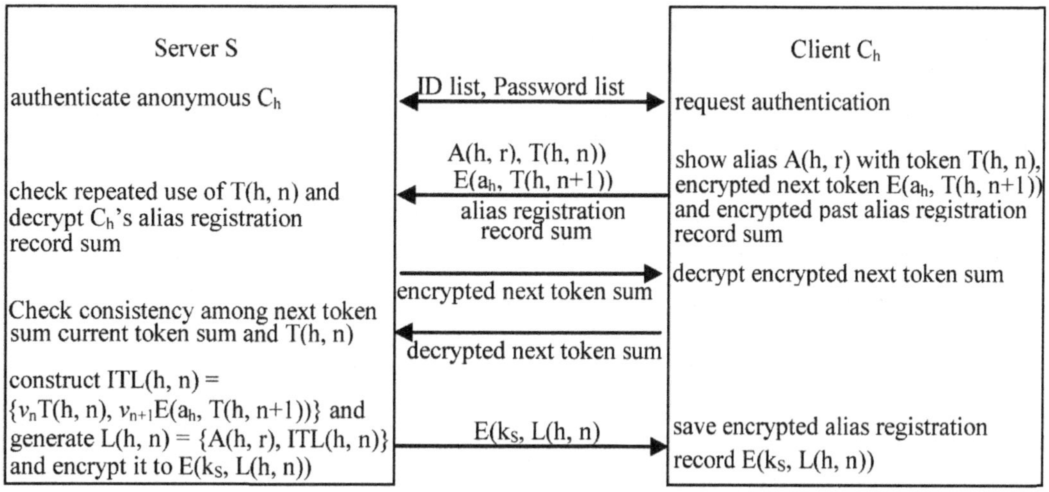

in ITL(h, n) is encrypted by C_h's secret key, no one except C_h can know the owner of A(h, r), or identify that T(h, n) and T(h, n+1) are the tokens assigned to the same client, i.e. the 1st requirement of the alias management mechanism is satisfied. Here, apparently C_h that uses alias A(h, r) is an authorized client because C_h had obtained it while being authenticated successfully based on the ID list based authentication mechanism; therefore C_h can request authentications also by using A(h, r). In the above, $E(a_h, x)$ and $E(k_s, y)$ are additive encryption functions of course.

At its m-th visit to S, C_h deletes its alias A(h, r) in the same way as it had generated A(h, r) except the 2 things, they are, firstly, S does not add A(h, r), instead it deletes A(h, r) from its database, and secondly, S constructs the deregistration record L(h, m) by calculating the negative of A(h, r), i.e. S constructs L(h, m) = {-A(h, r), v_mT(h, m), v_{m+1}E(a_h, T(h, m+1))}, where -A(h, r) is a bit string corresponding to the negative of alias A(h, r) when it is considered as a signed integer.

The important thing is that additive encryption functions $E(k_S, x)$ and $E(a_h, y)$ enable S to confirm that C_h had deleted its all aliases when it secedes from the system without knowing individual aliases of C_h. Namely, because A(h, r) generation and deletion are recorded as {A(h, r), v_nT(h, n), v_{n+1}E(a_h, T(h, n+1))} and {-A(h, r), v_mT(h, m), v_{m+1}E(a_h, T(h, m+1))}, respectively, S can know that C_h had deleted its all aliases, when the sum of aliases included in C_h's alias registration and deregistration records coincides with 0. Also, because these records are encrypted by additive encryption function $E(k_S, x)$, S can calculate the sum without knowing the individual records of C_h by decrypting the sum of encrypted records calculated by C_h itself, i.e. S can calculate $\sum_{p=0}^{p=N}${A(h, p)} by decrypting $\sum_{p=0}^{p=N}${E(k_S, L(h, p))} that is reported by C_h. Here, it is assumed that C_h carries out its seceding procedure at its (N+1)-th visit to S for alias registration and deregistration. On the other hand, because each L(h, n) is encrypted by S and tokens T(h, n) and T(h, n+1) in L(h, n) are multiplied by token concealers secret from C_h, C_h cannot delete, add, modify or forge registration or deregistration records of its aliases in unauthorized ways without being detected by S as discussed in section "Implicit Transaction Links," i.e. the 2nd requirement is satisfied.

S can protect the mechanism also from the threat that client C_j may delete aliases of other client C_h. Because each alias consists of a pair of alias ID and alias password, C_j cannot delete alias ID of other client without knowing the corresponding password. Of course it is possible for S to delete C_h's aliases without the permission of C_h; however C_h can prove that its aliases are deleted illegitimately by others by its maintaining records and its unused token, and when S deletes C_h's aliases dishonestly, S loses its reputation to continue its businesses.

It must be noted that clients must delete their aliases independent of their secessions. When C_h deletes its aliases just before it secedes from the system, S can expect that deleted aliases were owned by C_h. Especially when C_h deletes many aliases before its secession, this expectation becomes accurate. To conceal alias owners more successfully, clients must avoid consecutive deletions of their multiple aliases; instead, they must iterate new alias generations while deleting old ones. Of course, C_h cannot generate or delete multiple aliases at a time, when they are generated or deleted at a time S can easily know that these aliases are owned by a same anonymous client.

ANONYMOUS CREDENTIALS AND ANONYMOUS TAGS

Credentials are a kind of tokens but an important difference between usual tokens is that their validity can be verified by entities other than the servers that had issued them. Therefore although credentials are considered as extensions of tokens, ITL based mechanisms cannot be used for example, because secret keys of servers for encrypting and decrypting ITLs are required to generate and verify them. Let C_h, S_j and V_m be a client, a server and a verifier, respectively, where S_j issues credential $D_j(h)$ to C_h so that C_h can show V_m that it is an eligible entity authorized by S_j. Then, if C_h obtains credentials $D_1(h)$, $D_2(h)$, ---, $D_N(h)$ from servers S_1, S_2, ---, S_N, C_h can convince V_m that it is an eligible entity authorized by multiple servers S_{n1}, S_{n2}, ---, S_{nZ} by showing $D_{n1}(h)$, $D_{n2}(h)$, ---, $D_{nZ}(h)$ it had picked from $D_1(h)$, $D_2(h)$, ---, $D_N(h)$. For example, if $D_1(h)$ and $D_2(h)$ are credentials issued by a bank and a government office that ensure C_h had paid and the age of C_h is 25, respectively, C_h can convince a liquor shop that it is eligible to receive a bottle of whisky. Here, the amount that C_h had paid and age 25 in the credentials are called credential attribute values, and advanced anonymous credentials also enable their owners to prove their eligibilities without disclosing their exact attribute values and while combining multiple attribute values through predefined functions (Belenkiy, 2009, Cmamenisch, 2001, Shahandashti, 2009, Sudarsono, 2011).

Then as same as usual anonymous authentication mechanisms, anonymous credentials must satisfy requirements (1), (2), (3), (4), (5) and (6) in the introduction of this chapter, but to make anonymous credentials practical, an additional feature that enables entities to repeatedly use their (some) credentials becomes inevitable. Because C_h shows credentials issued by server S_j to verifiers instead of S_j itself, S_j cannot use token refreshing mechanisms, in which clients show their tokens in exchange for their new tokens, for issuing new credentials to clients. Therefore, if every credential is effective only once in the above example, client C_h must visit the government office to obtain a credential that proves its age every time it buys whisky, and the worse thing is that the government office may know C_h's privacy from the number of credentials that C_h had obtained. On the contrary, there are cases where servers must protect their credentials from being used too many times. Then, anonymous credentials must satisfy the following additional requirements, i.e.

7. A client can use its credential multiple times, and
8. A server that had issued a credential can limit the number of times the credential is effective.

The above features seem to contradict the 3rd requirement in the introduction that "no one except a client itself can link a sequence of its past authentication requests," but it is possible to implement anonymous credentials that satisfy requirements (1), (2), (3), (4), (5), (6), (7) and (8) except the 4th and the 5th ones. Although many schemes had been reported while extensively using zero knowledge proofs (ZKPs), this section implements them based on anonymous tags without exploiting complicated ZKPs (Tamura, 2008).

Issuing Anonymous Credentials

Anonymous credential $D_j(h)$ that client C_h obtains from server S_j is configured as $S(d, T_B^{D+Kg+K+1})$ $S(d, T^{R+Kg+k+1}) = S(d, T_B^{D+Kg+K+1}T^{R+Kg+K+1})$. Here as discussed in subsection "Anonymous Tokens based on Anonymous Tags," d is a secret signing key of S_j's RSA signing function $S(d, x) = x^d{}_{\bmod p}$, D is the attribute value of the credential (e.g. in the previous example, D represents the age of C_h), T_B and T are integers defined by S_j, R is a secret integer of C_h, K is a publicly disclosed integer common to all credentials, and g is S_j's secret integer. Then as shown in Figure 6, $S(d, T_B^{D+Kg+K+1})$ and $S(d, T^{R+Kg+K+1})$ constitute the attribute part and the token part values of $D_j(h)$, and $\{T_B, T_B^D\}$ and $\{T, T^R\}$ are anonymous tags, i.e. T_B and T are tag part values and T_B^D and T^R are associate tag part values.

C_h obtains $D_j(h)$ through the procedure shown in Figure 7. Firstly, C_h shows its identity with credential attribute value D so that S_j can verify C_h is eligible for value D, and if C_h is accepted as eligible, C_h calculates pairs $\{T_B, T_B^{D}\}$ and $\{T, T^R\}$ while generating its secret integer R. Where, integers T_B and T defined by S_j are unique to credential $S(d, T_B^{D+Kg+K+1}T^{R+Kg+K+1})$. Then, S_j verifies whether $\{T_B, T_B^{D}\}$ is calculated honestly or not, and finally, S_j signs on product $T_B^{D+Kg+K+1}T^{R+Kg+K+1}$ to generate $D_j(h) = S(d, T_B^{D+Kg+K+1}T^{R+Kg+K+1})$ to give it to C_h while attaching T_B^{g} and T^g.

In the above, S informs C_h of T_B^{g} and T^g so that C_h can convince anyone that $D_j(h)$ is valid. Also, although above credential $D_j(h) = S(d, T_B^{D+Kg+K+1}T^{R+Kg+K+1})$ includes only one attribute value D, it is possible to assign multiple attribute values to a single credential. For example, when S_j defines new integer T_F, it can assign expiration time F to $D_j(h)$ by constructing it as $D_j(h) = S(d, T_B^{D+Kg+K+1}T_F^{F+Kg+K+1}T^{R+Kg+K+1})$.

Verifying Anonymous Credentials

Client C_h shows its credential $D_j(h) = S(d, T_B^{D+Kg+K+1}T^{R+Kg+K+1})$ to verifier V_m in form $D_j(h)^W = S(d, T_B^{D+Kg+K+1}T^{R+Kg+K+1})^W$ together with set $\{D, T_B^{W}, T_B^{gW}, T^W, T^{gW}, T^{RW}\}$ while generating its secret integer W. Then, V_m confirms that $D_j(h)$ has the signature of S_j on the product of T_B^{W}, T_B^{KW}, T_B^{KgW}, T_B^{DW}, T^W, T^{KW}, T^{KgW}, T^{RW} and verifies the validity of anonymous tag $\{T^W, T^{RW}\}$. At the same time, C_h calculates used seal M^R to be maintained by V_m (in a case where $D_j(h)$ can be used repeatedly, C_h maintains pair $\{n, M(n)^R\}$, where, n is the number of authentication requests that C_h had made). Here, validity of tag $\{T_B^{W}, T_B^{DW}\}$ is automatically

Figure 6. Configuration of anonymous credential based on anonymous tags

Attribute part	Token part
$S(d, T_B^{D+Kg+K+1})$	$S(d, T^{R+Kg+K+1})$
Anomymous tag $\{T, T^D\}$	Anomymous tag $\{T, T^R\}$

Figure 7. Issuing anonymous credentials based on anonymous tags

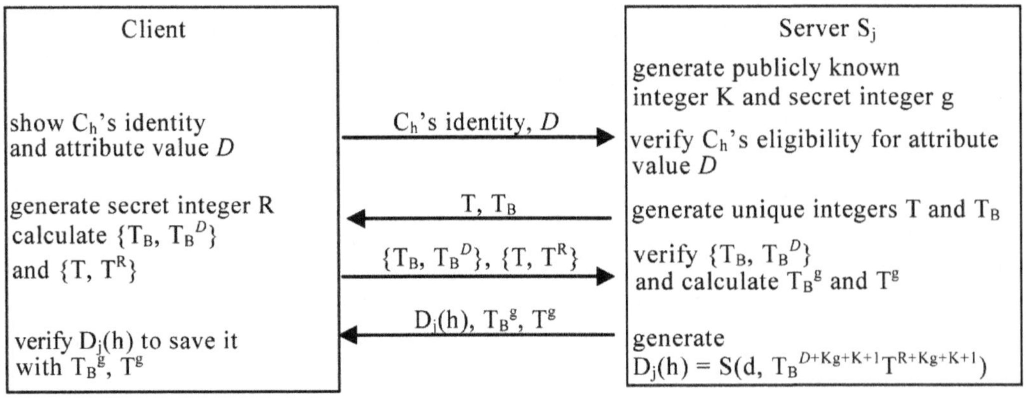

ensured, and the validity of $\{T^{W}, T^{RW}\}$ also can be verified without knowing C_h's secret R by the procedure in subsection "Anonymous Tokens based on Anonymous Tags" of Section 2.

It must be noted that attribute value D must be included in $D_j(h)$ in form $T_B^{D+Kg+K+1}$. If D is included in usual signed form S(d, D), $D_j(h)$ becomes $D_j(h)$ = S(d, D)S(d, $T^{R+Kg+K+1}$) = S(d, $DT^{R+Kg+K+1}$) (signing function S(d,x) is multiplicative). Then, at a time when C_h shows credential $D_j(h)^W$ = S(d, $DT^{R+Kg+K+1}$)^W, C_h can attach $\{D^P, (D^P)^Q, T^W, T^{gW}, T^{RW}\}$ instead of $\{D, D^W, T^W, T^{gW}, T^{RW}\}$ to the credential while defining P and Q so that relation PQ = W holds because V_m does not know W. Therefore, $(DT^{R+Kg+K+1})^W$ is regarded as the product of $(D^P)^Q$, T^{RW}, T^{KgW}, T^{KW} and T^W, and C_h can claim that the attribute value of $D_j(h)^W$ is D^P.

Performance of Anonymous Tag-Based Credentials

Anonymous credentials in the previous subsection satisfy requirements (1), (2), (3), (4), (5) and (6) listed in the introduction of this chapter except the 4th and the 5th ones as follow. About requirement (1), credential $D_j(h)$ convinces anyone that attribute value D is authorized by server S_j because only S_j that knows signing key d can generate consistent credentials, and as mentioned just above C_h cannot declare attribute value D dishonestly. In addition, other entity does not know C_h's secret R, therefore only client C_h, the owner of credential $D_j(h)$ = S(d, $T_B^{D+Kg+K+1}T^{R+Kg+K+1}$), can use $D_j(h)$. Although C_h can give $D_j(h)$ to other entity C_k together with its secret number R, in this case, C_h cannot use $D_j(h)$ anymore (in a case where $D_j(h)$ is allowed to be used multiple times, the number of times C_h can use it decreases). Namely, only authorized clients are successfully authenticated, and clients cannot give credentials to others without losing their eligibilities. But $D_j(h)$ cannot disable entities to steal it, i.e. when C_k steals $D_j(h)$ with secret number R, C_k can use it without being noticed by others.

Requirements (2),(3) and (6) are also satisfied as below, i.e. anyone except C_h cannot identify C_h from $D_j(h)$ or link a sequence of C_h's past visits even if it uses $D_j(h)$ repeatedly, because C_h uses $D_j(h)$ while transforming it to $D_j(h)^W$ by using its secret integer W that changes at every use. Nevertheless, S_j can identify C_h as the dishonest client if C_h had behaved dishonestly without revealing any privacy of honest clients, because C_h leaves used seals of the anonymous tag included in credential $D_j(h)$ based on its secret integer R. Namely as discussed in the section about anonymous tags in Part II, S can determine C_h that can calculate used seal M^R or $M(n)^R$ is dishonest, i.e. requirement (6) is satisfied.

About additional requirement (7) and (8), C_h can use $D_j(h)^W$ repeatedly while disabling others to identify the sequence of its authentication requests by changing values of its secret integer W as discussed already, and used seal $M(n)^R$ of anonymous tag based tokens that C_h had generated at its n-th authentication request disables C_h to use $D_j(h)$ more than N-times, where N is the limit that S_j defines in advance. In addition, used seal $M(n)^R$ can be used as the evidence that verifier V_m had accepted $D_j(h)^W$ as a valid credential, i.e. if V_m accepted $D_j(h)$ shown by other client C_k, the used seal generated by C_k is inconsistent because C_k does not know R, therefore, C_h can claim that someone other than C_h had used $D_j(h)$ and V_m had accepted it dishonestly. On the other hand when V_m maintains correct used seal $M(n)^R$, V_m can disable C_h to claim that its credential had been dishonestly accepted.

However, credential $D_j(h)$ cannot satisfy requirement (4) or (5), i.e. server S_j cannot immediately invalidate $D_j(h)$ even if it expels client C_h that owns $D_j(h)$, or it cannot reissue $D_j(h)$ when C_h

forgets its secrets. To satisfy these requirements, S_j must invalidate all credentials, or C_h must reveal its all privacies.

CONCLUSION

As anonymous authentication mechanisms, anonymous token, ITL and ID list based ones were discussed as well as an anonymous tag based credentials. Anonymous token and ITL based mechanisms have a substantial advantage in protecting secrets necessary in authentication processes, i.e. entities cannot give tokens necessary for authentication processes to others without losing their eligibilities. However, anonymous token based ones have difficulties in handling entities that are expelled or that forget their secrets. Regarding ITL based mechanisms, they disable entities not only to give their tokens to others but also to use tokens that they had stolen from others. In addition, ITL based mechanisms can handle expelled clients or clients that had lost their tokens when the number of those entities is not so large although they sacrifice the 3rd requirement of anonymous authentication schemes. Then, ITL based mechanisms can be considered as the best solution when the number of dishonest entities is not large. On the other hand, ID list based mechanisms can handle expelled and secret forgetting entities completely, however entities can tell their passwords to others without losing their eligibilities to enable other unauthorized entities to be authenticated successfully. Therefore, they can be considered as the best solution for systems in which eligible entities can receive any number of services at fixed prices during predefined periods.

Although it is expected that advantages of both ITL and ID list based anonymous authentication mechanisms can be exploited by combining them, simple combinations cannot work well. For example, although only entities that know passwords and have tokens are authenticated successfully when 2 mechanisms are combined, an expelled entity can still request authentications successfully by using its invalid token while being informed of a password of other eligible entity.

About a mechanism for anonymous credentials, when requirements for efficiently invalidating ineffective credentials and reissuing credentials to secret forgetting clients are abandoned, it was demonstrated that anonymous tags can successfully implement it.

REFERENCES

Belenkiy, M., Camenisch, J., Chase, M., Kohlweiss, M., Lysyanskaya, A., & Shacham, H. (2009). Randomizable proofs and delegatable anonymous credentials. *Proceedings of the 29th Annual International Cryptology Conference on Advances in Cryptology*, 16-20 August 2009, Santa Barbara, CA, (pp. 108-125).

Camenisch, J., & Lysyanskaya, A. (2001). An efficient system for non-transferable anonymous credential with optimal anonymity revocation. *Proceedings of EUROCRYPT'01, the International Conference on the Theory and Application of Cryptographic Techniques: Advances in Cryptography,* (pp. 93-118). London, UK: Springer-Verlag

Chaum, D. (1983). Blind signatures system. *Advances in Cryptology, CRYPTO, 83*, 153–156.

Kahn, D. (1996). *The codebreakers – The comprehensive history of secret communication from ancient times to the Internet – Revised and updated.* New York, NY: Scribner.

Shahandashti, S. F., & Safavi-Naini, R. (2009). Threshold attribute-based signatures and their application to anonymous credential systems. *Proceedings of the 2nd International Conference on Cryptology in Africa: Progress in Cryptology*. Berlin, Germany: Springer-Verlag.

Shigetomi, R., Otsuka, A., & Imai, H. (2003). *Refreshable tokens and its applications to anonymous loans*. SCIS2003.

Sudarsono, A., Nakanishi, T., & Funabiki, N. (2011). Efficient proofs of attributes in pairing-based anonymous credential system. *Springer Lecture Notes in Computer Science, 6794/2011*, (pp. 246-263).

Tamura, S., Kouro, K., Sasatani, S., Md. Rokibul, K. A., & Haddad, H. A. (2008). An information system platform for anonymous product recycling. *Journal of Software*, *3*(6), 46–56. doi:10.4304/jsw.3.6.46-56

Tamura, S., Kouro, K., & Yanase, T. (2006). Expenditure limits in anonymous credit card systems. *IEEE SMC, 2006*, 1238–1243.

Tamura, S., & Yanase, T. (2005). Information sharing among untrustworthy entities. *IEEJ Transactions in EIS*, *125*(11), 1767–1772. doi:10.1541/ieejeiss.125.1767

Tamura, S., & Yanase, T. (2007). A mechanism for anonymous credit card systems. *IEEJ Transactions in EIS*, *127*(1), 81–87. doi:10.1541/ieejeiss.127.81

Chapter 10
Electronic Payment Systems

ABSTRACT

An anonymous credit card system and an electronic cash (e-cash) system are developed while exploiting ITLs and anonymous tag based credentials. Both systems enable entities to make their purchases without disclosing their identities; also they disable anyone other than the entities themselves to link their consecutive purchases. Nevertheless, ITLs in the credit card system enable card companies to calculate correct total expenditure amounts of individual cardholders without invading any privacy of honest cardholders. Because of anonymous tag based credentials, entities in the developed e-cash system can also use e-cash that had been paid to them by others, and they can receive changes from others in e-cash, under both online and offline environments.

INTRODUCTION

Payment systems are the one of the most urgent applications those require anonymous security technologies. The reasons are on the one hand, they are the bases for developing other various important applications because many human activities in the real world include payments, and on the other hand, payments themselves are highly sensitive about privacies of people.

There are 2 types of payments, the one is credit transaction based and the other is cash transaction based, and corresponding to these types, anonymous electronic payment (e-payment) systems are also divided into 2 categories, i.e. anonymous credit card systems and electronic cash (e-cash) systems. Although requirements for both anonymous credit card and e-cash systems are almost the same, they attract interests of researchers in different ways. Regarding anonymous credit card systems, the main issue is how to calculate the total expenditure of each cardholder correctly without knowing its individual purchases. On the other hand about e-cash systems, interests are focused on the offline feature of cash, e.g. on mechanisms to disable entities to use their e-cash repeatedly without online databases of used e-cash or to pay changes by e-cash without attendances of the bank that issues e-cash.

DOI: 10.4018/978-1-4666-1649-3.ch010

This chapter shows that ITLs and anonymous tags discussed in Part II can satisfactory handle these issues, i.e. an anonymous credit card system and an e-cash system that satisfy all essential requirements are developed without assuming any absolutely trustworthy entity based on ITLs and anonymous tags, respectively.

ANONYMOUS CREDIT CARD SYSTEMS

Credit card systems are one of the most effective and efficient means for remote payments. For example, when the Internet and credit card systems are combined, people can buy anything without going out from their homes or offices, and as a consequence, development of highly efficient, convenient and environmentally friendly society becomes possible. However, all privacies of customers will be revealed, when credit card companies and Internet providers exchange information about their customers. Therefore, credit card systems must be endowed with anonymous features so that more people accept the systems and fully exploit their benefits.

Requirements for Anonymous Credit Card Systems

In the following, the server and clients denote the credit card company and cardholders, respectively. Then an anonymous credit card system must satisfy the following requirements, i.e.

1. The server can neither identify clients that carry out individual transactions nor link transaction records of same clients,
2. The server can calculate the total expenditures of individual clients at the end of its every service period (e.g. end of every month),
3. The server can identify clients that behaved dishonestly and charge them for correct amounts without information about other honest clients,
4. Clients can detect dishonest operations of the server, and
5. No absolutely trustworthy entity is assumed.

Firstly, although it is possible to enforce the server not to intentionally use the information of clients illegitimately as an organization, various attackers including malicious employees of the server may intrude in the server to acquire information about clients. Therefore, identities of clients that carry out individual transactions must be concealed from anyone including the server when clients desire. At the same time, links between consecutive transactions of same clients also must be concealed, since a transaction sequence of a client includes various suggestions for identifying the client. On the other hand, of course the server must be able to calculate the total expenditures of individual clients at the end of the server's every service period so that it can collect them from individual clients. Also in order to recover from inconsistent states caused by clients' intentional or accidental dishonest behaviors, the server must be able to identify exact clients that had caused the inconsistencies, and to charge them the correct amounts for their expenditures while maintaining identities of clients that had honestly carried out their transactions confidential. In the same way, clients must be able to detect inconsistent states of their transaction records in order to protect themselves from dishonest operations of the server.

Lastly, it is not desirable to assume the existence of absolutely trustworthy entities, such as tamper resistant memories or neutral organizations that are faithful both to the server and clients, because to assume the existence of these absolutely trustworthy entities is becoming difficult in the real world. Opportunities of intentional or accidental data disclosures become more likely as activities of servers and clients are expanding. These entities must maintain a lot of various and important information; also many sub-entities are becoming to be involved in carrying out individual transactions. Therefore, it is not realistic to develop anonymous credit card systems based on entities that are completely faithful to all relevant entities.

Different from e-cash systems discussed in the next section, only few anonymous credit card systems had been reported until now (Low, 1996, Androulaki, 2009). In addition, they maintain anonymity of clients by assuming anonymous bank accounts and distributing transaction records to multiple mutually independent banks, or they are developed based on e-cash systems. Therefore in the former case, systems become impractical, e.g. clients must make multiple accounts or anonymous accounts are not allowed in several countries, and more importantly, trusted entities that are faithful to all entities cannot be excluded completely, e.g. when identities of anonymous account holders are disclosed all privacies of clients will be revealed. In the latter case, clients cannot fully exploit benefits of credit card systems, e.g. they must buy e-cash before they make purchases although they may not be required to pay for the e-cash in advance. A scheme discussed in this chapter is based on ITLs and enables the development of complete anonymous credit card systems, i.e. credit card systems that satisfy all the above requirements, without assuming any absolutely trustworthy entity.

Development of an Anonymous Credit Card System

Overview of the System

The ITL based anonymous credit card system (Tamura, 2007) developed in this chapter consists of server S (the card company) and multiple clients (cardholders). In the followings except in subsection "Offline Anonymous Credit Card Systems" it is assumed that stores are connected always to server S and they can ask S to carry out every computation necessary for completing transactions, therefore individual stores can be considered as identical to server S. Then, the anonymous credit card system carries out transactions through 6 phases as shown in Figure 1. They are registration, token acquisition, initial transaction, transaction, account balancing and state recovery phases, and ITLs enable S to authenticate clients without knowing their identities and to force clients to maintain their transaction records honestly so that S can correctly calculate total expenditures of clients without knowing their individual purchases.

In the figure, each client C_h obtains open tokens T(h, n) and T(h, n+1) before its n-th visit to server S, and shows T(h, n) and $E(a_h, T(h, n+1))$ to be authenticated by S, then, S issues n-th transaction record TR(h, n) that includes ITL(h, n), the n-th ITL of client C_h. Here, as discussed in section "Implicit Transaction Links" of Part II, $E(a_h, x)$ is an additive encryption function implemented by linear equation based encryption scheme, a_h is C_h's secret encryption key, and ITL(h, n) is constructed as a pair of the current (n-th) and the encrypted next ((n+1)-th) tokens concealed by token concealers v_n and v_{n+1}, i.e. $ITL(h, n) = \{v_nT(h, n), v_{n+1}E(a_h, T(h, n+1))\}$ (as an exception, C_h's initial ITL has the form $ITL(h, 0) = \{v_0T(h, 0), v_0E(a_h, T(h, 0))+v_1E(a_h, T(h, 1))\}$. Also, token concealers are secret numbers of S that disable C_h to illegitimately modify transaction record TR(h, n), and values of token concealers are defined based on the number of visits that C_h had made before and declared by C_h itself. Therefore S can assign same v_{n+1} to values of the next token at C_h's n-th visit and the current token at its (n+1)-th visit. As mentioned in Part II, C_h cannot declare the number of visits it had made dishonestly, and the number of visits is initialized when it reaches a relatively small pre-defined value to conceal frequently visiting clients. Also actually, ITLs and encrypted next tokens are constructed as ex-

Figure 1. Six phases of anonymous credit card system

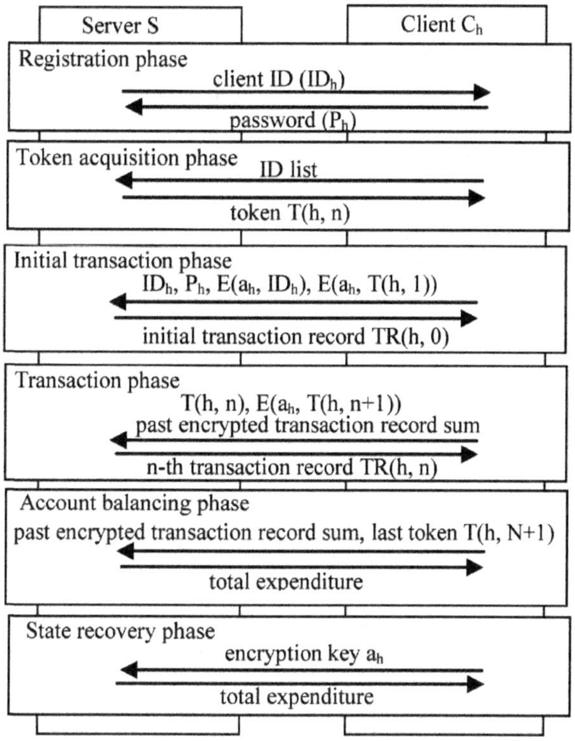

tended ITLs and extended next tokens to protect them from malicious entities including S and C_h.

In detail, before making purchases at stores, each client C_h must register itself as an authorized client of server S in the registration phase. As in usual registration procedures, C_h registers itself by obtaining ID_h as its identifier (ID) from S and defining its password P_h. In addition to that in this phase, C_h also defines its secret key a_h of encryption function E(a_h, x). The token acquisition phase is independent of other phases, and each client C_h obtains unique tokens through this phase in advance, where, C_h enters this phase without disclosing its identity based on the ID list based anonymous authentication mechanism discussed in the 1st chapter in this part and picks one open token from the token table prepared by S. Therefore, although anyone except C_h cannot identify the links between C_h and its obtaining tokens, the uniqueness of tokens is ensured, i.e. S does not give same tokens to clients. In the above, theoretically S does not need to authenticate C_h, because S authenticates C_h by ITLs in the transaction phase. A reason why S authenticates clients in this phase is to reduce the number of tokens it must prepare in the token table, i.e. unauthorized clients cannot pick tokens from the token table if their eligibilities are examined.

Then in the initial transaction phase, C_h visits S to receive its initial transaction record TR(h, 0) while showing {ID_h, P_h}, E(a_h, T(h, 1)) and E(a_h, T(h, ID_h)), therefore C_h is not anonymous in this phase. Where, T(h, 1) is a token that C_h had obtained through the token acquisition phase. Initial transaction record TR(h, 0) is a dummy one, and S generates it only for authorizing C_h's initial ITL (i.e. ITL(h, 0)) included in TR(h, 0). In more precisely, S defines the value of C_h's initial token as $T(h, 0) = ID_h$ and authorizes $E(a_h, T(h, 1))$ shown by C_h while including it together with $T(h, 0) = ID_h$ in $ITL(h, 0) = \{v_0T(h, 0), v_0E(a_h, T(h, 0)) + v_1E(a_h, T(h, 1))\}$ so that S can authenticate C_h by $T(h, 1)$ at its next visit. The important things are firstly $T(h, 0)$ and $E(a_h, T(h, 1))$ in $ITL(h, 0)$ are multiplied by token concealers secrets of S, and secondly, $T(h, 1)$ is encrypted to $E(a_h, T(h, 1))$ by C_h. Therefore, S can protect $ITL(h, 0)$ from illegitimate modifications by C_h, and C_h can make itself anonymous even if it shows $T(h, 1)$ to S at its next visit.

In the transaction phase, server S authenticates anonymous client C_h through the ITL based authentication scheme. In detail, C_h shows its token $T(h, n)$ at its n-th visit to S, and S confirms that $T(h, n)$ was not used before and verifies the consistency between $T(h, n)$ and past ITLs maintained by C_h itself. Namely, eligibility of C_h is ensured by the consistent relation between $T(h, n)$ and past ITLs C_h is maintaining. After that, C_h makes its purchases while exchanging information necessary for generating a draft of its n-th transaction record with server S, and C_h verifies the draft, encrypts its next token $T(h, n+1)$ to $E(a_h, T(h, n+1))$, then, finally S generates transaction record $TR(h, n)$ based on the draft and pair $\{T(h, n), E(a_h, T(h, n+1))\}$. Here, pair $\{T(h, n), E(a_h, T(h, n+1))\}$ sent from C_h is included in $ITL(h, n) = \{v_nT(h, n), v_{n+1}E(a_h, T(h, n+1))\}$ by S to be incorporated in $TR(h, n)$, therefore, C_h can make its next visit without disclosing its identity by showing $T(h, n+1)$ in the same way as it had used $T(h, 1)$ after its initial visit. But it must be noted that C_h must show $E(a_h, T(h, n+1))$ only after it verified the correctness of the draft transaction record. As mentioned in subsection "Homomorphic Anonymous Tokens," when dishonest events are detected about the transaction record accompanied by $ITL(h, n)$, S identifies C_h as a dishonest client when C_h consistently decrypts $E(a_h, T(h, n+1))$ included in $ITL(h, n)$, and this means that $ITL(h, n) = \{v_nT(h, n), v_{n+1}E(a_h, T(h, n+1))\}$ is regarded as C_h's approval of $TR(h, n)$. Therefore, if S knows $E(a_h, T(h, n+1))$ before C_h verifies the draft, S can generate $TR(h, n)$ at its will, e.g. S can include excessive expenditure amount in it.

In the account balancing phase, S calculates total expenditures of individual clients based on transaction records that it had generated in individual transaction phases, but to maintain anonymity of the clients, S stores individual records without knowing clients and it does not know linkages between consecutive transactions of same clients. Therefore, individual clients calculate their total expenditures by themselves based on transaction records they are maintaining. However, when responsibilities for calculating total expenditures are passed to anonymous clients, they can easily modify their transaction records to reduce the amounts that they must pay. Therefore, to protect transaction records from illegitimate modifications made by clients, S gives transaction records to each client C_h while encrypting them by its secret key.

Here, the important thing is that S encrypts transaction records by linear equation based additive encryption function, therefore it can know the total expenditure of C_h from the sum of encrypted transaction records calculated by C_h, in other words without knowing individual transaction records of C_h. This additive encryption function also protects S from dishonest reports of clients. Because the next token in $ITL(h, n)$ is the current token in $ITL(h, n+1)$, the sum of the current tokens and that of the next tokens included in C_h's past transaction records must be equal if C_h honestly maintains its all transaction records. Therefore, S can determine C_h is dishonest when its reporting sum of encrypted transaction records reveals different values as the sum of current tokens and that of next tokens.

The state recovery phase starts when dishonest events are detected in some transaction records so that server S can recover from damages caused by them. ITLs enable S also to identify dishonest entities liable for dishonest events without invading any privacy of honest clients, and once

C_h is determined as dishonest, S can trace all transactions of C_h by asking C_h to disclose its secret encryption key a_h (in this case encryption and decryption keys are the same). Here, S can enforce dishonest clients to reveal their secret keys, because clients are regarded as responsible for all damages corresponding to the discrepancy between the total sales amounts reported by all stores and total expenditure amounts reported by all clients if they do not disclose their keys.

Transaction Records

Different from usual systems, in the anonymous credit card system, individual clients are responsible for maintaining their transaction records. Therefore, a mechanism to disable each client C_h to modify or forge its maintaining transaction records is necessary, and also C_h must be protected from server S's dishonesty of course. To protect both C_h and S from dishonest events, S gives C_h 2-forms of TR(h, n), C_h's transaction record at its n-th visit. The one is the encrypted transaction record $E(k_s, TR(h, n))$ and the other is the signed transaction record $S(g_s, TR(h, n))$, where k_s and g_s are secret encryption and signing keys of S. Namely, C_h cannot illegitimately modify $E(k_s, TR(h, n))$ consistently because it does not know k_s. On the other hand, C_h can protect itself from S's forgeries or modifications of TR(h, n) by $S(g_s, TR(h, n))$. C_h can prove that S is dishonest when S forges or modifies TR(h, n), because its possessing $S(g_s, TR(h, n))$ is consistent with the record that C_h is maintaining, and $S(g_s, TR(h, n))$ can be generated only by S.

However, C_h cannot protect itself when S generates $E(k_s, TR(h, n))$ and $S(g_s, TR(h, n))$ dishonestly from the beginning. An anonymous record agreement protocol based on ITLs, in which $S(g_s, \{DR(h, n), S(g_s, E(b_h, E(a_h, T(h, n+1))))\})$, the tentative signed form of TR(h, n) that C_h obtains from S after it approved DR(h, n), disables S to generate the 2 forms of TR(h, n) dishonestly. Here, DR(h, n) is a draft of TR(h, n) and includes all information in TR(h, n) except ITL(h, n), and b_h is a secret encryption key of C_h. Therefore, $S(g_s, E(b_h, E(a_h, T(h, n+1))))$ is considered as the blind signature of S on $E(a_h, T(h, n+1))$. Namely, $S(g_s, E(b_h, E(a_h, T(h, n+1))))$ is decrypted to $S(g_s, E(a_h, T(h, n+1)))$ by C_h's secret decryption key b_h^{-1}. Then, C_h can extract DR(h, n) and the signature on $E(a_h, T(h, n+1))$ from the tentative signed form that can be generated only by S without disclosing the value of $E(a_h, T(h, n+1))$, and it becomes possible for C_h to claim that TR(h, n) must be consistent with DR(h, n) and it must be accompanied by ITL(h, n) that includes $v_{n+1}E(a_h, T(h, n+1))$ as its encrypted next token value even if S generates TR(h, n) dishonestly. Also, S cannot generate C_h's n-th transaction record without C_h's permission because S does not know $E(a_h, T(h, n+1))$ until C_h approves DR(h, n). This means that C_h can securely obtain its transaction records from S when a mechanism that enables C_h and S to agree about contents of DR(h, n) is available as explained later. In the above, encryption function $E(b_h, x)$ is different from $E(a_h, x)$, $E(a_h, x)$ is an additive encryption function as discussed later, but $E(b_h, x)$ is multiplicative. Also, $E(b_h, x)$ and $S(g_s, x)$ are commutative of course.

Client C_h's n-th transaction record TR(h, n) is configured as shown in Figure 2, i.e. it consists of plain token, token version, expenditure and ITL parts. The plain token part value Pt(h, n) represents token T(h, n) that was shown by C_h at its n-th visit, the token version part value Tv(h, n) is used for carrying out the above anonymous record agreement protocol, the expenditure part value is the amount that C_h must pay, and the ITL part value ITL(h, n) maintains a pair of the current and the encrypted next tokens of C_h multiplied by token concealers secrets of S, i.e. $ITL(h, n) = \{v_nT(h, n), v_{n+1}E(a_h, T(h, n+1))\}$. Here, although token T(h, n) is included in the ITL part it is concealed by v_n, therefore the plain token part Pt(h, n) is prepared separately so that C_h can verify the correctness of T(h, n) included in ITL(h, n).

Figure 2. Transaction record TR(h, n)

Plain token part	Token version part	Expenditure part	ITL part
Pt(h, n) = T(h, n)	Tv(h, n)	Ex(h, n)	ITL(h, n)

Although the above transaction record TR(h, n) is generated by S, S does not know the identity of C_h corresponding to TR(h, n), therefore, S must know the total expenditure of each client C_h from encrypted transaction records maintained by C_h itself, but to preserve privacies of C_h, S cannot decrypt individual records of course. To calculate the total expenditure amount of C_h without decrypting its individual transaction records, S encrypts transaction records of clients by additive encryption function $E(k_S, x)$ that is implemented based on the linear equation based encryption function discussed in Part I. Then, because the sum of encrypted forms $E(k_S, TR(h, 0))$, $E(k_S, TR(h, 1))$, ---, $E(k_S, TR(h, N))$ coincides with $E(k_S, \{TR(h, 0)+TR(h, 1)+ \text{---}\ TR(h, N)\})$, S can know the total expenditure Ex(h, 0)+Ex(h, 1)+ --- +Ex(h, N) by decrypting the sum of encrypted transaction records calculated by C_h itself without knowing individual transactions of C_h. On the other hand, C_h that does not know the encryption key k_S cannot illegitimately modify or forge its transaction records consistently.

However, clients can delete their transaction records easily even if they are encrypted. ITLs included in individual transaction records protect the records also from illegitimate deletions, and play important roles not only in forcing clients to honestly calculate their total expenditures but also in authenticating anonymous clients. Namely, because both encryption functions $E(k_s, x)$ and $E(a_h, x)$ are additive, the sum of encrypted next tokens in ITLs calculated based on the sum of encrypted transaction records C_h had reported must be decrypted to the sum of current tokens if C_h honestly maintains its past transaction records. In detail, when C_h is requested to decrypt the sum of its encrypted next tokens until its (n-1)-th visit the result must satisfy relation (1). Therefore, S can believe that the total expenditure calculated by C_h is correct when the accompanying sum of ITLs satisfies relation (1), where $\underline{T}(h, n-1)$ and $\underline{T}^*(h, n-1)$ are sums of current and next tokens included in past ITLs respectively, and S obtains $\underline{T}(h, n-1)$ and $E(a_h, \underline{T}^*(h, n-1))$ by decrypting the sum of transaction records reported by C_h, and C_h decrypts $E(a_h, \underline{T}^*(h, n-1))$ to $\underline{T}^*(h, n-1)$. As discussed in the previous chapter, S can convince itself that C_h is the authorized client when it shows T(h, n) that satisfies relation (1) at the same time. If C_h deletes some of its transaction records, or if T(h, n) is illegitimate, equation (1) does not hold.

$$\underline{T}^*(h, n) = E(a_h^{-1}, \{v_0 E(a_h, T(h, 0)) + v_1 E(a_h, T(h, 1)) + \text{---} + v_n E(a_h, T(h, n))\})$$

$$= v_n T(h, n) + \underline{T}(h, n-1) = v_n T(h, n) + \{v_0 T(h, 0) + v_1 T(h, 1) + \text{---} + v_{n-1} T(h, n-1)\} \quad (1)$$

In the above, token concealers secrets of S play the important role, i.e. they disable client C_h to adjust the sum of its current tokens and that of encrypted next tokens so that it can delete or modify its transaction records while maintaining values of the 2 sums consistent. On the other hand, although C_h shows its token and the sum of its past transaction records at its every visit, the transaction-wise ITL sum checking mechanism disables server S to link consecutive transaction records of C_h as discussed in the section about ITLs.

It must be noted that although linear equation based encryption functions are weak against plain text attacks S does not need to worry about it. S never discloses ITL(h, n) to others, therefore no one other than S can obtain plain text and encrypted form pairs of ITL values, i.e. plain text attacks are impossible. Although it is possible to obtain plain text and encrypted form pairs of other items in transaction records, C_h that had made its purchases by itself knows values of its tokens, expenditure amounts, etc. from the beginning, and it cannot obtain any benefit if it calculates them. Namely, ITL(h, n) and other items in TR(h, n) constitute the confidential part and the visible part of TR(h, n), respectively. C_h cannot modify or forge the encrypted form of TR(h, n) either. When C_h modifies or forges encrypted TR(h, n) by exploiting the additive property of encryption function $E(k_S, x)$, the value of the ITL part is generated in the way C_h cannot estimate, and the modified or forged results become inconsistent.

Behaviours in the Individual Phases

In the following, behaviors of individual phases are discussed in detail.

Registration Phase

In this phase, server S registers ID and password pair $\{ID_h, P_h\}$ of client C_h while verifying its eligibility by usual means. Different from usual client registration procedures, C_h also defines and registers its secret key a_h of encryption function $E(a_h, x)$. However to maintain the confidentiality of a_h, C_h decrypts a set of random bit string vectors given by S as $E(a_h, t_1)$, $E(a_h, t_2)$, ---, $E(a_h, t_C)$ to $check_1$, $check_2$, ---, $check_C$, the visible part values of their decrypted bit string vectors, by decryption keys a_h^{-1}, and registers pair $\{E(a_h, t_1), E(a_h, t_2), ---, E(a_h, t_C)\}$ and $\{check_1, check_2, ---, check_C\}$ instead of a_h. C_h can prove correctness of its encryptions and decryptions to S when required without disclosing a_h by using these encrypted forms and their decrypted results based on the homomorphism of $E(a_h, x)$, where, $E(a_h, x)$ is additive as mentioned before.

Token Acquisition Phase

At C_h's n-th transaction request, server S authenticate anonymous C_h based on its n-th token T(h, n) and authorizes its encrypted next token $E(a_h, T(h, n+1))$. This phase enables client C_h to obtain tokens T(h, n) and T(h, n+1) without disclosing its identity so that T(h, n) and T(h, n+1) do not suggest any information about C_h. Individual clients can enter this phase anytime regardless of the phases they are currently involved.

Firstly, S authenticates C_h without knowing C_h by ID list based anonymous authentication scheme discussed in the previous chapter. Here, although there are several different anonymous authentication schemes, ID list based one is suitable because of the following reasons i.e. it can handle clients that forget their passwords or that secede from the system. Also, the disadvantage of ID list based scheme that clients can give their passwords to others is not serious, because authorized clients can obtain any number of tokens from the beginning. Even if C_h tells its password to unauthorized client C_j and C_j obtains tokens, these tokens do not bring any benefit to C_j or C_h. Namely, the objective of client authentications in this phase is to maintain the number of tokens to be prepared in the table as small as possible by limiting the clients that can access it, and even when other client C_j obtains T(h, n) while impersonating C_h, C_j cannot use T(h, n) in the transaction phase. T(h, n) is examined whether it is consistent with past ITLs maintained by C_j in the transaction phase as discussed later.

After being authenticated successfully, C_h picks open token T(h, n) from the token table prepared by S and obtains signature of S on it (signatures of S on open tokens are not represented explicitly in this section). Therefore S cannot identify any link between C_h and T(h, n), but the uniqueness of T(h, n) is ensured, i.e. S does not sign on same tokens repeatedly, or S does not accept repeatedly used tokens in the transaction phase either. However, it must be noted that although C_h can obtain tokens anytime independent of other phases once it had been registered, it cannot obtain multiple tokens at a time. When it obtains T(h, n) and T(h, r) at a time, S can know that T(h, n) and T(h, r) are owned by the same anonymous client.

Initial Transaction Phase

In this phase server S authorizes C_h's encrypted token E(a_h, T(h, 1)) and generates the initial ITL so that C_h can prove its eligibility by T(h, 1) at its next visit to S without disclosing its identity. Client C_h enters this phase in non-anonymous way by showing its ID and password pair {ID_h, P_h}. After that C_h encrypts ID_h and token T(h, 1) to E(a_h, ID_h) and E(a_h, T(h, 1)), respectively by its secret encryption key a_h. Then, S constructs initial transaction record TR(h, 0) of C_h and registers it. Here, initial transaction record TR(h, 0) is a dummy one, and its plain token part and token version part values Pt(h, n) and Tv(h, 0) are defined as T(h, 0) = ID_h (i.e. ID_h is used as C_h's initial token) and 1, respectively, and ITL part value ITL(h, 0) is constituted as ITL(h, 0) = {v_0ID_h, v_0E(a_h, ID_h)+v_1E(a_h, T(h, 1))}, where v_0 and v_1 are token concealers. About expenditure part Ex(h, 0), value 0 is assigned to it of course. As a consequence, TR(h, 0) is defined as {Pt(h, 0) = ID_h, Tv(h, 0) = 1, Ex(h, 0) = 0, ITL(h, 0) = {v_0ID_h, v_0E(a_h, ID_h)+v_1E(a_h, T(h, 1))}}. After generating TR(h, 0), S calculates E(k_S, TR(h, 0)) and S(g_S, TR(h, 0)) as the encrypted form and the signed form of TR(h, 0) to give them to C_h.

Transaction Phase

At client C_h's n-th visit, server S and C_h carry out C_h's n-th transaction through 2 steps, i.e. the client authentication and the transaction execution steps as shown in Figure 3. As same as usual procedures, firstly at the client authentication step, S authenticates C_h. This authentication is carried out based on ITL based authentication scheme without knowing the identity of C_h, i.e. S examines if the n-th token T(h, n) shown by C_h is consistent with the sum of past transaction records C_h is maintaining. Then at the transaction execution step, C_h and S exchange necessary information about the transaction they are carrying out to generate DR(h, n), a draft of transaction record TR(h, n), and C_h approves DR(h, n) and informs S of its encrypted next token E(a_h, T(h, n+1)) so that S can generate complete transaction record TR(h, n) based on it.

Here, as a general threat to C_h, server S may generate TR(h, n) dishonestly. In usual transactions systems this kind of threats are removed by counter signatures of clients, i.e. clients approve their transaction records by their signatures, and the anonymous credit card system in this section removes them in the same way. However, signatures of C_h cannot be used in this case, because the signatures reveal the identity of C_h. Therefore instead of its signature, C_h discloses its encrypted next token E(a_h, T(h, n+1)) according to the ITL based anonymous record agreement protocol so that S can generate ITL(h, n) = {v_nT(h, n), v_{n+1}E(a_h, T(h, n+1))} as the evidence of C_h's approval of transaction record TR(h, n). Here, it is possible to regard ITL(h, n) in transaction record TR(h, n) as C_h's approval of TR(h, n), because consistent E(a_h, T(h, n+1)) in ITL(h, n) can be generated only by C_h, and on the other hand, S cannot generate TR(h, n) without ITL(h, n).

Client Authentication Step

Firstly, C_h shows its n-th token T(h, n) and the sum of encrypted transaction records it is maintaining to S. Then, S confirms that T(h, n) was not used before, and examines the consistency between T(h, n) and the sum of ITLs included in past transaction records that C_h had reported. Namely, S decrypts the sum of past transaction records reported by C_h to extract the sum of current tokens $\underline{T}$(h, n-1)

Figure 3. Steps in the transaction phase

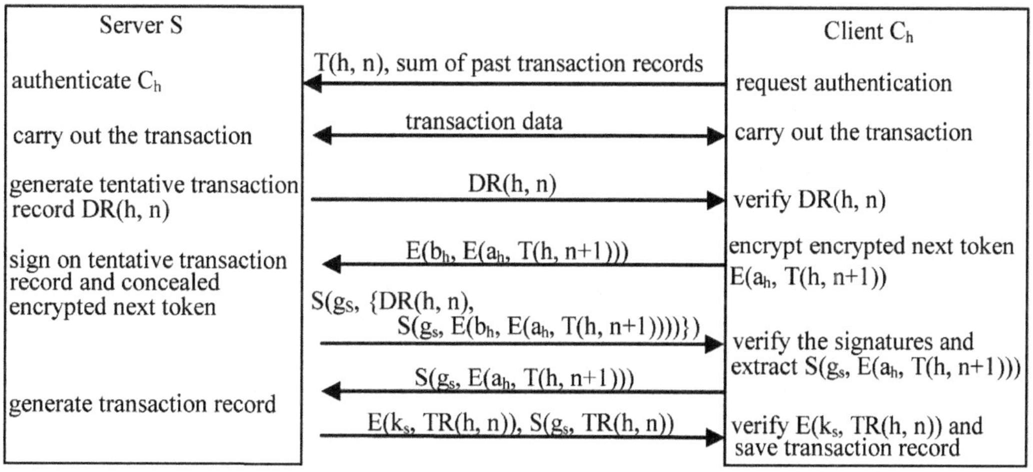

$= v_0T(h, 0) + v_1T(h, 1) + \cdots + v_{n-1}T(h, n-1)$ and the sum of encrypted next tokens $E(a_h, \underline{T}_*(h, n)) = \{E(a_h, v_0T(h, 0)) + E(a_h, v_1T(h, 1)) + \cdots + E(a_h, v_nT(h, n))\}$, and when $v_nT(h, n) + T(h, n-1)$ coincides with $E(a_h^{-1}, E(a_h, \underline{T}_*(h, n)))$, S decides that C_h is an authorized client. Here, if T(h, n) is invalid or C_h maintains its past transaction records dishonestly, C_h that does not know token concealers v_0, v_1, ---, v_n cannot decrypt $E(a_h, \underline{T}_*(h, n))$ consistently. As discussed in the previous chapter, this means that other client C_j cannot impersonate C_h while stealing T(h, n) from C_h. T(h, n) is consistent with only past transaction records maintained by C_h. On the other hand, because S verifies consistencies of sums of encrypted transaction records reported by individual clients thorough the transaction-wise ITL sum checking mechanism, although C_h reports sums of its past transaction records at its individual transaction requests, S cannot link consecutive transactions of C_h.

Transaction Execution Step

After client C_h has been authenticated successfully, C_h and server S exchange information necessary for completing C_h's purchases. Then, C_h and S carry out the procedure for ITL based anonymous record agreement protocol. Firstly, S constructs DR(h, n) = {Pt(h, n), Tv(h, n), Ex(h, n)}, the draft of transaction record at C_h's n-th visit while defining values of plain token, token version and expenditure parts of the transaction record. In detail, current token T(h, n) and value 1 are assigned to plain token part Pt(h, n) and token version part Tv(h, n), the value of expenditure part Ex(h, n) is defined according to the transaction amount of course. But, DR(h, n) does not include the ITL part, i.e. C_h does not inform S of $E(a_h, T(h, n+1))$ yet, therefore S cannot generate authorized transaction record TR(h, n) at this stage.

C_h that received DR(h, n) from S verifies its correctness, encrypts its encrypted (n+1)-th token $E(a_h, T(h, n+1))$ to $E(b_h, E(a_h, T(h, n+1)))$, and sends it back to S to obtain tentative signed record $Sig(DR(h, n)) = S(g_s, \{DR(h, n), S(g_s, E(b_h, E(a_h, T(h, n+1))))\})$ from S. In the tentative signed record, $S(g_s, E(b_h, E(a_h, T(h, n+1))))$ is the blind signature of S on $E(a_h, T(h, n+1))$, i.e. C_h can obtain signature of S on $E(a_h, T(h, n+1))$ without disclosing it by decrypting $S(g_s, E(b_h, E(a_h, T(h, n+1))))$. The blind signature mechanism can be implemented based on an RSA encryption function as discussed in section "Blind Signatures," i.e. provided that e_s is the public verification key corresponding to signing key g_s and b_h is a random number secret of C_h, $S(g_s, E(b_h, x))$ is calculated as $S(g_s, b_h^{es}x) = b_h^{(es)(gs)}x^{gs} = b_h x^{gs}$ and C_h can decrypt $S(g_s, E(b_h, x))$ to $S(g_s, x) = x^{gs}$ by dividing $b_h x^{gs}$ by its secret random number b_h.

Now after obtaining $S(g_s, E(a_h, T(h, n+1)))$, C_h sends it back to S, and S generates transaction record TR(h, n) by adding ITL(h, n) = $\{v_n T(h, n), v_{n+1} E(a_h, T(h, n+1))\}$ to DR(h, n). S also generates the encrypted and the signed forms of TR(h, n), i.e. $E(k_s$, TR(h, n) and $S(g_s$, TR(h, n)), so that C_h can maintain them and also C_h can make its next visit to S without disclosing its identity by using T(h, n+1). Here, although encryption key k_s is not known, C_h can verify the correctness of encrypted form $E(k_S$, TR(h, n)), because $E(k_S, x)$ is implemented by the linear equation based encryption function which is additive and verifiable, and also Pt(h, n), Tv(h, n) and Ex(h, n) are the visible parts of TR(h, n), i.e. C_h knows their values. Although C_h cannot verify the correctness of ITL(h, n) because T(h, n) and $E(a_h$, T(h, n+1)) in ITL(h, n) are multiplied by token concealers v_n and v_{n+1} that are secret of S and ITL(h, n) is in the confidential part of TR(h, n), disputes about incorrect encryptions of ITL part values can be resolved as discussed in the state recovery phase.

In the above procedure, C_h and S can agree on transaction records TR(h, n) as follows. Namely at a time when C_h receives incorrect tentative signed record Sig(DR(h, n)), because encrypted and signed forms $E(k_s$, TR(h, n) and $S(g_s$, TR(h, n)) are not generated yet, C_h can ask S to revise the tentative signed record. Here, C_h cancels the transaction when C_h and S cannot agree despite iterations of revisions, therefore although the cancellation may be against its will C_h can protect itself even if S does not agree on DR(h, n), i.e. C_h does not need to pay for the cancellation. Also, C_h can make another purchase by using token T(h, n) again because an entity that can use T(h, n) is only C_h even after T(h, n) is known to others. Then, after C_h and S agree on the revised tentative transaction record (including the cancelled record), C_h receives tentative signed record $Sig(DR_Q(h, n))$, the signature of S on pair $\{DR_Q(h, n) = \{Pt(h, n) = T(h, n), Tv(h, n) = Q, Ex(h, n) =$ expenditure amount$\}, E(b_h, E(a_h, T_Q(h, n+1)))\}$. Where, it is assumed that C_h and S agree after the tentative record was revised Q-times. Also, S increases the token version part value Tv(h, n) by 1 and C_h changes its next token value at each time when the tentative signed record is revised. As a consequence, the value of Tv(h, n) and the encrypted next token in $DR_Q(h, n)$ are defined as Q and $E(a_h, T_Q(h, n+1))$, respectively.

Once S and C_h had agreed on $DR_Q(h, n)$, this anonymous record agreement protocol protects S and C_h as follows. Firstly, C_h cannot claim that other transaction record TR(h, m) is invalid by using $Sig(DR_Q(h, n))$ because plain token part value T(h, n) included in $Sig(DR_Q(h, n))$ and T(h, m) included in TR(h, m) are different. However, $Sig(DR_1(h, n))$, $Sig(DR_2(h, n))$, ---, different versions of tentative signed records for TR(h, n), have the same plain token part value T(h, n). Therefore, provided that TR(h, n) was generated after C_h and S had agreed on $Sig(DR_Z(h, n))$ that is newer than $Sig(DR_Q(h, n))$ $(Z > Q)$, C_h can show $Sig(DR_Q(h, n))$ to claim that TR(h, n) is incorrect. Token version part values of TR(h, n) and $Sig(DR_Q(h, n))$ protect S from this dishonesty, i.e. token version part Tv(h, n) is defined so that $Sig(DR_Q(h, n))$ becomes effective for claiming incorrectness of TR(h, n) only when Tv(h, n) of $Sig(DR_Q(h, n))$ is not less than that of TR(h, n). Therefore, to accuse S that TR(h, n) is incorrect C_h must use $Sig(DR_Z(h, n))$ that S had used for generating TR(h, n), but TR(h, n) and $Sig(DR_Z(h, n))$ are consistent if S is honest.

On the other hand, S cannot reject C_h's claim with the latest version $Sig(DR_Q(h, n))$ even if it forges TR(h, n) while incorporating $E(a_h, T_Q(h, n+1)$ as its encrypted next token value and assigning Z $(Z>Q)$ to its token version part value. Because encrypted next token $E(a_h, T_Q(h, n+1)$ is bound to $Sig(DR_Q(h, n))$, S cannot include $E(a_h, T_Q(h, n+1)$ in TR(h, n) if its token version part value does not coincides with Q. Tentative signed record $Sig(DR_Q(h, n))$ protects C_h also from S's dishonesty, in which S does not give TR(h, n) to C_h or it gives incorrect TR(h, n) after C_h and S agreed on draft $DR_Q(h, n)$. Because pair $\{DR_Q(h, n), S(g_s, E(b_h, E(a_h, T_Q(h, n+1))))\}$ in $Sig(DR_Q(h, n))$ is equivalent to transaction record TR(h, n) and only S can sign on it, S must generate or correct TR(h, n) so that it becomes consistent with $Sig(DR_Q(h, n))$.

Here after having authorized TR(h, n), S can modify it to TR'(h, n) while copying consistent ITL part value from TR(h, n), but encrypted transaction record $E(k_s, TR(h, n))$ and signed transaction record $S(g_s, TR(h, n))$ maintained by C_h enable C_h to prove that TR'(h, n) is invalid as discussed in the state recovery phase. As another threat to C_h, S can generate transaction record $TR_{New}(h, n)$ without C_h's permission, but this dishonesty is also necessarily revealed because $TR_{New}(h, n)$ must include $E(a_h, T_{New}(h, n+1))$, encrypted form of next token $T_{New}(h, n+1)$, that is different from all tokens that C_h had used before. S that does not know C_h's encryption key a_h cannot generate $E(a_h, T_{New}(h, n+1))$ consistently, despite that $E(a_h, T_{New}(h, n+1))$ must be decrypted to visible part value *check* by decryption key a_h^{-1} (where *check* is a bit pattern added to tokens as their visible part values).

In the above, when S dishonestly generate transaction record TR(h, n) and correct it to TR'(h, n) according to C_h's claim, C_h can have 2 tokens $T_Q(h, n+1)$ and $T_Q'(h, n+1)$ as its (n+1)-th token, and $T_Q(h, n+1)$ is consistent with TR(h, n) and $T_Q'(h, n+1)$ is consistent with TR'(h, n). Therefore, provided that C_h had received a sequence of transaction records $E(k_s, TR'(h, n+1))$, $E(k_s, TR'(h, n+2))$, ---, $E(k_s, TR'(h, N))$ after having shown token $T_Q'(h, n+1)$ at its (n+1)-th visit, it can delete all transactions after its (n+1)-th visit by making its (n+1)-th visit again while showing $T_Q(h, n+1)$. Although $E(k_s, TR(h, n))$ was revised to $E(k_s, TR'(h, n))$ according to C_h's claim, C_h possesses $E(k_s, TR(h, n))$ and $T_Q(h, n+1)$, and $T_Q(h, n+1)$ is consistent with the early part of C_h's past transaction records $E(k_s, TR(h, 0))$, $E(k_s, TR(h, 1))$, ---, $E(k_s, TR(h, n))$, also S does not know the decrypted value of $E(a_h, T_Q(h, n+1))$. Therefore, S cannot notice even if C_h makes its (n+1)-the visit again by using $T_Q(h, n+1)$. However, these situations do not happen as long as S is honest.

Account Balancing Phase

At the end of every service period of server S, S asks all clients to calculate sums of their encrypted transaction records and to return the results with their newest unused tokens and their ID and password pairs, as shown in the upper part of Figure 4. Therefore, provided that client C_h had visited S N-times during the last service period of S, it returns $\underline{TR}^*(h, N) = E(k_S, TR(h, 0)) + E(k_S, TR(h, 1)) + \text{---} + E(k_S, TR(h, N))$ and T(h, N+1) to S. Then, because $E(k_S, x)$ is additive, S can calculate C_h's total expenditure $\underline{Ex}(h, N)$, and T(h, N) and $E(a_h, T^*(h, N+1))$ without knowing individual transaction records by decrypting $\underline{TR}^*(h, N)$. Here, T(h, n) and $E(a_h, T^*(h, n+1))$ represent the sum of current tokens $v_0T(h,0)+ v_1T(h,1)+ \text{---} +v_nT(h,n)$ and the sum of encrypted next tokens $v_0E(a_h, T(h, 0))+ v_1E(a_h, T(h, 1))+ \text{---} + v_{n+1}E(a_h, T(h, n+1))$.

S can know also T*(h, N+1), the sum of next tokens, by asking C_h to decrypt $E(a_h, T^*(h, N+1))$, and can verify the correctness of total expenditure $\underline{Ex}(h, N)$ extracted from $\underline{TR}^*(h, N)$, based on the fact that the sum of current tokens and that of next tokens are equal, i.e. when C_h honestly maintains its past transaction records, T*(h, N+1) that C_h calculated by decrypting $E(a_h, \underline{T}^*(h, N+1))$ must satisfies relation $\underline{T}^*(h, N+1) = T(h, N) + v_{N+1}T(h, N+1)$, where $v_{N+1}T(h, N+1)$ is calculated from T(h, N+1) reported by C_h as its last unused token. Namely, C_h cannot modify its maintaining encrypted transaction records while satisfying rela-

Figure 4. Account balancing and state recovery phases

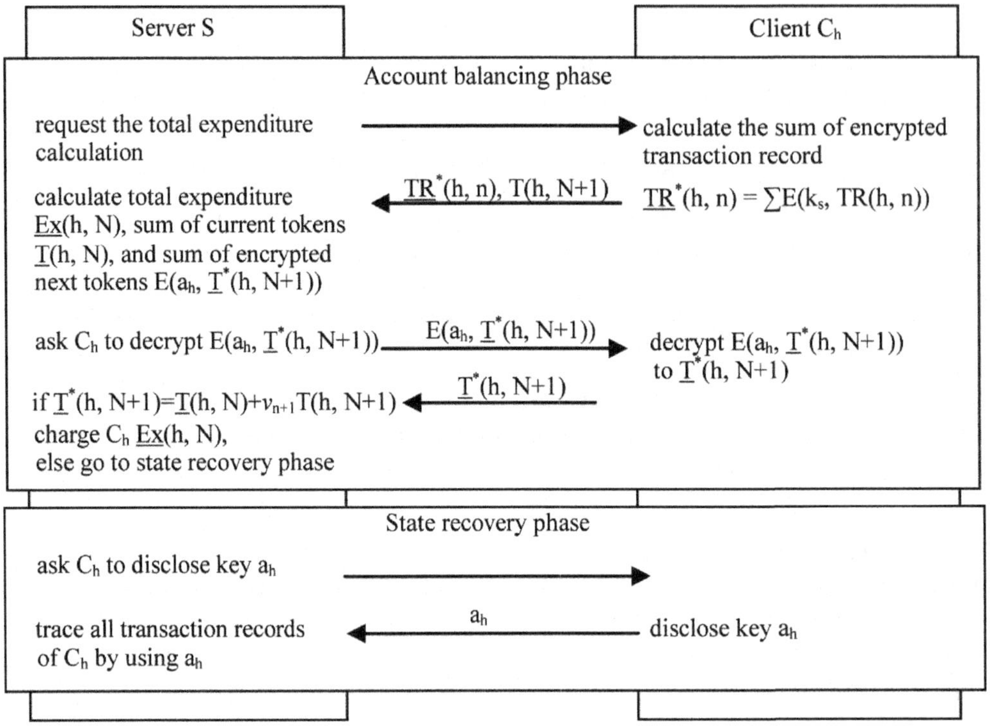

tion $\underline{T}^*(h,N+1)=\underline{T}(h,N)+v_{N+1}T(h,N+1)$, because it does not know either encryption key k_s or token concealers v_0, v_1, ---, v_{N+1}. On the other hand, C_h is requested to disclose only the sum of its past transaction records and its newest token T(h, N+1), therefore it can conceal its individual transactions from others including S.

State Recovery Phase

The state recovery phase is carried out only when dishonest events are detected in the transaction or the account balancing phase, and identifies entities liable for the dishonest events to correct relevant transaction records. Here, S detects dishonest events by examining sums of encrypted transaction records that are reported by individual clients as above. On the other hand, clients detect dishonest events caused by server S by comparing the expenditure amounts that are charged by S and those they calculate by themselves based on their maintaining signed transaction records. The important thing is that liable entities must be identified and inconsistent states caused by the dishonest events must be recovered while preserving privacies of honest clients, i.e. without examining transaction records of honest clients.

Protection of the Server

Client C_h may behave dishonestly in the following ways, firstly it may modify or delete its maintaining transaction records, and secondly it may report inconsistent value *X* to S as encrypted next token $E(a_h, T(h, n+1))$ at its n-th visit. In the 1st case, S detects dishonest behaviors of C_h during the account balancing phase as the violation of relation $\underline{T}^*(h, N+1) = \underline{T}(h, N) + v_{N+1}T(h, N+1)$, and S requests C_h to disclose its encryption key a_h (encryption key a_h and decryption key a_h^{-1} are the same) to calculate C_h's correct total expenditure. Here, although all privacies of C_h will be revealed C_h must disclose a_h, otherwise, C_h may be regarded as responsible for all damages including ones caused by other dishonest clients. Then, by using a_h, S can trace all transactions of C_h from its initial to its last transactions that are stored in S's own memory by decrypting encrypted next tokens in the ITLs as shown in the lower part of Figure 4.

Regarding the 2nd case, although C_h must show encrypted next token $E(a_h, T(n+1))$ so that it is decrypted to a consistent visible part value (i.e. *check* as mentioned before), it can complete its n-th transaction while dishonestly defining the confidential part value of $E(a_h, T(n+1))$. However, in this case C_h can complete its transactions only up to its n-th one, because its (n+1)-th transaction request is necessarily rejected, and this is also true for the account balancing phase. Namely, C_h is identified as dishonest client that cannot show its unused token that is consistent with its past transaction records, and C_h must disclose its encryption key a_h so that S can trace all transactions of C_h in the same way as discussed above. A case where C_h dishonestly reports T(h, N+1) in the account balancing phase is treated in totally the same way.

As another kind of dishonesties, S may find unpredictable dishonest events in transaction record TR(h, n). S can identify liable client C_h also in this case without knowing transactions of honest clients by exploiting the additive feature of encryption function $E(a_h, x)$. Namely, S asks all clients to decrypt $E(a_h, T(h, n+1))$ that is included in ITL of the dishonest record, then, the client that successfully decrypts $E(a_h, T(h, n+1))$ to consistent visible part value *check* is liable, in other words, other clients that do not know a_h cannot decrypt it consistently. Here, S can verify C_h's correct decryption of $E(a_h, T(h, n+1))$ based on its additive property by using encrypted forms $E(a_h, t_1)$, $E(a_h, t_2)$, ---, $E(a_h, t_C)$ and their decryption results $check_1$, $check_2$, ---, $check_C$ that had been registered in the client registration phase.

Protection of Clients

There are 2 kinds of threats to client C_h, i.e. firstly other anonymous client C_j may request a transaction by using C_h's token T(h, n), and secondly S may charge C_h excessively for its purchases in the account balancing phase.

As mentioned already the 1st threat can be removed. C_h does not suffer any damage even if C_j impersonates C_h by using T(h, n). The request of C_j is rejected because its past transaction records are not consistent with T(h, n). In a case where C_j conspires with S, S may give open token T(h, n) to C_j, and C_j's request with T(h, n) is accepted. But, S must accept also C_h's request with T(h, n) because T(h, n) is consistent with transaction records maintained by C_h. Also, C_h can prove that it did not use T(h, n) before as discussed just below, and this means S must compensate possible damages caused by repeatedly used T(h, n) by itself.

Clients can protect themselves also from S's dishonest total expenditure calculations by using their past signed transaction records. Namely, client C_h can detect dishonest total expenditure calculations of S by comparing the total expenditure, which C_h calculates based on its maintaining transaction records, with that S had calculated. After detecting the discrepancy between them, disputes between C_h and S can be resolved as below. Because transaction records in their signed forms can be generated only by S, S must agree that expenditure amounts of individual transaction records in the signed form are correct. Also, if C_h discloses its encryption key a_h, ITLs included in individual signed transaction records prove that C_h had certainly executed a sequence of transactions traced by them. Here, all privacies of C_h are revealed to S when C_h discloses its encryption key a_h, however S's dishonesty is finally revealed when C_h is honest. Therefore S cannot intentionally behave dishonestly if it has desires to continue its business.

As discussed in the previous chapter, ITL based anonymous authentication mechanisms have weaknesses in handling entities that are expelled or that forget tokens. Namely, when client C_h forgets its next token it must disclose its encryption key a_h or its past transaction records and all transactions it had made during the current service period are disclosed to S. However, it is not strange that responsibilities of clients for maintaining their secret information become much higher in anonymous environments than in usual non anonymous environments. About expelled clients, although the above authentication mechanism cannot disable them to carry out transactions, this is not the disadvantage specific to the anonymous credit card system in this section. Namely, clients can disappear without paying for their expenditures even in credit card systems that are operated currently. Damages of the card company can be reduced by the mechanism for limiting total expenditures of individual clients that will be discussed in the next subsection.

Limiting Expenditures

This subsection discusses the mechanism to enable server S to limit total expenditures of individual clients. Mechanisms for limiting expenditures of clients are essential for developing credit card systems. Clients may make purchases much more than they can afford and disappear without paying for them, and damages of the card company cannot be limited without the mechanisms. Here, it must be noted that clients must conceal not only their identities but also their current total expenditures from the server to preserve their privacies. Current total expenditures of individual clients help S extract transitions of expenditures of a client, and transitions of expenditures of a client suggest its identity. In the following, LT is the limit of the total expenditure of clients, Min is the S's secret number that is sufficiently large compared with LT, $\underline{TR}(h, n)$ is the sum of (decrypted) transaction records of C_h from its initial to current (n-th) transactions, and $\underline{Ex}(h, n)$ is the expenditure part value of $\underline{TR}(h, n)$ i.e. $\underline{Ex}(h, n)$ is the total expenditure of C_h until its n-th visit (current total expenditure of C_h at its n-th visit). Also, it is assumed for a while that client C_h can calculate $E(k_S, \underline{TR}(h, n)+Min^E)$ from its maintaining past transaction records. Here, x^E represents the transaction record that has x as its expenditure part value and 0 as values of other parts.

Conceptually the expenditure limiting mechanism detects overspendings of clients as shown in Figure 5 (Tamura, 2006). Firstly S assigns values Min or Max = Min+LT randomly to variable Q and generates Q^E to encrypt it to $E(k_S, Q^E)$. After that, client C_h, without knowing the value of Q, calculates $uE(k_S, P(h, Q, n))$ as shown in Equation (2) based on $E(k_S, Q^E)$ sent from S and the sum of past encrypted transaction records that C_h is maintaining, and S decrypts $uE(k_S, P(h, Q, n))$ to $uP(h, Q, n)$. Therefore, the expenditure part value $uP_{EX}(h, Q, n)$ of $uP(h, Q, n)$ must coincides with $u\{Q-(\underline{Ex}(h, n)+Min)\}$ as shown in Equation (3). In Equations (2) and (3), u is a random number secret of C_h and disables S to know the exact current total expenditure of anonymous client C_h. Actually, linear equation based encryption function $E(k_s, x)$ includes dummy secret terms that take different values in every encryption as discussed in Part I, therefore in the remainder of this subsection, $E(k_S, x)$ is represented also as $E(k_S, \{x, r\})$, where r represents the random secret terms.

$$uE(k_S, P(h, Q, n)) = uE(k_S, Q^E)\text{-}uE(k_S, \underline{TR}(h, n)+Min^E)$$

$$= uE(k_S, Q^E\text{-}\{\underline{TR}(h, n)+Min^E\}) \quad (2)$$

$$uP_{EX}(h, Q, n)= u\{Q\text{-}(\underline{Ex}(h, n)+Min)\} \quad (3)$$

Then, provided that C_h's secret random number u is positive, if the current total expenditure of C_h does not exceed limit LT, $uP_{EX}(h, Q, n)$ is positive when Q = Max, and it is negative when Q = Min. However, when C_h's expenditure exceeds LT, $uP_{EX}(h, Q, n)$ becomes negative even when Q = Max if C_h honestly calculates $uE(k_S, \{P(h, Q,$

Figure 5. Expenditure limiting mechanism

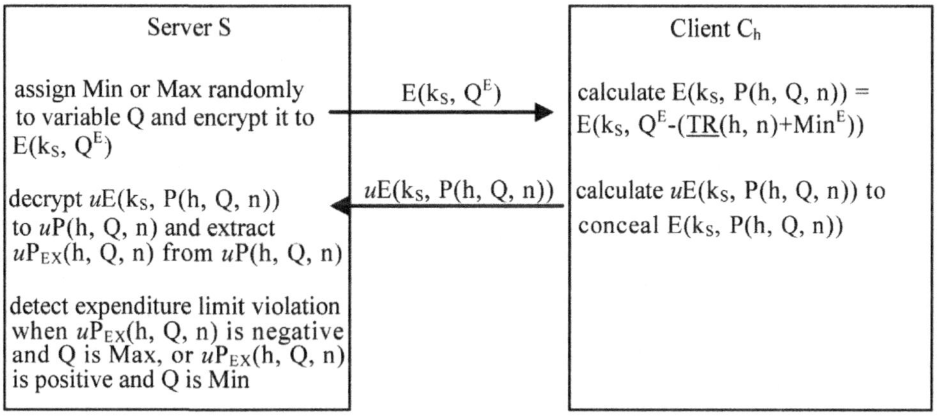

n), r_P}). On the other hand, if C_h dishonestly calculates it by multiplying $E(k_S, \underline{TR}(h, n)+Min^E))$ by z_1 ($z_1 < 1$) or multiplying $E(k_S, \{Q^E, r_Q\})$ by z_2 ($z_2 > 1$) to make $uP_{EX}(h, Q, n)$ positive when Q = Max so that S cannot detect its overspending, $uP_{EX}(h, Q, n)$ becomes positive even when Q = Min because Min is sufficiently large compared with $\underline{TR}(h, n)$. Therefore, S can detect overspending of C_h, that does not know the values of Q, with probability 1/2 by asking C_h to calculate $uP_{EX}(h, Q, n)$, and if it asks C_h to calculate $uP_{EX}(h, Q_1, n)$, $uP_{EX}(h, Q_2, n)$, ---, $uP_{EX}(h, Q_K, n)$ while generating K-different values $E(k_S, \{Q_1^E, r_{Q1}\})$, $E(k_S, \{Q_2^E, r_{Q2}\})$, ----, $E(k_S, \{Q_K^E, r_{QK}\})$, the probability can be increased to $1-1/2^K$, where for each j, Q_j = Max or Min and C_h does not know it.

It must be noted that C_h does not choose a negative number as the value of u, because $uP_{EX}(h, Q, n)$ becomes negative even if Q = Max, when u is negative. It is apparent that S cannot know the amount of C_h's current total expenditure from $u\{Q-(\underline{Ex}(h, n)+Min)\}$ because u is C_h's secret. Also, although S can behave maliciously while evaluating $u\{Q-(\underline{Ex}(h, n)+Min)\}$ reported by C_h dishonestly, a damage of C_h is not fatal, i.e. the only inconvenience C_h suffers from it is that C_h cannot make purchases temporally, and S's dishonesty will be eventually revealed.

Here, actually C_h can spend more than the limit, i.e. it can always adjust the value of $uE(k_S, \{P(h, Q, n), r_P\})$ so that $u\{Q-(\underline{Ex}(h, n)+Min)\}$ becomes positive or negative according to Q = Max or Q = Min. When C_h chooses number z in the interval $Min/(\underline{Ex}(h, n) + Min) < z < Max/(\underline{Ex}(h, n) + Min)$, $u\{Max-z(\underline{Ex}(h, n)+Min)\}$ is always positive, and $u\{Min-z(\underline{Ex}(h, n)+Min)\}$ is always negative. However, it is difficult for C_h to know the interval because Min is unknown, also Min is large and as a consequence the interval is very narrow. Therefore the possibility that C_h can successfully find values of z that exists within the interval is very low. In addition, S can ask C_h to calculate $uP(h, Q, n)$ for multiple different values of Min at a time.

However, although it is assumed that Min and Q are secrets of S in the above, encryption function $E(k_S, x)$ is weak against plain text attacks, and Min and Q are encrypted as expenditure part values that constitute the visible parts of transaction records. This means that C_h can obtain a plain text and its encrypted form pair at its every transaction request to try plain text attacks for calculating Min and Q, and once C_h knows their values, it can easily decide whether it must multiply $uE(k_S, \{TR(h, n)+Min^E\})$ by z or not so that it can spend more than the limit.

Figure 6. Extended transaction record

Plain token part	Token version part	Expenditure part	ITL part	1st accopmpanying expenditure	2nd accopmpanying expenditure
Pt(h, n) = T(h, n)	Tv(h, n)	Ex(h, n)	ITL(h, n)	Ae_1(h, n)	Ae_2(h, n)

Another thing that must be noted is, in the above, it is assumed that not only C_h calculates encrypted sum of its transaction records E(k_S, $\underline{TR}$(h, n)) honestly but also it does not calculate E(k_S, $\underline{TR}$(h, n)) and E(k_S, Min^E) separately. If C_h can calculate E(k_S, $\underline{TR}$(h, n)) dishonestly or can calculate E(k_S, $\underline{TR}$(h, n)) and E(k_S, Min^E) separately, it is trivial for it to dishonestly calculate uE(k_S, P(h, Q, n)) so that S does not notice its over spending. Namely, if the total expenditure of C_h is less than LT at its m-th visit and C_h calculates E(k_S, $\underline{TR}$(h, m)) instead of E(k_S, $\underline{TR}$(h, n)) (m < n), S cannot notice C_h's overspending at its n-th visit. Also, if C_h can obtain E(k_S, $\underline{TR}$(h, n)) and E(k_S, Min^E) separately, it can dishonestly calculate uE(k_S, P(h, Q, n)) as uE(k_S, Q^E)-zuE(k_S, $\underline{TR}$(h, n))+uE(k_S, Min^E) while multiplying uE(k_S, $\underline{TR}$(h, n)) by z that is small enough compared with 1 regardless that Q = Min or Max. Namely, by the above assumptions the only way for C_h to dishonestly calculate u{Q-($\underline{Ex}$(h, n)+Min)} consistently becomes the multiplication of E(k_S, Q^E) and z (>1) or that of E(k_S, $\underline{TR}$(h, n)+Min^E) and z (<1).

Now, according to these discussions, the following 2 problems must be solved to implement the above scheme. The one is to protect E(k_S, Q^E) and E(k_S, Min^E) from plain text attacks by C_h, and the other is to force C_h to calculate E(k_S, $\underline{TR}$(h, n)+Min^E) honestly and to disable it to know E(k_S, $\underline{TR}$(h, n)) and E(k_S, Min^E) separately. A solution of the 1st problem is as follow. That is to construct transaction record of C_h at its n-th visit as extended transaction record XR(h, n) that includes the 1st and the 2nd accompanying expenditure parts Ae_1(h, n) and Ae_2(h, n) in addition to already existing parts in $\underline{TR}$(h, n) as shown in Figure 6. Here, S assigns values to individual parts in XR(h, n) except Ae_1(h, n) and Ae_2(h, n) in the same way as it did for TR(h, n). An important thing is although values of Ae_1(h, n) and Ae_2(h, n) are defined so that S can calculate current total expenditures of C_h from them, Ae_1(h, n) and Ae_2(h, n) constitute confidential parts of XR(h, n). Therefore C_h that does not know values of Ae_1(h, n) or Ae_2(h, n) cannot try plain text attacks.

$$\underline{Ax}(h, n) = Ex(h, 0)^{1+\lambda}+Ex(h, 1)^{1+\lambda}+ \text{---} +Ex(h, n)^{1+\lambda} \quad (4)$$

$$\underline{Ax}_1(h, n) = Ae_1(h, 0)+Ae_1(h, 1)+ \text{---} +Ae_1(h, n)$$

$$\underline{Ax}_2(h, n) = Ae_2(h, 0)+Ae_2(h, 1)+ \text{---} +Ae_2(h, n) \quad (5)$$

$$\underline{Ax}_1(h, n) = Ax(h, n)+Min^{1+\lambda}, \text{ when n is even, and}$$

$$\underline{Ax}_2(h, n) = Ax(h, n)+Min^{1+\lambda}, \text{ when n is odd} \quad (6)$$

In more detail, while defining secret numbers Min and λ, S calculates Y_p = (Ex(h, n)$^{1+\lambda}$+Min$^{1+\lambda}$) and Y_m = (Ex(h, n)$^{1+\lambda}$-Min$^{1+\lambda}$), and assigns Y_p or Y_m to Ae_1(h, n) depending on n is even or odd, respectively. Contrarily, it defines value of Ae_2(h, n) as Y_m or Y_p depending on n is even or odd, but as an exception it assigns 0 to Ae_2(h, 0). Where, Ex(h, n) is the expenditure amount at C_h's n-th visit to S, Min is a sufficiently large number compared with expenditure limit LT as mentioned before, and λ is a positive number sufficiently small compared with 1. Therefore, $\underline{Ax}$(h, n) defined by Equation (4) and $\underline{Ax}_1$(h, n) and $\underline{Ax}_2$(h, n) defined by (5) satisfy relations shown in Equation (6).

Under these settings, S asks C_h to calculate u\{E($\underline{k}_S$, Q^E)-E($\underline{k}_S$, $\underline{XR}$(h, n))\} = uE($\underline{k}_S$, Q^E-$\underline{XR}$(h, n)) while informing C_h of E($\underline{k}_S$, Q^E), where, x^E represents the extended transaction record that has values x, \{(x+$Min^{1+\lambda}$), (x-$Min^{1+\lambda}$)\} or \{(x-$Min^{1+\lambda}$), (x+$Min^{1+\lambda}$)\}, and 0 as ones of its expenditure part, 1st and 2nd accompanying expenditure parts, and other parts, respectively, and k_S is a secret key of S for encrypting extended transaction record sum, $\underline{XR}$(h, n) = XR(h, 0)+XR(h, 1)+ --- +XR(h, n), and S randomly defines values of Q as $Min^{1+\lambda}$ or Max = $Min^{1+\lambda}$+$LT^{1+\lambda}$. Therefore, by decrypting uE($\underline{k}_S$, Q^E-$\underline{XR}$(h, n)), S can know value u\{Q-(Ax(h, n)+$Min^{1+\lambda}$)\} as the 1st or the 2nd accompanying expenditure part value of u\{Q^E-$\underline{XR}$(h, n)\}, and by using \{Q-($\underline{Ax}$(h, n)+$Min^{1+\lambda}$)\} as a substitute for \{Q-($\underline{Ex}$(h, n)+Min)\} in Equation (3), it can detect the overspending of C_h. Here, $\underline{Ex}$(h, n) may exceed LT even if \{Max-($\underline{Ax}$(h, n)+$Min^{1+\lambda}$)\} > 0 is satisfied because $a^{1+\lambda}+b^{1+\lambda} < (a+b)^{1+\lambda}$ when λ> 0, however, λ is small enough and S can allow the exceeding amount.

Then, although C_h knows its expenditures it cannot know Q, Min or λ, i.e. the accompanying expenditure parts constitute the confidential parts of XR(h, n), and C_h cannot try plain text attacks to calculate Q, Min or λ even if it gathers number of extended transaction records. On the other hand, C_h can maintain the value of $\underline{Ax}$(h, n) as its secret because S does not know secret number u, i.e. S can know only u\{Q-($\underline{Ax}$(h, n)+Min)\}. It must be noted that the accompanying expenditure part value cannot have the form (Ex(h, n)+Min) or (Ex(h, n)-Min) instead of (Ex(h, n)$^{1+\lambda}$+$Min^{1+\lambda}$) or (Ex(h, n)$^{1+\lambda}$-$Min^{1+\lambda}$). If XR(h, n) has (Ex(h, n)+Min) or (Ex(h, n)-Min) as its accompanying expenditure part value, although Min is unknown and consequently (Ex(h, n)+Min) or (Ex(h, n)-Min) is concealed from C_h, when C_h receives E($\underline{k}_S$, $\underline{XR}$(h, n_1)+Min^E) and E($\underline{k}_S$, $\underline{XR}$(h, n_2)+Min^E) from S (it is assumed that n_1 and n_2 are both even numbers), it can obtain E($\underline{k}_S$, XR(h, n_1)-$\underline{XR}$(h, n_2)). Therefore, C_h can have a plain text and its encrypted form pair \{$\underline{Ax}$(h, n_1)-$\underline{Ax}$(h, n_2) = $\underline{Ex}$(h, n_1)-$\underline{Ex}$(h, n_2), E($\underline{k}_S$, $\underline{XR}$(h, n_1)-$\underline{XR}$(h, n_2))\}, namely it knows the difference between total expenditure amounts at its n_1-th and n_2-th visits. Then, the accompanying expenditure parts cannot play roles of the confidential parts anymore.

When the extended transaction records are incorporated in the transaction-wise ITL sum checking mechanism that had been used in the client authentication step in the transaction phase, the 2nd problem also can be solved. In the mechanism, client C_h at its (n+1)-th visit generates random numbers \{0= y(0) < y(1) < y(2) < --- < y(P-1) < y(P) = n+1\}, and divides its past extended transaction records up to its n-th one based on these numbers. Namely, C_h generates subsequences Sq(h, 0) = \{E($\underline{k}_S$, XR(h, y(0))), E($\underline{k}_S$, XR(h, y(0)+1)), ---, E($\underline{k}_S$, XR(h, y(1)-1))\}, Sq(h, 1) = \{E($\underline{k}_S$, XR(h, y(1))), E($\underline{k}_S$, XR(h, y(1)+1)), ---, E($\underline{k}_S$, XR(h, y(2)-1))\}, ---, Sq(h, P-1) = \{E($\underline{k}_S$, XR(h, y(P-1))), E($\underline{k}_S$, XR(h, y(P-1)+1)), ---, E($\underline{k}_S$, XR(h, y(P)-1))\}. Where, y(1), y(2), ---, y(P-1) are defined so that relation $\underline{Ax}_1$(j) = Ae_1(h, y(j))+ Ae_1(h, y(j+1))+ --- + Ae_1(h, y(j+1)-1) = Ex(h, y(j))$^{1+\lambda}$+ --- +Ex(h, y(j+1)-1)$^{1+\lambda}$+$Min^{1+\lambda}$ or $\underline{Ax}_2$(j) = Ae_2(h, y(j))+ Ae_2(h, y(j+1))+ --- + Ae_2(h, y(j+1)-1) = Ex(h, y(j))$^{1+\lambda}$+ --- +Ex(h, y(j+1)-1)$^{1+\lambda}$+$Min^{1+\lambda}$ holds for every j (according to the definitions of accompanying expenditure part values C_h always can define them in this way).

By using the above subsequences of C_h's past transaction records, S detects overspendings of C_h as shown in Figure 7. Firstly for each Sq(h, j), C_h calculates E($\underline{k}_S$, Sq(h, j)) = E($\underline{k}_S$, XR(h, y(j)))+ --- +E($\underline{k}_S$, XR(h, y(j+1)-1)) and $\underline{Ex}$(j) = Ex(h, y(j))+ --- +Ex(h, y(j+1)-1), the sum of encrypted extended transaction records and that of expenditures during a period from y(j) to y(j+1)-1 (C_h can calculate $\underline{Ex}$(j) because it knows its past expenditures), and for each j, defines LT(j) so

Figure 7. Augmented expenditure limiting procedure

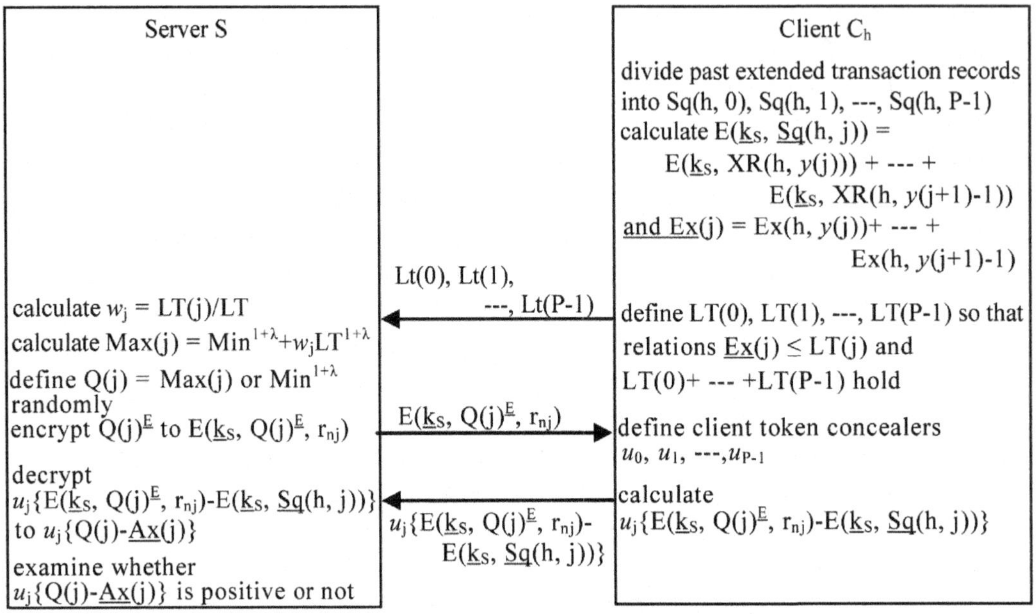

that relations $Ex(j) \leq LT(j)$ and LT(0)+LT(1)+ --- +LT(P-1) = LT hold (apparently C_h can define LT(j) in this way when its current total expenditure does not exceed expenditure limit LT). After that, S that receives LT(0), LT(1), ---, LT(P-1) from C_h calculates w_j = LT(j)/LT, defines Q(j) as $Q(j) = Max(j) = Min^{1+\lambda}+w_jLT^{1+\lambda}$ or $Q(j) = Min^{1+\lambda}$ randomly, and encrypts it to $E(k_S, Q(j)^E, r_{nj})$ while defining r_{nj} unique to j as secret random terms for encrypting Q(j). Then, C_h defines client token concealers $u_0, u_1, ---, u_{P-1}$ and calculates $u_j\{E(\underline{k}_S, Q(j)^E, r_{nj})-E(k_S, \underline{Sq}(h, j))\}$ for each j, and finally, S decrypts each $u_j\{E(\underline{k}_S, Q(j)^E, r_{nj})-E(\underline{k}_S, \underline{Sq}(h, j))\}$ to the 1st or the 2nd accompanying expenditure part value to extract $u_j\{Q(j)-\underline{Ax}(j)\}$, where $\underline{Ax}(j) = Ex(h, y(j))^{1+\lambda}+ --- +Ex(h, y(j+1)-1)^{1+\lambda}+Min^{1+\lambda}$.

In the above, provided that C_h's current total expenditure does not exceed LT, apparently the sign of each $\{Q(j)-\underline{Ax}(j)\}$ is positive when $Q(j) = Max(j)$, and it is negative when $Q(j) = Min^{1+\lambda}$ because $Ex(j) \leq LT(j) = w_jLT$. On the other hand if the current total expenditure of C_h exceeds the limit, C_h cannot make all $\{Q(0)-\underline{Ax}(0)\}$, ---, $\{Q(P-1)-\underline{Ax}(P-1)\}$ positive even when Q(0), ---, Q(P-1) are Max(0), ---, Max(P-1), provided that C_h calculates each $u_j\{E(\underline{k}_S, Q(j)^E, r_{nj})-E(\underline{k}_S, \underline{Sq}(h, j))\}$ honestly. Therefore, S can detect the overspending of C_h by examining sign of each $u_j\{Q(j)-\underline{Ax}(j)\}$. Namely, the total expenditure of C_h exceeds the limit when at least one of $u_j\{Q(j)-Ax(j)\}$ is negative even if Q(j) is Max(j).

S can detect the overspending of C_h even if C_h calculates $u_j\{E(\underline{k}_S, Q(j)^E, r_{nj})-E(\underline{k}_S, \underline{Sq}(h, j))\}$ dishonestly. The important thing is because the accompanying expenditure part value of $E(k_S, Sq(h, j))$ is calculated as $\underline{Ax}(j) = Ex(h, y(j))^{1+\lambda}+ --- +Ex(h, y(j+1)-1)^{1+\lambda}+Min^{1+\lambda}$, C_h cannot know $E(\underline{k}_S, Ex(h, y(j))^{1+\lambda}+ --- +Ex(h, y(j+1)-1)^{1+\lambda})$ or $E(\underline{k}_S, Min^{1+\lambda E})$ separately. Therefore, the only way for C_h to calculate $u_j\{E(\underline{k}_S, Q(j)^E, r_{nj})-E(\underline{k}_S, \underline{Sq}(h, j))\}$ dishonestly is to multiply $E(\underline{k}_S, Q(j)^E, r_{nj})$ or $E(\underline{k}_S, \underline{Sq}(h, j))$ by z. In addition, ITLs included in extended transaction records disable C_h to report each $u_j\{E(\underline{k}_S, Q(j)^E, r_{nj})+ E(\underline{k}_S, \underline{Sq}(h,$

j))} while deleting some of transactions it had made, as discussed in the section about ITLs in Part II. Then, even if C_h calculates $u_j\{E(\underline{k}_S, Q(j)^E, r_{nj})-E(\underline{k}_S, \underline{Sq}(h, j))\}$ dishonestly, S can detect that because $u_j\{Q(j)-\underline{Ax}(j)\}$ becomes positive despite Q(j) is $Min^{1+\lambda}$.

On the other hand, S cannot know the current total expenditure of C_h because C_h informs S of each $\{E(\underline{k}_S, Q(j)^E, r_{nj})+ E(\underline{k}_S, \underline{Sq}(h, j))\}$ while multiplying it by client token concealer u_j secret from S.

Offline Credit Card Systems

In the previous section it is assumed that all stores are always connected to server S, therefore complete information about past transactions of all clients maintained by S is available at each transaction of client C_h. Also stores can encrypt and decrypt transaction records without knowing secret keys of S by asking S to carry out all encryption and decryption operations. Although this assumption is practical enough in the recent networked societies, it is more convenient when individual stores can process transactions independent of S, e.g. scales of software and hardware necessary for communications between S and individual stores will be reduced substantially. Offline anonymous credit card systems enable this.

However there are at least 2 problems in developing offline anonymous credit card systems. They are, firstly individual stores cannot check repeated uses of tokens because they do not maintain records of transactions carried out at different stores; only S maintains all transaction records. Secondly, stores cannot encrypt or decrypt transaction records because only S knows its encryption and decryption keys. If S informs stores of them, stores can behave dishonestly. The followings are approaches to solve these problems.

The 1st problem is not so difficult if delays for detecting repeated uses of tokens are allowed, e.g. S can easily detect multiple uses of tokens, and as in the procedure for the state recovery phase discussed in the previous subsection, it can also identify clients that had used tokens repeatedly at ends of its individual service periods by asking all clients to decrypt encrypted next tokens that are included in the transaction records corresponding to repeatedly used tokens. The clients that successfully decrypt the encrypted next tokens are liable. However, stores that do not know the encryption and decryption keys of server S cannot use the ITL based anonymous authentication scheme, because they cannot encrypt transaction records or verify consistencies between tokens shown by clients and their maintaining past encrypted transaction records. To use ITL based authentication scheme, the 2nd problem must be solved.

Although the 2nd problem is difficult to solve completely, even a partial solution can reduce interactions between S and stores (or clients) substantially. In the partial solution, transaction procedures are divided into 2 parts, one is offline where interactions between S and stores are not necessary, and the other is online where the interactions are inevitable. For example, if a process in which a client and a store carry out a transaction is divided into 2 stages, i.e. the purchase stage in which the client makes its purchases and the store generates a transaction record, and the record registration stage in which server S authorizes the transaction records reported by the client and the store, the purchase stage can be carried out as an offline process without being connected to S. Then, volume of interactions between stores and server S at individual purchases of clients can be reduced.

ELECTRONIC CASH (E-CASH) SYSTEMS

The most distinctive aspects that make cash and credit cards different are the universality and the transferability of cash. For example, a cardholder in a credit card system is a trusted privileged entity, and can make purchases by its credit card more than it can afford, but by cash a person cannot buy an article of which price is more than the amount of the each. People may think cash is inconvenient for this reason, but at the same time, people think cash is more convenient because any people can use cash, and they do not need to worry about overspendings. Also, people can give cash to others, without worrying about their misuses. Namely, different from credit cards that can be used only by people who are trusted by card companies, anyone can obtain, use and exchange cash while convincing itself that its uses of cash do not cause damages more than the amount of the cash. Therefore, it is expected that people are encouraged to use e-cash systems as same as anonymous credit card systems.

This section firstly develops an online e-cash system based on anonymous tag based credentials (Tamura, 2008), then, it is extended to an offline e-cash system. Different from anonymous credit card systems, since the untraceable electronic cash system had been reported based on blind signature scheme (Chaum, 1988), many e-cash systems are being proposed and they satisfy essential requirements of e-cash discussed in the next subsection (Brands, 1994, Canard, 2007, Davida, 1997, Eslami, 2011, Ferguson, 1994, Otsuka, 2002). However, many of them extensively use ZKPs that make e-cash not practical enough. Anonymous tag based credentials used here do not exploit ZKPs, and enable e-cash systems more practical.

Here, it must be noted that advantages of e-cash systems that even untrustworthy entities can use e-cash and people can safely give e-cash to others is spoiled in offline environments although the offline feature is one of the most desirable properties of e-cash systems. Namely, to substitute e-cash for real cash, e-cash systems must enable people to use (pay or exchange) e-cash at anytime and anyplace (e.g. at homes) without the attendance of banks that issue e-cash. But universality and transferability of e-cash and offline features totally contradict each other at least under the currently available technologies. For example, in offline environments, banks cannot immediately detect an entity that pays more than the issue price of its e-cash and excessively used e-cash are detected later (in this section "excessively used e-cash" is used to denote e-cash, by which entities paid more than its issue price), therefore if e-cash holders are not trustworthy, no one ensure that the e-cash holders will pay for their excessive uses. E-cash holders may have disappeared when excessive uses of their e-cash are detected. Then, although it is possible to develop offline e-cash systems, offline e-cash systems can be used only among trusted people as same as credit card systems.

Requirements for E-Cash Systems

In the following, bank B denotes an entity that issues e-cash and clients C_1, C_2, ---, C_M denote e-cash holders that use and exchange their e-cash. Then, requirements for e-cash systems are summarized as below, i.e.

1. No one including a bank that issues e-cash can identify clients that use the e-cash,
2. A client can return its e-cash to a bank to correctly receive its amount,
3. A client can use e-cash even if it is the one that it had received from others,
4. A client can receive changes from other clients by e-cash,
5. A bank can disable a client to pay more than the issue price of its e-cash or can identify a client that use its e-cash excessively, without information about other honest clients, and
6. No absolutely trustworthy entity is assumed.

Among the above requirements, ones except 3 and 4 are essential. As same as anonymous credit card systems, e-cash systems must satisfy the first requirement to preserve privacies of clients. The 2nd and the 5th ones are also essential of course, and as same as for anonymous credit card systems, the 6th requirement is practically essential because absolutely trustworthy entities

Figure 8. Configuration of e-cash

$S(d, T_{Bi}^{e(i)+KGi+K+1})$	$S(d, T_{Hi}^{Rh(i)+KGi+K+1})$
Price-tag part	Holder-tag part

do not exist in the real world. About requirements 3 and 4, they are highly desirable to make e-cash convenient enough, i.e. clients must be able to use e-cash that they had received from others as same as real cash. Also, if clients can receive changes only in real cash, clients must carry e-cash always together with real cash, and benefits of e-cash vanish.

Development of an Online E-cash System

If banks can attend every e-cash exchanging between e-cash holders, an e-cash system that satisfies the requirement in the previous subsection can be developed easily by exploiting anonymous tag based tokens, i.e. when credential attribute value *D* in the previous chapter is considered as the issue price of cash, an anonymous credential automatically becomes e-cash.

Let $e(i)$ be the issue price of cash, T_{Bi}, T_{Hi}, K and G_i be integers defined by bank B, and $R_{h(i)}$ be client C_h's secret integer, then anonymous credential $E(h, i) = S(d, T_{Bi}^{e(i)+KGi+K+1})S(d, T_{Hi}^{Rh(i)+KGi+K+1}) = S(d, T_{Bi}^{e(i)+KGi+K+1}T_{Hi}^{Rh(i)+KGi+K+1})$ discussed in the previous chapter is C_h's i-th e-cash that had been issued by B. Here, $S(d, x)$ is an RSA signing function (therefore, $S(d, x) = x^d$ is multiplicative), d is a secret signing key of B, T_{Bi}, T_{Hi} and $R_{h(i)}$ are unique to E(h, i), K is a publicly known integer common to all e-cash and G_i is B's secret integer.

Conceptually, e-cash E(h, i) consists of price-tag part $S(d, T_{Bi}^{e(i)+KGi+K+1})$ and holder-tag part $S(d, T_{Hi}^{Rh(i)+KGi+K+1})$ as shown in Figure 8, and each part constitutes an anonymous tag based token signed by B. Therefore, by generating secret integer W^i and showing $E(h, i)^{Wi}$ while attaching $\{e(i), T_{Bi}^{Wi}, T_{Bi}^{GiWi}, T_{Hi}^{Wi}, T_{Hi}^{GiWi}, T_{Hi}^{Rh(i)Wi}\}$, C_h can convince anyone that it is the owner of $E(h, i)^{Wi}$ and $E(h, i)^{Wi}$ had been issued by B, as a consequence, issue price $e(i)$ embedded in it is ensured when $T_{Bi}^{e(i)Wi}$ is extracted form $T_{Bi}^{(e(i)+KGi+K+1)Wi}$ as $T_{Bi}^{(e(i)+KGi+K+1)Wi}/T_{Bi}^{Wi}T_{Bi}^{WiK}T_{Bi}^{WiKGi}$. Nevertheless, no one including B can identify C_h from $E(h, i)^{Wi}$ even if C_h had shown its identity for obtaining E(h, i), because $R_{h(i)}$ and W_i are C_h's secrets, i.e. e-cash E(h, i) satisfies the 1st requirement.

About the 5th requirement, at a time when E(h, i) is used, bank B can memorize used seal $M^{Rh(i)}$ that C_h calculates based on anonymous tag $\{T_{Hi}^{Wi}, T_{Hi}^{Rh(i)Wi}\}$ included in $E(h, i)^{Wi}$ without knowing $R_{h(i)}$ itself as discussed in subsection "Limiting Multi-time Uses of Anonymous Tag based Tokens" of Part II. Therefore B can disable excessive uses of E(h, i) by asking the client that is paying E(h, i) to calculate its used seal $M^{Rh(i)}$ and finding $M^{Rh(i)}$ in its memory to reject $E(h, i)^{Wi}$ when $M^{Rh(i)}$ appears repeatedly. Here, B can make C_h's secret integer $R_{h(i)}$ unique to E(h, i) so that used seal $M^{Rh(i)}$ becomes unique in the system as discussed also in Part II.

Satisfying from the 2nd to the 4th requirements is straightforward. Because clients cannot forge or modify signed e-cash or use same e-cash repeatedly, B must pay C_h correct amount when C_h returns $E(h, i)^{Wi}$. Also, at a time when C_h shows (pays) $E(h, i)^{Wi}$ to other client C_v, B can issue new e-cash to C_v as the amount that C_h is going to pay, because clients are always connected to B. Here, it must be noted that an entity except C_h cannot use e-cash E(h, i) even if it steals E(h, i) because it does not know C_h's secret integer $R_{h(i)}$. Finally, it is apparent that there is no absolutely trustworthy entity, i.e. the 6th requirement is satisfied.

The procedure in which client C_h buys its i-th e-cash E(h, i) from bank B is summarized in Figure 9. In the procedure, after verifying C_h's eligibility (this verification process can be removed in the online e-cash system) and receiving amount *e*(i), B generates integers T_{Bi} and T_{Hi}, and C_h calculates $T_{Bi}^{e(i)}$ and $T_{Hi}^{Rh(i)}$ while generating its secret integer $R_{h(i)}$, then finally, B generates e-cash E(h, i) = S(d, $T_{Bi}^{e(i)+KGi+K+1}T_{Hi}^{Rh(i)+KGi+K+1}$) of issue price *e*(i) to give it to C_h while attaching T_{Bi}^{Gi} and T_{Hi}^{Gi}.

Development of an Offline E-cash System

Theoretically, it is not difficult to extend the above online e-cash system to an offline system. Namely, although entities can use same e-cash excessively and they can use forged e-cash or copies of e-cash if bank B does not attend e-cash exchanges between clients, these dishonesties and their liable entities can be detected and identified.

An offline system developed in this subsection differs from the online system in 2 aspects; firstly, client C_h obtains its e-cash E(h, i) = S(d, $T_{Bi}^{e(i)+KGi+K+1}T_{Hi}^{Rh(i)+KGi+K+1}$) from bank B necessarily while disclosing its identity and also it must receive the signature of B on tag constructor {*e*(i), T_{Bi}^{Wi}, T_{Bi}^{GiWi}, T_{Hi}^{Wi}, T_{Hi}^{GiWi}, $T_{Hi}^{Rh(i)Wi}$} while leaving used seal $M^{Rh(i)}$ of tag {T_{Hi}^{Wi}, $T_{Hi}^{Rh(i)Wi}$} after it obtained E(h, i) and before it uses E(h, i). Namely, C_h obtains E(h, i) while disclosing its identity, and after that it calculates $E_*(h, i) = E(h, i)^{Wi}$ = S(d, $(T_{Bi}^{e(i)+KGi+K+1}T_{Hi}^{Rh(i)+KGi+K+1})^{Wi}$) and receives S(d, {*e*(i), T_{Bi}^{Wi}, T_{Bi}^{GiWi}, T_{Hi}^{Wi}, T_{Hi}^{GiWi}, $T_{Hi}^{Rh(i)Wi}$}), signed tag constructor of $E_*(h, i)$, from B without disclosing its identity. Here, the tag constructor enables C_h to show that $E_*(h, i)$ is the signature on the product of $T_{Bi}^{e(i)}$, T_{Bi}^{KGiWi}, T_{Bi}^{KWi}, T_{Bi}^{Wi}, $T_{Hi}^{Rh(i)Wi}$, T_{Hi}^{KGiWi}, T_{Hi}^{GiWi}, T_{Hi}^{Wi} and used seals disable C_h to obtain multiple tag constructors for its single e-cash while using random integers different from W_i, in other words, C_h can use E(h, i) only in form $E_*(h, i) = E(h, i)^{Wi}$. Also, because W_i is C_h's secret integer, C_h can make itself anonymous even if it shows $E_*(h, i)$ or its signed tag constructor.

As the 2nd difference, bank B issues also anonymous credentials to a client in addition to e-cash so that the client can re-issue new e-cash from its owning e-cash by itself. In detail, client C_v obtains credential D(v, q) = S(d, $T_{Dq}^{e*(q)+KGq+K+1}$ $T_{Pq}^{Rv(q)+KGq+K+1}$) and calculates $D_*(v, q)$ = S(d, $(T_{Dq}^{e*(q)+KGq+K+1}T_{Pq}^{Rv(q)+KGq+K+1})^{Wq}$ and receives signed

Figure 9. E-cash buying procedure

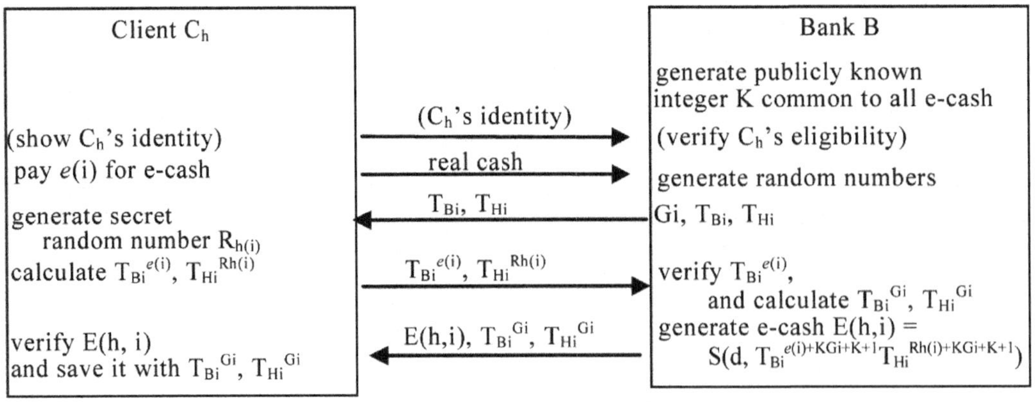

tag constructor $S(d, \{e^*(q), T_{Dq}^{Wq}, T_{Dq}^{GqWq}, T_{Pq}^{Wq}, T_{Pq}^{GqWq}, T_{Pq}^{Rv(q)Wq}\})$ while generating its secret integer W^q in the same way as C_h generates $E_*(h, i)$ and its tag constructor. Here, as same as in e-cash $E_*(h, i)$, $e^*(q)$ represents the issue price of $D_*(v, q)$, T_{Dq} and T_{Pq} are defined by B as unique integers to $D(v, q)$, and G_q is B's secret integer. But, although issue price $e^*(q)$ is embedded in credential $D_*(v, q)$, $D_*(v, q)$ itself does not have any value. Therefore, $e^*(q)$ is constructed as a concatenation of $e(q)$ and $r(q) (> 0)$ to be put in the credential and the corresponding tag constructor so that anyone can discriminate between $E_*(h, i)$ and $D_*(v, q)$, where, $e(q)$ denotes the real issue price of $D_*(v, q)$ and $r(q)$ denotes the round number explained later.

Under the above settings, at a time when C_h pays amount $e(q)$ to other client C_v by e-cash $E_*(h, i) = E(h, i)^{Wi}$, C_h re-issues its q-th new e-cash $E_*(h, i, q)$ of issue price $e(q)$ to C_v as product of C_v's credential $D_*(v, q)$ and C_h's e-cash $E_*(h, i)$. Namely, $E_*(h, i, q) = D_*(v, q)E_*(h, i) = S(d, (T_{Dq}^{e^*(q)+KGq+K+1}T_{Pq}^{Rv(q)+KGq+K+1})^{Wq}(T_{Bi}^{e(i)+KGi+K+1}T_{Hi}^{Rh(i)+KGi+K+1})^{Wi})$ consists of current holder part $D_*(v, q)$ and old cash part $E_*(h, i)$ as shown in Figure 10, where, $D_*(v, q)$ represents $E_*(h, i, q)$ is owned by C_v that knows $R_{v(q)}$ and the issue price of $E_*(h, i, q)$ is $e(q)$, on the other hand, $E_*(h, i)$ represents $E_*(h, i, q)$ had been generated by C_h that knows $R_{h(i)}$ based on its e-cash $E_*(h, i)$ of issue price $e(i)$. Then, when C_v informs C_h of signed tag constructor $S(d, \{e^*(q), T_{Dq}^{Wq}, T_{Dq}^{GqWq}, T_{Pq}^{Wq}, T_{Pq}^{GqWq}, T_{Pq}^{Rv(q)Wq}\})$,

C_h can generates a cash-history of $E_*(h, i, q)$ as shown in Figure 11 that includes also signed tag constructor $S(d, \{e(i), T_{Bi}^{Wi}, T_{Bi}^{GiWi}, T_{Hi}^{Wi}, T_{Hi}^{GiWi}, T_{Hi}^{Rh(i)Wi}\})$, and based on the cash-history C_h and C_v can confirm that $D_*(v, q)$ and $E_*(h, i)$ in $E_*(h, i, q)$ are signatures of B on products of $\{T_{Dq}^{Wq}, T_{Dq}^{KWq}, T_{Dq}^{KGqWq}, T_{Dq}^{e^*(q)Wq}, T_{Pq}^{Wq}, T_{Pq}^{KWq}, T_{Pq}^{KGqWq}, T_{Pq}^{Rv(q)Wq}\}$ and $\{T_{Bi}^{Wi}, T_{Bi}^{KWi}, T_{Bi}^{KGiWi}, T_{Bi}^{e(i)Wi}, T_{Hi}^{Wi}, T_{Hi}^{KWi}, T_{Hi}^{KGiWi}, T_{Hi}^{Rh(i)Wi}\}$, respectively. As a consequence, C_h that knows $R_{h(i)}$ can convince C_v that it has e-cash $E_*(h, i)$ of issue price $e(i)$ that is not less than $e(q)$, on the other hand C_v that knows $R_{v(q)}$ can convince C_h that C_h is paying amount $e(q)$ to an entity registered by B. In addition, provided that $E_*(h, i, q)$ is accompanied by its cash-history, anyone can know that $E_*(h, i, q)$ is the signature of B on the product of $\{T_{Dq}^{Wq}, T_{Dq}^{KWq}, T_{Dq}^{KGqWq}, T_{Dq}^{e^*(q)Wq}, T_{Pq}^{Wq}, T_{Pq}^{KWq}, T_{Pq}^{KGqWq}, T_{Pq}^{Rv(q)Wq}, T_{Bi}^{Wi}, T_{Bi}^{KWi}, T_{Bi}^{KGiWi}, T_{Bi}^{e(i)Wi}, T_{Hi}^{Wi}, T_{Hi}^{KWi}, T_{Hi}^{KGiWi}, T_{Hi}^{Rh(i)Wi}\}$, and consequently, C_v that knows $R_{v(q)}$ can convince anyone that C_v is the owner of $E_*(h, i, q)$ and issue price $e(q)$ of $E_*(h, i, q)$ is not greater than $e(i)$, the amount of $E_*(h, i)$ from which $E_*(h, i, q)$ was generated.

Figure 11 shows the configuration of a cash-history of e-cash $E_*(*)$ that was initially re-issued by C_h to C_v as $E_*(h, i, q) = D_*(v, q)E_*(h, i)$ based on $E_*(h, i)$. Here, re-issued e-cash $E_*(h, i, q)$ also can be defined as an old cash part value, as a consequence a general form of re-issued e-cash is constituted as the product of credentials of multiple clients and an e-cash originally issued

Figure 10. Configuration of re-issued e-cash

Current holder part $D_*(v, q)$		Old cash part $E_*(h, i)$	
$S(d, T_{Dq}^{e^*(q)+KGq+K+1})^{Wq}$	$S(d, T_{Pq}^{Rv(q)+KGq+K+1})^{Wq}$	$S(d, T_{Bi}^{e(i)+KGi+K+1})^{Wi}$	$S(d, T_{Hi}^{Rh(i)+KGi+K+1})^{Wi}$
Price-tag part	Holder-tag part	Price-tag part	Holder-tag part

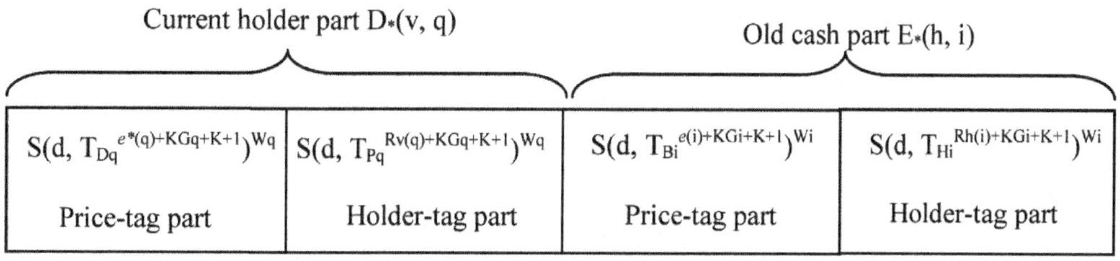

Figure 11. Configuration of cash-history

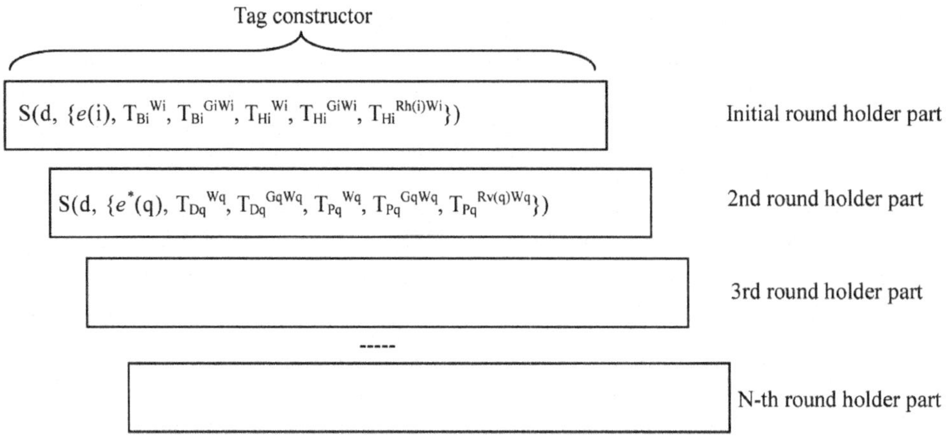

by bank B, and corresponding to these credentials of multiple clients, a cash-history attached to $E_*(*)$ is constituted as a chain of multiple holder parts. Here, to disable entities to place individual tag constructors at illegitimate holder part positions, issue price $e^*(q)$ of credential $D_*(v, q)$ is accompanied by round number $r(q)$, i.e. anyone can know that the tag constructor corresponding to credential $D_*(v, q)$ must be placed at the $r(q)$-th round holder part. This means that each client must prepare credentials for multiple rounds, but this fact does not bring clients serious problems, clients can obtain any number of credentials at a time without payments.

Then, the cash history in Figure 11 that includes tag constructors corresponding to past cash holders enables entities to verify the validity of e-cash $E_*(*)$ as follows. Namely, by decrypting $E_*(*)$ while using public verification key d^{-1}, by decomposing the result into individual anonymous tags, and by examining price-tags and holder-tags of e-cash $E_*(h, i)$ and individual credentials, anyone can convince that issue price $e(z)$ in $e^*(z)$ of z-th round credential does not exceed $e(z-1)$, the issue price of the previous round credential, and anonymous client C_* that knows secret integer R_* embedded in the latest round credential is the owner of $E_*(*)$.

Figure 12 is the procedure in which client C_h pays client C_v e-cash $E_*(h, i)$ while re-issuing $E_*(h, i, q)$. Here, it must be noted that although C_v that obtains new e-cash $E_*(h, i, q)$ through this procedure can know that $e(i)$, the issue price of $E_*(h, i)$ included in $E_*(h, i, q)$, is not less than $e(q)$ included in $e^*(q)$, it cannot know about e-cash that C_h had issued or will issue to other clients from $E_*(h, i)$, i.e. C_v cannot confirm that total amount of e-cash $E_*(h, i, 1)$, $E_*(h, i, 2)$, ---, $E_*(h, i, n)$ re-issued from single e-cash $E_*(h, i)$ does not exceed the issue price of $E_*(h, i)$. On the other hand, C_v that knows its credential $D_*(v, q)$ can extract $E_*(h, i)$ from new e-cash $E_*(h, i, q)$, and can forge different e-cash $E_*(h, i, z) = D_*(v, z)E_*(h, i)$ without permission from C_h. Also C_h or C_v can simply use $E_*(h, i)$ or $E_*(h, i, q)$ excessively. To detect these dishonesties and to identify liable entities, in the figure, C_v calculates $D_*(v, q)^{Rv(q)}$ while using its secret $R_{v(q)}$, and based on it C_h generates payer's seal $(D_*(v, q)^{Rv(q)})^{Rh(i)}$ (used seal of anonymous tag $\{T_{Hi}^{Wi}, T_{Hi}^{R(hi)Wi}\}$) to be saved by C_v. Mechanisms in the next subsection that identify dishonest entities exploit the property of payer's seal $(D_*(v, q)^{Rv(q)})^{Rh(i)}$ that it can be generated only through the collaboration between C_v and C_h and it is unique to $D_*(v, q)$ but C_h does not know C_v's secret $R_v(q)$.

Figure 12. E-cash exchanging procedure

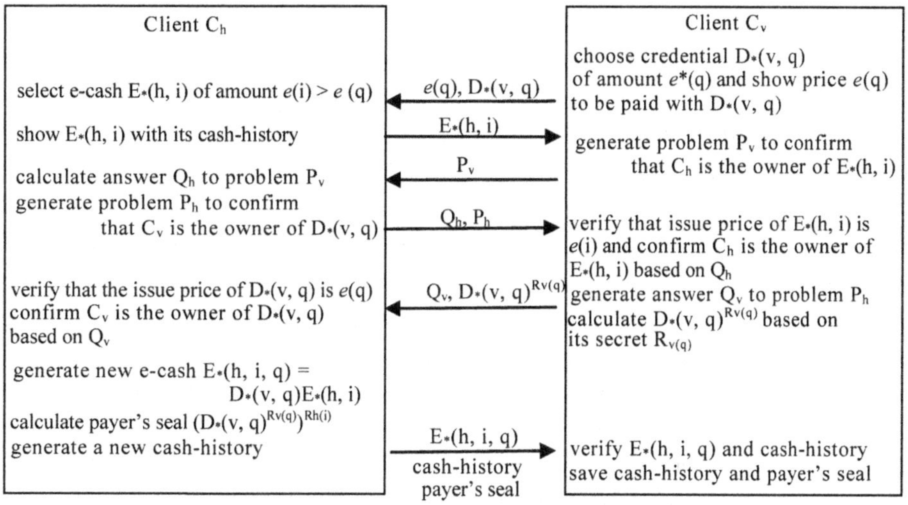

Detection of Illegitimate E-Cash and Identification of Liable Clients

Firstly, to pay e-cash $E_*(*)$ or to exchange it for real cash, client C_z that owns $E_*(*)$ must show $E_*(*)$ with a cash-history that includes consistent sequence of signed tag constructors, namely, $E_*(*)$ must be decomposed into consistent credentials and an original e-cash according to the attached cash-history. Here, only C_z knows secret integer R_* embedded in the holder-tag part of the last round credential, therefore other client or bank B that receives $E_*(*)$ can convince itself that C_z is the owner of $E_*(*)$, also issue prices of individual credentials and e-cash included in the cash-history ensures that the issue price of $E_*(*)$ does not exceed those of credentials and the original e-cash included in $E_*(*)$.

However, clients and or bank B can illegitimately generate consistent e-cash and accompanying cash-history through the following ways. Namely, 1) client C_z or bank B can generate consistent e-cash by making copies of other e-cash, 2) C_z can generate consistent new e-cash as the product of its credential and old cash part of e-cash that it had received (e.g. C_v in the previous subsection can generate $D_*(v, q')E_*(h, i)$ if it obtains $E_*(h, i, q) = D_*(v, q)E_*(h, i)$) from C_h). Also B can generate e-cash by arbitrarily combining credentials and e-cash it had issued, and 3) from its legitimate e-cash $E_*(*)$, C_z can re-issue multiple e-cash more than the issue price of $E_*(*)$. The offline e-cash system in this subsection detects excessive uses of e-cash and illegitimate e-cash, and it also identifies liable entities without invading any privacy of irrelevant clients as shown below.

To detect excessive uses of e-cha and illegitimate e-cash, for each e-cash $E_*(*)$ that is included in ones returned from clients as their old e-cash part values, firstly B enumerates e-cash that had been re-issued based on $E_*(*)$ (e.g. in a case where $E_*(*)$ is e-cash $E_*(h, i)$ originally issued to client C_h by B, B enumerates $E_*(h, i, 1)$, $E_*(h, i, 2)$, ---, $E_*(h, i, n)$ from returned e-cash), calculates the total amount of the enumerated e-cash, and compare the calculated total amount with the issue price of $E_*(*)$. If the total amount exceeds the issue price, the holder of $E_*(*)$ had overspent it or some of e-cash that include $E_*(*)$ are illegitimate ones. Now, B identifies liable clients as follows.

Let $D_*(k_m, p_m)$ be a credential that constitute enumerated e-cash $D_*(k_m, q_m)D_*(k_{m-1}, q_{m-1})$---$D_*(k_1, q_1)E_*(k_0, q_0)$, therefore e-cash $E_*(*)$ is constituted as $D_*(k_{m-1}, q_{m-1})D_*(k_{m-2}, p_{m-2})$ --- $D_*(k_1, q_1)E_*(k_0, q_0)$), then B asks all clients whether they know secret integer R_{km} or $R_{k(m-1)}$ embedded in holder-tag part values of $D_*(k_m, q_m)$ or $D_*(k_{m-1}, q_{m-1})$ so that B can identify C_m and C_{m-1}, owners of $D_*(k_m, q_m)$ and $D_*(k_{m-1}, q_{m-1})$. After that B asks C_m to show payer's seal $(D_*(k_m, q_m)^{Rm})^{R(m-1)}$ that C_{m-1} had calculated, and determines that C_m is dishonest when it does not have the consistent seal. Namely, client C_m had received e-cash $E_*(*)$ without obtaining the consistent payer's seal and nevertheless it had used it. On the other hand, when all clients that had received $E_*(*)$ possess consistent seals, B determines that C_{m-1} had excessively used $E_*(*)$, because only C_{m-1} can calculate the payer's seals consistently (this case includes the one in which C_m and C_{m-1} had conspired with each other).

In the above, at a time when C_{m-1} pays e-cash $E_*(*)$, it cannot calculate payer's seal $(D_*(k_m, q_m)^{Rm})^{R(m-1)}$ dishonestly as discussed in Part II in conjunction with anonymous tag based tokens, e.g. when C_{m-1} pays C_m e-cash $E_*(*)$, C_{m-1} that does not know value $D_*(k_m, q_m)^{Rm}$ cannot discriminate it from other values that are used for verifying secret integer R_{m-1}, i.e. if C_{m-1} calculates $(D_*(k_m, q_m)^{Rm})^{R(m-1)}$ dishonestly $E_*(*)$ is rejected by C_m. B can find C_m and C_{m-1} and force them to honestly calculate their payer's seals in the same way. Also, C_m cannot modify the payer's seal. When C_m modifies the seal, later B regards it as a dishonest client. Finally, dishonesties of bank B itself are detected as ones of which liable entities cannot be identified.

As discussed in the above, the offline e-cash system successfully detects excessively used and illegitimately generated e-cash and identifies liable entities without invading privacies of irrelevant clients. Namely, the offline e-cash system satisfies the all requirements. However, it must be noted that clients relevant to illegitimate e-cash include even honest clients, e.g. in the process to identify dishonest client C_m or C_{m-1} in the above, B knows both C_m and C_{m-1}, despite that one of them may be honest. Also, anyone can know that re-issued e-cash $E_*(h, i, 1)$, $E_*(h, i, 2)$, $E_*(h, i, n)$ were used by the same client C_h although C_h is still anonymous. Finally to make the above e-cash system practical enough the following 2 aspects must be considered. The 1st one is that although the length of e-cash itself does not change even if the e-cash is exchanged many times, the size of the accompanying cash-history grows as many clients exchange the e-cash, and the 2nd one is that bank B cannot detect illegitimate e-cash or identify liable entities until all e-cash had been returned to B in the worst case. Among them, the 1st aspect is not serious, i.e. if bank B declares it does not buy e-cash that was exchanged more than N-times, clients may return their e-cash to B before lengths of cash-histories exceed N. But the 2nd aspect is serious. Although it is easy to define expiration times to individual e-cash, these expiration times must be long enough, and it may not be rare that detection of dishonest e-cash are too late, also some clients never return their e-cash to B. Therefore as mentioned in the beginning of this section, offline e-cash systems make sense only when they are used within small number of rather trustworthy clients.

CONCLUSION

While aiming at the establishment of anonymous electronic payment mechanisms, requirements for anonymous credit card systems and e-cash systems were identified, and an anonymous credit card system and an e-cash system were developed based on ITLs and anonymous tags, respectively.

The developed anonymous credit card system satisfies the identified requirements as follow. Namely except in the account balancing phase, card holder C_h uses its credit card without showing its identity through ITL based anonymous authentication scheme, C_h shows only its open tokens and the sum of its past transaction records. Also, anyone except C_h itself cannot identify links between its consecutive transactions, because C_h shows next tokens for its future credit card uses in their encrypted forms. On the other hand, although the total expenditure of cardholder C_h is calculated by C_h itself, transaction-wise ITL sum checking mechanism ensures card company S honest calculations of C_h, i.e. C_h is forced to honestly maintain and report its transaction records. ITLs also enable card company S and card holders to detect dishonest transactions and identify their liable entities. In addition, the developed system does not include any neutral and absolutely trustworthy entity. Also because cardholders cannot modify their transaction records illegitimately, tamper resistant devices like IC cards are not necessary; therefore all programs that must be executed by card holders can be implemented on state of the art PCs with sufficient performances.

However, although it is the drawback of every kind of existing credit card systems, the developed system is defenseless against transaction record forgeries executed by entities that have complete information about both the credit card company and cardholders. These cases occur when the credit card company steals tokens and encryption keys from cardholders. Also, there should be big arguments over anonymous credit card systems, e.g. they may encourage money launderings. Regulations, in which authorities can force a cardholder to disclose its encryption key if necessary, is a solution to mitigate these worries. Authorities can trace all transaction records of the cardholder when its encryption key is disclosed; then various undesirable side effects of anonymity can be reduced.

The online and offline e-cash systems developed based on anonymous tags also satisfy the identified requirements, i.e. anonymous tags enable e-cash holder C_h to re-issue new e-cash provided that the total amount of the new e-cash does not exceed the issue price of the old e-cash. Then, C_h can pay other client C_v any amount (of course it cannot exceed the issue price of its owning e-cash) by generating new e-cash without disclosing its identity, and C_v can use the received new e-cash to pay other client, and any client that possesses legitimate e-cash can exchange it for real cash at bank B. Also, payer's seals of e-cash enable bank B to detect illegitimate e-cash and excessively used e-cash and identify dishonest entities without invading privacies of irrelevant entities.

However, a serious problem remains to make the offline e-cash system practical enough. That is, bank B cannot detect excessively used or illegitimately generated e-cash until all e-cash is returned to it. Therefore, an entity can spend infinite amount while making copies of its e-cash and disappear. This problem can be solved or mitigated if e-cash is exchanged only among trusted entities and bank B defines expiration times on individual e-cash. But this solution ruins the advantage of e-cash systems over credit card systems totally. Therefore at least under the currently available technologies, advantages of e-cash systems over credit card systems can be exploited only in online environments.

REFERENCES

Androulaki, E., & Bellovin, S. (2009). An anonymous credit card system. *Proceedings of the 6th International Conference: Trust, Privacy and Security in Digital Business*, 3-4 September 2009, New York, (pp. 42-51). Linz, Austria: Springer.

Brands, S. (1994). Untraceable off-line cash in wallets with observers. *Proceedings of CRYPTO, 93*, 302–318.

Canard, S., & Gouget, A. (2007). Lecture Notes in Computer Science: *Vol. 4515. Divisible e-cash systems can be truly anonymous. Advances in Cryptology - EUROCRYPT* (pp. 482–497). Berlin, Germany: Springer-Verlag.

Chaum, D., Fiat, A., & Naor, M. (1988). Untraceable electronic cash. *Proceedings of CRYPTO, 88*, 319–327.

Davida, D., Frankel, Y., Tsiounis, Y., & Yung, M. (1997). Anonymout control in e-cash systems. *Advances in Cryptology -Financial Cryptology '97* [Springer-Verlag.]. *LNCS, 1318*, 1–16.

Eslami, Z., & Talebi, M. (2011). A new untraceable off-line electronic cash system. *Electronic Commerce Research and Applications, 10*(1), 59–66. doi:10.1016/j.elerap.2010.08.002

Ferguson, N. (1994). Single term off-line coins. *Advances in Cryptography -EUROCRYPTO'93*, (pp. 318-328).

Low, S. H., Nicholas, F., & Sanjoy, P. (1996). Anonymous credit cards and their collusion analysis. *IEEE/ACM Transactions on Networking, 4*(6), 809–816. doi:10.1109/90.556339

Otsuka, A., Hanaoka, G., Shikata, J., & Imai, H. (2002). An unconditionally secure electronic cash scheme with computational untraceability. *IEICE Transactions, Fundamentals . E (Norwalk, Conn.), 85-A*(1), 140–148.

Tamura, S., Kouro, K., Sasatani, S., Md. Rokibul, K. A., & Haddad, H. A. (2008). An information system platform for anonymous product recycling. *Journal of Software, 3*(6), 46–56. doi:10.4304/jsw.3.6.46-56

Tamura, S., Kouro, K., & Yanase, T. (2006). Expenditure limits in anonymous credit card systems. *IEEE SMC, 2006*, 1238–1243.

Tamura, S., & Yanase, T. (2007). A mechanism for anonymous credit card systems. *IEEJ Transactions in EIS, 127*(1), 81–87. doi:10.1541/ieejeiss.127.81

Chapter 11
Electronic Procurement Systems

ABSTRACT

As elements that constitute electronic procurement systems, anonymous auction, object delivery, and object monitoring systems are developed based on ITLs, anonymous tags and anonymous memories, respectively. The developed anonymous auction system enables entities to securely sell and/or buy their articles without disclosing their identities, and the anonymous object delivery system enables them to send or receive their articles to or from other entities also without disclosing their identities. The object monitoring system monitors running states of objects (e.g. home appliances) so that they can be used efficiently, safely, and environmentally friendlily while preserving privacies of their users. It also detects dishonest users (e.g. that discords their objects illegitimately) without invading privacies of honest users. Here, anonymous memories used in the monitoring system are memory sections by which users can securely and efficiently maintain their data without disclosing their identities.

INTRODUCTION

In this chapter, auction, object delivery and object monitoring systems are developed as components of electronic procurement (e-procurement) systems, in which people connected by networks sell or buy articles, transportation service providers deliver articles to their buyers, and monitoring stations remotely monitor running states of articles such as home appliances to enable individual users to use them efficiently, safely, and environmentally friendlily. Here, although this kind of e-procurement systems not only make our societies efficient, convenient and safe but also enable effective and efficient recycling of products and materials, to encourage more people to accept these systems, privacies of individual sellers, buyers or users involved must be preserved. Therefore, anonymous e-procurement systems supported by security and service components discussed in Section 2 play important roles.

DOI: 10.4018/978-1-4666-1649-3.ch011

Figure 1 depicts the overall configuration of the anonymous e-procurement system (Tamura, 2008). In the figure, participants sell or buy articles to or from other participants, and among the participants, some of them sell or buy articles without disclosing their identities and in these cases payments are carried out through anonymous credit card systems discussed in the previous chapter, but some others (e.g. established manufacturers) sell or buy articles while disclosing their exact identities. Here, an anonymous auction mechanism is one of schemes in which people sell and buy articles without disclosing their identities. Then once articles are bought by buyers, buyers e.g. auction winners, receive articles through anonymous object delivery systems from sellers (they may be also anonymous) without disclosing their identities, and monitoring stations monitor running states of articles such as home appliances while preserving privacies of their owners or users. When monitoring stations detect that the articles are used inadequately they warn the anonymous users of the dangers, or when the articles are discarded illegitimately they identify the liable users without invading any privacy of other users.

ANONYMOUS AUCTION SYSTEMS

Although there are many kinds of auction protocols this section discusses 2 of them i.e. English and Vickrey auction schemes (Yokoo, 2006). Both English and Vickrey auction schemes consist of sellers S_1, S_2, ---, S_M, buyers B_1, B_2, ---, B_N, auctioneer A and BBs (bulletin boards) as shown in Figure 2. In the figure, each seller S_j brings its article to auctioneer A, A conducts auctions, in which buyers B_1, B_2, ---, B_N bid prices to buy the article brought by S_j, and auction results and if necessary states of the auction processes are disclosed in BBs. Here, when auctions are anonymous each B_h can make bids and pay for its winning articles without disclosing its identity to others including auctioneer A and seller S_j that had brought the article. Also, each seller S_j can bring its articles and be paid for them while concealing its identity from others. Here, anonymous networks enable sellers and buyers to access the auction system without disclosing their identities, anonymous credit card systems enable anonymous buyers and sellers to conduct their payment processes, and anonymous object delivery systems enable sellers and buyers to bring their owning articles and to

Figure 1. Configuration of anonymous e-procurement system

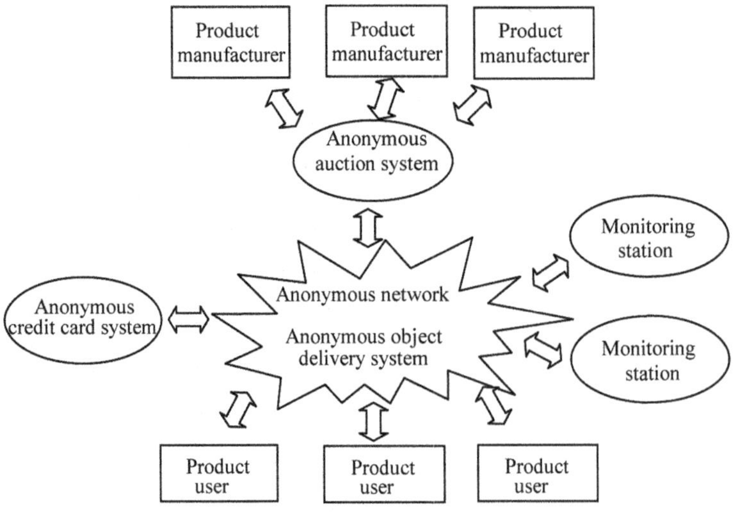

Figure 2. Anonymous auction system

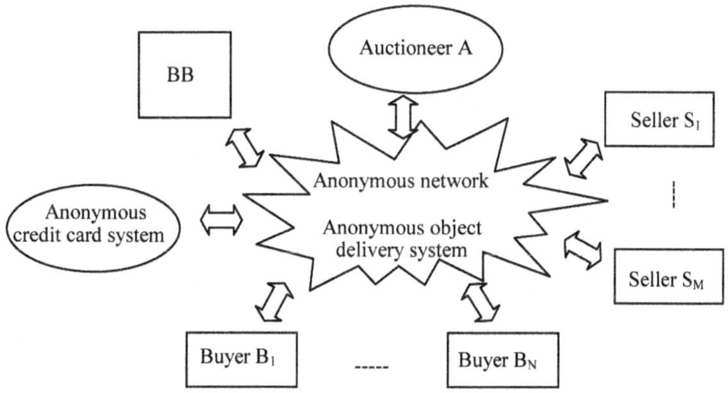

receive their winning articles without disclosing their identities to others.

In an English auction scheme, firstly auctioneer A declares the initial price of the article brought by seller S_j as the current price, and buyer B_h among B_1, B_2, ---, B_N that wants to buy the article makes a bid with price higher than the current one. Then, the current price is replaced by the new price declared by B_h. In the same way, other buyer B_j makes a bid with price higher than the current one if it wants to buy the article, and this process is repeated until no buyer appears that makes a bid. The auction winner is the buyer that had made the highest bid of course, and it buys its winning article at the highest bid price. On the other hand, in a Vickrey auction scheme, all buyers make bids at the same time while concealing their bid prices. Then, auctioneer discloses the prices of all buyers, and the auction winner is determined as the buyer who had made the highest bid, however, the winning price is determined as the 2nd highest price. Here, the Vickrey auction scheme is regarded as the one in which winning prices reflect values of articles most truly or directly.

In the following subsections, an anonymous English auction scheme is developed without assuming any absolutely trustworthy entity, i.e. the entity that each participant can trust is only itself. On the other hand, an anonymous Vickrey auction scheme is developed while distributing trusts to multiple auctioneers, i.e. privacies of participants are preserved at least one of the auctioneers is honest.

Requirements for Anonymous Auctions

Auction systems in this chapter consist of sellers S_1, S_2, ---, S_M, buyers B_1, B_2, ---, B_N and auctioneer A. Then, requirements for anonymous auction systems can be summarized as follows, i.e.

1. Only authorized entities can participate in auctions as sellers or buyers,
2. Each participant can conceal its identity from others, i.e. when the participant is a buyer, no one can identify the correspondence between it and its bids, and when the participant is a seller, no one can identify the correspondence between it and its bringing articles,
3.
   a. no one except buyer B_j itself can link a sequence of bids made by B_j in case of an English auction scheme,

   b. in case of a Vickrey auction scheme, no one can know the bid prices of other buyers except the 2nd highest ones,
4. Auction winners can obtain their winning articles from anonymous sellers at the prices determined by the auctions without disclosing their identities,
5. Sellers can force anonymous auction winners to buy their winning articles and collect exact amounts from them without revealing their identities to others, and
6. No absolutely trustworthy entity is assumed.

The 1st requirement concerns with the safe operations of auctions, i.e. in order to protect sellers, buyers and auctioneers from various threats caused by unauthorized entities only registered entities must be allowed to bring and buy articles to or from auctions so that liable entities can be identified when dishonest events occur. However, privacies of honest sellers and buyers must be preserved as stated in the 2nd requirement. About the 3rd requirement, in cases of English auctions, individual bids made by a same buyer also must be protected from being linked, because a sequence of bids made by a same buyer may suggest the identity of the buyer. On the other hand in cases of Vickrey auctions, if buyers know individual bid prices of other anonymous buyers even after auction winners had been decided, buyers may use this information for their future auctions and consequently the advantage of Vickrey auctions that winning prices reflect values of articles most truly is depraved. For example, when the highest bid price P_H is known to buyers in addition to the 2nd highest one, a buyer who absolutely wants to buy a same kind of article may bid with the price higher than P_H in the future auction, then the winning price does not truly reflect the value of the article anymore.

To satisfy only these 3 requirements is trivial, e.g. simple deployments of anonymous security and service components disable participants of English auctions not only to know individual buyers but also to link bids made by same buyers. Also, simple re-encryption schemes enable participants of Vickrey auctions to decide winners without disclosing individual bid prices except the 2nd highest ones. The difficult thing is that the other remaining requirements must be satisfied at the same time. Namely as the 4th requirement, anonymous auction schemes must ensure that although sellers are anonymous auction winners can buy their winning articles with the prices determined by the auctions, in other words, sellers cannot sell their articles to buyers except the auction winners. On the other hand as shown in the 5th requirement, sellers must be ensured that they can force auction winners to buy their winning articles and can collect the exact amounts from them despite that auction winners are anonymous.

Finally as the 6th requirement, to convince sellers and buyers that their identities are not revealed, it is desirable that absolutely trustworthy entities are completely excluded; because no entity exists that is absolutely trustworthy in the real world. The English auction scheme developed in the next subsection satisfies this requirement, but in the Vickrey auction scheme, sellers and buyers can believe that they are anonymous when at least one of multiple authorities is honest.

Despite that various anonymous auction schemes had been proposed already (Franklin, 1996, Naor, 1999, Nguyen, 2000, Stajano, 2002) they do not satisfy the above requirements for anonymous auctions completely or they require complicated computations. Although a mechanism used in (Stajano, 2002) does not assume any absolutely trustworthy entity, it can neither force auction winners to buy their winning articles nor to force sellers to sell their articles to auction winners. In this section, ITLs are used to develop anonymous auction systems that satisfy all of the above requirements (Hassan, 2006, Tamura, 2008).

Development of Anonymous Auction Systems

As same as clients of the anonymous credit card system in the previous chapter, sellers and buyers in anonymous auction systems developed in this section firstly register themselves as members of auction systems while showing their explicit identities and their encrypted next tokens to auctioneer A. For example, buyer B_h shows its ID and password pair $\{ID_h, PW_h\}$ and its encrypted next token $E(a_h, T(h, 1))$ to A, and obtains its encrypted and signed initial bid records $E(k_A, BR(h, 0))$ and $S(g_A, BR(h, 0))$. Then at its next visit to A, it can prove its eligibility without disclosing its identity by using T(h, 1). Where, k_A and g_A are secret encryption and signing keys of A, and a_h is the secret encryption key of buyer B_h, and encryption functions $E(k_A, x)$ and $E(a_h, y)$ are additive ones based on linear equations. T(h, 1) is the open token, and B_h obtains its tokens from the token table prepared by A in advance without disclosing its identity through ID list based anonymous authentication scheme, but as an exception B_h does not pick its initial token T(h, 0) from the token table, value of T(h, 0) is defined as ID_h, the ID of B_h. In the above registration process, B_h also decrypts a set of bit string vectors $\{E(a_h, t_{A1}(h)), E(a_h, t_{A2}(h)), ---, E(a_h, t_{Az}(h))\}$ given by A to visible part values $\{check_{A1}(h), check_{A2}(h), ---, check_{Az}(h)\}$ and registers them as encrypted test bit strings and their decrypted forms in addition to $\{ID_h, PW_h\}$.

Each buyer B_h's n-th bid record BR(h, n) consists of plain token, token version, bid price, article and ITL parts as shown in Figure 3. Here, plain token part Pt(h, n), token version part Tv(h, n) and ITL Section 1TL(h, n) include the same information as those in transaction record TR(h, n) of the anonymous credit card system did. Namely, at B_h's n-th access to auctioneer A, A assigns B_h's n-th token T(h, n) to Pt(h, n) as its value, Tv(h, n) is used in the procedures for anonymous record agreement protocol between B_h and A, and the value of ITL(h, n) is defined as $\{v_n T(h, n), v_{n+1} E(a_h, T(h, n+1))\}$, a pair of current token T(h, n) and the encrypted next token T(h, n+1) multiplied by token concealers v_n and v_{n+1} secrets of A. Price part Pr(h, n) and article part Ar(h, n) represent the bid price and the identifier of the article to be sold, respectively.

Here, as same as in previous chapters ITLs enable auctioneer A to authenticate buyers without knowing them, i.e. after the (n-1)-th bid record BR(h, n-1) of buyer B_h that includes ITL(h, n-1) = $\{v_{n-1} T(h, n-1), v_n E(a_h, T(h, n))\}$ had been registered as encrypted and signed forms $E(k_s, BR(h, n-1))$ and $S(g_s, BR(h, n-1))$, B_h can prove its eligibility to make its n-th access to A without disclosing its identity by showing T(h, n), in detail, A convinces itself that B_h is an authorized buyer when T(h, n) and the sum of past ITLs that B_h maintains are consistent. A authenticates seller S_j in the same way, and a record corresponding to an event that a seller brings its article to A also has the form shown in Figure 3 and is called as a bid record, although price part value Pr(j, k) does not have meanings in this case.

ITLs play important roles not only in authenticating anonymous buyers and sellers but also in

Figure 3. Bid record

Plain token part	Token version part	Price part	Article part	ITL part
Pt(h, n) = T(h,n)	Tv(h, n)	Pr(h, n)	Ar(h, n)	ITL(h, n)

fairly conducting auctions, i.e. they force sellers to sell their articles to auction winners and at the same time they force buyers to buy their winning articles from sellers as discussed later. To fairly conduct auctions, anonymous auction systems developed in this section also disclose all states of auctions e.g. the current bid prices and tokens accompanying them in English auction systems, in the public bulletin board (BB) except cases where they are secrets of some entities, and all participants of auctions can share auction states in real-time. Where only auctioneer A can write date on the BB, but anyone can read them at any-time; therefore A cannot modify data in the BB illegitimately without being noticed by entities that are watching the BB.

As mentioned before, sellers and buyers can access auctioneer A without disclosing their identities through anonymous networks discussed in Section 2, the anonymous object delivery system discussed in the next section enables sellers and buyers to bring and receive their articles without revealing their identities to others, and they can conduct their payment processes anonymously through the anonymous credit card system developed in the previous chapter.

English Auction

Figure 4 describes the behavior of the anonymous English auction scheme developed in this subsection, where buyers show their unused tokens to make their individual bids. Firstly, the initial price of the article brought by seller S_j is disclosed as the current price in the BB by auctioneer A, and the current price is increased by several buyers, then buyer B_h makes its bid with price that is higher than the current one while showing its n-th token T(h, n) to A (it is assumed that B_h makes its bid at its n-th visit to A). Auctioneer A accepts B_h's bid price if T(h, n) was not used before and it is consistent with the sum of past ITLs of B_h, and it discloses the price declared by B_h as the new current price in the BB together with token T(h, n). At the same time B_h informs S of its encrypted (n+1)-th token E(a_h, T(h, n+1)), and based on it, S authorizes BR(h, n), n-th bid record of B_h that includes ITL(h, n) = {v_nT(h, n), v_{n+1}E(a_h, T(h, n+1))}, as encrypted and signed forms E(k_s, BR(h, n)) and S(g_s, BR(h, n)), and gives them to B_h. This process is repeated until no buyer appears to make bid, and the auction winner is determined as the one that had made the highest bid. Although it is not described to simplify the explanation, actually to securely conduct the bid record construction process, auctioneer A gives buyer B_h a signed tentative bid record before authorizing each BR(h, n) according to the anonymous record agreement protocol as same as in the anonymous credit card system discussed in the previous chapter.

Then the requirements of anonymous auctions listed in the previous subsection are satisfied as below. Firstly, only authorized sellers and buyers can participate in the auction, because auctioneer A registers sellers or buyers while identifying them, and sellers or buyers can access the auction system only when they show tokens that are consistent with their past bid records that had been authorized by A at the sellers' or buyers' previous accesses to A. Also, it is apparent that ITL based authentication scheme ensures anonymities of sellers and buyers. In addition, ITL based authentication scheme disables any entity except buyer B_h or seller S_j to link individual bids of B_h or individual articles brought by S_j, because B_h or S_j shows its next token T(h, n+1) or T(j, k+1) only in its encrypted form at a time when it shows its current token T(h, n) or T(j, k).

Auction winner B_h can force A to sell its winning article to it by showing its token T(h, n), the token that is attached to the winning bid. Although T(h, n) is disclosed in the BB already and any entity can show T(h, n) to A, A can determine that T(h, n) is the token of B_h when T(h, n) is consistent with the sum of past ITLs maintained by B_h. However, A must ask B_h to calculate the sum of its past ITLs while using client token concealers different from the ones that B_h had

Figure 4. Behavior of English anonymous auction

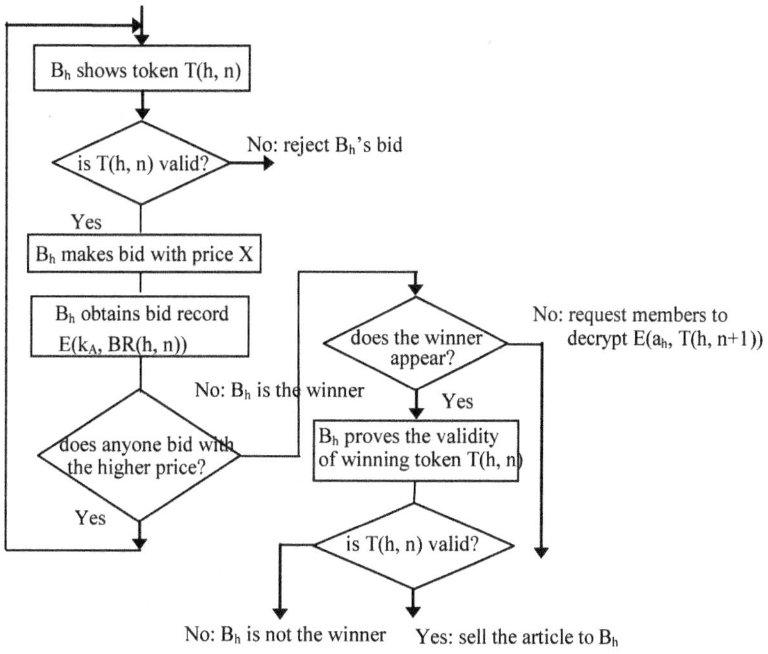

used for the winning bid, i.e. B_h must inform A of the different values as the sums. Because B_h had already reported the sums at a time when it made the winning bid, even entities other than B_h can calculate the sums consistently if A allows B_h to use the same client token concealers.

As the simpler way A can give signed token $S(g_A, T(h, n))$ to B_h at B_h's every bid, however in this case an entity that stole $S(g_A, T(h, n))$ from B_h can buy the article on behalf of B_h. More serious problem about $S(g_A, T(h, n))$ is that B_h that had obtained its winning article already can claim that auctioneer A had illegitimately generated its signature and sold B_h's winning article to other entity. Different from simple signatures, ITLs enable buyers not to worry even if their tokens are stolen, and at the same time rather more importantly, they enable the auctioneer not to worry about disputes between it and buyers. Because the authenticity of token T(h, n) is verified while being compared with past bid records of B_h itself, entities other than B_h cannot use it, and this means that auctioneer A can resolve a dispute between it and B_h by recording triple $\{T(h, n), T(h, n\text{-}1), E(a_h, \underline{T}^*(h, n))\}$ at a time when B_h obtains the article, where $\underline{T}(h, n\text{-}1)$ is the sum of current tokens and $E(a_h, \underline{T}^*(h, n))$ is the sum of encrypted next tokens that B_h had shown for receiving its winning article at its n-th access to A. Namely, $\{T(h, n), \underline{T}(h, n\text{-}1), E(a_h, \underline{T}^*(h, n))\}$ proves that B_h had obtained the article because $E(a_h, \underline{T}^*(h, n))$ that is decrypted to $\underline{T}^*(h, n) = \underline{T}(h, n\text{-}1)+v_n T(h, n)$ by key a_h can be generated only by B_h, in other words, if A had actually sold the article to other entity, A cannot show triple $\{T(h, n), \underline{T}(h, n\text{-}1), E(a_h, \underline{T}^*(h, n))\}$ so that $E(a_h, \underline{T}^*(h, n))$ is decrypted to $\underline{T}(h, n\text{-}1)+v_n T(h, n)$ by a_h. Here, B_h cannot dishonestly decrypt $E(a_h, \underline{T}^*(h, n)$ because encryption function $E(a_h, x)$ is additive and verifiable as discussed just below.

About the 5th requirement, even when auction winner B_h that had made the highest bid with token T(h, n) and encrypted next token $E(a_h, T(h, n+1))$ does not appear to buy its winning article, auctioneer A can force it to buy the article by asking all buyers to decrypt $E(a_h, T(h, n+1))$. Namely, only winner B_h that knows encryption key a_h can decrypt $E(a_h, T(h, n+1))$ to a consistent value. Also, test bit strings and their encrypted forms registered with B_h's identity force B_h to honestly decrypt $E(a_h, T(h, n+1))$ as discussed in subsection "Homomorphic Anonymous Tokens." Here, auctioneer A can ask all buyers to decrypt $E(a_h, T(h, n+1))$ without disturbing them if it carries out the inquiry in conjunction with payment processes at the end of its every service period, e.g. at the end of every month.

However, buyer B_h can continue to participate in auctions before the inquiry even if it did not buy its winning articles. Auctioneer A can disable B_h, which does not buy its winning article, to participate in auctions even before the inquiries, if it issues bid record $E(k_A, BR(h, n))$ and $S(g_A, BR(h, n))$ only after the appearance of other buyer that makes the higher bid than B_h's n-th one or B_h's appearance for receiving its winning article (Hassan, 2006). Namely, when B_h is the auction winner and it does not buy the article, it cannot make its (n+1)-th bid because it does not have its n-th bid record BR(h, n) and consequently its (n+1)-th token T(h, n+1) is not effective.

Vickrey Auction

Anonymous Vickrey auction systems also can be developed easily when one of re-encryption schemes discussed in subsection "Homomorphic, Probabilistic, Commutative and Verifiable Encryption Functions" of Section 1 is used. As same as the previous English auction scheme, the Vickrey auction scheme developed in this subsection is also based on the ITL based anonymous authentication scheme, i.e. at its n-th visit to auctioneer A, anonymous buyer B_h makes its bid with its n-th token T(h, n) and its (n+1)-th encrypted token $E(a_h, T(h, n+1))$. Figure 5 shows the procedure, where auctioneer A is configured as a set of mutually independent multiple authorities A_1, A_2, ---, A_Q, and each buyer B_h repeatedly encrypts its bid price P_h to $E(k_Q, E(k_{Q-1}, ---, E(k_1, C^{Ph}{}_{\text{mod } p})$---$)) = E(k_*, C^{Ph}{}_{\text{mod } p})$ while using publicly known encryption key k_j of A_j, and puts $E(k_*, C^{Ph}{}_{\text{mod } p})$ at a randomly selecting place in the BB with its token T(h, n) and encrypted next token $E(a_h, T(h, n+1))$. Here, if a secret key based re-encryption scheme is adopted, B_h must ask authorities A_1, A_2, ---, A_N, to repeatedly encrypt P_h while concealing it by its secret key and decrypt the result by itself because encryption keys k_1, k_2, ---, k_N are secrets of the individual authorities.

Figure 5. Behavior of Vickrey anonymous auction

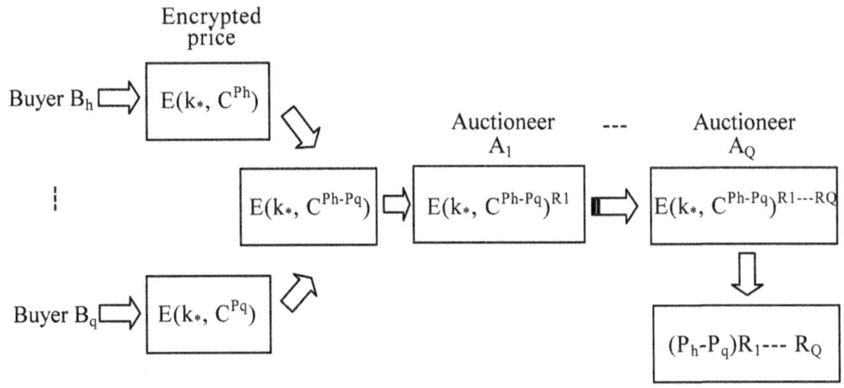

In the above, C and p are appropriate constant integers, and encryption function $E(k_*, x)$ is assumed to be multiplicative. Then, $E(k_*, C^{Ph}{}_{\bmod p})$ becomes additive when it is considered as the encrypted form of P_h as discussed in subsections "RSA" and "ElGamal" in Section 1, i.e. $E(k_*, C^{Ph}) E(k_*, C^{Pq}) = E(k_*, C^{Ph}C^{Pq}) = E(k_*, C^{Ph+Pq})$ is decrypted to P_h+P_q. In addition to the additive feature, each encryption function $E(k_q, x)$ is assumed to be probabilistic, therefore B_h can conceal its bid price even from buyers who had made their bids with the same price as B_h. In the following, auctioneer A is the representative of multiple authorities A_1, A_2, ---, A_Q, and the base of modulo arithmetic p is omitted.

After bids from all buyers had been put in the BB, auctioneer A calculates $E(k_*, C^{Ph})/E(k_*, C^{Pq}) = E(k_*, C^{Ph-Pq})$ for each encrypted bid price pair $\{E(k_*, C^{Ph}), E(k_*, C^{Pq})\}$ of anonymous buyers B_h and B_q, and A_1, A_2, ---, A_Q repeatedly calculate $E(k_*, C^{Ph-Pq})^{R1}$, $E(k_*, C^{Ph-Pq})^{R1R2}$, ---, $E(k_*, C^{Ph-Pq})^{R1R2---RQ}$ while disclosing all interim results in the BB by generating random number R_j that is a secret of A_j. Here, each A_j generates different numbers as values of R_j for different encrypted bid price pairs. Then, A_Q, A_{Q-1}, ---, A_1 repeatedly decrypt each $E(k_*, C^{Ph-Pq})^{R1R2---RQ}$ to disclose the result $(P_h-P_q)R_1$--- R_Q in the BB; therefore, anyone can determine whether price P_h is higher than P_q or not by the sign of $(P_h-P_q)R_1$--- R_Q ($-P_q$ is represented as a complement of P_q), however no one can know exact values of P_h or P_q unless all A_1, A_2, ---, A_Q conspire, because each R_j is known only to A_j. As a consequence, all participants can know the token of the auction winner i.e. the token of the buyer who had made the highest bid. Also they can know the price of the article, when A_Q, A_{Q-1}, ---, A_1 repeatedly decrypt the encrypted 2nd highest bid price (therefore as an exception, all participants can know the 2nd highest bid). However, it must be noted that all integers are regarded as signed integers, i.e. the left most bit of $(P_h-P_q)R_1$--- R_Q is regarded as sign bit, therefore integer p and random secret numbers R_1, R_2, ---, R_Q must be defined so that product $P_hR_1R_2$---R_Q does not exceed p/2 for any P_h. When $P_hR_1R_2$---R_Q or $P_qR_1R_2$---R_Q exceeds p/2, $(P_h-P_q)R_1R_2$---R_Q may become negative even when (P_h-P_q) is positive for example.

Then, the above scheme satisfies the 3rd requirement. Namely, no one except buyer B_h itself can know bid price P_h of B_h when it is not the 2nd highest bid price. Other requirements are satisfied totally in the same way as in the English auction scheme. Here, authorities may calculate $E(k_*, C^{Ph-Pq})^{R1R2---RQ}$ from $E(k_*, C^{Ph-Pq})$ or decrypt $E(k_*, C^{Ph-Pq})^{R1R2---RQ}$ to $(P_h-P_q)R_1R_2$---R_Q dishonestly, also B_h may bid invalid $E(k_*, C^{Ph})$ (e.g. $E(k_*, C^{Ph})$ may be decrypted to a negative value). Authorities and buyers also protect themselves from these dishonesties as follows. Firstly, to disable authorities A_1, A_2, ---, A_Q to calculate $E(k_*, C^{Ph-Pq})^{R1R2---RQ}$ dishonestly, anonymous B_h is allowed to ask its choosing authority A_j to disclose its secret number R_j. Therefore, anyone can verify that A_j had honestly calculated $E(k_*, C^{Ph-Pq})^{R1R2---Rj}$ from $E(k_*, C^{Ph-Pq})^{R1R2---R(j-1)}$ by examining the disclosed $E(k_*, C^{Ph-Pq})^{R1R2---R(j-1)}$ and $E(k_*, C^{Ph-Pq})^{R1R2---Rj}$ in the BB. Then, because A_j is chosen by B_h at random, entities can convince themselves that other A_i also had calculated $E(k_*, C^{Ph-Pq})^{R1R2---R(i-1)Ri}$ from $E(k_*, C^{Ph-Pq})^{R1R2---R(i-1)}$ honestly. However, no one can know the value of $(P_h-P_q)R_1R_2$---R_Q because remaining R_1, R_2, --, R_{j-1}, R_{j+1}, --, R_Q are still not known.

Also, multiplicative feature of encryption function $E(k_j, x)$ protects buyers from dishonest decryptions of authorities; anyone can verify A_j's correct decryption of $E(k_j, x)$, in other words and more importantly, each A_j can prove its correct decryption of $E(k_j, x)$ without disclosing decryption key k_j^{-1} or the random numbers to make $E(k_j, x)$ probabilistic. About the threat that buyer B_h may bid with invalid price, the invalid encrypted bid price does not bring any damage to entities except B_h itself. Namely, encrypted bid $E(k_*, C^{Ph})$ of B_h is decrypted to a some bid price, and when $E(k_*, C^{Ph})$ is decrypted to a small value e.g. a negative value, the result is that B_h cannot obtain the article even if it is wanting to buy it. On the other hand when $E(k_*, C^{Ph})$ is decrypted to a large value, B_h is forced to buy the article even if it does not want.

Identifying Dishonest Sellers

Dishonest seller S_j is a one that brings counterfeits or inferior goods as its articles. Although sellers are anonymous, auctioneer A also can identify S_j without revealing any privacy of honest sellers or buyers by the same procedure that it had identified buyers who did not by their winning articles. Namely, when A asks all participants to decrypt the encrypted next token $E(a_j, T(j, k+1))$ that had been shown by S_j at the time when the article was brought, the only entity that can decrypt it consistently is S_j that knows encryption key a_j.

ANONYMOUS OBJECT DELIVERY AND MONITORING SYSTEMS

This section develops mechanisms to deliver objects to unknown entities or receive objects from unknown entities and to monitor states of objects e.g. running states of home appliances without knowing identities of their owners or users. Although buyers in the previous auction systems could bid for articles without disclosing their identities, their identities will be revealed at times when the auctioneer sends the objects to auction winners. The former mechanism solves this problem, i.e. buyers can receive their winning articles while completely concealing their identities; and consequently more people are encouraged to participate in auctions. The latter mechanism enables monitoring stations to suggest the ways to use objects more safely, efficiently and environmentally friendlily to their users without knowing any privacy of them. It also enables the identifications of liable users when dishonest events, e.g. illegitimate disposals of home appliances, are detected while preserving privacies of honest users.

The next subsection discusses requirements for these systems, and a mechanism for anonymous memories is introduced as one of bases for developing systems that satisfy these requirements. Then, based on the anonymous memory together with anonymous tags and ITLs, an anonymous object delivery system and an anonymous object monitoring system are developed. In developing anonymous object monitoring systems, anonymous statistics calculation mechanisms discussed in Section 2 are also exploited. In this section, entities that send, receive or use objects are called clients, and ones that deliver or monitor objects are called stations.

Requirements for Anonymous Object Delivery and Monitoring Systems

Anonymous object delivery and monitoring systems must satisfy the following requirements, i.e.

1. Client C_h can send an object to client C_j that receives the object without disclosing its identity to others including stations and receiver C_j, and/or C_j can receive an object from sender C_h without disclosing its identity to others including stations and C_h,
2. C_h that sends an object or C_j that receives an object is able to not only trace the object during it is being transported through the anonymous object delivery system but also detect troubles on it and can identify stations liable for the troubles while concealing its identity and without knowing any secret (e.g. secret key) of stations,
3. Monitoring station S can monitor running states of an object without knowing the client that uses or owns the object,
4. Monitoring station S can calculate statistics of the running states of an object without knowing individual states,
5. Monitoring station S can inform clients of its monitoring results without knowing their identitics, and

6. When S detects a dishonest event about an object it is monitoring, it can identify the client liable for the event without invading any privacy of honest clients.

The 1st and the 3rd requirements are apparent; they are the most fundamental requirements for anonymous object delivery and monitoring systems, respectively. Here although C_h or C_j is anonymous, the object delivery system also must ensure that the only entity, which can send the object or can receive the object is client C_h or C_j. Regarding the 2nd requirement, different from messages in anonymous networks, individual objects in the anonymous object delivery system require much longer durations until they successfully arrive at their receivers because they are physical objects. Also it is not easy to resend physical objects when some troubles happen on them. Therefore, client C_h or C_j that sends or receives the object must be endowed with capabilities to trace its object in the delivery system; also it must be able to detect troubles on its object and to identify entities that had caused the troubles. Here, the important thing is that C_h or C_j must trace its objects, detect troubles and identify liable entities without knowing secrets of stations that transport the object, e.g. their encryption keys, because if C_h or C_j requires secrets of stations to trace its objects, the object delivery system must stop operations to replace their old secrets with new ones every time when clients trace their objects.

From the 4th to the 6th requirements relate to the object monitoring system. Namely, frequently station S is required to calculate statistics based on time series of running states of objects used by anonymous clients e.g. to diagnose troubles of home appliances, however, usually these time series include suggestions to estimate the clients, then the 4th requirement becomes important. Also, to notify clients about troubles of their home appliances, or to suggest ways to use them more safely, efficiently and environmentally friendlily to clients without revealing their privacies, monitoring systems must satisfy the 5th requirement. Then finally, to protect systems from malicious events, monitoring systems must be able to identify clients that behaved dishonestly, e.g. when they had illegitimately discarded their home appliances, without invading any privacy of honest clients.

The following subsection discusses anonymous memories, then, the anonymous object delivery and monitoring systems are developed.

Anonymous Memory

An anonymous memory is a set of memory sections that are owned by anonymous clients, and clients can maintain their sensitive information securely while concealing their identities from others including managers of the memory by storing the information in their owing sections. Figure 6 shows the configuration of the anonymous memory (Tamura, 2009). It consists of anonymous clients, multiple memory sections that are assigned to individual clients, and the memory manager. All operations on these sections, such as reading data and writing data, are carried out by the memory manager, i.e. clients access their memory sections through the manager. Functions of the memory manager include registration, access control, memory access, error detection and accounting, i.e. the memory manager registers/deregisters clients, authenticates clients to protect the memory system from being accessed by unauthorized entities, carries out read/write operations on memory sections, detects illegitimate memory accesses, and charges clients for their memory uses through these functions. Here, to enable clients to access their memory sections while concealing their identities, clients and the memory manager are connected through anonymous networks discussed in Section 2.

To store information securely while maintaining anonymity of clients, the anonymous memory must be endowed with the following features. In the remainder of this section, M denotes the

Figure 6. Configuration of anonymous memories

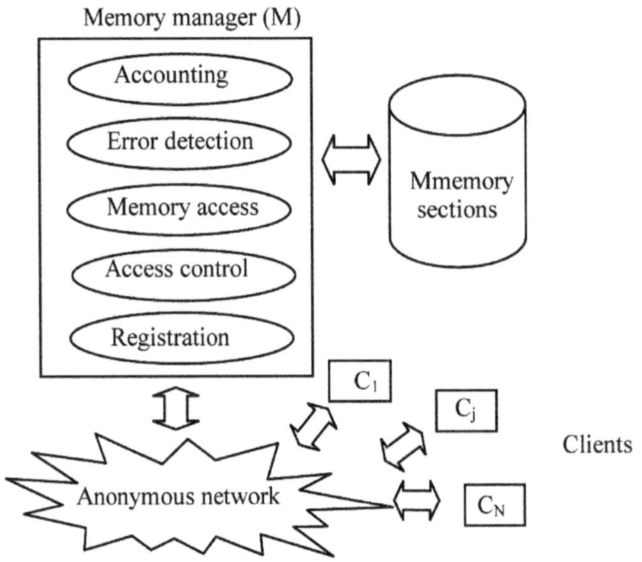

manager of the anonymous memory and C_1, C_2, ---, C_N denote clients. The required features are,

1. Client C_h can obtain and release its memory sections in the anonymous memory without disclosing its identity,
2. C_h can read/write data from/to its memory sections without disclosing its identity,
3. Only authorized entities are allowed to access their memory sections,
4. Although C_h is anonymous, it can force manager M to read/write data from/to its memory sections successfully,
5. Disputes between C_h and M about disruptions of date in memory sections assigned to C_h can be resolved without disclosing any privacy of honest clients, and
6. M can charge clients correct amounts for using their memory sections without knowing their identities.

Firstly to enable clients to anonymously access their memory sections, not only the 2nd but also the 1st requirements are necessary. Namely, if client C_h reveals its identity for acquiring or deleting its memory sections, its every access to them also will be revealed because the entity that can access the memory sections acquired by C_h is only C_h. The 3rd requirement is for protecting the anonymous memory system from unauthorized accesses, i.e. clients other than C_h must be disabled to access the memory sections acquired by C_h even they are anonymous. The 4th and the 5th requirements relate to secure maintenance of data in the anonymous memory. Anonymous memories are more vulnerable to various kinds of dishonest events than usual memories because clients are anonymous. For example, although manager M usually can be assumed to be honest, it may modify the data in memory sections without permissions of the memory section owners while counting the difficulty of finding liable entities in environments where entities are anonymous, and on the other hand, this possibility enables clients to intentionally put invalid data in their memory sections and impute liabilities for data disruptions to M. To prevent data from various threats and to protect managers from dishonest claims of clients, the anonymous memory system must be able to detect dishonest events and to identify liable entities for the events also without invading any privacy of honest clients. An additional important thing is that the volume of records that should be maintained by clients as the evidences for resolving disputes between clients and manager M about the above kind of dishonest events must be reduced as much as possible. When the volume of these records is large, clients may use their private memories to keep their data instead of ones in the anonymous memory. Lastly, manager M must be able to charge clients fees for their uses of memory sections during its every service period without knowing their identities.

Although not so many mechanisms had been reported yet, anonymous memories can be implemented rather straightforwardly while exploiting already discussed anonymous security and service components as below. Namely, anonymous authentication schemes enable clients to acquire and access their memory sections without disclosing their identities, and ITLs enable manager M to securely manage memory sections that are acquired and released by anonymous clients in the same way as they had enabled management of aliases generated and discarded by anonymous clients in the ID list based anonymous authentication scheme. Also ITLs, hash functions and homomorphic anonymous tokens provide clients and manager M with practical solutions to resolve disputes between them about disruptions of data in memory sections, i.e. clients and manager M can detect dishonest events in the anonymous memory system, also they can identify entities liable for the events while maintaining volumes of memory access records that must be kept by clients at the minimum. Lastly, anonymous credit card systems enable M to charge anonymous clients fees for their memory uses.

Figure 7 shows the phases through which client C_h accesses the anonymous memory system. Firstly, C_h registers itself as a member of the system while disclosing its identity in the registration phase, and it generates anonymous accounts for acquiring and deleting its memory sections in the account generation phase without disclosing its identity. After generating its accounts, C_h acquires or releases its memory sections in the memory acquisition phase, and reads or writes data from or to its memory sections in the memory access phase, also without disclosing its identity of course. Then finally, manager M charges C_h for its memory section uses in the payment phase without knowing the identity of C_h.

In the above, manager M and client C_h are connected through anonymous networks so that C_h can conceal itself from M as mentioned before, and M authenticates anonymous C_h based on the ITL based anonymous authentication scheme in the account generation, the memory acquisition, the memory access, and the payment phases. In more detail, client C_h obtains open tokens from token tables prepared in advance, and shows tokens for generating accounts, acquiring and accessing memory sections, and paying for its memory uses. However, generally tokens used in different phases belong to different categories. In the remaining of this section, account token $T_A(h, m)$, memory token $T_M(h, n)$, payment token $T_P(h, q)$ represent tokens that are used in account generation, memory acquisition and access, and payment phases, respectively. Then, payment tokens independent of others enable clients to use anonymous memory systems and anonymous credit card systems operated by different organizations more easily. When the payment tokens and the account tokens are unified, combinations of 2 organizations that manage anonymous memory systems and credit card systems must be fixed for example. Also, account tokens independent of memory tokens enable clients to easily manage their memory sections, e.g. when C_h generates multiple accounts and assigns different kind of memory tokens for accessing memory sections in different accounts, it can manage memory sections in individual accounts according to their properties specific to them.

In the followings, behaviors of individual phases are discussed in detail.

Figure 7. Phases for using anonymous memory systems

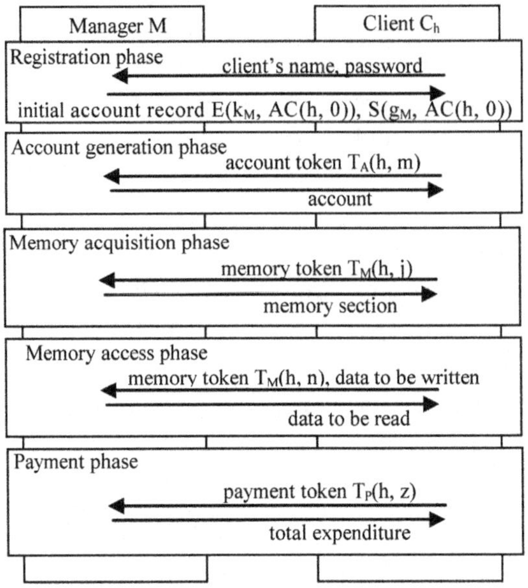

Registration

First of all, client C_h requests manager M to register itself as a member of the anonymous memory system while disclosing its identity, i.e. identifier $ID(C_h)$ of C_h, together with its encrypted next account token $E(a_h, T_A(h, 1))$, and M generates a set of random bit string vectors $\{\underline{t}_{A1}(h), \underline{t}_{A2}(h), ---, \underline{t}_{AZ}(h)\}$. Then, C_h decrypts them to test bit strings $\{E(a_h^{-1}, \underline{t}_{A1}(h)) = check_{A1}(h), E(a_h^{-1}, t_{A2}(h)) = check_{A2}(h), ---, E(a_h^{-1}, t_{AZ}(h)) = check_{AZ}(h)\}$ so that M can memorize pair $\{check_{A1}(h), check_{A2}(h), ---, check_{AZ}(h)\}$ and $\{\underline{t}_{A1}(h), \underline{t}_{A2}(h), ---, \underline{t}_{AZ}(h)\}$ as the identity information of C_h in addition to $ID(C_h)$, where each $check_{Aq}(h)$ represents the visible part value of $E(a_h^{-1}, t_{Aq}(h))$. After that, M generates C_h's initial account record $AC(h, 0)$ that includes $E(a_h, T_A(h, 1))$, and its encrypted and signed forms $E(k_M, AC(h, 0))$ and $S(g_M, AC(h, 0))$ to be maintained by C_h, therefore C_h can make its next visit for generating or deleting its account without disclosing its identity by using account token $T_A(h, 1)$. Here, $E(a_h, x)$ and $E(k_M, y)$ are linear equation based additive encryption functions, a_h is an encryption key secret of C_h, and k_M and g_M are secret encryption and signing keys of M. $T_A(h, m)$ is an account token that enables C_h to show its eligibility to generate or to delete its accounts without disclosing its identity at its m-th visit to M, and the value of $T(h, 0)$ is defined as $ID(C_h)$. Also, M uses bit string vectors $\{check_{A1}(h), check_{A2}(h), ---, check_{AZ}(h)\}$ and $\{\underline{t}_{A1}(h), \underline{t}_{A2}(h), ---, \underline{t}_{AZ}(h)\}$ to identify C_h as the liable client when C_h behaves dishonestly about its account generations or deletions without invading any privacy of other honest clients.

Account record $AC(h, m)$ consists of plain token part $Pt(h, m)$, token version part $Tv(h, m)$, ID Section $1d(h, m)$, and ITL Section $1TL_A(h, m)$ as shown in Figure 8. Here, as same as transaction records in the anonymous credit card system discussed in the previous chapter, $Pt(h, m)$ is the token that C_h shows at its m-th visit to M for generating or deleting its accounts, and $Tv(h, m)$ is used for carrying out procedures of the anonymous record agreement protocol between C_h and M, i.e. for securely constructing the account record. $ITL_A(h, n)$ is pair $\{v_{Am}T_A(h,$

m), $v_{A(m+1)}E(a_h, T_A(m+1))\}$, C_h's current and encrypted next account tokens multiplied by token concealers v_{Am} and $v_{A(m+1)}$ secrets of M. Id(h, m) represents the identifier of the account that C_h is generating or deleting as will be discussed in the account generation phase, and at this stage it has no meaning. As a consequence, values of initial account record AC(h, 0) of C_h are set as Pt(h, 0) = ID(C_h), Tv(h, 0) = 1, Id(h, 0) = 0, $ITL_A(h, 0) = \{v_{A0}ID(C_h), v_{A0}E(a_h, ID(C_h))+v_{A1}E(a_h, T_A(h, 1))\}$. As same as in the anonymous credit card system, encrypted initial token $v_{A0}E(a_h, ID(C_h))$ is added to $v_{A1}E(a_h, T_A(h, 1))$ as an exception to construct an encrypted next token value of initial ITL.

Account Generation

Clients generate or delete their accounts by showing their account tokens without disclosing their identities so that they can acquire and release their memory sections as anonymous account holders, where a client can generate multiple accounts if necessary. Namely, at its m-th visit to memory manager M for generating or deleting its accounts, anonymous C_h requests account generation or deletion while showing its m-th account token T_A(h, m), and M constructs C_h's m-th account record AC(h, m). Here, C_h shows $E(a_h, T_A(h, m+1))$ as the encrypted next token value of ITL_A(h, m) in AC(h, m) to make its next visit without disclosing its identity by using account token T_A(h, m+1). In addition when the request is account generation, M defines the ID part value of AC(h, m) as T_A(h, m), and it authorizes memory token T_M(h, 1) that is encrypted and shown by C_h while creating ITL_M(h, 0) = $\{v_{M0}T_A(h, m), v_{M0}E(a_h, T_A(h, m)+v_{M1}E(a_h, T_M(h, 1))\}$, therefore M and C_h can identify account Act(h, m) that C_h had generated by T_A(h, m), and C_h can acquire its 1st memory sections as an anonymous holder of account Act(h, m) while showing memory token T_M(h, 1) that is implicitly connected to account token T_A(h, m). Here, a_h is a secret encryption key of C_h for encrypting its memory tokens, and in this subsection, notation Act(h, m) is used for representing the account that C_h generates at its m-th visit.

At a time when C_h deletes account Act(h, m) at its p-th visit to M (m < p), it can designate the account by identifier T_A(h, m), but when C_h secedes from the anonymous memory system, M must confirm that all accounts of C_h had been deleted without examining C_h's individual accounts to preserve privacies of C_h. To satisfy this requirement, as same as in the alias management procedure of ID list based anonymous authentication scheme, M constructs account record AC(h, p) while defining -T_A(h, m) as its ID part value. Then, M can know whether C_h had deleted all of its accounts or not from the sum of C_h's past account records without knowing C_h's individual accounts. When M decrypts the sum of encrypted account records reported by C_h, the ID part value of the decryption result becomes 0 if C_h had deleted all of its accounts. On the other hand, if C_h did not delete all accounts, the sum of ID part values remains positive. Also in this account record sum calculation, ITLs included in individual records disable C_h to report the sums dishonestly. At a time when

Figure 8. Account record

Plain token part	Token version part	ID part	ITL part
Pt(h, m) = T(h,m)	Tv(h, m)	Id(h, m)	ITL_A(h, m)

C_h deletes account Act(h, m), M must confirm all memory sections acquired under Act(h, m) also had been released, and M can achieve this by the same mechanism as discussed just above.

The following is the account generation and deletion procedure.

1. To generate or delete its account, client C_h at its m-th visit to manager M shows its m-th account token T_A(h, m) and the sum of its encrypted past account records from its initial visit to its (m-1)-th visit.
2. If T_A(h, m) shown by C_h was not used before and it is consistent with the sum of past account records, M accepts the visit, and C_h requests M to generate or delete its account. If the request is account generation, C_h shows its initial encrypted next memory token E($\underline{a}_h$, $T_M(T_A$(h, m), 1)) so that it can acquire and release memory sections as an anonymous holder of the newly generated account Act(h, m) by using memory token $T_M(T_A$(h, m), 1). Also, M generates a set of random bit string vectors {$\underline{t}_{M1}(T_A$(h, m)), $\underline{t}_{M2}(T_A$(h, m)), ---, $\underline{t}_{MZ}(T_A$(h, m))} to be decrypted to {E($\underline{a}_h^{-1}$, $\underline{t}_{M1}(T_A$(h, m))) = $check_{M1}(T_A$(h, m)), E($\underline{a}_h^{-1}$, $\underline{t}_{M2}(T_A$(h, m))) = $check_{M2}(T_A$(h, m)), ---, E($\underline{a}_h^{-1}$, $\underline{t}_{MY}(T_A$(h, m))) = $check_{MY}(T_A$(h, m))} by C_h ($check_{Mq}(T_A$(h, m)) is the visible part value of E($\underline{a}_h^{-1}$, $\underline{t}_{Mq}(T_A$(h, m))). Where, E($\underline{a}_h$, *x*) is a linear equation based additive encryption function and a_h is the secret key of C_h for encrypting memory tokens. Then, M can identify a liable entity when dishonest events are detected about memory sections generated under account Act(h, m) by using pair {$check_{M1}(T_A$(h, m)), $check_{M2}(T_A$(h, m)), ---, $check_{MY}(T_A$(h, m))} and {$\underline{t}_{M1}(T_A$(h, m)), $\underline{t}_{M2}(T_A$(h, m)), ---, $\underline{t}_{MZ}(T_A$(h, m))} while preserving privacies of honest clients. It must be noted that although a_h differs from a_h that C_h uses for generating and deleting its accounts, M can identify C_h when dishonest events occur about memory sections acquired under Act(h, m), i.e. M identifies account Act(h, m) by pair {$check_{Mq}(T_A$(h, m)), $\underline{t}_{Mq}(T_A$(h, m))} and identifies account holder C_h by pair {$check_{Aq}$(h), $\underline{t}_{Aq}$(h)}.

On the other hand, if C_h requests to delete its account Act(h, p), C_h shows T_A(h, p) with $\underline{AC}$*(h, p-1), the account token that it had used for generating Act(h, p) and the sum of its past encrypted account records until its (p-1)-th visit, as the identifier of Act(h, p) and the evidence for proving the ownership of Act(h, p), and M examines whether C_h had released all memory sections acquired under account Act(h, p) or not. Here, C_h can prove its ownership of Act(h, p), because $\underline{AC}$*(h, p-1) is consistent with T_A(h, p). Also as discussed in the memory acquisition phase, M can know if C_h had released all memory sections or not without knowing individual memory sections in the account, and if memory sections are remaining M rejects the request of course.

3. According to the request from C_h, M generates a draft of account record DA(h, m) that does not include the ITL parts, i.e. the draft is constructed as DA(h, m) = {Pt(h, m), Tv(h, m), Id(h, m)}. Where, Pt(h, m) = T_A(h, m), Tv(h, m) = 1, and as the value of Id(h, m), T_A(h, m) is assigned when the request is account generation, and -T_A(h, p) is assigned when the request is account deletion.
4. After examining DA(h, m), C_h encrypts its encrypted (m+1)-th token E(a_h, T_A(h, m+1)) to E(b_h, E(a_h, T_A(h, m+1))) and shows the result to M. Where, b_h is a secret encryption key of C_h different from a_h, and encryption function E(b_h, *x*) is not additive, instead it is constructed so that E(b_h, *x*) and signing function S(g_M, *x*) become commutative as shown in the next step (where g_M is a signing key of M).
5. Based on E(b_h, E(a_h, T_A(h, m+1))), M generates tentative signed record Sig(DA(h, m)) = S(g_M, {DA(h, m), S(g_M, E(b_h, E(a_h, T_A(h,

m+1))))}), then because E(b_h, *x*) and S(g_M, *x*) are commutative, C_h can calculate S(g_M, E(a_h, T_A(h, m+1))), a signature of M on E(a_h, T_A(h, m+1)), from Sig(DA(h, m)) without disclosing E(a_h, T_A(h, m+1)).

6. C_h that verified the validity of Sig(DA(h, m)) sends its (m+1)-th encrypted token E(a_h, T_A(h, m+1)) to M, and based on it, M calculates ITL_A(h, m) to generate account record AC(h, m) by adding it to DR(h, m). M also generates E(k_M, AC(h, m)) and S(g_M, AC(h, m)), the encrypted and the signed forms of account record AC(h, m).
7. When the request is account generation, M generates new account Act(h, m), and associates test bit string vector and their encrypted form pairs {*check*$_{M1}$(T_A(h, m)), *check*$_{M2}$(T_A(h, m)), ---, *check*$_{MY}$(T_A(h, m))} and {$\underline{t}_{M1}$(T_A(h, m)), $\underline{t}_{M2}$(T_A(h, m)), ---, $\underline{t}_{MY}$(T_A(h, m))} with it. M also generates MA(T_A(h, m), 0), the initial memory access record of account Act(h, m), and its encrypted form E(k_M, MA(T_A(h, m), 0)) and signed form S(g_M, MA(T_A(h, m), 0)). Here as defined in the memory acquisition phase, as a part of its ITL part value, MA(T_A(h, m), 0) includes encrypted next memory token E($\underline{a}_h$, T_M(T_A(h, m), 1)) that was declared by C_h at step 2, therefore C_h, anonymous account holder of Act(h, m), can anonymously make its next visit for acquiring and releasing its memory sections by showing T_M(T_A(h, m), 1). On the other hand when the request is account deletion, M deletes the account corresponding to T_A(h, p).
8. C_h saves E(k_M, AC(h, m)) and S(g_M, AC(h, m)) in its private memory, and when its requests is an account generation, C_h also saves encrypted and signed initial memory access records E(k_M, MA(T_A(h, m), 0)) and S(g_M, MA(T_A(h, m), 0)).

As same as in the transaction phase of the anonymous credit card system, C_h can cancel its request when M does not issue correct tentative signed record Sig(DA(h, m)) = S(g_M, {DA(h, m), S(g_M, E(b_h, E(a_h, T_A(h, m+1))))}). Also, C_h can force M to generate correct account record AC(h, m) once C_h and M had agreed on Sig(DA(h, m)).

Now, the above procedure satisfies the requirements for anonymous memory systems as follows. Namely, no one except C_h can identify the owner of its accounts, because C_h shows only T_A(h, m), E(a_h, T_A(h, m+1)) and the sum of its encrypted past account records as the information that proves its eligibility. Also, next token T_A(h, m+1) is encrypted by C_h's secret key a_h, therefore anyone except C_h cannot know linkages between accounts that C_h had generated or deleted either. On the other hand, the ITL based anonymous authentication scheme allows only authorized clients to generate or delete their accounts. C_h also can disable other anonymous entity C_j to delete its account Act(h, p) corresponding to account token T_A(h, p). When, M asks C_j to show the sum of its past account records until its (p-1)-th visit, the result is not consistent with T_A(h, p). Namely, the only entity that can show the sum of its past account records that is consistent with T_A(h, p) is C_h itself. Although it is possible for manager M to delete accounts of C_h without the permission of C_h, C_h can notice it, and disputes about the liability are resolved as discussed later in "Protections of Memory Sections."

Memory Acquisition

In the following, it is assumed that client C_h generates or release memory sections as an anonymous holder of account Act(h, m) that it had generated in the account generation phase by showing account token T_A(h, m). As same as in the account generation phase, C_h visits memory manager M

Figure 9. Memory access record

Plain token part	Token version part	Size part	Location part	Data part	ITL part
$Pt(T_A(h, m), n) = T_M(T_A(h, m), n)$	$Tv(T_A(h, m), n)$	$S_Z(T_A(h, m), n)$	$L_C(T_A(h, m), n)$	$H_S(T_A(h, m), n)$	$ITL_M(T_A(h, m), n)$

anonymously while showing its memory tokens, i.e. ITLs enable C_h to acquire and release its memory sections without disclosing its identity or links between its acquiring memory sections to others. On the other hand, also while being supported by ITLs, manager M can force C_h to release all memory sections that C_h had acquired at a time when it deletes account Act(h, m) and also to pay M for uses of all memory sections in Act(h, m) through the anonymous credit card system. Here, all memory tokens that account holder C_h uses are linked implicitly to account token $T_A(h, m)$ by ITLs, i.e. at step 3 of the account generation phase, an initial memory token of the account holder of Act(h, m) was defined as account token $T_A(h, m)$.

The memory acquisition phase proceeds in the same way as the account generation phase. At C_h's n-th visit to M for acquiring its memory section, firstly M authenticates C_h based on memory token $T_M(T_A(h, m), n)$ shown by C_h, and finds unoccupied memory section $Sec(T_A(h, m), n)$ in the anonymous memory. Then, M assigns $T_M(T_A(h, m), n)$ to $Sec(T_A(h, m), n)$ as its anonymous owner, and generates memory access record $MA(T_A(h, m), n)$, its encrypted form $E(k_M, MA(T_A(h, m), n))$ and signed form $S(g_M, MA(T_A(h, m), n))$ to be maintained by C_h.

Here, memory access record $MA(T_A(h, m), n)$ consists of 6 parts as shown in Figure 9, and plain token part $Pt(T_A(h, m), n)$ maintains memory token $T_M(T_A(h, m), n)$ that C_h is showing to M (in this case for acquiring or releasing its memory section), and size part $S_Z(T_A(h, m), n)$ is the size of the acquired memory section. As same as in the account generation phase, token version part $Tv(T_A(h, m), n)$ is used to carry out procedures for the anonymous record agreement protocol between C_h and M, and $ITL_M(T_A(h, m), n)$ is a pair of the current and the encrypted next memory tokens that disables C_h to calculate sums of its past encrypted memory access records dishonestly, i.e. $ITL_M(T_A(h, m), n) = \{v_{Mn}T_M(T_A(h, m), n), v_{M(n+1)}E(\underline{a}_h, T_M(T_A(h, m), n+1))\}$, where, v_{Mn} and $v_{M(n+1)}$ are the token concealers secrets of M. Although location part $L_C(T_A(h, m), n)$ and data part $H_S(T_A(h, m)\ n)$ do not have meanings at this stage because C_h does not access any memory section yet, $L_C(T_A(h, m), n)$ is the identifier of the memory section C_h accesses (token that C_h had shown for acquiring the corresponding memory section is used as its identifier) and data part $H_S(T_A(h, m), n)$ is the hash value of the data stored in it. As an exception, initial memory access record $MA(T_A(h, m), 0)$ is constructed at a time when C_h generates account Act(h, m) corresponding to $T_A(h, m)$, and individual values of $MA(T_A(h, m), 0)$ are defined as $Pt(T_A(h, m), 0) = T_A(h, m)$, $Tv(T_A(h, m), 0) = 1$, $Sz(T_A(h, m), 0) = 0$, $Lc(T_A(h, m), 0) = 0$, and $ITL_M(T_A(h, m), 0) = \{v_{M0}T_A(h, m), v_{M0}E(\underline{a}_h, T_A(h, m))+v_{M1}E(\underline{a}_h, T_M(T_A(h, m), 1))\}$.

C_h releases memory section $Sec(T_A(h, m), q)$ that it had acquired at its q-th visit as an anonymous account holder of Act(h, m) by showing memory token $T_M(T_A(h, m), q)$ in the same way, i.e. at C_h's n-th visit ($q < n$), M authenticates C_h by its n-th memory token $T_M(T_A(h, m), n)$, generates memory access record $MA(T_A(h, m), n)$, its encrypted form $E(k_M, MA(T_A(h, m), n))$ and signed form $S(g_M, MA(T_A(h, m), n))$ to give them to C_h. But different from cases for memory acquisitions, firstly in addition to $T_M(T_A(h, m), n)$ and $\underline{MA}^*(T_A(h, m), n-1)$, the sum of its past encrypted memory access records until its (n-1)-th (current) visit, C_h shows $T_M(T_A(h, m), q)$ and $\underline{MA}^*(T_A(h, m), q-1)$, the sum of its past encrypted memory access records until its (q-1)-th visit, as the identifier of memory section $Sec(T_A(h, m), q)$ to be released and as the evidence for proving the ownership of $Sec(T_A(h, m), q)$, i.e. C_h shows its ownership of $Sec(T_A(h, m), q)$ by the consistent relation between $T_M(T_A(h, m), q)$ and $\underline{MA}^*(T_A(h, m), q-1)$ as same as in the account generation phase.

Secondly, manager M assigns $-S_Z(T_A(h, m), q)$ (negative of the memory section size) as the size part value of $MA(T_A(h, m), n)$ so that the sum of the size part values of its past memory access records becomes 0 when C_h releases all memory sections in account Act(h, m). But it must be noted that S cannot know whether last unused memory token $T_M(T_A(h, m), n)$ corresponds to account Act(h, m) or not at a time when C_h deletes Act(h, m). To solve this problem, M asks C_h to calculate $\underline{MA}^-(T_A(h, m), n-1)$, the sum of its past encrypted memory access records from the 2nd to the (n-1)-th visit and show it with $MA(T_A(h, m), 0)$. Then, M calculates $\underline{MA}^*(T_A(h, m), n-1)$ as $\underline{MA}^*(T_A(h, m), n-1) = MA(T_A(h, m), 0)+\underline{MA}^-(T_A(h, m), n-1)$. As a consequence, consistency of last unused memory token $T_M(T_A(h, m), n)$ is examined with combination $\{MA(T_A(h, m), 0), \underline{MA}^-(T_A(h, m), n-1)\}$, and M can know the correspondence between token $T_M(T_A(h, m), n)$ and account Act(h, m) because M maintains initial memory access record $MA(T_A(h, m), 0)$ that includes account token $T_A(h, m)$. Here, as same as in account generation phase, C_h does not need to worry even when memory token $T_M(T_A(h, m), q)$ is stolen by other entities. Although manager M can release any memory section at its will, C_h also can detect M's dishonesty when M releases $Sec(T_A(h, m), q)$ dishonestly, as discussed later in "Protecting Memory Sections."

The above procedure satisfies the requirements for anonymous memory section acquiring and releasing in the same way as the account generation procedure did for account generations and deletions. Namely, C_h shows only $T_M(T_A(h, m), n)$, $E(\underline{a}_h, T_M(T_A(h, m), n+1))$ and the sum of its past memory access records, therefore, no one except C_h can identify the owner of $Sec(T_A(h, m), n)$, and because next token $T_M(T_A(h, m), n+1)$ is encrypted by C_h's secret key $\underline{a}_h$, anyone except C_h cannot know the linkage between $Sec(T_A(h, m), n)$ and $Sec(T_A(h, m), n+1)$ acquired by C_h either. On the other hand, ITL based anonymous authentication scheme allows only authorized clients to acquire their memory sections. Also, by decrypting the sum of C_h's past memory access records, M can know whether C_h had released all memory sections in account Act(h, m) or not without knowing individual memory sections when C_h deletes Act(h, m), i.e. when the sum of encrypted memory access records is decrypted, its size part value coincides with the difference between the total size of memory sections that C_h had acquired and that it had released. M can also charge C_h for its uses of all memory sections without knowing their exact locations by using this size. Here, ITLs included in individual memory access records disable C_h to dishonestly report sums of its encrypted memory access records as discussed already.

Memory Access

At its n-th visit to manager M as an anonymous account holder of Act(h, m), client C_h accesses its memory section Sec(T_A(h, m), q) while showing its q-th memory token T_M(T_A(h, m), q), which is the token that C_h used to have acquired Sec(T_A(h, m), q), i.e. the identifier of Sec(T_A(h, m), q). Here, although M or an entity that conspires with M can access Sec(T_A(h, m), q) without C_h's permission, C_h can protect the information in Sec(T_A(h, m), q) from illegitimate modifications as discussed just below. About confidentiality of data in Sec(T_A(h, m), q), C_h can conceal them from others by simply encrypting them; an entity that does not know the decryption key cannot understand the data even if it illegitimately access Sec(T_A(h, m), q).

The memory access phase proceeds as same as in the account generation and the memory acquisition phases. Namely at its n-th visit to M, firstly to prove its eligibility and its ownership of Sec(T_A(h, m), q), C_h shows T_M(T_A(h, m), n), T_M(T_A(h, m), q) and the sums of its encrypted memory access records until its (n-1)-th visit and its (q-1)-th visit to M, i.e. C_h is eligible when T_M(T_A(h, m), n) is consistent with $\underline{MA}$*(T_A(h, m), n-1) and it is the owner of Sec(T_A(h, m), q) when T_M(T_A(h, m), q) is consistent with $\underline{MA}$*(T_A(h, m), q-1). But, M must ask C_h to define different client token concealers for every access to Sec(T_A(h, m), q) to disable malicious entities to access Sec(T_A(h, m), q) by using T_M(T_A(h, m), q) and $\underline{MA}$*(T_A(h, m), q-1) that the entities had obtained while having eavesdropped on the communication between C_h and M on the one hand, and on the other hand to disable C_h to dishonestly claim that M informed other entities of T_M(T_A(h, m), q) and $\underline{MA}$*(T_A(h, m), q) that C_h had used at its past access. After that, M and C_h exchange information necessary for reading or writing data from or to Sec(T_A(h, m), q), M constructs tentative memory access record DM(T_A(h, m), n), and after verifying the validity of DM(T_A(h, m), n), C_h shows its encrypted (n+1)-th memory token E(a_{1i}, T_M(T_A(h, m), n+1)). Then, M reads or writes data from or to Sec(T_A(h, m), q) on behalf of C_h, and generates memory access record MA(T_A(h, m), n), its encrypted form E(k_M, MA(T_A(h, m), n)) and signed form S(g_M, MA(T_A(h, m), n)) to be saved by C_h.

However, different from the other phases where C_h does not access its memory section, in this phase, it actually reads and/or writes data. Therefore, the location part Lc(T_A(h, m), n) and data part Hs(T_A(h, m), n) in memory access record MA(T_A(h, m), n) have meanings, and M defines their values as Lc(T_A(h, m), n) = T_M(T_A(h, m), q) and Hs(T_A(h, m), n) = (hash value of data in Sec(T_A(h, m), q)), so that C_h can claim if data in Sec(T_A(h, m), q) are modified without its permission. Namely, when the data in Sec(T_A(h, m), q) were modified illegitimately, at a time when C_h accesses Sec(T_A(h, m), q), it can easily detect the inconsistency between the data in it and the hash part value H_Z(T_A(h, m), q_1) of memory access record MA(T_A(h, m), q_1), because it is practically impossible to modify the data in Sec(T_A(h, m), q) while maintaining the consistency between hash value H_Z(T_A(h, m), q_1), where, it is assumed that C_h had made its last access to Sec(T_A(h, m), q) at its q_1-th visit to M. Also, It is possible to identify the entity liable for the modifications as discussed later in "Protecting Memory Sections," and the data in Sec(T_A(h, m), q) can be reconstructed. Here, the entity liable for illegitimate modifications is only M or C_h itself, because data in Sec(T_A(h, m), q) is written by M at the request of C_h.

Then as same as in the account generation and the memory acquisition phases, the above memory access procedure satisfies all the requirements for the anonymous memory system. However, it must be noted that different from cases in anonymous credit card systems where cardholder C_h can conceal not only its identity but also links between its consecutive transaction records, client C_h in the anonymous memory system cannot conceal its consecutive memory accesses to same memory section Sec(T_A(h, m), q), because Sec(T_A(h, m), q) can be accessed only by its owner.

Protecting Memory Sections

In the account generation, memory acquisition and memory access phases, client C_h may secedes from the system without deleting all accounts that it had generated, may delete its account without releasing all memory sections that it had acquired under the account, and may disrupt data in its memory sections to impute the liability to manager M. On the other hand, M may delete accounts of C_h, may release C_h's memory sections and may modify data in memory sections of C_h without permissions of C_h. ITLs enable M and C_h to detect these dishonesties and also to identify liable entities while preserving privacies of honest clients as follows.

Regarding deletions of accounts and releases of memory sections, manager M can detect existences of not deleted accounts or not released memory sections and their owners by decrypting sums of encrypted account records or sums of encrypted memory access records reported by clients when they secede from the system or when they delete accounts, i.e. if the sum of the ID part values in account records of C_h is positive at a time when C_h shows its last unused account token $T_A(h, m)$ to secedes from the anonymous memory system, M can determine that C_h did not delete all accounts that it had generated. Also, if the sum of the size part values in memory access records of C_h is positive at a time when C_h shows its last unused memory token $T_M(T_A(h, m), n)$ to delete its account, M can determine that the anonymous account holder did not release all memory sections.

In a case where C_h did not delete all of its accounts, it is trivial for M to identify C_h, because C_h shows its identity when it secedes from the anonymous memory system or M knows C_h when it expels C_h. M also can know remaining accounts of C_h by asking C_h to disclose its secret key a_h. Although C_h does not show its identity for deleting its individual accounts, M also can identify C_h that deletes its account Act(h, m) without releasing its all memory sections. Namely, if the communication channel between C_h and M is still not disconnected, C_h is forced to disclose its secret key a_h for encrypting its memory tokens, and once a_h is disclosed M can know all remaining memory sections in account Act(h, m). M also can know account token $T_A(h, m)$ as the owner of account Act(h, m), and can force account holder $T_A(h, m)$ to disclose its secret key a_h for encrypting its account tokens to identify client C_h if necessary. On the other hand if the communication channel had been disconnected, C_h does not have effective unused memory token, and when M asks all clients to show their unused memory tokens C_h cannot show it. Then, M can force C_h to show its secret key $\underline{a}_h$ and consequently a_h. Here, M cannot force C_h to disclose $\underline{a}_h$ or a_h when C_h is honest, because M's dishonesty is necessarily revealed after C_h's disclosure of $\underline{a}_h$ or a_h.

About illegitimate modifications of data *D* in memory section $Sec(T_A(h, m), q)$ owned by C_h, at a time when C_h accesses $Sec(T_A(h, m), q)$ it can detects them by comparing data *D* in $Sec(T_A(h, m), q)$ with the memory access record that C_h had received at its last access to $Sec(T_A(h, m), q)$. Namely, provided that C_h had made its last access to $Sec(T_A(h, m), q)$ by showing its memory token $T_M(h, q_1)$ and after that someone had illegitimately modified *D*, data part value $Hz(T_A(h, m), q_1)$ of signed memory access record $S(g_M, MA(T_A(h, m), q_1))$ that C_h is maintaining is not consistent with *D*. Then, C_h can claim that *D* had been changed without its permission by showing $S(g_M, MA(T_A(h, m), q_1))$. However, C_h may dishonestly claim that *D* was modified illegitimately, i.e. C_h claims that $Hz(T_A(h, m), q_1)$ in $S(g_M, MA(T_A(h, m), q_1))$ is inconsistent with *D* while having changed *D* at its q_2-th visit to M (here, $q_2 > q_1$ of course).

This dispute between C_h and M can be resolved as follows. Firstly, manager M finds memory access record $MA(h_*, x)$ that correspond to the last access to memory section $Sec(T_A(h, m), q)$ from its database, and extracts encrypted next token $E(\underline{a}_{h*}, T_x)$ from the ITL part value of $MA(h_*, x)$ to ask all clients to decrypt $E(\underline{a}_{h*}, T_x)$. Here if C_h

is dishonest, M can find $MA(T_A(h, m), q_2)$ that satisfies $q_2 > q_1$ and its data part value $Hz(T_A(h, m), q_2)$ is consistent with *D*, also $MA(T_A(h, m), q_2)$ includes $E(\underline{a}_h, T_M(T_A(h, m), q_2))$, memory token encrypted by C_h, as a part of its ITL value, and C_h that knows a_h can decrypt $E(\underline{a}_h, T_M(T_A(h, m), q_2))$ into consistent value, but other clients that do not know a_h cannot decrypt $E(\underline{a}_h, T_M(T_A(h, m), q_2))$ consistently, then C_h is determined as dishonest. In the same way as before, M can force C_h to honestly decrypt $E(\underline{a}_{h*}, T_x)$ by using a set of test bit string vector $\{check_{M1}(T_A(h, m)), check_{M2}(T_A(h, m)), ---, check_{MY}(T_A(h, m))\}$ and their encrypted forms $\{\underline{t}_{M1}(T_A(h, m)), \underline{t}_{M2}(T_A(h, m)), ---, \underline{t}_{MY}(T_A(h, m))\}$ attached to account Act(h, m) under which memory section $Sec(T_A(h, m), q)$ was obtained.

On the other hand when C_h is honest, the above last memory access record $MA(h_*, x)$ must be $MA(T_A(h, m), q_1)$, and its data part value $Hz(T_A(h, m), q_1)$ is not consistent with *D*; therefore M is determined as dishonest. If M forges memory access record $MA(h_*, x)$ that is different from $MA(T_A(h, m), q_1)$, C_h decrypts encrypted next token $E(\underline{a}_{h*}, T_x)$ extracted from the ITL part of $MA(h_*, x)$ into an inconsistent value because M that does not know a_h cannot forge $E(a_{h*}, T_x)$ consistently, as a consequence M cannot prove C_h is dishonest. Although it may be possible for M to construct $MA(h_*, x)$ by using $E(\underline{a}_h, T_M(T_A(h, m), w+1))$ that was used by C_h before, C_h maintains signed memory access records $S(g_M, MA(T_A(h, m), w))$ that includes $E(\underline{a}_h, T_M(T_A(h, m), w+1))$ in its ITL part value, and C_h can prove that $S(g_M, MA(T_A(h, m), w))$ is not consistent with $MA(h_*, x)$. In a case where M claims that Sec $(T_A(h, m), q)$ is not owned by C_h, C_h can prove its ownership by disclosing its encryption key a_h and tracing memory sections that it had acquired based on ITLs included in its memory access records signed by M. In this case privacies of C_h are revealed, but M cannot behave in this manner because its dishonesty is necessarily revealed.

Then, disputes between manager M and clients can be resolved successfully. The important thing here is that client C_h is not required to maintain large volume of evidences to resolve these disputes, C_h needs to maintain only encrypted and signed memory access records $E(k_M, MA(T_A(h, m), n))$ and $S(g_M, MA(T_A(h, m), n))$ for each n.

Payment

It is straightforward to apply anonymous credit card systems discussed in the previous chapter to payments in anonymous memory systems. However, although it is possible to automatically register C_h as a client of the anonymous memory system at a time when it is registered as a client of the anonymous credit card system (in this case C_h's token $T_P(h, n)$ for the credit card system is used also as account token $T_A(h, n)$ for generating accounts for the anonymous memory system), clients can use anonymous memories more conveniently when account token $T_A(h, n)$ are prepared separately from payment token $T_P(h, m)$ as discussed at the beginning of this section. Namely, clients can combine different kinds of anonymous credit card systems and anonymous memory systems flexibly. Anyway regardless that account and payment tokens are unified or not, anonymous memory system manager M can collect memory access fees from clients without knowing their owning memory sections, i.e. fees for individual memory sections of a client are aggregated as the total expenditure that includes all other purchases that the client had made.

About memory token, it is also possible but not desirable to use payment token $T_P(h, n)$ for accessing memories. The reason is that sequences of requests of client C_h in anonymous memory systems are necessarily linked because memory sections owned by C_h can be accessed only by C_h, and these links give entities clues for connecting other transaction records. However, sequences of transactions of same cardholders must be concealed, because these sequences are strong supports to identify cardholders.

An Example of Anonymous Memory Applications

As one of applications of anonymous memories different from the anonymous object monitoring system that will be developed later in this chapter, here tamper resistant memories are discussed. A tamper resistant memory section is a memory section that can protect the data in it from being modified by unauthorized entities. IC cards are typical example of tamper resistant memories, i.e. only privileged entities that know inner structures of the IC cards can write data in them without permissions of their owners therefore data in them can be protected. Another form of a tamper resistant memory section is a duplicated one, a memory section that has multiple copies. When it is assumed that accessing multiple copies at the same time is difficult for unauthorized entities, data owners can detect illegitimate modifications of their data by comparing different copies, i.e. the data are illegitimately modified when data in multiple copies are not consistent. Data owners also can recover the consistent data along the majority decision principle. However, the above 2 mechanisms are not sufficient, i.e. entity that know the inner mechanisms of the IC cards can easily modify the data in them without permissions of their owners. Also, managers of duplicated memory systems can easily modify the multiple copies consistently.

A tamper resistant memory based on the anonymous memory enhances the security of the above duplicated memory sections. Namely, different from normal duplicated memory sections where privileged entities, e.g. system managers, can modify data consistently without permissions of the data owners by modifying data in all copies, it is extremely difficult to illegitimately modify data in anonymous memory based duplicated memory sections. Because owners of individual memory sections are anonymous, entities other than the data owners cannot know locations of the copies. However, it must be noted that asynchronous and fake memory access mechanisms must be implemented to make the tamper resistant memory more secure, because entities can identify locations of anonymous copies by eavesdropping on simultaneous memory accesses. Also, data in different copies must be encrypted by different keys, in order to disable other entities to identify locations of copies by comparing their contents.

Development of an Anonymous Object Delivery System

An anonymous object delivery system is a one that transport parcels from their initial places to their destinations so that no one except the senders can identify the senders of the parcels, or no one except the receivers can identify the receivers of them. Although things to be transferred in anonymous networks are different from ones transferred in anonymous object delivery systems, an approach of Mix-net for concealing senders of messages can be used also for anonymous object delivery systems. In this subsection an anonymous object delivery system is developed based on this approach. Namely, the anonymous object delivery system consists of multiple stations that transport parcels, and senders or receivers encrypt addresses of receivers by encryption keys of multiple stations to be decrypted by those multiple stations just as same as in Mix-net. The difference is that anonymous tags discussed in Section 2 are also attached to parcels so that clients that had sent or will receive the parcels can trace them.

As same as other systems discussed in this part, the anonymous object delivery system also authenticates anonymous clients that send or receive parcels through the ITL based anonymous authentication mechanism. Namely, the manager of the object delivery system S_{A1} (the representative of stations that transport parcels) authenticates anonymous client C_h that sends or receives its parcel by examining $T_D(h, n)$, the latest unused delivery system token of C_h that C_h had obtained from the token table prepared by S_{A1} in

Figure 10. Anonymous object delivery system

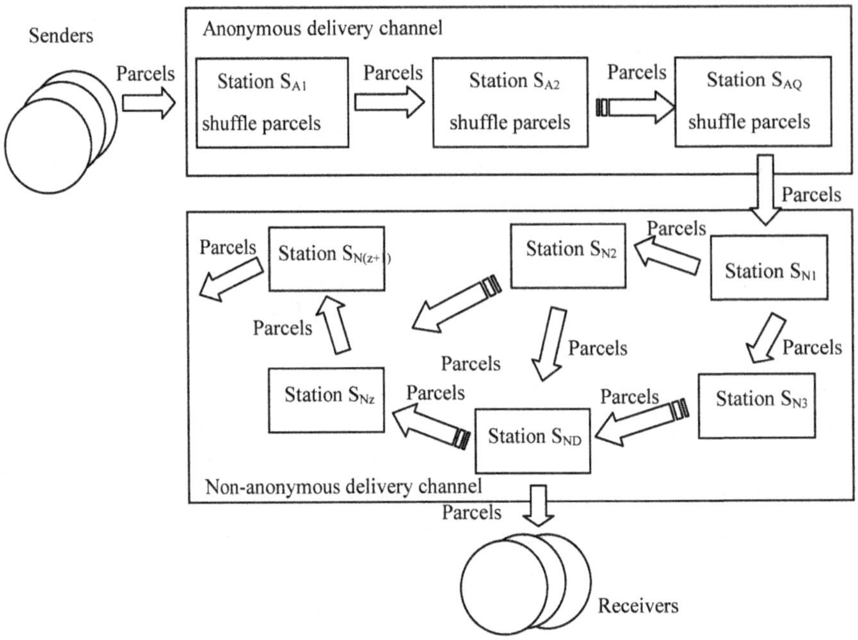

advance. Here, S_{A1} registers C_h as an authorized client while storing a set of data $ID(C_h)$, $E(a_h, T_D(h, 1))$, $\{check_{D1}(h), check_{D2}(h), ---, check_{DZ}(h)\}$ and $\{\underline{t}_{D1}(h), \underline{t}_{D2}(h), ---, \underline{t}_{DZ}(h)\}$ as same as in other systems discussed before, where $ID(C_h)$ is the identifier of C_h, $E(a_h, T_D(h, 1))$ is the encrypted next token of C_h, and each $t_{Dj}(h)$ is an encrypted test bit string vector generated by the manager and $check_{Dj}(h)$ is the visible part value of its decrypted form, and $E(a_h, T_D(h, 1))$ enables C_h to make its next visit to the delivery system without disclosing its identity by using token $T_D(h, 1)$, each pair $\{check_{Dj}(h), t_{Dj}(h)\}$ is used to identify liable entities when dishonest events occur about parcels. Manager S_{A1} also constructs C_h's initial parcel record PR(h, 0) and gives its encrypted form $E(k_D, PR(h, 0))$ and signed form $S(g_D, PR(h, 0)$ to C_h as the registration record. In the above, a_h is a secret encryption key of C_h, k_D and g_D are secret encryption and signing keys of S_{A1}, and $E(a_h, x)$ and $E(k_D, x)$ are additive encryption functions based on linear equations. Also, provided that v_{D0} and v_{D1} are token concealers secret of S_{A1}, initial parcel record PR(h, 0) includes $v_{D0}ID(C_h)$ and $v_{D1}E(a_h, T_D(h, 1))$ as its ITL part value (the configuration of parcel record PR(h, n) will be discussed later).

Figure 10 shows the configuration of the anonymous object delivery system developed in this subsection. It consists of the anonymous delivery channel and the non-anonymous delivery channel. Where, the anonymous delivery channel is a sequence of stations, and conceals correspondences between parcels and their senders or receivers as Mix-net conceals correspondences between messages and their senders or receivers. Namely, anonymous clients bring parcels to the 1st station in the anonymous delivery channel, and each station in the anonymous delivery channel shuffles its receiving parcels to forward them to the station next to it. On the other hand, the non-anonymous delivery channel is a usual object-transportation channel, and anonymous clients visit stations nearest to them in this channel to receive their parcels.

There are 2 types of object transportations, the one is sender initiative and the other is receiver initiative, and only clients that had sent parcels can trace them in sender initiative cases. On the other hand in receiver initiative cases, clients that can trace parcels are only the ones that receive them. In both cases, destinations of objects are designated by addresses of stations in the non-anonymous delivery channel nearest to their receivers, and senders may know the receiver addresses only in forms that are encrypted by encryption keys of multiple stations in the anonymous delivery channel. Here, encryption functions of individual stations in the anonymous delivery channel are probabilistic of course, and receivers inform senders of their repeatedly encrypted addresses through anonymous communication networks discussed in Section 2 if they want to hide their identities from the senders.

Delivering Objects

At its n-th visit to the anonymous object delivery system, client C_h brings its n-th parcel P(h, n) to S_{A1}, the 1st station in the anonymous delivery channel and the representative of the system, while showing its n-th token T_D(h, n), encrypted (n+1)-th token E(a_h, T_D(h, n+1)) and the sum of its past encrypted parcel records, together with anonymous tag Tg(h, n) and repeatedly encrypted address A_{ND} of station S_{ND} in the non-anonymous delivery channel, which is nearest to client C_j that receives P(h, n). Here, sender C_h can conceal its identity because T_D(h, n) is anonymous, and when E(a_h, T_D(h, n+1)) is successfully included in C_h's n-th parcel record PR(h, n), it also can make its next visit anonymously by showing T_D(h, n+1).

The correspondence between parcel P(h, n) and its sender or receiver is concealed in the same way as in Mix-net, namely, address A_{ND} of parcel P(h, n) is repeatedly encrypted to E(k_*, A_{ND}) = E(k_1, E(k_2, ---, E(k_Q, A_{ND}) ---)) by encryption keys of multiple stations in the anonymous delivery channel, and each station in the channel decrypts it so that address A_{ND} is finally revealed, where k_q is the encryption key of station S_{Aq} and encryption functions E(k_1, x), E(k_2, x), ---, E(k_Q, x) are probabilistic. Sender C_h can calculate E(k_*, A_{ND}) on behalf of C_j in a case where receiver C_j is not anonymous, however if C_j wants to hide its identity, C_j must inform C_h of E(k_*, A_{ND}) through anonymous networks while calculating it by itself. The important difference from Mix-net is that anonymous tag Tg(h, n) is also attached to P(h, n) in addition to E(k_*, A_{ND}) so that C_h or C_j can trace P(h, n) travelling in the anonymous and non-anonymous delivery channel. About encryption algorithms used in the anonymous delivery channel, encryption and decryption overheads are not so serious compared with anonymous networks where electronic signals are transferred. Therefore, various mechanisms such as RSA based Mix-net described in Section 2 can be adopted in addition to ESEBM.

Now, S_{A1} that receives P(h, n) from sender C_h generates parcel record PR(h, n) as the representative of all stations in the anonymous delivery channel, and calculates its encrypted form E(k_D, PR(h, n)) and signed form S(g_D, PR(h, n)) to give them to C_h. Here, parcel record PR(h, n) consists of plain token part Pt(h, n), token version part Tv(h, n), receipt part Rc(h, n), and ITL Section ITL_D(h, n) as shown in Figure 11, and anonymous tag Tg(h, n) attached to P(h, n) is put as the value of Rc(h, n). As same as in previous subsections, token T_D(h, n) shown by C_h is assigned to Pt(h, n) as its value, Tv(h, n) is used for carrying out procedures of the anonymous record agreement protocol between C_h and S_{A1}, and ITL_D(h, n) is C_h's current and the encrypted next token pair {$v_{Dn}T_D$(h, n), $v_{D(n+1)}$E(a_j, T_D(h, n+1))} multiplied by token concealers v_{Dn} and $v_{D(n+1)}$ secrets of S_{A1}.

Anonymous tag Tg(h, n) is generated by C_h itself in a sender initiative case, i.e. C_h defines integers G_h and p_h, and generates pair {G_h, G_h^{ph}} while maintaining p_h as its secret. Here, G_h and G_h^{ph} constitute the tag part and the associate tag part of Tg(h, n), respectively, as shown in Figure

Figure 11. Parcel record

Plain token part	Token version part	Receipt part	ITL part
Pt(h, n) = T_D(h,n)	Tv(h, n)	Rc(h, n) = Tg(h, n)	ITL_D(h, n)

Figure 12. Anonymous tag

Tag part	Associate tag part
G(h, n) (G_h or G_j)	$G(h, n)^{hn}$ (G_h^{ph} or G_j^{pj})

12. On the other hand in a receiver initiative case, C_j defines integers G_j and p_j, and generates pair $\{G_j, G_j^{pj}\}$ while maintaining p_j as C_j's secret, i.e. Tg(h, n) is generated by C_j, and G_j and G_j^{pj} constitute the tag part and the associate tag part of Tg(h, n). Therefore in receiver initiative cases, C_j must inform C_h of not only encrypted address $E(k_*, A_{ND})$ but also anonymous tag Tg(h, n). In the following, pair $\{G(h, n), G(h, n)^{hn}\}$ is also used for representing the value of Tg(h, n) instead of $\{G_h, G_h^{ph}\}$ or $\{G_j, G_j^{pj}\}$.

After issuing the encrypted and signed parcel record to C_h, the 1st station S_{A1} in the anonymous delivery channel packs parcel P(h, n) into a box that has the same shape and the colour with the ones for other parcels, makes weight of P(h, n) equal to all other parcels by adding dummy weights to it if necessary, and attaches encrypted station address $E(k_*, A_{ND})$ and anonymous tag Tg(h, n) to P(h, n). Then, S_{A1} decrypts encrypted station address $E(k_*, A_{ND}) = E(k_1, E(k_2, ---, E(k_Q, A_{ND})---))$ to $E(k_2, E(k_3, ---, E(k_Q, A_{ND})---))$ by its secret decryption key k_1^{-1}, transforms $Tg(h, n) = \{G(h, n), G(h, n)^{hn}\}$ to $\{G(h, n)^{z1}, G(h, n)^{(hn)(z1)}\}$ while generating its secret number z_1, waits for arrivals of predefined number of other parcels, shuffle parcels, and transfer all parcels to station S_{A2} next to it. Other stations in the anonymous delivery channel perform in the same way, and when the last station S_{AQ} in the anonymous delivery channel completes its operations, encrypted station address $E(k_*, A_{ND})$ is decrypted to A_{ND}, therefore, stations in the non-anonymous delivery channel that receive P(h, n) can transport it to S_{ND}, the station nearest to receiver C_j. About the value of anonymous tag Tg(h, n), it changes from $\{G(h, n), G(h, n)^{hn}\}$ to $\{G(h, n)^{z1}, G(h, n)^{(hn)(z1)}\}$, $\{G(h, n)^{(z1)(z2)}, G(h, n)^{(hn)(z1)(z2)}\}$, ---, $\{G(h, n)^{(z1)(z2)---(zQ)}, G(h, n)^{(hn)(z1)(z2)---(zQ)}\}$ in the anonymous delivery channel.

Then, no one except C_h can identify the correspondence between it and parcel P(h, n) in the sender initiative case, but C_h can identify P(h, n) in the anonymous and non-anonymous delivery channel without knowing any secret key of stations. On the other hand in the receiver initiative case, no one except C_j can identify the correspondence between C_j and P(h, n), but C_j can identify P(h, n) without knowing any secret key of stations. Namely as same as in Mix-net, anyone (including C_h and C_j) cannot identify P(h, n) from the encrypted station address attached to it unless all stations conspire, because each station S_q does not know decryption key k_p^{-1} of other station S_p. Nevertheless, anonymous tag Tg(h, n) attached to P(h, n) enables C_h or C_j to identify P(h, n) in the delivery system. Depending on the sender or the receiver initiative case, C_h or C_j that knows its secret number h_n can identify P(h, n) by comparing the associate tag part value $G(h, n)^{(hn)(z1)(z2)\cdots(zq)}$ with the h_n-th power of the tag part value $G(h, n)^{(z1)(z2)\cdots(zq)}$ (i.e. $(G(h, n)^{(z1)(z2)\cdots(zq)})^{hn}$). However, other entities including stations in the anonymous delivery channel cannot identify it.

Receiving Objects

In the sender initiative case, client C_h that had sent parcel P(h, n) can know its arrival at station S_{ND} nearest to C_j that receives P(h, n) by checking anonymous tags of all parcels arrived at S_{ND}, i.e. parcel P_x, of which anonymous tag {X, Y} satisfies relation $X^{hn} = Y$, is P(h, n). Therefore, C_h informs C_j of the arrival of P(h, n) at S_{ND} through anonymous networks. In the same way in the receiver initiative case C_j can know the arrival of P(h, n), but in this case C_j does not need to inform anyone about that because C_j itself receives P(h, n). Now, after knowing the arrival of P(h, n), C_j must convince S_{ND} that it is the authorized receiver of P(h, n) in both cases, and this can be achieved also by anonymous tag Tg(h, n) = {X, Y} attached to P(h, n) as shown below.

Firstly, client C_j visits station S_{ND} to receive parcel P(h, n) while showing its eligibility to S_{A1}, the representative of all stations, by its latest unused token $T_D(j, s)$ and the sum of its past encrypted parcel records, and when $T_D(j, s)$ is verified successfully, S_{ND} generates its secret number y, and calculates pair $\{X^y, Y^y\}$ from anonymous tag {X, Y} attached to P(h, n). Here, it must be noted that relation $Y^y = X^{(y)(hn)}$ holds because $Y = X^{hn}$. Then in the receiver initiative case, S_{ND} convinces itself that C_j is the receiver if C_j can calculate Y^y from X^y, i.e. other entity that does not know h_n or y cannot calculate Y^y from X^y. In the sender initiative case C_j asks C_h to calculate $Y^y = X^{(y)(hn)}$ from X^y through anonymous networks, and S_{ND} convinces itself that C_j is the receiver in the same way as in the receiver initiative case. In both cases, S_{ND} generates parcel record PR(j, s) and representative S_{A1} generates its encrypted and signed forms $E(k_D, PR(j, s))$ and $S(g_D, PR(j, s))$ to give them to C_j, where, receipt part Rc(j, s) and ITL Section $1TL_D(j, s)$ of parcel record PR(j, s) have values {X, Y} and $\{v_{Ds}T_D(j, s), v_{D(s+1)}E(a_j, T_D(j, s+1))\}$, respectively. It must be noted that if secret number h_n is disclosed even after C_j had received P(h, n), any entity can trace P(h, n) in the anonymous object delivery system, i.e. anyone can identify P(h, n) in each station's parcel records by examining anonymous tags attached to individual parcels. The advantage of anonymous tag Tg(h, n) is that C_h or C_j does not need to disclose its secret number h_n.

However, S_{ND} knows y and {X, Y} and can calculate Y^y, therefore C_j can claim that P(h, n) was stolen by someone who had been informed of Y^y from S_{ND}, even if C_j had received P(h, n) already. ITLs disable C_j to behave in this manner. When C_j claims that its parcel P(h, n) had been stolen while showing anonymous tag {X, Y}, representative S_{A1} finds parcel record PR(j, s), of which receipt part value Rc(j, s) coincides with {X, Y}, from its database, and asks all clients to decrypt encrypted next token $E(a_j, T(j, s+1))$ in the ITL part of PR(j, s). Then S_{A1} can reject C_j's claim in a case where C_j decrypts the encrypted next token successfully. Namely, if C_j had received P(h, n) already, encrypted next token included in the ITL part value of PR(h, n) is $E(a_j, T(j, s+1))$, and C_j that knows decryption key a_j^{-1} can decrypt it to a consistent visible part value. On the other hand, other entities including stations do not know a_j^{-1} and cannot decrypt $E(a_j, T(j, s+1))$ to any consistent value. Here, test bit string vectors and their encrypted forms registered as identity information of clients disable clients to dishonestly encrypt tokens or decrypt encrypted next tokens, as discussed in subsection "Homomorphic Anonymous Tokens."

Two different situations happen in a case where P(h, n) actually had been stolen. In the 1st situation, no client can decrypt the encrypted next token consistently, and S_{ND} is regarded that it had stolen P(h, n) without having generated an effective parcel record. In the 2nd situation, client C_v other than C_j successfully decrypts the encrypted token, and this implies that C_v is the authorized receiver or C_v had received P(h, n) illegitimately while having being informed of Y^y from S_{ND}, therefore disputes between C_j and C_v must be resolved. Anonymous tags resolve also these disputes. When C_v does not know the secret number h_n, C_j can prove C_v is dishonest by calculating X^w from X and asking C_v to calculate $Y^w = X^{w(hn)}$. Here, W is an integer secret of C_j, therefore C_v that does not know h_n cannot calculate Y^w from X^w. If C_v is honest, it can prove C_j's dishonesty in the same way. Although there are cases where both C_j and C_v know h_n, however this case occurs only when C_v or C_j had stolen h_n from C_j or C_v, and C_j or C_v is responsible for stolen h_n, and the dispute must be resolved between C_j and C_v without station S_{A1}.

Identifying Entities Liable for Lost Objects

When parcel P(h, n) is lost during it is being transported from S_{A1} in the anonymous delivery channel to S_{ND} in the non-anonymous delivery channel, C_h or C_j can identify the liable station without disclosing their identities and without knowing any secret of stations. To enable clients to detect troubles in their parcels and to identify liable stations, each station S_{Aq} in the anonymous delivery channel maintains anonymous tag conversion records, i.e. for each receiving parcel P_r, S_{Aq} maintains pair $\{X_r, Y_r\}$ and $\{X_r^{zq}, Y_r^{zq}\}$ in its anonymous tag conversion table, where, $\{X_r, Y_r\}$ is the anonymous tag of P_r at the time when S_{Aq} had received it from $S_{A(q-1)}$, $\{X_r^{zq}, Y_r^{zq}\}$ is that of P_r at the time when S_{Aq} had forwarded it to station $S_{A(q+1)}$ next to it, and z_q is the secret number of S_{Aq}. Also every station S_{Aq} in the anonymous delivery channel signs on anonymous tag $\{X_r, Y_r\}$ and gives the result to station $S_{A(q-1)}$ as a receipt when it receives P_r from $S_{A(q-1)}$.

Now when parcel P(h, n) disappears in the anonymous delivery channel, anonymous C_h or C_j can identify the liable station as follows. Firstly, C_h or C_j shows parcel record PR(h, n) it received from S_{A1} when it had brought parcel P(h, n) to S_{A1} (in the receiver initiative case, C_j obtains PR(h, n) by asking C_h). Then, from PR(h, n), S_{A1} extracts receipt part value $Tg(h, n) = \{G(h, n), G(h, n)^{hn}\}$, the anonymous tag initially attached to P(h, n), and finds pair $[\{G(h, n), G(h, n)^{hn}\}, \{G(h, n)^{z1}, G(h, n)^{(hn)(z1)}\}]$ in its anonymous tag conversion table. After that, S_{A1} shows signature of S_{A2} on $\{G(h, n)^{z1}, G(h, n)^{(hn)(z1)}\}$ to S_{A2}, and based on it S_{A2} finds $\{G(h, n)^{(z1)(z2)}, G(h, n)^{(hn)(z1)(z2)}\}$ that corresponds to $\{G(h, n)^{z1}, G(h, n)^{(hn)(z1)}\}$ in its anonymous tag conversion table. The remaining stations in the anonymous delivery channel perform in the same way, therefore, if station S_{Aq} is liable, it is identified as the station that gave receipt $\{G(h, n)^{(z1)(z2)---(zq-1)}, G(h, n)^{(hn)(z1)(z2)---(zq-1)}\}$ to $S_{A(q-1)}$ but could not obtain receipt $\{G(h, n)^{(z1)(z2)---(zq)}, G(h, n)^{(hn)(z1)(z2)---(zq)}\}$ from $S_{A(q+1)}$. Namely, $S_{A(q-1)}$ can prove that it had transported P(h, n) to S_{Aq} by the signature of S_{Aq} on $\{G(h, n)^{(z1)(z2)---(zq-1)}, G(h, n)^{(hn)(z1)(z2)---(zq-1)}\}$, but S_{Aq} cannot prove that it had transported it to $S_{A(q+1)}$ because it does not have signature of $S_{A(q+1)}$ on $\{G(h, n)^{(z1)(z2)---(zq)}, G(h, n)^{(hn)(z1)(z2)---(zq)}\}$. Here, S_{Aq} cannot show the signature of $S_{A(q+1)}$ on other tag $\{G(y, m)^{(z1)(z2)---(zq)}, G(y, m)^{(ym)(z1)(z2)---(zq)}\}$, because $(G(y, m)^{(z1)(z2)---(zq)})^{hn} \neq G(y, m)^{(ym)(z1)(z2)---(zq)}$.

Stations in the non-anonymous delivery channel liable for disappearances of parcels can be identified more easily. Because stations in the non-anonymous delivery channel do not change anonymous tags or shuffle parcels that they receive, any entity can detect stations where parcels disappear by observing anonymous tags attached to input and output parcels of individual stations. It must be noted that C_h or C_j does not need to disclose its identity to find a station liable for the lost parcel P(h, n), i.e. parcel record PR(h, n) does not include any information about C_h or C_j. Stations are not required to disclose their encryption or decryption keys either. Therefore, all clients can preserve their privacies, and each station S_{Aq} does not need to change its encryption key k_q even if clients claim that their parcels had diapered. About collisions among secret integers, C_h can define h_n unique to it as discussed in subsection "Anonymous Tokens based on Anonymous Tags" in Section 2.

Then, the anonymous object delivery system discussed in this section satisfies all the requirements. Namely, depending on the sender initiative or the receiver initiative cases, only client C_h that sends parcel P(h, n) or client C_j that receives P(h, n) can identify and trace P(h, n) in the system. Also, C_h and C_j can force station S_{ND} to deliver P(h, n) only to receiver C_j, and stations liable for disappearing parcels can be identified without disclosing identities of clients or secrets of stations. As a typical example, when auction winners receive their winning articles through the anonymous object delivery system in the receiver initiative mode, anyone other than the auction winners including stations and auctioneers cannot identify the correspondences between articles and their winners or the stations where the articles arrive at. However in the sender initiative mode, senders can identify the stations nearest to the receivers by tracing anonymous tags attached to the parcels although senders cannot identify exact receivers.

Payments

It is trivial to apply the anonymous credit card system discussed in the previous chapter to enable clients to pay for their sending or receiving of parcels thorough the anonymous object delivery system without disclosing their identities to others.

Development of Anonymous Object Monitoring System

Object monitoring systems monitor running states of objects such as home appliances and alert clients (users) to emergent states of the objects or suggest optimal (e.g. more efficient, safe or environmentally friendly) conditions for operating the objects to clients (Djurdjanovic, 2003). They also detect dishonest events on the objects, e.g. their illegitimate disposals, and identify liable clients. Anonymous object monitoring systems perform the above functions without invading privacies of honest clients, e.g. without knowing identities of honest clients or without knowing individual running states of objects owned by honest clients.

In this subsection, an anonymous object monitoring system is developed based on anonymous memories and anonymous networks (Tamura, 2008). Here, it is assumed that clients become the members of the anonymous object monitoring system when they had registered themselves as members of the anonymous auction system developed in the previous section, therefore monitoring stations can authenticate client C_h at its n-th visit to them by C_h's n-th auction system token T(h, n) without knowing its identity, also they can identify object P_h without knowing the identity of C_h that is using P_h from article part value Ar(h, m) of bid record BR(h, m) that C_h received from the auctioneer when it had obtained P_h.

Figure 13 shows a configuration of the anonymous object monitoring system. It consists of monitoring stations, clients (users of objects) and anonymous memories, and clients put running states of their objects in the memory sections of the anonymous memory assigned to them through anonymous networks, then, monitoring stations fetch the running states of the objects from these memory sections to detect dangerous conditions, to calculate optimal running conditions, to detect dishonest events and to identify their liable entities. Therefore, clients can conceal their identities from anyone except themselves, i.e. anonymous

Figure 13. Anonymous object monitoring system

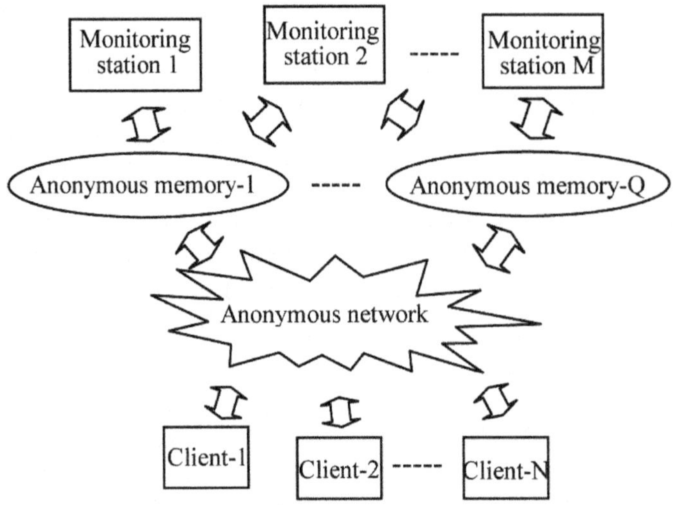

networks conceal identities of clients that put states of their objects in anonymous memories, and anonymous memories disable monitoring stations to know clients corresponding to individual memory sections.

To enable C_h to maintain running states of object P_h and at the same time to enable monitoring stations to identify P_h without knowing client C_h that is using P_h, C_h assigns its memory section in the anonymous memory to its owning P_h, in detail, at a time when it obtains P_h through the auction, C_h acquires a memory section in the anonymous memory, puts IDs of P_h and its anonymous user in it, and informs monitoring stations of the memory section address. Here, the memory section corresponding to P_h is configured as shown in Figure 14. Object ID is used for identifying P_h, and article part value Ar(h, m) of bid record BR(h, m) that C_h received from the auction system when it had bought P_h is assigned as its value. User ID is used for identifying C_h when dishonest events occur on P_h, and T(h, m), the token part value of BR(h, m) is assigned as its value. Then, monitoring stations informs C_h of suggestions or cautions for using object P_h through the message part. The message Section Is also used by client C_h to ask monitoring stations questions about using or maintaining P_h. The state part maintains history of running states of P_h reported by client C_h.

Here, there is at least one advantage to use the anonymous memory in the above, i.e. not to connect clients to monitoring stations directly through anonymous networks. That is the possibility that peak loads of anonymous communication channels are decreased. In cases where clients and monitoring stations are connected directly through anonymous networks, messages exchanged between clients and monitoring stations concentrate during monitoring stations carry out their monitor-

Figure 14. Data structure of states of an object

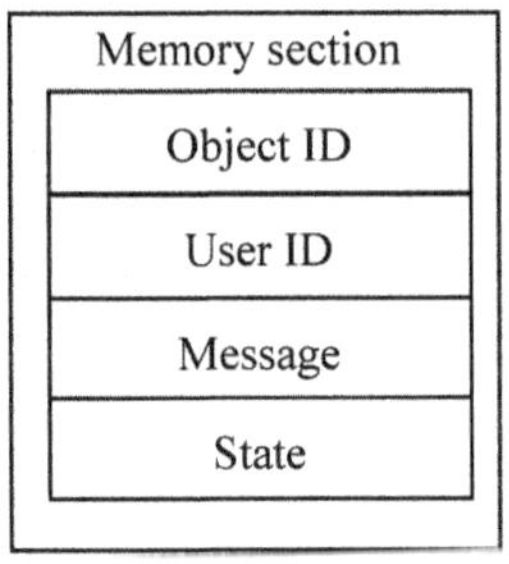

ing tasks despite that anonymous networks are not efficient enough as usual non anonymous ones. These volumes further increase if monitoring tasks require conversations between clients and monitoring stations. On the other hand when anonymous memories are used, clients can send running states of their objects in advance independent of the monitoring tasks, and monitoring stations can gather state information through usual non anonymous networks without worrying about limited capacities of anonymous networks.

Monitoring Objects Used by Anonymous Entities

A problem in developing the anonymous monitoring system is in many cases histories of running states of object P_h are good clues for estimating the identity of client C_h that is using P_h, despite that these histories are essential to provide C_h with valuable suggestions for using and maintaining P_h. This problem becomes more serious when a client and an object are a manufacturing company and its possessing manufacturing machine for example, i.e. in several cases it is not so difficult to identify a company from the correlation between operation histories of its machines and transitions of its sales amounts, and in these cases monitoring stations can know production strategies of the company that may be its top secret. To cope with this difficulty, a client of the monitoring system divides running states of its object into 2 groups, the one is the emergent group and the other is the non-emergent group. Namely, states in the emergent group are essential for monitoring stations to determine whether the object is in normal states or in emergent states; and the client informs monitoring stations of exact values of states in this group (of course these values may be encrypted by encryption keys of the monitoring stations to protect them from wiretappings). On the other hand, states in the non-emergent group strongly relate to privacies of the client, e.g. histories of these states include many clues to estimate the client that is using the object; therefore the client reports only aggregated values of these states to the monitoring station.

Then, to monitor states in the emergent group is straightforward, i.e. a monitoring station can complete its task for monitoring object P_h by gathering exact sates of P_h in the anonymous memory. On the other hand, a monitoring station must carry out monitoring tasks about states in the non-emergent group of P_h based on their aggregated values e.g. averages, variances, and auto and/or cross correlations, without knowing their individual values. However, kinds of aggregations that are used for monitoring P_h or algorithms for efficiently and accurately calculating these values may be secrets of the monitoring station, or client C_h may not desire to install programs for calculating these values in its own computers. In these cases the monitoring station must calculate these aggregated values by itself without knowing values of individual states, and this can be achieved by exploiting anonymous statistics calculation schemes discussed in Section 2.

For example, to calculate the cross correlation of $\{x(t_1), x(t_2), ---, x(t_z)\}$ and $\{y(t_1), y(t_2), ---, y(t_z)\}$, time series of 2 different states of object P_h used by client C_h, without knowing their individual values, firstly, C_h encrypts them to $\{E(a_h, x(t_1)), E(a_h, x(t_2)), ---, E(a_h, x(t_z))\}$, $\{E(a_h, y(t_1)), E(a_h, y(t_2)), ---, E(a_h, y(t_z))\}$ and $\{E(b_h, x(t_1)), E(b_h, x(t_2)), ---, E(b_h, x(t_z))\}$, $\{E(b_h, y(t_1)), E(b_h, y(t_2)), ---, E(b_h, y(t_z))\}$ to put them in memory section Sec(h) of the anonymous memory assigned to P_h, where a_h and b_h are secret encryption keys of C_h, $E(a_h, x)$ is an additive encryption function and $E(b_h, y)$ is a both additive and multiplicative encryption function as discussed in chapter "Anonymous Statistics Calculations." After that, the monitoring station reads the encrypted states in Sec(h) to calculate the encrypted cross correlation, and put the result in Sec(h) so that C_h can decrypt it. Then, the monitoring station examines the decrypted results in Sec(h) to generate suggestions about optimal, safe or environmentally friendly uses of object P_h. However to keep its identity secret, C_h cannot read the data in Sec(h) immediately, because other entities can identify C_h by the times when the monitoring station puts the encrypted calculation results and C_h reads them; therefore C_h must accept time lags for knowing monitoring results, but this time lag does not cause any serious problem because events about states in the non-emergent group are not urgent.

Here, there exist tradeoffs between categorizing a given state into the emergent group and the non-emergent one. When the state is in the emergent group, privacies of the client become more vulnerable although the client can use the object safely, on the other hand, when the state is in the non-emergent group, the client must risk its safety.

Identifying Dishonest Entities

When a dishonest event on an object is detected, a liable client can be identified without revealing any privacy of honest clients in the same way as identifying liable clients in the anonymous auction system in the previous chapter (Tamura, 2010). Let us assume that monitoring station S_j detects a dishonest event on object P_h that anonymous client C_h had obtained by the bid in the auction accompanied by token T(h, n). Then, the corresponding bid record BR(h, n) includes $E(a_h, T(h, n+1))$ as the encrypted next token value in its ITL part. Therefore, S_j can identify liable client C_h by asking all clients to decrypt $E(a_h, T(h, n+1))$. Namely, C_h that knows decryption key a_h^{-1} and can decrypt $E(a_h, T(h, n+1))$ to consistent visible part value is regarded as the liable client.

Monitoring stations also can identify clients that bought articles through auctions without registering them in the monitoring system. Namely, when C_h does not register object P_h that corresponds to article part value Ar(h, n) of bid record BR(h, n), monitoring stations can know that because no section in the anonymous memory includes Ar(h, n), and they can identify C_h by asking all clients to decrypt $E(a_h, T(h, n+1))$ in the ITL part value of BR(h, n). Here, S_j can ask decryptions of $E(a_h, T(h, n+1))$ to individual clients in conjunction with processes to collect fees for monitoring tasks not to disturb honest clients every time when a dishonest event is detected.

Payments

The monitoring system can collect fees from anonymous clients through anonymous credit card systems in the same way as the anonymous object delivery system did in the previous subsection.

CONCLUSION

As discussed in this chapter it is not difficult to implement anonymous auction systems, i.e. ITLs, bulletin boards and re-encryption schemes satisfactory enable sellers and buyers to participate auctions while protecting their privacies. Fairness of auctions also can be achieved without invading privacies of participants, i.e. it is ensured that auction winners can buy their winning articles from their sellers and sellers can sell their articles to auction winners at the prices determined by the auctions. In addition, buyers can pay anonymous sellers their bid prices for winning articles and sellers can be paid without disclosing their identities through the anonymous credit card systems. Also, buyers can receive their winning articles without being noticed by others when anonymous object delivery systems are exploited.

About the anonymous object delivery and the object monitoring systems developed in this chapter, the former enables objects to be securely transported without revealing any privacy of their owners, and the latter enables monitoring stations to monitor states of objects while preserving privacies of their owners or users. Then, together with the anonymous auction systems, they are expected to encourage more people to use e-procurement systems and consequently to reuse their objects (e.g. home appliances) and to use them more efficiently, safely and environmentally friendlily. They also reduce anxiety about various services provided by environments such as cloud computing, i.e. people or organizations can exploit services provided through cloud computing without worrying that their privacies or secrets are revealed. As a consequence, it becomes possible to share various resources and efforts among different people and organizations to make use of them more efficiently and effectively.

About future works, the anonymous delivery system in this chapter enables senders or receivers to trace their parcels according to whether transportation modes are sender initiative or receiver initiative; as a consequence senders or receivers can identify the receivers or the senders. To preserve privacies of both senders and receivers, mechanisms for anonymous tags must be enhanced so that both senders and receivers are disabled to trace their parcels without permissions of the receivers or the senders. These mechanisms can be implemented by defining secret key h of anonymous tag $\{G, G^h\}$ as the product of secret keys h_1 and h_2 of sender C_1 and receiver C_2. Namely, when anonymous tag $\{G, G^{(h1)(h2)}\}$ is attached to object P, it can be identified as the one attached to P only when C_1 and C_2 jointly calculate G^{h1} and $G^{(h1)(h2)} = G^h$ or G^{h2} and $G^{(h2)(h1)} = G^h$. It is also possible for C_1 to send P in the sender initiative mode while attaching the encrypted address of the 1st station S_{A1} in the anonymous delivery channel and to change the mode to receiver initiative while attaching the encrypted address of the receiver C_2. In this case, C_2 cannot trace P while P is being transported in the sender initiative mode, and C_1 cannot trace P after the mode is changed to receiver initiative. These mechanisms can be applied also to anonymous networks in Section 2.

To make the anonymous object monitoring systems more reliable at least 2 problems must be solved. Firstly, to calculate various values necessary for efficiently and safely operating objects without knowing individual states of the objects is not easy. Currently available schemes can handle only limited forms of functions, e.g. sums and/or products of data, and their auto and cross correlations as discussed in the chapter "Anonymous Statistics Calculation." To make the anonymous object monitoring system more practical, i.e. to enable calculations of various kinds of functions of data that are required in practical applications, more effective and efficient mechanisms are necessary.

The 2nd problem to be considered is how to reliably detect dishonest events that are caused by anonymous entities in remote places. Various kinds of dishonest events exist, e.g. using objects at inhibited places or periods, lending objects to unauthorized entities, and discarding objects without carrying out defined disposal procedures. Although many elaborate sensors are already available, e.g. position sensors imbedded in IC cards can disable clients to dishonestly report places where their objects are located, or monitoring stations can detect illegitimate disposals of objects by analysing places where the devices attached to them emit alive-signals, clients can easily detach these devices from their objects to deceive monitoring stations that they are in the right places or they are alive. To protect objects from being used or discarded in inappropriate manners, more sophisticated mechanisms to acquire and analyze their running states are necessary.

REFERENCES

Djurdjanovic, D., Lee, J., & Ni, J. (2003). Watchdog agent - An infotronics based prognostics approach for product performance assessment and prediction. *International Journal of Advanced Engineering Informatics . Special Issue on Intelligent Maintenance Systems, 17*(3-4), 109–125.

Franklin, M., & Reiter, M. (1996). The design and implementation of a secure auction service. *IEEE Transactions on Software Engineering, 22*, 302–312. doi:10.1109/32.502223

Hassan, K., Tamura, S., & Yanase, T. (2006). A mechanism for anonymous auction. *Proceedings of Asian Simulation Conference (Systems Modeling and Simulation),* Springer, (pp. 233-237).

Naor, M., Pinkas, B., & Sumner, R. (1999). Privacy preserving auctions and mechanism design. *Proceedings of the 1st ACM Conference on Electronic Commerce*, (pp. 129-139).

Nguyen, K., & Traore, J. (2000). An online public auction protocol protecting bidder privacy. *5th Australasian Conference on Information Security and Privacy, ACISP'00*, (pp. 427-442).

Stajano, F. (2002). *Security for ubiquitous computing*. John Wiley & Sons. doi:10.1002/0470848693

Tamura, S., Haddad, H. A., Tsurugi, H., & Md. Rokibul, A. K. (2009). Mechanisms for anonymous memories. *IEEE InternationalConference on Industrial Tecnology, ICIT, 09*, 398–403.

Tamura, S., Kouro, K., Sasatani, S., Md. Rokibul, K. A., & Haddad, H. A. (2008). An information system platform for anonymous product recycling. *Journal of Software, 3*(6), 46–56. doi:10.4304/jsw.3.6.46-56

Tamura, S., Ohashi, Y., Tanigichi, S., & Yanase, T. (2010). Detection of dishonest entities. *SMC2010, Proceedings of IEEE International Conference on System, Man and Cybernetics,* (pp. 906-911).

Chapter 12
Electronic Governance Systems

ABSTRACT

As one of applications in electronic governance, this chapter develops an electronic voting (e-voting) system. After discussing requirements for e-voting systems and reviewing existing approaches, an e-voting system is developed based on confirmation numbers and signature pairs. Here, e-voting systems must satisfy requirements intrinsically contradicting each other, e.g. they must convince anyone that votes from only and all eligible voters had been counted, but at the same time to protect voters from a coercer that forces voters to choose its supporting candidate, correspondences between voters and their votes must be concealed from anyone including election authorities and voters themselves. The developed e-voting system successfully satisfies these requirements. However, it must be noted that these requirement are satisfied under the assumption that at least one of mutually independent multiple authorities is honest.

INTRODUCTION

Electronic governance (e-governance) systems are governmental systems supported by information and communication technologies, and because of features of information included, as same as e-payment systems they are most privacy sensitive systems. Among various mechanisms about e-governance systems, this chapter develops mechanisms for electronic voting (e-voting) systems, as ones, in which anonymous features are essential (e.g. if correspondences between voters and their votes are identified, an entity can easily force other entities to choose a candidate that the entity is supporting), while exploiting several schemes discussed in Part I and II. Anonymous features are also essential in electronic poll (e-poll) systems that enable government offices to collect opinions from citizens quickly, accurately and environmentally friendlily, but requirements for e-poll systems are almost the same as e-voting systems. Therefore, this chapter does not discuss them; they can be developed in the same way as e-voting systems.

Here, it must be noted that although many individual governmental tasks are intrinsically non-anonymous, i.e. they cannot be accomplished without knowing identities of individuals, there are many opportunities for anonymous security

DOI: 10.4018/978-1-4666-1649-3.ch012

technologies also in these systems. For example, although people inevitably must disclose their identities to register their cars and estates, they may not want that their cars and estates are linked by others.

In the following, after discussing requirements for e-voting systems and existing approaches for satisfying them, the e-voting system is developed and performances of the system are evaluated. In the developed e-voting system, the election administrator consists of multiple independent authorities, and it works under the assumption that at least one of the authorities is honest, i.e. nothing can make the system unreliable if at least one of the authorities is honest.

REQUIREMENTS FOR E-VOTING SYSTEMS

E-voting is one of anonymous security applications that attract most researchers because of its difficult challenges, i.e. to develop e-voting systems various requirements that intrinsically contradict each other must be satisfied. In practical aspect, e-voting systems are also one of most important applications. Namely in e-voting systems, voters cast their votes as electronic signals and votes are tallied by computers, therefore voting and tallying processes become efficient and accurate. In addition because ballot papers are replaced by electronic signals, physical resources required for voting can be reduced substantially, and moreover, supported by computer networks voters in remote places can participate in elections more easily. However, different from paper based voting systems where physically sealed ballot boxes and publicly disclosed tallying processes ensure the legitimate voting, in e-voting systems, everything is processed by computer programs that cannot be seen physically, and as a consequence, people cannot convince themselves that voting is legitimate, e.g. even when the computer program replaces some votes with different ones no one except the computer can notice that. Therefore simple mechanisms ruin all the above benefits of e-voting systems.

Here, ideal e-voting systems must preserve privacies of individual voters, must be able to convince people that the voting is accurate and fair, must disable any entity to coerce voters to choose a candidate it is supporting, and must be able to resolve disputes between voters and election administrators. Also, they must be robust against various intentional or accidental troubles, must be applicable to large-scale elections, and must be supported by practical assumptions. However, some of these requirements completely contradict each other, e.g. individual votes must be linked to their voters to convince people that all votes are legitimate, but these links reveal privacies of voters, also they enable an entity to coerce voters to choose its supporting candidate more reliably. To protect a voter from being coerced by other entities, any link between a voter and its vote must be concealed even from the voter itself.

Requirements for e-voting systems are summarized as follows.

1. Privacy

Choices of voters must be concealed from others including election authorities. Here, it must be noted that the choice of a voter includes the abstention from the voting. A solution in paper based voting systems is easy when abstentions are not considered, i.e. sealed ballot boxes of which insides are not visible from the outside satisfy the requirement. At a time when a ballot box is opened, anyone (even voters themselves) cannot identify correspondences between voters and their votes, because votes in the box are shuffled. However, in e-voting systems, it is not trivial to convince voters that computer programs had actually shuffled votes in the way that no one including election authorities can know the shuffling results. Also even for paper based systems, it is not easy to preserve privacies of voters who abstain from the voting.

2. Accuracy and Verifiability

Voting results are called accurate when the final tally includes only and all votes from eligible voters; and a voting system is called verifiable when anyone including voters and third parties can verify the accuracy. Paper based voting systems achieve this property by the above sealed ballot boxes and publicly opened tallying processes. Namely, seals of ballot boxes convince all voters and third parties that all votes from only eligible voters are included in them, and publicly opened tallying processes ensure that election authorities cannot count votes in the boxes dishonestly. However, the privacy and the accuracy are usually traded in simple e-voting systems. Namely, when it is allowed to publicly disclose correspondences between voters and their votes, developing an accurate e-voting system is trivial. On the other hand, it is easy to conceal correspondences between voters and their votes if accuracy is not required. In some literatures, notion of verifiability is divided into universal verifiability and individual verifiability, where, while the universal verifiability enables any one including the third parties to verify the accuracy of elections, individually verifiable elections can only convince each voter that its own vote is certainly counted. Therefore, accuracy of elections is ensured when all voters confirm that their votes are counted and the number of confirmed votes coincides with that of voters. Apparently the universal verifiability is inevitable to conduct real elections.

3. Fairness

Fairness relates to the ability of a voting system to disable anyone to know interim election results before the end of the election. Interim election results strongly influence ways voters choose candidates; therefore to conduct elections fairly, voting systems must conceal interim results from anyone including election authorities. In paper based voting systems, fairness is ensured by sealed ballot boxes, i.e. when seals of the boxes are not breached until the end of the election anyone can believe that no one know interim tallying results.

4. Incoercibility

Incoercibility is the ability of a voting system to protect voter V from coercer Ce who forces V to choose a candidate in a way Ce designates. There are 3 types of ways to force V, the 1st type is forced abstention, in which Ce forces V to abstain from the voting, the 2nd type is to force V to choose candidate X that Ce is supporting, and the 3rd type is to force V to cast an invalid vote.

It is easy to protect voter V from the 2nd threat in paper based voting systems. Because election authorities check eligibilities of individual voters coercer Ce itself cannot participate in the election on behalf of V. Ce cannot know whether V actually chose candidate X it is supporting either because the correspondence between V and its vote is not known to anyone other than V itself. However, it must be noted that this is true only when there is at least one voter who had chosen X, i.e. Ce can easily know that V did not behave as it had asked if votes finally disclosed at the tallying stage do not include X. This situation becomes plausible when X is replaced by an invalid vote unique to V, i.e. Ce can know if V actually had cast invalid vote X or not by examining the tallying results. Therefore, even for paper based voting systems to protect voters from threats of the 3rd type is not possible. Paper based systems cannot protect voters from the 1st type threats either; authorities can know if voter V had abstained from voting or not and tell that to coercer Ce. Then, e-voting schemes may have advantages in protecting voters from these threats. Actually, the e-voting system developed in this chapter removes all types of threats including the 2nd type ones under environments where no voter chooses the candidate that the coercer designates as discussed later.

5. Receipt-freeness

Receipt-freeness is an essential feature of e-voting systems to achieve incoercibility. Different from in paper based voting systems where election authorities can convince voter V that its vote had been certainly put in a ballot box without a receipt, in e-voting systems, authorities cannot convince V that computers had actually accepted V's vote without a receipt. However, the receipt enables entity Ce that is coercing V to confirm that V actually chose the candidate Ce had designated, and helps Ce coerce voters more effectively. It must be noted that receipt-freeness requires not only to exclude receipts but also to disable individual voters to identify their votes in the vote set disclosed as the tallying results, i.e. if voter V can identify its vote in the disclosed vote set, coercer Ce can know the vote of V by forcing V to show its vote. Then receipt-freeness requires election authorities to convince voters that their votes are registered without disclosing correspondences between voters and their registered votes, and makes developments of e-voting systems difficult.

6. Dispute-freeness

When voters claim that election authorities are dishonest or election authorities detect dishonest voters, disputes between the authorities and voters about liability for the dishonesties must be resolved without revealing any privacy of honest voters. The important thing is that the election authorities cannot reveal any of their secrets. For example, when the authorities reveal their encryption or decryption keys, votes of other honest voters also may be disclosed.

7. Robustness

Various kinds of dishonest events may happen in an actual election, but to conduct the election again because of these events is difficult, e.g. choices of voters may be influenced by the previous results. Robustness relates to this issue, namely, a voting system must be able to complete the election even when dishonest events occur. Here to complete voting processes, the voting system must recover from dishonest events without any help of entities liable for the events. If it requires helps from dishonest entities, it cannot complete the election when they disappear, for example.

8. Scalability

One of expected advantages of e-voting systems over paper based ones is they can handle many votes from many different voting sites in short time. Therefore to encourage election administrators to adopt e-voting systems, they must be extended easily to satisfy requirements for large scale elections.

9. Practicality

To apply e-voting systems to real elections, they must be developed under practical assumptions and constraints. For example, necessity of single absolutely trustworthy authorities must be excluded, and e-voting systems must be able to handle various kinds of vote forms, e.g. t out of n choices and freely chosen write-in ballots.

Classification of Existing Approaches

Existing e-voting schemes can be classified into 3 categories, i.e. hidden vote, hidden voter, and hidden voter with hidden vote schemes (Sampigethaya, 2006). All schemes assume mutually independent multiple election authorities to satisfy the requirements listed in the previous subsection, i.e. schemes satisfy requirements about privacy, accuracy, etc. when at least one of the authorities is honest. In other words, currently available technologies including the scheme developed in this chapter cannot completely exclude trusted entities faithful to all relevant participants.

Hidden Voter

In e-voting systems of the hidden voter scheme, although individual votes are publicly disclosed in their plain forms in BBs (bulletin boards), voters hide their identities to cast their votes. Then, no one except voters themselves can know links between voters and their votes, i.e. privacies of voters are preserved. Multiple mutually independent voting authorities of a typical hidden voter scheme constitute a decryption type Mix-net, and the voting process proceeds as follow (Chaum, 1981, Sako, 1995).

1. Token generation stage

Voter V_j generates its secret encryption and decryption key pair $\{a_j, a_j^{-1}\}$ and encrypts a_j^{-1} to $E(k_*, a_j^{-1}) = E(k_Q, E(k_{Q-1}, ---, E(k_1,a_j^{-1})---))$, where k_q is a public encryption key of the q-th server of the Mix-net and each $E(k_q, x)$ is a probabilistic encryption function. Then, the 1st server of the Mix-net authenticates V_j while examining V_j's identity, and blindly signs on a_j^{-1} shown by V_j, therefore later on, V_j can prove its eligibility to cast its vote anonymously by showing the signature on a_j^{-1}, i.e. a_j^{-1} works as an anonymous token. V_j also shows $E(k_*, a_j^{-1})$ to the 1st server, and receives the signature on $E(k_*, a_j^{-1})$ as a receipt.

2. Verification stage

The Mix-net decrypts encrypted decryption keys of individual voters and put the results in BB-1, so that each V_j can confirm that its showing $E(k_*, a_j^{-1})$ is correctly decrypted to a_j^{-1}. Here, if V_j cannot find a_j^{-1} in BB-1, it can prove dishonesties of the Mix-net by its receipt.

3. Voting stage

V_j encrypts its vote v_j to $E(a_j, v_j)$ by its encryption key a_j and generates $E(k_*, \{E(a_j, v_j), a_j^{-1}\})$ by encrypting $\{E(a_j, v_j), a_j^{-1}\}$ while using public encryption keys of the Mix-net. After that, V_j anonymously proves its eligibility by showing the signature on a_j^{-1} and sends $E(k_*, \{E(a_j, v_j), a_j^{-1}\})$ to the 1st server in the Mix-net. Then, the 1st server puts $E(k_*, \{E(a_j, v_j), a_j^{-1}\})$ in BB-2, issues the receipt to V_j, and the Mix-net decrypts $E(k_*, \{E(a_j, v_j), a_j^{-1}\})$ to $\{E(a_j, v_j), a_j^{-1}\}$ and discloses it in BB-3 with other votes.

In the above scheme, V_j can identify its vote in BB-3 based on a_j^{-1} provided that encryption key a_j is ensured as unique to voter V_j, anyone can calculate vote v_j from $\{E(a_j, v_j), a_j^{-1}\}$ disclosed in BB-3, and no one except V_j can generate $E(a_j, v_j)$ that is successfully decrypted to v_j by publicly disclosed decryption key a_j^{-1} because only V_j knows a_j. Therefore, V_j who had cast $E(k_*, \{E(a_j, v_j), a_j^{-1}\})$ can convince itself that its vote is certainly counted. Namely, the scheme is individually verifiable. In addition, because V_j is authenticated by the signature on its token a_j^{-1} that had been generated through the blind signature scheme and each server shuffles its decryption result of $E(k_*, a_j^{-1})$ with other results, anyone except V_j cannot identify the correspondence between V_j and a_j^{-1} or V_j and its vote v_j, i.e. the scheme satisfies requirements about privacy. Also, when $E(k_*, \{E(a_j, v_j), a_j^{-1}\})$ is decrypted to $\{E(a_j, v_j), a_j^{-1}\}$ only after votes from all eligible voters had been cast, no one can know interim tallying results, i.e. the scheme satisfies fairness.

Drawbacks of the scheme is that it cannot ensure the universal verifiability, i.e. voters other than V_j cannot determine whether $\{E(a_j, v_j), a_j^{-1}\}$ in BB-3 is actually the vote of an eligible voter or it is the one forged by the authorities. For example, the 1st server S_Q in the Mix-net can replace the encrypted vote received from V_j with its forging vote $\{X, a_j^{-1}\}$ because S_Q knows a_j^{-1} and encryption keys of other servers are publicly known. Although $E(a_j^{-1}, X)$ may be invalid because S_Q does not know a_j, no one can notice that $\{X, a_j^{-1}\}$ is the replaced one when V_j that had put $\{E(a_j, v_j), a_j^{-1}\}$ does not verify its vote. Also, existence of the signature on a_j^{-1} makes the scheme coercible (not incoercible); a coercer can confirm that V_j actually behaved as it had asked by forcing V_j to show a_j^{-1}.

About the fairness, usually it is difficult to satisfy it for hidden voter schemes. Because votes are disclosed in their plain forms, voters may know partial tallying results, and when reelection is required because of accidents, e.g. when some voters claim that their votes had been illegitimately modified or deleted, choices of voters may be influenced. However, despite that the scheme discloses votes in their plain forms, it satisfies the fairness provided that base encryption functions are homomorphic and votes are decrypted after all voters had cast their votes, i.e. when authorities are honest, authorities can reject claims of voters because votes cannot be modified without being noticed by someone else once they had been put in the BB-2 and authorities can prove the correctness of their decryptions without disclosing their decryption keys (i.e. while preserving privacies of other voters) based on the verifiability of the encryption functions with homomorphic properties.

Hidden Vote

In a typical hidden vote scheme, voter V_j, of which eligibility is verified through a usual non-anonymous authentication scheme, casts its vote v_j in its encrypted form at the section assigned to it in the publicly disclosed BB. However election authorities do not decrypt individual votes in the BB, instead, while exploiting the homomorphism of the encryption functions they count votes in their encrypted forms and finally decrypt the counted results (Cohen (Benaloh), 1985, Cramer, 1997, Schoenmakers, 1999). Therefore, although anyone can know the correspondences between voters and their encrypted votes, voters can preserve their privacies. A scheme shown below is an example. In the example, threshold ElGamal is assumed as the base encryption mechanism. Where, although the example accepts only yes/no votes (i.e. it is for elections with 2 pre-specified candidates), it is possible to apply the scheme also to elections with more than 2 pre-specified candidates if increase of computation volume is allowed.

1. Announcement stage

Each S_q in a set of Q-election authorities generates its secret decryption key x_q and public encryption key $y_q = g^{xq}$, and common public encryption key y_* is defined as $y_* = y_1 y_2 \text{---} y_Q = g^{x1+x2+ \text{---} +xQ}$.

2. Pre-voting stage

Each voter V_j encrypts its vote v_j to $\{g^{aj}, B^{vj}y_*^{aj}\}$ while using its secret random number a_j, and the authorities verify the consistency of the encryption through ZKP (zero knowledge proof) processes. Here, B is an adequate constant integer and vote v_j takes 0 (no) or 1 (yes) as its value, therefore when the product of all encrypted votes is decrypted the result reveals the number of yes votes as discussed in the section "ElGamal" in Part I (the product of encrypted forms of B^{vj} and B^{vh} is decrypted to the sum of v_j and v_h). In the above, it must be noted that verification of $\{g^{aj}, B^{vj}y_*^{aj}\}$ is essential. If $\{g^{aj}, B^{vj}y_*^{aj}\}$ is not decrypted to 0 or 1, e.g. when $\{g^{aj}, B^{vj}y_*^{aj}\}$ is decrypted to a negative integer or an integer greater than 1, the decryption result of the product does not reveal the number of yes votes.

3. Voting stage

V_j proves its eligibility while showing its identity and casts its encrypted vote at the position in the BB assigned to it.

4. Tallying stage

A representative of the authorities calculates the product of encrypted votes in the BB. Then, t-authorities selected from the Q-authorities jointly decrypt the product to reveal the sum of yes votes, while proving their honesty by using ZKP or by exploiting the homomorphic feature of ElGamal encryption functions.

Because individual voters encrypt their votes by themselves and they are not decrypted individually, privacies of voters are preserved. ZKP processes or verifiable features of ElGamal encryption functions convince anyone that all t-authorities had honestly counted the sum of yes votes, namely the scheme is universally verifiable. Also, the scheme obviously achieves fairness; no interim tallying result is disclosed. About the receipt-freeness, although the scheme does not issue receipts explicitly it is not receipt-free, $\{g^{aj}, B^{vj}y_*^{aj}\}$ put at the position in the BB assigned to voter V_j works as a receipt. Namely, entity C that is coercing V_j can know whether V_j actually behaved as it had asked or not by forcing V_j to disclose a_j and v_j and calculate $\{g^{aj}, B^{vj}y_*^{aj}\}$ again by itself.

A drawback of this scheme is firstly ZKP processes for verifying correct encryptions of individual votes require tremendous computations. Also, it is applicable only to elections with pre-specified candidates, i.e. the scheme cannot accept free write-in ballots, because the number of votes for each candidate must be counted without decrypting individual votes. In addition, although it can accept not only yes/no votes but also all kind of votes for pre-specified candidates, the required computation volume increases as the number of candidates.

Hidden Voter with Hidden Vote

Hidden voter with hidden vote schemes are mixtures of hidden voter schems and hidden vote schemes, and combine their advantages (Fujioka, 1993, Golle, 2002, Park, 1994). Namely, they can satisfy requirements about privacy, universal verifiability and fairness without limiting elections to those for pre-specified candidates. Although several additional mechanisms are required they can also satisfy the receipt-freeness. A typical hidden voter with hidden vote scheme based on homomorphic encryption functions proceeds as below. As same as the previous hidden vote scheme, threshold ElGamal encryption functions are used also in this scheme, but votes are assumed as free write in ballots.

1. Announcement stage

Each S_q in a set of Q-election authorities generates its secret decryption key x_q and public encryption key $y_q = g^{xq}$, and common public key y_* is defined as $y_* = y_1y_2 \text{---} y_Q = g^{x1+x2+ \text{---} +xQ}$.

2. Pre-Voting stage

Each voter V_j encrypts its vote v_j to $\{g^{aj}, v_jy_*^{aj}\}$, where a_j is a random number secret of V_j.

3. Voting stage

V_j proves its eligibility while showing its identity and casts its vote at the position assigned to it in the 1st BB (BB-1), and the multiple authorities that constitute re-encryption type Mix-net encrypt it to $\{g^{aj+k1+k2+ \text{----} +kQ}, v_jy_*^{aj+k1+k2+ \text{----} +kQ}\}$ while shuffling it with other votes to disclose the results in the 2nd BB (BB-2). The authorities also prove their honest encryptions through ZKP processes.

4. Tallying stage

t-authorities selected from the Q-authorities jointly decrypt individual votes in BB-2 to reveal the election results, while proving their honest decryptions through ZKP processes.

As mentioned before hidden voter with hidden vote schemes combine advantages of the hidden voter scheme and the hidden vote scheme, therefore many of the requirements listed in the beginning of this section are satisfied by them while making vote forms flexible, e.g. not limiting elections to ones for pre-specified candidates. The main difference between the above scheme and the previous hidden vote scheme is that authorities in this scheme encrypt votes that had been encrypted by voters again at the voting stage while shuffling them. As a consequence, although voters show their identity and individual encrypted votes are finally decrypted in BB-2, links between voters and their votes can be concealed, i.e. voters can conceal not only their identities but also their votes.

However, authorities must prove their correct encryptions and decryptions through ZKP processes that require large volume of computations. Also, although it is possible to make the scheme receipt-free, they cannot satisfy complete incoercibility despite that incoercibility is an essential requirement for e-voting systems. Namely, different from conventional paper based voting systems where additional efforts are required for coercer Ce to confirm that voter V certainly behaved as it had asked, in e-voting systems, Ce can confirm that without fail if the underlying scheme is not incoercible. However, satisfying incoercibility is extremely difficult because they intrinsically contradict the verifiability, and although several e-voting systems achieve receipt-freeness and incoercibility, they require tremendous volume of computations, and they are also based on assumptions not practical enough.

DEVELOPMENT OF AN E-VOTING SYSTEM

In this section an e-voting system is developed based on probabilistic, commutative and verifiable re-encryption scheme supported by confirmation numbers (CNs) and signature pairs discussed in Part-II (Tamura, 2009). The developed system can be classified as a kind of hidden voter with hidden vote schemes and satisfies all the requirements for e-voting systems, i.e. it satisfies requirements about privacy, accuracy, verifiability, fairness, receipt-freeness, dispute-freeness, and robustness, under the assumption that at least one of multiple election authorities is honest. Also it is practical and scalable, it can handle any kind of vote forms including free write in ballots and does not include any ZKP process that requires tremendous computations. About the incoercibility, provided that there is at least one inferior candidate that can obtain apparently less votes compared with other candidates and also it is possible to force all voters to cast their votes (voters abstain from the election by casting invalid votes in this case), the scheme can protect voters from type-1, type-2 and type-3 threats even in elections that accept free write in ballots, although to exclude these threats is considered almost impossible if free write in ballots are accepted as discussed before. This chapter firstly develops an e-voting system that protects voters from type-1 and type-2 threats under the assumption that for every possible candidate X there is at least one voter who chooses it. An e-voting system that excludes this assumption and copes with also type-3 threats is developed after that.

Here, mechanisms that enable the scheme to efficiently satisfy the mutually contradicting requirements of e-voting systems are confirmation numbers (CNs) and signature pairs of multiple election authorities. CNs are registered and publicly disclosed unique numbers that are assigned to individual voters, and multiple election authorities repeatedly encrypt them so that no one can generate the encrypted forms illegitimately or know their decrypted forms unless all the authorities conspire. Therefore anyone including third parties can convince itself the authenticity of votes when decrypted forms of CNs attached to the votes reveal registered numbers. Also, by comparing CNs attached to votes with the registered ones disclosed in advance, anyone can confirm that only and all votes from eligible voters are counted. Nevertheless any link between voters and their votes is removed because no one including voters themselves knows the decrypted forms of CNs assigned to voters. Signature pairs of multiple election authorities on encrypted votes prove the authenticity of votes even when their decrypted forms reveal invalid candidates. Namely, anyone can convince itself that a vote with an invalid value was meaningless from the beginning when 2 different signatures on it reveal the same value, because no one can forge 2 different signatures consistently without conspiring with all authorities. The important thing is that different from schemes based on ZKP, the scheme based on CNs and signature pairs is simple enough, it requires much less computations for individual entities, i.e. it enables the development of e-voting systems that satisfy all the requirements while maintaining its scalability and practicality.

System Configuration

The e-voting system developed in this section consists of voters, multiple election authorities, and multiple BBs (bulletin boards) as shown in Figure 1, where the election authorities include voting manager VM, multiple mutually independent tallying managers TM_1, TM_2, ---, TM_Q, and vote disruption detection manager DM, and BBs include VoterList, TokenList, ConfNoList, ActiveTokenList, VotingPanel and TallyingPanel. Roles of voters and election authorities are as below.

Voter: voter V_j is characterized by its identifier ID_j and password PW_j, and has secret encryption and secret decryption key pair $\{a_j, \underline{a}_j\}$ for concealing its vote v_j from others at a time when it casts v_j.

Voting manager: Voting manager VM is responsible for authenticating voters, for issuing tokens so that voters can anonymously ask VM to cast and approve their votes, for assigning CNs and unknown random numbers to voters, and for casting encrypted votes in VotingPanel on behalf of voters. It can be constructed by multiple independent entities to distribute its trustworthiness if necessary.

Tallying managers: Tallying managers are responsible for encrypting votes to be cast in VotingPanel so that correspondences between voters and their votes are concealed, for signing on encrypted votes to ensure the accuracy of elections, and for decrypting encrypted votes to disclose the results in TallyingPanel. They also blindly sign on tokens shown by voters.

For $q > Z$, each tallying manager TM_q has 2 secret encryption and secret decryption key pairs $\{k_q, k_q^{-1}\}$ and $\{g_q, g_q^{-1}\}$ of encryption functions $E(k_q, x) = x^{kq}{}_{\text{mod p1}}$ and $E(g_q, y) = y^{gq}{}_{\text{mod p2}}$. For $q \leq Z$, TM_q has 2 secret signing and public verification key pairs $\{h_{1q}, \underline{h}_{1q}\}$ $\{h_{2q}, \underline{h}_{2q}\}$ of signing functions $S(h_{1q}, z)$ and $S(h_{2q}, z)$, and 4 secret signing and secret verification key pairs $\{s_{q1}, s_{q1}^{-1}\}$, $\{s_{q2}, s_{q2}^{-1}\}$, $\{t_{q1}, t_{q1}^{-1}\}$, $\{t_{q2}, t_{q2}^{-1}\}$ of signing functions $S(s_{q1}, x) = x^{s(q1)}{}_{\text{mod p1}}$, $S(s_{q2}, x) = x^{s(q2)}{}_{\text{mod p1}}$, $S(t_{q1}, y) = y^{t(q1)}{}_{\text{mod p2}}$ and $S(t_{q2}, y) = y^{t(q2)}{}_{\text{mod p2}}$. By keys h_{1q} and h_{2q}, TM_q ($q \leq Z$) blindly signs on tokens of voters. Encryption keys $\{k_Q, g_Q\}$, ---, $\{k_{Z+1}, g_{Z+1}\}$ of TM_Q, ---, TM_{Z+1} are used to encrypt votes to be cast in VotingPanel. TM_Z, ---, TM_1 sign on encrypted votes in VotingPanel by 2 signing key pairs $\{(s_{Z1}, t_{Z1}), (s_{Z2}, t_{Z2})\}$, ---, $\{(s_{11}, t_{11}), (s_{12}, t_{12})\}$, and decryption keys $\{k_{Z+1}^{-1}, g_{Z+1}^{-1}\}$, ---, $\{k_Q^{-1}, g_Q^{-1}\}$ of TM_{Z+1}, ---, TM_Q decrypt them to be disclosed in TallyingPanel. Then finally, 2 verification key pairs $\{(s_{11}^{-1}, t_{11}^{-1}), (s_{12}^{-1}, t_{12}^{-1})\}$, ---, $\{(s_{Z1}^{-1}, t_{Z1}^{-1}), (s_{Z2}^{-1}, t_{Z2}^{-1})\}$ of TM_1, ---, TM_Z are disclosed so that anyone can know the tallying results. Here, encryption and signing functions $E(k_{z+1}, x)$, ---, $E(k_Q, x)$, $S(s_{11}, x)$, ---, $S(s_{Z1}, x)$, $S(s_{12}, x)$, ---, $S(s_{Z2}, x)$ and also $E(g_{z+1}, x)$, ---, $E(g_Q, x)$, $S(t_{11}, x)$, ---, $S(t_{Z1}, x)$, $S(t_{12}, x)$, ---, $S(t_{Z2}, x)$ are commutative.

Vote disruption detection manager: Vote disruption detection manager DM detects inconsistent votes in TallyingPanel, and when inconsistencies are detected it identifies the entities liable for the inconsistencies.

Figure 1. Configuration of e-voting system

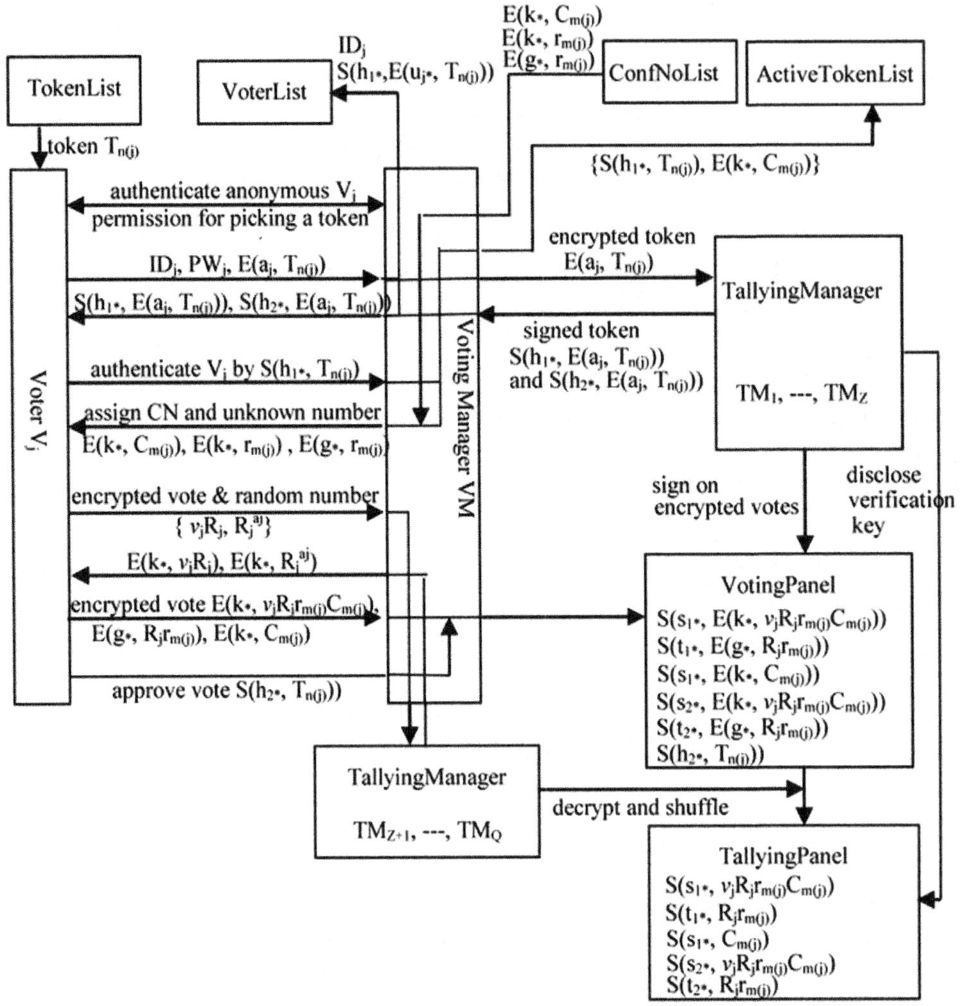

These entities behave through the following 6 stages.

1. Preliminary stage: Objectives of this stage are to prepare CNs and unknown random numbers. Namely, confirmation numbers C_1, C_2, ---, C_N and their repeatedly encrypted forms $E(k_*, C_1), E(k_*, C_2)$, ---, $E(k_*, C_N)$ calculated by multiple tallying managers TM_Q, TM_{Q-1}, ---, TM_{Z+1} are disclosed in the ConfNoList in the way that no one can know the correspondence between each C_j and $E(k_*, C_j)$. Tallying managers also generate $\{E(k_*, r_1), E(g_*, r_1)\}, \{E(k_*, r_2), E(g_*, r_2)\}$, ---, $\{E(k_*, r_N), E(g_*, r_N)\}$, repeatedly encrypted form pairs of random numbers r_1, r_2, ---, r_N so that no one can know their decrypted values. Here, N is the number of voters, and $E(k_*, x) = E(k_{Z+1}, E(k_{Z+2}, \text{---} E(k_Q, x) \text{---}))$ and $E(g_*, x) = E(g_{Z+1}, E(g_{Z+2}, \text{---} E(g_Q, x) \text{---}))$.
2. Token acquisition stage: An objective of this stage is to assign token $T_{n(j)}$ which is unique in the system to voter V_j so that V_j can behave anonymously later on. First of all, V_j obtains $T_{n(j)}$ from TokenLIst in advance without disclosing its identity, where,

$n(j)$ means that V_j had picked $n(j)$-th token from TokenList. Then, voting manager VM, while verifying the eligibility of V_j based on its ID and password pair $\{ID_j, PW_j\}$, asks each tallying manager TM_q $(1 \leq q \leq Z)$ to blindly sign on $T_{n(j)}$ by its 2 signing keys h_{1q} and h_{2q} so that V_j can obtain the 1st and the 2nd signatures $S(h_{1q}, T_{n(j)})$ and $S(h_{2q}, T_{n(j)})$ by decrypting the encrypted signatures. At the same time, VM discloses ID_j and the 1st encrypted signed token of V_j in VoterList. Therefore, anyone including third parties can know that V_j had obtained signatures on its token, but no one except V_j can know $T_{n(j)}$, because the signature disclosed in VoterList is encrypted by V_j itself. Nevertheless, by showing sets of signatures $S(h_{1*}, T_{n(j)}) = \{S(h_{11}, T_{n(j)}), ---, S(h_{1Z}, T_{n(j)})\}$ and $S(h_{2*}, T_{n(j)}) = \{S(h_{21}, T_{n(j)}), ---, S(h_{2Z}, T_{n(j)})\}$, V_j can prove its eligibility for casting and approving its vote without disclosing its identity, because signature sets $S(h_{1*}, T_{n(j)})$ and $S(h_{2*}, T_{n(j)})$ cannot be generated illegitimately unless all TM_1, ---, TM_Z conspire.

3. Pre-voting stage: Objectives of this stage are to assign encrypted CNs and unknown random numbers to individual voters and to disclose the assignment in ActiveTokenList. Namely, each voter V_j obtains encrypted confirmation number $E(k_*, C_{m(j)})$ and $E(k_*, r_{m(j)})$, $E(g_*, r_{m(j)})$, 2-encrypted forms of unknown random number $r_{m(j)}$, from voting manager VM while proving its eligibility by showing its 1st signed token $S(h_{1*}, T_{n(j)})$. Then VM discloses pair $\{S(h_{1*}, T_{n(j)}), E(k_*, C_{m(j)})\}$ in ActiveTokenList, therefore, although V_j is anonymous anyone can know that $E(k_*, C_{m(j)})$, $E(k_*, r_{m(j)})$ and $E(g_*, r_{m(j)})$ are assigned to a single and eligible voter. However, no one can identify V_j from $C_{m(j)}$ or $r_{m(j)}$ at a time when $E(k_*, C_{m(j)})$, $E(k_*, r_{m(j)})$ and $E(g_*, r_{m(j)})$ are decrypted, because no one knows decrypted values of $E(k_*, C_{m(j)})$, $E(k_*, r_{m(j)})$, or $E(g_*, r_{m(j)})$ unless all tallying managers TM_{Z+1}, ---, TM_Q conspire. Here, notation $m(j)$ means that VM had assigned the $m(j)$-th encrypted CN and encrypted unknown random number to V_j.

4. Voting stage: Objectives of this stage are to enable voters to cast their votes while concealing their vote values, and to make individual votes verifiable. Here, a verifiable vote means that anyone including third parties can confirm that the vote is the one certainly cast by an eligible voter. Firstly, each voter V_j generates its secret number R_j and encrypts its vote v_j to triple $\{E(k_*, v_jR_jr_{m(j)}C_{m(j)}), E(g_*, R_jr_{m(j)}), E(k_*, C_{m(j)})\}$ while asking tallying managers TM_Q, ---, TM_{Z+1} without disclosing v_j itself by concealing it as v_jR_j (every encryption or signing function is multiplicative, therefore V_j can multiply the encryption result of v_jR_j by $E(k_*, C_{m(j)})$, $E(k_*, r_{m(j)})$ and $E(g_*, r_{m(j)})$ to construct $\{E(k_*, v_jR_jr_{m(j)}C_{m(j)}), E(g_*, R_jr_{m(j)}), E(k_*, C_{m(j)})\}$), therefore, no one except V_j can know v_j. After that, VM puts the encrypted vote in VotingPanel, and tallying managers TM_Z, ---, TM_1 repeatedly sign on the triple to generate $\{S(s_{*1}, E(k_*, v_jR_jr_{m(j)}C_{m(j)})), S(t_{*1}, E(g_*, R_jr_{m(j)})), S(s_{*1}, E(k_*, C_{m(j)})), S(s_{*2}, E(k_*, v_jR_jr_{m(j)}C_{m(j)})), S(t_{*2}, E(g_*, R_jr_{m(j)}))\}$ by using their 4 signing keys, where for j = 1, 2, $S(s_{*j}, x) = S(s_{1j}, S(s_{2j}, ---, S(s_{Zj}, x)---))$, $S(t_{*j}, y) = S(t_{1j}, S(t_{2j}, ---, S(t_{Zj}, y)---))$. Then finally after verifying its vote, V_j puts its 2nd signed token $S(h_{2*}, T_{n(j)})$ in VotingPanel as its approval. Here, as mentioned already every encryption or signing function is homomorhic (multiplicative) and consequently verifiable, therefore individual voters can verify their votes in VotingPanel without knowing encryption or signing keys of tallying managers. As a consequence, anyone can convince that all votes in VotingPanel are legitimate when they are attached by 2nd signed tokens of voters, despite that no

one can know decrypted forms of votes in VotingPanel.

5. Tallying stage: Objectives of this stage are to decrypt all encrypted votes in VotingPanel and to disclose the results in TallyingPanel. Namely, multiple independent tallying managers TM_{Z+1}, ---, TM_Q repeatedly decrypt encrypted votes while shuffling their interim decryption results, and TM_1, ---, TM_Z disclose their verification keys, therefore, no one can know correspondences between encrypted votes cast by individual voters in VotingPanel and decrypted votes in TallyingPanel, i.e. between voters and their votes. Nevertheless, it is ensured that the tallying is accurate. Anyone can know plain forms of individual votes by the disclosed verification keys, and unique and registered confirmation numbers attached to individual decrypted votes and consistent signature pairs on them convince anyone that the tallying includes only and all votes cast by eligible voters.
6. Disrupted vote detection stage: If inconsistent votes are disclosed in TallyingPanel, the liable entities for the inconsistencies are identified while maintaining the privacies of honest voters.

As shown in the above, information exchanged between entities in individual stages is disclosed in the corresponding BBs listed below so that no one can modify the information illegitimately without being noticed by others once it had been approved by relevant entities.

A. VoterList: It consists of the ID and the token parts. The ID part maintains IDs of eligible voters, and as the token part value corresponding to V_j's ID, VM puts the 1st signatures of tallying managers TM_Z, ---, TM_1 on token $T_{n(j)}$ of voter V_j encrypted by V_j itself as shown in Figure 2 (a). Therefore anyone can know voters who had acquired signatures on their tokens. However no one except voters themselves can know their tokens.
B. TokenList: TokenList consists of the token and the flag parts, and enables voters to acquire tokens without collision. The token part maintains open tokens, and when voter V_j picks unused token $T_{n(j)}$ from this table anonymously, VM makes the corresponding flag part used as shown in Figure 2 (b).
C. ConfNoList: It consists of the plain CN, the encrypted CN and the random number parts, and for N-voters, N-different numbers C_1, C_2, ---, C_N are generated as the registered CNs and arrayed in the plain CN part. Then, each C_j is repeatedly encrypted to $E(k_*, C_j)$ by tallying managers TM_Q, ---, TM_{Z+1} while being shuffled with other encrypted CNs to be cast at a random position in the encrypted CN part. At the same time, TM_Q, ---, TM_{Z+1} generate a pair of repeatedly encrypted forms $\{E(k_*, r_j), E(g_*, r_j)\}$ of unknown random number r_j to be attached to $E(k_*, C_j)$ as shown in Figure 2 (c).
D. ActiveTokenList: It consists of the token and the CN parts, and enables anyone to know anonymous voters to whom VM had assigned encrypted CNs. The n(j)-th position of the token part maintains the 1st signed form of the n(j)-th token $T_{n(j)}$ i.e. $S(h_{1*}, T_{n(j)})$. The corresponding CN part maintains $E(k_*, C_{m(j)})$ assigned to the voter who had obtained $T_{n(j)}$ as shown in Figure 2 (d). Then, by comparing items in ActiveTokenList, ConfNoList and VoterList, anyone can verify that CNs were assigned only to eligible voters who had obtained signed tokens, and VM did not misuse or add any extra CN illegitimately.
E. VotingPanel: VotingPanel consists of the vote and the approval parts, and enables anyone to know that voters had certainly approved their votes disclosed in it. The vote part corresponding to the n(j)-th position maintains 2 signed forms of $\{E(k_*, v_jR_jr_{m(j)}C_{m(j)}),$

$E(g_*, R_j r_{m(j)})$, $E(k_*, C_{m(j)})$}, the encrypted vote of anonymous voter V_j that possesses token $T_{n(j)}$. Namely it maintains {$S(s_{*1}, E(k_*, v_j R_j r_{m(j)} C_{m(j)}))$, $S(t_{*1}, E(g_*, R_j r_{m(j)}))$, $S(s_{*1}, E(k_*, C_{m(j)}))$, $S(s_{*2}, E(k_*, v_j R_j r_{m(j)} C_{m(j)}))$, $S(t_{*2}, E(g_*, R_j r_{m(j)}))$}, and the approval part maintains $S(h_{2*}, T_{n(j)})$, the 2nd signed form of $T_{n(j)}$ as shown in Figure 2 (e).

F. TallyingPanel: TallyingPanel consists of the vote part and the CN part and enables anyone to know the election results. It maintains decrypted data of those in VotingPanel i.e. for each vote v_j, vote part maintains {$S(s_{*1}, v_j R_j r_{m(j)} C_{m(j)})$, $S(t_{*1}, R_j r_{m(j)})$, $S(s_{*2}, v_j R_j r_{m(j)} C_{m(j)})$, $S(t_{*2}, R_j r_{m(j)})$} and the CN part maintains $S(s_{*1}, C_{m(j)})$ as shown in Figure 2 (f). Here, anyone can know v_j from its signed forms in TallyingPanel when Tallying managers TM_Z, ---, TM_1 disclose their verification keys.

In the above, V_j encrypts its vote v_j by its secret key before multiple tallying managers repeatedly encrypt it. Also individual tallying managers that do not know decryption keys of other managers repeatedly decrypt encrypted votes while shuffling them. In addition, no one knows the value of $R_j r_{m(j)}$ or $C_{m(j)}$ attached to v_j. Therefore, no one other than V_j itself can know vote v_j, even V_j itself cannot know the correspondence between its encrypted vote in VotingPanel and the decrypted vote in TallyingPanel either. Nevertheless, accuracy of decrypted votes in TallyingPanel is ensured. Firstly, although votes in Voting Panel are encrypted by tallying managers, verifiable encryption and signing functions enable anyone to convince itself that individual votes in VotingPanl that were verified by voters themselves are valid when they are accompanied by 1st signed tokens of voters, and secondly, anyone can convince itself that only and all votes in VotingPanel are disclosed in TallyingPanel when all votes in TallyingPanel are accompanied by different registered CNs and all registered CNs appear, because no one can generate repeatedly signed forms of CNs illegitimately. In addition, consistent signature pairs ensure that even meaningless votes are valid ones.

However it must be noted that token $T_{n(j)}$ cannot disable entities to know whether V_j had abstained from the election or not although $T_{n(j)}$ is anonymous. Entity Ce that is coercing V_j can ask V_j to disclose its token $T_{n(j)}$, and can confirm that V_j had actually abstained or not. Therefore, kind of regulations to force all voters to cast their votes are necessary to protect voters from type-1 threats, and in this case, V_j can abstain from the election without being noticed by others by casting a meaningless vote.

Following subsections describe the details of individual stages.

Preliminary Stage

Voting manager VM and mutually independent multiple tallying managers TM_Q, ---, TM_{Z+1} prepare repeatedly encrypted CNs and unknown random numbers through the following steps.

1. VM generates N unique numbers C_1, C_2, ---, C_N (N is the number of voters) and discloses them in the plain CN part of ConfNoList.
2. TM_Q, ---, TM_{Z+1} repeatedly encrypt C_1, C_2, ---, C_N by their secret encryption keys k_Q, ---, k_{Z+1} while shuffling their interim encryption results to put the final results at random positions in the encrypted CN part of ConfNoList.
3. Each TM_q ($Z+1 \leq q \leq Q$) generates its secret numbers r_{1q}, ---, r_{Nq}, and encrypts them by its encryption key k_q and g_q to $E(k_q, r_{1q})$, ---, $E(k_q, r_{Nq})$ and $E(g_q, r_{1q})$, ---, $E(g_q, r_{Nq})$ to send them to TM_Q, ---, TM_{q+1}, TM_{q-1}, ---, TM_{Z+1}.
4. TM_Q, ---, TM_{q+1}, TM_{q-1}, ---, TM_{Z+1} that receive $E(k_q, r_{1q})$, ---, $E(k_q, r_{Nq})$ and $E(g_q, r_{1q})$, ---, $E(g_q, r_{Nq})$ from TM_q repeatedly encrypt them to $E(k_*, r_{1q})$, ---, $E(k_*, r_{Nq})$ and $E(g_*, r_{1q})$, ---, $E(g_*, r_{Nq})$.

Figure 2. BBs in e-voting system

ID	token
ID_1	$S(h_{1*}, E(u_{u1*}, T_{n(1)}))$
ID_2	$S(h_{1*}, E(u_{u2*}, T_{n(2)}))$
⋮	⋮

(a)VoterList

token	flag
T_1	unused
T_2	used
⋮	⋮

(b) TokenList

plainCN	encryptedCN	random number
C_1	$E(k_*, C_{p1})$	$E(k_*, r_{p1}), E(g_*, r_{p1})$
C_2	$E(k_*, C_{p1})$	$E(k_*, r_{p2}), E(g_*, r_{p2})$
⋮	⋮	⋮

(c) ConfNoList

token	CN
$S(h_{1*}, T_1)$	$E(k_*, C_{q1})$
$S(h_{1*}, T_2)$	$E(k_*, C_{q2})$
⋮	⋮

(d) ActiveTokenList

Vote	approval
$S(s_{*1},E(k_*,v_{h1}R_{h1}r_{q1}C_{q1}))$, $S(t_{*1},E(g_*,R_{h1}r_{q1}))$, $S(s_{*1},E(k_*,C_{q1}))$, $S(s_{*2},E(k_*,v_{h1}R_{h1}r_{q1}C_{q1}))$, $S(t_{*2},E(g_*,R_{h1}r_{q1}))$	$S(h_{2*}, T_1)$
$S(s_{*1},E(k_*,v_{h2}R_{h2}r_{q2}C_{q2}))$, $S(t_{*1},E(g_*,R_{h2}r_{q2}))$, $S(s_{*1},E(k_*,C_{q2}))$, $S(s_{*2},E(k_*,v_{h2}R_{h2}r_{q2}C_{q2}))$, $S(t_{*2},E(g_*,R_{h2}r_{q2}))$	$S(h_{2*}, T_2)$
⋮	⋮

(e) VotingPanel

Vote	CN
$S(s_{*1},v_{g1}R_{g1}r_{w1}C_{w1})$, $S(t_{*1},R_{g1}r_{w1})$, $S(s_{*2},v_{g1}R_{g1}r_{w1}C_{w1})$, $S(t_{*2},R_{g1}r_{w1})$	$S(s_{*1},C_{w1})$
$S(s_{*1},v_{g2}R_{g2}r_{w2}C_{w2})$, $S(t_{*1},R_{g2}r_{w2})$, $S(s_{*2},v_{g2}R_{g2}r_{w2}C_{w2})$, $S(t_{*2},R_{g2}r_{w2})$	$S(s_{*1},C_{w2})$
⋮	⋮

(f) TallyingPanel

5. TM_{Z+1}, the representative of TM_Q, ---, TM_{Z+1}, calculates $E(k_*, r_{j(Z+1)})E(k_*, r_{j(Z+2)})$---$E(k_*, r_{jQ}) = E(k_*, r_{j(Z+1)}r_{j(Z+2)}$---$r_{jQ}) = E(k_*, r_j)$ and $E(g_*, r_{j(Z+1)})E(g_*, r_{j(Z+2)})$---$E(g_*, r_{jQ}) = E(g_*, r_{j(Z+1)}r_{j(Z+2)}$---$r_{jQ}) = E(g_*, r_j)$ for each j (j = 1, 2, ---, N) while exploiting the homomorphism of $E(k_*, x)$ and $E(g_*, x)$, and puts it at a random position in the random number part of ConfNoList.

In the above, CN_j changes its form $E(k_Q, C_j)$ to $E(k_{Q-1}, E(k_Q, C_j))$, ---, $E(k_*, C_j)$ while being shuffled with other encrypted CNs, and each TM_q does not know encryption or decryption keys of other tallying managers, therefore no one can know correspondences between individual CNs and their encrypted forms unless all tallying managers conspire. By the same reason, no one can know the decrypted value of each $E(k_*, r_j)$ or

$E(g_{*}, r_j)$ when at least one TM_q is honest. Security problems at this stage can be solved as follows.

A. Tallying managers may encrypt CNs dishonestly: It is not necessary to verify the correct encryptions of each C_j at this stage. At the later stage $E(k_{*}, C_j)$ is signed by TM_Z, ---, TM_1 to generate $S(s_{*1}, E(k_{*}, C_j))$, and TM_Q, ---, TM_{Z+1} decrypt $S(s_{*1}, E(k_{*}, C_j))$ to $S(s_{*1}, C_j)$, where $S(s_{*1}, C_j)$ cannot be generated illegitimately provided that at least one of TM_Z, ---, TM_1 is honest (i.e. at least one of tallying managers does not reveal its secret signing key). Therefore, $E(k_{*}, C_j)$ is not an honest encrypted form if decryption result $S(s_{*1}, C_j)$ does not reveal any confirmation number defined in ConfNoList or $S(s_{*1}, C_j)$ appears multiple times in TallyingPanel. In a case when $E(k_{*}, C_j)$ is determined as illegitimate, liable tallying managers can be identified at the disrupted vote detection stage.

B. Tallying managers may encrypt unknown random numbers dishonestly: When one of TM_Q, ---, TM_{Z+1} calculates $E(k_{*}, r_{jq})$ and $E(g_{*}, r_{jq})$ in the way that they are decrypted to different values, a vote of the voter to whom unknown random number $r_j = r_{j(Z+1)}r_{j(Z+2)}$---$r_{jQ}$ is assigned may become invalid. However, individual voters verify correct encryptions of their unknown random numbers at the pre-voting stage; therefore, verifications of their correct encryptions are not necessary at this stage.

Token Acquisition Stage

Token acquisition stage consists of the following 8 steps.

1. Voting manager VM authenticates anonymous voter V_j through an appropriate anonymous authentication scheme, and V_j picks unused token $T_{n(j)}$ from TokenList prepared by VM.
2. V_j proves its eligibility by showing its ID and password pair $\{ID_j, PW_j\}$.
3. V_j encrypts $T_{n(j)}$ to $E(u_{j*}, T_{n(j)}) = \{u_{j1}h^{11}T_{n(j)}, u_{j2}h^{12}T_{n(j)}, ---, u_{jZ}h^{1Z}T_{n(j)}\}$ and $E(w_{j*}, T_{n(j)}) = \{w_{j1}h^{21}T_{n(j)}, w_{j2}h^{22}T_{n(j)}, ---, w_{jZ}h^{2Z}T_{n(j)}\}$ by multiplying $T_{n(j)}$ by $\{u_{j1}h^{11}, u_{j2}h^{12}, ---, u_{jZ}h^{1Z}\}$ and $\{w_{j1}h^{21}, w_{j2}h^{22}, ---, w_{jZ}h^{2Z}\}$, where $\{u_{j1}, u_{j2}, ---, u_{jZ}\}$ and $\{w_{j1}, w_{j2}, ---, w_{jZ}\}$ are random numbers secret of V_j (secret key of V_j), and $\{h_{1q}, \underline{h}_{1q}\}$and $\{h_{2q}, \underline{h}_{2q}\}$ are secret signing and public verification key pairs of TM_q, therefore they satisfy relations $x^{h1}qh1q = 1$ and $x^{h2}qh2q = 1$ for any x.
4. Each TM_q ($1 \leq q \leq Z$) signs on each $E(u_{jq}, T_{n(j)}) = u_{jq}{}^{h1q}T_{n(j)}$ and $E(w_{jq}, T_{n(j)}) = w_{jq}h2^{q}T_{n(j)}$ by its signing key h_{1q} and h_{2q}, i.e. it calculates $S(h_{1q}, E(u_{jq}, T_{n(j)})) = u_{jq}{}^{(h1q)(h1q)}T_{n(j)}{}^{h1q} = u_{jq}T_{n(j)}{}^{h1q}$ and $S(h_{2q}, E(u_{jq}, T_{n(j)})) = w_{jq}{}^{(h2q)(h2q)}T_{n(j)}{}^{h2q} = w_{jq}T_{n(j)}{}^{h2q}$.
5. VM gathers signatures $S(h_{11}, E(u_{j1}, T_{n(j)}))$, ---, $S(h_{1Z}, E(u_{jZ}, T_{n(j)}))$ and $S(h_{21}, E(w_{j1}, T_{n(j)}))$, ---, $S(h_{2Z}, E(w_{jZ}, T_{n(j)}))$ from TM_1, ---, TM_Z to construct $S(h_{1*}, E(u_{j*}, T_{n(j)})) = \{S(h_{11}, E(u_{j1}, T_{n(j)}))$, ---, $S(h_{1Z}, E(u_{jZ}, T_{n(j)}))\}$ and $S(h_{2*}, E(w_{j*}, T_{n(j)})) = \{S(h_{21}, E(w_{j1}, T_{n(j)}))$, ---, $S(h_{2Z}, E(w_{jZ}, T_{n(j)}))\}$.
6. VM discloses pair $\{ID_j, S(h_{1*}, E(u_{j*}, T_{n(j)}))\}$ in VoterList.
7. For each q, V_j decrypts $S(h_{1q}, E(u_{jq}, T_{n(j)}))$ and $S(h_{2q}, E(w_{jq}, T_{n(j)}))$ to $S(h_{1q}, T_{n(j)})$ and $S(h_{2q}, T_{n(j)})$, i.e. divides each $u_{jq}T_{n(j)}{}^{h1q}$ and $w_{jq}T_{n(j)}{}^{h2q}$ by u_{jq} and w_{jq} to generate $T_{n(j)}{}^{h1q}$ and $T_{n(j)}{}^{h2q}$. As a consequence, V_j obtains $S(h_{1*}, T_{n(j)})$ and $S(h_{2*}, T_{n(j)})$, 2 different signatures of TM_1, ---, TM_Z on $T_{n(j)}$.
8. V_j verifies the correctness of signatures on $T_{n(j)}$.

About step 1, voting manager VM prepares TokenList filled by different tokens in advance. Here, tokens in TokenList are open tokens and signatures of VM on them are only for maintaining the uniqueness of tokens, i.e. they become effective after step 4. Therefore, theoretically VM does not need to authenticate V_j. The reason why VM authenticates voters at step 1 is to make TokenList as small as possible, i.e. this authentication process disables unauthorized entities to request tokens. However, eligible voters may pick multiple tokens because voters are anonymous, therefore VM must prepare more than N-tokens (N is the number of eligible voters). Here, although VM signs on open token $T_{n(j)}$ at step 1, this signature is omitted from notations in this chapter.

From step 3 to 7 are procedures for the blind signature scheme, i.e. tallying managers sign on $T_{n(j)}$ without knowing its value, therefore, later on V_j can prove its eligibility to cast and approve its vote by showing signed tokens $S(h_{1*}, T_{n(j)})$ and $S(h_{2*}, T_{n(j)})$ without revealing its identity. Here, pair $\{ID_j, S(h_{1*}, E(u_{j*}, T_{n(j)}))\}$ disclosed in VoterList enables anyone including third parties to know voters who had obtained signatures on their tokens. It must be noted that anyone cannot generate consistent signatures $S(h_{1*}, T_{n(j)})$ or $S(h_{2*}, T_{n(j)})$ illegitimately unless all TM_1, ---, TM_Z conspire. Nevertheless, V_j can verify the validity of $S(h_{1*}, T_{n(j)})$ or $S(h_{2*}, T_{n(j)})$ easily because verification keys are publicly known.

Security problems of this stage are solved as below.

A. Voter V_j may pick multiple open tokens from TokenList: Because only tokens with signatures of tallying managers are effective, and tallying managers sign on an open token after the eligibility of V_j is confirmed at step 2, V_j can use only a single token even it obtains multiple open tokens.

B. Voting manager VM may reject requests from V_j to access TokenList: Because multiple tokens cause no inconvenience as mentioned just above, voter V_j can pick tokens repeatedly until it successfully obtains a token.

C. An entity other than V_j may request signatures on open token $T_{n(j)}$ picked by V_j: Because open tokens shown by voters are encrypted by voters themselves, tallying manages may sign on same open token $T_{n(j)}$ repeatedly, and when voter V_i uses $S(h_{1*}, T_{n(j)})$ before V_j, V_j cannot participate in the election. However, V_i can obtain $T_{n(j)}$ that V_j had already picked from TokenList only when it is conspiring with voting manager VM. Therefore if necessary, this threat can be removed by constructing VM as a set of multiple mutually independent authorities, i.e. V_i can obtain $T_{n(j)}$ that had been picked by V_j only when all authorities that constitute VM are conspiring.

D. V_j cannot obtain correct signed token $S(h_{1*}, T_{n(j)})$ or $S(h_{2*}, T_{n(j)})$ from VM: It is possible for VM to put $\{ID_j, X\}$ in VoterList instead of $\{ID_j, S(h_{1*}, E(u_{j*}, T_{n(j)}))\}$ without the permission of V_j. In this case, V_j is regarded as a voter who had already obtained its signed token, and as a consequence, it cannot obtain signed token $S(h_{1*}, T_{n(j)})$ to participate in the election. This dishonesty can be disabled also by constituting VM as a set of multiple independent authorities.

Pre-Voting Stage

To assign CNs and unknown random numbers to anonymous voters, voter V_j and voting manager VM interact through the following steps.

1. V_j asks VM to assign a CN and an encrypted unknown random number to it.
2. VM gives unused encrypted CN and encrypted unknown random number $E(k_*, C_{m(j)})$, $E(k_*, r_{m(j)})$ and $E(g_*, r_{m(j)})$ to V_j.
3. V_j verifies the correctness of $E(k_*, r_{m(j)})$ and $E(g_*, r_{m(j)})$.
4. V_j shows signed token $S(h_{1*}, T_{n(j)})$ to VM, and VM verifies the validity of $S(h_{1*}, T_{n(j)})$.
5. VM puts pair $\{S(h_{1*}, T_{n(j)}), E(k_*, C_{m(j)})\}$ in ActiveTokenList.

At step 4, VM can verify the eligibility of V_j by checking the signatures on $T_{n(j)}$ that was not used before without identifying V_j, because only eligible voters can obtain tokens signed by tallying managers. Also at step 3, V_j can verify that $E(k_*, r_{m(j)})$ and $E(g_*, r_{m(j)})$ are encrypted forms of a same unknown random number by asking tallying managers TM_{Z+1}, ---, TM_Q to decrypt randomly selecting encrypted number pair $\{E(k_*, r_{m(j)q}), E(g_*, r_{m(j)q})\}$ that were generated by tallying manager TM_q to constitute $\{E(k_*, r_{m(j)}), E(g_*, r_{m(j)})\}$, i.e. when both $E(k_*, r_{m(j)q})$ and $E(g_*, r_{m(j)q})$ are decrypted to same value $r_{m(j)q}$, V_j can convince itself that other pair $\{E(k_*, r_{m(j)h}), E(g_*, r_{m(j)h})\}$ $(h \neq q)$ that constitute $\{E(k_*, r_{m(j)}), E(g_*, r_{m(j)})\}$ is also decrypted to same value $r_{m(j)h}$, because to encrypt them dishonestly TM_h must take a risk that its dishonesty is revealed when V_j asks to decrypt pair $\{E(k_*, r_{m(j)h}), E(g_*, r_{m(j)h})\}$. In this process each tallying manager TM_q cannot decrypt $\{E(k_*, r_{m(j)q}), E(g_*, r_{m(j)q})\}$ dishonestly because $E(k_*, x)$ and $E(g_*, y)$ are verifiable.

Security problems of this stage are as follows.

A. Voter V_j, to whom $E(k_*, C_{m(j)})$, $E(k_*, r_{m(j)q})$, $E(g_*, r_{m(j)q})$ had been assigned already, may illegitimately obtain $E(k_*, C_x)$, $E(k_*, r_x)$, $E(g_*, r_x)$ while disconnecting communication channel between it and VM before step 4: VM registers $S(h_{1*}, T_{n(1)})$ and $E(k_*, C_{m(j)})$ that V_j legitimately obtained in ActiveTokenList and V_j cast its vote in the voting stage while showing both $S(h_{1*}, T_{n(1)})$ and $E(k_*, C_{m(j)})$, therefore, VM can reject V_j's vote accompanied by $S(h_{1*}, T_{n(1)})$ and illegitimate $E(k_*, C_x)$, $E(k_*, r_x)$, $E(g_*, r_x)$.

B. VM may put signed tokens in ActiveTokenList before V_j: When VM that can access ActiveTokenList puts $\{S(h_{1*}, T_{n(1)}), E(k_*, C_x)\}$ without V_j's permission, VM can cast a vote by using $S(h_{1*}, T_{n(1)})$ and $E(k_*, C_x)$ on behalf of V_j, as a consequence V_j cannot participate in the election. However, VM knows neither secret keys $\{u_{j1}, ---, u_{jZ}\}$, $\{w_{j1}, ---, w_{jZ}\}$ nor signing keys of TM_1, ---, TM_Z, therefore it cannot generate consistent signatures $S(h_{1*}, T_{n(1)})$ until V_j discloses it. Namely, it is impossible for VM to put consistent signatures in ActiveTokenList without V_j's permission unless it conspires with all TM_1, ---, TM_Z.

C. V_j cannot obtain encrypted $E(k_*, C_{m(j)})$ or $\{E(k_*, r_{m(j)}), E(g_*, r_{m(j)})\}$: There is no inconvenience to assign identical $E(k_*, C_{m(j)})$, $E(k_*, r_{m(j)})$ and $E(g_*, r_{m(j)})$ to V_j repeatedly, because all encrypted confirmation numbers and unknown random numbers are publicly disclosed in ConfNoList and all assignment results are disclosed in ActiveTokenList. This means that V_j that possesses consistent $S(h_{1*}, T_{n(j)})$ can ask VM to assign $E(k_*, C_{m(j)})$ and $\{E(k_*, r_{m(j)}), E(g_*, r_{m(j)})\}$ repeatedly until it successfully obtains them.

D. VM gives incorrect $E(k_*, C_{m(j)})$ or $\{E(k_*, r_{m(j)}), E(g_*, r_{m(j)})\}$ to V_j: Because $E(k_*, C_{m(j)})$, $E(k_*, r_{m(j)})$ and $E(g_*, r_{m(j)})$ are publicly disclosed in ConfNoList, VM cannot give non-registered $E(k_*, C_{m(j)})$ or $\{E(k_*, r_{m(j)}), E(g_*, r_{m(j)})\}$ to a voter, or give same $E(k_*, C_{m(j)})$ or $\{E(k_*, r_{m(j)}), E(g_*, r_{m(j)})\}$ to different voters. Although it is possible for tallying managers to encrypt $C_{m(j)}$ incorrectly, this dishonesty and the liable entities are detected at the disrupted vote detection stage. Also, V_j can detect incorrect encryptions of $E(k_*, r_{m(j)})$ and $E(g_*, r_{m(j)})$ at step 3.

Voting Stage

The voting stage consists of 5 steps, and they proceed as follows.

1. Voter V_j generates its secret random number R_j to calculate v_jR_j and R_j^{aj} and asks TM_Q, ---, TM_{Z+1} to encrypt them into $E(k_*, v_jR_j)$ and $E(g_*, R_j^{aj})$. After that, V_j decrypts $E(g_*, R_j^{aj})$ to $E(g_*, R_j)$, i.e. based on the homomorphism of $E(g_*, x)$, it calculates $E(g_*, R_j^{aj})^{aj} = E(g_*,$

$R_j^{a_j a_j}$) = E(g_*, R_j), where a_j and a_j are the secret encryption and decryption key pair of V_j, i.e. $y^{a_j a_j} = 1$ for any *y*. As a consequence, V_j obtains pair {E(k_*, v_jR_j), E(g_*, R_j)}.

2. V_j verifies the correctness of {E(k_*, v_jR_j), E(g_*, R_j)}, and calculates E(k_*, v_jR_j)E(k_*, $r_{m(j)}$) E(k_*, $C_{m(j)}$) = E(k_*, $v_jR_jr_{m(j)}C_{m(j)}$) and E(g_*, R_j) E(g_*, $r_{m(j)}$) = E(g_*, $R_jr_{m(j)}$) while exploiting the homomorphism of E(k_*, *x*) and E(g_*, *x*) to construct its vote as triple {E(k_*, $v_jR_jr_{m(j)}C_{m(j)}$), E(g_*, $R_jr_{m(j)}$), E(k_*, $C_{m(j)}$)}. Then, VM casts V_j's vote at the position in VotingPanel corresponding to token $T_{n(j)}$.
3. Each tallying manager TM_q (1≤ q≤ Z) repeatedly signs on {E(k_*, $v_jR_jr_{m(j)}C_{m(j)}$), E(g_*, $R_jr_{m(j)}$), E(k_*, $C_{m(j)}$)} in VotingPanel by its 1st signing keys s_{q1} and t_{q1} to generate {S(s_{*1}, E(k_*, $v_jR_jr_{m(j)}C_{m(j)}$)), S(t_{*1}, E(g_*, $R_jr_{m(j)}$)), S(s_{*1}, E(k_*, $C_{m(j)}$))}.
4. After verifying the correctness of signatures on its vote in VotingPanel, V_j approves it by putting S(h_{2*}, $T_{n(j)}$), its token signed by the 2nd signing keys of tallying managers, in VotingPanel.
5. Each tallying manager TM_q (1≤q≤Z) repeatedly signs on E(k_*, $v_jR_jr_{m(j)}C_{m(j)}$) and E(g_*, $R_jr_{m(j)}$) in VotingPanel by its 2st signing keys s_{q2} and t_{q2} to generate S(s_{*2}, E(k_*, $v_jR_jr_{m(j)}C_{m(j)}$)) and S(t_{*2}, E(g_*, $R_jr_{m(j)}$)), and V_j verifies the signatures. Then, the final vote form of V_j disclosed in VotingPanel becomes {S(s_{*1}, E(k_*, $v_jR_jr_{m(j)}C_{m(j)}$)), S(t_{*1}, E(g_*, $R_jr_{m(j)}$)), S(s_{*1}, E(k_*, $C_{m(j)}$)), S(s_{*2}, E(k_*, $v_jR_jr_{m(j)}C_{m(j)}$)), S(t_{*2}, E(g_*, $R_jr_{m(j)}$))}.

At step 1 voter V_j asks tallying managers to encrypt v_jR_j instead of v_j while generating its secret random number R_j, therefore other entities including tallying managers cannot know vote v_j, i.e. privacy of V_j is preserved and the fairness of the election is achieved. Also encrypted v_jR_j is further multiplied by the encrypted form of unknown random number $r_{m(j)}$ at step 2, therefore even V_j cannot identify its vote at the tallying stage. Regarding the correctness of encryptions and signings of tallying managers about vote v_j at step 4 and 5, the homomorphism of encryption and signing functions of tallying managers enables V_j to verify them without knowing any key of tallying managers. Finally about the approval of vote v_j at step 5, no one except V_j knows S(h_{2*}, $T_{n(j)}$) even after the 1st signed token S(h_{1*}, $T_{n(j)}$) had been disclosed, because no one knows the 2nd signing keys of all tallying managers TM_1, TM_2, ---, TM_Z. Then, only V_j can approve its vote, and consequently after its approval, V_j cannot claim that any of election authorities is dishonest about its vote in VotingPanel.

Security problems at this stage are solved as follows.

A. Voter V_j may cast a meaningless vote to disrupt the election: Even when V_j casts a meaningless vote in VotingPanel, any entity except V_j itself cannot determine whether its encrypted vote in VotingPanel is meaningless or not until the tallying stage is completed. As a consequence, V_j can claim that its vote was disrupted during the tallying stage while having cast a meaningless vote from the beginning. Confirmation numbers and signature pairs on individual votes prevent this kind of dishonesties as discussed in the tallying stage.

B. Voter V_j may use E(k_*, $C_{m(h)}$) assigned to other voter: Vote form {E(k_*, $v_jR_jr_{m(j)}C_{m(j)}$), E(g_*, $R_jr_{m(j)}$), E(k_*, $C_{m(j)}$)} of V_j explicitly includes E(k_*, $C_{m(j)}$) and encrypted CN assigned to V_j is disclosed in ActiveTokenList. Therefore, VM can easily check the correctness of E(k_*, $C_{m(h)}$).

C. Voting manager VM may not put vote or put incorrect vote in VotingPanel: Because signed token S(h_{1*}, $T_{n(j)}$) that cannot be generated illegitimately is open to the public, V_j can repeatedly cast its vote before its approval, therefore VM cannot reject V_j's request. If VM puts incorrect vote, V_j can disapprove it.

D. Someone may modify votes in VotingPanel: Because VotingPanel is publicly disclosed, no one can modify or delete votes in it without being detected by others.

Tallying Stage

Mutually independent tallying managers carry out the following steps.

1. Tallying managers TM_{Z+1}, ---, TM_Q repeatedly decrypt encrypted votes in VotingPanel while shuffling their interim decryption results, and put final decrypted forms at randomly selected positions in TallyingPanel.
2. TM_1, ---, TM_Z disclose their verification keys so that anyone can know the election results.

In the above, because interim decryption results are shuffled by each tallying manager, no one including tallying managers and voters themselves can identify correspondences between votes in VotingPanel and TallyingPanel, in other words between voters and their votes.

Security problems in this stage also can be solved as follows:

A. Tallying managers may modify vote v_j of voter V_j while decrypting $\{S(s_{*1}, E(k_*, v_jR_jr_{m(j)}C_{m(j)})), S(t_{*1}, E(g_*, R_jr_{m(j)})), S(s_{*1}, E(k_*, C_{m(j)})), S(s_{*2}, E(k_*, v_jR_jr_{m(j)}C_{m(j)})), S(t_{*2}, E(g_*, R_jr_{m(j)}))\}$ dishonestly: As discussed in subsection "Unlinkable Signatures with Confirmation Numbers and Signature pairs" in Part II, there may exist 5 ways for tallying managers to modify votes, but all possibilities are disabled as follows.
   1. The 1st way is to replace vote v_j by v_i, a vote legitimately cast by other voter, however, anyone can detect this replacement because the modified vote is accompanied by the same CN as original vote v_i is.
   2. The 2nd way is to multiply encrypted v_j by other encrypted vote v_i. Because encryption and signing functions are homomorphic, multiplication result $\{S(s_{*1}, E(k_*, v_jv_iR_jr_{m(j)}R_ir_{m(i)}C_{m(j)}C_{m(i)})), S(t_{*1}, E(g_*, R_jr_{m(j)}R_ir_{m(i)})), S(s_{*1}, E(k_*, C_{m(j)}C_{m(i)})), S(s_{*2}, E(k_*, v_jv_iR_jr_{m(j)}R_ir_{m(i)}C_{m(j)}C_{m(i)})), S(t_{*2}, E(g_*, R_jr_{m(j)}R_ir_{m(i)}))\}$ constitutes the encrypted form of v_jv_i with consistent signatures of tallying managers. However, accompanying $C_{m(j)}C_{m(i)}$ is inconsistent, i.e. $C_{m(j)}C_{m(i)}$ is not a registered one, it is a repeatedly used one, or it is an unused one. Here, unused CNs are ones that are not assigned to any voter, and can be detected by decrypting and disclosing all unused CNs. Tallying managers also can disrupt v_j consistently by replacing $\{S(s_{*1}, E(k_*, v_jR_jr_{m(j)}C_{m(j)})), S(t_{*1}, E(g_*, R_jr_{m(j)})), S(s_{*1}, E(k_*, C_{m(j)})), S(s_{*2}, E(k_*, v_jR_jr_{m(j)}C_{m(j)})), S(t_{*2}, E(g_*, R_jr_{m(j)}))\}$ with $\{S(s_{*1}, E(k_*, v_jR_jr_{m(j)}C_{m(j)}))^H, S(t_{*1}, E(g_*, R_jr_{m(j)}))^H, S(s_{*1}, E(k_*, C_{m(j)}))^H, S(s_{*2}, E(k_*, v_jR_jr_{m(j)}C_{m(j)}))^H, S(t_{*2}, E(g_*, R_jr_{m(j)}))^H\}$, where H is an arbitrary integer. But $C_{m(j)}{}^H$ attached to it is not the registered one, it is the repeatedly used one, or it is an unused one as same as the above.

B. The 3rd way is to modify $S(s_{*1}, E(k_*, v_jR_jr_{m(j)}C_{m(j)}))$ to $S(s_{*1}, E(k_*, v_iR_ir_{m(i)}C_{m(j)}))$. Namely, when 2 encrypted form pairs $\{S(s_{*1}, E(k_*, v_jR_jr_{m(j)}C_{m(j)})), S(s_{*1}, E(k_*, C_{m(j)}))\}$ and $\{S(s_{*1}, E(k_*, v_iR_ir_{m(i)}C_{m(i)})), S(s_{*1}, E(k_*, C_{m(i)}))\}$ are given, where both are legitimate votes of voters V_j and V_i respectively, it is possible to calculate $S(s_{*1}, E(k_*, v_iR_ir_{m(i)}))$ as $S(s_{*1}, E(k_*, v_iR_ir_{m(i)})) = S(s_{*1}, E(k_*, v_iR_ir_{m(i)}C_{m(i)}))/S(s_{*1}, E(k_*, C_{m(i)}))$, then $S(s_{*1}, E(k_*, v_jR_jr_{m(j)}C_{m(j)}))$ can be modified to $S(s_{*1}, E(k_*, v_iR_ir_{m(i)}C_{m(j)}))$ with unique and registered $CN_{m(j)}$ by multiplying $S(s_{*1}, E(k_*, v_iR_ir_{m(i)}))$ and $S(s_{*1}, E(k_*, C_{m(j)}))$. However, no one can generate consistent signature $S(s_{*2}, E(k_*, v_iR_ir_{m(i)}C_{m(j)}))$ illegitimately because $S(s_{*2}, E(k_*, C_{m(j)}))$ is not disclosed different from $S(s_{*1}, E(k_*, C_{m(j)}))$. Therefore, anyone can detect also this dishonesty as an inconsistent signature pair.

C. The 4th way is to disrupt v_j, i.e. it is easy to replace $\{S(s_{*1}, E(k_*, v_jR_jr_{m(j)}C_{m(j)})), S(t_{*1}, E(g_*, R_jr_{m(j)})), S(s_{*1}, E(k_*, C_{m(j)})), S(s_{*2}, E(k_*, v_jR_jr_{m(j)}C_{m(j)})), S(t_{*2}, E(g_*, R_jr_{m(j)}))\}$ with $\{X_1, S(t_{*1}, E(g_*, R_jr_{m(j)})), S(s_{*1}, E(k_*, C_{m(j)})), X_2, S(t_{*2}, E(g_*, R_jr_{m(j)}))\}$, where X_1 and X_2 are arbitrary bit strings. Signature pairs also disable this dishonesty, i.e. no one can generate X_1 and X_2 so that they are decrypted to the signed forms of the same vote, unless all tallying managers conspire.

D. The 5th way is the deletion of $\{S(s_{*1}, E(k_*, v_jR_jr_{m(j)}C_{m(j)})), S(t_{*1}, E(g_*, R_jr_{m(j)})), S(s_{*1}, E(k_*, C_{m(j)})), S(s_{*2}, E(k_*, v_jR_jr_{m(j)}C_{m(j)})), S(t_{*2}, E(g_*, R_jr_{m(j)}))\}$, however, anyone can detect the deletion by counting the numbers of votes in Voting Panel and Tallying Panel.

When illegitimate votes are detected in TallyingPanel, liable entities are identified in the disrupted vote detection stage without revealing any privacy of honest voters.

E. Tallying managers may add votes: Anyone can detect the added votes by checking CNs attached to them, i.e. the attached CNs are duplicated ones, not registered ones or they are unused ones.

F. Voter V_j may cast an invalid vote to disrupt the election: V_j cannot claim that its vote is disrupted even its vote is meaningless because disclosed $C_{m(j)}$ is valid and the signature pair on its vote is consistent.

Disrupted Vote Detection Stage

If inconsistent votes are found in TallyingPanel, vote disruption detection manager DM identifies liable entities as follows.

1. When inconsistent vote v is found, DM asks tallying managers to encrypt $\underline{v}$ again in the reverse order of the tallying stage. Namely, each TM_q encrypts $S(s_{*1}, E(k_{q+1}, E(k_{q+2}, ---, E(kQ\underline{vRrC})---)))$ that receives from TM_{q+1} to $S(s_{*1}, E(k_q, E(k_{q+1}, ---, E(kQ\underline{vRrC})---)))$. Where, R, r, and C are values of secret random numbers and CN attached to v, and other elements of the encrypted vote i.e. $S(s_{*1}, E(g_*, \underline{Rr}))$, $S(s_{*1}, E(k_*, \underline{C}))$, $S(s_{*2}, E(k_*, \underline{vRrC}))$ and $S(s_{*2}, E(g_*, \underline{Rr}))$ are omitted to simplify the description.
2. When $S(s_{*1}, E(k_q, E(k_{q+1}, ---, E(kQ\underline{vRrC})---)))$ does not coincide with any input that TM_q had received from TM_{q-1} in the Tallying stage, TM_q is dishonest.

It must be noted that TM_q cannot encrypt votes dishonestly at step 1 because encryption function $E(k_q, x)$ is homomorphic, i.e. anyone can verify the correctness of encryptions without knowing key k_q. Also, if v is a vote that had been cast legitimately by an eligible voter, the dishonest manager is identified before the chain for finding inputs of individual tallying managers reaches VotingPanel. Therefore privacies of honest voters are preserved.

Performance of the E-Voting System

The scheme described in previous subsections satisfies the all requirements of e-voting systems as follows.

1. Privacy

Voter V_j whose eligibility is checked by its token $T_{n(j)}$ asks mutually independent multiple tallying managers to repeatedly encrypt its vote v_j

while concealing it by a random number secret of V_j to be put in VotingPanel, and votes in VotingPanel are decrypted by each tallying manager to be disclosed in TallyingPanel while being shuffled with other votes. Therefore, provided that at least one tallying manager is honest, no one except V_j can know the vote of V_j regardless that token $T_{n(j)}$ is anonymous or not. The secret random number assigned to V_j also makes encryptions probabilistic, therefore even voters who had chosen same candidate v_j cannot know the decrypted form of V_j's vote in VotingPanel. In a case where V_j is not coerced by others, it can conceal its abstention by simply not casting its vote because token $T_{n(j)}$ is anonymous. However, entity Ce that coerces V_j can know whether it had cast its vote or not by forcing V_j to disclose its token $T_{n(j)}$. Therefore, Ce can effectively coerce V_j not to participate in the election. A way to protect voters from this kind of threats is discussed in conjunction with the incoercibility.

2. Accuracy and universal verifiability

Each voter V_j shows its ID and password pair at a time when it obtains signatures of tallying managers on its token, and signatures on the token cannot be generated illegitimately unless all tallying managers conspire, therefore ineligible entities cannot cast their votes. V_j cannot cast its vote multiple times either, because V_j's vote is put at the position in VotingPanel corresponding to token $T_{n(j)}$ assigned to it. Also, all votes in VotingPanel were verified by voters themselves, and CNs and signature pairs attached to individual votes in TallyingPanel ensure that tallying managers honestly decrypted only and all votes in VotingPanel.

3. Fairness

Votes in VotingPanel cannot be decrypted unless all tallying managers conspire. Also as in discussions about dispute-freeness, disputes between voters and election authorities about dishonest events on votes are necessarily solved; therefore re-election is not necessary. Then, provided that votes in VotingPanel are decrypted only after the deadline of the election, voting results are kept unknown from anyone including election authorities until the completion of the election.

4. Receipt-freeness

Voters know their tokens, encrypted votes, encrypted CNs and encrypted unknown random numbers, but all of them cannot be linked to their votes in TallyingPanel, i.e. the scheme is receipt-free. Namely, although voter V_j that knows its token can identify the encrypted form of its vote v_j in VotingPanel, it can tell others that v_j in VotingPanel corresponds to any vote disclosed in TallyingPanel.

5. Incoercibility

Provided that there are regulations that inhibit voters to skip the voting stage, voters can protect themselves from the 1st type threats (forced abstentions), and even in this case voters can abstain from the election by casting invalid votes. Also, because no one can identify correspondences between votes in VotingPanel and TallyingPanel, coercers who had forced voters to abstain from the election cannot know whether the voters actually had cast invalid votes or not. However, it must be noted that without the regulations, V_j cannot protect itself from coercers. Namely, coercer Ce can know $S(h_{1*}, T_{n(j)})$, signed token V_j had obtained, by asking V_j, and $S(h_{1*}, T_{n(j)})$ disclosed in ActiveTokenList and an encrypted vote at the position corresponding to $S(h_{1*}, T_{n(j)})$ in VotingPanel enable Ce to know whether V_j had cast its vote or not. Fortunately, it is rather easy to force voters to cast their votes regardless that their votes are consistent or meaningless, when voters can cast their votes remotely.

About the 2nd type threats, receipt-freeness of the system disables entity Ce, which is coercing V_j, to identify the correspondence between V_j and its vote; therefore V_j can choose a candidate by its own decision without being noticed by Ce provided that TallyingPanel includes at least one vote for v_C, the candidate that Ce is supporting. It must be noted that v_C may be an invalid candidate that is unique to V_j, and in this case, v_C does not appear in TallyingPanel if V_j had chosen a different candidate. But, it is also possible to disable Ce to know whether V_j had chosen v_C or not even when v_C does not appear in TallyingPanel as discussed in the next subsection, and this means that the scheme protects voters also from the 3rd type threats. As a consequence, the scheme achieves the complete incoercibility, provided that there are regulations that inhibit voters to skip the voting stage.

6. Dispute-freeness

CNs and signature pairs ensure one to one correspondences between voters and their votes in TallyingPanel; therefore voters cannot claim about the accuracy of the election once they had approved their votes in VotingPanel provided that election authorities are honest. When election authorities had illegitimately modified votes, modifications are detected as duplicated CNs, unauthorized CNs or inconsistent signature pairs. Election authorities liable for the detected modifications also can be identified when the modified votes are encrypted again without revealing any privacy of voters. About approvals of votes, voters cannot claim that election authorities are dishonest, because voters can recast their votes until they satisfy with the ones in VotingPanel.

7. Robustness

Voters can disrupt only their votes by casting invalid votes. Either voting manager or tallying managers cannot disrupt votes. Namely, the correctness of votes in VotingPanel is ensured because voters approve their votes by themselves, and when tallying managers decrypt votes dishonestly, the liable entities are identified at the disrupted vote detection stage and correct election results can be revealed by simply forcing tallying managers that behaved dishonestly to decrypt disrupted votes again.

8. Scalability

CNs and signature pairs reduce volumes of computations required for voters, election authorities and third parties substantially, while satisfying requirements such as accuracy, fairness, incoercibility, etc. To compare the performance of the e-voting system developed in this chapter with that of ZKP based systems (ZKPs are used for verifying correct encryptions and decryptions of election entities), a simulation system had been developed that consisted of 6 tallying managers, where TM_4, TM_5 and TM_6 repeatedly encrypted individual votes to put them in VotingPanel and TM_1, TM_2 and TM_3 signed on encrypted votes. According to the simulation results, the confirmation number based system (Md Rokibul, 2010) had reduced the time required for processing each vote at the tallying stage to less than 1/100 times of that required by a ZKP based scheme (Weber, 2006).

9. Practicality

The scheme is based on weaker assumptions about trustworthiness of entities i.e. nothing can make the scheme unreliable unless all multiple election authorities conspire. Also, the scheme accepts any form of votes including free write in ballots.

Satisfying Incoercibility

About the incoercibility, when tallying managers TM_{Z+1}, ---, TM_Q are divided into 2 groups {TM_{Z+1}, TM_{Z+2}, ---, TM_P} and {TM_{P+1}, TM_{P+2}, ---, TM_Q} as shown in Figure 3, the previous e-voting system

Figure 3. Configuration of incoercible voting scheme

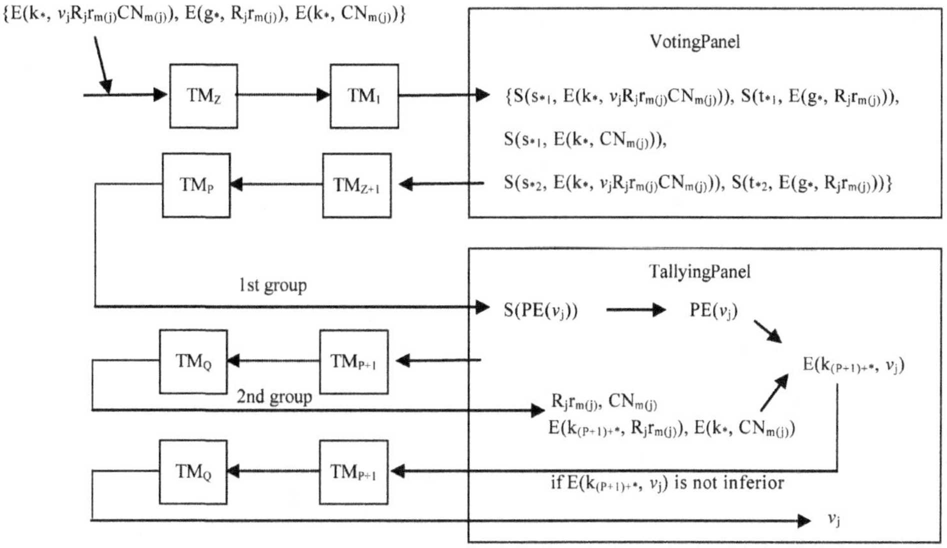

$S(PE(v_j)) = \{S(s_{*1}, E(k_{(P+1)+*}, v_jR_jr_{m(j)}CN_{m(j)})), S(t_{*1}, E(g_{(P+1)+*}, R_jr_{m(j)})), S(s_{*1}, E(k_{(P+1)+*}, CN_{m(j)})),$

$S(s_{*2}, E(k_{(P+1)+*}, v_jR_jr_{m(j)}CN_{m(j)})), S(t_{*2}, E(g_{(P+1)+*}, R_jr_{m(j)}))\}$

can protect voter V_j from type-1, type-2 and type-3 threats even in cases where coercer Ce forces V_j to cast vote v_C which is unique to V_j, (v_C may be an invalid vote) provided that there is at least one inferior candidate who apparently obtains less votes than other candidates.

In the figure, entities in the election behave in the same way as in the previous subsections until the voting stage, i.e. TM_Q, ---, TM_{Z+1} repeatedly encrypt votes shown by voters to put the results in VotingPanel, and TM_Z, ---, TM_1 repeatedly sign on them. But at the tallying stage, encrypted vote $\{S(s_{*1}, E(k_*, v_jR_jr_{m(j)}C_{m(j)})), S(t_{*1}, E(g_*, R_jr_{m(j)})), S(s_{*1}, E(k_*, C_{m(j)})), S(s_{*2}, E(k_*, v_jR_jr_{m(j)}C_{m(j)})), S(t_{*2}, E(g_*, R_jr_{m(j)}))\}$ in VotingPanel is decrypted only by tallying managers in the 1st group while being shuffled with other decrypted results, and partially decrypted form $S(PE(v_j)) = \{S(s_{*1}, E(k_{(P+1)*}, v_jR_jr_{m(j)}C_{m(j)})), S(t_{*1}, E(g_{(P+1)*}, R_jr_{m(j)})), S(s_{*1}, E(k_{(P+1)*}, C_{m(j)})), S(s_{*2}, E(k_{(P+1)*}, v_jR_jr_{m(j)}C_{m(j)})), S(t_{*2}, E(g_{(P+1)*}, R_jr_{m(j)}))\}$ is disclosed in TallyingPanel instead of $\{S(s_{*1}, v_jR_jr_{m(j)}C_{m(j)}), S(t_{*1}, R_jr_{m(j)}), S(s_{*1}, C_{m(j)}), S(s_{*2}, v_jR_jr_{m(j)}C_{m(j)}), S(t_{*2}, R_jr_{m(j)})\}$, where, $E(k_{(P+1)*}, x) = E(k_{P+1}, E(k_{P+2}, ---, E(k_Q, x) ---))$ and $E(g_{(P+1)*}, x) = E(g_{P+1}, E(g_{P+2}, ---, E(g_Q, x) ---))$. Then, TM_1, ---, TM_Z disclose their verification keys, and triple $PE(v_j) = \{E(k_{(P+1)*}, v_jR_jr_{m(j)}C_{m(j)}), E(g_{(P+1)*}, R_jr_{m(j)}), E(k_{(P+1)*}, C_{m(j)})\}$ is attached to the partially decrypted vote $S(PE(v_j))$ in TallyingPanal. Here, anyone can calculate $\{E(k_{(P+1)*}, v_jR_jr_{m(j)}C_{m(j)}), E(g_{(P+1)*}, R_jr_{m(j)}), E(k_{(P+1)*}, C_{m(j)})\}$ from $S(PE(v_j))$ when verification keys of TM_1, TM_2, ---, TM_Z are disclosed, and 2 signed forms $\{S(s_{*1}, E(k_{(P+1)*}, v_jR_jr_{m(j)}C_{m(j)})), S(t_{*1}, E(g_{(P+1)*}, R_jr_{m(j)}))\}$ and $\{S(s_{*2}, E(k_{(P+1)*}, v_jR_jr_{m(j)}C_{m(j)})), S(t_{*2}, E(g_{(P+1)*}, R_jr_{m(j)}))\}$ reveal same partially decrypted result $\{E(k_{(P+1)*}, v_jR_jr_{m(j)}C_{m(j)}), E(g_{(P+1)*}, R_jr_{m(j)})\}$ if TM_{Z+1}, ---, TM_P had decrypted the repeatedly encrypted vote honestly.

After that, TM_{P+1}, ---, TM_Q decrypts only $E(g_{(P+1)*}, R_jr_{m(j)})$ and $E(k_{(P+1)*}, C_{m(j)})$ to $R_jr_{m(j)}$ and $C_{m(j)}$ (i.e. $E(k_{(P+1)*}, v_jR_jr_{m(j)}C_{m(j)})$ is not decrypted) without shuffling it with other decryption results, and they repeatedly encrypt $R_jr_{m(j)}$ to $E(k_{(P+1)*},$

$R_j r_{m(j)}$) again. Then, anyone can calculate E($k_{(P+1)*}$, v_j) by dividing E($k_{(P+1)*}$, $v_j R_j r_{m(j)} C_{m(j)}$) by E($k_{(P+1)*}$, $R_j r_{m(j)}$) and E($k_{(P+1)*}$, $C_{m(j)}$) while exploiting the homomorphism of encryption function E($k_{(P+1)*}$, x). Therefore, {S(PE(v_j)), E($k_{(P+1)*}$, $v_j R_j r_{m(j)} C_{m(j)}$), E($g_{(P+1)*}$, $R_j r_{m(j)}$), E($k_{(P+1)*}$, $R_j r_{m(j)}$), E($k_{(P+1)*}$, $C_{m(j)}$), E($k_{(P+1)*}$, v_j), $C_{m(j)}$, $R_j r_{m(j)}$} is disclosed in Tallying-Panel, and anyone can identify votes for inferior candidates even they are encrypted. Namely, E($k_{(P+1)*}$, v_j) is an encrypted form of an inferior candidate that could have obtained apparently less votes than other candidates, if TallyingPanal includes only small number of E($k_{(P+1)*}$, v_j). Then, because inferior candidates cannot be election winners, TM_{P+1}, ---, TM_Q decrypt only votes for non-inferior candidates. Consequently, as the complete decrypted form of V_j's vote, combination {S(PE(v_j)), E($k_{(P+1)*}$, $R_j r_{m(j)}$), E($k_{(P+1)*}$, v_j), $C_{m(j)}$, $R_j r_{m(j)}$} or {S(PE(v_j)), E($k_{(P+1)*}$, $R_j r_{m(j)}$), v_j, $C_{m(j)}$, $R_j r_{m(j)}$} is disclosed in TallyingPanel depending on v_j is a vote for an inferior candidate or not.

Provided that at least one inferior candidate exists, the above scheme protects voters from the 1st, the 2nd and the 3rd type threats about incoercibility even when there is no vote for the candidates that coercers are asking to choose. Namely, TallyingPanel includes at least one vote v_h that is for an inferior candidate, and v_h appears in TallyingPanel only in the form E($k_{(P+1)*}$, v_h), and no one knows that E($k_{(P+1)*}$, v_h) corresponds to v_h. This means that if voter V_j is coerced to cast vote v_C by coercer Ce, V_j can tell Ce that its vote in TallyingPanel is E($k_{(P+1)*}$, v_h). No one including V_j itself knows the confirmation number C_j or unknown random number $R_{m(j)} r_{m(j)}$ assigned to V_j, or anyone does not know the decrypted form of E($k_{(P+1)*}$, v_h) either.

On the other hand, anyone can convince itself that election winners determined by decrypting and counting votes only for non-inferior candidates are legitimate, i.e. apparently inferior candidates cannot be election winners.

CONCLUSION

An e-voting system that preserves privacies of individual voters and ensures accuracies of elections has been developed. Although it cannot exclude trusted entities faithful to all relevant entities completely, the above features are satisfied at least one of multiple election authorities is honest. Also, when there is a regulation that forces all voters to cast their votes (but voters can cast invalid votes) and at least one inferior candidate that obtains apparently less votes than other candidates exists, the system also can protect voters from coercers completely, i.e. voter V_j who is coerced by other entity Ce to abstain from the election or to cast vote v_C that Ce is supporting, can cast its vote by its own decision without being noticed by Ce, even if v_C is an invalid vote unique to V_j. Most importantly, while being supported by CNs and signature pairs of authorities, the scheme achieves desirable features of e-voting systems in a simple and efficient way. Unlike complicated ZKP based systems, the simplified computational requirements of individual election entities make the scheme practical and scalable.

Different from other systems where occurrences of small dishonest events are allowed (e.g. credit card systems can accept dishonest events when the amount of the losses is small), in many cases, even tiny dishonest events are not allowed to occur in e-voting systems. Namely, a claim from only one voter about inaccuracy of the election result may disrupt the whole election. Here, it must be noted that a dishonest event caused by even a voter may be imputed to election authorities if the e-voting system cannot prove its honesty. Therefore, e-voting systems are required to completely disable entities to behave dishonestly. Then as the future works, combinations of various different schemes must be investigated so that disadvantages of individual schemes are compensated by advantages of other schemes.

REFERENCES

Chaum, D. (1981). Untraceable electronic mail, return address and digital pseudonyms. *Communications of the ACM, 24*(2), 84–90. doi:10.1145/358549.358563

Cohen (Benaloh). J., & Fiischer, M. (1985). A robust and verifiable cryptographically secure election scheme. *Proceedings of 26th Symposium on Foundation of Computer Science,* (pp. 372-382).

Cramer, R., Gennaro, R., & Schoenmakers, B. (1997). A secure and optimally efficient multi-authority election scheme. *Advances in Cryptology - EUROCRYPTO'97* [Springer-Verlag.]. *LNGS, 1233*, 103–118.

Fujioka, A., Okamoto, T., & Ohta, K. (1993). A practical secret voting scheme for large scale elections. *AUSCRYPT'92* [Springer-Verlag.]. *LNCS, 718*, 248–259.

Golle, S., & Zhong, D. Boneh, Jakobsson, M., & Juels, A. (2002). An optimistic mixing for exit-polls. *ASIACRYPTO'02, LNGS, 2501*, (pp. 451-465). Springer-Verlag.

Md Rokibul, K. A., Tamura, S., Taniguchi, S., & Yanase, T. (2010). An anonymous voting scheme based on confirmation numbers. *IEEJ Transactions in EIS, 130*(11), 2065–2073. doi:10.1541/ieejeiss.130.2065

Park, G., Ito, K., & Kurosawa, K. (1994). Efficient anonymous channel and all/nothing election scheme. *Advances in Cryptology - EUROCRYPTO'93* [Springer-Verlag.]. *LNGS, 765*, 248–259.

Sako, K., & Killian, J. (1995). Receipt-free mix-type voting scheme - a practical solution to the implementation of a voting booth. *Advances in Cryptology - EUROCRYPTO'95* [Springer-Verlag.]. *LNGS, 921*, 393–403.

Sampigethaya, K., & Poovendran, R. (2006). A framework and taxonomy for comparison of electronic voting schemes. *Elsevier Computers and Security, 25*, 137–153.

Schoenmakers, B. (1999). A simple publicly verifiable secret sharing scheme and its applications to electronic voting. *Advances in Cryptology - CRYPTO'99* [Springer-Verlag.]. *LNGS, 1666*, 148–164.

Tamura, S. Md. Rokibul, A. K., & Haddad, H. A. (2009). A probabilistic and commutative re-encryption scheme. *Proceedings of Asia Simulation Conference 2009.*

Weber, S. (2006). *A coercion-resistant cryptographic voting protocol - Evaluation and prototype implementation*. Diploma thesis, Darmstadt University of Technology.

Compilation of References

Abe, M. (2000). Universally verifiable Mix-net with verification work independent of the number of mix-servers. *IEICE Trans. Fundamentals. E (Norwalk, Conn.)*, *83-A*(7), 1431–1440.

Amoroso, E. (1994). *Fundamentals of computer security technology*. Prentice Hall.

Anderson, R. (2001). *Security engineering - A guide to building dependable distributed systems*. John Wiley & Sons.

Androulaki, E., & Bellovin, S. (2009). An anonymous credit card system. *Proceedings of the 6th International Conference: Trust, Privacy and Security in Digital Business*, 3-4 September 2009, New York, (pp. 42-51). Linz, Austria: Springer.

Belenkiy, M., Camenisch, J., Chase, M., Kohlweiss, M., Lysyanskaya, A., & Shacham, H. (2009). Randomizable proofs and delegatable anonymous credentials. *Proceedings of the 29th Annual International Cryptology Conference on Advances in Cryptology*, 16-20 August 2009, Santa Barbara, CA, (pp. 108-125).

Blum, M., Feldman, P., & Micali, S. (1988). Non-interactive zero-knowledge and its applications. *Proceedings of the 20th Annual ACM Symposium on Theory of Computing* (pp. 103-112).

Boneh, D., & Golle, P. (2002). *Almost entirely correct mixing with applications to voting* (pp. 68–77). ACM Conferences on Computer and Communications Security.

Brands, S. (1994). Untraceable off-line cash in wallets with observers. *Proceedings of CRYPTO*, *93*, 302–318.

Bruschi, D., Fovino, I., & Lanzi, A. (2005). A protocol for anonymous and accurate e-polling. *Proceedings of the International Conference on E-Government: Towards Electronic Democracy,* (pp. 112-121).

Camenisch, J., & Lysyanskaya, A. (2001). An efficient system for non-transferable anonymous credential with optimal anonymity revocation. *Proceedings of EUROCRYPT'01, the International Conference on the Theory and Application of Cryptographic Techniques: Advances in Cryptography,* (pp. 93-118). London, UK: Springer-Verlag

Canard, S., & Gouget, A. (2007). Lecture Notes in Computer Science: *Vol. 4515. Divisible e-cash systems can be truly anonymous. Advances in Cryptology - EUROCRYPT* (pp. 482–497). Berlin, Germany: Springer-Verlag.

Chaum, D. (1981). Untraceable electronic mail, return address and digital pseudonyms. *Communications of the ACM*, *24*(2), 84–90. doi:10.1145/358549.358563

Chaum, D. (1983). Blind signatures system. *Advances in Cryptology, CRYPTO*, *83*, 153–156.

Chaum, D. (1988). The dining cryptographers problem: Unconditional sender and recipient untraceability. *Journal of Cryptology*, *1*, 65–75. doi:10.1007/BF00206326

Chaum, D., Fiat, A., & Naor, M. (1988). Untraceable electronic cash. *Advances in Cryptology, - . CRYPTO*, *88*, 319–327.

Cohen (Benaloh). J., & Fiischer, M. (1985). A robust and verifiable cryptographically secure election scheme. *Proceedings of 26th Symposium on Foundation of Computer Science,* (pp. 372-382).

Cormen, T., Leiserson, C., Rivest, R., & Stein, C. (2001). *Introduction to algorithms*. MIT Press and McGraw-Hill.

Cramer, R., Gennaro, R., & Schoenmakers, B. (1997). A secure and optimally efficient multi-authority election scheme. *Advances in Cryptology - EUROCRYPTO'97* [Springer-Verlag.]. *LNGS*, *1233*, 103–118.

Desmedt, Y., & Frankel, Y. (1990). *Threshold cryptosystems. Proceedings of Advances in Cryptology - CRYPTO'89, LNCS 435* (pp. 307–315). Springer-Verlag.

Dingledine, R., & Mathewson, N. (2004). Tor: The second-generation onion router. *Proceedings of the 13th USENIX Security Symposium,* (pp. 303-320).

Djurdjanovic, D., Lee, J., & Ni, J. (2003). Watchdog agent - An infotronics based prognostics approach for product performance assessment and prediction. *International Journal of Advanced Engineering Informatics. Special Issue on Intelligent Maintenance Systems*, *17*(3-4), 109–125.

Elgamal, T. (1985). A public-key cryptosystem and a signature scheme based on discrete logarithms. *IEEE Transactions on Information Theory*, *31*(4), 469–472. doi:10.1109/TIT.1985.1057074

Eslami, Z., & Talebi, M. (2011). A new untraceable off-line electronic cash system. *Electronic Commerce Research and Applications*, *10*(1), 59–66. doi:10.1016/j.elerap.2010.08.002

Ferguson, N. (1994). Single term off-line coins. *Advances in Cryptography -EUROCRYPTO'93*, (pp. 318-328).

FIPS. (1977). *Data encryption standard. FIPS pub 46*. FIPS.

Franklin, M., & Reiter, M. (1996). The design and implementation of a secure auction service. *IEEE Transactions on Software Engineering*, *22*, 302–312. doi:10.1109/32.502223

Fujioka, A., Okamoto, T., & Ohta, K. (1993). A practical secret voting scheme for large scale elections. *AUSCRYPT'92* [Springer-Verlag.]. *LNCS*, *718*, 248–259.

Furukawa, J., & Sako, K. (2001). An efficient scheme for proving a shuffle. *CRYPTO 2001*. *LNCS*, *2139*, 368–387.

Goldreich, O., Micali, M., & Wigderson, A. (1987). How to play any mental game. *Proceedings of 19th ACM Symposium on Theory of Computing,* (pp. 218-229).

Goldwasser, S., Micali, S., & Rackoff, C. (1989). The knowledge complexity of interactive proof system. *SIAM Journal on Computing*, *18*(1), 291–304. doi:10.1137/0218012

Golle, P., & Jakobsson, M. (2003). Reusable anonymous return channels. *Proceedings of the 2003 ACM Workshop on Privacy in the Electronic Society, WPES '03*, (pp. 94-100). ACM.

Golle, S., & Zhong, D. Boneh, Jakobsson, M., & Juels, A. (2002). An optimistic mixing for exit-polls. *ASIACRYPTO'02, LNGS, 2501*, (pp. 451-465). Springer-Verlag.

Haddad, H., Tamura, S., Taniguchi, S., & Yanase, T. (2011). Development of anonymous networks based on symmetric key encryptions. *Journal of Networks*, *6*(11), 1533–1542. doi:10.4304/jnw.6.11.1533-1542

Hamming, R. W. (1980). *Coding and information theory*. Prentice-Hall.

Hassan, K., Tamura, S., & Yanase, T. (2006). A mechanism for anonymous auction. *Proceedings of Asian Simulation Conference (Systems Modeling and Simulation),* Springer, (pp. 233-237).

Ingledine, R., Freedman, M. J., Hopwood, D., & Molnar, D. (2001). A reputation system to increase MIX-net reliability. *Proceedings of the 4th International Workshop on Information Hiding, LNCS 2137,* (pp. 126-141). Springer-Verlag.

Jakobsson, M., Juels, A., & Rivest, R. (2002). Making mix nets robust for electronic voting by randomized partial checking. *USENIX Security*, *02*, 339–353.

Kahn, D. (1996). *The codebreakers – The comprehensive history of secret communication from ancient times to the Internet – Revised and updated*. New York, NY: Scribner.

Katz, J., & Lindell, Y. (2007). *Introduction to modern cryptography*. Boca Raton, FL: CRC Press.

Koblitz, N. (1994). *A course in number theory and cryptography* (2nd ed., p. 114). New York, NY: Springer-Verlag Graduate Texts in Mathematics.

Krawczyk, H., Bellare, B., & Canetti, R. (1997). *HMAC: Keyed-hashing for message authentication. RFC 2104*. IETF.

Low, S. H., Nicholas, F., & Sanjoy, P. (1996). Anonymous credit cards and their collusion analysis. *IEEE/ACM Transactions on Networking, 4*(6), 809–816. doi:10.1109/90.556339

Md Rokibul, K. A., Tamura, S., Taniguchi, S., & Yanase, T. (2010). An anonymous voting scheme based on confirmation numbers. *IEEJ Transactions in EIS, 130*(11), 2065–2073. doi:10.1541/ieejeiss.130.2065

Menezes, A. J., van Oorschot, P. C., & Vanstone, S. A. (1996). *Handbook of applied cryptography*. CRC Press.

Naor, M., Pinkas, B., & Sumner, R. (1999). Privacy preserving auctions and mechanism design. *Proceedings of the 1st ACM Conference on Electronic Commerce*, (pp. 129-139).

National Institute of Standards and Technology. (1993). *Secure hash algorithm*. FIPS180-1.

Nguyen, K., & Traore, J. (2000). An online public auction protocol protecting bidder privacy. *5th Australasian Conference on Information Security and Privacy, ACISP '00*, (pp. 427-442).

Nguyen, L., Sahavi-Naimi, R., & Kurosawa, K. (2004). Verifiable shuffles: S formal model and a Paillier-based efficient construction with provable security. *ACNS 2004 . LNCS, 3089*, 61–75.

Otsuka, A., Hanaoka, G., Shikata, J., & Imai, H. (2002). An unconditionally secure electronic cash scheme with computational untraceability. *IEICE Transactions, Fundamentals . E (Norwalk, Conn.), 85-A*(1), 140–148.

Park, G., Ito, K., & Kurosawa, K. (1994). Efficient anonymous channel and all/nothing election scheme. *Advances in Cryptology - EUROCRYPTO '93* [Springer-Verlag.]. *LNGS, 765*, 248–259.

Pieprzyk, J., Hardjono, T., & Seberry, J. (2003). *Fundamentals of computer security*. Springer-Verlag.

Reed, M. G., Syverson, P. F., & Goldschlag, D. M. (1998). Anonymous connections and onion routing. *Selected Areas in Communications, 16*(4), 482–494. doi:10.1109/49.668972

Reiter, K., & Rubin, A. D. (1998). Crowds: Anonymity for web transactions. *ACM Transactions on Information and System Security, 1*(1), 66–92. doi:10.1145/290163.290168

Rivest, R., Shamir, A., & Adleman, L. (1978). A method for obtaining digital signatures and public-key cryptosystems. *Communications of the ACM, 21*(2), 294–299. doi:10.1145/359340.359342

Sako, K., & Killian, J. (1995). Receipt-free mix-type voting scheme - a practical solution to the implementation of a voting booth. *Advances in Cryptology - EUROCRYPTO '95* [Springer-Verlag.]. *LNGS, 921*, 393–403.

Sampigethaya, K., & Poovendran, R. (2006). A framework and taxonomy for comparison of electronic voting schemes. *Elsevier Computers and Security, 25*, 137–153.

Schoenmakers, B. (1999). A simple publicly verifiable secret sharing scheme and its applications to electronic voting. *Advances in Cryptology - CRYPTO '99* [Springer-Verlag.]. *LNGS, 1666*, 148–164.

Shahandashti, S. F., & Safavi-Naini, R. (2009). Threshold attribute-based signatures and their application to anonymous credential systems. *Proceedings of the 2nd International Conference on Cryptology in Africa: Progress in Cryptology*. Berlin, Germany: Springer-Verlag.

Shamir, A. (1979). How to share a secret. *Communications of the ACM, 22*(11), 612–613. doi:10.1145/359168.359176

Shigetomi, R., Otsuka, A., & Imai, H. (2003). *Refreshable tokens and its applications to anonymous loans*. SCIS2003.

Stajano, F. (2002). *Security for ubiquitous computing*. John Wiley & Sons. doi:10.1002/0470848693

Sudarsono, A., Nakanishi, T., & Funabiki, N. (2011). Efficient proofs of attributes in pairing-based anonymous credential system. *Springer Lecture Notes in Computer Science, 6794/2011*, (pp. 246-263).

Tamura, S. Md. Rokibul, A. K., & Haddad, H. A. (2009). A probabilistic and commutative re-encryption scheme. *Proceedings of Asia Simulation Conference 2009*.

Tamura, S., Kouro, K., & Yanase, T. (2006). Expenditure limits in anonymous credit card systems. *Proc. of IEEE SMC 2006*, (pp. 1238-1243).

Tamura, S., Ohashi, Y., Tanigichi, S., & Yanase, T. (2010). Detection of dishonest entities. *SMC2010, Proc. of IEEE International Conference on System, Man and Cybernetics*, (pp. 906-911)

Tamura, S., Ohashi, Y., Taniguchi, S., & Yanase, T. (2010). Detection of dishonest entities. *SMC2010, Proc. of IEEE International Conference on System, Man and Cybernetics*, (pp. 906-911).

Tamura, S., Haddad, H. A., Tsurugi, H., & Md. Rokibul, A. K. (2009). Mechanisms for anonymous memories. *IEEE InternationalConference on Industrial Tecnology, ICIT*, *09*, 398–403.

Tamura, S., Kouro, K., Sasatani, M., Md. Rokibul, K. A., & Haddad, A. S. (2008). An information system platform for anonymous product recycling. *Journal of Software*, *3*(6), 46–56. doi:10.4304/jsw.3.6.46-56

Tamura, S., Kouro, K., & Yanase, T. (2006). Expenditure limits in anonymous credit card systems. *IEEE SMC*, *2006*, 1238–1243.

Tamura, S., & Yanase, T. (2005). Information sharing among untrustworthy entities. *IEEJ Transactions in EIS*, *125*(11), 1767–1772. doi:10.1541/ieejeiss.125.1767

Tamura, S., & Yanase, T. (2007). A mechanism for anonymous credit card systems. *IEEJ Trans. EIS*, *127*(1), 81–87. doi:10.1541/ieejeiss.127.81

Trappe, W., & Washington, L. C. (2005). *Introduction to cryptography with coding theory*. Englewood Cliffs, NJ: Prentice-Hall.

Vaudenay, S. (2006). *A classical introduction to cryptography, applications for communication security*. New York, NY: Springer-Verlag.

Weber, S. (2006). *A coercion-resistant cryptographic voting protocol - Evaluation and prototype implementation*. Diploma thesis, Darmstadt University of Technology.

Yao, A. C. (1986). *How to generate and exchange secrets*. Proc. of the 27th IEEE Symposium on Fo

About the Author

Shinsuke Tamura received the B.S., M.S., and Dr.(Eng.) degrees in Control Engineering from Osaka University in 1970, 1972, and 1991, respectively. From 1972 to 2001 he worked for Toshiba Corporation, and had been developing information systems for various applications including mechanical CAD systems, system engineering tools, manufacturing systems, power systems, railway control systems, and building, factory and office automation systems. He is currently a Professor of Graduate School of Engineering, University of Fukui. His current research interests include distributed system architecture, system development methods, information security, path planning algorithms (for manipulators), and manufacturing scheduling algorithms.

Index

G

H

I

L

M

N

O

P

R

S

T

U

V

W

Z